F I F T H   E D I T I O N

ORGANIZATION DEVELOPMENT AND TRANSFORMATION

Managing Effective Change

Edited by

Wendell L. French
Graduate School of Business Administration
University of Washington

Cecil H. Bell, Jr.
Graduate School of Business Administration
University of Washington

Robert A. Zawacki
Graduate School of Business Administration
University of Colorado and
Management Technology Group, Inc.

Irwin
McGraw-Hill

Boston   Burr Ridge, IL   Dubuque, IA   Madison, WI   New York   San Francisco   St. Louis
Bangkok   Bogotá   Caracas   Lisbon   London   Madrid
Mexico City   Milan   New Delhi   Seoul   Singapore   Sydney   Taipei   Toronto

McGraw-Hill Higher Education

A Division of The **McGraw-Hill** Companies

ORGANIZATION DEVELOPMENT AND TRANSFORMATION:
MANAGING EFFECTIVE CHANGE

This book is printed on acid-free paper.

1 2 3 4 5 6 7 8 9 0 FGR/FGR 9 0 9 8 7 6 5 4 3 2 1 0 9

ISBN 0-256-24116-3

Vice president/Editor-in-chief: *Michael W. Junior*
Publisher: *Craig S. Beytien*
Senior sponsoring editor: *John E. Biernat*
Editorial coordinator: *Erin Riley*
Marketing manager: *Kenyetta Giles Haynes*
Project manager: *Kimberly Moranda*
Manager, new book production: *Melonie Salvati*
Freelance design coordinator: *Mary Christianson*
Compositor: *Electronic Publishing Services, Inc.*
Typeface: *10.5/12 Bembo*
Printer: *Quebecor Printing Book Group/Fairfield*

Library of Congress Cataloging-in-Publication Data

Organization development and transformation : managing effective change / edited by Wendell L. French, Cecil H. Bell, Jr., Robert A. Zawacki. — 5th ed.
  p. cm.
  Includes index.
  ISBN 0-256-24116-3
  1. Organizational change.   I. French, Wendell L., 1923–
II. Bell, Cecil, 1935–   .   III. Zawacki, Robert A.
HD58.8.O724   2000
658.4'06—dc21   99-27906

http://www.mhhe.com

From Wendell to
Andy, Tom, and Amy

From Cecil to
Dianne

From Bob to
Jimmie

Organization development is an organizational improvement strategy that uses behavioral science principles and practices to increase individual and organizational effectiveness. The field of organization development (or OD as it is called) continues to gain practitioners, clients, theorists, researchers, and new technologies. It is applied in a wide range of settings and has become a preferred strategy for facilitating change in organizations.

What began as isolated experiments for improving organizational dynamics and management practices in the 1950s evolved into the coherent discipline we know today as organization development. And the field of OD continues to evolve. For example, in the 1980s as the pace and scope of environmental changes increased, new theories and techniques were developed to help leaders direct large-scale, systemwide changes. These efforts, called "organizational transformation," (OT) represent a variant of OD in which organizations are transformed in fundamental ways. These transformations often involve paradigm shifts—radical changes in management philosophy, ways of organizing the work, and ways of relating to employees and customers. Organization development and transformation focus on how people *and* organizations and people *in* organizations function, and how to make them function better.

The field of organization development offers a prescription for improving the "goodness of fit" between individuals and organizations and between organizations and environments. Ingredients of that prescription include a focus on the organization's culture and processes; guidelines for designing and implementing action programs; conceptualizing the organization and its environment in system theory terms; and creating change processes that empower individuals through involvement, participation, and commitment.

OD is the applied domain of organizational psychology and sociology. It is the engineering side of the organizational sciences. Planned change involves common sense; hard work applied diligently over time; a systematic and goal-oriented approach; and valid knowledge about organizational dynamics and how to change them. The valid knowledge comes from basic and applied behavioral science. The total prescription comes from four decades of practice in discovering what works in organizations and why.

The aim of organization development and transformation is to help individuals and organizations function better in today's increasingly interdependent, complex, and competitive world. The aim of this book is to present a clear, comprehensive picture of organization development and transformation so that you may acquire the knowledge and skill to manage change more effectively.

We wish to thank the authors whose writings we have included. We acknowledge our debt to the hundreds of talented contributors to the field of OD.

Wendell L. French
Cecil H. Bell, Jr.
Robert A. Zawacki

What Is Organization Development

Organization development (OD) is a powerful set of concepts and techniques for improving organizational effectiveness and individual well-being that had its genesis in the behavioral sciences and was tested in the laboratory of real-world organizations. OD addresses the opportunities and problems involved in managing human dynamics in organizations. It offers solutions that have been shown to work. Organization development consists of intervention techniques, theories, principles, and values that show how to take charge of planned change efforts and achieve success.

What Is Organization Transformation

Organization transformation (OT) is a recent extension of organization development that seeks to create massive changes in an organization's structures, processes, culture, and orientation to its environment. Organization transformation is the application of behavioral science theory and practice to effect large-scale, paradigm-shifting organizational change. An organizational transformation usually results in totally new paradigms or models for organizing and performing work. Organization transformation has been referred to as "second-generation organization development." The demands on today's organizations for constant change and adaptation are so great that new behavioral science responses were required. OT represents one of those responses. But simultaneously improving organizational effectiveness and individual well-being is still the goal. Both OD and OT are means to accomplish that goal.

Why Study Organization Development

Understanding what OD is and how it is practiced is important for several reasons. **First,** it works. Organization development programs can improve individual performance, create better morale, and increase organizational profitability. Many chronic problems or organizations can be cured by OD techniques.

Second, the use of organization development is growing. The approach and methods of OD are applied throughout the gamut of today's organizations and industries. Manufacturing and service companies, high-technology and low-technology organizations, and public-and private-sector institutions all have sponsored successful OD programs.

Third, it is now recognized that the most important assets of organizations are human assets—the men and women who produce the goods and make the decisions. Finding ways to protect, enhance, and mobilize human assets doesn't just make good human-relations sense, it makes good economic sense. OD offers a variety of methods to strengthen the human side of organizations to the benefit of both the individual and the organization.

Fourth, OD is a critical managerial tool. We believe that the concepts and techniques of organization development will soon be as much a part of the well-trained manager's repertoire as knowledge of accounting, marketing, and finance. We predict that a significant period of transition lies just ahead in which the charter and boundaries of organization development will be expanded; specifically, the practice of OD will be incorporated within the art and science of management. Organization development offers a set of generic tools available to any managers and members of organizations who want to improve goal achievement. Today's managers manage change, and OD is a prescription for managing change. Managers need to know what OD is and how to use it. A good understanding or organization development has great practical value for present and future managers and leaders.

This collection of readings tells the story of OD's and OT's theory, practice, and research foundations. Articles by prominent authors in the field present a comprehensive portrait that we hope will be useful to managers, students of organizational dynamics, and professionals in the fields of human resource management and organization development and transformation.

The field of organization development is fun and exciting. We hope this anthology will convey some of that sense of excitement.

This fifth edition differs substantially from its predecessors. We added 16 new articles while retaining 30 articles from previous editions. This reflects our goal of presenting both classic statements about the field and recent developments showing where the field is going. This edition adds articles on empowerment, trust, creating transformational change, "centers of excellence," and the like. The field of organization development and transformation is evolving, and this anthology evolves with it.

Part I, Mapping the Territory, provides an introduction and overview of the field. Early definitions and descriptions of organization development along with an historical look at the origins of OD begin the story. Next, the concepts of change and changing are examined, followed by a description of changes taking place in the field in the mid-1980s. A comprehensive review of organization development and organization transformation presents a state-of-the-art description of theory and practice. Finally, an examination of the research on OD concludes that organization development techniques produce positive results in most situations.

Part II, Foundations of Organization Development and Transformation, shows some of the theoretical and practice underpinnings of the field. Articles on intervention theory, intergroup problems in organizations, and organizational culture focus on important aspects of OD. A new article on the principles of sociotechnical systems theory explains how this major approach to organizational change works.

Most of the actual work in organization development consists of structuring sets of activities, called "interventions," so that learning and change take place.

The interventions in **Part III, Fundamental Interventions,** have been around for a long time; are designed to improve diagnosis, role clarification, intergroup relations, decision making, planning procedures, and the like; and have demonstrated their effectiveness.

The interventions in **Part IV, Cutting-Edge Change Strategies,** are of more recent vintage and address problems posed by the information age with its turbulent environment and rapid, chaotic change. This section presents techniques for self-directed teams, organizational and individual learning, appreciative inquiry, visioning alternative futures, and effecting large-scale, systemwide change. These interventions reflect the continuing evolution of OD and OT; and they work.

Part V, Implementation Guidelines and Issues, offers suggestions for increasing the chances that consultants and clients will be successful in their change programs. What are the ingredients of successful OD and OT consulting? What are the critical success factors in managing long-term change projects? These questions are answered in this section. We have added new articles on trust, creating readiness for change, power, and facilitating transformational change.

We always enjoy creating the section of the book that reports on actual case studies and the varieties of settings where OD can be used. In **Part VI, Examples and Special Situations,** we present three informative cases and several articles about the relevance of OD for entrepreneurial firms and for turnaround situations.

Part VII, Challenges and Opportunities for the Future, completes the anthology. We selected articles on empowerment, ethics, managing discontinuous change, implementing effective human resource practices, the search for "community" in organizations, and a proposed agenda for OD in the near-term future. There are plenty of challenges and opportunities for the field, but if the past is a good predictor of the future, new theories and techniques will be developed, tested, and proven—and these will show up in future editions of this book.

The need for organization development and transformation has never been greater. We believe organization development offers a way to achieve organizational and individual effectiveness in a rapidly changing world. Again, we express our thanks to the authors of these articles for their insights. The "present" is an exciting time, and organization development is an exciting field.

CONTENTS

I   MAPPING THE TERRITORY

The subject matter of this book is organization development and transformation, a relatively specific kind of planned change effort aimed at helping members of organizations do the things they want to do—better. We have attempted to fashion a systematic examination of organization development to help the reader determine the applicability, utility, and viability of this particular approach as a means of organization improvement.

Organization development (OD) focuses primarily on the human and social aspects of organizations; it views organizational behavior as consisting essentially of the coordinated goal-directed activities of a number of people. Other possible approaches to understanding and intervening in organizations exist—one can focus exclusively on organization structure and design, technology and task design, or organization-environment congruence, for example. Organization development programs attend to these issues, but the principal emphasis is on *all* the human aspects of the organization conceived as a social system.

In Part I we begin at the beginning—mapping the territory of organization development and transformation. What is OD? What characteristics differentiate OD from other improvement programs? What are some of the varieties of OD and organization transformation (OT)?

Toward a Definition of Organization Development

The words *organization development* refer to something about organizations and developing them. According to Edgar Schein, "An organization is the planned coordination of the activities of a number of people for the achievement of some common explicit purpose or goal, through division of labor and function, and through a hierarchy of authority and responsibility."[1] Organizations are social systems possessing characteristics described by Schein, and OD efforts are directed toward organizations or major subparts of them.

Development is the act, process, result, or state of being developed—which, in turn, means to advance, to promote the growth of, to evolve the possibilities of, to further, to improve, or to enhance *something*. Two elements of this definition seem important: first, development may be an act, process, or end state; second, development refers to "bettering" something.

Combining these words suggests that organization development is the act, process, or result of furthering, advancing, or promoting the growth of an organization. According to these definitions, organization development is anything done to "better" an organization. But this definition is too broad and all-inclusive. It can refer to almost anything done in an organizational context that enhances the organization—hiring a person with needed skills, firing an incompetent, merging with another organization, installing a computer, removing a computer, buying a new plant, and so on. This definition serves neither to identify and specify nor to delimit (perhaps something done to "worsen" an organization would be ruled out). The term *organization development* must be given added meaning, must refer to something more specific, if productive discourse on the subject is desired.

Another way of defining organization development is to examine the following definitions, which have been suggested in the early OD literature:

Organization development is an effort (1) *planned,* (2) *organizationwide,* and (3) *managed* from the *top,* to (4) *increase organization effectiveness* and *health* through (5) *planned interventions* in the organization's "processes," using *behavioral-science* knowledge.[2]

Organization development (OD) is a response to change, a complex educational strategy intended to change the beliefs, attitudes, values, and structure of organizations so that they can better adapt to new technologies, markets, and challenges, and the dizzying rate of change itself.[3]

Organization development is the strengthening of those human processes in organizations which improve the functioning of the organic system so as to achieve its objectives.[4]

Organization renewal is the process of initiating, creating, and confronting needed changes so as to make it possible for organizations to become or remain viable, to adapt to new conditions, to solve problems, to learn from experiences, and to move toward greater organizational maturity.[5]

OD can be defined as a planned and sustained effort to apply behavioral science for system improvement, using reflexive, self-analytic methods.[6]

Organization development is a process of planned change—change of an organization's culture from one which avoids an examination of social processes (especially decision making, planning, and communication) to one which institutionalizes and legitimizes this examination.[7]

In the behavioral science, and perhaps ideal, sense of the term, *organization development is a long-range effort to improve an organization's problem-solving and renewal processes, particularly through a more effective and collaborative management of organization culture—with special emphasis on the culture of formal work teams—with the assistance of a change agent, or catalyst, and the use of the theory and technology of applied behavioral science, including action research.*[8] [Italics in the original.]

Analysis of these definitions suggests that organization development is *not* just "anything done to better an organization"; it is a particular kind of change process designed to bring about a particular kind of end result. In Figure 1 the definitions are dissected and put into an analytic framework to discover the particular kind of change processes and the particular kind of end results desired.

Examination of Figure 1 suggests the following conclusion. Organization development (OD) is a prescription for a process of planned change in organizations in which the key prescriptive elements relate to (1) the nature of the effort or program (it is a long-range, planned, systemwide process); (2) the nature of the change activities (they utilize behavioral science interventions of an educational, reflexive, self-examining, learn-to-do-it-yourself nature); (3) the targets of the change activities (they are directed toward the human and social processes of organizations, specifically individuals' beliefs, attitudes, and values, the culture and processes of work groups—viewed as basic building blocks of the organization—and the processes and culture of the total organization); and (4) the desired outcomes of the change activities (the goals are *needed changes* in the targets of the interventions that cause the organization to be better able to adapt, cope, solve its problems, and renew itself). Organization development thus represents a unique strategy for system change, a strategy largely based in the theory and research of the behavioral sciences, and a strategy having a substantial prescriptive character. Organization development is thus a normative discipline; it prescribes how planned change in organizations should be approached and carried out if organization improvement is to be obtained.

In summary, organization development is a process of planned system change that attempts to make organizations (viewed as social-technical systems) better able to attain their short- and long-term objectives. This is achieved by teaching the organization members to manage their organization processes, structures, and culture more effectively. Facts, concepts, and theory from the behavioral sciences are utilized to fashion both the process and the content of interventions. A basic belief of OD theorists and practitioners is that for effective, lasting change to take place, the system members must grow in the competence to master their own fates.

Let us examine in detail some of the distinguishing characteristics of OD.

Distinguishing Characteristics of Organization Development

Perusal of the many descriptions and definitions of organization development in the literature leads to the conclusion that most authors believe OD is a unique change strategy possessing the characteristics described in this section. Two of us (French and Bell) have been concerned with the issue of identifying and specifying the nature of organization development for some time now. In an earlier publication we stated:

> We see eight characteristics that we think differentiate organization development interventions from more traditional interventions:
>
> 1. An emphasis, although not exclusively so, on group and organizational processes in contrast to substantive content.
> 2. An emphasis on the work team as the key unit for learning more effective modes of organizational behavior.
> 3. An emphasis on the collaborative management of work-team culture.

FIGURE 1

An analysis of selected definitions of organization development

Components of the Organization Development Process

Author	Nature and Scope of the Effort	Nature of Activities/Interventions	Targets of Interaction/Activities	Knowledge Base	Desired Goals, Outcomes, or End States of Organization Development Effort
Beckard	Planned. Organizationwide. Managed from the top.	Planned interventions in the organization's "processes."	Total organization. Organization's "processes."	Behavioral science knowledge.	Increased organization effectiveness and health.
Bennis	Complex educational strategy. A response to change.	Educational. Change-oriented.	Beliefs, attitudes, values, and structures of organizations.		Better ability to adapt to new technologies, markets, and challenges, and the dizzying rate of change itself.
Gordon Lippitt (on OD)		Designed to strengthen human processes in organizations.	Those human processes in organizations that improve the organic system.		Enable the organization to achieve its objectives (through improved functioning of the organic system).
Gordon Lippitt (on organization renewal)	A process.	A process of initiating, creating, and confronting needed changes.	[Implied] total organization.		Enhance the ability of the organization to: Become or remain viable. Adapt to new conditions. Solve problems. Learn from experience. Move toward greater organizational maturity.

Schmuck and Miles	A planned and sustained effort.	Apply behavioral science for system improvement. Using reflexive, self-analytic methods.	Total system (organization).	Behavioral science.	System improvement. [implied] continued self-analysis and reflection.
Burke and Hornstein	A process of planned change.	Change-oriented and self-examining oriented; specifically change of an organization's culture from one which avoids an examination of social processes in organization ...to one which institutionalizes and legitimizes this examination.	The organization's culture and the social processes in organization, especially decision making, planning, and communication.		[Self-examination] of social processes in organization, especially decision making, planning, and communication.
French and Bell	A long-range effort.	Designed to bring about a more effective and collaborative management of organization culture; using assistance of change agent, or catalyst.	Organization culture. Culture of formal work teams. Organization's problem-solving and renewal processes.	The theory and technology of applied behavioral science, including action research.	Improve an organization's problem-solving and renewal processes.

4. An emphasis on the management of the culture of the total system.
5. Attention to the management of system ramifications.
6. The use of the action research model.
7. The use of a behavioral scientist-change agent, sometimes referred to as a "catalyst" or "facilitator."
8. A view of the change effort as an ongoing process.

Another characteristic, number 9, a primary emphasis on human and social relationships, does not necessarily differentiate OD from other change efforts, but it is nevertheless an important feature.[9]

While we still believe these characteristics describe organization development efforts, let us add another means of identifying OD.

An Organization Development Program Is a Long-Range, Planned, and Sustained Effort That Unfolds According to a Strategy

The key elements here are long range, planned and sustained, and strategy. There is a long-range time perspective on the part of both the client system and the consultant in OD programs. Both parties envision an ongoing relationship of one, two, or more years together if things go well in the program. A one-shot intervention into the system is thus not organization development according to this criterion, even though the intervention may be one that is used in OD efforts. Thus, the dozens of case studies reporting a three-day or week-long T-group (T for training) experience for system members do not constitute OD as we see it, if the T-group experience was the only intervention of the program.

The reasons for OD practitioners and theorists conceptualizing OD programs in long-range terms are several. First, changing a system's culture and processes is a difficult, complicated, and long-term matter if lasting change is to be effected. OD programs envision that the system members become better able to manage their culture and processes in problem-solving and self-renewing ways. Such complex new learning takes time. Second, the assumption is made that organizational problems are multifaceted and complex. One-shot interventions probably cannot solve such problems, and they most assuredly cannot teach the client system to solve them in such a short time period.

OD programs are planned and sustained efforts. They are planned, not accidental—they represent a deliberate entry of either an OD consultant or OD activities into the client system. And they are sustained. The assumption is made that follow-up and sustained effort and energy are needed in order to solve organization problems. These points are fairly straightforward. There is, however, a related point that is a source of some confusion. When some good management practices are taking place in an organization without an OD program—for example, a manager has worked out effective ways to manage team and intergroup culture and processes—is that organization development? We do not think so. OD practitioners try to inculcate good management practices in organizations; that is, they try to help organization members learn to manage themselves and others better. But many managers and many organizations are competently managing their affairs without help from organization development consultants and OD programs; what they are doing would not be called OD even though they may be using some techniques found in the OD technology. OD practitioners did not invent good management practices; OD practitioners are not the sole source for learning good management practices; and finally, the term *organization development* is not synonymous with the term *good management*.

Organization development programs unfold according to a strategy. A part of the planned nature of OD programs almost always involves an overall strategy even though the strategy may be only dimly obvious and articulable, and even though the strategy may emerge and change shape over time. (From our experience, the more viable OD efforts have a fairly clear and openly articulated strategy.) Consultants and clients develop overall goals and paths to goals in organization development programs, and these guide the programmatic activities. It is preferable and usual for the strategy to be developed out of the diagnosed problems and opportunities of the client system, the client system's desires and capabilities, and the consultant's capabilities and insights into client system needs.

The Organization Development Consultant Establishes a Unique Relationship with Client System Members

Probably the most fundamental differences between organization development programs and other organization improvement programs are found in the role and behavior of the consultant vis-à-vis the client system. In OD the consultant seeks and maintains a collaborative relationship of relative equality with the organization members. Collaboration means "to labor together"—essentially it implies that the consultant does not do all the work while the client system passively waits for solutions to its problems; and it means that the client system does not do all the work while the consultant is a disinterested observer. In organization development, consultant and client co-labor.

A second distinguishing feature of the consultant-client relationship is that it is one of relative equality—the two parties come together as relative equals, each possessing knowledge and skills different from but needed by the other. The client group is encouraged to critique the consultant's program and his or her effectiveness in terms of meeting client system needs and wants. In OD the consultant's role is generally that of a facilitator, not an expert on matters of content; the consultant acts primarily as a question-asker, and secondarily as an answer-giver.

The consultant's role is often described as nondirective and that is partially true, but the rationale behind this nondirective posture is less well understood. The OD consultant role rests on three beliefs. The first belief is simply an affirmation of the efficacy of division of labor and responsibility: let the consultant be responsible for doing what he or she does best (structuring activities designed to solve certain problems); and let the client system do what it does best (bring to bear its special knowledge and expertise on the problem and alternative solutions). The second belief is derived from the question: Where is the best solution to this problem likely to be found? In situations where the consultant is in an expert role, the answer to the question is that the best solution is in the consultant's head due to that person's education, experience, and expertise. Both clients and consultant believe this. In organization development situations where the consultant is playing an enabling and facilitating role, the answer is that the best solution is in the heads of the client members and the challenge is to structure situations to allow it to become known. The third belief is that the responsibility for changing something rests ultimately in the client system members, not in the consultant. Therefore the members of the client system must "own" the problem and the solution, and that is best done when they generate both the problems and the solutions. This belief no doubt rests on Lewin's conceptualization of "own" and "induced" forces. Lewin believed, and demonstrated, that an individual's own forces toward a particular behavior were more powerful in determining the behavior than forces/motives/pushes induced by some outside agent.

The consultant is both expert and directive on matters relating to the best ways to facilitate/enable the client group to approach, diagnose, and solve its problems. In organization development, it is this expertise that the clients expect from the consultant—the expertise to offer the clients effective *ways* to work on problems, not *answers* to problems.

The Nature of the Intervention Activities Differentiates OD from Other Improvement Strategies

OD consultants fashion, conduct, or cause to happen, interventions—structured sets of activities and events in the life of the organization designed to achieve certain outcomes. As indicated in Figure 1, the nature of these interventions is that they are reflective, self-analytical, self-examining, proactive, diagnostically oriented, and action oriented. Further, they focus on the organization culture and its human processes. OD consultants try to inculcate diagnostic skills, self-analytical skills, and reflexive skills in organization members, based on the belief that the organization's members must be able to diagnose situations accurately in order to arrive at successful solutions. But there are several additional beliefs hidden in this statement. Diagnosis and self-reflection are necessary skills to have for problem solution—that is a belief of OD consultants. But *who* should possess those skills? "The client system members," answer OD consultants; "me," answer expert consultants. This is a key difference in the OD prescription. Another belief involved here is that both the problems and the solutions to the problems abound in the client system members. Teaching the client system to diagnose and solve problems and take corrective actions is the goal of the OD consultant. The overriding goal is that the client system members learn to do it themselves. This tenet derives from nondirective therapy notions suggesting that responsibility for improvement and change rests in the individual (organization) that needs to change, not some outside agent. This is supported by most discussions of normalcy and maturity in psychotherapy that include the patient's ability to solve problems, adapt effectively, and cope effectively as criteria for a healthy organism. Many authors, including Gordon Lippitt, speak of the organization "learning from experience," and the OD literature suggests that "learning how to learn" is a desired outcome of OD interventions. This is what is being discussed: that the client system become expert in self-examination, diagnosis, and corrective action taking.

Planning, problem solving, and self-renewal are also mentioned as important processes for the client system to be reflexive about. The same overriding goal applies here: the client system members must learn to manage these processes effectively by themselves. There is thus a unique character to the nature of OD interventions: the intent that the client system becomes proficient in solving its own problems—present and future—*by itself.* The ancient Chinese proverb seems to describe the underlying rationale: Give a man a fish, and you have given him a meal; teach a man to fish, and you have given him a livelihood.

The Targets of OD Interventions Differentiate OD from Other Improvement Strategies

The OD prescription calls for certain configurations of people as targets of OD interventions—intact work groups, two or more work-related groups, subsystems of organizations, and total organizations. Katz and Kahn speak of "role sets," the offices (positions) and people an individual interacts with while performing role-relevant behavior in an organization. They state:

> Each member of an organization is directly associated with a relatively small number of others, usually the occupants of offices adjacent to his in the work-flow structure or in the hierarchy of authority. They constitute his role set and typically include his immediate supervisor (and perhaps his supervisor's immediate superior), his subordinates, and certain members of his own or other departments with whom he must work closely. These offices are defined into his role set by virtue of the work-flow, technology, and authority structure of the organization.[10]

Many of an individual's values, norms, and perceptions of organization reality are derived from contact with role-set members. Role-enactment problems derive from interaction with role-set members. A person's immediate work group, immediate superior, and immediate subordinates are immensely important factors for an individual's effectiveness in an organization. OD interventions concentrate on work-relevant constellations of people in the belief that these groups have inherent in them considerable power to determine individual and group behavior and also contain many of the sources of organizational problems and opportunities.

What goes on *between* units is also of vital importance in organizational effectiveness. OD goes beyond intact work teams and also focuses on enhancing key interdependencies across units and levels. For example, data are typically collected about the degree of cooperation versus dysfunctional competition between the various units, and identified problems are then worked on with members of the relevant groups present. Thus intergroup configurations are a second major target of OD interventions.

A third target of OD interventions is the organization's processes and culture. In a sense, OD is a comprehensive long-term effort to collaboratively manage the culture of an organization (since processes can be considered part of organization culture). As shown in Figure 1, some of the authors mention culture and some mention human and social processes as the targets of OD interventions. Problem-solving, planning, self-renewal, decision-making, and communications processes are identified as important processes. This focus on culture and processes is simply a part of the bet/hypothesis/belief system that OD consultants have: culture and processes are important strategic leverage points in an organization for bringing about organization improvement and change. Other consultants and practitioners make different bets on the best strategic leverage points—the technology of the organization, the strategy of the organization, its design, and so forth. OD consultants, because they are working with a behavioral science knowledge base, focus on culture, structure and processes. And the OD prescription suggests that these targets are important ingredients in the process of planned organizational change.

OD Consultants Utilize a Behavioral Science Base

This is a characteristic of the practice of OD, but it is shared by many different improvement strategies. We will not discuss this point extensively. Perhaps it is sufficient to say that the behavioral science knowledge base of the practice of OD contributes to its distinctive gestalt. OD is an applied field in which theories, concepts, and practices from sociology, psychology, social psychology, education, economics, psychiatry, and management are brought to bear on real organizational problems.

The Desired Outcomes of OD Are Distinctive in Nature

The desired outcomes of OD efforts are both similar to other improvement strategies, and different from other improvement strategies. OD programs and efforts are designed to produce organizational effectiveness and health, better system functioning, greater ability to achieve objectives, and so forth, as shown in some of the definitions in Figure 1. But some of the definitions point to additional desired outcomes: outcomes relating to a changed organization culture, to changed processes (especially renewal and adaptation processes) and to the establishing of norms of continual self-study and proaction.

Michael Beer lists the aims of OD as "(1) enhancing congruence between organizational structure, processes, strategy, people, and culture; (2) developing new and creative organizational solutions; and (3) developing the organization's self-renewing capacity."[11] It is these self-renewal outcomes that seem particularly distinctive in the OD process.

Summary of the Distinctive Features of Organization Development

We believe that organization development is a particular kind of organization improvement strategy possessing distinguishing characteristics as follows:

1. An OD program is a long-range, planned, and sustained effort that is based on an overall strategy.
2. A consultant (one or more) is used, and that consultant establishes a unique relationship with the client system: the consultant seeks and maintains a collaborative relationship of relative equality with the organization members.

3. OD interventions are distinctive in their nature: they are reflexive, self-analytical, self-skill-building in nature. Another way of saying this is that a pervasive use of a collaborative action-research model underlies most OD interventions.

4. OD interventions assume that work-related groups of individuals and work-related intergroup configurations are more important leverage points for change than are other configurations; they also assume that organization culture and organizational processes are strategic leverage points for effecting organizational change.

5. OD utilizes a behavioral science base.

6. The desired outcomes of organizational effectiveness and health are supplemented in OD with the goal that organization culture and processes be changed in order that the organization continue to be reflexive and self-examining.

This overview provides a broad outline of the field. The rest of the book will expand on these themes, will add details and implications, and will make clearer what organization development is and what it can do.

The Emergence of Organization Transformation (OT)

The preceding discussion describes classical organization development, which began in the mid-1950s and continues to the present. Over the years the practice of OD has evolved and matured, clarifying its values, theories, methods, and interventions, as well as adding new values, theories, and so forth. Beginning in the 1980s, articles and books appeared that described change programs designed to cause large-scale, radical, and fundamental changes in organizations. These paradigm-shifting changes were referred to as "organization transformation" or "organizational transformation." Some authors believe OT is an extension of OD; others believe OT represents a new discipline in its own right. It is too early to categorize organization transformation; for now, we see it as an extension of OD. Some forces leading to the emergence of OT can be identified, however.

In the 1960s and 1970s OD focused on improving the internal workings of organizations through the use of role clarification, improved communication, team building, intergroup team building, and the like. The organization was conceptualized as an open system in interaction with its environment, but primary attention was directed toward making the parts and the whole function better. In the 1970s new work arrangements were tested in the form of sociotechnical systems theory experiments and quality of work life experiments. Sociotechnical systems theory (STS) postulates that an organization is comprised of both a social system and a technical system, and that these two systems must be jointly optimized for best results.[12] One result of STS experimentation was the discovery that "autonomous work groups" (similar to today's self-managed teams and self-directed teams) constituted a better working arrangement than the usual isolated individuals with a boss to tell them what to do. This was an important discovery, and autonomous work groups and self-managed teams proliferated in a variety of settings. Quality of work life experiments led to similar discoveries about the value of self-directed teams, and they additionally produced new ways for labor and management to work together to lessen adversarial relations.[13] These experiments and others in work redesign and reorganization called into question old paradigms (beliefs and assumptions) about working arrangements and authority relations in organizations.

In the 1980s strategic management achieved prominence in managerial thinking, and attention was directed toward the fit between the environment with its "threats" and "opportunities" and the organization with its "strengths" and "weaknesses." Considerable effort was directed toward defining the mission, purpose, vision, and strategy of organizations. OD practitioners developed interventions to facilitate strategic management by the organization's executives. It was soon realized that a clear, articulated vision was a powerful component of organizational effectiveness.

Also in the 1980s the demands on organizations intensified: competition increased; customers demanded better products and services; the total quality movement created winners and losers; information technology exploded; economic and political changes occurred. Organizations had to change—fast—to survive. The old ways of doing things were no longer good enough; the old belief systems were no longer adequate. Organizations had to be transformed, not just "tweaked." Paradigms had to be changed, not just adjusted. All these conditions and more gave rise to explorations in the theory and practice of organization transformation.

Porras and Silvers state in Reading 5: "Planned change interventions can be divided into two general types. The first comprises the more traditional approach, Organization Development (OD), which until recently was synonymous with the term *planned change*. The second, Organization Transformation (OT), is the cutting edge of planned change and may be called 'second generation OD.'" These authors emphasize the importance of "vision," "guiding beliefs and principles," "purpose," and "mission" as major features of OT interventions.

Cummings and Worley describe OT as follows:

> Organization transformations can occur in response to or in anticipation of major changes in the organization's environment or technology. In addition, these changes are often associated with significant alterations in the firm's business strategy, which, in turn, may require modifying corporate culture as well as internal structures and processes to support the new direction. Such fundamental change entails a new paradigm for organizing and managing organizations. It involves qualitatively different ways of perceiving, thinking, and behaving in organizations.[14]

They suggest three interventions to facilitate organization transformations: culture change, strategic change, and self-designing organizations.

Clearly the phenomenon of organization transformation is important, real, and here to stay. The task for OD and OT practitioners is to develop behavioral science theories, models, practices, and interventions to facilitate the transformations.

Readings in Part I

The readings in this part range from early statements about the nature and characteristics of organization development to recent articles describing both OD and organization transformation.

The first selection is by Richard Beckhard, an early OD practitioner and theorist. Beckhard asks and answers the question: What is organization development? His operational definition, operational goals of OD, and characteristics of OD efforts combine to make this one of the best statements available on what OD is all about. He is pithy, to the point, and right on target. He identifies several distinguishing features about OD that are not found in other organizational change approaches. This selection is taken from his little book titled *Organization Development: Strategies and Models* that appeared in 1969. In that year Addison–Wesley Publishing Company published six little paperback books on OD, all packaged together. These came to be known as "The Addison-Wesley OD Six Pack" among practitioners. Collectively these books defined the field of OD at that time. Other authors and titles in the "Six Pack" were Warren Bennis, *Organization Development: Its Nature, Origins, and Prospects;* Paul Lawrence and Jay Lorsch, *Developing Organizations: Diagnosis and Action;* Edgar Schein, *Process Consultation: Its Role in Organization Development;* Richard Walton, *Interpersonal Peacemaking: Confrontations and Third-Party Consultation;* and Robert Blake and Jane Srygley Mouton, *Building a Dynamic Corporation through Grid Organization Development.*

The roots, birth, and major milestones in the development of the field or organization development are described in the next article. Wendell French has been intrigued with tracing the history of OD for many years. The selection was written by him; it appears in a book on organization development by Wendell French and Cecil Bell.[15] French points to the importance of Kurt Lewin as a prime contributor to events leading up to the emergence of OD, and to four mainstreams of activities as precursors of OD—laboratory training, survey research and feedback, action research, and the sociotechnical and socioclinical approaches of the Tavistock Clinic in England. Early projects and the people involved in them are described, using as source materials both published accounts and extensive correspondence with the individuals who were in the forefront of the new applied behavioral science developments at that time—Robert Blake, Herbert Shepard, Ronald Lippitt, Eva Schindler-Rainman, Richard Beckhard, and others.

An article on the history of OD by Michael McGill, not included in this reader, gives a somewhat different view of early events.[16] McGill goes back to just after World War II to search for the beginnings of OD and, in so doing, finds reason to include the activities, writings, and conceptualizations of Leland Bradford and Neely Gardner as important foundations. Both Bradford and Gardner were engaged in training and development activities in large organizations and conceived the necessity to develop *both* the individual and the organization. Bradford has been intimately involved with most of the applied behavioral science developments in the United States because he was the director of the National Training Laboratory in Group

Development (NTL) from its inception in 1947 to his retirement in 1970. NTL (now the NTL—Institute for Applied Behavioral Science) was both a source of support for the fledgling organization development movement and also a source of most of the OD practitioners.[17]

The article by Robert Chin and Kenneth D. Benne describes three broad general strategies for effecting changes in human systems—the empirical-rational strategy, the normative-reeducative strategy, and the power-coercive strategy. This elegant and erudite essay was written for the book *The Planning of Change,* edited by Warren Bennis, Kenneth Benne, and Robert Chin. The historical development of the three strategies of change is traced in detail and examples of each strategy in operation are given. It is our opinion that organization development rests primarily on a normative-reeducative strategy and secondarily on an empirical-rational strategy. For this reason, understanding the three general strategies for change is important for the OD practitioner as well as for leaders who may be interested in OD efforts in their organizations.

The selection by Marvin Weisbord sets the stage for thinking about organization transformations and how a consultant can help. Weisbord ponders the differences between traditional organization development thinking and practice and the thinking and practice required in a "third-wave" world as described by futurist Alvin Toffler. New times require new paradigms. Weisbord supplies some. His "four useful practices" suggest new ways consultants can facilitate organization transformation. His discussion of the "four-room apartment" provides great insights. These are important issues for leaders, managers, and OD consultants.

The selection by Jerry Porras and Robert Silvers is taken from the *Annual Review of Psychology.* About every four years the latest developments in the field of OD (and now, OT) are summarized by prominent theorists/practitioners in that publication. This article represents the first time that organization transformation was featured. An especially important contribution of this reading is its model of planned change. Organization development and transformation need better theoretical underpinnings, and this article addresses that deficiency. Porras and Silvers present a thorough review of contemporary research and thinking in the field of organization development and transformation.

Robert Golembiewski, Carl Proehl, and David Sink report on a comprehensive review of the OD research literature. The authors analyzed 574 studies conducted over a 35-year period to determine the types of OD programs in use and the effects of those programs. Their results are promising: a wide variety of programs are in use; OD efforts have been directed toward both public sector and private sector organizations; and positive results were found in the vast majority of programs with very few negative effects reported. Reviews such as this are useful for taking stock of where OD is as a field and pointing the way toward needed future research efforts.

These selections should give the reader a good understanding of what organization development and transformation are all about. Subsequent sections of the book will develop these themes in detail.

Endnotes

1. Edgar H. Schein, *Organizational Psychology,* 3rd ed. (Englewood Cliffs, N.J.: Prentice Hall, 1980), p. 15.

2. Richard Beckhard, *Organization Development: Strategies and Models* (Reading, Mass.: Addison-Wesley Publishing, 1969), p. 9.

3. Warren G. Bennis, *Organization Development: Its Nature, Origins, and Prospects* (Reading, Mass.: Addison-Wesley Publishing, 1969), p. 2.

4. Gordon L. Lippitt, *Organization Renewal* (New York: Appleton-Century-Crofts, 1969), p. 1.

5. Ibid., p. 4.

6. Richard Schmuck and Matthew Miles, *Organization Development in Schools* (Palo Alto, Calif.; National Press Books, 1971), p. 2.

7. Warner Burke and Harvey A. Hornstein, *The Social Technology of Organization Development* (Fairfax, Va.: Learning Resources Corp., 1972), p. xi.

8. Wendell L. French and Cecil H. Bell, Jr., *Organization Development,* 2nd ed. (Englewood Cliffs, N.J.: Prentice Hall, 1978), p. 14.

9. Ibid., p. 18.

10. Daniel Katz and Robert L. Kahn, *The Social Psychology of Organizations* (New York: John Wiley & Sons, 1966), p. 174.

11. Michael Beer, *Organization Change and Development* (Santa Monica, Calif.: Goodyear Publishing, 1980), p. 10.

12. E. Trist and K. Bamforth, "Some Social and Psychological Consequences of the Longwall Method of Coal-Getting," *Human Relations* 4 (January 1951), pp. 1–38.

13. R. E. Walton, "Quality of Working Life: What Is It?" *Sloan Management Review,* Fall 1973, pp. 11–21.

14. T. G. Cummings and C. G. Worley, *Organization Development and Change,* 5th ed. (Minneapolis, Minn.: West Publishing Co., 1993), p. 520.

15. Wendell L. French and Cecil H. Bell, Jr., *Organization Development: Behavioral Science Interventions for Organizational Improvement,* 6th ed. (Upper Saddle River, N.J.: Prentice Hall, 1999).

16. Michael E. McGill, "The Evolution of Organization Development: 1947–1960," *Public Administration Review,* March–April 1974, pp. 98–105.

17. Leland P. Bradford, *National Training Laboratories—Its History: 1947-1970.* Copyright 1974 by Leland P. Bradford, Bethel, Maine.

READING 1
WHAT IS ORGANIZATION DEVELOPMENT?

Richard Beckhard

Definition. Organization development is an effort (1) *planned,* (2) *organizationwide,* and (3) *managed* from the *top,* to (4) increase *organization effectiveness* and *health* through (5) *planned interventions in* the organization's "processes," using *behavioral-science* knowledge.

1. It is a *planned change* effort.

An OD program involves a systematic diagnosis of the organization, the development of a strategic plan for improvement, and the mobilization of resources to carry out the effort.

2. It involves the total *"system."*

An organization development effort is related to a total organization change such as a change in the culture or the reward systems or the total managerial strategy. There may be tactical efforts which work with subparts of the organization but the "system" to be changed is a total, relatively autonomous organization. This is not necessarily a total corporation, or an entire government, but refers to a system which is relatively free to determine its own plans and future within very *general* constraints from the environment.

3. *It is managed from the top.*

In an organization development effort, the top management of the system has a personal investment in the program and its outcomes. They actively participate in the *management* of the effort. This does not mean they must participate in the same *activities* as others, but it does mean that they must have both knowledge and *commitment* to the goals of the program and must actively support the methods used to achieve the goals.

Source: Richard Beckhard, *Organization Development; Strategies and Models,* pp. 9, 10, 14. © 1969 Addison Wesley Longman Inc. Reprinted by permission of Addison Wesley Longman.

4. It is designed to *increase organization effectiveness* and *health.*

To understand the goals of organization development, it is necessary to have some picture of what an "ideal" effective, healthy organization would look like. What would be its characteristics? Numbers of writers and practitioners in the field have proposed definitions which, although they differ in detail, indicate a strong consensus of what a healthy operating organization is. Let me start with my own definition. An effective organization is one in which:

a. The total organization, the significant subparts, and individuals, manage their work against *goals* and *plans* for achievement of these goals.

b. Forms follows function (the problem, or task, or project, determines how the human resources are organized).

c. Decisions are made by and near the sources of information regardless of where these sources are located on the organization chart.

d. The reward system is such that managers and supervisors are rewarded (and punished) comparably for:
   Short-term profit or production performance.
   Growth and development of their subordinates.
   Creating a viable working group.

e. Communication laterally and vertically is *relatively* undistorted. People are generally open and confronting. They share all the relevant facts including feelings.

f. There is a minimum amount of inappropriate win/lose activities between individuals and groups. Constant effort exists at all levels to treat conflict, and conflict situations, as *problems* subject to problem-solving methods.

g. There is high "conflict" (clash of ideas) about tasks and projects, and relatively little energy spent in clashing over *interpersonal* difficulties because they have been generally worked through.

h. The organization and its parts see themselves as interacting with each other *and* with a *larger* environment. The organization is an "open system."

i. There is a shared value, and management strategy to support it, of trying to help each person (or unit) in the organization maintain his (or its) integrity and uniqueness in an interdependent environment.

j. The organization and its members operate in an "action-research" way. General practice is to build in *feedback mechanisms* so that individuals and groups can learn from their own experience.

Another definition is found in John Gardner's set of rules for an effective organization. He describes an effective organization as one which is *self-renewing* and then lists the rules:

The *first rule* is that the organization must have an effective program for the recruitment and development of talent.

The *second rule* for the organization capable of continuous renewal is that it must be a hospital environment for the individual.

The *third rule* is that the organization must have built-in provisions for self-criticism.

The *fourth rule* is that there must be fluidity in the internal structure.

The *fifth rule* is that the organization must have some means of combating the process by which men become prisoners of their procedures.[1]

Edgar Schein defines organization effectiveness in relation to what he calls "the adaptive coping cycle," that is, an organization that can effectively adapt and cope with the changes in its environment. Specifically, he says:

The sequence of activities or processes which begins with some change in the internal or external environment and ends with a more adaptive, dynamic equilibrium for dealing with the change, is the organization's "adaptive coping cycle." If we identify the various stages or processes of this cycle, we shall also be able to identify the points where organizations typically may fail to cope adequately and where, therefore, consultants and researchers have been able in a variety of ways to help increase organization effectiveness.[2]

The organization conditions necessary for effective coping, according to Schein, are:

The ability to take in and communicate information reliably and validly.

Internal flexibility and creativity to make the changes which are demanded by the information obtained (including structural flexibility).

Integration and commitment to the goals of the organization from which comes the willingness to change.

An internal climate of support and freedom from threat, since being threatened undermines good communication, reduces flexibility, and stimulates self-protection rather than concern for the total system.

Miles et al. (1966) define the healthy organization in three broad areas—those concerned with task accomplishment, those concerned with internal integration, and those involving mutual adaptation of the organization and its environment. The following dimensional conditions are listed for each area:

In the task-accomplishment area, a healthy organization would be one with (1) reasonably clear, accepted, achievable and appropriate goals; (2) relatively understood communications flow; (3) optimal power equalization.

In the area of internal integration, a healthy organization would be one with (4) resource utilization and individuals' *good fit* between personal disposition and role demands; (5) a reasonable degree of cohesiveness and "organization identity," clear and attractive enough so that persons feel actively connected to it; (6) high morale. In order to have growth and active changefulness, a healthy organization would be one with innovativeness, autonomy, adaptation, and problem-solving adequacy.[3]

Lou Morse, in his recent thesis on organization development, writes that:

> The commonality of goals are cooperative group relations, consensus, integration, and commitment to the goals of the organization (task accomplishment), creativity, authentic behavior, freedom from threat, full utilization of a person's capabilities, and organizational flexibility.[4]

5. Organization development achieves its goals through *planned interventions* using behavior science knowledge.

A strategy is developed of intervening or moving into the existing organization and helping it, in effect, "stop the music," examine its present ways of work, norms, and values, and look at alternative ways of working, or relating, or rewarding. . . . The interventions used draw on the knowledge and technology of the behavioral sciences about such processes as individual motivation, power, communications, perception, cultural norms, problem solving, goal setting, interpersonal relationships, intergroup relationships, and conflict management.

Some Operational Goals in an Organization-Development Effort

To move toward the kind of organization conditions described in the above definitions, OD efforts usually have some of the following operational goals:

1. To develop a self-renewing, *viable system* that can organize in a variety of ways depending on tasks. This means systematic efforts to change and loosen up the way the organization operates, so that it organizes differently depending on the nature of the task. There is movement toward a concept of "form follows function," rather than that *tasks* must *fit* into existing structures.

2. To optimize the effectiveness of both the stable (the basic organization chart) and the temporary systems (the many projects, committees, et cetera, through which much of the organization's work is accomplished) by built-in, *continuous improvement mechanisms.* This means the introduction of procedures for analyzing work tasks and resource distribution, and for building in continuous "feedback" regarding the way a system or subsystem is operating.

3. To move toward *high collaboration* and *low competition* between interdependent units. One of the major obstacles to effective organizations is the amount of dysfunctional energy spent in inappropriate competition—energy that is not, therefore, available for the accomplishment of tasks. If all of the energy that is used by, let's say, manufacturing people disliking or wanting to "get those sales people," or vice versa, were available to improve organization output, productivity would increase tremendously.

4. To create conditions where conflict is brought out and managed. One of the fundamental problems in unhealthy (or less than healthy) organizations is the amount of energy that is dysfunctionally used trying to work around, or avoid, or cover up, conflicts which are inevitable in a complex organization. The goal is to move the organization towards seeing conflict as an inevitable condition and as problems that need to be *worked* before adequate decisions can be made.

5. To reach the point where decisions are made on the basis of information source rather than organizational role. This means the need to move toward a *norm* of the *authority of knowledge* as well as the authority of role. It does not only mean that decisions should be moved down in the organization; it means that the organization manager should determine which is the best source of information (or combination of sources of information) to work a particular problem, and it is there that the decision making should be located.

Endnotes

1. J. W. Gardner, "How to Prevent Organizational Dry
   Rot," *Harper's Magazine,* October 1965.
2. E. H. Schein, *Organizational Psychology* (Englewood
   Cliffs, N.J.: Prentice Hall, 1965.)
3. M. B. Miles et al., "Data Feedback and Organization
   Change in a School System." (Paper given at a
   meeting of the American Sociological Association,
   August 27, 1966.)
4. L. H. Morse, "Task-Centered Organization
   Development." (Master's thesis, Sloan School
   of Management, MIT, June 1968.)

READING 2
A HISTORY OF ORGANIZATION DEVELOPMENT

Wendell L. French
Cecil H. Bell, Jr.

The history of organization development is rich with the contributions of behavioral scientists and practitioners, many of whom are well known, as well as the contributions of many people in client organizations. Even if we were aware of all the significant contributors, which we are not, we could not do justice to the richness of this history in a short essay. Therefore, all we can do is write about what we believe to be the central thrusts of that history, based on our research to date, and hope that the many people who are not mentioned will not be offended by our incompleteness. Our focus will be largely the origins of OD plus some discussion of current trends and the current extent of application.

Systematic organization development activities have a recent history and, to use the analogy of a mangrove tree, have at least four important trunk stems. One trunk stem consists of innovations in applying laboratory training insights to complex organizations. A second major stem is survey research and feedback methodology. Both stems are intertwined with a third, the emergence of action research. Paralleling these stems, and to some extent linked, is a fourth stem—the emergence of the Tavistock sociotechnical and socioclinical approaches. The key actors in these stems interact with each other and are influenced by experiences and concepts from many fields, as we will see.

The Laboratory Training Stem

The T-Group. Laboratory training, essentially unstructured small-group situations in which participants learn from their own actions and the

group's evolving dynamics, began to develop about 1946 from various experiments in using discussion groups to achieve changes in behavior in back-home situations. In particular, an Inter-Group Relations workshop held at the State Teachers College in New Britain, Connecticut, in the summer of 1946 influenced the emergence of laboratory training. This workshop was sponsored by the Connecticut Interracial Commission and the Research Center for Group Dynamics, then at MIT.

The Research Center for Group Dynamics (RCGD) was founded in 1945 under the direction of Kurt Lewin, a prolific theorist, researcher, and practitioner in interpersonal, group, intergroup, and community relationships.[1] Lewin had been recruited to MIT largely through the efforts of Douglas McGregor of the Sloan School of Management, who had convinced MIT President Carl Compton of the wisdom of establishing a center for group dynamics. Lewin's original staff included Marian Radke, Leon Festinger, Ronald Lippitt, and Dorwin Cartwright.[2] Lewin's field theory and his conceptualizing about group dynamics, change processes, and action research profoundly influenced the people associated with the various stems of OD.

Through a series of events at the New Britain workshop of 1946, what was later to be called the "T-group" ("T" for "training") began to emerge. The workshop staff consisted of Kurt Lewin, Kenneth Benne, Leland Bradford, and Ronald Lippitt. The latter three served as leaders of "learning groups" (sometimes called "L-groups"). Each group, in addition to group members and a leader, had an observer who made notes about interactions among members. At the end of each day, the observers met with the staff and reported what they had seen. At the second or third evening session,

Source: Wendell L. French and Cecil H. Bell, Jr., *Organization Development: Behavioral Science Interventions for Organization Improvement,* 6th ed. (Upper Saddle River, N.J.: Prentice Hall, 1999), pp. 32–61. Copyright © 1999. Reprinted by permission of Prentice Hall.

three members of the workshop asked if they could sit in on the reporting session, and were encouraged to do so. One woman disagreed with the observer about the meaning of her behavior during the day's sessions, and a lively discussion ensued. The three workshop members then asked to return to the next reporting session, and, because of the lively and rich discussion, Lewin and the staff enthusiastically agreed. By the next evening, about half of the 50–60 members of the workshop attended the feedback session. These sessions soon became the most significant learning experiences of the conference.[3]

This experience led to the National Training Laboratory in Group Development, organized by Benne, Bradford, and Lippitt (Lewin died in early 1947). They held a three-week session during the summer of 1947 at the Gould Academy in Bethel, Maine.[4] Participants met with a trainer and an observer in Basic Skill Training Groups (later called T-groups) for a major part of each day. The 1947 laboratory was sponsored by the Research Center for Group Dynamics (MIT), the National Education Association (NEA), Teachers College of Columbia University, University of California at Los Angeles (UCLA), Springfield College, and Cornell University. The work of that summer evolved into the National Training Laboratory, later called NTL Institute for Applied Behavioral Science, and into contemporary T-group training. Out of the Bethel experiences and NTL grew a significant number of laboratory training centers sponsored by universities. One of the first was the Western Training Laboratory, headed by Paul Sheats and sponsored by UCLA. The Western Training Laboratory offered its first program in 1952.

In addition to Lewin and his work, extensive experience with role playing and Moreno's psychodrama influenced Bradford, Lippitt, and Benne's invention of the T-group and the subsequent emergence of OD.[5] Further, Bradford and Benne were influenced by John Dewey's philosophy of education, including concepts about learning and change and about the transactional nature of humans and their environment.[6] Benne, in collaboration with

R. Bruce Raup and others, built on Dewey's philosophy, focusing on the processes by which people who differ reach policy agreements.[7] In addition, Benne was influenced by the works of Mary Follett, an early management theorist, including her ideas about integrative solutions to problems in organizations.[8]

As a footnote to the emergence of the T-group, the widespread use of flip-chart paper as a convenient way to record, retrieve, and display data in OD activities and in training sessions was invented by Ronald Lippitt and Lee Bradford during the 1946 New Britain sessions. Lippitt reports,

> The blackboards were very inadequate, and we needed to preserve a lot of the material we produced. So I went down to the local newspaper and got a donation of the end of press runs. The paper was still on the rollers. We had a "cutting bee" of Lee, Ken, myself and several others to roll the sheets out and cut them into standard sizes that we could put up in quantity with masking tape on the blackboards and walls of the classrooms. We took the practice back to MIT and I had the shop make some boards with clamps across the top. We hung them in our offices and the seminar room, and Lee did the same thing at the NEA in Washington. . . . The next summer at Bethel we had a large supply of cut newsprint and used some of the boards on easels, as well as using the walls.[9]

Bradford also reports that he and Ronald Lippitt used "strips of butcher paper" in their early work with organizations.[10]

In a sense, the T-group emerged from an awareness that had been growing for a decade or more, awareness of the importance of helping groups and group leaders focus on group and leadership *processes*. This growing awareness was particularly evident in adult education and group therapy.[11] As the use of the laboratory method evolved, stated goals of T-group experiences tended to include such statements as "(1) self-insight . . . , (2) understanding the conditions which inhibit or facilitate group functioning, (3) understanding interpersonal operations in groups, and (4) developing skills for diagnosing individual, group, and organizational behavior."[12]

While these insights and skills were practical and relevant for most participants, one driving force for the rapidly growing popularity of T-groups was probably their spiritual and therapeutic (therapy for normals) aspects. Art Kleiner captures these aspects:

> . . . toward the end of the two weeks (or three, or one), something wonderful and unfathomable would happen. It was rarely written down in the voluminous scholarly literature that NTLers created about T-Groups, but it kept drawing people back, session after session, and it prodded some participants to drop out of their management jobs to become educators and psychologists. After two or three weeks of soul-baring in a group of soul-barers, each person in the room would reach a moment when he or she discovered some core of redemption, some inner worth, deep within. The same feeling surged in those moments that, perhaps, surged when crowds gathered around Pelagius in Rome, and that surges whenever people gather to understand the deepest ties they hold in common.
>
> Some of the NLT participants described the experience as "unconditional love"; others, as "pure joy"; others, as a kind of mystical breakthrough or peak experience. . . . After you experienced that peak, you knew that the unconscious was not a Freudian cesspool spewing forth bitter legacies of childhood traumas. It was a source of Pelagian grace and hidden value, terrifying in its power and yet delightful in its beauty. It could only come forward when peopled learned, in a trusting, empathic environment like a T-Group, how to break free of their old ways of talking and thinking.
>
> A few NLT participants never felt the Pelagian grace rise within them. They sat in their T-Groups, puzzled and mildly disappointed, while everyone around them was swept up in a contact conversational high.[13]

Over the next decade, as trainers began to work with social systems of more permanency and complexity than T-groups, they began to experience considerable frustration in transferring laboratory behavioral skills and insights of individuals into solving problems in organizations. Personal skills learned in the "stranger" T-groups setting were difficult to transfer to complex organizations. However, the training of "teams" from the same organization emerged early at Bethel and undoubtedly was a link to the total organizational focus of Douglas McGregor, Herbert Shepard, Robert Blake, and Jane Mouton and subsequently the focus of Richard Beckhard, Chris Argyris, Jack Gibb, Warren Bennis, Eva Schindler-Rainman, and others.[14] All had been T-group trainers in NTL programs.

Robert Tannenbaum. Some of the earliest sessions of what would now be called "team building" were conducted by Robert Tannenbaum in 1952 and 1953 at the U.S. Naval Ordnance Test Station at China Lake, California.[15] According to Tannenbaum, the term *vertically structured groups* was used with groups dealing with "personal topics (such as departmental sociometrics, interpersonal relationships, communication, and self-analysis), and with organizational topics (such as deadlines, duties and responsibilities, policies and procedures, and—quite extensively—with interorganizational-group relations)."[16] These sessions, which stimulated a 1954 *Personnel* article by Tannenbaum, Kallejian, and Weschler, were conducted "with all managers of a given organizational unit present."[17] The more personally oriented dynamics of such sessions were described in a 1955 *Harvard Business Review* article by the same authors.[18]

Tannenbaum, along with Art Shedlin, also led what appears to be the first nondegree training program in OD, the Learning Community in Organizational Development at UCLA. This annual program was first offered as a full-time, ten-week, residential program, January–March 1967.[19]

Tannenbaum, who held a Ph.D. in Industrial Relations from the School of Business at the University of Chicago, was influenced early by Mary Parker Follett in management theory, V. V. Anderson's *Psychiatry in Industry,* Roethlisberger and Dickson's *Management and the Worker,* and Burleigh Gardner's *Human Relations in Industry.* He was on the planning committee for the Western Training Laboratory (WTL) and a staff member for the first session (1952). During that first session he co-trained with a psychiatric social worker who had attended a Bethel program, and in subsequent sessions, in his words, "co-trained with a psychiatrist, an educator, a clinical psychologist . . . and I learned much from them."[20]

Chris Argyris. In 1957, Chris Argyris, then a faculty member at Yale University (later at Harvard), was one of the first to conduct team building sessions with a CEO and the top executive team. Two of Argyris's early clients were IBM and Exxon. His early research and interventions with a top executive group are reported in his 1962 book *Interpersonal Competence and Organizational Effectiveness.*[21]

In 1950, while working on a Ph.D. at Cornell University, Argyris visited Bethel as a member of NTL's research staff in order to study T-groups. In his words, "I became fascinated with what I saw, and wanted to become a trainer. Several years later . . . I was invited to become a staff member."[22]

Argyris was later to make extensive contributions to theory and research on laboratory training, OD, and organizational learning. One of his several books on OD, *Intervention Theory and Method,* stands as a classic in the field.[23]

According to Argyris, three people had the greatest impact on his early career:

> Number one was Kurt Lewin.[24] . . . I was at Clark, finishing my undergraduate degree. I would go over (to MIT) and sit in on his seminars.[25] . . . But his writings . . . had the greatest impact.[26] Next came Roger Barker, and his studies on psychological ecology and behavioral settings. I worked with Roger for several years. His greatest impact was not only on helping me to understand how to study behavioral settings more rigorously, but his whole approach to knowledge, which was to explore, to enquire, and to experiment. Finally, there was Bill Whyte at Cornell University, with whom I received my Ph.D. (in organizational behavior). Bill was not only a very thoughtful and encouraging advisor, but he was very smart and learned about field work. He had a sensitivity for what it meant to be an ethnographer that helped me to learn a lot about what to do in the field.[27]

Argyris interacted with many of the early leaders in the T-group and OD fields. For example, in referring to Douglas McGregor, he states, "I had many wonderful discussions with him in the advanced president's programs at Bethel and in Florida." In referring to Bradford, with whom he worked numerous times from 1950 on, he states that "he was, without any doubt, the person who helped make NTL come alive."[28]

Douglas McGregor. Beginning about 1957, Douglas McGregor, as a professor-consultant, working with Union Carbide, was one of the first behavioral scientists to address the transfer problem and to talk systematically about and to help implement the application of T-group skills in complex organizations.[29] John Paul Jones, who had come up through industrial relations at Union Carbide, in collaboration with McGregor and with the support of a corporate executive vice president and director, Birny Mason, Jr. (later president of the corporation), established a small internal consulting group. In large part, this group used behavioral science knowledge to help line managers and their subordinates learn how to be more effective in groups. McGregor's ideas were a dominant force in this consulting group; other behavioral scientists who influenced Jones's thinking were Rensis Likert and Mason Haire. Jones's organization was later called an "organization development group."[30]

Among the many influences on Douglas McGregor, of course, was Kurt Lewin, a colleague at MIT whom McGregor had helped recruit. It is also clear that he was influenced by Leland Bradford, Edwin Boring, Irving Knickerbocker, Jay Forrester, and Gordon Allport.[31] McGregor also must have been influenced by Carl Rogers, the leading theorist and practitioner in client-centered therapy, because McGregor assigned Rogers' writings to his classes at MIT.[32] McGregor's classic work, *The Human Side of Enterprise,* which has had a great impact on managers since its publication in 1960, cites an extensive list of psychologists, sociologists, and management theorists, including Peter Drucker.[33] (See the discussion of Richard Beckhard, which refers to the influence of McGregor's consulting work at General Mills on *The Human Side of Enterprise.*) (As a historical footnote, McGregor was president of Antioch College from 1948 to 1954 after his first tour as a professor at MIT. Subsequent to this college presidency, McGregor returned to MIT to start a program in organizational studies.[34])

Herbert Shepard. During the same year, 1957, introductions by Douglas McGregor led to Herbert Shepard's joining the employee relations department of Esso Standard Oil (now Exxon) as a research associate. Shepard was to have a major impact on the emergence of OD. Although we will focus mainly on Shepard's work at Esso, we also want to note that Shepard was later involved in community development activities and, in 1960, at the Case Institute of Technology, founded the first doctoral program devoted to training OD specialists.

Before joining Esso, Shepard had completed his doctorate at MIT and stayed for a time as a faculty member in the Industrial Relations Section. Among influences on Shepard were Roethlisberger and Dickson's *Management and the Worker* (1939) and a biography of Clarence Hicks. (As a consultant to Standard Oil, Hicks had helped develop participative approaches to personnel management and labor relations.) Shepard was also influenced by Farrell Toombs, who had been a counselor at the Hawthorne plant and had trained under Carl Rogers. In addition, Shepard was heavily influenced by the writings of Kurt Lewin and others of NTL. He attended an NTL lab in 1950 and subsequently was a staff member in many of its programs.[35]

In 1958 and 1959 Shepard launched three experiments in organization development at major Esso refineries: Bayonne, New Jersey; Baton Rouge, Louisiana; and Bayway, Texas. At Bayonne, he conducted an interview survey that was discussed with top management. The survey was followed by a series of three-day laboratories for all members of management.[36] Paul Buchanan, who had worked earlier at the Naval Ordnance Test Station and more recently had been using a somewhat similar approach in Republic Aviation, collaborated with Shepard at Bayonne and subsequently joined the Esso staff.

Herbert Shepard and Robert Blake.   At Baton Rouge, Robert Blake joined Shepard, and the two initiated a series of two-week laboratories attended by all members of "middle" management. At first, they tried to combine the case method with the laboratory method, but their designs soon emphasized T-groups, organizational exercises, and lectures. One innovation in this training program was an emphasis on intergroup as well as interpersonal

relations. Although working on interpersonal problems affecting work performance was clearly an organizational effort, between-group problem solving had even greater organization development implications because it involved a broader and more complex segment of the organization.

At Baton Rouge, efforts to involve top management failed, and as a result follow-up resources for implementing organization development were not available. By the time the Bayway program started, two fundamental OD lessons had been learned: the requirement for top management's active involvement in and leadership of the program and the need for on-the-job application.

Bayway brought two significant innovations. First, Shepard, Blake, and Murray Horwitz used the instrumental laboratory, which Blake and Jane Mouton had been developing in social psychology classes at the University of Texas and which they later developed into the Managerial Grid approach to organization development.[37] (An essential dimension of the instrumental lab is feedback based on measurements of group and individual behavior during sessions.[38]) Second, at Bayway more resources were devoted to team development, consultation, intergroup conflict resolution, and so forth than were devoted to laboratory training of "cousins," that is, organization members from different departments. As Robert Blake stated, "It was learning to *reject* T-group stranger-type labs that permitted OD to come into focus," and it was intergroup projects, in particular, that "triggered real OD."[39]

Robert Blake and Jane Mouton.   Several influences on Robert Blake up to that point were important in the emergence of OD. While at Berea College majoring in psychology and philosophy (later an M.A., University of Virginia, and a Ph.D., University of Texas), Blake was strongly influenced by the works of Korzybski and the general semanticists and found that "seeing discrete things as representative of a continuous series was much more stimulating and rewarding than just seeing two things as 'opposites.'" This thinking contributed in later years to Blake's conceptualization of the

Managerial Grid with Jane Mouton and to their intergroup research on win-lose dynamics. This intergroup research and the subsequent design of their intergroup conflict management workshops were also heavily influenced by Muzafer Sherif's fundamental research on intergroup dynamics.[40] Jane Mouton's influence on Blake's thinking and on the development of the Grid stemmed partly, in her words, "from my undergraduate work (at Texas) in pure mathematics and physics which emphasized the significance of measurement, experimental design, and a scientific approach to phenomena."[41] (Mouton later attained an M.A. from the University of Virginia and a Ph.D. from the University of Texas.)

During World War II, Blake served in the Psychological Research Unit of the Army Air Force where he interacted with many behavioral scientists, including sociologists. This experience contributed to his interest in "looking at the system rather than the individuals within the system on an isolated one-by-one basis."[42] (This system-wide approach is probably one of many links between systems concepts or systems theory and OD.)

Another major influence on Blake was the work of John Bowlby, a medical member of the Tavistock Clinic in London, who was working in family group therapy. After completing his Ph.D. work in clinical psychology, Blake went to England for 16 months in 1948 and 1949 to study, observe, and do research at Tavistock. As Blake states it,

> Bowlby had the clear notion that treating mental illness of an individual out of context was an . . . ineffective way of aiding a person. . . . As a result, John was unprepared to see patients, particularly children, in isolation from their family settings. He would see the intact family: mother, father, siblings. . . . I am sure you can see from what I have said that if you substitute the word organization for family and substitute the concept of development for therapy, the natural next step in my mind was organization development.[43]

Among others at Tavistock who influenced Blake were Wilfred Bion, Henry Ezriel, Eric Trist, and Elliott Jaques.

After returning from Tavistock and taking an appointment at Harvard, Blake joined the staff for the summer NTL programs at Bethel. His first assignment was joint responsibility for a T-group with John R. P. French. Blake was a member of the Bethel staff from 1951 to 1957 and continued after that with NTL labs for managers at Harriman House, Harriman, New York. Among other influences on Blake were Jacob Moreno's action orientation to training through the use of psychodrama and sociodrama and E. C. Tolman's notions of purposive behavior in humans.[44]

Richard Beckhard.   Richard Beckhard, another major figure in the emergence and extension of the OD field, came from a career in the theater. In his words,

> I came out of a whole different world—the theater—and went to NTL in 1950 as a result of some discussions with Lee Bradford and Ron Lippitt. At that time they were interested in improving the effectiveness of the communications in large meetings and I became involved as head of the general sessions program. But I also got hooked on the whole movement. I made a career change and set up the meetings organization, "Conference Counselors." My first major contact was the staging of the 1950 White House conference on children and youth. . . . I was brought in to stage the large general sessions with six thousand people. . . . I had been doing a lot of large convention participative discussion type things and had written on the subject. . . . At the same time I joined the NTL summer staff. . . . My mentors in the field were Lee Bradford, in the early days, and Ron Lippitt and later, Ren Likert, and very particularly, Doug McGregor, who became both mentor, friend, father figure . . . and in the later years, brother. Doug had left MIT and was at Antioch as president. . . . Doug and I began appearing on similar programs. One day coming back on the train from Cincinnati to Boston, Doug asked if I was interested in joining MIT. . . .
>
> In the period 1958–63, I had worked with him (McGregor) on two or three projects. He brought me to Union Carbide, where I replaced him in working with John Paul Jones, and later, George Murray and the group. We (also) worked together at . . . Pennsylvania Bell and . . . at General Mills.[45]

Beckhard worked with McGregor at General Mills in 1959 or 1960, where McGregor was working with Dewey Balsch, vice president of personnel and industrial relations, in an attempt to facilitate "a total organizational culture change program which today might be called quality of work life or OD." Beckhard goes on to say, "The issues that were being worked were relationships between workers and supervision; roles of supervision and management at various levels; participative management for real. . . . This experience was one of the influences on Doug's original paper, 'The Human Side of Enterprise' . . . and from which the book emerged a year or so later."[46]

Beckhard developed one of the first major non-degree training programs in OD, NTL's Program for Specialists in Organizational Training and Development (PSOTD). The first program was an intensive four-week session held in the summer of 1967 at Bethel, Maine, the same year that UCLA launched its Learning Community in OD. Core staff members the first year in the NTL program were Beckhard as dean, Warner Burke, and Fritz Steele. Additional resource persons the first year were Herbert Shepard, Sheldon Davis, and Chris Argyris.

In addition, Beckhard along with McGregor, Rensis Likert, Chris Argyris, Robert Blake, Lee Bradford, and Jack Gibb, founded NTL's Management Work Conferences. These conferences are essentially laboratory training experiences for middle managers. As an extension of this program, Beckhard was also active in developing and conducting NTL's senior executive conferences and presidents' labs.[47]

Warren Bennis.   One of the major figures associated with the evolution of the OD field has been Warren Bennis. As described in Art Kleiner's book, *The Ages of Heretics,* Warren Bennis has been a " . . . lecturer, professor, essayist, university president, author of prominent books on leadership, dreamer of grand visions, and the only NTLer to actually take the helm of a large organization and try to reshape it from the top." Bennis had been an industrial management professor in Douglas McGregor's department at MIT, a T-group trainer, and a participant in a number of the early major OD consulting projects, including one at the U.S. State Department.[48]

During his career, Bennis became vice president for academic affairs at State University of New York at Buffalo, and then president of the University of Cincinnati. His associates and mentors, particularly in the earlier years, included Douglas McGregor, Ed Schein, Mason Haire, Abraham Maslow, Carl Rogers, Kenneth Benne, Herb Shepard, Leland Bradford, Peter Drucker, and Robert Chin.[49] He was also influenced by the labor economist George Schultz (later to be Secretary of Labor and Secretary of State), Elton Mayo, and Henry Stack Sullivan. Some of his more notable publications include the book *The Planning of Change,*[50] written with Kenneth Benne and Robert Chin, and the essay "Democracy Is Inevitable,"[51] coauthored with Philip Slater.

Eva Schindler-Rainman.   Probably one of the first persons to be an NLT staff member doing OD work and having been trained almost exclusively in the social work field was Eva Schindler-Rainman. Schindler-Rainman was awarded both a masters and doctorate from the University of Southern California with specialties in group work, organizational behavior, and community organization. While employed as director of personnel and training for the Los Angeles Girl Scouts Council, in the early 1950s she attended one of the first events of the Western Training Laboratory. Her T-group trainers there were Gordon Hearn and Marguerite Vanderworker.

About 1959, Schindler-Rainman was on the staff of an NTL-sponsored Community Development Laboratory at UCLA's Arrowhead Conference Center where she was a T-group co-trainer with Leland Bradford. Others on the staff were Warren Schmidt, Kenneth Benne, and Max Birnbaum.

Reflecting on transferring her social work, community development experiences, and T-group training to the emerging field of OD, Schindler-Rainman observes

> . . . I would say that I began consciously doing OD work when I was the Director of Training and Personnel for the Girl Scouts. . . . I did OD-type work with school districts, organizing a coordinating council that made it possible to bring in-service classes from UCLA to teachers from all of those districts.[52]

Schindler-Rainman goes on to describe her work with the Health Department in Los Angeles, and the Education Extension department at UCLA where she was at one time assistant director. Along with Charles Ferguson, she later became one of the associate directors of the Department of Conferences at UCLA, headed by Warren Schmidt. She also worked with Robert Tannenbaum, Irv Weschler, Joan Lasko, and Jerry Reisel. In addition, she worked with Richard Beckhard, who was doing a series of interventions with the California Cancer Society.

Schindler-Rainman's formal link to NTL came with a staff assignment at Bethel about 1966. Ronald Lippitt was the dean. Other staff members included Dorothy Mial, Cyril Mill, and Matthew Miles. Some of the other women with whom Schindler-Rainman worked, in addition to Dorothy Mial, were Edith Seashore, Miriam Ritvo, and Peggy Lippitt. Referring to the women in the field, Schindler-Rainman recounts, "Edie [Edith Seashore] was the person doing more OD interventions than anybody else as far as I know."[53] (For more on Edith Seashore, see Kleiner, *The Age of Heretics*.[54])

Schindler-Rainman worked with a wide range of clients, both in the United States and internationally. A few of her well-known publications are *The Creative Volunteer Community: A Collection of Writings,*[55] *Building the Collaborative Community,*[56] *The Volunteer Community,*[57] and *Team Training for Community Change.*[58] (The latter three were coauthored with Ronald Lippitt.) Schindler-Rainman's extensive professional training, her collaboration with a number of key men and women in the early days of NTL and the OD movement, and her early and extensive contribution to the community development movement clearly identify her as one of the pioneers in the laboratory training stem of OD.

The Term *Organization Development.*

It is not entirely clear who coined the term *organization development,* but the term likely emerged more or less simultaneously in two or three places through the works of Robert Blake, Herbert Shepard, Jane Mouton, Douglas McGregor, and Richard Beckhard.[59] The phrase *development group* had been used earlier by Blake and Mouton in connection with human relations training at the University of Texas, and it appeared in their 1956 document distributed for use in the Baton Rouge experiment.[60] The same phrase appeared in a Mouton and Blake article first published in the journal *Group Psychotherapy* in 1957.[61]) The Baton Rouge T-groups run by Shepard and Blake were called *development groups,*[62] and this program of T-groups was called "organization development" to distinguish it from the complementary management development programs already underway.[63]

Referring to his consulting with McGregor at General Mills, Beckhard gives this account of the term emerging there:

> At that time we wanted to put a label on the program at General Mills. . . . We clearly didn't want to call it management development because it was total organization-wide, nor was it human relations training although there was a component of that in it. We didn't want to call it organization improvement because that's a static term, so we labeled the program "Organization Development," meaning system-wide change effort.[64]

Thus, the term emerged as a way of distinguishing a different mode of working with organizations and as a way of highlighting its developmental, systemwide, dynamic thrust.

The Role of Human Resources Executives.

It is of considerable significance that organization development efforts in three of the first corporations to be extensively involved, Union Carbide, Esso, and General Mills, included human resources people seeing themselves in new roles. At Union Carbide, John Paul Jones, in industrial relations, now saw himself as a behavioral science consultant to other managers.[65] At Esso, the headquarters human relations research division began to view itself as an internal consulting group offering services to field managers rather than as a research group developing reports for top management.[66] At General Mills, the vice president of personnel and industrial relations, Dewey Balsch, saw his role as including leadership in conceptualizing and coordinating changes in the culture of the total organization.[67] Thus, in the history of OD we see both external consultants and internal staff departments departing from their traditional roles and collaborating in a new approach to organization improvement.

The Survey Research and Feedback Stem.

Survey research and feedback,[68] a specialized form of action research (see Chapter 7) constitutes the second major stem in the history of organization development. The history of this stem revolves around the techniques and approach developed over a period of years by staff members at the Survey Research Center (SRC) of the University of Michigan.

Rensis Likert.

The SRC was founded in 1946 after Rensis Likert, director of the Division of Program Surveys of the Federal Bureau of Agricultural Economics, and other key members of the division moved to Michigan. Likert held a Ph.D. in psychology from Columbia, and his dissertation, *A Technique for the Measurement of Attitudes,* was the classic study that developed the widely used five-point Likert scale. After completing his degree and teaching at Columbia for awhile, Likert worked for the Life Insurance Agency Management Association. There he conducted research on leadership, motivation, morale, and productivity. He then moved to the U.S. Department of Agriculture, where his Division of Program Surveys furthered a more scientific approach to survey research in its work with various federal departments, including the Office of War Information.[69] In 1948 after helping to develop and direct the Survey Research Center, Likert became the director of a new Institute for Social Research, which included both the SRC and the Research Center for Group Dynamics. The latter had moved to Michigan from MIT after Lewin's death.

Floyd Mann, Rensis Likert, and Others.

Part of the emergence of survey research and feedback was based on refinements made by SRC staff members in survey methodology. Another part was the evolution of feedback methodology. As related by Rensis Likert,

In 1947, I was able to interest the Detroit Edison Company in a company-wide study of employee perceptions, behavior, reactions and attitudes which was conducted in 1948. Floyd Mann, who had joined the SRC staff in 1947, was the study director on the project. I provided general direction. Three persons from D.E.: Blair Swartz, Sylvanus Leahy and Robert Schwab with Mann and me worked on the problem of how the company could best use the data from the survey to bring improvement in management and performance. This led to the development and use of the survey-feedback method. Floyd particularly played a key role in this development. He found that when the survey data were reported to a manager (or supervisor) and he or she failed to discuss the results with subordinates and failed to plan with them what the manager and others should do to bring improvement, little change occurred. On the other hand, when the manager discussed the results with subordinates and planned with them what to do to bring improvement, substantial favorable changes occurred.[70]

Another aspect of the Detroit Edison study was the process of feeding back data from an attitude survey to the participating departments in what Mann calls an "interlocking chain of conferences."[71] Additional insights are provided by Baumgartel, who participated in the project and who drew the following conclusions from the Detroit Edison study:

> The results of this experimental study lend support to the idea that an intensive, group discussion procedure for utilizing the results of an employee questionnaire survey can be an effective tool for introducing positive change in a business organization. It may be that the effectiveness of this method, in comparison to traditional training courses, is that it deals with the system of human relationships as a whole (superior and subordinate can change together) and it deals with each manager, supervisor, and employee in the context of his own job, his own problems, and his own work relationships.[72]

Links between the Laboratory Training Stem and the Survey Feedback Stem.

As early as 1940, links occurred between people who were later to be key figures in the laboratory training stem of OD and people who were to be key figures in the survey feedback stem. These links, which continued over the years, were undoubtedly of significance in the evolution of both stems. Of particular interest are the links between Likert and Lewin and between Likert and key figures in the laboratory training stem of OD. As Likert states, "I met Lewin at the APA annual meeting at State College, Pa., I believe in 1940. When he came to Washington during the War, I saw him several times and got to know him and his family quite well."[73] In 1944 Likert arranged a dinner at which Douglas McGregor and Kurt Lewin explored the feasibility of a group dynamics center at MIT.[74]

Likert further refers to McGregor: "I met McGregor during the war and came to know him very well after Lewin had set up the RCGD at MIT. After the War, Doug became very interested in the research on leadership and organizations that we were doing in the Institute for Social Research. He visited us frequently and I saw him often at Antioch and at MIT after he returned." Likert goes on to refer to the first NTL lab for managers held at Arden House in 1956: "Douglas McGregor and I helped Lee Bradford launch it.... Staff members in the 1956 lab were: Beckhard, Benne, Bradford, Gordon Lippitt, Malott, Shepard and I. Argyris, Blake and McGregor joined the staff for the 1957 Arden House lab."[75]

Argyris refers to Likert:

Rensis Likert was also a leader in the field when I was a graduate student, and I had the highest respect for him and his commitment to trying to connect theory with practice. Indeed, I've always been a bit sad to see how many of his colleagues, who saw themselves as mere researchers, at times would downplay Rensis' commitment to practice. They saw him as being too . . . committed to the world of practice. I never felt that. I felt that it was the combination of practice and theory that made him an important member of our community. I would put Lewin first on that dimension, and Ren Likert and Doug McGregor next, each in his own way making important contributions.[76]

Links between group dynamics and survey feedback people were extensive, of course, after the RCGD moved to Michigan with the encouragement of Rensis Likert and members of the SRC.

Among the top people in the RCGD who moved to Michigan were Leon Festinger, Dorwin Cartwright, Ronald Lippitt, and John R. P. French, Jr. Cartwright, selected by the group to be the director of the RCGD, was particularly knowledgeable about survey research, since he had been on the staff of the Division of Program Surveys with Rensis Likert and others during World War II.[77]

The Action Research Stem

In earlier chapters we briefly described action research as a collaborative, client-consultant inquiry. Chapter 7 describes four versions of action research, one of which, participant action research, is used with the most frequency in OD. The laboratory training stem in the history of OD has a heavy component of action research; the survey feedback stem is the history of a specialized form of action research; and Tavistock projects have had a strong action research thrust, as we will discuss shortly.

Because we will treat the history of action research in some detail later, we will mention only a few aspects here. For example, William F. Whyte and Edith L. Hamilton used action research in their work with Chicago's Tremont Hotel in 1945 and 1956; John Collier, commissioner of Indian Affairs, described action research in a 1945 publication; Kurt Lewin and his students conducted numerous action research projects in the mid-1940s and early 1950s. The work of these and other scholars and practitioners in inventing and utilizing action research was basic in the evolution of OD.

The Sociotechnical and Socioclinical Stem

A fourth stem in the history of OD is the evolution of socioclinical and sociotechnical approaches to helping groups and organizations. Parallel to the work of the RCGD, the SRC, and NTL was the work of the Tavistock Clinic in England. The clinic was founded in 1920 as an outpatient facility to provide psychotherapy based on psychoanalytic theory and insights from the treatment of battle neurosis in World War I. A group focus emerged early in the work of Tavistock in the context of family therapy in which the child and the parent received treatment simultaneously.[78] (See the reference earlier in this chapter to John Bowlby's influence on Robert Blake and, in turn, the emergence of the concept of "organization development.") The action research mode also emerged at Tavistock in attempts to give practical help to families, organizations, and communities.

W. R. Bion, John Rickman, and Others.   The professional staff of the Tavistock Clinic was extensively influenced by such innovations as World War II applications of social psychology to psychiatry, the work of W. R. Bion and John Rickman and others in group therapy, Lewin's notions about the "social field" in which a problem was occurring, and Lewin's theory and experience with action research. Bion, Rickman, and others had been involved with the six-week "Northfield Experiment" at a military hospital near Birmingham during World War II. In this experiment each soldier was required to join a group that performed some tasks such as handicraft or map reading as well as discussed feelings, interpersonal relations, and administrative and managerial problems. Insights from this experiment carried over into Bion's theory of group behavior.[79]

Eric Trist.   A clear historical and conceptual connection can be made between the group dynamics field and the sociotechnical approaches to assisting organizations. Tavistock's sociotechnical approach is particularly significant in that it grew out of Eric Trist's 1947 visit to a British coal mine at Haighmoor; his insights as to the relevance of Lewin's work on group dynamics and Bion's work on leaderless groups resulted in a new approach to solving mine problems.[80] Trist was also influenced by the systems concepts of Von Bertalanffy and Andras Angyal.[81]

At Haighmoor, Trist observed miners working in teams—teams that the miners themselves had organized—which was in stark contrast to the typical assembly-line structure in the mines of that day. According to Kleiner, each team ran the job and sold the coal, and would take care of team member's families in the case of an accident. Each miner might handle several different jobs, and

team members were compensated on the basis of the team tonnage produced. The results of the team approach were remarkable in terms of safety and productivity.[82]

Trist's subsequent experiments in work design and the use of semiautonomous work teams in coal mining were the forerunners of other work redesign experiments in various industries in Europe, India, Australia, and the United States. In these experiments, terms such as *industrial democracy, open systems,* and *sociotechnical systems* were used by Trist and his colleagues, including Fred Emery.[83] (Emery's extensive collaboration with Eric Trist includes the development of "Search Conferences," to be discussed later.)

Tavistock–U.S. Links.   Tavistock leaders, including Trist and Bion, had frequent contact with Kurt Lewin, Rensis Likert, Chris Argyris, and others in the United States. One product of this collaboration was the decision to publish the journal *Human Relations* as a joint publication between Tavistock and MIT's Research Center for Group Dynamics.[84] Some Americans prominent in the emergence and evolution of the OD field, for example, Robert Blake, as we noted earlier, and Warren Bennis,[85] studied at Tavistock. Chris Argyris held several seminars with Tavistock leaders in 1954.[86]

The sociotechnical approach focused on the nonexecutive ranks of organizations and especially the redesign of work. The focus on teams and the use of action research and participation was consistent with evolving OD approaches. Some contemporary quality of work life (QWL) and some total quality management (TQM) programs are amalgamations of OD, sociotechnical, and other approaches.

The Changing Context

Even though it is important to understand how OD emerged, it is also important to understand the changing milieu in which contemporary OD activities are occurring. That context has changed dramatically throughout the 1980s and 1990s. As authors are prone to say, the environment has become increasingly "turbulent." In the United

States, the pace of technological innovation, company mergers, acquisitions, leveraged buyouts, bankruptcies, success stories, downsizings, and changes in law has intensified. At the same time, thousands of small companies are born each year. Globalization of companies is commonplace. Worldwide, many previously centralized and autocratic societies are moving toward creating democratic institutions and privatizing business and industry. These changes create opportunities for OD applications, but also stretch the capabilities of leaders and OD practitioners to the utmost.

In this context what might be called *second-generation OD* is evolving. Practitioners still rely on the first-generation techniques of OD that are highly relevant to adaptive, incremental change, such as action research, a focus on teams, team building, the use of facilitators, process consultation, survey feedback, intergroup problem solving, sociotechnical systems approaches to job design, and participative management. Indeed, theory building and/or research as well as application relative to all of these OD basics is growing. But the field is reaching far beyond these first-generation approaches in the sense that many applications of OD are now more complicated and more multifaceted.

Second-Generation OD

Practitioners and researchers are giving considerable attention to emerging concepts, interventions, and areas of application that might be called second-generation OD. Each, to some extent, overlaps with some or all of the others. Second-generation OD, in particular, has a focus on organizational transformation.

Interest in Organizational Transformation.
More and more, practitioners and scholars are talking and writing about "organizational transformation." Amir Levy and Uri Merry give one of the most complete explorations of this topic in their book, *Organizational Transformation*. They define the term as follows: "Second-order change (organization transformation) is a multi-dimensional, multi-level, qualitative, discontinuous, radical organizational change involving a paradigmatic shift."[87]

Increasingly, OD professionals distinguish between the more modest, or evolutionary, efforts toward organization improvement and those that are massive and, in a sense, revolutionary. For example, Nadler and Tushman refer to "transitions" on the one hand, and "frame bending" on the other.[88] Goodstein and Burke contrast "fine tuning" and "fundamental, large-scale change in the organization's strategy and culture."[89] Barczak, Smith, and Wilemon differentiate "adaptive, incremental change" from "large-scale change."[90] Beckhard and Pritchard contrast "incremental" change strategies and "fundamental" change strategies.[91] Organizational transformation is seen as requiring more demands on top leadership, more visioning, more experimenting, more time, and the simultaneous management of many additional variables.

Interest in Organizational Culture.
Efforts to define, measure, and change organizational culture have become more sophisticated. Schein in particular has written extensively about culture.[92] He has devised interventions to help leaders and employees identify those cultural assumptions that will assist the organization in attaining its goals and those that hinder goal attainment. Making such distinctions is done through a joint exploration to identify sequentially the organization's *artifacts,* such as office layout and status symbols; the *values* underlying these artifacts; and the *assumptions* behind those values.[93] Others have helped organizations focus on culture through the use of questionnaires aimed at identifying actual and desired norms. Participants then make agreements about new norms and how to monitor and reinforce the changes.[94] (For greater detail, see chapter 11.)

Interest in the Learning Organization.
The works of Argyris,[95] Argyris and Schon,[96] and Senge have stimulated considerable interest in the conditions under which individuals, teams, and organizations learn. Argyris, for example, has focused on the defensive routines of organizational members, or "master programs in their heads that tell them how to deal with embarrassment and threat." Basically, according to Argyris, individuals tend to follow these rules:

1. Bypass embarrassment and threat whenever possible.
2. Act as though you are not bypassing them.
3. Don't discuss steps 1 and 2 while they are happening.
4. Don't discuss the undiscussability of the undiscussable.[97]

Workshops with top management teams are designed to tackle simultaneously major tasks such as strategy formulation plus learning how to recognize defensive routines that hinder improvements in communications and the quality of team decision making.[98]

Senge writes extensively about the importance of systems thinking ("the fifth discipline") in organizations, and about the learning disabilities that plague organizations. One learning disability, for example, is focusing on one's own job exclusively with little sense of responsibility for the collective product. Another is blaming the "enemy out there" for things that are wrong, whether it's another department in the same organization or a competitor overseas.[99] Senge is noted for workshops in which he uses games and exercises to create an awareness of these disabilities and to develop different ways of thinking about complex problems.[100]

Intensified Interest in Teams. A focus on intact work teams and other team configurations has been central to OD since the emergence of the field, but recent years have seen a widening and deepening interest in teams, especially what are called high-performance teams, cross-functional teams, and self-managed teams. Interest has intensified particularly in self-managed or self-directed teams. This interest has accelerated due to converging pressures on organizations to improve quality, to become more flexible, to reduce layers of management, and to enhance employee morale.[101]

Laboratory training methods have proved highly useful in training team members in effective membership and leadership behaviors, and in training supervisors and managers in the arts of delegation and empowerment. Furthermore, many organizations use team-building approaches to help self-

managed teams and cross-functional teams get started. In addition, as self-managed teams have assumed many functions previously performed by management, supervisors and middle managers have used team-building approaches within their own ranks to help reconceptualize their own roles.

Interest in Total Quality Management (TQM). The past decade has seen a mushrooming of interest in total quality management worldwide, and then perhaps some decline in application as both successes and failures have been reported. Applications that have been successful appear to have some ingredients in common with OD efforts.

Ciampa, who acknowledges the pioneering contributions of Joseph Juran, W. Edwards Deming, and Armand Feigenbaum to the development of TQM,[102] provides a clear statement on the relationship between TQM and OD. First, his definition: "Total Quality is typically a companywide effort seeking to install and make permanent a climate where employees continuously improve their ability to provide on demand products and services that customers will find of particular value."[103] He then goes on to say that one element that separates successful TQ efforts from less successful ones is

> . . . a particular set of values about the individual and the individual's role in the organization. TQ efforts in these companies encourage true employee involvement, demand teamwork, seek to push decision-making power to lower levels in the company, and reduce barriers between people. . . . These values are at the core of Organization Development (OD), as well.[104]

Burke also comments on the contribution OD can make to TQM efforts. Focusing on the OD practitioner, he states: " . . . the quality movement, to be successful, is highly dependent on effective process—and process is the OD practitioner's most important product."[105] (For more on OD and TQM, see Chapter 12.)

Interest in Visioning and Future Search. Interventions designed to help organizational members look to the future—visioning—are not new to OD, but renewed interest has developed using interventions to look at trends projected into the future and their organizational implications. Marvin Weisbord, for example, has built on the work and experience of Ronald Lippitt and Edward Lindaman,[106] Ronald Fox, Ronald Lippitt, and Eva Schindler-Rainman,[107] and Eric Trist and Fred Emery[108] to develop "future search conferences." In a two- or three-day conference, participants are asked to "(a) build a data base, (b) look at it together, (c) interpret what they find, and (d) draw conclusions for action."[109] This last part of the conference asks participants to develop next action steps and a structure for carrying them out, including task forces and specific assignments.[110]

Senge believes that "the origin of the vision is much less important than the process whereby it comes to be shared." He strongly urges that "shared visions" be based on encouraging organizational members to develop and share their own personal visions, and he claims that a vision is not truly shared "until it connects with the personal visions of people throughout the organization."[111] This type of connection obviously requires OD-like processes to implement.

Rediscovering Large Meetings and Getting the "Whole System" in the Room. As described earlier, one contributing factor in the emergence of the OD movement was the experience of people such as Leland Bradford, Ronald Lippitt, and Richard Beckhard in improving the effectiveness of large meetings. Early on, Beckhard wrote an article entitled "The Confrontation Meeting," which was really about getting the total management group of an organization together in a one-day session to diagnose the state of the system and to make plans for quickly improving conditions.[112] In recent years, Marvin Weisbord and others have written about the importance of OD consultants "getting the whole system in the room." For example, with reference to future search conferences, he advises that such conferences involve all of top management and "people from as many functions and levels as feasible." Again, the final products are action plans and specific assignments to carry the process forward.[113]

Other Directions and Areas of Interest. Several other areas are notable in second-generation OD. Assistance in developing diversity awareness workshops and in "managing" and "valuing" diversity has been much in evidence recently. Expanded interest in sociotechnical systems design, interrelated with interest in self-managed teams and in total quality management, has been apparent. OD applications to quality of work life (QWL) programs have continued but are less evident because of the heightened attention to TQM. Partially as a result of a focus on teams and teamwork, a great deal of attention has been directed toward developing congruent reward systems, including productivity gainsharing plans and skills-based pay plans. Research and conceptualizing about action research, process consultation, and third-party roles have continued and perhaps increased. There is renewed interest in the concept of community as well as spirituality relative to organizational transformation and high-performance organizations. Considerable work has been done with "appreciative inquiry" workshops. (In these sessions, participants focus on the best of "what is" and use these themes as a springboard for focusing on "what might be.")[114] Interest in physical settings continues among OD practitioners.

Widespread business and media interest in *reengineering*—called by various names such as *business process reengineering* and *core process redesign*[115]—has caught the attention of OD practitioners and theorists. OD processes and values appear *not* to underly most reengineering efforts, and the almost-stampede by business and industry to embrace reengineering raises a number of issues pertaining to the role that OD practitioners should or should not play relative to this phenomenon. (See Chapter 12.)

All these areas are fruitful areas for OD theory, research, and practice. However, with the diffusion of OD techniques into so many areas, identifying what is and what is not OD becomes more difficult. Thus, the importance of examining the assumptions and the processes underlying various improvement efforts cannot be overstated—not because OD or the term "OD" is inherently sacred—because the fundamental building blocks of OD as defined in this book are vital ingredients, we believe, to long-term organizational effectiveness and to participant satisfaction and development.

Extent of Application

Applications emerging from one or more of the stems described previously are evident in contemporary organization development efforts occurring in many countries, including England, Japan, Norway, Italy, Belgium, Switzerland, Canada, Sweden, Germany, Finland, Australia, New Zealand, the Philippines, Mexico, France, Venezuela, and the Netherlands, as well as in the United States. Among the large number of organizations in America that have at one time or another embarked on organization development efforts are Union Carbide and Exxon (the first two companies), Connecticut General Insurance Company, Hewlett-Packard, Tektronix, Graphic Controls, Equitable Life Assurance Company, Digital Equipment Corporation, Procter & Gamble, Microelectronics and Computer Technology Corporation (MCC), Mountain Bell Telephone, Searle Laboratories, the Boeing Company, Bankers Trust, Ford Motor Company, Heinz Foods, Polaroid, Sun Oil, and TRW Inc.

Applications have varied, with the total organization involved in many instances, but with only some divisions or plants in others. Further, some efforts have moved ahead rapidly, only to flounder at a later time. In many situations, OD approaches have become an ongoing way of managing with little program visibility and under different terminology. Thus, the extent of application is sometimes difficult to report with any precision.

Applications at TRW Space & Electronics Group (S&EG) were of major significance in the emergence and history of OD. Among the key figures in the beginnings of OD there in the early 1960s (then called TRW Systems Group) were Jim Dunlap, director of industrial relations; Shel Davis, who was later promoted to that position; Ruben Mettler, president; and Herb Shepard. T-group labs conducted by internal trainers, NTL, and UCLA staff members were also important in providing

impetus to the effort in its early phases. Early applications of OD at TRW Systems included team building, intergroup team building, interface laboratories between departments and between company and customers, laboratory training, career assessment workshops, and organization redesign and structuring for improved productivity and quality of working life.[116] (For more on the life of Shel Davis and his contribution to the OD field, see the essay by Celeste A. Coruzzi. In that essay, Warner Burke refers to him as "the pioneer internal OD consultant."[117])

After successful applications in the 1960s, OD activities at TRW declined during the 1970s and 1980s. However, according to Michael Thiel, director of leadership and organization effectiveness at S&EG, "radical structural change within the defense industry has forced TRW (and other defense contractors) to critically examine and shift basic operating paradigms."[118] Thiel goes on to say:

> This has led to the rebirth of "OD-like" activities as part of cultural change and organization transformation efforts. Since 1989, S&EG has been actively pursuing the creation/implementation of a total quality culture, incorporating continuous process improvement, employee empowerment, performance management, and the use of concurrent engineering/-integrated product development with cross-functional teams. OD methodologies such as organizational diagnosis, values clarification, offsite meetings, sensing, etc. have been used where appropriate in these activities. Other tools include team facilitation, team-based experimental education and survey/feedback systems.
>
> Most of these "organization effectiveness" interventions are spearheaded by the Human Resources organization, either HR generalists, or specialists from my office. In addition, there are a number of line/technical managers involved in various facets (specifically team facilitation/process improvement, and self-managed work teams).[119]

Business and industrial organizations are by no means the only kinds of institutions involved. Applications can be made, for example, in public school systems; colleges; medical schools; social welfare agencies; police departments; professional associations; governmental units at the local, county, state, and national levels; the White House;[120] various health care delivery systems; churches; Native American tribes; and the U.S. military.

The history of OD in the U.S. military is beyond the scope of this book, but OD activities in the military services have been extensive. For example, at one time, the Army ran an Organizational Effectiveness Center at Fort Ord, California, and graduated some 1,702 officers as internal consultants between 1975 and 1985.[121] In 1977, the Navy was utilizing 300 full-time OD specialists.[122] Further, during that period, the Naval Postgraduate School offered a masters degree in human resources management, which was essentially a masters degree in OD. Students in that program included active duty officers from the Air Force, Coast Guard, and Army in addition to Navy officers.[123]

Some community development strategies share a number of elements in common with organization development, such as the use of action research, the use of a change agent, and an emphasis on facilitating decision-making and problem-solving processes.[124] Undoubtedly, some of the commonality stems from OD practitioners working in the community development field. For example, in 1961 Herbert Shepard conducted community development laboratories at China Lake, California, sponsored by the Naval Ordnance Test Station. These one-week labs involved military persons and civilians of all ages and socioeconomic levels. Outcomes included the resolution of some community and intercommunity issues.[125] In later years, such conferences have been called *search conferences* or *future search conferences*.

In addition to emphasizing the diversity of systems using OD consultants, we want to emphasize that intraorganization development efforts have not focused on just top management teams, although the importance of top management involvement will be discussed in later chapters. The range of occupational roles that have been involved in OD is almost limitless and has included production workers,[126] managers, soldiers, military officers, miners, scientists and engineers, ministers, psychologists, geologists, lawyers, accountants, nurses, physicians, teachers, computer specialists,

foresters, technicians, secretaries, clerical employees, board members, and flight crews.

The emergence and growth of the OD Network indicates the widespread application of organization development concepts. The OD Network began in 1964 and by 1998 had a membership of about 34,000 and 46 regional networks. Most members either have major roles in the OD efforts of organizations or are scholar-practitioners in the OD field. Although most network members reside in the United States, in 1998 the Network included 184 international members, the majority from Canada. Thirty-one countries were represented in addition to the United States.

The OD Network began with discussions at the Case Institute of Technology between Herbert Shepard, Sheldon Davis of TRW Systems, and Floyd Mann of the University of Michigan,[127] and through the initiative of Leland Bradford and Jerry Harvey of NTL and a number of industrial people who had attended labs at Bethel. Among the industrial founders of the organization, originally called the Industrial Trainers Network, were Sheldon Davis of TRW Systems, George Murray of Union Carbide, John Vail of Dow Chemical, and Carl Albers of the Hotel Corporation of America. Other early members were from Procter & Gamble, Weyerhaeuser, Bankers Trust, West Virginia Pulp and Paper Company, The U.S. State Department, the U.S. National Security Agency, Pillsbury, Eli Lilly, Polaroid, Esso, Parker Pen, American Airlines, Goodrich-Gulf Chemicals, RCA, Sandia, National Association of Manufacturers, General Foods, Armour & Company, Heublein, and Du Pont. Jerry Harvey was the first secretary/coordinator of the emerging organization, and Warner Burke assumed that role in 1967 shortly after joining NTL full-time. At that time the Network had fewer than 50 members; when Warner Burke stepped aside as executive director in 1975, it had approximately 1,400 members.[128] That same year the OD Network became independent of NTL.

The Academy of Management, whose members are mostly professors in management and related areas, established a Division of Organization Development within its structure in 1971. This unit, renamed The Division of Organization Development and Change, had 1,601 members by 1998. The OD Forum of the American Society for Training and Development had 11,374 members the beginning of that year. The Society of Industrial-Organizational Psychology of the American Psychological Association has held workshops on organization development at the annual APA conventions; several annual conventions going back at least to 1965 have included papers or symposia on organization development or related topics.[129] In 1974 the *Annual Review of Psychology* for the first time devoted a chapter entirely to a review of research on organization development.[130] Chapters on OD have appeared at other times, for example, 1977,[131] 1982, 1987,[132] and 1991.[133] The 1982 chapter was written by authors from the Netherlands and France, indicative of OD's international applications.[134]

The first doctoral program devoted to training OD specialists was founded by Herbert Shepard in 1960 at the Case Institute of Technology. Originally called The Organizational Behavior Group, this program is now part of the Department of Organizational Behavior, School of Management, Case Western Reserve University. UCLA also has a program at the doctoral level. Pepperdine offers Doctor of Education in Organization Change (EdDOC), and Benedictine University offers a Ph.D. in Organization Development.

Masters degree programs in organization development or masters programs with concentrations in OD have been offered in recent years by several universities, including New York University, Brigham Young, Pepperdine, Loyola, Bowling Green, New Hampshire, Central Washington University, Columbia, Case Western Reserve, Antioch, University of South Florida, University of San Francisco, Sonoma State University, California School of Professional Psychology, Fielding Institute, Eastern Michigan University, and Sheffield Polytechnic in England. The American University and NTL Institute jointly offers a master of science in organization development. The John F. Kennedy University and NTL cosponsor a masters program that has organization development and change as a major component. Many other major U.S. universities, if not most, now have graduate courses concentrating on organization development, including UCLA, Stanford, Harvard, University of Washington, University of Southern California, Hawaii, Oklahoma, Colorado, Indiana, and Purdue. In England, such courses are found at the University of Manchester Institute of Science and Technology and the University of Bath.[135]

This rapid growth in OD interest and attention has been given impetus by special programs in OD, particularly NTL Institute's Program for Specialists in OD (PSOD), now called Integrating OD Theory and Practice. Other NTL OD programs include such offerings as What is OD?, Facilitating and Managing Complex Systems Change, Consultation Skills, Diversity and OD, Group Process Consultation, Team Building, Managing Conflict, and Creating and Sustaining High-Performing Teams. Another strong source of OD education and training is Teachers College at Columbia University. As part of its organizational psychology program, Columbia offers both a two-part Principles of Organization Development Program and a three-part Advanced Program in Organization Development and Human Resources Management. Another organization, the Organization Development Institute, offers numerous workshops, and sponsors an Organization Development World Congress held in a different country each year. Other professional programs in OD have been or are now being offered in the United States, Canada, the United Kingdom, Australia, New Zealand, and elsewhere under the sponsorship of universities, foundations, professional associations, and other institutions.

Concluding Comments

Organization development emerged largely from applied behavioral sciences and has four major stems: (1) the invention of the T-group and innovations in the application of laboratory training insights to complex organizations, (2) the invention of survey feedback technology, (3) the emergence of action research, and (4) the evolution of the Tavistock sociotechnical and socioclinical approaches.

Key figures in this early history interacted with each other across these stems and were influenced by concepts and experiences from a wide variety of disciplines and settings. These disciplines included social psychology, clinical psychology, family group therapy, ethnography, military psychology and psychiatry, the theater, general semantics, social work, systems theory, mathematics and physics, philosophy, psychodrama, client-centered therapy, survey methodology, experimental and action research, human resources management, organizational behavior, general management theory, and large conference management.

The context for applying OD approaches has changed to an increasingly turbulent environment. While practitioners still rely on OD basics, they are giving considerable attention to new concepts, interventions, and areas of application. Among the directions of interest in second-generation OD are organizational transformation, organizational culture, the learning organization, high-performance teams, total quality management, "getting the whole system in the room," future search, and the role OD practitioners should play in reengineering.

The field of OD is emergent in that a rapidly increasing number of behavioral scientists and practitioners are building on the research and insights of the past as well as rediscovering the utility of some of the earlier insights. These efforts, often under different terminology, are now expanding and include a wide range of organizations, types of institutions, occupational categories, and geographical locations.

In the chapters that follow, the assumptions, theory, and techniques of organization development, as well as problems with implementing OD processes, will be examined in considerable depth. We will also speculate on the future viability of OD or OD-like processes.

Endnotes

1. The phrase *group dynamics* was coined by Kurt Lewin in 1939. See Warren Bennis, address to the Academy of Management, San Diego, California, August 3, 1981.
2. This and the next paragraph are based on Kenneth D. Benne, Leland P. Bradford, Jack R. Gibb, and Ronald O. Lippitt, eds., *The Laboratory Method for Changing and Learning: Theory and Application* (Palo Alto, CA: Science and Behavior Books, 1975), pp. 1–6; and Alfred J. Marrow, *The Practical Theorist: The Life and Work of Kurt Lewin* (New York: Basic Books, 1969), pp. 210–214. For additional history, see Leland P. Bradford, "Biography of an Institution," *Journal of Applied Behavioral Science,* 3 (April–June 1967), pp. 127–143; and Alvin Zander, "The Study of Group Behavior during Four Decades," *Journal of Applied Behavioral Science,* 15 (July–September 1979), pp. 272–282. We are indebted to Ronald Lippitt for his correspondence, which helped to clarify this and the following paragraph.
3. Jerrold I. Hirsch, *The History of the National Training Laboratories 1947–1986* (New York: Peter Lang publishing, 1987), pp. 17–18; and address by Ronald Lippitt, Academy of Management annual conference, Chicago, Illinois, August 1986. For more on Bradford, see David L. Bradford, "A Biography of Leland P. Bradford," *Journal of Applied Behavioral Science,* 26, no. 1 (1990), p. viii.
4. See also Nancie Coan, "A History of NTL Institute in Bethel," *NTL Institute News & Views* (February 1991), pp. 11–15.
5. Peter B. Smith, ed., *Small Groups and Personal Change* (London: Methuen & Co. 1980), pp. 8–9.
6. Robert Chin and Kenneth D. Benne, "General Strategies for Effecting Changes in Human Systems," in Warren G. Bennis, Kenneth D. Benne, and Robert Chin, eds., *The Planning of Change,* 2d ed. (New York: Holt, Rinehardt and Winston, 1969), pp. 100–102.
7. Correspondence with Kenneth Benne. Raup was Benne's Ph.D. major professor at Columbia. Benne states that he was also influenced by Edward Lindeman. For more on Benne, see Paul Nash, "Biography of Kenneth D. Benne," *Journal of Applied Behavioral Science,* 28 (June 1992), p. 167.
8. Chin and Benne, op cit., p. 102.
9. Correspondence with Ronald Lippitt.
10. Conversation with Lee Bradford, conference on current theory and practice in organization development, San Francisco, March 16, 1978.
11. See, for example, S. R. Slavson, *An Introduction to Group Therapy* (New York: The Commonwealth Fund, 1943); and S. R. Slavson, *Creative Group Education* (New York: Association press, 1937), especially Chapter 1.
12. Edgar H. Schein and Warren G. Bennis, *Personal and Organizational Change through Group Methods: The Laboratory Approach* (New York: John Wiley & Sons, 1965), p. 35.

13. Art Kleiner, *The Age of Heretics* (New York: Currency and Doubleday, 1996), pp. 41–42.

14. Based largely on correspondence with Ronald Lippitt. According to Lippitt, as early as 1945 Bradford and Lippitt were conducting "three-level training" at Freedman's Hospital in Washington, D.C., in an effort "to induce interdependent changes in all parts of the same system." Lippitt also reports that Leland Bradford very early was acting on a basic concept of "multiple entry," that is, simultaneously training and working with several groups in the organization.

15. Correspondence with Robert Tannenbaum.

16. Tannenbaum correspondence; memorandum of May 12, 1952, U.S. Naval Ordnance Test Station from E. R. Toporeck to "Office, Division and Branch Heads, Test Department," and "Minutes, Test Department Management Seminar, 5 March 1953."

17. Robert Tannenbaum, Verne Kallejian, and Irving R. Weschler, "Training Managers for Leadership," *Personnel*, 30 (January 1954), p. 3.

18. Verne J. Kallejian, Irving R. Weschler, and Robert Tannenbaum, "Managers in Transition," *Harvard Business Review*, 33 (July–August 1955), pp. 55–64.

19. Tannenbaum correspondence.

20. Ibid.

21. Correspondence with Chris Argyris; and Chris Argyris, *Interpersonal Competence and Organizational Effectiveness* (Homewood, IL: Richard D. Irwin, 1962).

22. Argyris correspondence.

23. Chris Argyris, *Intervention Theory and Method* (Reading, MA: Addison-Wesley, 1970).

24. Argyris correspondence.

25. Donald D. Bowen, "Competence and Justice: A Conversation with Chris Argyris," p. 4.2 of a manuscript accepted for publication in the 1988 *OD Annual*.

26. Argyris correspondence.

27. Ibid. Argyris's Ph.D. in organizational behavior may have been the first ever awarded.

28. Argyris correspondence.

29. See Richard Beckhard, W. Warner Burke, and Fred I. Steele, "The Program for Specialists in Organization Training and Development," p. ii, mimeographed paper (NTL Institute for Applied Behavioral Science, December 1967); and John Paul Jones, "What's Wrong with Work?" in *What's Wrong with Work?* (New York: National Association of Manufacturers, 1967), p. 8. According to correspondence with

Rensis Likert, the link between McGregor and John Paul Jones occurred in the summer of 1957. Discussion took place between the two when Jones attended one of the annual two-week seminars at Aspen, Colorado, organized by Hollis Peter of the Foundation for Research on Human Behavior and conducted by Douglas McGregor, Mason Haire, and Rensis Likert.

30. Gilbert Burck, "Union Carbide's Patient Schemers," *Fortune,* 72 (December 1965), pp. 147–149. For McGregor's account, see "Team Building at Union Carbide," in Douglas McGregor, *The Professional Manager* (New York: McGraw-Hill, 1967), pp. 106–110.

31. See the Editor's Preface to Douglas McGregor, *The Professional Manager* (New York: McGraw-Hill, 1967), p. viii.

32. Conversation with George Strauss, Western Division of the Academy of Management conference, San Diego, California, March 1985. For a brief overview of Rogers's life and career, see "Carl Rogers (1902–1987)," *American Psychologist,* 43 (February 1988), pp. 127–128. Carl Rogers was also on the staff of several NTL president's labs in the early days. Seminar with Carl Rogers, Western Division of the Academy of Management conference, San Diego, California, March 1985.

33. Douglas McGregor, *The Human Side of Enterprise* (New York: McGraw-Hill, 1960). For more on McGregor, see Marvin R. Weisbord, *Productive Workplaces* (San Francisco: Jossey-Bass Publishers, 1987), pp. 106–122.

34. Warren Bennis, *An Invented Life: Reflections on Leadership and Change* (Reading, MA: Addison-Wesley, 1993), p. 14.

35. This paragraph is based on interviews with Herbert Shepard, August 3, 1981. For a brief discussion of the career of Clarence Hicks, see Wendell French, *The Personnel Management Process,* 6th ed. (Boston: Houghton Mifflin, 1987), Chap. 2.

36. Much of the historical account in this paragraph and the following three paragraphs is based on correspondence and interviews with Herbert Shepard, with some information added from correspondence with Robert Blake.

37. Correspondence with Robert Blake and Herbert Shepard. For further reference to Murray Horowitz and Paul Buchanan, as well as to comments about the innovative contributions of Michael Blansfield,

see Herbert A. Shepard, "Explorations in Observant Participation," in Bradford, Gibb, and Benne, eds., *T-Group Theory,* pp. 382–383. See also Marshall Sashkin, "Interview with Robert R. Blake and Jane Srygley Mouton," *Group and Organization Studies,* 3 (December 1978), pp. 401–407.

38. See Robert Blake and Jane Srygley Mouton, "The Instrumented Training Laboratory," in Irving R. Weschler and Edgar M. Schein, eds., *Selected Readings Series Five: Issues in Training* (Washington, DC: National Training Laboratories, 1962), pp. 61–85. In this chapter, Blake and Mouton credit Muzafer and Carolyn Sherif with important contributions to early intergroup experiments. Reference is also made to the contributions of Frank Cassens of Humble Oil and Refinery in the early phases of the Esso program. For a brief description of the development of the two-dimensional Managerial Grid, see Robert Blake and Jane Srygley Mouton, *Diary of an OD Man* (Houston: Gulf 1976), pp. 332–336. For more on Sherif, see O. J. Harvey, "Muzafer Sherif (1906–1988)," *American Psychologist,* 44 (October 1989), pp. 1325–1326.

39. Based on correspondence with Robert Blake. See also Robert R. Blake and Jane Srygley Mouton, "Why the OD Movement is 'Stuck' and How to Break It Loose," *Training and Development Journal,* 33 (September 1979), pp. 12–20.

40. Blake correspondence.

41. Mouton correspondence.

42. Blake correspondence.

43. Ibid. For more on Bowlby, see Mary D. Salter Ainsworth, "John Bowlby (1907–1993)," *American Psychologist,* 47 (May 1992), p. 668.

44. Blake correspondence.

45. Correspondence with Richard Beckhard.

46. Ibid.

47. Based on Beckhard correspondence and other sources.

48. Kleiner, *The Age of Heretics,* p. 223.

49. Bennis, *An Invented Life: Reflections on Leadership and Change* pp. 15–29.

50. Warren G. Bennis, Kenneth D. Benne, and Robert Chin, *The Planning of Change,* 2d ed. (Holt, Rinehart and Winston, 1969).

51. Warren G. Bennis and Philip Slater, "Democracy Is Inevitable," *Harvard Business Review* (September–October 1990).

52. The previous three paragraphs and the following three are based on correspondence with Eva Schindler-Rainman. For additional material, see Anthony J. Reilly, "Interview" (with Eva Schindler-Rainman and Ron Lippitt) *Group & Organization Studies,* 2 (September 1977), pp. 265–281.

53. For more on Edith Seashore, see Charleen Alderfer, "A Biography of Edith Whitfield Seashore," *Journal of Applied Behavioral Science,* 28 (March 1992), pp. 7–8.

54. Kleiner, *The Age of Heretics,* pp. 223–225.

55. Eva Schindler-Rainman, *The Creative Volunteer Community: A Collection of Writings by Eva Schindler-Rainman, D.S.W.* (Vancouver, BC: Vancouver Volunteer Centre, 1987).

56. Eva Schindler-Rainman and Ronald Lippitt, *Building the Collaborative Community: Mobilizing Citizens for Action* (Riverside, CA: University of California Extension, 1980.) (Third printing available through ENERGIZE, 5450 Wissahickon Avenue, Philadelphia, PA 19144.)

57. Eva Schindler-Rainman and Ronald Lippitt, *The Volunteer Community: Creative Use of Human Resources,* 2d ed. (San Diego: University Associates, 1975.) (Available through ENERGIZE.)

58. Eva Schindler-Rainman and Ronald Lippitt, *Team Training for Community Change: Concepts, Goals, Strategies and Skills* (Bethesda, MD: Development Publications, 1972). (Third printing, 1993, available through Dr. Eva Schindler-Rainman, 4267 San Rafael Avenue, Los Angeles, CA 90042.)

59. Interpretations of Blake correspondence, Shepard interview, Beckhard correspondence, and Larry Porter, "OD: Some Questions Some Answers— An Interview with Beckhard and Shepard," *OD Practitioner,* 6 (Autumn 1974), p. 1.

60. Blake correspondence.

61. Jane Srygley Mouton and Robert R. Blake, "University Training in Human Relations Skills," *Selected Readings Series Three: Forces in Learning* (Washington DC: National Training Laboratories, 1961), pp. 88–96, reprinted from *Group Psychotherapy,* 10 (1957), pp. 342–345.

62. Shepard and Blake correspondence.

63. Interview with Herbert Shepard, San Diego, California, August 3, 1981.

64. Beckhard correspondence.

65. Burck, "Union Carbide's Patient Schemers," p. 149.

66. Harry D. Kolb, "Introduction" to *An Action Research Program for Organization Improvement* (Ann Arbor, MI: Foundation for Research on Human Behavior, 1960), p. i. The phrase *organization development* is used

several times in this monograph based on a 1959 meeting about the Esso programs and written by Kolb, Shepard, Blake, and others.

67. Based on Beckhard correspondence.

68. This history is based largely on correspondence with Rensis Likert and partially on "The Career of Rensis Likert," *ISR Newsletter* (Winter 1971); and *A Quarter Century of Social Research,* Institute for Social Research (1971). See also Charles Cannell and Robert Kahn, "Some Factors in the Origins and Development of The Institute for Social Research, The University of Michigan," *American Psychologist,* 39 (November 1984), pp. 1256–1266.

69. "Rensis Likert," *ISR newsletter,* p. 6.

70. Likert correspondence. Floyd Mann later became the first director of the Center for Research on the Utilization of Scientific Knowledge (CRUSK) when the center was established by ISR in 1964. See also Floyd C. Mann, "Studying and Creating Change," in Bennis, Benne, and Chin, eds., *Planning of Change,* pp. 605–613.

71. Mann, "Studying and Creating Change," p. 609.

72. Howard Baumgartel, "Using Employee Questionnaire Results for Improving Organizations: The Survey (Feedback) Experiment," *Kansas Business Review,* 12 (December 1959), pp. 2–6.

73. Likert correspondence.

74. Marrow, *The Practical Theorist,* p. 164. This book about the life and work of Kurt Lewin is rich with events that are important to the history of OD.

75. Likert correspondence.

76. Argyris correspondence.

77. Likert correspondence.

78. H. V. Dicks, *Fifty Years of the Tavistock Clinic* (London: Routledge & Kegan Paul, 1970), pp. 1, 32.

79. Based on ibid., 5, 7, 133, 140; and Robert DeBoard, *The Psychoanalysis of Organizations* (London: Tavistock 1978), pp. 35–43.

80. Eric Trist and Marshall Sashkin, "Interview," *Group & Organization Studies,* 5 (June 1980), pp. 150–151; and Kleiner, *The Age of Heretics,* pp. 63–64.

81. Trist and Sashkin, p. 155. See also William A. Pasmore and Guruder S. Khalsa, "The Contributions of Eric Trist to the Social Engagement of Social Science," *Academy of Management Review,* 18 (July 1993), pp. 546–569.

82. Kleiner, p. 64.

83. Ibid., p. 65.

84. Trist and Sashkin, pp. 144–151.

85. Bennis address, Academy of Management, August 3, 1981.

86. Argyris correspondence.

87. Amir Levy and Uni Merry, *Organizational Transformation* (New York: Praeger Publishers, 1986), p. 5.

88. David A. Nadler and Michael L. Tushman, "Organizational Frame Bending: Principles for Managing Reorientation," *The Academy of Management Executive,* 3 (August 1989), pp. 194–204.

89. Leonard D. Goodstein and W. Warner Burke, "Creating Successful Organization Change," *Organizational Dynamics,* 19 (Spring 1991), pp. 5–17.

90. Gloria Barczak, Charles Smith, and David Wilemon, "Managing Large-Scale Organizational Change," *Organizational Dynamics* (Autumn 1987), pp. 23–35.

91. Richard Beckhard and Wendy Pritchard, *Changing the Essence* (San Francisco: Jossey-Bass Publishers, 1992), p. 3; and Richard Beckhard, "Choosing and Leading a Fundamental Change," *Academy of Management ODC Newsletter* (Summer 1993), pp. 6–8.

92. Edgar H. Schein, *Organizational Culture and Leadership* (San Francisco: Jossey-Bass Publishers, 1985).

93. Edgar H. Schein, "Organization Development and the Study of Organizational Culture," *Academy of Management OD Newsletter* (Summer 1990), pp. 3–5.

94. Ralph H. Kilmann, "Five Steps for Closing Culture-Gaps," pp. 351–369; and Robert F. Allen, "Four Phases for Bringing about Cultural Change," pp. 332–350 in Ralph H. Kilmann, Mary J. Saxton, and Roy Serpa, eds. *Gaining Control of the Corporate Culture* (San Francisco: Jossey-Bass Publishers, 1985). See also William G. Ouchi and Raymond L. Price, Hierarchies, Clans, and Theory Z: A New Perspective on Organization Development," *Organizational Dynamics,* 21 (Spring 1993), pp. 62–70.

95. Chris Argyris, *Overcoming Organizational Defensive Routines* (Boston: Allyn and Bacon, 1990).

96. Chris Argyris and Donald Schon, *Organizational Learning* (Reading, MA: Addison-Wesley, 1976).

97. Chris Argyris, "Strategy Implementation and Experience in Learning," *Organizational Dynamics,* 18 (Autumn 1989), pp. 8, 9.

98. Ibid., pp. 5–15; and Chris Argyris, "Teaching Smart People How to Learn," *Harvard Business Review,* 69 (May–June 1991), pp. 99–109.

99. Peter M. Senge, *The Fifth Discipline: The Art and Practice of the Learning Organization* (New York: Doubleday/Currency, 1990), pp. 12, 18, 19, 44.

100. John A. Byrne, "Management's New Gurus," *Business Week,* August 31, 1992, pp. 44–52.

101. For more on teams, see Jon R. Katzenbach and Douglas K. Smith, *The Wisdom of Teams* (Boston: Harvard Business School Press, 1993); Richard S. Wellins, William C. Byham, and Jeanne M. Wilson, *Empowered Teams* (San Francisco: Jossey-Bass Publishers, 1991); David Barry, "Managing the Bossless Team: Lessons in Distributed Leadership," *Organizational Dynamics,* 20 (Summer 1991), pp. 31–46; Eric Sundstrom, Kenneth P. De Meuse, and David Futrell, "Work Teams Applications and Effectiveness," *American Psychologist,* 45 (February 1990), pp. 120–133. Glenn M. Parker, *Team Players and Teamwork* (San Francisco: Jossey-Bass Publishers, 1990); and Larry Hirschhorn, *Managing in the New Team Environment* (Reading, MA: Addison-Wesley Publishing Company, 1991).

102. Dan Ciampa, *Total Quality* (Reading, MA: Addison-Wesley Publishing Company, 1992), p. xxi. See also Marshall Sashkin and Kenneth J. Kiser, *Total Quality Management* (Seabrook, MD: Ducochon Press, 1991).

103. Ciampa, *Total Quality*, p. xxii.

104. Ibid., p. xxiv.

105. W. Warner Burke, *Organization Development: A Process of Learning and Changing* (Reading, MA: Addison-Wesley Publishing Company, 1994), p. 199.

106. Edward Lindaman and Ronald Lippitt, *Choosing the Future You Prefer* (Washington, DC: Development Publications, 1979).

107. Ronald Fox, Ronald Lippitt, and Eva Schindler-Rainman, *The Humanized Future: Some New Images* (LaJolla, CA: University Associates, 1973).

108. Merrelyn Emery, *Searching: For New Directions, in New Ways for New Times* (Canberra: Centre for Continuing Education, Australian National University, 1982).

109. Marvin R. Weisbord, "Future Search: Toward Strategic Integration," in Walter Sikes, Allan Drexler, and Jack Gant, eds., *The Emerging Practice of Organization Development* (Alexandria, VA: NTL Institute for Applied Behavioral Science, and San Diego, CA: University Associates, 1989), p. 171; and Marvin R. Weisbord, "Future Search: Innovative Business Conference," *Planning Review,* 12 (July 1984), pp. 16–20.

110. Marvin R. Weisbord, *Productive Workplaces* (San Francisco: Jossey-Bass Publishers, 1987), pp. 289–292.

111. Senge, *The Fifth Discipline,* p. 214.

112. Richard Beckhard, "The Confrontation Meeting," *Harvard Business Review,* 45 (March-April 1967), pp. 149–155. See also W. Warner Burke and Richard Beckhard, *Conference Planning,* 2d ed. (San Diego: University Associates, 1970).

113. Marvin R. Weisbord, "Toward Third-Wave Managing and Consulting," *Organizational Dynamics,* 15 (Winter 1987), pp. 19–20.

114. See Frank J. Barrett and David L. Cooperrider, "Generative Metaphor Intervention: A New Approach for Working with Systems Divided by Conflict and Caught in Defensive Perception," *Journal of Applied Behavioral Science,* 26, no. 2 (1990), 219–239; and Rita F. Williams, "Survey Guided Appreciative Inquiry: A Case Study," *OD Practitioner,* 28, nos. 1, 2 (1996), pp. 43–51.

115. Gerard Burke and Joe Peppard, *Examining Business Process Re-Engineering: Current Perspectives and Research Directions* (London: Kogan Page, 1995), p. 25.

116. Interview with Sam Shirley, February 4, 1982; correspondence with Sheldon A. Davis; Sheldon A. Davis, "An Organic Problem-Solving Method of Organizational Change," *Journal of Applied Behavioral Science,* 3 (November 1, 1967), pp. 3–21; and the case study of the TRW Systems Group in Gene Dalton, Paul Lawrence, and Larry Greiner, *Organizational Change and Development* (Homewood, IL: Irwin-Dorsey, 1970), pp. 4–153.

117. Celeste A. Coruzzi, "Remembering Shel Davis," *OD Practitioner,* 27, nos. 2, 3 (1995), pp. 19–21.

118. Correspondence with Michael Thiel, June 1993.

119. Ibid.

120. *The Wall Street Journal*, March 5, 1993, p. B7A.

121. Mel R. Spehn, "Reflections on the Organizational Effectiveness Center and School," mimeographed paper, compiled in the summer/fall of 1985, Fort Ord, CA, p. 3.

122. Ibid., p. 11.

123. Correspondence from Ray L. Forbes, Jr., Franklin University Graduate School of Business, June 5, 1995; and Raymond L. Forbes, Jr., "Organization Development: An Analysis of the U.S. Navy Experience," a human resource management working paper, Department of Administrative Sciences, Naval Postgraduate School, Monterey, California, June 30, 1977.

124. See Eva Schindler-Rainman, "Community Development Through Laboratory Methods," in Benne, Bradford, Gibb, and Lippitt, eds., *Laboratory*

Method of Changing and Learning, pp. 445–463. See also John W. Selsky, "Lessons in Community Development," *Journal of Applied Behavioral Science,* 27 (March 1991), pp. 91–115.

125. Shepard correspondence. Starting in 1967, Herbert Shepard was involved in the applications of OD to community problems in Middletown, CT.

126. See Scott Myers, "Overcoming Union Opposition to Job Enrichment," *Harvard Business Review,* 49 (May–June 1971), pp. 37–49; and Robert Blake, Herbert Shepard, and Jane Mouton, *Managing Intergroup Conflict in Industry* (Houston: Gulf, 1964), pp. 122–138.

127. Shepard correspondence.

128. Correspondence with W. Warner Burke and memoranda and attendance lists pertaining to 1967–1969 Network meetings furnished by Burke.

129. For example, the following topics were included in the program of the 1965 convention: "Strategies for Organization Improvement: Research and Consultation," "Managerial Grid Organization Development," and "The Impact of Laboratory Training in Research and Development Environment," *American Psychologist,* 20 (July 1965), pp. 549, 562, 565.

130. Frank Friedlander and L. Dave Brown, "Organization Development," *Annual Review of Psychology,* 25 (1974), pp. 313–341.

131. Clay Alderfer, "Organization Development," *Annual Review of Psychology,* 28 (1977), pp. 197–223.

132. Michael Beer and Anna Elise Walton, "Organizational Change and Development," *Annual Review of Psychology,* 38 (1987), pp. 339–367.

133. Jerry I. Porras and Robert C. Silvers, "Organization Development and Transformation," *Annual Review of Psychology,* 42 (1991), pp. 51–78.

134. Claude Faucheux, Gilles Amada, and André Laurent, "Organizational Development and Change," *Annual Review of Psychology,* 33 (1982), pp. 343–370.

135. D. D. Warrick, ed., *OD Newsletter,* OD Division, Academy of Management (Spring 1979), p. 7. Also various sources, including "Academic Program Reviews," *OD Practitioner,* 28, nos. 1, 2 (1996), pp. 61–67.

READING 3
GENERAL STRATEGIES FOR EFFECTING CHANGES IN HUMAN SYSTEMS

Robert Chin
Kenneth D. Benne

Discussing general strategies and procedures for effecting change requires that we set limits to the discussion. For, under a liberal interpretation of the title, we would need to deal with much of the literature of contemporary social and behavioral science, basic and applied.

Therefore we shall limit our discussion to those changes which are planned changes—in which attempts to bring about change are conscious, deliberate, and intended, at least on the part of one or more agents related to the change attempt. We shall also attempt to categorize strategies and procedures which have a few important elements in common but which, in fact, differ widely in other respects. And we shall neglect many of these differences. In addition, we shall look beyond the description of procedures in commonsense terms and seek some genotypic characteristics of change strategies. We shall seek the roots of the main strategies discussed, including their variants, in ideas and idea systems prominent in contemporary and recent social and psychological thought.

One element in all approaches to planned change is the conscious utilization and application of knowledge as an instrument or tool for modifying patterns and institutions of practice. The knowledge or related technology to be applied may be knowledge of the nonhuman environment in which practice goes on or of some knowledge-based "thing technology" for controlling one or another feature of the practice environment. In educational practice, for example, technologies of communication and calculation, based upon new knowledge of electronics—audiovisual devices,

television, computers, teaching machines—loom large among the knowledges and technologies that promise greater efficiency and economy in handling various practices in formal education. As attempts are made to introduce these new thing technologies into school situations, the change problem shifts to the human problems of dealing with the resistances, anxieties, threats to morale, conflicts, disrupted interpersonal communications, and so on, which prospective changes in patterns of practice evoke in the people affected by the change. So the change agent, even though focally and initially concerned with modifications in the thing technology of education, finds himself in need of more adequate knowledge of human behavior, individual and social, and in need of developed "people technologies," based on behavioral knowledge, for dealing effectively with the human aspects of deliberate change.

The knowledge which suggests improvements in educational practice may, on the other hand, be behavioral knowledge in the first instance—knowledge about participative learning, about attitude change, about family disruption in inner-city communities, about the cognitive and skill requirements of new careers, and so forth. Such knowledge may suggest changes in school grouping, in the relations between teachers and students, in the relations of teachers and principals to parents, and in counseling practices. Here change agents, initially focused on application of behavioral knowledge and the improvement of people technologies in school settings, must face the problems of using people technologies in planning, installing, and evaluating such changes in educational practice. The new people technologies must be experienced, understood, and accepted by teachers and administrators before they can be used effectively with students.

Source: "General Strategies for Effecting Changes in Human Systems" from *The Planning of Change,* 3rd ed., by Warren G. Bennis, Kenneth D. Benne, Robert Chin, and Kenneth E. Corey, copyright © 1976 by Holt, Rinehart, and Winston, Inc. Reprinted by permission of the publisher.

This line of reasoning suggests that, whether the focus of planned change is in the introduction of more effective thing technologies or people technologies into institutionalized practice, processes of introducing such changes must be based on behavioral knowledge of change and must utilize people technologies based on such knowledge.

Types of Strategies for Changing

Our further analysis is based on three types or groups of strategies. The first of these, and probably the most frequently employed by men of knowledge in America and Western Europe, are those we call empirical-rational strategies. One fundamental assumption underlying these strategies is that men are rational. Another assumption is that men will follow their rational self-interest once this is revealed to them. A change is proposed by some person or group which knows of a situation that is desirable, effective, and in line with the self-interest of the person, group, organization, or community which will be affected by the change. Because the person (or group) is assumed to be rational and moved by self-interest, it is assumed that he (or they) will adopt the proposed change if it can be rationally justified and if it can be shown by the proposer(s) that he (or they) will gain by the change.

A second group of strategies we call normative-reeducative. These strategies build upon assumptions about human motivation different from those underlying the first. The rationality and intelligence of men are not denied. Patterns of action and practice are supported by sociocultural norms and by commitments on the part of individuals to these norms. Sociocultural norms are supported by the attitude and value systems of individuals— normative outlooks which undergird their commitments. Change in a pattern of practice or action, according to this view, will occur only as the persons involved are brought to change their normative orientations to old patterns and develop commitments to new ones. And changes in normative orientations involve changes in attitudes, values, skills, and significant relationships, not just changes in knowledge, information, or intellectual rationales for action and practice.

The third group of strategies is based on the application of power in some form, political or otherwise. The influence process involved is basically that of compliance of those with less power to the plans, directions, and leadership of those with greater power. Often the power to be applied is legitimate power or authority. Thus the strategy may involve getting the authority of law or administrative policy behind the change to be effected. Some power strategies may appeal less to the use of authoritative power to effect change than to the massing of coercive power, legitimate or not, in support of the change sought.[1]

Empirical-Rational Strategies.   A variety of specific strategies are included in what we are calling the empirical-rational approach to effecting change. As we have already pointed out, the rationale underlying most of these is an assumption that men are guided by reason and that they will utilize some rational calculus of self-interest in determining needed changes in behavior.

It is difficult to point to any one person whose ideas express or articulate the orientation underlying commitment to empirical-rational strategies of changing. In Western Europe and America, this orientation might be better identified with the general social orientation of the enlightenment and of classical liberalism than with the ideas of any one man. On this view, the chief foes of human rationality and to change or progress based on rationality were ignorance and superstition. Scientific investigation and research represented the chief ways of extending knowledge and reducing the limitations of ignorance. A corollary of this optimistic view of man and his future was an advocacy of education as a way of disseminating scientific knowledge and of freeing men and women from the shackles of superstition. Although elitist notions played a part in the thinking of many classic liberals, the increasing trend during the 19th century was toward the universalization of educational opportunity. The common and universal school, open to all men and women, was the principal instrument by which knowledge would replace ignorance and superstition in the minds of people and become a principal agent in the spread of reason, knowledge, and knowledge-based action and practice (progress) in human society. In American experience, Jefferson may be taken as a principal, early advocate of research and of education as agencies of human progress. And Horace Mann may be taken as the prophet of progress through the institutionalization of universal education opportunity through the common school.[2]

Basic Research and Dissemination of Knowledge through General Education.   The strategy of encouraging basic knowledge building and of depending on general education to diffuse the results of research into the minds and thinking of men and women is still by far the most appealing strategy of change to most academic men of knowledge and to large segments of the American population as well. Basic researchers are quite likely to appeal for time for further research when confronted by some unmet need. And many people find this appeal convincing. Both of these facts are well illustrated by difficulties with diseases for which no adequate control measure or cures are available—polio-myelitis, for example. Medical researchers asked for more time and funds for research and people responded with funds for research, both through voluntary channels and through legislative appropriations. And the control measures were forthcoming. The educational problem then shifted to inducing people to comply with immunization procedures based on research findings.

This appeal to a combination of research and education of the public has worked in many areas of new knowledge-based thing technologies where almost universal readiness for accepting the new technology was already present in the population. Where such readiness is not available, as in the case of fluoridation technologies in the management of dental cavities, the general strategy of basic research

plus educational (informational) campaigns to spread knowledge of the findings do not work well. The cases of its inadequacy as a single strategy of change have multiplied, especially where "engineering" problems, which involve a divided and conflicting public or deep resistances due to the threat by the new technology to traditional attitudes and values, have thwarted its effectiveness. But these cases, while they demand attention to other strategies of changing, do not disprove the importance of basic research and of general educational opportunity as elements in a progressive and self-renewing society.

We have noted that the strategy under discussion has worked best in grounding and diffusing generally acceptable thing technologies in society. Some have argued that the main reason the strategy has not worked in the area of people technologies is a relative lack of basic research on people and their behavior, relationships, and institutions and a corresponding lack of emphasis upon social and psychological knowledges in school and college curricula. It would follow in this view that increased basic research on human affairs and relationships and increased efforts to diffuse the results of such research through public education are the ways of making the general strategy work better. Auguste Comte, with his emphasis on positivistic sociology in the reorganization of society, and Lester F. Ward in America may be taken as late 19th-century representatives of this view. And the spirit of Comte and Ward is by no means dead in American academia or in influential segments of the American public.

Personnel Selection and Replacement.   Difficulties in getting knowledge effectively into practice may be seen as lying primarily in the lack of fitness of persons occupying positions with job responsibilities for improving practice. The argument goes that we need the right person in the right position, if knowledge is to be optimally applied and if rationally based changes are to become the expectation in organizational and societal affairs. This fits with the liberal reformers' frequently voiced and enacted plea to drive the unfit from office and to replace them with those more fit as a condition of social progress.

That reformers' programs have so often failed has sobered but by no means destroyed the zeal of those who regard personnel selection, assessment, and replacement as a major key to program improvement in education or in other enterprises as well. This strategy was given a scientific boost by the development of scientific testing of potentialities and aptitudes. We will use Binet as a prototype of psychological testing and Moreno as a prototype in sociometric testing, while recognizing the extensive differentiation and elaboration which have occurred in psychometrics and sociometrics since their original work. We recognize, too, the elaborated modes of practice in personnel work which have been built around psychometric and sociometric tools and techniques. We do not discount their limited value as actual and potential tools for change, while making two observations on the way they have often been used. First, they have been used more often in the interest of system maintenance rather than of system change, since the job descriptions personnel workers seek to fill are defined in terms of system requirements as established. Second, by focusing on the role occupant as the principal barrier to improvement, personnel selection and replacement strategies have tended not to reveal the social and cultural system difficulties which may be in need of change if improvement is to take place.

Systems Analysts as Staff and Consultants. Personnel workers in government, industry, and education have typically worked in staff relations to line management, reflecting the bureaucratic, line-staff form of organization which has flourished in the large-scale organization of effort and enterprise in the 20th century. And other expert workers— systems analysts—more attuned to system difficulties than to the adequacies or inadequacies of persons as role occupants within the system, have found their way into the staff resources of line management in contemporary organizations.

There is no reason why the expert resources of personnel workers and systems analysts might not be used in nonbureaucratic organizations or in processes of moving bureaucratic organizations toward nonbureaucratic forms. But the fact remains that their use has been shaped, for the most part, in the image of the scientific management of bureaucratically organized enterprises. So we have placed the systems analysts in our chart under Frederick Taylor, the father of scientific management in America.

The line management of an enterprise seeks to organize human and technical effort toward the most efficient service of organizational goals. And these goals are defined in terms of the production of some mandated product, whether a tangible product or a less tangible good or service. In pursuing this quest for efficiency, line management employs experts in the analysis of sociotechnical systems and in the laying out of more efficient systems. The experts employed may work as external consultants or as an internal staff unit. Behavioral scientists have recently found their way, along with mathematicians and engineers, into systems analysis work.

It is interesting to note that the role of these experts is becoming embroiled in discussions of whether or not behavioral science research should be used to sensitize administrators to new organizational possibilities, to new goals, or primarily to implement efficient operation within perspectives and goals as currently defined. Jean Hills has raised the question of whether behavioral science when applied to organizational problems tends to perpetuate established ideology and system relations because of blinders imposed by their being "problem centered" and by their limited definition of what is "a problem."[3]

We see an emerging strategy, in the use of behavioral scientists as systems analysts and engineers, toward viewing the problem of organizational change and changing as a wide-angled problem, one in which all the input and output features and components of a large-scale system are considered. It is foreseeable that with the use of high-speed and high-capacity computers, and with the growth of substantial theories and hypotheses about how parts of an educational system operate, we shall find more and more applications for systems analysis and operations research in programs of educational change. In fact, it is precisely the quasi-mathematical character of these modes of research that will make possible the rational analysis of qualitatively different aspects of educational work and will bring them into the range of rational planning—masses of students, massive problems of poverty and educational and cultural deprivation, and so on. We see no necessary incompatibility between an ideology which emphasizes the individuality of the student and the use of systems analysis and computers in strategizing the problems of the total system. The actual incompatibilities may lie in the limited uses to which existing organizers and administrators of educational efforts put these technical resources.

Applied Research and Linkage Systems for Diffusion of Research Results.   The American development of applied research of a planned system for linking applied researchers with professional practitioners and both of these with centers for basic research and with organized consumers of applied research has been strongly influenced by two distinctive American inventions—the land-grant university and the agricultural extension system. We, therefore, have put the name of Justin Morrill, author of the land-grant college act and of the act which established the cooperative agricultural extension system, on our chart. The land-grant colleges or universities were dedicated to doing applied research in the service of agriculture and the mechanic arts. These colleges and universities developed research programs in basic sciences as well and experimental stations for the development and refinement of knowledge-based technologies for use in engineering and agriculture. As the extension services developed, county agents—practitioners—were attached to the state land-grant college or university that received financial support from both state and federal governments. The county agent and his staff developed local

organizations of adult farm men and women and of farm youth to provide both a channel toward informing consumers concerning new and better agricultural practices and toward getting awareness of unmet consumer needs and unsolved problems back to centers of knowledge and research. Garth Jones has made one of the more comprehensive studies of the strategies of changing involved in large-scale demonstration.[4]

All applied research has not occurred within a planned system for knowledge discovery, development, and utilization like the one briefly described above. The system has worked better in developing and diffusing thing technologies than in developing and diffusing people technologies, though the development of rural sociology and of agricultural economics shows that extension workers were by no means unaware of the behavioral dimensions of change problems. But the large-scale demonstration, through the land-grant university cooperative extension service, of the stupendous changes which can result from a planned approach to knowledge discovery, development, diffusion, and utilization is a part of the consciousness of all Americans concerned with planned change.[5]

Applied research and development is an honored part of the tradition of engineering approaches to problem identification and solution. The pioneering work of E. L. Thorndike in applied research in education should be noted on our chart. The processes and slow tempo of diffusion and utilization of research findings and inventions in public education are well illustrated in studies by Paul Mort and his students.[6] More recently, applied research, in its product development aspect, has been utilized in a massive way to contribute curriculum materials and designs for science instruction (as well as in other subjects). When we assess this situation to find reasons why such researches have not been more effective in producing changes in instruction, the answers seem to lie both in the plans of the studies which produced the materials and designs and in the potential users of the findings. Adequate linkage between consumers and researchers was frequently not established. Planned and evaluated demonstrations and experimentations connected with the use of materials were frequently slighted. And training of consumer teachers to use the new materials adaptively and creatively was frequently missing.

Such observations have led to a fresh spurt of interest in evaluation research addressed to educational programs. The fear persists that this, too, may lead to disappointment if it is not focused for two-way communication between researchers and teachers and if it does not involve collaboratively the ultimate consumers of the results of such research—the students. Evaluation researches conducted in the spirit of justifying a program developed by expert applied researchers will not help to guide teachers and students in their quest for improved practices of teaching and learning, if the concerns of the latter have not been taken centrally into account in the evaluation process.[7]

Recently, attempts have been made to link applied research activities in education with basic researchers on the one hand and with persons in action and practice settings on the other through some system of interlocking roles similar to those suggested in the description of the land-grant extension systems in agriculture or in other fields where applied and development researches have flourished.

The linking of research-development efforts with diffusion-innovation efforts has been gaining headway in the field of education with the emergence of federally supported research and development centers based in universities, regional laboratories connected with state departments of education, colleges and universities in a geographic area, and with various consortia and institutes confronting problems of educational change and changing. The strategy of change here usually includes a well-researched innovation which seems feasible to install in practice settings. Attention is directed to the question of whether or not the innovation will bring about a desired result, and with what it can accomplish, if given a trial in one or more practice settings. The questions of *how* to get a fair trial and *how* to install an innovation in

an already going and crowded school system are ordinarily not built centrally into the strategy. The rationalistic assumption usually precludes research attention to these questions. For, if the invention can be rationally shown to have achieved desirable results in some situations, it is assumed that people in other situations will adopt it once they know these results and the rationale behind them. The neglect of the above questions has led to a wastage of much applied research effort in the past.

Attention has been given recently to the roles, communication mechanisms, and processes necessary for innovation and diffusion of improved education practices.[8] Clark and Guba have formulated very specific processes related to and necessary for change in educational practice following upon research. For them, the necessary processes are: *development,* including invention and design; *diffusion,* including dissemination and demonstration; *adoption,* including trial, installation, and institutionalization. Clark's earnest conviction is summed up in this statement: "In a sense, the education research community will be the educational community, and the route to educational progress will self-evidently be research and development."[9]

The approach of Havelock and Benne is concerned with the intersystem relationships between basic researchers, applied researchers, practitioners, and consumers in an evolved and evolving organization for knowledge utilization. They are concerned especially with the communication difficulties and role conflicts that occur at points of intersystem exchange. These conflicts are important because they illuminate the normative issues at stake between basic researchers and applied researchers, between applied researchers and practitioners (teachers and administrators), between practitioners and consumers (students). The lines of strategy suggested by their analysis for solving role conflicts and communication difficulties call for transactional and collaborative exchanges across the lines of varied organized interests and orientations within the process of utilization. This brings their analysis into the range of normative-reeducative strategies to be discussed later.

The concepts from the behavioral sciences upon which these strategies of diffusion rest come mainly from two traditions. The first is from studies of the diffusion of traits of culture from one cultural system to another, initiated by the American anthropologist, Franz Boas. This type of study has been carried on by Rogers in his work on innovation and diffusion of innovations in contemporary culture and is reflected in a number of recent writers, such as Katz and Carlson.[10] The second scientific tradition is in studies of influence in mass communication associated with Carl Hovland and his students.[11] Both traditions have assumed a *relatively passive recipient of input* in diffusion situations. And actions within the process of diffusion are interpreted from the standpoint of an observer of the process. Bauer has pointed out that scientific studies have exaggerated the effectiveness of mass persuasion since they have compared the total number in the audience to the communications with the much smaller proportion of the audience persuaded by the communication.[12] A clearer view of processes of diffusion must include the actions of the receiver as well as those of the transmitter in the transactional events which are the units of diffusion process. And strategies for making diffusion processes more effective must be transactional and collaborative by design.

Utopian Thinking as a Strategy of Changing.   It may seem strange to include the projection of utopias as a rational-empirical strategy of changing. Yet inventing and designing the shape of the future by extrapolating what we know of in the present is to envision a direction for planning and action in the present. If the image of a potential future is convincing and rationally persuasive to men in the present, the image may become part of the dynamics and motivation of present action. The liberal tradition is not devoid of its utopias. When we think of utopias quickened by an effort to extrapolate from the sciences of man to a future vision of society, the utopia of B. F. Skinner comes to mind.[13] The title of the Eight State Project, "Designing Education for the Future," for which this paper was prepared, reveals a utopian intent and aspiration and illustrates an attempt to employ utopian thinking for practical purposes.[14]

Yet it may be somewhat disheartening to others as it is to us to note the absence of rousing and beckoning normative statements of what both can and ought to be in man's future in most current liberal-democratic utopias, whether these be based on psychological, sociological, political, or philosophical findings and assumptions. The absence of utopias in current society, in this sense, and in the sense that Mannheim studied them in his now classical study,[15] tends to make the forecasting of future directions a problem of technical prediction, rather than equally a process of projecting value orientations and preferences into the shaping of a better future.

Perceptual and Conceptual Reorganization through the Clarification of Language.   In classical liberalism, one perceived foe of rational change and progress was superstition. And superstitions are carried from man to man and from generation to generation through the agency of unclear and mythical language. British utilitarianism was one important strand of classical liberalism, and one of utilitarianism's important figures, Jeremy Bentham, sought to purify language of its dangerous mystique through his study of fictions.

More recently, Alfred Korzybski and S. I. Hayakawa, in the general semantics movement, have sought a way of clarifying and rectifying the names of things and processes.[16] While their main applied concern was with personal therapy, both, and especially Hayakawa, were also concerned with bringing about changes in social systems as well. People disciplined in general semantics, it was hoped, would see more correctly, communicate more adequately, and reason more effectively and thus lay a realistic common basis for action and changing. The strategies of changing associated with general semantics overlap with our next family of strategies, the normative-reeducative, because of their emphasis upon the importance of interpersonal relationships and social contexts within the communication process.

Normative-Reeducative   Strategies   of Changing.   We have already suggested that this family of strategies rests on assumptions and hypotheses about man and his motivation which contrast significantly at points with the assumptions and hypotheses of those committed to what we have called rational-empirical strategies. Men are seen as inherently active, in quest of impulsive and need satisfaction. The relation between man and his environment is essentially transactional, as Dewey[17] made clear in his famous article on "The Reflex-Arc Concept." Man, the organism, does not passively await given stimuli from his environment in order to respond. He takes stimuli as furthering or thwarting the goals of his ongoing action. Intelligence arises in the process of shaping organism-environmental relations toward more adequate fitting and joining of organismic demands and environmental resources.

Intelligence is social, rather than narrowly individual. Men are guided in their actions by socially funded and communicated meanings, norms, and institutions, in brief by a normative culture. At the personal level, men are guided by internalized meanings, habits, and values. Changes in patterns of action or practice are, therefore, changes, not alone in the rational information equipment of men, but at the personal level, in habits and values as well and, at the sociocultural level, changes are alterations in normative structures and in institutionalized roles and relationships, as well as in cognitive and perceptual orientations.

For Dewey, the prototype of intelligence in action is the scientific method. And he saw a broadened and humanized scientific method as man's best hope for progress, if men could learn to utilize such a method in facing all of the problematic situations of their lives. *Intelligence,* so conceived, rather than *reason* as defined in classical liberalism, was the key to Dewey's hope for the invention, development, and testing of adequate strategies of changing in human affairs.

Lewin's contribution to normative-reeducative strategies of changing stemmed from his vision of required interrelations between research, training, and action (and, for him, this meant collaborative relationships, often now lacking, between researchers, educators, and activists) in the solution of human problems, in the identification of needs for change, and in the working out of improved knowledge, technology, and patterns of action in meeting these needs. Man must participate in his own reeducation if he is to be reeducated at all. And reeducation is a normative change as well as a cognitive and perceptual change. These convictions led Lewin[18] to emphasize action research as a strategy of changing, and participation in groups as a medium of reeducation.

Freud's main contributions to normative-reeducative strategies of changing are two. First, he sought to demonstrate the unconscious and preconscious bases of man's actions. Only as a man finds ways of becoming aware of these nonconscious wellsprings of his attitudes and actions will he be able to bring them into conscious self-control. And Freud devoted much of his magnificent genius to developing ways of helping men to become conscious of the main springs of their actions and so capable of freedom. Second, in developing therapeutic methods, he discovered and developed ways of utilizing the relationships between change agent (therapist) and client (patient) as a major tool in reeducating the client toward expanded self-awareness, self-understanding, and self-control. Emphasis upon the collaborative relationship in therapeutic change was a major contribution by Freud and his students and colleagues to normative-reeducative strategies of changing in human affairs.[19]

Normative-reeducative approaches to effecting change bring direct interventions by change agents, interventions based on a consciously worked out theory of change and of changing, into the life of a client system, be that system a person, a small group, an organization, or a community. The theory of changing is still crude, but it is probably as explicitly stated as possible, granted our present state of knowledge about planned change.[20]

Some of the common elements among variants within this family of change strategies are the following. First, all emphasize the client system and his (or its) involvement in working out programs of change and improvement for himself (or itself). The way the client sees himself and his problem must be brought into dialogic relationship with the way in which he and his problem are seen by the change agent, whether the latter is functioning as researcher, consultant, trainer, therapist, or friend in relation to the client. Second, the problem confronting the client is not assumed a priori to be one which can be met by more adequate technical information, though this possibility is not ruled out. The problem may lie rather in the attitudes, values, norms, and the external and internal relationships of the client system and may require alteration or reeducation of these as a condition of its solution. Third, the change agent must learn to intervene mutually and collaboratively along with the client into efforts to define and solve the client's problem(s). The here and now experience of the two provide an important basis for diagnosing the problem and for locating needs for reeducation in the interest of solving it. Fourth, nonconscious elements which impede problem solution must be brought into consciousness and publicly examined and reconstructed. Fifth, the methods and concepts of the behavioral sciences are resources which change agent and client learn to use selectively, relevantly, and appropriately in learning to deal with the confronting problem and with problems of a similar kind in the future.

These approaches center in the notion that people technology is just as necessary as thing technology in working out desirable changes in human affairs. Put in this bold fashion, it is obvious that for the normative-reeducative change agent, clarification and reconstruction of values is of pivotal importance in changing. By getting the values of various parts of the client system, along with his own, openly into the arena of change, and by working through value conflicts responsibly, the change agent seeks to avoid manipulation and indoctrination of the client, in the morally reprehensible meanings of these terms.

We may use the organization of the National Training Laboratories (NTL) in 1947 as a milestone in the development of normative-reeducative approaches to changing in America. The first summer laboratory program grew out of earlier collaborations among Kurt Lewin, Ronald Lippitt, Leland Bradford, and Kenneth Benne. The idea behind the laboratory was that participants, staff, and students would learn about themselves and their back-home problems by collaboratively building a laboratory in which participants would become both experimenters and subjects in the study of their own developing interpersonal and group behavior within the laboratory setting. It seems evident that the five conditions of a normative-reeducative approach to changing were met in the conception of the training laboratory. Kurt Lewin died before the 1947 session of the training laboratory opened. Ronald Lippitt was a student of Lewin's and carried many of Lewin's orientations with him into the laboratory staff. Leland Bradford and Kenneth Benne were both students of John Dewey's philosophy of education. Bradford had invented several technologies for participative learning and self-study in his work in WPA adult education programs and as training officer in several agencies of the federal government. Benne came out of a background in educational philosophy and had collaborated with colleagues prior to 1943 in developing a methodology for policy and decision making and for the reconstruction of normative orientations, a methodology which sought to fuse democratic and scientific values and to translate these into principles for resolving conflicting and problematic situations at personal and community levels of human organization.[21] Benne and his colleagues had been much influenced by the work of Mary Follett,[22] her studies of integrative solutions to conflicts in settings of public and business administration, and by the work of Karl Mannheim[23] on the ideology and methodology of planning changes in human affairs, as well as by the work of John Dewey and his colleagues.

The work of the National Training Laboratories has encompassed development and testing of various approaches to changing in institutional settings, in America and abroad, since its beginning.

One parallel development in England which grew out of Freud's thinking should be noted. This work developed in efforts at Tavistock Clinic to apply therapeutic approaches to problems of change in industrial organizations and in communities. This work is reported in statements by Elliot Jaques[24] and in this volume by Eric Trist. Another parallel development is represented by the efforts of Roethlisberger and Dickson to use personal counseling in industry as a strategy of organizational change.[25] Roethlisberger and Dickson had been strongly influenced by the pioneer work of Elton Mayo in industrial sociology[26] as well as by the counseling theories and methodologies of Carl Rogers.

Various refinements of methodologies for changing have been developed and tested since the establishment of the National Training Laboratories in 1947, both under its auspices and under other auspices as well. For us, the modal developments are worthy of further discussion here. One set of approaches is oriented focally to the improvement of the problem-solving processes utilized by a client-system. The other set focuses on helping members of client systems to become aware of their attitude and value orientations and relationship difficulties through a probing of feelings, manifest and latent, involved in the functioning and operation of the client system.[27] Both approaches use the development of "temporary systems" as a medium of reeducation of persons and of role occupants in various ongoing social systems.[28]

Improving the Problem-Solving Capabilities of a System.   This family of approaches to changing rests on several assumptions about change in human systems. Changes in a system, when they are reality oriented, take the form of problem solving. A system to achieve optimum reality orientation in its adaptations to its changing internal and external environments must develop and institutionalize its own problem-solving structures and processes. These structures and processes must be tuned both to human problems of relationship and morale and to technical problems of meeting the system's task requirements, set by its goals of production, distribution, and so on.[29] System problems are typically not social *or* technical but actually sociotechnical.[30] The problem-solving structures and processes of a human system must be developed to deal with a range of sociotechnical difficulties, converting them into problems and organizing the relevant processes of the data collection, planning, invention, and tryout of solutions, evaluation and feedback of results, replanning, and so forth, which are required for the solution of the problems.

The human parts of the system must learn to function collaboratively in these processes of problem identification and solution and the system must develop institutionalized support and mechanisms for maintaining and improving these processes. Actually, the model of changing in these approaches is a cooperative, action-research model. This model was suggested by Lewin and developed most elaborately for use in educational settings by Stephen M. Corey.[31]

The range of interventions by outside change agents in implementing this approach to changing is rather wide. It has been most fully elaborated in relation to organizational development programs. Within such programs, intervention methods have been most comprehensively tested in industrial settings. Some of these more or less tested intervention methods are listed below. A design for any organizational development program, of course, normally uses a number of these in succession or combination.

1. Collection of data about organizational functioning and feedback of data into processes of data interpretation and of planning ways of correcting revealed dysfunctions by system managers and data collectors in collaboration.[32]

2. Training of managers and working organizational units in methods of problem solving through self-examination of present ways of dealing with difficulties and through development and tryout of better ways with consultation by outside and/or inside change agents. Usually, the working unit

leaves its working place for parts of its training. These laboratory sessions are ordinarily interspersed with on-the-job consultations.

3. Developing acceptance of feedback (research and development) roles and functions within the organization, training persons to fill these roles, and relating such roles strategically to the ongoing management of the organization.

4. Training internal change agents to function within the organization in carrying on needed applied research, consultation, and training.[33]

Whatever specific strategies of intervention may be employed in developing the system's capabilities for problem solving, change efforts are designed to help the system in developing ways of scanning its operations to detect problems, of diagnosing these problems to determine relevant changeable factors in them, and of moving toward collaboratively determined solutions to the problems.

Releasing and Fostering Growth in the Persons Who Make Up the System to Be Changed.   Those committed to this family of approaches to changing tend to see the person as the basic unit of social organization. Persons, it is believed, are capable of creative, life-affirming, self- and other-regarding and respecting responses, choices, and actions, if conditions which thwart these kinds of responses are removed and other supporting conditions developed. Rogers has formulated these latter conditions in his analysis of the therapist–client relationship—trustworthiness, empathy, caring, and others.[34] Maslow has worked out a similar idea in his analysis of the hierarchy of needs in persons.[35] If lower needs are met, higher need-meeting actions will take place. McGregor[36] has formulated the ways in which existing organizations operate to fixate persons in lower levels of motivation and has sought to envision an organization designed to release and support the growth of persons in fulfilling their higher motivations as they function within the organizations.

Various intervention methods have been designed to help people discover themselves as persons and commit themselves to continuing personal growth in the various relationships of their lives.

1. One early effort to install personal counseling widely and strategically in an organization has been reported by Roethlisberger and Dickson.[37]

2. Training groups designed to facilitate personal confrontation and growth of members in an open, trusting, and accepting atmosphere have been conducted for individuals from various back-home situations and for persons from the same back-home setting. The processes of these groups have sometimes been described as "therapy for normals."[38]

3. Groups and laboratories designed to stimulate and support personal growth have been designed to utilize the resources of nonverbal exchange and communication among members along with verbal dialogue in inducing personal confrontation, discovery, and commitment to continuing growth.

4. Many psychotherapists, building on the work of Freud and Adler, have come to use groups, as well as two-person situations, as media of personal reeducation and growth. Such efforts are prominent in mental health approaches to changing and have been conducted in educational, religious, community, industrial, and hospital settings. While these efforts focus primarily upon helping individuals to change themselves toward greater self-clarity and fuller self-actualization, they are frequently designed and conducted in the hope that personal changes will lead to changes in organizations, institutions, and communities as well.

We have presented the two variants of normative-reeducative approaches to changing in a way to emphasize their differences. Actually, there are many similarities between them as well, which justify placing both under the same general heading. We have already mentioned one of these similarities. Both frequently use temporary systems—a residential laboratory or workshop, a temporary group with special resources built in, an ongoing system which incorporates a change agent (trainer, consultant, counselor, or therapist) temporarily—as an aid to growth in the system and/or in its members.

More fundamentally, both approaches emphasize experience-based learning as an ingredient of all enduring changes in human systems. Yet both accept the principle that people must learn to learn from their experiences if self-directed change is to be maintained and continued. Frequently, people have learned to defend against the potential lessons of experience when these threaten existing equilibria, whether in the person or in the social system. How can these defenses be lowered to let the data of experience get into processes of perceiving the situation, of constructing new and better ways to define it, of inventing new and more appropriate ways of responding to the situation as redefined, of becoming more fully aware of the consequences of actions, of rearticulating value orientations which sanction more responsible ways of managing the consequences of actions, and so forth? Learning to learn from ongoing experience is a major objective in both approaches to changing. Neither denies the relevance or importance of the noncognitive determinants of behavior—feelings, attitudes, norms, and relationships—along with cognitive-perceptual determinants, in effecting behavioral change. The problem-solving approaches emphasize the cognitive determinants more than personal growth approaches do. But exponents of the former do not accept the rationalistic biases of the rational-empirical family of change strategies, already discussed. Since exponents of both problem-solving and personal growth approaches are committed to reeducation of persons as integral to effective change in human systems, both emphasize norms of openness of communication, trust between persons, lowering of status barriers between parts of the system, and mutuality between parts as necessary conditions of the reeducative process.

Great emphasis has been placed recently upon the releasing of creativity in persons, groups, and organizations as requisite to coping adaptively with accelerated changes in the conditions of modern living. We have already stressed the emphasis which personal growth approaches put upon the release of creative responses in persons being reeducated. Problem-solving approaches also value creativity, though they focus more upon the group and organizational conditions which increase the probability of creative responses by persons functioning within those conditions than upon persons directly. The approaches do differ in their strategies for releasing creative responses within human systems. But both believe that creative adaptations to changing conditions may arise *within* human systems and do not have to be imported from *outside* them as in innovation-diffusion approaches already discussed and the power-compliance models still to be dealt with.

One developing variant of normative-reeducative approaches to changing, not already noted, focuses on effective conflict management. It is, of course, common knowledge that differences within a society which demand interaccommodation often manifest themselves as conflicts. In the process of managing such conflicts, changes in the norms, policies, and relationships of the society occur. Can conflict management be brought into the ambit of planned change as defined in this volume? Stemming from the work of the Sherifs in creating intergroup conflict and seeking to resolve it in a field-laboratory situation,[39] training in intergroup conflict and conflict resolution found its way into training laboratories through the efforts of Blake and others. Since that time, laboratories for conflict management have been developed under NTL and other auspices and methodologies for conflict resolution and management, in keeping with the values of planned change, have been devised. Blake's and Walton's work represents some of the findings from these pioneering efforts.[40]

Thus, without denying their differences in assumption and strategy, we believe that the differing approaches discussed in this section can be seen together within the framework of normative-reeducative approaches to changing. Two efforts to conceptualize planned change in a way to reveal the similarities in assumptions about changing and in value orientations toward change underlying these variant approaches are those by Lippitt, Watson, and Westley and by Bennis, Benne, and Chin.[41]

Another aspect of changing in human organizations is represented by efforts to conceive human organization in forms that go beyond the bureaucratic form which captured the imagination and fixed the contours of thinking and practice of organizational theorists and practitioners from the latter part of the 19th through the early part of the 20th century. The bureaucratic form of organization was conceptualized by Max Weber and carried into American thinking by such students of administration as Urwick.[42] On this view, effective organization of human effort followed the lines of effective division of labor and effective establishment of lines of reporting, control, and supervision from the mass base of the organization up through various levels of control to the top of the pyramidal organization from which legitimate authority and responsibility stemmed.

The work of industrial sociologists like Mayo threw doubt upon the adequacy of such a model of formal organization to deal with the realities of organizational life by revealing the informal organization which grows up within the formal structure to satisfy personal and interpersonal needs not encompassed by or integrated into the goals of the formal organization. Chester Barnard may be seen as a transitional figure who, in discussing the functions of the organizational executive, gave equal emphasis to his responsibilities for task effectiveness and organizational efficiency (optimally meeting the human needs of persons in the organization).[43] Much of the development of subsequent organizational theory and practice has centered on problems of integrating the actualities, criteria, and concepts of organizational effectiveness and of organizational efficiency.

A growing group of thinkers and researchers have sought to move beyond the bureaucratic model toward some new model of organization which might set directions and limits for change efforts in organizational life. Out of many thinkers, we choose four who have theorized out of an orientation consistent with what we have called a normative-reeducative approach to changing.

Rensis Likert has presented an intergroup model of organization. Each working unit strives to develop and function as a group. The group's efforts are linked to other units of the organization by the overlapping membership of supervisors or managers in vertically or horizontally adjacent groups. This view of organization throws problems of delegation, supervision, and internal communication into a new light and emphasizes the importance of linking persons as targets of change and reeducation in processes of organizational development.[44]

We have already stressed McGregor's efforts to conceive a form of organization more in keeping with new and more valid views of human nature and motivation (Theory Y) than the limited and false views of human nature and motivation (Theory X) upon which traditional bureaucratic organization has rested. In his work he sought to move thinking and practice relevant to organization and organizational change beyond the limits of traditional forms. "The essential task of management is to arrange organizational conditions and methods of operation so that people can achieve their own goals best by directing their own efforts toward organizational objectives."[45]

Bennis has consciously sought to move beyond bureaucracy in tracing the contours of the organizations of the future.[46] And Shephard has described an organizational form consistent with support for continual changing and self-renewal, rather than with a primary mission of maintenance and control.[47]

Power-Coercive Approaches to Effective Change.   It is not the use of power, in the sense of influence by one person upon another or by one group upon another, which distinguishes this family of strategies from those already discussed. Power is an ingredient of all human action. The differences lie rather in the ingredients of power on which the strategies of changing depend and the ways in which power is generated and applied in processes of effecting change. Thus what we have called rational-empirical approaches depend on knowledge as a major ingredient of power. in this view, men of knowledge are legitimate sources of power and the desirable flow of influence or power is from men who know to men who don't know through processes of education and of dissemination of valid information.

Normative-reeducative strategies of changing do not deny the importance of knowledge as a source of power, especially in the form of knowledge-based technology. Exponents of this approach to changing are committed to redressing the imbalance between the limited use of behavioral knowledge and people technologies and the widespread use of physical-biological knowledge and related thing technologies in effecting changes in human affairs. In addition, exponents of normative-reeducative approaches recognize the importance of noncognitive determinants of behavior as resistances or supports to changing—values, attitudes, and feelings at the personal level and norms and relationships at the social level. Influence must extend to these noncognitive determinants of behavior if voluntary commitments and reliance on social intelligence are to be maintained and extended in our changing society. Influence of noncognitive determinants of behavior must be exercised in mutual processes of persuasion within collaborative relationships. These strategies are oriented against coercive and nonreciprocal influence, both on moral and on pragmatic grounds.

What ingredients of power do power-coercive strategies emphasize? In general, emphasis is upon political and economic sanctions in the exercise of power. But other coercive strategies emphasize the utilization of moral power, playing upon sentiments of guilt and shame. Political power carries with it legitimacy and the sanctions which accrue to those who break the law. Thus getting a law passed against racial imbalance in the schools brings legitimate coercive power behind efforts to desegregate the schools, threatening those who resist with sanctions under the law and reducing the resistance of others who are morally oriented against breaking the law. Economic power exerts coercive influence over the decisions of those to whom it is applied. Thus federal appropriations granting funds to local schools for increased emphasis upon science instruction tend to exercise coercive influence over the decisions of local school officials concerning the emphasis of the school curriculum. In general, power-coercive strategies of changing seek to mass political and economic power behind the change goals which the strategists of change have decided are desirable. Those who oppose these goals, if they adopt the same strategy, seek to mass political and economic power in opposition. The strategy thus tends to divide the society when there is anything like a division of opinion and of power in that society.

When a person or group is entrenched in power in a social system, in command of political legitimacy and of political and economic sanctions, that person or group can use power-coercive strategies in effecting changes which they consider desirable, without much awareness on the part of those out of power in the system that such strategies are being employed. A power-coercive way of making decisions is accepted as in the nature of things. The use of such strategies by those in legitimate control of various social systems in our society is much more widespread than most of us might at first be willing or able to admit. This is true in educational systems as well as in other social systems.

When any part of a social system becomes aware that its interests are not being served by those in control of the system, the coercive power of those in control can be challenged. If the minority is committed to power-coercive strategies, or is aware of no alternatives to such strategies, how can they make headway against existing power relations within the system? They may organize discontent against the present controls of the system and achieve power outside the legitimate channels of authority in the system. Thus teachers' unions may develop power against coercive controls by the central administrative group and the school board in a school system. They may threaten concerted resistance to or disregard of administrative rulings and board policies or they may threaten work stoppage or a strike. Those in control may get legislation against teachers' strikes. If the political power of organized teachers grows, they may get legislation requiring collective bargaining between organized teachers and the school board on some range of educational issues. The power struggle then shifts to the negotiation table, and compromise between competing interests may become the expected goal of the intergroup exchange. Whether the augmented power of new, relevant knowledge or the generation of common power through joint collaboration and deliberation are lost in the process will depend on the degree of commitment by all parties to the conflict and to a continuation and maintenance of power-coercive strategies for effecting change.

What general varieties of power-coercive strategies, to be exercised either by those in control as they seek to maintain their power or to be used by those now outside a position of control and seeking to enlarge their power, can be identified?

Strategies of Nonviolence. Mahatma Gandhi may be seen as the most prominent recent theorist and practitioner of nonviolent strategies for effecting change, although the strategies did not originate with him in the history of mankind, either in idea or in practice. Gandhi spoke of Thoreau's *Essay on Civil Disobedience* as one important influence in his own approach to nonviolent coercive action. Martin Luther King was perhaps America's most distinguished exponent of nonviolent coercion in effecting social change. A minority (or majority) confronted with what they see as an unfair, unjust, or cruel system of coercive social control may dramatize their rejection of the system by publicly and nonviolently witnessing and demonstrating against it. Part of the ingredients of the power of the civilly disobedient is in the guilt which their demonstration of injustice, unfairness, or cruelty of the existing system of control arouses in those

exercising control or in others previously committed to the present system of control. The opposition to the disobedient group may be demoralized and may waver in their exercise of control, if they profess the moral values to which the dissidents are appealing.

Weakening or dividing the opposition through moral coercion may be combined with economic sanctions—like Gandhi's refusal to buy salt and other British manufactured commodities in India or like the desegregationists' economic boycott of the products of racially discriminating factories and businesses.

The use of nonviolent strategies for opening up conflicts in values and demonstrating against injustices or inequities in existing patterns of social control has become familiar to educational leaders in the demonstrations and sit-ins of college students in various universities and in the demonstrations of desegregationists against de facto segregation of schools. And the widened use of such strategies may be confidently predicted. Whether such strategies will be used to extend collaborative ways of developing policies and normative-reeducative strategies of changing, or whether they will be used to augment power struggles as the only practical way of settling conflicts, will depend in some large part upon the strategy commitments of those now in positions of power in education systems.

Use of Political Institutions to Achieve Change. Political power has traditionally played an important part in achieving changes in our institutional life. And political power will continue to play an important part in shaping and reshaping our institutions of education as well as other institutions. Changes enforced by political coercion need not be oppressive if the quality of our democratic processes can be maintained and improved.

Changes in policies with respect to education have come from various departments of government. By far the most of these have come through legislation on the state level. Under legislation, school administrators have various degrees of discretionary powers, and policy and program changes are frequently put into effect by administrative rulings. Judicial decisions have played an important part in shaping educational policies, none more dramatically than the Supreme Court decision declaring laws and policies supporting school segregation illegal. And the federal courts have played a central part in seeking to implement and enforce this decision.

Some of the difficulty with the use of political institutions to effect changes arises from an over-estimation by change agents of the capability of political action to effect changes in practice. When the law is passed, the administrative ruling announced, or the judicial decision handed down legitimizing some new policy or program or illegitimizing some traditional practice, change agents who have worked hard for the law, ruling, or decision frequently assume that the desired change has been made.

Actually, all that has been done is to bring the force of legitimacy behind some envisioned change. The processes of reeducation of persons who are to conduct themselves in new ways still have to be carried out. And the new conduct often requires new knowledge, new skills, new attitudes, and new value orientations. And, on the social level, new conduct may require changes in the norms, the roles, and the relationship structures of the institutions involved. This is not to discount the importance of political actions in legitimizing changed policies and practices in educational institutions and in other institutions as well. It is rather to emphasize that normative-reeducative strategies must be combined with political coercion, both before and after the political action, if the public is to be adequately informed and desirable and commonly acceptable changes in practice are to be achieved.

Changing through the Recomposition and Manipulation of Power Elites.
The idea or practice of a ruling class or of a power elite in social control was by no means original with Karl Marx. What was original with him was his way of relating these concepts to a process and strategy of fundamental social change. The composition of the ruling class was, of course, for Marx those who owned and controlled the means and processes of production of goods and services in a society. Since, for Marx, the ideology of the ruling class set limits to the thinking of most intellectuals and of those in charge of educational processes and of communicating, rationales for the existing state of affairs, including its concentration of political and economic power, is provided and disseminated by intellectuals and educators and communicators within the system.

Since Marx was morally committed to a classless society in which political coercion would disappear because there would be no vested primate interests to rationalize and defend, he looked for a counterforce in society to challenge and eventually to overcome the power of the ruling class. And this he found in the economically dispossessed and alienated workers of hand and brain. As this new class gained consciousness of its historic mission and its power increased, the class struggle could be effectively joined. The outcome of this struggle was victory for those best able to organize and maximize the productive power of the instruments of production—for Marx this victory belonged to the now dispossessed workers.

Many of Marx's values would have put him behind what we have called normative-reeducative strategies of changing. And he recognized that such strategies would have to be used after the accession of the workers to state power in order to usher in the classless society. He doubted if the ruling class could be reeducated, since reeducation would mean loss of their privileges and coercive power in society. He recognized that the power elite could, within limits, accommodate new interests as these gained articulation and power. But these accommodations must fall short of a radical transfer of power to a class more capable of wielding it. Meanwhile, he remained committed to a power-coercive strategy of changing until the revolutionary transfer of power had been effected.

Marxian concepts have affected the thinking of contemporary men about social change both inside and outside nations in which Marxism has become the official orientation. His concepts have tended to bolster assumptions of the necessity of power-coercive strategies in achieving fundamental redistributions of socio-economic power or in recomposing or manipulating power elites in a society. Democratic, reeducative methods of changing have a place only after such changes in power allocation have been achieved by power-coercive methods. Non-Marxians as well as Marxians are often committed to this Marxian dictum.

In contemporary America, C. Wright Mills has identified a power elite, essentially composed of industrial, military, and governmental leaders, who direct and limit processes of social change and accommodation in our society. And President Eisenhower warned of the dangerous concentration of power in substantially the same groups in his farewell message to the American people. Educators committed to democratic values should not be blinded to the limitations to advancement of those values, which are set by the less than democratic ideology of our power elites. And normative-reeducative strategists of changing must include power elites among their targets of changing as they seek to diffuse their ways of progress within contemporary society. And they must take seriously Marx's questions about the reeducability of members of the power elites, as they deal with problems and projects of social change.

The operation of a power elite in social units smaller than a nation was revealed in Floyd Hunter's study of decision making in an American city. Hunter's small group of deciders, with their satellite groups of intellectuals, front men, and implementers, is in a real sense a power elite. The most common reaction of educational leaders to Hunter's "discovery" has been to seek ways in which to persuade and manipulate the deciders toward support of educational ends which educational leaders consider desirable—whether bond issues, building programs, or anything else. This is non-Marxian in its acceptance of power relations in a city or community as fixed. It would be Marxian if it sought to build counter power to offset and reduce the power of the presently deciding group where this power interfered with the achievement of desirable educational goals. This latter strategy, though not usually Marxian inspired in the propaganda sense of that term, has been more characteristic of organized teacher effort in pressing for collective bargaining or of some student demonstrations and sit-ins. In the poverty program, the federal government in its insistence on participation of the poor in making policies for the program has at least played with a strategy of building countervailing power to offset the existing concentration of power in people not identified with the interests of the poor in reducing their poverty.

Those committed to the advancement of normative-reeducative strategies of changing must take account of present actual concentrations of power wherever they work. This does *not* mean that they must develop a commitment to power-coercive strategies to change the distribution of power except when these may be necessary to effect the spread of their own democratically and scientifically oriented methods of changing within society.

FIGURE 1

Strategies of deliberate changing

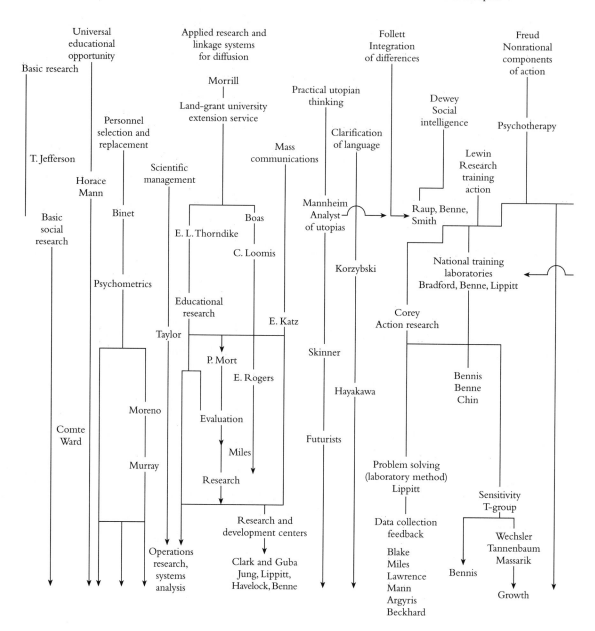

A. Rational-Empirical
Views of the enlightenment and classical liberalism

B. Normative
Views of therapists

FIGURE 1

(concluded)

Endnotes

1. Throughout our discussion of strategies and procedures, we will not differentiate these according to the size of the target of change. We assume that there are similarities in processes of changing, whether the change affects an individual, a small group, an organization, a community, or a culture. In addition, we are not attending to differences among the aspects of a system, let us say an educational system, which is being changed—curriculum, audiovisual methods, team teaching, pupil grouping, and so on. Furthermore, because many changes in communities or organizations start with an individual or some small membership group, our general focus will be upon those strategies which lead to and involve individual changes.

   We will sidestep the issue of defining change in this paper. As further conceptual work progresses in the study of planned change, we shall eventually have to examine how different definitions of change relate to strategies and procedures for effecting change. But we are not dealing with these issues here.

2. We have indicated the main roots of ideas and idea systems underlying the principal strategies of changing and their subvariants on a chart which appears as Figure 1 at the end of this essay. It may be useful in seeing both the distinctions and the relationships between various strategies of changing in time perspective. We have emphasized developments of the past 25 years more than earlier developments. This makes for historical foreshortening. We hope this is a pardonable distortion, considering our present limited purpose.

3. Jean Hills, "Social Science, Ideology and the Purposes of Educational Administration," *Education Administration Quarterly,* Autumn 1965, pp. 23–40.

4. Garth Jones, "Planned Organizational Change, a Set of Working Documents," Center for Research in Public Organization, School of Public Administration (Los Angeles: University of Southern California, 1964).

5. For a review, see Ronald G. Havelock and Kenneth D. Benne, "An Exploratory Study of Knowledge Utilization," in *The Planning of Change,* 2nd ed. Warren G. Bennis, Kenneth D. Benne, and Robert Chin (New York: Holt, Rinehart & Winston, 1969), chap. 3, p. 124.

6. Paul R. Mort and Donald R. Ross, *Principles of School Administration* (New York: McGraw-Hill, 1957). Paul R. Mort and Francis G. Cornell, *American Schools in Transition: How Our Schools Adapt Their Practices to Changing Needs* (New York: Bureau of Publications, Teachers College, Columbia University Press, 1941).

7. Robert Chin, "Research Approaches to the Problem of Civic Training," in *The Adolescent Citizen,* ed. F. Patterson (New York: Free Press, 1980).

8. Matthew B. Miles, *Some Propositions in Research Utilization in Education* (March 1965), in press. Kenneth Wiles, paper for seminar on Strategies for Curriculum Change (Columbus: Ohio State University, 1965). Charles Jung and Ronald Lippitt, "Utilization of Scientific Knowledge for Change in Education," in *Concepts for Social Change* (Washington, D.C.: National Educational Association, National Training Laboratories, 1967). Havelock and Benne, "Exploratory Study of Knowledge Utilization," in Bennis et al., *Planning of Change,* chap. 3, p. 124. David Clark and Egon Guba, "An Examination of Potential Change Roles in Education," seminar on Innovation in Planning School Curricula (Columbus: Ohio State University, 1965).

9. David Clark, "Educational Research and Development: The Next Decade," in *Implications for Education of Prospective Changes in Society,* a publication of "Designing Education for the Future—an Eight State Project" (Denver, Colo., 1967).

10. Elihu Katz, "The Social Itinerary of Technical Change: Two Studies on the Diffusion of Innovation," in Bennis et al., *Planning of Change,* chap. 5, p. 230. Richard Carlson, "Some Needed Research on the Diffusion of Innovations" (paper at the Washington Conference on Educational Change, Columbus, Ohio, Ohio State University). Everett Rogers, "What Are Innovators Like?" in *Change Process in the Public Schools,* Center for the Advanced Study of Educational Administration (Eugene: University of Oregon, 1965). Everett Rogers, *Diffusion of Innovations* (New York: Free Press, 1962).

11. Carl Hovland, Irving Janis, and Harold Kelley, *Communication and Persuasion* (New Haven, Conn.: Yale University Press, 1953).

12. Raymond Bauer, "The Obstinate Audience: The Influence Process from the Point of View of Social Communication," in Bennis et al., *Planning of Change,* chap. 9, p. 507.

13. B. F. Skinner, *Walden Two* (New York: Crowell-Collier and Macmillan, 1948).

14. "Designing Education for the Future—an Eight State Project" (Denver, Colo., 1967).

15. Karl Mannheim, *Ideology and Utopia* (New York: Harcourt Brace Jovanovich, 1946).

16. Alfred Korzybski, *Science and Sanity,* 3rd ed. (International Non-Aristotelian Library Publishing

Company, 1948). S. I. Hayakawa, *Language in Thought and Action* (New York: Harcourt Brace Jovanovich, 1941).

17. John Dewey, *Philosophy, Psychology and Social Practice,* ed. Joseph Ratner (New York: Capricorn Books, 1967).

18. Kurt Lewin, *Resolving Social Conflicts* (New York: Harper & Row, 1948). Kurt Lewin, *Field Theory in Social Science* (New York: Harper & Row, 1951).

19. For Freud, an interesting summary is contained in Otto Fenichel, *Problems of Psychoanalytic Technique* (Albany: NT Psychoanalytic Quarterly, 1941).

20. W. Bennis, K. Benne, and R. Chin, *The Planning of Change,* 1st ed. (New York: Holt, Rinehart & Winston, 1961). R. Lippitt, J. Watson, and B. Westley, *The Dynamics of Planned Change* (New York: Harcourt Brace Jovanovich, 1958). W. Bennis, *Changing Organizations* (New York: McGraw-Hill, 1966).

21. Raup, Benne, Smith, and Axtelle, *The Discipline of Practical Judgment in a Democratic Society,* Yearbook No. 28 of the National Society of College Teachers of Education (Chicago: University of Chicago Press, 1943).

22. Mary Follett, *Creative Experience and Dynamic Administration* (New York: David McKay, 1924).

23. Karl Mannheim, *Man and Society in an Age of Reconstruction* (New York: Harcourt Brace Jovanovich, 1940).

24. Elliot Jaques, *The Changing Culture of a Factory* (New York: Holt, Rinehart & Winston, 1952).

25. William J. Dickson and F. J. Roethlisberger, *Personal Counseling in an Organization: A Sequel to the Hawthorne Researchers* (Boston: Harvard Business School, 1966).

26. Elton Mayo, *The Social Problems of an Industrial Civilization* (Cambridge, Mass.: Harvard University Press, 1945).

27. Leland Bradford, Jack R. Gibb, and Kenneth D. Benne, *T-Group Theory and Laboratory Methods* (New York: John Wiley & Sons, 1964).

28. Matthew B. Miles, "On Temporary Systems," in *Innovation in Education,* ed M. B. Miles (New York: Bureau of Publications, Teachers College, Columbia University Press, 1964), pp. 437–92.

29. Robert R. Blake and Jane S. Mouton, *The Managerial Grid* (Houston: Gulf Publishing, 1961).

30. Jay W. Lorsch and Paul Lawrence, "The Diagnosis of Organizational Problems," in Bennis et al., *Planning of Change,* chap. 8, p. 468.

31. Stephen M. Corey, *Action Research to Improve School Practices* (New York: Bureau of Publications, Teachers College, Columbia University Press, 1953).

32. See contributions by Miles et al., "Data Feedback and Organizational Change in a School System," in Bennis et al., *Planning of Change,* chap. 8, p. 457; and Lorsch and Lawrence, "Diagnosis of Organizational Problems," in Bennis et al. *Planning of Change,* chap. 8, p. 468.

33. C. Argyris, "Explorations in Consulting-Client Relationships," in Bennis et al., *Planning of Change,* chap. 8, p. 434. See also Richard Beckhard, "The Confrontation Meeting," in Bennis et al., *Planning of Change,* chap. 8, p. 478.

34. Carl Rogers, "The Characteristics of a Helping Relationship," in Bennis et al. *Planning of Change,* chap. 4, p. 153.

35. Abraham Maslow, *Motivation and Personality* (New York: Harper & Row, 1954).

36. Douglas M. McGregor, "The Human Side of Enterprise," in W. Bennis et al., *The Planning of Change,* 1st ed. (New York: Holt, Rinehart & Winston, 1961), pp. 422–31.

37. Dickson and Roethlisberger, *Personal Counseling in an Organization.*

38. James V. Clark "A Healthy Organization," in Bennis et al., *Planning of Change,* chap. 6, p. 282. Irving Weschler, Fred Massarik, and Robert Tannenbaum, "The Self in Process: A Sensitivity Training Emphasis," in *Issues in Training,* ed I. R. Weschler and E. Schein. Selected Reading Series No. 5 (Washington, D.C.: National Training Laboratories).

39. Muzafer and Carolyn Sherif, *Groups in Harmony and Tension* (New York: Harper & Row, 1953).

40. Robert Blake et al., "The Union Management Inter-Group Laboratory," in Bennis et al., *Planning of Change,* chap. 4, p. 176. Richard Walton, "Two Strategies of Social Change and Their Dilemmas," in Bennis et al., *Planning of Change,* chap. 4, p. 167.

41. Lippitt et al., *Dynamics of Planning Change.* Bennis et al., *Planning of Change,* 1st ed.

42. Lyndall Urwick, *The Pattern of Management* (Minneapolis: University of Minnesota Press, 1956).

43. Chester I. Barnard, *The Functions of the Executive* (Cambridge, Mass.: Harvard University Press, 1938).

44. Rensis Likert, *New Patterns of Management* (New York: McGraw-Hill, 1961).

45. McGregor, "Human Side of Enterprise," pp. 422–31.

46. W. G. Bennis, "Changing Organizations," in Bennis et al., *Planning of Change,* chap. 10, p. 568.

47. H. A. Shephard, "Innovation-Resisting and Innovation-Producing Organizations," in Bennis et al., *Planning of Change,* chap. 9, p. 519.

READING 4
TOWARD THIRD-WAVE MANAGING AND CONSULTING

Marvin R. Weisbord

The results of this generalized speedup of the corporate metabolism are multiple: shorter product life cycles, more leasing and renting, more frequent buying and selling, more ephemeral consumption patterns, more fads, more training time for workers (who must continually adjust to new procedures), more frequent changes in contracts, more negotiations and legal work, more pricing changes, more job turnover, more dependence on data, more ad hoc organization. . . . Under these escalating pressures, it is easy to see why so many businessmen, bankers, and corporate executives wonder what exactly they are doing and why. Brought up with Second-Wave certainties, they see the world they knew tearing apart under the impact of an accelerating wave of change.

Alvin Toffler
The Third Wave, 1980

We live in the midst of a historic global revolution—from physical to knowledge work, mechanical to process technologies, manufacturing to service economies, cultural sameness to greater diversity. Future-thinker Alvin Toffler calls this sea change "the third wave" to differentiate it from the agricultural and industrial revolutions of centuries past. Above all, it is a social revolution. Quality of working life (QWL)—meaning quality of products, services, and work itself—has become a worldwide aspiration. QWL is also an umbrella for every sort of "change" program—from quality circles, organization development, statistical quality control, sociotechnical systems design, and cultural transformation.

In this article I want to suggest another "bottom line" for the widespread interest in QWL. I see a hunger everywhere for community among people alienated from work and each other by new technologies and global economics. *Community,* as I use it here, means a workplace where people produce goods or services for a living. A productive community is one where people find dignity, meaning, and security in contributing to the whole.

My purpose is as old as the industrial revolution. More than 40 years ago, Elton Mayo, founder of industrial human relations, noted how "science and industry put an end to the individual's feeling of identification with his group, of satisfaction in his work." We still seek constructive responses to Mayo's diagnosis. Consider the historic 1986 agreement between the United Steelworkers of America and National Steel Corporation. Management, despite economic hard times, promised employment security. The union offered greater job flexibility to increase output. That deal marked a radical break with adversarial traditions. Both parties will be a long time, however, learning to make it work. Yet it exactly embodies the spirit of productive community.

A Practice Theory for Managers and Consultants

Here I offer some spadework toward a "third-wave" practice theory of managing and consulting grounded in these values. My ideas apply to what I know best—reorganizations and work redesign to improve output, quality, and customer focus. They synthesize my work as manager and consultant for more than 25 years with my observations of the uneasy relationship between engineering and psychology in this century. I seek a coherent way of reorganizing under what management professor Peter Vaill calls conditions of "permanent white water."

I want to shift my gaze away from "problems" like cost control *or* interpersonal conflict, that are symptomatic of needs, toward productive community—based on purposes, missions, strategies, and structures worthy of our aspirations, cooperation, and sweat. What can we do today—right now—to make work more secure and improve quality? If you had only a few hours or a few weeks, how would you use your time?

The need to build workplace communities, I'm convinced, is closely tied to preserving democratic values as global economic pressures mount and new hardware, software, and robots pump into the workplace at a furious rate. These developments encompass at once the best and the scariest aspects of American individualism. We revere entrepreneurial behavior and self-actualization. We always have been ambivalent about commitments to each other across levels, functions, lines of status, ethnicity, and class.

"We insist, perhaps more than ever before, on finding our true selves independent of any cultural or social influence," Robert Bellah and partners write in *Habits of the Heart*. "Yet we spend much of our time navigating through immense bureaucratic structures—multiversities, corporations, government agencies—manipulating and being manipulated by others."

We want things every which way. We demand freedom, equal opportunity, and the right to run our own lives, making good Jefferson's Declaration of Independence for "life, liberty, and the pursuit of happiness." We also covet personal security, dignity, support—as promised in the Constitution and Bill of Rights. In the workplace this sometimes plays out as a demand that management "give" people these qualities, when, in fact, all management has the power to do is join in searching for ways to preserve them.

We are driven together again out of necessity. Work methods change so fast now they cannot be controlled by traditional management systems. Social scientists Fred Emery and Eric Trist observed in the 1960s that firms were in increasingly "turbulent fields"—making prediction and control impossible. In *Beyond the Stable State* (1971), Donald Schon saw technology disrupting all "anchors for personal identity." Now the top is spinning faster. Companies, agencies, institutions that used to reorganize every five years now rearrange themselves annually. Many change work sites, job content, titles, and product and service concepts in a perpetual redirection of technologies and markets. How shall we manage these chaotic transactions among economics, technology, and people in the workplace? I suggest that the only steady beacons in such stormy seas are aspirations for dignity and meaning—the wellsprings of motivation—in work.

Invoking Science

For more than 100 years the image of science has been invoked as the key to human motivation. This holy grail was pursued by Frederick Taylor, "the father of scientific management," long before management became a profession. It was pursued with equal intensity by social psychologist Kurt Lewin, "the practical theorist" who invented "force field analysis," discovered participative management, and laid the intellectual groundwork for organization development (OD) in the 1940s.

Taylor, a self-taught engineer, realized that managers awash in the "the second wave" could not motivate factory workers. In 1893 he invented a new profession, "consulting engineer," linking cost accounting, time study, wage incentives, and planning into a system that today influences nearly every workplace in the industrial world. Taylor sought to squeeze human discretion from work. He raised wages dramatically if people would do things "the one best way" specified by his engineers.

Taylor today is reviled for his rigid methods. His values, lost in the mists, were quite contemporary. A pacifist as a child, he hated conflict. He wanted to increase labor-management cooperation, cut out authoritarian supervision, reduce job stress, give people more equitable pay for jobs challenging their highest abilities. Taylor made industrial engineers third-party arbiters between labor and management. They devised the "correct" methods for cooperation and conflict resolution. Both organization development and sociotechnical systems design (STS), guided by Kurt Lewin's action research theories, adopted similar purposes. OD managers became the industrial engineers of group development, prescribing self-awareness and interpersonal skills and/or self-managing work teams instead of time and motion study for taking the arbitrariness out of work.

Taylor fell from grace when his descendants divorced his values and married his techniques. Similarly, many OD practitioners, seduced by social technologies, lost sight of Lewin's values—the spirit of inquiry, cooperation, and democratic principles. They were mesmerized by an innovative bag of tricks for diagnosis and intervention—survey feedback, team building, inter-group problem solving, experiential training. Like time study, these could be shoehorned into organizations without dignity, meaning, or worker commitment. In the ultimate absurdity, people were sent wholesale to learn free choice and commitment—whether they wanted to or not.

A Trip through the Forests of Change Theory

To appreciate why I want to redefine the playing field, I would like you to join me on a trip through the thickets of organizational change theory. OD case studies for 25 years have reflected two *different* theories of improvements, coexisting uneasily. One was a theory of "process" diagnosis based on the expert's data-collecting abilities, what I call "snap-shooting." Another was Lewin's brilliant theory of participative change-oriented action— "movie-making" in my lingo, but very different from Hollywood's. Most practitioners know that the two theories are really one—that how we take the snapshot determines the quality of the movie. Yet all of us have one foot in what Eric Trist, the originator of sociotechnical thinking, calls the "old paradigm"—Taylor's cause-effect reasoning.

Diagnosis and Action

All consultants advocate expert diagnosis and action-taking. Engineers and behavioral scientists alike have diagnoses of organizational conflict and prescriptions for solving it. *Diagnosis* is medical jargon for the gap between sickness and health. As biology exploded in the late 19th century, the human body, like the workplace, was divided into manageable components, too. Doctors became the industrial engineers of the human physique. Their claim to expertise was based on their ability to factor in every relevant "variable" and thus heal the sick.

It is no surprise that early psychologists thought the same way about mental processes. Indeed, until the biologist Ludwig von Bertalanffy proposed a general systems theory, people educated in Western industrial nations could hardly think any other way. Diagnosis, conceived as identifying and closing gaps between how things are and how they should be, used all the tools of science and technology. It was the ultimate expression of the industrial revolution.

Lewin added a new dimension to the medical model. He highlighted processes unseen through 19th-century eyes because nobody had a conceptual lens powerful enough. Lewin's force fields allowed the taking of "process" snapshots—the feelings, motives, intentions, and other intangibles accompanying "results." Lewin portrayed diagnostic gaps in dynamic terms, as an interaction of social forces—personal, group, company-wide, societal. Who are the gatekeepers, asked Lewin, whose behavior must change to assure constructive action? What forces prevent or accelerate their involvement? Answers could be found through "action research"—a collaboration between activist scholars and social institutions to bring about constructive personal change.

Two Core Concepts

From Lewin I inherited two core concepts that made my consulting practice possible. Human systems, Lewin believed, were almost, but not quite, static and resistant to change. The consulting goal was to help organizations "unfreeze," "move," and

Musings on Getting "Whole Systems" in a Room

1. I don't like one-shot events. School boards and town councils meet repeatedly. A one-shot conference is not adequate to the tasks of productive community in a workplace, either.

2. In planning workshops, I seek to *reduce* dynamic tensions. A decision to work with groups of 12 is a decision to train group leaders or facilitators—a step away from self-management. Subteams of three or four work well for many tasks, in which mode 100 people can easily work in one room on their own. I suggest that people make time for small groups to review each other's work and for whole system reviews—so all task forces or departments find out what the others are up to.

3. I contract to manage time boundaries and task structures. In self-managed conferences, I suggest that people monitor their own processes and be responsible for output.

4. I do better organizing the search than "the data." I don't withhold my observations, perspectives, or knowledge. But I don't want to make them the center of the action, either. I like to see "task structures"—worksheets, lists, hints, glossaries, exercises, bibliographies, handouts, overheads—devised with client help. I wish to keep them simple and use

them sparingly. I aspire to give people information when they can use it, or call for it, not all at once. This does not square with what some people want from consultants. I am unable to help people who are convinced there's a lot more.

5. I aspire to keep the task front and center, directed toward output, and to shift focus to "process" only to get the task back on track. I am not against struggle, anxiety, or bewilderment. We have to go through Confusion to get to Renewal. I tend to become more involved if asked and/or when I see people running away from the task or fighting with each other. I do not always know what to do. Fortunately, someone else usually does.

6. I want to help set norms for productive learning. I reduce my involvement as people get past initial anxiety and take over the work. I have found Merrelyn Emery's advice to avoid attaching to a particular subgroup and becoming its (informal) leader a useful discipline for managing large group events.

7. I like rooms with windows and plenty of light. Hotel "dungeon rooms" depress groups and make productive community very difficult.

8. None of these practices are "the" answer to anything—except how one consultant and ex-manager seeks meaning in work.

"refreeze." Like all OD consultants, I learned to take diagnostic pictures that would make people want to act—to melt the ice of indifference, ignorance, or uncertainty and unfreeze the system. Once melted, it would follow more natural channels until cooled

enough to refreeze in more functional patterns. All OD case studies fit that framework. At the heart of this diagnostic act was a confrontation: The client must "own" the incongruity between what is said and what is done—the demon to be exorcised before healing could begin. It was not necessary to assume sickness to use Lewin's model. However, it was not easy to avoid it either for those of us socialized to view life as one long medical model.

A second concept goes by the name of the "task/process" relationship—the subtle chicken/egg interplay between ends and means, methods and goals. A task is something concrete, observable, and thing-oriented. It can be converted into criteria, measurements, targets, and deadlines—just the way Taylor did. A task—group dynamics people were fond of saying—refers to *what* is to be done.

Process refers to *how*. It reflects perceptions, attitudes, reasoning. Process diagnosticians ask, "Why aren't we making progress?" Or, "Who feels committed to this?" They don't ask when, where, and how many but why, how, and whether. Task/process thinking can be likened to the famous visual paradox of the Old Woman/Young Woman, reproduced below. Do you see a young beauty with her head turned or a wizened crone in profile?

You can't see both at once. By some mental gyration, you can learn to shift between them. Does one picture "cause" the other? Cause-effect thinking that gave rise both to Taylorism and the medical model led to a relentless propensity to see one form of task only as *the* "task." Western industrial managers developed an exquisite "left-brain"—linear, rational, A causes B, three steps, nine phases, finish by Tuesday, get to the bottom line. Diagnosis, even of "processes," requires

structure and precision. Whether your categories are "hard" or "soft," listing and prioritizing puts the left brain into high gear.

Action, on the other hand, reflects pure process. We guide it largely on automatic pilot, fueled by little explosions of energy in the right brain—of creativity, insight, synthesis—that can't be quantified or specified as "targets." Lewin ingeniously expanded left-brain thinking. He shifted the diagnostician's viewpoint to the other picture—*processes* always present and not previously visible because nobody was looking for them. From his work came my simple practice theory: "Process" issues *always* block work on tasks."

Through trained observation, you can diagnose ingenious linkages between task and process. When work stalls, for example, determine what is *not* being talked about—the gap between word and deed, the all-too-human shortfall between aspiration and action. You must shift attention the way a pilot scans instruments—from compass to altimeter to air speed indicator—to keep task and process synchronized. That requires skills few of us learn in school.

Unfortunately, left-brain diagnostic thinking—perfected by scientists for more than 100 years—leads people to pay attention to the compass and to consider the altimeter a frill. The diagnoser is assumed to stand outside, impartial, "objective," and aloof from what is observed. If you add to this our propensity to defer to authority—parents, bosses, experts—you have a setup for disappointment. For the authority/dependency relationship *itself* becomes a "process" issue, especially when the person invested with magical abilities lacks satisfactory "answers." Group dynamics' great contribution to management was its relentless gaze at the process picture as inseparable from the task, the diagnoser inseparable from the diagnosis, a leader's effectiveness inseparable from follower contributions.

Unfreezing, Etc.

Now, let us visit the connection between the task/process interplay and "unfreezing, moving, and refreezing." This linkage made the OD profession possible. Unresolved "process" issues accumulate in organizations like junk in an attic. People "freeze" in dysfunctional patterns—nobody listens, appreciates, communicates. Output and quality suffer. Reacting to crises drives out planning. Lewin sought to "unfreeze" this self-perpetuating ice storm over corporate headquarters with action research.

If the stored-up stuff could be got out in the open, if "undiscussable" topics could be talked about, energy would be released. People would become aware of their own contributions to their problems. New behavior would emerge, accelerated by explicit skill training. Unfrozen people could evolve strategy, policy, procedure, systems, relationships, and norms more to their liking. Implementing new action plans would refreeze the system into more functional patterns. Shifting your gaze between task and process could become a "way of life." Results could be feedback loops. When you had new dilemmas, you would realize how your own assumptions contributed. You would be more inclined, for example, to involve others previously left out. This is called "learning how to learn"—studying a situation in which you assume responsibility by taking account of "data" previously ignored.

Consulting Skills and Cultural Change

In the 1950s, people began working out a new form of third-party behavior, "consulting skills," to encourage this form of learning. Technical experts diagnosed and prescribed without involving others in their analyses. Behavioral science consultants made a different deal. They proposed a "scientific" method of data collection, arrangement, and discussion derived from Lewin's insights that people are more likely to act on solutions they have helped develop. It included a minor fiction—that questions, methods of inquiry, data presentation, analysis, and action steps would be jointly planned. I say "fiction" because the methods inevitably belonged to the consultants, and so did the theories of task/process, unfreezing, etc. The "feedback meeting" became a pivotal point of social change—the payoff for action research. There the data was "owned," the system melted, and

movement initiated. Those were the OD change assumptions so far as the "movie" was concerned.

As for the "snapshot," the OD consultant may have been an open-systems dreamer, but the practice did not reflect the aspiration. It was too attached to feelings, perceptions, and communications, too separated from technology, economics, and structural relations. "Social researchers," wrote William H. Whyte in *Learning from the Field,* "tended to concentrate almost exclusively on human relations. We gave lip service to the importance of technology but tended to treat it as a constant instead of as a variable, which could be changed along with changes in human relations."

However, many "sociotechnical systems" practitioners who saw technology and people as one system lost sight of the participatory process. They prescribed complex methods of analysis and change that only trained consultants could apply. They evolved analytical tools that belied the movie's basic simplicity. Yet STS was not an "expert" invention. In 1949 Eric Trist found a British coal mine where union workers and a mine manager, driven by a change in roof-control technology, had worked out a system of self-managing teams.

Trist and Emery worked out some simple procedures embodying what they had learned—about redundant skills, managing boundaries, and full participation. In no time their successors had added checklists, analytical tools, exercises, procedures, steps, principles, team building, and other "have tos" enough to deter even the most dedicated clients. Thus we have the central paradox of the changeover from industrial to postindustrial societies—how to encourage people to solve their own problems when every simple new idea can be elaborated endlessly by specialists. What becomes of dignity, community, and meaning in work if you can't reorganize yourself without three years of full-time study? Traditional science has no answers for that paradox.

Yet second-wave ODers thought they had found one. They added up the three stages—unfreezing by third parties, movement by principals and third parties together, refreezing by the principals—that made up a "cultural change strategy." Science could be mobilized to beat back authoritarianism and bureaucracy. What made this different from Taylorism were the psychological content and participative techniques—learning to do things with others, not to them or for them.

The Snapshot Sets Up the Movie

For decades OD diagnoses were based on what might be called Lewin's law. The "snapshot" focused attention on discrepancies and pinpointed ways to close gaps. In *Productive Communities,* I recount four OD projects from 1969 to 1980 based on Lewinian action research methods. Two involved surveys and feedback of structured data and two interviews, group diagnosis, and problem-solving task forces. One project led to a reduction in employee turnover in food service cafeterias, another to a more focused research and development effort in a chemical firm, the third to production improvements in a pill factory, the fourth to strategic redirection in a solar energy company.

In all four, the consultants—with client acceptance—supplied the methods, collected and summarized data, prepared reports, created situation "maps," facilitated discussions. Eventually client groups took over, planned, and implemented changes with consulting help. Reviewing these now, I detect a subtle shift in my practice—from classical action research, based on consultant-centered problem diagnosis, toward much greater client involvement in looking at the whole system regardless of the problem. Why diagnostic technologies for systems change? The reason is not far to seek. We have assumed since Lewin that only accurate "data" and thorough analyses will "unfreeze" structures, procedures, relationships, and norms. Anything less would be unprofessional and unscientific. That is precisely what Taylor assumed about lathes and drillpresses.

Rethinking Lewin

I find my old-practice theory unsatisfying from two perspectives now. First, global markets, technologies, and worker expectations change so fast that a frozen workplace is a temporary phenomenon.

Today, change goes more like a bullet train than a melting iceberg. The rate of change has accelerated since Kurt Lewin died in 1947. It occurs too fast for experts to pin down, even the "process" kind. Conventional diagnoses may serve many useful functions, but "unfreezing" systems is not one of them.

Second, we change our behavior when we are ready to do it, not because of a force field (or any) analysis. The first law of techniques is: Everything works; nothing works. Nobody is skilled enough to push the river. That is supported by consulting experiences clear back to Frederick Taylor. The best a consultant can do is create opportunities for people to discover and do what they want to do anyway. When we apply the "bag of tricks" in a linear way, without informed cooperation and self-control, *only* the content differs from Taylor's. The process comes out uncomfortably the same.

If you accept that proposition, you will see why I worry more about responding to needs for dignity and meaning in work—which means *solving your own problems*—than about supplying "right" answers. There is considerable anxiety and confusion everywhere. I think it is wrong to assume our mutual dilemmas mean "sickness," as if only the diagnostician is whole and in control. Nothing holds still long enough to be diagnosed and "changed" anyway. So consultant-centered diagnostic activities intended to unfreeze systems, even when welcomed by clients willing to defer to authority, may inadvertently distract people from taking charge of their own lives.

Building on Lewin

To honor Lewin now, we must go beyond him. But how? We need new processes for managing and consulting that I do not fully understand. I'm conscious of profound paradoxes. I have at my fingertips diagnostic techniques for every "issue" in the cosmos. On my bookshelf I find more models for fixing things than there are starts in the galaxy. Yet I am strangely undernourished by this intellectual cornucopia. My objective, I keep reminding myself, is not to diagnose and heal "sickness," but to help people manage their work lives better—to enact productive community.

The consultants' dilemma is that we always arrive in the middle of somebody else's movie and leave before the end. It usually has many subplots and informal directors. The consultant negotiates a role—sometimes major, sometimes minor—but always limited by the willingness of others to play along. My view of the consultant's role has turned upside down from what I once thought it was. I imagine it now as helping people discover a more whole view of what they are doing than any one "discipline" or perspective can provide, *including mine.*

I find that proposition fraught with uncertainty. Is it "doable"? To the extent that I can help people integrate worthy values and tasks, I make an important contribution. Yet that means being at some level an "expert" and accepting people's projections of authority, even when I don't act the authoritarian. None of us knows, exactly, how to be both an expert and just one of the gang—when we are dedicated more to collaboration and mutual learning than to being "right." There is no substitute for learning. That any of us can teach others to "learn how to learn" is, in my opinion, a theory full of iffiness.

Toward Assessing Possibilities

We come at last to the heart of it: It is not always practical or desirable to negotiate a consulting role that, at its simplest, is helping people do what they are going to do anyway. The consultant's task in the movie is to see confusion and anxiety through to energy for constructive action and to learn along with everybody else. That has an odd ring to somebody, like me, who grew up in the "second wave." I find myself thinking that assessing conditions under which such an unusual client/consultant partnership is feasible should be the first task of consultation. I wouldn't be deciding how to help, but whether to even make the offer. That means a different kind of snapshot from the "unfreezing" variety.

Diagnosis, the gap between sickness and health, is not the right word for what I mean. The third wave of change is not a sickness, although some consequences can be. Anxiety is not a sickness. It is a sign of learning and potential energy. We need another term. Maybe *assessment* will do. Third-wave mangers need simple ways for assessing the potential for action, unifying themes to focus attention, methods to help people learn together about the whole contraption. That is quite different from having a consultant build a "problem list" and prioritize it. I am not against expertise—only the assumption that the specialist (or boss, or consultant) knows *everything* required to resolve the situation defined by his or her expertise or authority without having to do anything new or risky. This is especially true in the complex activity called "reorganizing." That's a developmental task—a great deal of it governed by the right brain and not amenable, except in small details, to ordinary problem solving.

Moreover, we should not mistake "human resources management" for third-wave practices. A major limitation on action is the belief that a human resources department on the 8th floor, just like the strategic planning department on the 14th, somehow makes us immune from reductionistic, linear, rigid solutions. Staff-centered activity is not necessarily conducive to productive community, whether named "participative management," or "dynamic synergistic wholistic transformation." It doesn't matter what you call it. If people don't join in the process of planning their own work, it's old Fred Taylor all over again, only with sociopsychological window dressing instead of his time-and-motion study.

Whose Movie Is It?

It is terribly important to grasp this point if you wish to enact a productive community. An effective snapshot, seen as a dual image—task/process—portrays the whole system in relation to a worthy purpose. It can only do that accurately when the whole system, to the extent possible, takes it, appears in it, and looks it over together. When the whole system is in perpetual motion, every relationship changing, it's impossible for one person to take a coherent picture. As soon as people start making a collective self-portrait, it is no longer a snapshot. *Voilà,* it's part of the ongoing movie, a form of *cinéma vérité,* as messy as life itself.

Only those most involved can make such a movie. The best role a consultant can hope for is stage manager. Kurt Lewin showed that during World War II when he discovered participative management by having Iowa housewives decide whether to change their food habits. Nobody has improved on the principle—that the wisest decisions, given as much information as we can get, are the ones we make for ourselves. People benefit most, I'm convinced, from talking with each other and deciding what to do. I'm for any consulting methods that enhance the dialog.

Thoughts on Stage Managing Third-Wave Movies

To be part of a good movie—to influence committed action—we need a practice theory that (1) respects the past, (2) enhances productive community, and (3) is responsive to the sea change of the third wave. Such a theory requires imagining under what conditions people will work together, which is the manager's dilemma, and under what conditions a consultant can help. "Ninety percent of living," comedian Woody Allen once said, "is just showing up." Just making it possible for the right people to show up may also be 90 percent of consultation. The other 10 percent is helping people focus on worthy purposes they identify for themselves.

My task as consultant is to do the minimum needed to accomplish those objectives. I want to use my data-collecting skills to identify *essential starting conditions* rather than to codify problems. I want to move away from discrepancies between words and deeds—an act of verbal abstraction which, in my view, has very little motivating power—and focus on people's willingness to be responsible for doing important tasks together. In short, I'm more interested in figuring out whether I can make a contribution to this movie than I am in being seen as a brilliant snap-shooter. I am not saying that this is the best consultation, only that I find it compatible with my faith in the metaphor of productive community.

Four Useful Practices

In reviewing my projects over 25 years, I find recurring patterns—related to leadership, energizing situations, and energizing people—under which I do better work. The leaders I have learned most from seem to me to have certain knacks. They *focus attention* on worthy aspirations; they *mobilize energy* by involving others; they seem *willing to face the unknown* without "answers."

My leadership observation underlies the first of four "useful practices" I have been experimenting with in evolving a third-wave practice theory. The other three depend on the outcome of the first. I consider these practices plausible (though far from trouble free) alternatives to more traditional consultation for reorganizing large companies and restructuring work. The four practices are to (1) assess the potential for action, (2) get the whole system into the room, (3) focus on the future, and (4) structure tasks that people can do for themselves. They focus on enacting productive community as the backdrop for finding appropriate solutions in "permanent white water." They seem to be well-known among current practitioners, though not well articulated.

Many of us—we can hardly avoid it—continue to mix them indiscriminately with "second-wave" procedures. I believe that as we use these and similar practices more confidently we will enable "third-wave" reorganizations and work redesigns in the spirit of productive community. Yet moving away from traditional uses of expertise and authority takes us down paths riddled with potholes and pitfalls, for which there are no easy "how tos." Perhaps an explanation of each of the four third-wave practices along with examples will make things easier.

Useful Practice 1: Assess the Potential for Action. Instead of diagnosing "gaps," I find myself asking under what conditions I could make a contribution. That leads me away from problem lists toward an assessment of leadership, business opportunities, and sources of energy.

Condition 1: committed leadership. Does the person authorized to hire me have itches he or she wants to scratch badly enough to put his or her own rear end on the line? Consultants make better contributions when a person in authority says, "I think this is so important that I'm willing to take a risk, too." I'm wary of requests to fix somebody else or to supply unilateral "expert" answers.

Condition 2: good business opportunities. Good business opportunities come in packages labeled economics and technology—the glue of productive community. So I listen sympathetically to the "people problem" list, but I don't focus on it. Rather, I focus on the opportunities for cooperative action—chances to innovate products/services and/or ways of making/delivering them. These occur most dependably in mergers, acquisitions, reorganizations, declining markets, overhead crises, structures that don't function, new technologies, the need to save jobs.

The Medical Products Division of Atomic Energy of Canada, Ltd., for example, in 1985 rescued itself from economic disaster and mass layoffs by assuring jobs for a year and employing much of its workforce in market studies, work redesign, and new employment opportunities. The payoff was a viable, $30-million-a-year business, managed participatively by employees.

These two conditions—a leader and a promising dilemma—can't be "behavioral-scienced" in, nor "engineered." Frederick Taylor understood their importance in 1900. He did not know as much as we do, though, about commitment and support. Taylor assumed that only the expert's diagnosis and prescription counted. Thanks to action research, we know a great deal more about commitment and support than our grandparents did. We have many choices about how we focus attention and mobilize energy. We know that every task needs a viable process, that every process exists only in relation to a worthy task. We also know that task and process cannot be integrated *for* people. Thus underlying theory—pure Lewin—is that involving those most affected leads to better solutions and quicker actions. Yet participative techniques, or economic ones for that matter, are useless in the absence of leadership and purposeful goals.

Condition 3: energized people. The third dimension is a little trickier. We all drag our feet some days and burst with energy on others. What can a consultant do about this? Ches Jannssen, a Swedish social psychologist, has devised a simple tool for visualizing potential energy. Each person, group, department, company, says Janssen, lives in a "four-room apartment."

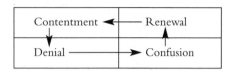

We move from room to room, depending on perceptions, feelings, and aspirations triggered by external events. The rooms represent cyclical phases, not unlike the process of death and dying. Indeed, change represents a "little death," a letting go of the past to actualize a desired future. We change rooms as we grow. However, it's not an ever upward spiral where things only get better. It's a circle game. Our feelings and behavior go up and down as outside pressures impinge on our own "life space." How much energy we have for support and commitment depends upon which room we're in.

In Contentment, we like the status quo. When that changes—through merger, reorganization, new leader, new system, market crisis, job threat—we move into Denial. We stay there until we own up to fear or anxiety. That moves us through the door into Confusion. Mucking about in Confusion, sorting our bits and pieces, opens the door to Renewal. The passage to Renewal leads from Denial through Confusion. You can't get there from Contentment by any other route.

Anxiety, in Gestalt terminology "blocked excitement," is the emotional décor of the Confusion room. Far from a state to be avoided, it signifies readiness to learn. Anxiety is the place we store energy while deciding whether to invest it. Every new project, course correction, major change requires optimal anxiety. If there's too much, we are paralyzed; too little, unmotivated.

In every Confusion room there are people already taking constructive action. It is they who will carry the movie forward—if they can be brought together to learn how their initiatives integrate with the whole. So I seek to assess which room people live in right now, and how they are acting there. That helps me decide how I can act constructively in the situation. (See Figure 1.)

People in Contentment or Denial are not "frozen." Events will move them soon enough. Little can be done to hasten the day, though rational problem solving can certainly delay it. We can make our presence felt and accepted by acting appropriately with people in those rooms—supporting their right to stay there as long as they wish. To mobilize energy, we need to be with people in Confusion or Renewal. I believe if someone were to revisit OD cases from this perspective, they would see that "failure" correlates closely with action-research methods foisted onto people living in Contentment or Denial. The seeds of success are sown in Confusion and sprout in Renewal. Those are the rooms where people welcome flip charts, models, and OD techniques.

Even that is too simple. Any task—at some point—may shake people into Denial when the going gets rough. When that happens I don't know what to do except keep talking and wait it out. They won't be ready to work toward any changes until they have moved from the Denial room to Confusion or Renewal.

The urge to hold on—to old habits, familiar patterns, relationships, and structures (whether they satisfy or not)—is as old as human history. Robert Tannenbaum and Robert Hanna have pointed out the powerful losses change represents for each of us—of identity, of certainty, of meaning itself. Under these conditions no "unfreezing" techniques are likely to help. According to Tannenbaum and Hanna, "Realistic patience and a sense of an appropriate time scale must underlie and guide the change process itself." We can help by giving people a chance to come together, to experience their mutual dilemmas more fully, to make their own choices about when and how to move.

Hooking together many activities requires only a little linear planning. If we provide the right container, people will fill it with the right elixir. This

FIGURE 1

Action-taking in the four-room apartment

Contentment Room	Renewal Room
What clients say: "I like it just the way it is."	*What clients say:* "We've got more possibilities that we can ever use. I don't know what to do first."
What a consultant should do: Leave people alone, unless you think the building's on fire.	*What a consultant should do:* Offer assistance through simple, mutually arranged tasks.
Denial Room	Confusion Room
What clients say: "What, me worry?! Everything's fine—I think . . . ."	*What clients say:* "This is the damnedest mess I ever saw. Helllppp!"
What a consultant should do: Ask questions. Give support. Heighten awareness. Do *not* offer advice.	*What a consultant should do:* Structure tasks. Focus on the future. Get people together. Ask for/offer help.

happens spontaneously as the other practices—getting the system in the room, focusing on the future, constructing doable tasks—are applied. I think it is more likely to happen when we work on important tasks, mutually defined, that improve our chances for survival and self-control.

"Should We/Shouldn't We" Discussions.   The activities I like best—because they involve whole systems—are joint planning of business strategy (external focus), work redesign (internal focus), and reorganizations that embody both strategy and structure. In each mode the people most affected help devise and test various structural models, using consulting help. I don't mean to make this sound easy as pie. I usually find myself in long "should we/shouldn't we" dialogs—hours or days of hashing out the pros and cons of opening the action to many others, whether there's time to do it all, whether short-term results will suffer, what good alternatives exist. Above all, each of us uses the dialogs to decide whether to become personally involved.

So I look for a leader, a business opportunity, and a "should we/shouldn't we" discussion. If we decide to team up, I help people plan how to raise a crowd, structure a task, and provide some (left brain) methods for getting started. As right brains are activated, they take care of what can't be planned in advance.

Useful Practice 2: Get the "Whole System" in the Room.   There are many ways to get a "whole system" together. A system can be there, for example, in your head—a conceptual rather than logistical feat that most people can master. Try the "All-Purpose Viewing Lens" in Figure 2, and see how fast you can become a "systems" thinker.

However, knowing what's going on is not the same as enacting productive community. People need shared perceptions to make their contributions. That means getting together to *live* the open system. How many functions, levels, managers, operators, staff, lines can be mustered to work on their own organization all at once? Could customers and suppliers be involved? My inclination

is to push for "more" and let others say what's "realistic." I confess I don't know how to involve a cast of thousands all at once. Yet keeping that as a benchmark helps me remember what I set out to do. Systems get better when the members cooperate on joint tasks. When people from top and bottom meet across lines of status, function, sex, race, and hierarchy, and when "problems" can be seen as systemic rather than discrete, wonderful new (and unpredictable) things happen. These can't be "planned" except in the sense of making them more probable. Such happenings lead to more creative and committed actions, more secure and engaging work. Let's look at some examples.

In the merger that created Sovran Bank, the largest financial services institution in Virginia, the operations departments used an interlocking chain of team-development conferences, starting with three top executives from each bank, cascading to the next two levels, culminating in a mass meeting of several hundred people. People planned their own roles and divided up work—an exercise many believed was impossible.

Bethlehem Steel's Sparrows Point plate mill reorganized during a two-week training marathon attended by 80 people—managers, supervisors, and staff—who specified, in advance, which problems they wished to manage better. Together they studied every aspect of the mill—it's internal dynamics, the marketplace, corporate connections, and relationships across levels and functions. They visited "suppliers" in steel-making and customers in distant cities. As workshop "inputs" linked to their own experience, they quickly changed mill practices to serve customers better. They could do this because of an unusual business opportunity—the annual maintenance shutdown. The key new management behavior: paying people to come in and learn instead of taking a two-week vacation.

A fast-growing software development company, McCormack & Dodge, lacked the structure to implement a new strategic plan. Top management convened four conferences for 50 people representing all levels and functions. Design teams organized by product line analyzed the system and

FIGURE 2

An all-purpose viewing lens

	Inside Picture	*Outside Picture*
Economics	Are costs up or down?	Is revenue up or down?
Technology	Do systems work as intended?	How are products/services being improved?
People	How do people feel about their work?	How do customers feel about the company?

Note: Each question can be followed by a "why," and each person who answers these questions will provide a new slant.

created new organization designs. They included in the "design specs" a 1990 strategy, their own values about employees and customers, and their analysis of how to close information gaps, improve career paths and develop more accountability and self-control. Then came the unpredictable part: Twenty-four hours into the first meeting they began making changes to existing practices as information gaps were discovered. Long before a design was "finalized" people were already acting in ways neither planned for nor diagnosed in advance. As a design emerged, the 50 talked over implementation issues with 1,000 other employees.

There is a further benefit to having a whole system present. New patterns of action that are achieved in the room are often carried outside of it *because* all the relevant parties enacted them together. There is less "sell" needed when three or four levels are able to come to the same conclusion at the same time.

Useful Practice 3: Focus on the Future.
This practice derives from work by the late Ronald Lippitt, the coiner, with Kurt Lewin, of the term *group dynamics* 40 years ago. In 1949 Lippitt began tape-recording planning meetings. The tapes revealed that people's voices grew softer, more stressed, depressed, as problems were listed and prioritized. You could hear the energy drain away as the lists grew longer.

In the 1950s Lippitt started using "images of potential," rather than gripes, as springboards for change. In the 1970s he created new workshops merging group dynamics with future thinking. He has people visualize *preferred futures* in rich detail— as they wish things to be two, three, and even five years into the future. This simple concept has enormous power. While untangling present problems leads to depression, imagining scenarios energizes common values. Taking a stand for a desired future provides purposeful guidance for goal setting, planning, and skill building. Successful entrepreneurs, notes Charles Garfield in *Peak Performers,* are uniquely skilled at projecting alternative futures. They get "feed-forward" from their imagination, which is a qualitatively different experience from feedback on past behavior.

This concept—"visioning" is one name for it— is so attractive that most people want to go out and run a group through a visioning training session. This technique *will not work* in the absence of committed leadership, a business opportunity, and some energized people. But don't take my word for it. Try it anyway.

Useful Practice 4: Structure Tasks That People Can Do for Themselves.   What structures make it possible for people to learn, focus on the future, and action plan for themselves (when leadership, opportunity, and energy exist)? A conference series designed by clients and consultants together is one way to bring the productive community alive. These are task-focused, working conferences to reorganize work or refocus effort; they shouldn't serve as add-ons or data dumps.

For consultants to manage such events, they need, first of all, sanction from credible parties. If that can be got, then any plausible "bag of tricks" will do. It is here—at the very last—we get to OD (or any) techniques. If the other signals say "go," then we need few of what Richard Hackman in *Work Design* calls "task performance strategies." One example (out of hundreds) is "responsibility charting," which is a simple way of symbolizing whether people are expected to be active or passive vis-à-vis a decision. Other examples include simple worksheets—which are derived from sociotechnical analysis—to help people with the process of analyzing and redesigning their own work.

Merrelyn Emery, a leading advocate of this perspective, points out that the purpose of consulting technique is to create a learning climate, not solutions. This is a subtle and important distinction. It is essential that we do nothing that would reinforce the idea—both undemocratic and unscientific— "that people cannot make sense of their own experience." Creating a learning climate, points out Emery, results in "an almost immediate increase in energy, common sense, and goodwill."

Summary Observations

Working in these ways, I find myself doing things which don't "come naturally." I have had to shift my focus—a real mental wrench—away from "content" diagnoses and problem lists, even of "process issues." I need to *understand* what a company is up against in the marketplace, what it takes to create committed customers. But I help more and faster when I can assess the potential for action rather than dictate the solution required. So I look for a leader, a business opportunity, some energized employees—conditions no consultant should leave home without. When they exist, I have faith that I can make a contribution to the most complicated reorganizations, despite my concerns that I always do too little or too much.

I have stopped fantasizing that one or two "experts"—even the process kind—are smart enough to figure out on their own the right learning structures. That's 1950s thinking. Anybody who offers to sell you an exemption from the clarifying experience of muddling through to renewal is a charlatan. The more we experts know about our own specialty, the less likely we are to see our favorite solution's impact on a system. When the "whole system" gets into one room, when people have valued tasks to accomplish, I believe the right diagnoses and action steps occur in "real time." Designing somebody else's work is not in any way, shape, or form an expert task.

Nor do I imagine that I can take away, by any known magical mystery trick, technique, system, jargon, book, speaker, or dog-and-pony show, the travail, confusion, chaos, and anxiety that are as natural to our species as breathing. These conditions fertilize growth, excitement, creativity, joy, energy, and commitment. As a consultant I am often invested with the power to grant people exemptions from states of denial and confusion. Alas, like the Wizard of Oz (who knew he was a fraud pretending that his technologies "worked"), I can't do it.

Instead, I seek to reduce anxiety (my own and others') through simple procedures that allow people to sort through and use their own experience. I help those who wish to design their own futures. I hate to hear anxious people labeled "change resisters," as if the natural cycle of human experience is an evil legion to be defeated by superior methodological firepower on the force fields of organizational strife. Resistance is as natural as eating. I am learning to accept my own resistance, too, especially to client expectations I cannot meet.

In sum, I believe that elaborate, consultant-centered diagnoses are unnecessary to reorganize workplaces flooded by tides of change. As the author of a widely used "six-box" diagnostic model, I expect some fans will be startled by my statement. That model served its function for me long ago—translating process language into managerial tasks. I'm delighted that so many still modify and use it, for it shows that they own it—and this is a development consistent with my theory.

With or without a model, I have learned to expect frustration and anxiety, not smooth sailing, in every white-water voyage. I greet them as familiar traveling companions. I try to rejoin them each time with good humor and to forgive myself when I can't. I recall Rudyard Kipling's poem about keeping your head "when others all about you are losing theirs and blaming it on you." The productive community for me is an anchor point for dignity and meaning in democratic societies. We need to preserve, enhance, and extend it for reasons at once pragmatic, moral, humanistic, ethical, economic, technical, and social.

QWL—far from "cultural change"—can be seen as a serious effort to conserve our culture's deepest values against erosion by narrow economic and technocratic thinking. That for me is the song and dance of restructuring workplaces. I am interested in preserving economic stability beyond quarterly dividends because I believe that democratic societies depend on creating employment. Moreover, I would like to find new ways to help people manage economic and technical innovation so that all of us, myself included, find dignity and meaning in work.

In 1900, Taylor had experts solve problems for people—"scientific management." In 1950, Lewin's descendants started "everybody" solving their own problems—participative management. About 1960, experts discovered "systems" thinking—and began improving whole systems *for* other people. Now, we are learning how to get "everybody" improving whole systems. The most successful third-wave managers and consultants will be those who learn to do that soonest.

References

The "generalized speedup of the corporate metabolism" has been documented with increasing frequency since World War II. Donald A. Schon celebrated it in *Beyond the Stable State* (Random House, 1971). Alvin Toffler describes it as a historic global shift in human consciousness in *The Third Wave* (Bantam Books, 1980),

detailing the impact of new technologies on families, work, lifestyles, and human societies. Toffler's conclusion—more direct democracy is an imperative for survival in a high-tech age—will come as no surprise to this journal's readers.

The negative impact of technology on human aspirations for dignity, meaning, and community has been observed repeatedly form the dawn of history as an antidote to paeans of progress. Elton Mayo's *The Social Problems of an Industrial civilization* (Harvard University Division of Research, 1945) remains a vivid statement of our own primacy over machines—although why we need to keep asserting this when people devised the contraptions to begin with troubles me. My quote is from Chapter 1, "The Seamy Side of Progress." Donald A. Schon makes the same point in *Beyond the Stable State* (Random House, 1971), adding that organizations and people have to become "learning systems" if they wish to prosper.

The tension between individualism and community in American life predates industrialization. Alexis de Tocqueville, the awed French critic of U.S. democracy, fingered this issue more than 150 years ago. For a contemporary update on his observation see *Habits of the Heart: Individualism and Commitment in American Life* (University of California, 1985) by Robert N. Bellah, Richard Madsen, William M. Sullivan, Anne Swidler, and Steven M. Tipton. This is "must reading" for anybody who cares about the future of interdependence on a shrinking planet, an old-fashioned sociology of real people above statistics in a scholarly genre I haven't seen for 20 years.

Frederick W. Taylor's values have resurfaced in a powerful way in the 1980s, even while we bury his methods for good. *The Principles of Scientific Management,* first published in 1911, is still available in paperback (W. W. Norton, 1967). It's as readable as your newspaper and just as contemporary—perhaps the earliest treatise on collaborative techniques of human resources management. If you ever believed it was anything else, you should read it for yourself—as a reminder that "participation," "commitment," and "excellence" are just as liable to "taylorization" as time-and-motion study.

For evidence of that, look what happened to Kurt Lewin's change concepts. Lewin started with a startling observation—that you can't understand a person's behavior without knowing more about the present situation he or she is in, and vice versa, embodied in "field theory." He talked "psychological ecology" before such a term was fashionable. He believed (not unlike Taylor) that an exact science could be made of human behavior. His original writings are full of obscure mathematical formulae (he used topological geometry to map social-psychological problems). It was only a short jump for appliers of his thinking to imagine (old paradigm) that "unfreezing" techniques could be divined to accelerate human development. I recommend Alfred Marrow's *The Practical Theorist* (Basic Books, 1969), an admiring, intimate, readable account of Lewin's life. In *Productive Communities,* I show Lewin's vast influence on management and the similarity of his interests to Taylor's. I think his most readable work is in *Resolving Social Conflicts: Selected Papers on Group dynamics* (Harper & Row, 1948) edited by Gertrud Weiss Lewin.

The clearest-eyed antidote I know to megalomania about change techniques is the work of Robert Tannenbaum and Robert Hanna, accessible in "Holding On, Letting Go, and Moving On: Understanding a Neglected Perspective on Change," Chapter 6 in *Human Systems Development,* by Robert Annenbaum, Newton Margulies, Fred Massarik and Associates (Jossey-Bass, 1985). They make the point that we can't purport to change organizations if we don't appreciate the importance of the human need to hold onto certainty, even the unpleasant kind. Their practice theory supports my belief that Douglas McGregor's Theories X and Y are not so much opposing assumptions about human nature as they are an internal dialog in each of us between our need for control and our wish to be free—a major theme of *Productive Communities.*

For consulting skills—in all areas of experience—I know of no better guide than Peter Block's *Flawless Consulting* (Learning Concepts, 1981). Block's readable follow-up, *The Empowered Manager* (Jossey-Bass, 1986) describes the choices available to those who would take initiative and risk to make their organizations great—a

beacon for those who would "let go" of old assumptions and create their own futures.

There is no way to overstate the contributions of Fred Emery, Eric Trist, and colleagues to the revamping of the work world—a history I take up in my book. The best overview I know is Trist's *The Evolution of Socio-Technical Systems: A Conceptual Framework and an Action Research Program* (Ontario Quality of Working Life Centre, June 1981). These concepts will one day be seen as the most revolutionary in human history. That they are not better known now is partly a function of their dense vocabulary (e.g., "causal texture," "turbulent social field") and partly our slowness to recognize how the "new paradigm"—of necessity—is replacing the old in the same way that autos replaced buggies. To extend the analogy, our 1986 understanding of sociotechnical design in the workplace corresponds now to 1917 in the development of the car. Many people have heard of it, far fewer have seen it in action, relatively few have one, not everybody is sure they want one, and those who own one find it cranky, unpredictable, and needing constant maintenance. Eventually everybody will take new paradigm practices for granted.

The "future-oriented" book that has most influenced my practice of workplace improvements is *Building the Collaborative Community: Mobilizing Citizens for Action* (University of California Extension, 1980), by Eva Schindler-Rainman and the late Ronald Lippitt. It describes the methods used to get whole systems in the room to focus on the future and do the job for themselves in 88 community conferences for cities and states all over North America—involving thousands from all walks of life. This book is so diffident its title does not appear on the spine, making it hard to pick off a bookshelf. It deals with voluntary community action, not business firms. It shows more concretely than any work I know that what people can imagine, people can do.

READING 5
ORGANIZATION DEVELOPMENT AND TRANSFORMATION

Jerry I. Porras
Robert C. Silvers

Introduction

Rapidly changing environments demand that organizations generate equally fast responses in order to survive and prosper. Planned change that makes organizations more responsive to environmental shifts should be guided by generally accepted and unified theories of organizations and organizational change—neither of which currently exists. Yet despite this absence of clear conceptual underpinnings, the field continues to evolve and grow.

In this chapter, we review recent research that improves our understanding of planned change theory and practice. We begin by proposing a new model of the change process rooted in a conception of organizations presented by Porras (1987) and Porras et al. (1990). This change model organizes our understanding of the field and guides the discussion of research presented in the second half of the chapter.[1]

A Model of Planned Change

Organizational change is typically triggered by a relevant environmental shift that, once sensed by the organization, leads to an intentionally generated response. This intentional response is "planned organizational change" and consists of four identifiable, interrelated components: (a) a change intervention that alters (b) key organizational target variables that then impact (c) individual organizational members and their on-the-job behaviors resulting in changes in (d) organizational outcomes. These broad components of planned change are shown at the top of Figure 1. The lower part of the figure adds more

detail to each component and graphically summarizes our Planned Process Model;[2] we discuss each component below.

Change Interventions. Planned change interventions can be divided into two general types. The first comprises the more traditional approach. Organization Development (OD), which until recently was synonymous with the term *planned change*. The second, Organization Transformation (OT), is the cutting edge of planned change and may be called "second-generation OD." At present, OD is relatively well defined and circumscribed in terms of its technologies, theory, and research. OT, on the other hand, is emerging, ill-defined, highly experimental, and itself rapidly changing.[3]

Organization Development. Organization development is defined as:

1. A set of behavioral science theories, values, strategies, and techniques

2. aimed at the planned change of organizational work settings

3. with the intention of generating alpha, beta, and/or gamma (A) cognition change in individual organizational members, leading to behavioral change and thus

4. creating a better fit between the organization's capabilities and its current environmental demands, or

5. promoting changes that help the organization to better fit predicted future environments.

OD often occurs in response to modest mismatches with the environment and produces relatively moderate adjustments in those segments of

Source: Jerry Porras and Robert Silvers, "Organization Development and Transformation," *Annual Review of Psychology* 42 (1991), pp. 51–78. With permission, from the *Annual Review of Psychology*, Volume 42, © 1991, by Annual Reviews.

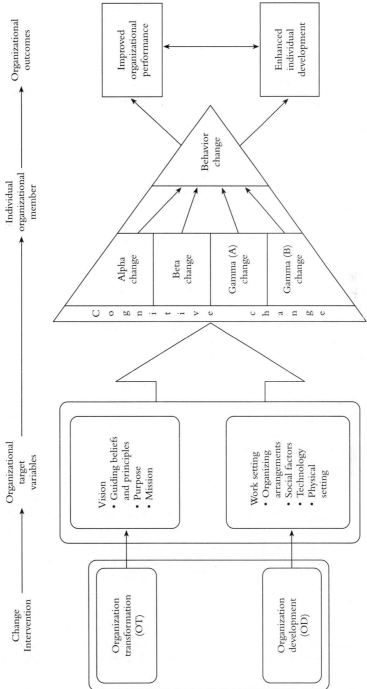

FIGURE 1

the organization not congruent with the environment. This form of OD results in individuals' experiencing only alpha and beta cognition change, with a correspondingly limited change in behaviors.

Additionally, OD is triggered not only by current environmental mismatches but also by an organization's desire to fit into future desirable environmental niches. This results in the creation of new modes of functioning and impacts substantial segments of the organization. This second type of OD leads to alpha, beta, and gamma(A) cognition change in organizational members, and behavioral changes are broader.[4]

In summary, then, OD concentrates on work-setting changes that either help an organization better adapt to its current environment or improve its fit into expected future environments. This approach to planned change produces appreciable, not radical, change in individual employees' cognitions as well as behaviors.

Organization Transformation. Organization transformation is:

1. A set of behavioral science theories, values, strategies, and techniques

2. aimed at the planned change of organizational vision and work settings

3. with the intention of generating alpha, beta, gamma (A) and/or gamma (B) cognition change in individual organizational members, leading to behavioral change and thus

4. promoting paradigmatic change that helps the organization better fit or create desirable future environments.

OT is also planned and primarily directed at creating a new vision for the organization. Vision change occurs most effectively when an organization develops the capability for continuous self-diagnosis and change; a "learning organization" evolves—one that is constantly changing to more appropriately fit the present organizational state and better anticipate desired futures. This set of interventions leads to alpha, beta, gamma(A), and gamma(B) cognition change in organizational members, and concomitant radical change in their behaviors.

Organizational Target Variables. Planned change interventions impact two major types of organizational variables: organizational vision and the work setting. Taken together, these create the internal organizational environment in which individual employees function.

Vision consists of three main factors: *(a)* the guiding beliefs and principles of the organization; *(b)* the enduring organizational purpose that grows out of these beliefs; and *(c)* a catalyzing mission that is consistent with organizational purpose and, at the same time, moves the organization toward the achievement of that purpose (Collins & Porras, 1989).

The work setting consists of many dimensions and, as such, requires a parsimonious framework to organize our understanding of it. From our perspective, the organizational work setting can be subdivided into four major streams of variables: *(a)* organizing arrangements, *(b)* social factors, *(c)* technology, and *(d)* physical setting (Porras, 1987). Table 1 lists the subvariables that constitute each of these streams. These four streams of variables are themselves shaped by the organization's vision, which gives them coherence and direction.

Individual Organizational Members. Individual organizational members must change their on-the-job behaviors in order for the organization to change over a longer term. The complex environment surrounding individuals at work is the primary catalyst for behaviors on the job (moderated, as discussed below, by cognitive change). Organizational behaviors are generated by individuals behaving in response to the signals received directly from their work setting and indirectly from organizational vision. Therefore, successful planned change efforts must alter these two components of the internal organizational environment such that new signals influence individuals to produce new

TABLE 1

Organizational components in the stream organizational model

Organizing Arrangements (OA)	Social Factors (SF)	Technology (T)	Physical Setting (PS)
A. goals	A. culture	A. tools, equipment, & machinery	A. space configuration
B. strategies	1. basic assumptions		1. size
C. formal structure	2. values	B. technical expertise	2. shape
D. administrative policies & procedures	3. norms	C. job design	3. relative locations
E. administrative systems	4. language & design	D. work flow design	B. physical ambiance
F. formal reward systems	5. rituals	E. technical policies & procedures	1. light
1. evaluation system	6. history	F. technical systems	2. heat
2. pay systems	7. stories		3. noise
3. benefits packages	8. myths		4. air quality
G. ownership	9. symbols		5. cleanliness
	B. interaction processes		C. interior design
	1. interpersonal		1. decorations
	2. group		2. furniture
	3. intergroup		3. window coverings
	C. social patterns & networks		4. floor coverings
	1. communication		5. colors
	2. problem solving/ decision making		a. floors
	3. influence		b. walls
	4. status		c. ceilings
	D. individual attributes		D. architectural design
	1. attitudes & beliefs		
	2. behavioral skills		
	3. feelings		
	E. management style		

Source: Adapted from Porras, J. I. 1987. *Stream Analysis.* Reading, Mass.: Addison-Wesley: p. 52, Table 3–1.

behaviors. Employees consciously process work setting cues and modify their behavior as a result.

Individual Cognition and Planned Change. The types of individual cognitive change that occur as a result of planned change activities have been discussed in the management and organization literature for over four decades (e.g. Lindblom, 1959; Vickers, 1965; Greiner, 1972; Sheldon, 1980). For our purposes, the most useful conceptualization appeared in the OD literature 15 years ago when Golembiewski and his colleagues proposed alpha, beta, and gamma change as the three possible measurable outcomes of OD interventions (Golembiewski et al., 1976):

1. "Alpha change involves a variation in the level of some existential state, given a constantly calibrated measuring instrument related to a constant conceptual domain" (p. 134).

2. "Beta change involves a variation in the level of some existential state complicated by the fact that some intervals of the measurement continuum associated with a constant conceptual domain have been recalibrated" (p. 135).

3. "Gamma change involves a redefinition or reconceptualization of some domain, a major change in the perspective or frame

of reference within which phenomena are perceived and classified, in what is taken to be some relevant slice of reality" (p. 135).

This perspective is primarily oriented toward framing change in the context of measurement issues, but it highlights some important principles. Alpha change is a perceived change in objective circumstances, while beta change is that type of change coupled with changing standards of individual interpretation. Gamma change is a radical shift in an individual's assumptions about causal relationships, the values attached to various dimensions of reality, and the interpretive frameworks that describe reality. In other words, gamma change describes a "paradigm shift" in organizational members' mental constructs (Kuhn, 1970).

The notion of paradigm is useful for conceptualizing the change process. An organizational paradigm may be defined as:

> a prevailing world-view or collective belief system. The fundamental set of beliefs or organizing principles which are unquestioned and unexamined assumptions about the nature of reality (Adams, 1984, p. 278).[5]

Integrating the construct of organizational paradigm with the notions of alpha, beta, and gamma change is a useful way to develop a new typology that conceptualizes individual cognitive change processes. The focus here is not on measurement but on broad categories of individual cognitive change. This leads to the following four types:

1. Alpha change: change in the perceived levels of variables within a paradigm without altering their configuration (e.g. a perceived improvement in skills).

2. Beta change: change in people's view about the meaning of the value of any variable within an existing paradigm without altering their configuration (e.g. change in standards).

3. Gamma(A) change: change in the configuration of an existing paradigm without the addition of new variables (e.g. changing the central value of a

"production-driven" paradigm from "cost containment" to "total quality focus"; this results in the reconfiguration of all variables within this paradigm).

4. Gamma(B) change: the replacement of one paradigm with another that contains some or all new variables (e.g. replacing a "production-driven" paradigm with a "customer-responsive" paradigm).

Each of these cognitive changes leads to corresponding changes in behavior. As an illustration, a change in standards (the example given above for beta change) causes behavior to change in order to meet these new standards. As another example, a paradigm shift from "production-driven" to "customer-responsive" alters existing behaviors, creates new behaviors, and gives individual employees a totally new way of viewing their work. The level and depth of behavior change will therefore correspond to the shift in individual cognitions.

Organizational Outcomes.   Two kinds of organizational outcomes are central to our model. The first is organizational performance, captured in such factors as productivity, profitability, efficiency, effectiveness, quality, and so on. The second is individual development, an actualization of the self that occurs as individuals alter their world views, expand their repertoire of behaviors, and/or improve their skills and abilities.

Summary.   The Change Process Model identifies the key components of a change process and organizes them in a way that improves one's understanding of the field as a whole. We use this model to categorize our review of recent research by analyzing articles according to the intervention approach used, the variables targeted for change, the type of individual cognitive change that occurs, and the organizational outcomes derived from the intervention activity. Unfortunately, much of the research does not give enough detail to fully analyze work by the last two above-mentioned categories, so we categorize articles primarily by intervention approach and target variables.

Research Findings

This review examines articles concerning OD and OT that were published between 1985 and 1989 in journals with an organizational behavior and/or organization development focus (e.g., the *Journal of Applied Behavioral Science, Human Relations, Group and Organizational Studies, Journal of Applied Psychology, Academy of Management Journal, Academy of Management Review, Organizational Dynamics,* and more). Because little literature on OT was found in these sources, we reviewed books and other journals that do contain work on OT (e.g., Levy & Merry, 1986; Adams, 1984).

Organization Development. We first focus our discussion on OD research and structure our comments using the change targets (i.e., organizing arrangements, social factors, technology, and physical space) as subcategories in our review. Articles that do not fit these categories are reviewed at the end of this section.

Organizing Arrangements. Research on a variety of interventions focuses on this stream of target variables. Quality circles (QCs), gainsharing interventions, and other forms of employee involvement are the topics most prevalent in the period reviewed. Some research also focused on other OA dimensions, such as alternative work schedules, new design tools, and new design options. We review the key articles that further our understanding of these various interventions and/or discuss innovative practices and ideas.[6]

Quality circles. Generally, the literature on QCs lacks empirical and statistical rigor. One important cause of this appears to be the absence of a clear theoretical foundation to guide research. Initial attempts at theory have been made that primarily classified QCs as focusing on work technology, with productivity as its end target (Steel & Shane, 1986). Later attempts to strengthen QC theory provided a more detailed model of the QC process, focusing on both structural and processual variables. However, the empirical evidence supporting these models has been mixed (Steel & Lloyd, 1988).

Other additions to QC theory emphasize the conditions leading to failure in QC implementation. One approach views disappointments with QCs as due to flawed assumptions (e.g., that groups always outperform individuals) and a lack of understanding regarding the cultural differences between the United States and Japan (Ferris & Wagner, 1985). Another proposes that a myriad of organizational factors hamper QC success, such as supervisory resistance, lack of volunteers, departmental transfer of employees (leading to less QC continuity), unskilled meeting facilitation, et cetera (Meyer & Stott, 1985). A third suggests that QCs are an employee-involvement strategy leading to minimal changes in organizational power and should be used primarily when conditions are not favorable for more extensive employee involvement (Lawler & Mohrman, 1987; Lawler, 1988). These perspectives all imply that changes in both structure and process are necessary to improve QC success rates.

Additional empirical research investigating QC efficacy has focused on assessing the impact of QC interventions on a variety of attitudinal and perceptual variables. QC membership significantly affects attitudes specific to QC functioning, such as communication, participation (Marks et al., 1986), and influence (Rafaeli, 1985); changes in more general attitudes, such as satisfaction and commitment, have also been found (Griffin, 1988).[7]

Findings on the effects of QCs on task perceptions have been contradictory. Rafaeli (1985) showed significant effects from QC membership on task perceptions while, in a similar study, Head et al. (1986) did not. Overall, the evidence regarding QCs is most positive for attitudinal and behavioral impacts directly related to QC functioning; the evidence is contradictory about QC impact on task perceptions.

Gainsharing. Theory and research on gainsharing has emphasized its motivational effects on performance. Although the theory base for this approach is relatively weak, there have been recent attempts at strengthening it. For example, Florkowski (1987) proposed a theoretical model explaining the connection between profit sharing and behavioral and attitudinal outcomes. Drawing on expectancy theory and labor relations theory, he hypothesizes that profit sharing is a motivator for individual employees to the extent that it is a salient and important part of earnings and/or based on subunit performance.

Empirical investigations of this motivation dimension have not yielded highly positive findings. For example, Pearce et al. (1985) found that merit pay for federal agency managers had no effect on improved performance in the manager's units. Jordan (1986) examined the effects of performance-contingent rewards and found that this type of pay for social service workers decreased intrinsic motivation and did not affect satisfaction with pay. However, positive effects were reported in a study of a manufacturing firm that had employed the Scanlon Plan for approximately a decade. Miller & Schuster (1987) found that the plan had statistically significant effects on employment stability along with positive effects on productivity and labor-management cooperation.

The negative empirical findings regarding gainsharing theory appear to be derived from change projects of more limited scope and duration. On the other hand, much more positive findings seem to obtain when gainsharing is part of a long-term, broad-based program (i.e., the Scanlon Plan study). It appears that gainsharing has the greatest effect when it is part of a larger-scale and more extensive change process.

Employee ownership. Research on employee ownership is expanding and developing a stronger theory base. Some of the most substantial work in this arena was done by Klein (1987), who tested three competing models relating employee stock ownership to employee attitudes. She found that the financial benefits and influence opportunities of ownership most strongly impacted attitudes. This evidence supported extrinsic and instrumental models of ownership, but not an intrinsic model where ownership is satisfying in and of itself.

Regarding the influence effects of employee ownership, some research contradicts the "expected" link between employee ownership and desire for influence in organizational policies. For example, French (1987) characterized employees as investors who only seek influence when it is in their best financial interests to do so. As a consequence, he concludes that ownership may not be a solution for increasing power equalization within the firm.

In summary, research on employee ownership has grown and illustrates a promising and innovative approach to organizing in this country. However, it still lacks a strong theory base, one that is much needed to guide both practice and research.

Alternative work schedules. Researchers here have primarily investigated the impact of alternative work schedules on attitudes and productivity. Attitude changes about the schedule and free time have been found to be a primary effect of work schedule changes, with smaller impacts on general attitudes and effectiveness (Dunham et al., 1987). The process used to implement alternative work schedules is also important. As would be expected, the greater the participation in the implementation process, the more favorable the attitudes toward the change (Latack & Foster, 1985).[8] Regarding only the relationship between alternative work schedules and productivity, positive effects of flextime on productivity occur when resources are scarce and productivity is measured at the group level (Ralston et al., 1985).

In summary, although this approach to organizational improvement has existed for over a decade, there has been little research on it. Alternative schedules appear to improve attitudes and performance, but more research is needed to determine the conditions under which these effects extend beyond variables specific to the intervention.

Organizational structure. Changes in organizational structure have been discussed in the literature from a variety of perspectives. One approach has focused on the development of new structural options. Ackoff (1989) proposed the "circular organization," where each manager reports to a "board of directors" consisting of his or her immediate superiors, subordinates, and important peers or outsiders. These boards are responsible for planning and coordination with other units, and, in some cases, for evaluating managerial performance. This approach to organization structure highlights one way that democracy and responsiveness need not conflict in modern organizations.

A second perspective focuses on new tools for design, rather than the final design itself. Two such tools have been proposed by McDaniel et al. (1987) and Nelson (1988). The former examined the usefulness of decision analysis for interventions involving organizational design. They found this tool helped participants to identify problems and resolve them productively. The latter discussed the uses of "blockmodeling" (a form of network analysis found primarily in sociology) for structural diagnosis, coalition identification, and intergroup relations analysis. Network analysis uncovers groupings and patterns not easily identified by traditional OD diagnostic methods. These two approaches to the problem of organization design are creative and should set the stage for additional (and much needed) development in this area.[9]

Summary. While it is encouraging to see more theory related to organization-level issues and structural interventions, most of the above research consists of "little studies." Although these further knowledge of a specific intervention and its particular effects, no attempt is made to explore multifaceted interventions and systemic outcomes. Intervention research in this and other areas would be more profitable if it explored broader and more complex system change and its outcomes (e.g., the effects of gainsharing on social factors variables, such as culture). In addition, research needs to expand its focus from direct effects to more pervasive and indirect impacts in order to assess the overall effectiveness of organizing arrangement interventions.

Social Factors. The social factors (SF) variables have historically been the most frequent targets of OD in organizations, but research in this area has decreased somewhat in recent years. In addition, the particular dimensions of interest have shifted; team interventions and group variables (which used to be the primary focus of this area) do not dominate the more current literature.

We begin our discussion with interventions oriented toward the alteration of individual attributes, next review research on group change, and then treat work focusing on culture change.

Personality theory. An exciting development in the SF area is the increased integration of personality theory with OD. Personality theory research reported in the period reviewed has been applied to all levels of analysis: to the individual employee, the manager, the small group, and the overall organization.

At the individual level, personality theory has been applied to identifying traits that might moderate the acceptance and effects of planned change. One that has been identified is the employee's "focus of attention" (Gardner et al., 1987). Employees may either focus on the job, the work unit, or off-the job; each focus leads to different effects from various interventions. It was hypothesized that job design interventions would positively affect individuals focused on their jobs, with similar types of predictions made for the other foci. Empirical evidence indicated that job focus and job change impacted hard measures, whereas work unit focus and job change impacted soft measures. Off-the-job focus impacted both types of measures negatively.

An important application of personality theory to the understanding of manager behavior has been made by Fisher et al. (1987), who drew on developmental psychology to create a four-stage model of the managerial life cycle. Their research showed that few managers have reached the final two stages (which emphasize a tolerance for ambiguity and "transformational" leadership); therefore, problems in the organization may indicate a mismatch between organizational needs and managers' development. This framework could be useful as a diagnostic tool to identify dysfunctional matches.

Krantz (1985) used a Tavistock Institute approach to explore how unconscious group processes, such as defenses against anxiety, serve to create a specific organizational structure and culture. Examples of organizational decline were used to elucidate this process. This analysis provides an innovative method for understanding resistance to change and implementing effective organizational designs.

These three articles further our understanding of the impact of individual differences on intervention efficacy. They also highlight the link between organizational form and individual personality. However, this area (like many others) needs substantially more attention than it has been given. Other personality factors should be explored, and a more comprehensive model of personality related to OD should be developed.

Team Building. We found relatively few studies of team building. Those we identified were clustered into three broad groups: one that investigated the effects of team building on group process variables, a second that explored the impact of team building on the productivity or performance of the group, and a third that presented new perspectives on team building dynamics and appropriate research methods.

The impact of team building interventions on process measures was explored in two studies by Eden (1985, 1986a). Working with Israel Defense Forces (IDF) officers, Eden found that team building significantly affected self-perceptions of the efficacy of the intervention but did not effect actual changes (as rated by subordinates). A follow-up study (Eden, 1986a) showed significant effects on teamwork, conflict handling, and information about plans but not on other variables less directly related to the intervention itself (such as challenge, officer support, and so on). These studies provide only mixed evidence for the efficacy of the team building intervention.

The impact of team building on performance measures was examined in three different investigations. Bottger & Yetton (1987) studied the impact of individual training in problem solving on group performance and found significantly positive effects. Mitchell (1986) showed that revealing one's "internal frame of reference" leads to improved task accomplishment. However, these results were not significantly better than a traditional team building intervention. Research by Buller & Bell (1986) examined a team building/goal setting intervention with miners and found only marginally significant effects on outcomes such as productivity. It appears that narrowly focused team building interventions have a positive effect on performance. This suggests that the creative combination of some of these more narrowly focused intervention techniques could produce a substantially greater impact.

Contributions to the theory base of team building were made by Buller (1986), who utilized concepts from force-field analysis and participative decision making to develop a more precise definition of team building. He proposed that the effect of "team building–problem solving" on task performance occurs due to a variety of individual, group, task, and organizational factors. Finally, Buller suggests that team building research can be substantially improved through the development of clear operational definitions of variables, clear conceptualization of causal mechanisms, increased use of experimental designs, and the development of objective performance measures. We agree with these recommendations, except for the use of experimental designs. The reality of field research often precludes the use of true experiments; in addition, there are strong arguments against the use of these types of designs in OD (Bullock & Svyantek, 1987).

Multilevel issues. Social factor interventions that attempt to affect more complex organizational problems or arenas were reported in two studies. The first (Evans, 1989) dealt with multinational corporate development, where there has been a shift from structural to processual approaches. This is because the major challenge faced today by multinational corporations is to couple global integration with local responsiveness. For OD to be relevant in this arena, it must focus more on macro/substantive issues and become more culturally sensitive.

In contrast to the multinational setting, Golembiewski et al. (1987) discussed an intervention within a large company where the human resources staff was experiencing high levels of burnout. Both the sources and solutions to the situation were multilevel and required that a complex set of actions be undertaken. Active intervention into the culture, processes, and structure of the unit not only reduced the incidence of burnout but also improved working conditions.

New tools. An interesting new tool in OD demonstrates the time-honored principle that the sounder the theory base, the more potent any tool derived from it will be. Bernstein & Burke (1989) began with a theory of meaning systems in organizations; an implication of this theory is that belief systems must change in order to produce behavioral change in organizations. The authors used survey data and multivariate methods to uncover basic belief structures held by individuals and groups within organizations, and stated that making beliefs explicit allows for their conscious change. We encourage the use of new tools in OD, especially when these tools are derived from a sound theoretical base.

Technology. Research focusing on interventions in the technology area has utilized primarily sociotechnical systems (STS) and quality of work life (QWL) approaches. These approaches have, over time, been more broadly applied to change of entire organizations or major subsystems. A more recent variant of these two approaches uses parallel organizations (POs) as a key mechanism to implement change. We begin our discussion by focusing on studies where POs were used.

Parallel organizations. Research on POs focuses on the contingencies and outcomes associated with their success or failure. Scholars such as Herrick (1985) view POs as a "metapractice" of STS theory. If successful, POs serve as models leading to the implementation of STS concepts across the whole organization. Bushe (1987) studied a QWL intervention involving POs and found that they were more effective when a permanent middle-management problem-solving group was also created; these groups led to greater feelings of empowerment and security for the managers, who were then less threatened by changes in employees' power. Shani & Eberhardt (1987) examined the implementation of the PO in a hospital, and employees who were a part of the PO became highly involved with organizational issues and suggestions for change. Ironically, this very interest proved threatening to top management, and this aspect of POs must be carefully managed in order to ensure their effective use. Bushe (1988), in a later study, examined the implementation of five QWL projects within a large organization and showed that QWL projects utilizing POs outperformed projects involving QCs.[10]

Quality of work life. Bocialetti (1987) examined a QWL intervention in a unionized metals processing plant and found younger workers more satisfied with the intervention because it allowed them to circumvent both the seniority system and the adversarial relations between management and older workers. Ondrack & Evans (1987) examined the effects of QWL in both greenfield and redesigned plants in the petrochemical industry in Canada. No differences were found in either job enrichment or satisfaction between traditional and QWL plants. Sorenson et al. (1985) examined the effects of QWL on a small organization and found positive changes in attitudes and performance over a four-year period. These results suggest that QWL interventions frequently have positive effects on attitudes but that performance effects are somewhat more mixed.

Sociotechnical systems. Two studies explored theoretical issues about STS interventions. Kolody & Stjernberg (1986) drew upon case studies to develop a model of the STS process that highlights specific organizational subsystems as important to design efforts in plant settings. Susman & Chase (1986) explored the technical and social challenges that computer-integrated manufacturing poses for traditional STS plan design. The authors suggest changes in the STS process that will result in more successful implementation. Unfortunately, no subsequent research appears to be guided by either approach.

Other research explored STS interventions in a variety of settings. Pasmore et al. (1986) found that negative results from an STS intervention in a health care setting were due to the consultants' lack of sensitivity to the unique dynamics of this setting. Wall et al. (1986) instituted an autonomous workgroup design in a greenfield plant site and found positive effects only for intrinsic job satisfaction. Other individual-level measures showed no positive and/or lasting effects. Conversely, Taylor (1986) created an STS intervention in a computer operations department that did not involve semiautonomous work groups (a mainstay of typical STS interventions). Positive effects on turnover and production were demonstrated.

Reviewing the technology interventions as a whole, we are heartened that, by and large, they increasingly focus on whole-system issues and change. At the same time, the mixed success of these interventions means that their theoretical base still needs more refinement. Questions regarding the appropriateness of STS to different settings as well as the efficacy of QWL arrangements in creating both satisfaction and productivity are prime targets for further examination.

Physical Setting. Although planned change interventions focusing on physical settings have been part of the OD literature for over 15 years (e.g., Steele, 1973), we located only two more recent studies that focused on this intervention strategy. Oldham, one of the more active researchers in this area, investigated the effects of changing from a normal open office plan to either a more spacious open office plan or partitioned cubicles (Oldham, 1988). Both approaches resulted in positive effects on variables specific to the change (such as privacy satisfaction); individual differences in privacy needs and stimulus screening were significant moderators of these relations. In a somewhat similar study, Zalesny & Farace (1987) examined the effects of moving from closed offices to an open office plan for governmental employees. Symbolic theory (i.e., that work environments communicate information symbolically) best explained the results because those with higher positions were less satisfied (i.e., managers felt losing their offices indicated a loss of position).

Other Areas of Interest. A substantial amount of theory and research in OD focuses on general processes and issues.

New settings for OD. Gray & Hay (1986) extended political analysis to interorganizational domains to explicate the necessary conditions and actions for successful interventions in this arena. For interventions to be successful, powerful and legitimate stakeholders must participate in domain definition and action. Key environmental forces must also be successfully managed. Some have focused on how well OD might fit with other cultures. Boss & Mariono (1987) examined the history and practice of OD in Italy and showed that it has primarily occurred in large organizations that train their own professionals. Italian work culture

appears to be oriented more toward role-oriented and structural interventions than does the United States. Jaeger (1986) drew upon Hofstede's work (1980) on national values to determine the fit of OD with various cultures. He concluded that some areas, such as Scandinavia, have values very consonant with OD; while others, such as Latin America, do not.[11] The author suggests that the success of OD in other nations will be determined by its adaptation to the dominant local values.

The applicability of OD to settings other than traditional corporate ones has also been examined. Leitko & Szczerbacki (1987) found that applying traditional OD strategies in professional bureaucracies (such as found in human service organizations) often fails. Traditional OD typically uses interpersonal interventions that loosen the constraints imposed by the "machine" bureaucracies found in industry. However, as the authors note, professional bureaucracies are often loosely integrated, and interventions that create more bounded systems are more appropriate here. Shamir & Salomon (1985) investigated telecommuting (i.e., work at home employing computer technology) and concluded that home work is not a panacea for the problems of modern organization. Thus research needs to consider carefully both the problems and benefits of home work before it is suggested as a desirable alternative. These studies explore the role of OD in situations that require the development of new concepts and new techniques for intervention.

Research methods. Methodology issues in OD have also been researched. One controversy in this area concerns the appropriateness of different measurement approaches. Bullock & Svyantek (1987) argued persuasively that evaluating OD interventions using random strategies fundamentally contradicts the need for collaboration and participation found in effective OD. Therefore the authors suggest the use of more appropriate research methods such as case meta-analysis (discussed below). Eden (1986b) suggested that rigorous research designed to eliminate "expectation effects" associated with interventions is misguided. He argues that these effects are an important part of OD's success and should be studied and clarified, rather than removed from research. Woodman (1989) takes the position that research should be useful to both practitioners and academics, and therefore should require both "thick" description and generalizable propositions. He proposes a "combined paradigm" approach (using both qualitative and quantitative methods), with stream analysis (Porras, 1987) and appreciative inquiry (Cooperrider & Srivasta, 1987) as possible examples for this.

Appreciative inquiry is an exciting new method of inquiry that deserves mention. Cooperrider & Srivasta view action research as impotent in generating alternative forms for organizing that can lead to social betterment. They propose appreciative inquiry as a revitalization of action research that both improves practice and generates theory. It does this by highlighting areas where an organization "works" and, using collaborative inquiry processes, determines directions for growth and renewal. This approach is distinct from the organizational pathology model implicit in most OD.

Stream analysis is also an important new intervention method. Porras (1987) has developed a graphical tool that maps organizational problems into the four streams (OA, SF, T, and PS), and then diagrams the links between them. By doing this, core problems are identified and targeted for change. A stream diagram is then developed mapping out the intervention's time-line and targets. This approach is a simple yet powerful way to diagnose and intervene in organizational issues.

Research in this period has also focused on better measurement of the Golembiewski et al. (1976) typology. Millsap & Hartog (1988) propose a methodology based on factorial structures within a structural equation framework to determine whether either gamma or beta change has occurred. Van de Vliert et al. (1985) propose a method to distinguish between alpha and beta change in which, once gamma change is ruled out (by examining the construct validity of pre- and post-test measures), dynamic correlations are used to separate alpha and beta change.

An exciting innovation in OD research is the use of both quantitative and case meta-analysis to combine results across many different studies. Case meta-analysis (Bullock & Tubbs, 1987) integrates OD case studies (still the most prevalent form of OD research) by coding study variables and then performing correlational analysis on them. Quantitative meta-analysis uses the statistics provided in more quantitative research and determines "effect sizes" due to interventions on outcome variables.

Guzzo et al. (1985) performed a meta-analysis that examined the effects of psychologically based interventions on "hard" measures. Interventions such as team building showed strong effects on productivity (in contrast to the team building research cited above) but not on withdrawal or disruption (e.g., absenteeism, grievances, et cetera). Beekun (1989) conducted a meta-analysis of STS interventions and demonstrated generally positive effects on productivity and withdrawal behaviors. Several moderator variables were also important to STS success but, interestingly enough, workgroup autonomy was not one of them. This again indicates the need for some rethinking of STS theory. Finally, Newman et al. (1989) conducted a meta-analysis of OD interventions on attitudinal outcomes. The authors find the primary effects on attitudes to be due to human processual, not technostructural interventions.

Some authors have investigated measures to improve OD research. Porras & Hoffer (1986) conducted a survey of leading OD professionals and found substantial agreement among them on a set of nine behaviors that correlate with successful interventions. Hoffer (1986) operationalized the behaviors into a questionnaire that she then used to explore the relationship between them and hard measures of organizational performance. Her results showed a highly significant relationship between an index representing the entire set of behaviors and various hard measures of organizational performance, such as sales levels, market share, costs, profits, et cetera. This indicates that these behaviors hold promise for providing a common base upon which to aggregate findings from disparate change studies.

Nicholas & Katz (1985) also focused on the same "aggregation" issue. They reviewed OD research from 1948 to 1982 and suggested a set of reporting standards to make cross-study comparison much more effective. It is clear that one of the challenges facing OD research is to find ways to aggregate the research findings of the field. In turn, this aggregation process will help to improve the quality of theory found in OD.

The generation of theory and new methodology in OD should be encouraged. At the same time, much of this research is fragmented and does not build on work done by other authors laboring in a similar arena. More effort should be directed at the development of a paradigm for OD, and thus researchers must build more consciously on each other's work.

Organization Transformation

OT has emerged over the last decade as a distinct form of planned change. It is an advancement over OD owing to its focus on precipitating more profound change in organizations. This occurs because the variables targeted by OT approaches (organizational beliefs, purpose, and mission, the components of organizational vision) affect a "deeper" level in the organization than those traditionally targeted for change by OD (i.e., work setting variables).

First we examine interventions focused on organizational vision. We then discuss the practice of industrial democracy in Norway. This type of intervention has not usually been considered part of OT, but recent developments indicate that the types of change pursued here are transformational. Finally, we survey other areas of interest in the OT field. The literature on OT was quite limited, reflecting the newness of this area.

Organizational vision. Organizational-level views of vision examine the processes through which organizations are able to change and learn. Individual-level perspectives assume that organizational transformation is dependent upon individual workers radically shifting their typical ways of thinking and doing.

Levy & Merry (1986) identify two distinct approaches to individual consciousness change: reframing (which draws from theory in family therapy—e.g., Watzlawick et al., 1974) and consciousness raising (which has many roots—e.g., Harrison, 1984). Reframing consists of organizational interventions that change an organization member's perceptions of reality. Reframing does not change current organizational reality; instead, it alters the way individuals view the world. This new worldview leads to corresponding changes in attitudes and behaviors, and organizational transformation follows.

Consciousness raising, on the other hand, makes the processes of transformation visible to organization members. Thought is viewed as the source of both existing circumstances and potential change; therefore, individuals with more awareness of transformative processes are better able to guide them. Theory here has been primarily adapted form transpersonal psychology (e.g., Walsh & Vaughan, 1980). Techniques such as meditation and creativity exercises are suggested as practice interventions in this approach.

Other work on organizational transformation focuses on creating organizations that understand how (and when) to initiate radical change and have strategies and structures in place to produce this change. Beer (1987) examined three cases of organizational transformation where successful change included the concurrent development of a vision of the future and a heightened dissatisfaction with the status quo throughout the whole organization. These factors, coupled with a well-managed change process, led to successful transformation. Nadler & Tushman (1989) developed a model of the transformation process similar to Beer's; however, these authors also stressed diagnosis and provided more detail regarding implementation steps. For example, they stress the need for a "magic leader," who serves as a focus for the change effort, followed by a diffusion of energy for change throughout the organization.

Bartunek & Moch (1987) and Levy & Merry (1986) examined transformation caused by changing the organizational "paradigm." Transformation is accomplished here by increasing the system's ability to analyze and change current paradigms, as well as to envision desirable future paradigms. Lundberg (1989) discussed organizational learning in OD and proposed a cyclical process of learning occurring at three successively deeper levels: organizational change, development, and transformation. His model provides a useful set of analytical tools for implementing transformative processes.

The differences between the micro and macro approaches to organizational vision reflect a "top-down" versus "bottom-up" orientation. Organizational-level approaches typically view top management as the catalyst for changes in organizational vision; these changes then spread throughout the whole organization. Individual-level approaches view vision change as decentralized; when enough organizational members change their consciousness, organizational change occurs. We believe that whether an intervention focuses on the macro or micro level matters less than how effective it is at producing change; it is also likely that interventions combining both strategies will have the greatest impact.

Industrial Democracy.   The theory and practice of industrial democracy developed outside the United States and has not been generally considered part of either OD or OT. However, the change processes initiated by this approach result in paradigm shifts. The techniques that constitute the industrial democracy change strategy all relate to the shifting of power in the organization toward the end goal of democratizing the work setting. The intervention techniques used in this approach have their roots in STS and QWL concepts and technology but have evolved to the point where they focus primarily on gamma(A) and gamma(B) change.

Perhaps the most interesting and innovative work in this area has occurred in Norway and increasingly centers on "local theory" (Gustavsen & Engelstad, 1986). Local theory evolved when

change projects based on general OD, STS, and QWL theory were not successful. This led to the realization that theories of democracy not generated by employees themselves are, in some sense, not democratic. Thus generative capacity (i.e., the ability of people to develop solutions to their own organizational problems) is most important, and interventions should be designed to increase this capacity. Gustavsen & Engelstad view "the conference" (an off-site meeting involving managers and employees from several companies) as an ideal setting for the practice of industrial democracy. Successes at such conferences can then be translated into practices appropriate for individuals' home organizations.

Elden (1986), in a very insightful piece, discussed how these ideas have become a part of public policy in Norway. Empowering participation is the key phrase in the Norwegian efforts; workers shape the actual conditions of their work through participatory STS activity. Participation is seen as second-order [gamma (A) and gamma (B)] change in this new framework. In this way, the change thrust has moved from empowerment through structure (e.g., instituting autonomous work groups) to empowerment through process (workers making local-level decisions about appropriate work practices). Some necessary conditions for empowering participation include institutional and political support at higher levels, participatory research, researchers as co-learners, empowering the less powerful, and rejecting conventional OD and STS.

Other Areas of Interest.   An interesting area of OT research examines disequilibrium models, where transformation is the rule, rather than the exception. Gemmill & Smith (1985) developed a dissipative structure model of transformation, where turbulent conditions prevent organizations from damping change and reaching equilibrium. When this happens, old forms of organizing break down and experimentation with many new forms occurs. Eventually, the most successful experiment reorganizes the system at a higher functional level. Leifer (1989) also proposed a dissipative structure model but stressed that a vision of the future is needed to mobilize the energy for experimentation. The premise of these articles is that organizations move from transformation to transformation, with only brief periods of stability (characterized by efficiency concerns) in between.

Several other authors have proposed intervention methods appropriate for OT work. Argyris et al. (1985) described "action science," an approach that attempts to catalyze double-loop learning [roughly equivalent to gamma(B) change] in individuals and organizations. The theoretical underpinning of this work parallels work discussed above on individual consciousness change and paradigm shifts. Pava (1986) proposed the concept of "normative incrementalism," an intervention method appropriate when both high complexity and high conflict exist in organizations (a condition ripe for transformation). These conditions only allow for interventions that are incremental and not threatening to current interests. This intervention therefore introduces some general theme (such as "quality of working life") without specifying how this translates into day-to-day organizational practice. However, this theme triggers employees to engage in activities that begin to clarify it retrospectively. This is a dialectic process that leads to the reformulation of values and ultimately to major organizational change.

After reviewing the breadth of ideas in OT, it is apparent how much vitality exists in this emerging approach to planned change. Although the broad outlines of the field may be sketched (e.g., focus on vision, consciousness change, et cetera), there is still considerable diversity in this area and consequently many different directions for future development. It is therefore difficult to predict where the field will be in 10 years, but we are certain that it will still be generating excitement and interest for both scholars and practitioners.

Summary

There was much research on OD in the period reviewed, while relatively little published literature exists in the area of OT. OD is still vigorous, as judged by the number of publications in this area, but the field has moved (since the late 1960s) from an energetic adolescence to a somewhat sedate maturity. In categorizing OD intervention approaches and target variables, we noticed two interesting patterns (noted only regarding the OA and SF streams). First of all, SF interventions dominated OD in the 1960s and early 1970s. However, in the period reviewed there had been a definite shift in emphasis from interventions emphasizing individual and group processes to interventions focusing on structural arrangements and reward systems (i.e., a shift from SF to OA research). OD research has, over time, increasingly emphasized organizational-level factors, and this is reflected by the increased volume of work on OA interventions.

The second pattern we noted concerned the target variables of research. OA research, although examining newer types of interventions in OD, typically focuses on "traditional" variables. These include participation (e.g., Marks et al., 1986), motivation (e.g., Jordan, 1986), task perceptions (e.g., Rafaeli, 1985), etc. In addition, OA research typically investigates the connection between these variables and outcomes such as productivity (e.g. Ralston et al 1985). In contrast, SF research has focused on a more innovative set of variables. These include internal frames of reference (Mitchell, 1986), managerial life cycles (Fisher et al, 1987), organizational embodiments of ego defenses (Krantz, 1985), et cetera. OA research seems to "lag" SF research in its choice of variables, and we suggest more integration of organizational-level intervention research with newer variables. At the same times, SF research can be criticized for not more explicitly theorizing and researching the link between innovative target variables and organizational outcomes (Buller's 1986 study was an exception).

Although there are some innovative areas of OD research in the period reviewed, no fundamental new paradigms have been developed and embraced by the field, and major new insights are rare. OT, on the other hand, is exciting precisely because it involves dramatically new premises for planned change. OT draws on more recent developments in psychology, transpersonal psychology, and systems theory, and often challenges traditional concepts in OD regarding models and methods. However, since this area is so underdeveloped, it is our hope that an increasing amount of rigorous theory development and research will appear in the near future.

Future Directions in Planned Change

Our analysis of the last five years of organizational change research has led us to a series of conclusions about where the field should head.

An important arena for future research concerns organizational paradigms. Paradigms are a key concept in OT work, but no clear conceptualization or research strategy for them has been developed. Specifying the mechanisms and boundaries of paradigm change is also important.

Organizational vision is another crucial area where research could improve OT theory and practice. Collins & Porras (1989) discuss vision and its component parts (guiding beliefs, purpose, mission) in detail, but more work needs to be done. The role of vision in maintaining organizational coherence should be explored, as should the dynamics of vision change in organizational change.

Concepts from Asian philosophy underlie some types of OT practice (e.g., the use of medication as a tool for consciousness change). However, these concepts are not rigorously integrated into OT theory, and more theory development exploring Eastern conceptions of individual and group change should be done.

Planned change theory in general also needs much more development. The Change Process Model is one attempt to improve this area, but we encourage other attempts at developing theoretical models of change. In addition to general models of change, research should focus on how interventions impact important organizational variables and how change in these variables cascades throughout the organizational system.

The dynamics and effects of new organizational forms need much more research. Exploring Ackoff's

(1989) circular organization, parallel organizations, and other innovations will increase the knowledge bases of both OD and OT. Another important area of research concerns changes in ownership, rather than in governance. More employee ownership research on ESOPs and their outcomes is needed, as well as research on organizations that are fully employee owned.

Finally, as mentioned above, more research is needed on the direct effects of physical-setting change. Beyond that, exploring the interrelationship of physical setting and other organizational factors (such as structure and culture) has important implications for change theory and practice. Research should investigate the contingencies that make different types of physical setting optimal under different conditions.

There are also some important directions in which research methods and measures should head. Of course theory building that results in testable models is a key to improving research. Such models are the best guides for research, and can lead to more productive exploration of OD and OT issues.

In addition to better theory, developing a common set of variables upon which to aggregate findings is important. Meta-analysis provides the analytical tools for cross-study comparison, but meaningful comparisons can only be made when common measures are employed. We believe that the behaviors of individual organizational members are a useful and easily measured set of variables that could serve this function. The set of behaviors proposed by Porras & Hoffer (1986) are an example of this.

The Golembiewski et al. (1976) typology of alpha, beta, and gamma change would be another way to develop a common set of measures. Given the amount of interest generated by this typology in the last 15 years, it was shocking to find no studies in our review that used these measures. One reason may be that methodologists are still exploring the optimal way to measure these types of change (e.g. Millsap & Hartog 1988); however, several such measures already exist, and this typology provides another common metric for more integration of research. Better reporting standards (Nicholas & Katz 1985) also would aid in promoting cross-study comparison. All in all, better theory coupled with more integration of findings would immeasurably improve the effectiveness of planned change interventions.

Endnotes

1. The six previous major reviews of the field (Friedlander & Brown, 1974; Beer, 1976; Alderfer, 1977; Faucheux et al., 1982; Beer & Walton, 1987; Porras et al., 1990) each used different frameworks to organize their discussions—frameworks based on change targets, strategies, functions, or theories. None, however, was based on a model of the change process itself. We hope our attempt to model the change process will interest others in doing the same. The field sorely needs a clear model of change to guide research and action.

2. This perspective is rooted in the Stream Organization Model, a model of organizations proposed by Porras (1987) and Porras et al. (1990) as a conceptual base for planned change work. Its key assumptions include these: that individual behavior is central to producing organizational outcomes; that individual work behavior is mostly driven by the context (work setting) of individual employees; that organizational vision provides the basic rationale for the design of the work setting; and that two major outcomes, organizational performance and individual development, derive from collective behaviors.

3. Each of these two intervention approaches will be defined in terms of subsequent sections of the Change Process Model. As such, these definitions may not be completely clear to the reader at this point. We ask the reader to bear with us until all components are discussed.

4. While this type of change is primarily caused by OD, some OT interventions focus on the work setting and also produce this pattern of change.

5. Kuhn (1970) defined a knowledge paradigm as "the collection of ideas within the confines of which scientific inquiry takes place, the assumed definition of what are legitimate problems and methods, the accepted practice and point of view with which the student prepares for membership in the scientific community, the criteria for choosing problems to attack, the rules and standards of scientific practice" (p. 11). This definition of paradigm, which is widely cited in both the natural and social sciences, is consistent with Adam's definition, which focuses specifically on organizations.

6. This same criteria will be applied to each of the following sections.

7. It should be noted, however, that these findings were reported for the second and third years of a longitudinal study. By the fourth year, the measures of these indicators did not differ from the first year.

8. Latack & Foster (1985) also propose an interesting unanticipated consequence of altering work schedules—that if they are compressed schedules they will tend to lead to job enrichment, since workers on duty at any one time will have to perform more tasks.

9. It is useful to note that, irrespective of the technique used to design organizational structures, their implementation is strongly enhanced through the use of employee involvement and process consultation work. Stebbins & Shani (1989) reviewed four major approaches to organizational design (Galbraith's Information Processing Model; MacKenzie's ABCE model and OA&A process: Kilmann's MAPS technology; and Sociotechnical Systems consulting) and found that while all four methods varied in their foci and key variables, they all incorporated process consultation and employee involvement principles in their implementation process.

10. Bushe also found the evidence mixed regarding the usefulness of traditional QWL theory and proposed intergroup theory as a better way to understand QWL.

11. Faucheux et al. (1982), in their review of OD, also emphasized the substantial differences in change approaches between Latin and Anglo-Saxon countries.

References

Ackoff, R.L. 1989, "The Circular Organization: An Update." *Acad. Mange. Exec.* 3:11–16.

Adams, J.D., ed. 1984. *Transforming Work: A Collection of Organizational Transformation Readings.* Alexandria, VA: Miles River Press.

Alderfer, C. P. 1977. "Organization Development." *Annu. Rev. Psychol.* 28:197–223.

Argyris, C.; Putnam, R.; Smith, D. M. 1985. *Action Science.* San Francisco: Jossey-Bass.

Bartunek, J. M.; Moch, M. K. 1987. "First-Order, Second-Order, and Third-Order Change and Organization Development Interventions: A Cognitive Approach." *J. Appl. Behav. Sci.* 23:483–500.

Beekun, R. I. 1989. "Assessing the Effectiveness of Sociotechnical Intervention: Antidote or Fad?" *Hum. Relat.* 42:877–97.

Beer, M. 1976. "The Technology of Organization Development." In *Handbook of Industrial and Organizational Psychology,* ed. M. Dunnette. Chicago: Rand McNally College Publishing.

Beer, M. 1987. "Revitalizing Organizations: Change Process and Emergent Model." *Acad. Manage. Exec.* 1:51–55.

Beer, M., Walton, A. E. 1987. "Organization Change and Development." *Annu. Rev. Psychol.* 38:339–67.

Bernstein, W. M.; Burke, W. W. 1989. "Modeling Organizational Meaning Systems." See Woodman & Pasmore, 1989, pp. 117–59.

Bocialetti, G. 1987. "Quality of Work Life: Some Unintended Effects on the Seniority Tradition of an Industrial Union." *Group Organ. Stud.* 12:386–410.

Boss, R. W., Mariono, M. V. 1987. "Organization Development in Italy." *Group Organ. Stud.* 12:245–56.

Bottger, P. C., Yetton, P. W. 1987. "Improving Group Performance by Training in Individual Problem Solving." *J. Appl. Psychol.* 72:651–57.

Buller, P. F. 1986. "The Team Building-Task Performance Relation: Some Conceptual and Methodological Refinements." *Group Organ. Stud.* 11:147–68.

Buller, P. F., Bell, C. H., Jr. 1986. "Effects of Team Building and Goal Setting on Productivity: A Field Experiment." *Acad. Manage. J.* 29:305–28.

Bullock, R. J., Svyantek, D. J. 1987. "The Impossibility of Using Random Strategies to Study the Organization Development Process." *J. Appl. Behav. Sci.* 23:255–62.

Bullock, R. J., Tubbs, M. E. 1987. "The Case Meta-Analysis Method for OD." See Woodman & Pasmore, 1987, pp. 171–228.

Bushe, G. R. 1987. "Temporary or Permanent Middle-Management Groups? Correlates with Attitudes in QWL Change Projects." *Group Organ. Stud.* 12:23–37.

Bushe, G. R. 1988. "Developing Cooperative Labor-Management Relations in Unionized Factories: A Multiple Case Study of Quality Circles and Parallel Organizations within Joint Quality of Work Life Projects," *J. Appl. Behav. Sci.* 24:129–50.

Collins, J. C., Porras, J. I. 1989. "Making Impossible Dreams Come True." *Stanford Bus. Sch. Mag.* 57:12–19.

Cooperrider, D. L., Srtivasta, S. 1987. "Appreciative Inquiry in Organizational Life." See Woodman & Pasmore, 1987, pp. 129–69.

Dunham, R. B.; Pierce, J. L.; Castaneda, M. B. 1987. "Alternative Work Schedules: Two Field Experiments." *Personnel Psychol.* 40:215–41.

Eden, D. 1985. "Team Development: A True Field Experiment at Three Levels of Rigor." *J. Appl. Psychol.* 70:94–100.

Eden, D. 1986a. "Team Development: Quasi-Experimental Confirmation among Combat Companies." *Group Organ. Stud.* 11:133–46.

Eden, D. 1986b. "OD and Self-Fulfilling Prophecy: Boosting Productivity by Raising Expectations." *J. Appl. Behav. Sci.* 22:1–13.

Elden, M. 1986. "Sociotechnical Systems Ideas as Public Policy in Norway: Empowering Participation through Worker-Managed Change," *J. Appl. Behav. Sci.* 22:239–55.

Evans, P. A. L. 1989. "Organizational Development in the Transnational Enterprise." See Woodman & Pasmore, 1989, pp. 1–39.

Faucheux, C., Amado, G., Laurent, A. 1982. "Organizational Development and Change." *Annu. Rev. Psychol.* 33:343–70.

Ferris, G. R., Wagner, J. A. III. 1985. "Quality Circles in the United States: A Conceptual Reevaluation." *J. Appl. Behav. Sci.* 21:155–67.

Fisher, D.; Merron, K.; Torbert, W. R. 1987. "Human Development and Managerial Effectiveness." *Group Organ. Stud.* 12:257–73.

Florkowski, G. W. 1987. "The Organizational Impact of Profit Sharing." *Acad. Manage. Rev.* 12:622–36.

French, J. L. 1987. "Employee Perspectives on Stock Ownership: Financial Investment or Mechanism of Control?" *Acad. Manage. Rev.* 12:427–35.

Friedlander, F., Brown, L. D. 1974. "Organization Development." *Annu. Rev. Psychol.* 25:313–41.

Gardner, D. G.; Dunham, R. B.; Cummings, L. L.; Pierce, J. L. 1987. "Employee Focus of Attention and Reactions to Organizational change." *J. Appl. Behav. Sci.* 23:351–70.

Gemmill, G., Smith, C. 1985. "A Dissipative Structure Model of Organizational Transformation." *Hum. Relat.* 38:751–66.

Golembiewski, R. T.; Billingsley, K.; Yeager, S. 1976. "Measuring Change and Persistence in Human

Affairs: Type of Change Generated by OD Designs." *J. Appl. Behav. Sci.* 12:133–57.

Golembiewski, R. T.; Hilles, R.; Daly, R. 1987. "Some Effects of Multiple OD Interventions on Burnout and Work Site Features." *J. Appl. Behav. Sci.* 23:295–313.

Gray, B., Hay, T. M. 1986. "Political Limits to Interorganizational Consensus and Change." *J. Appl. Behav. Sci.* 22:95–112.

Greiner, L. 1972. "Evolution and Revolution as Organizations Grow." *Harv. Bus. Rev.* 50:39–46.

Griffin, R. W. 1988. "Consequences of Quality Circles in an Industrial Setting: A Longitudinal Assessment." *Acad. Manage. J.* 31:388—58.

Gustavsen, B., Engelstad, P. H. 1986. "The Design of Conferences and the Evolving Role of Democratic Dialogue in Changing Work Life." *Hum. Relat.* 39:101–16.

Guzzo. R. A.; Jette, R. D.; Katzell, R. A. 1985. "The Effects of Psychologically Based Intervention Programs on Worker Productivity: A Meta-Analysis." *Personnel Psychol.* 38:275–91.

Harrison, R. 1984. "Leadership and Strategy for a New Age." In *Transforming Work,* ed. J. Adams. Alexandria, VA: Miles River Press.

Head, T. C.; Molleston, J. L.; Sorenson, P. F., Jr.; Gargano, J. 1986. "The Impact of Implementing a Quality Circle Intervention on Employee Task Perceptions." *Group Organ. Stud.* 11:360–73.

Herrick, N. Q. 1985. "Parallel Organizations in Unionized Settings: Implications for Organizational Research." *Hum. Relat.* 38:963–81.

Hoffer, S. J. 1986. *Behavior and Organizational Performance: An Empirical Study."* PhD thesis. Stanford Univ. Grad. Sch. Educ.

Hofstede, G. 1980. *Culture's Consequences: International Differences in Work Related Values.* Beverly Hills, CA: Sage.

Jaeger, A. M. 1986. "Organization Development and National Culture: Where's the Fit?" *Acad. Manage. Rev.* 11:178–90.

Jordan, P. C. 1986. "Effects of an Extrinsic Reward on Intrinsic Motivation: A Field Experiment." *Acad. Manage. J.* 29:405–12.

Klein, K. J. 1987. "Employee Stock Ownership and Employee Attitudes: A Test of Three Models." *J. Appl. Psychol.* 72:319–32.

Kolodny, H.; Stjernberg, T. 1986. "The Change Process of Innovative Work Designs: New Design and Redesign in Sweden, Canada, and the U.S." *J. Appl. Behav. Sci.* 22:287–301.

Krantz, J. 1985. "Group Processes under Conditions of Organizational Decline." *J. Appl. Behav. Sci.* 21:1–17.

Kuhn, T. 1970. *The Structure of Scientific Revolution.* Chicago: Univ. Chicago Press. 2nd ed.

Latack, J. C.; Ooster, L. W. 1985. "Implementation of Compressed Work Schedules: Participation and Job Redesign as Critical Factors for Employee Acceptance." *Personnel Psychol.* 38:75–92.

Lawler, E. E. III. 1988. "Choosing an Involvement Strategy." *Acad. Manage. Exec.* 2:197–204

Lawler, E. E. III; Mohrman, S. A. 1987. "Quality Circles: After the Honeymoon." *Organ. Dyn.* 15:42–54.

Leifer, R. 1989. "Understanding Organizational Transformation Using a Dissipative Structure Model." *Hum. Relat.* 42:899–916.

Leitko, T. A.; Szczerback, D. 1987. "Why Traditional OD Strategies Fail in Professional Bureaucracies." *Organ. Dyn.* 15:52–65.

Levy, A.; Merry, U. 1986. *Organizational Transformation.* New York: Praeger.

Lindblom, C. 1959. "The Science of Muddling Through." *Public Admin. Rev.* 21:78–88.

Lundberg, C. C. 1989. "On Organizational Learning: Implications and Opportunities for Expanding Organizational Development." See Woodman & Pasmore, 1989, pp. 61–82.

Marks, M. L.; Mirvis, P. H.; Hackett, E. J.; Grady, J. F. Jr. 1986. "Employee Participation in a Quality Circle Program: Impact on Quality of Work Life, Productivity, and Absenteeism." *J. Appl. Psychol.* 71:61–69.

McDaniel, R. R. Jr.; Thomas, J. B.; Ashmos, D. P.; Smith, J. P. 1987. "The Use of Decision Analysis for Organizational Design: Reorganizing a Community Hospital." *J. Appl. Behav. Sci.* 23:337–50.

Meyer, G. W., Stoff, R. G. 1985. "Quality Circles: Panacea or Pandora's Box?" *Organ. Dyn.* 13:34–50.

Miller, C. S., Schuster, M. 1987. "A Decade's Experience with the Scanlon Plan: A Case Study." *J. Occup. Behav.* 8:167–74.

Millsap, R. E.; Hartog, S. B. 1988. "Alpha, Beta, and Gamma Change in Evaluation Research: A Structural Equation Approach." *J. Appl. Psychol.* 73:574–84.

Mitchell, R. 1986. "Team Building by Disclosure of Internal Frame of Reference." *J. Appl. Behav. Sci.* 22:15–28.

Nadler, D. A.; Tushman, M. L. 1989. "Organizational Frame Bending: Principles for Managing Reorientation." *Acad. Manage. Exec.* 3:194–204.

Nelson, R. E. 1988. "Social Network Analysis as an Intervention Tool: Examples from the Field." *Group Organ. Stud.* 13:39–58.

Neuman, G. A.; Edwards, J. E.; Raju, N. S. 1989. "Organization Development Interventions: A Meta-Analysis of Their Effects on Satisfaction and Other Attitudes." *Personnel Psychol.* 42:461–89.

Nicholas, J. M.; Katz, M. 1985. "Research Methods and Reporting Practices in Organization Development: A Review and Some Guidelines." *Acad. Manage. Rev.* 10:737–49.

Oldham, G. R. 1988. "Effects of Changes in Workspace Partitions and Spatial Density on Employee Reactions: A Quasi-Experiment." *J. Appl. Psychol.* 73:253–58.

Ondrack, D. A.; Evans, M. G. 1987. "Job enrichment and Job Satisfaction in Greenfield and Redesign QWL Sites." *Group Organ. Stud.* 12:5–22.

Pasmore, W.; Petee, J.; Bastian, R. 1986. "Sociotechnical Systems in Health Care: A Field Experiment." *J. Appl. Behav. Sci.* 22:329–39.

Pava, C. 1986. "New Strategies of Systems Change: Reclaiming Nonsynoptic Methods." *Hum. Relat.* 39:615–33.

Pearce, J. L.; Stevenson, W. B.; Perry, J. L. 1985. "Managerial Compensation Based on Organizational Performance: A Time Series Analysis of the Effects of Merit Pay." *Acad. Manage. J.* 28:261–78.

Porras, J. I., 1987. *Stream Analysis: A Powerful New Way to Diagnose and Manage Change.* Reading, MA: Addison-Wesley.

Porras, J. I.; Hoffer, S. J. 1986. "Common Behavior Changes in Successful Organization Development Efforts." *J. Appl. Behav. Sci.* 22:477–94.

Porras, J. I.; Robertson, P.; Goldman, L. 1990. "Organization Development." In *Handbook of Industrial and Organizational Psychology,* ed. M. Dunnette. Palo Alto, CA: Psychological Press.

Rafaeli, A. 1985. "Quality Circles and Employee Attitudes." *Personnel Psychol.* 38:603–15.

Ralston, D. A.; Anthony, W. P.; Gustafson, D. J. 1985. "Employees May Love Flextime, But What Does It Do to the Organization's Productivity?" *J. Appl. Psychol.* 70:272–79.

Shamir, B.: Salomon, I. 1985. "Work-at-Home and the Quality of Working Life." *Acad. Manage. Rev.* 10:455–64.

Shani, A. B.; Eberhardt, B. J. 1987. "Parallel Organization in a Health Care Institution." *Group Organ. Stud.* 12:147–73.

Sheldon, A. 1980. "Organizational Paradigms: A Theory of Organizational Change." *Organ. Dyn.* 8:61–80.

Sorenson, P. F. Jr.; Head, T. C.; Stotz, D. 1985. "Quality of Work Life and the Small Organization: A Four-Year Case Study." *Group Organ. Stud.* 10:320–39.

Stebbins, M. W.; Shani, A. B. 1989. "Organization Design: Beyond the Mafia Model." *Organ. Dyn.* 17:18–30.

Steel, R. P.; Lloyd, R. F. 1988. "Cognitive, Affective, and Behavioral Outcomes of Participation in Quality Circles: Conceptual and Empirical Findings." *J. Appl. Behav. Sci.* 24:1–17.

Steel, R. P.; Shane, G. S. 1986. "Evaluation Research on Quality Circles: Technical and Analytical Implications." *Hum. Relat.* 39:449–68.

Steele, F. I. 1973. *Physical Settings and Organization Development.* Reading, MA: Addison-Wesley.

Susman, G. I.; Chase, R. B. 1986. "A Sociotechnical Analysis of the Integrated Factory." *J. Appl. Behav. Sci.* 22:257–70.

Taylor, J. C. 1986. "Long-Term Sociotechnical Systems Change in a Computer Operations Department." *J. Appl. Behav. Sci.* 22:303–13.

Van de Vliert, E.; Huismans, S. E.; Stok, J. J. L. 1985. "The Criterion Approach to Unraveling Beta and Alpha Change." *Acad. Manage. Rev.* 10:269–74.

Vickers, G. 1965. *The Art of Judgment.* New York: Basic Books.

Wall, T. D.; Kemp, N. J.; Jackson, P. R.; Clegg, C. W. 1986. "Outcomes of Autonomous Workgroups: A Long-Term Field Experiment." *Acad. Manage. J.* 29:280–304.

Walsh, R. N.; Vaughan, F. 1980. *Beyond Ego. Transpersonal Dimensions in Psycology.* Los Angeles: J. P. Tarcher.

Watzlawick, P.; Weakland, J; Fisch, R. 1974. *Change.* New York: W. W. Norton.

Woodman, R. W. 1989. "Evaluation Research on Organizational Change: Arguments for a 'Combined Paradigm' Approach." See Woodman & Pasmore, 1989, pp. 161–80.

Woodman, R. W.; Pasmore, W. A., eds. 1987. *Research in Organizational Change and Development,* vol. 1. Greenwich, CT: JAI Press.

Woodman, R. W.; Pasmore, W. A., eds. 1989. *Research in Organizational Change and Development,* vol. 3. Greenwich, CT: JAI Press.

Zalesny, M. E.: Farace, R. V. 1987. "Traditional versus Open Offices: A Comparison of Sociotechnical, Social Relations, and Symbolic Meaning Perspectives." *Acad. Manage. J.* 30:240–59.

READING 6
ESTIMATING THE SUCCESS OF OD APPLICATIONS

Robert T. Golembiewski
Carl W. Proehl, Jr.
David Sink

One of the better topics over the years for inspiring argument has involved assessing the state of organization development (OD). In more recent days, however, a curious agreement has developed. Friend and foe alike tend to have real doubts about OD's future. Critics point to a range of problems—theoretical, methodological, and ethical.[1] Many historic supporters see OD at a critical life-state—as an adolescent, with quite definite signs of lacking those qualities associated with "most likely to succeed."[2] Other supporters see a kind of academic and applied aging, with the memories of early hopes still alive but with a growing sense that the "heydays" are all over.[3] We have in mind a recent academic symposium of OD "afficionados," who had for several hours zestfully played "can you top this" with pronouncements concerning the deficiencies and all-but-inevitable doom facing OD—poor research, inadequate underlying theory, and so on.

Three Base-Line Minima

This article seeks to provide needed perspective for ardent supporters, convinced critics, and zestful flagellants alike, specifically by rooting this argument in three base-line minima about which broad and even universal consensus exists.

First, without doubt, OD still shows many of the signs of a burgeoning area of activity. We will be selective only, but illustrations suffice to make the case. Thus OD texts[4] and books of readings[5] find a ready market. Professional associations with thousands of members have developed in the last decade.[6] The catalog of public or business organizations having had at least a flirtation with OD is very long and growing. Degree programs in OD have proliferated. It is certainly noteworthy that the largest employers of OD perspectives, designs, and personnel include the U.S. military services,[7] whose base-values provide a very difficult target for penetration by OD perspectives and technologies.

Second, both major interpretations of this business rest on similar bases that are palpably inadequate and may be wrong as well. That is, the business implies to some that OD "works." Others see a kind of "market high" just before an inevitable and formidable sell-off. Commonly, however, neither conclusion rests on satisfactory *and* comprehensive documentation of OD's efficacy, or lack thereof.

Note that this second base-line conclusion refers to satisfactory *and* comprehensive documentation, rather than to the absence of documentation. Documentation exists. Indeed, several comparative studies[8] suggest an appreciable success rate for various OD applications, but such work has two major limitations for present purposes. The databases for such summary studies tend to be small, on the order of scores of cases. For example, the study by Porras deals with 35 cases.[9] Morrison's methodological overview involves 26 cases.[10] In addition, only a small fraction of such databases refers to public sector applications, which are widely regarded as posing unusually difficult problems for OD and, by implication at least, as having low success rates. Perhaps 10–15 percent represents the usual proportion of public applications in available databases, and

Source: Robert T. Golembiewski, Carl W. Proehl, Jr., and David Sink, "Estimating the Success of OD Applications," *Training & Development Journal* 36, no. 4 April 1982, pp. 86–95.

one-tenth of a small database does not provide a very solid foundation for generalizations.

Third, these information gaps have not often deterred enthusiasts or critics. They seem to *know,* absent the required documentation. Artfully, for example, some observers see the OD intervener as a kind of contemporary shaman,[11] while (at least to these authors) also conveying the distinct impression that more rattle-shaking than technology and theory are involved in OD applications. Generally, in addition, the state of affairs is presented as being worse in the public sector. Drawing on his experience as both a designer and a student of OD interventions, for example, Giblin concludes that the "unique constraints imposed on public organizations appear to render them almost immune from conventional OD interventions."[12] Others conclude that public sector OD—if defined as something more than "tinkering with the system"—will be very difficult, if not palpably impossible, for a broad range of reasons.

Burke concludes that: "Most OD consultants find working with bureaucracies, especially public ones, to be difficult at best.... Apparently, most OD consultants either become more pragmatic and realistic or they have given up when it comes to working with large bureaucratic organizations."[13]

The Present Database

What do the data imply about OD applications? Specifically, this article reports an effort to transcend the all-but-universal limitations of the literature, based on a very intensive search for OD applications in both business and government contexts. Five basic sources are used to develop a database of OD applications that could support useful conclusions about effects: [14]

- Seven specialized bibliographies.

- Searches of the several relevant computerized listings (e.g., ERIC) of publications in social science journals over the past 20 years.

- A review of the last 20 years of studies reported in 88 journals, including 10 from overseas.

- More than 100 books surveyed for bibliographic items as well as for reports of interventions.

- Personal letters sent to 50 well-known change agents, especially soliciting unpublished materials, such as internal memos, dissertations or theses, and so on.

Appropriate citations occurred as early as 1945, and the search extended into mid-1980 when it was closed to analyze data. This search-process has two gaps, neither of which is seen as damning, but which all may wish did not exist. First, journals unavailable in English were searched only selectively, but 17 percent of the total batch of interventions were accomplished in non-American settings. This leaves our database with a dominant locus and a distinct cosmopolitan flavor.

Second, the search did not encompass the twice-yearly meetings of the Organization Development Network or of the OD Division of ASTD. Until recently, neither interest group published proceedings. Many interventions reported at these meetings, however, got into our database, either after being published or because they were forwarded by our 50 personal contacts. Through mid-1980, these two gaps notwithstanding, our search uncovered a substantial number of OD applications—574 cases, to be exact.[15]

We make only two claims about this set of cases. First, there seems almost no question that public sector applications get adequate representation. Indeed, the very number of such applications—270—may itself constitute a major finding, since most sources emphasize the paucity of public sector applications.[16] In contrast, public sector cases constitute over 47 percent of the present batch of OD studies.

Second, we propose, a little more tentatively, that the 574 cases provide a reasonable replica of all OD activity. Early published work has some bias toward "successful" applications, but we include a broad range of unpublished sources. Moreover, the 35-year collection period and the large number of cases should substantially compensate for any early but artifactual hopes. Hence we propose that the 574 cases provide a credible source for seeking answers to two major questions concerning OD:

- What is the range and diversity of interventions or applications?
- What is the probability that an intervention will be successful?

Range and diversity

The range of the 574 interventions is broad, with major representation from all the major classes of interventions associated with OD. Let us build toward this conclusion by providing useful detail.

Most observers see OD as one of the major derivatives of the "laboratory approach"—a major way of learning to learn. Globally, the laboratory approach to OD has at least six distinguishing features:[17]

- Rootedness in a definite set of values, which emphasize openness, trust, and collaborative effort.
- Seeking to simultaneously meet individual needs and the needs of several levels of systems—small groups, large organizations, and so on.
- Grounding in immediate experiences as they occur: this often gets expressed as a here-and-now orientation and is reflected in "process analysis" of the panoply of personal and institutional forces acting on individuals and groups.
- Emphasis on feelings and emotions, as well as on ideas and concepts.
- Preeminence of the individual's involvement and participation—as subject and object, as generator of data as well as responder to those data—in an "action-research" sense.
- Heavy reliance on group contexts for choice and change; to validate data, to develop and

enforce norms, and to provide emotional support and identification.

The laboratory approach had its first major technological expression in the T-group or sensitivity training group. The T-group was typically composed of strangers meeting on a "cultural island" and focused on learning from each other about (for example) "how we are seen by others and how we see them."[18] Such work sparked major attention to interaction-centered OD designs.

In a decade or so, OD became the major extension of such early work. It commonly came to encompass not only interaction-centered designs but those focused on structure and policies/procedures. Basically, the core values and central dynamics of the laboratory approach were built into several classes of learning designs, appropriate for choice or change in large aggregates. Each OD application will be unique to an extent and typically will combine several basic designs. As a first-cut, however, these alternative designs can be classified in terms of eight "activities." The classes are listed here, roughly in order of their complexity and subtlety:

- *Process analysis activities,* or applications of behavioral science perspectives to understand complex and dynamic situations. These perspectives can be simple—for example, as in routine retrospection among task-group members who ask: How do we feel about what we just did? The perspectives also can be complex, as in seeking to understand interpersonal conflict as an expression of differing predispositions.
- *Skill-building activities,* or various designs for gaining facility with behaviors consistent with OD values, as in giving/receiving feedback, listening, resolving conflict, and so on.
- *Diagnostic activities,* which often include process analysis, but which also may employ interviews, psychological instruments, or opinion surveys to generate data from and for members of some social systems. These data get fed back into that system, to serve

as the raw material for action-research sequences: diagnosis, prescription of changes, implementation, and evaluation.

- *Coaching/counseling activities,* which seek to apply OD values in intimate situations, as between a pair-in-conflict in an organization via "third-party consultation."
- *Team-building activities,* or efforts to increase the efficiency and effectiveness of intact task-groups. Variants may use T-group or sensitivity training modes, as well as one or more of the activities listed here.
- *Intergroup activities,* which seek to build effective and satisfying linkages between two or more task-groups, such as departments in a large organization.
- *Technostructural activities,* which seek to build need-satisfying roles, jobs, and structures. Typically, these activities rest on a "growth psychology," such as that of Maslow, Argyris, or Herzberg. These structural or policy approaches—job enlargement, flexi-time, and so on—often are coupled with other OD activities.
- *System-building or system-renewal activities,* which seek comprehensive changes in a large organization's climate and values, using complex combinations of the seven activities sketched above, and having time spans in the three to five year range.

These eight activities fit with varying precision into three basic OD modes: interaction-centered, structure, and policies or procedures. Process analysis, skill-building, and coaching/counseling are basically interaction-centered. Technostructural and system-building emphasize structure, although not to the exclusion of the other two modes. Team-building and intergroup activities often have dominant interaction emphases, but also deal with structure and especially policies or procedures.

What is the distribution of our 574 cases among these classes of activities? Table 1 implies that our population covers the field of interventions. The most narrow designs—diagnostic activities and process analysis—constitute the dominant intervention mode in *less* than 5 percent of the cases. OD interventions tend to hunt bigger game. To illustrate, nearly 40 percent of the private sector cases can be categorized as emphasizing the most complex intervention modes—system-building or renewal and technostructural activities. Reading the individual case reports in the public sector also reinforces that impression. The applications there seem to give substantial attention to the tough cases, on balance. Hence, the common emphases on racial tension; conflict between individuals, specialties, and organization units; community conflict between police and minorities; and basic reorganization. OD applications seem to respect this difficult prescription: *Intervene where the pain is felt!*

The 574 cases imply similar reliance on dominant OD modes in both public and business settings. In most cases, the probabilities of using the eight classes of activities vary in a very narrow range only. Technostructural activities constitute the most prominent exception, perhaps because public structures/policies/procedures are more likely to be set by distal authorities, especially legislatures. Therefore, these activities would more often be out of convenient reach. Even so, technostructural activities constitute the dominant OD mode in nearly one of every five public sector cases.

In sum, the 574 cases do not constitute a collection of easy pieces, and the database suggests no huge differences between the reliance on specific modes of OD interventions in public and business sectors. Consequently, the database should provide a real test of the efficacy of OD techniques and perspectives, of how often, and to what degree they tend to "work," within and between the private and public sectors.

The classification of the 574 published OD reports by dominant mode of intervention has a high reliability. Two independent observers classified all cases and had a very high degree of agreement. A 10 percent sample (approximately) places that agreement at nearly 98 percent of the cases. These few differences were reconciled before summation in Table 1.

TABLE 1

Incidence of eight classes of OD activities in public and private sectors

Class of OD Design	Individual Applications Classified by Dominant Design			
	Public Sector		Private Sector	
	No.	%	No.	%
Process analysis activities	10	4%	6	2%
Skill-building activities	65	24	57	19
Diagnostic activities	14	5	18	6
Coaching/counseling activities	19	7	30	10
Team-building activities	51	19	56	18
Intergroup activities	38	14	18	6
System-building or system-renewal activities	29	11	35	11
Technostructural activities	44	16	84	28
	N = 270	100%	N = 304	100%

High interobserver reliability was not crucial in this case. The efficacy of OD interventions was uniform over the full range of dominant modes.

Two Estimates of Success

How can we estimate specifically the efficacy of OD interventions? Do public-sector interventions have a lower success rate than their counterparts in business organizations? Two approaches to answers will be sketched here and tested against business and government OD applications. The approaches may be labeled "global" and "multiple indicators."

Global Estimate of Efficacy. A few details provide needed perspective on the "global" evaluation of OD interventions. Two independent readers reviewed each of the 574 interventions and assigned each set of effects to one of four categories whose content the observers had discussed and illustrated in detail. The evaluative categories include:

- *Highly positive and intended effects* on the efficacy and effectiveness of some relatively discrete system, as in improving the ability of individuals to hear one another without distortion, or in reducing the degree of hostility between conflicting actors or units.

- *Definite balance of positive and intended effects,* defined in terms of mixed but generally favorable effects—e.g., most but not all intended effects were achieved on a number of variables; or major positive effects occurred in one system, while some negative but not counterbalancing effects occurred in another system.

- *No appreciable effect.*

- *Negative effects,* or a case in which substantial reductions occurred in the efficiency and effectiveness of some subsystem or of some broader system of which it was a part.

What did this laborious rating and cross-checking reveal? Four points summarize the major findings. First, by and large, the observers saw the same effects. Specifically, the observers' ratings correlated 0.78, which indicates substantial agreement between raters. Almost all cases of disagreement involved the first two rating categories. Some differences were reconciled after this reliability check, but in all cases, the ratings of one observer are

TABLE 2

Global estimate of the success of 574 OD applications

	Individual Applications Classified by Degree of Effects			
	Public Sector		**Private Sector**	
Rating Categories	*No.*	*%*	*No.*	*%*
Highly positive and intended effects	110	41%	122	40%
Definite balance of positive and intended effects	116	43	148	49
No appreciable effect	18	7	14	5
Negative effects	26	9	20	6
	N = 270	100%	N = 304	100%

reflected in Table 2. One can then conclude with some confidence that *in this population of studies* more than 80 percent of the interventions had at least a definite balance of positive and intended effects.

Third, global estimates of the efficacy of OD interventions do not vary much between the public and business sectors. Table 2 implies that major point.

Fourth, global estimates of success vary somewhat by dominant mode of intervention. Table 3 summarizes the experience for private sector interventions, which do not differ markedly from public sector experience. Except for two classes of OD activities—process analysis and diagnostic—the efficacy estimates are all 83 percent or greater for at least a definite balance of positive and intended effects.

Multiple Indicators Estimate Efficacy.
Another approach to estimating the efficacy of OD interventions relies on numerous multiple indicators which comprise 308 variables. Proehl[19] coded each of the 574 cases in the present batch of studies, in terms of the comprehensive set of indicators developed by Porras and Berg.[20] Proehl describes his procedure in these terms:

> each of the . . . studies in this research's database was searched for the 308 variables developed by Porras

and Berg. When one of the variables was found, it was coded according to whether it had improved (0) or not improved (1) during the course of the change project. Once all of the variables present in each study were identified and coded, the *"percentage of positive reported change"* was calculated for each organizational level (individual, leader, group, or organization) or study. This was accomplished by dividing the number of positive variables by the total number of variables in which change was desired in each organizational level of each study. For example, a change effort which sought to change five individual-level variables and reported three of them as having changed positively was given a score of 60 percent. Scores ranged from zero percent in a change effort which failed to produce any positive change in process and outcome variables to 100 percent for a case in which positive change was reported in all variables for which change was desired.

The reliability of these assignments was estimated by a limited, if random, process. Three independent observers each rated two randomly selected variables, and agreement existed on 228 of 240 cases. This interobserver reliability of 95 percent is taken to be representative of the record on the other variables, and it seems an acceptable level of reliability of assignments on which to base analysis.

The "percentage of positive reported change" was 70.5 percent, overall, when the 574 cases were

TABLE 3

Global estimates of efficacy, private sector cases only, N = 304

	Estimated Effects in Percent*			
Class of OD Design	Highly Positive and Intended Effects	Definite Balance of Positive and Intended Effects	No Appreciable Effects	Negative Effects
Process analysis activities	16.7%	50.0%	16.7%	16.7%
Skill-building activities	40.4	52.6	3.5	3.5
Diagnostic activities	33.3	44.4	5.6	16.7
Coaching/counseling activities	40.0	46.7	6.7	6.7
Team-building activities	39.3	51.8	3.6	5.4
Intergroup activities	44.4	39.0	5.6	11.1
System-building or system-renewal activities	45.7	40.0	5.7	8.7
Technostructural activities	40.5	51.2	3.6	4.8

*Due to rounding, totals may accumulate to > 100%.

scored for all of the 308 Porras/Berg variables applicable in each case. The efficacy of the 574 applications also can be arrayed according to levels of analysis, four of which were distinguished by Porras and Berg. The specific percentages of positive reported change are:

- Individual: 78.1 percent for 243 cases.
- Leader: 68.1 percent for 173 cases
- Group: 77.9 percent for 161 cases.
- Organization: 72.4 percent for 206 cases.

We conclude that, as the best-informed possible estimate from the standpoint of multiple indicators, at least 7 of 10 variables show a balance of positive effects resulting from OD applications. Because not all of the same variables are considered in the two comparisons above, the success rate at the four levels of analysis surpasses 70 percent by a noticeable margin. In addition, no major differences distinguish public vs. business applications.

Five Perspectives on Success

These results confirm a substantial success rate for a large batch of OD interventions. To be conservative, the two approaches to an estimate imply a success ratio of at least 7 in 10 cases. The more

ebullient might choose to give credence to the global bottom-line estimate of efficacy, which approximates an 85 percent success rate.

These data powerfully imply that both critics and previously pessimistic supporters of OD must "sing a different tune" in the future, or at least a more complicated one. Such adaptation must take cognizance of at least five factors. First, these results are reinforced in other studies, although with databases that are small fractions of the size of the present batch. To sample only:

- Eight percent of Morrison's 26 cases deal with "failures."[21]
- In Dunn and Swierczek's 67 cases, 65–70 percent were considered "effective."[22]
- In Porras's 35 cases selected for high degrees of methodological rigor, variables changed in the predicted directions in about 50 percent of the cases.[23]
- Margulies and his associates rated 73 percent of 30 applications as "positive," with 10 percent "mixed," 24 percent "no change," and 3 percent as "negative."[24]

Second, These favorable success rates do not mean that all OD problems have been recognized, let alone solved to such a degree that designs and perspectives can be applied following a cookbook approach. Positively, these results imply that whatever exists in the organizational world can be accommodated, most of the time, by the kind of OD interveners who research and write up their experiences. Diagnosis is critical.

Third, the results do not imply that public sector OD is easier than "in business," more difficult, or the same. To restate the previous point, the results here only imply that the unique constraints existing in various organizations, whether governmental or business, can be accommodated by the written experiences of appropriate OD interventions.

This is no cute conclusion. In fact, we know quite a bit about how to develop such accommodations to the specific characteristics of agencies in the public sector. This is not the place, however, to detail that experience and theory, which has been accomplished elsewhere.[25]

Fourth, greater specificity will be required for finer-tuned analyses than the one attempted here. To illustrate, future comparative analysis will require a more precise typology of interventions, as well as a more complex differentiation of hosts or targets for such interventions. This consciousness has been raised recently,[26] but much remains to be done. In the present case, for example, interventions are distinguished only in gross terms. Targets/hosts are differentiated only as "public" and "business." A more satisfactory typology of OD systems will eventually take into explicit account the full range of differences/similarities usually encapsulated in the short-hand "public vs. private"; and it seems just as clear that this typology also will encompass those equally significant differences/similarities *within* "public" and "business" sectors.

Fifth, and finally, this analysis may be faulted by a major contaminant. As some observers emphasize,[27] published materials may be biased toward reporting "positive results." If this bias characterizes the present database, that would obviously account for some part of the high success rate. Our procedures provide only partial protection against such a bias. Note the effort to solicit unpublished materials—consultant reports, in-house memos, theses, and dissertations; this implies a counterbalance to

any bias toward "positive results" in published work. Presumably, unpublished materials would be less contaminated in this regard.

These five concluding points encompass the present analysis, rather than nullify it. The present results may be considered the best available comprehensive estimate of the efficacy of OD efforts.

Endnotes

1. Warner Woodworth, Gordon Meyer, and N. Smallwood. "A Critical Assessment of Organization Development Theory and Practice." Unpublished MS, Department of Organizational Behavior, Brigham Young University, 1980.

2. Frank Friedlander. "OD Reaches Adolescence." *Journal of Applied Behavioral Science* 12, no. 7 (January 1976).

3. W. Warner Burke. "Organization Development in Transition," *Journal of Applied Behavioral Science* 12, no. 24 (January 1976); W. Warner Burke, "Organization Development and Bureaucracies in the 1980s." *Journal of Applied Behavioral Science* 16, no. 423 (July 1980).

4. Wendell F. French and Cecil H. Bell, Jr. *Organization Development,* Prentice Hall, Englewood Cliffs, NJ, 1978. Robert T. Golembiewski, *Approaches to Planned Change,* 2 vols., Marcel Dekker, New York, 1979. Edgar F. Huse, *Organization Development and Change,* West Publishing, St. Paul, Minn., 1980.

5. Wendell F. French, Cecil H. Bell, Jr., and Robert A Zawacki, eds. *Organization Development: Theory, Practice and Research.* Business Publications, Inc., Dallas, TX, 1975. And Robert T. Golembiewski and William Eddy, eds., 2 vols., *Organization Development in Public Administration,* Marcel Dekker, New York, 1978.

6. The Organization Development Network is the most prominent professional association, achieving nearly 5,000 members in less than two decades of existence. Its energy level is reflected in its two yearly meetings, each lasting nearly a week.

7. *Southern Review of Public Administration* 1, no. 406 (March 1978).

8. Peggy Morrison. "Evaluation in OD: A Review and An Assessment." *Group and Organization Studies* 3, no. 42 (March 1978). Jerry Porras, "The Comparative Impact of Different OD Techniques and Intervention Intensities." *Journal of Applied Behavioral Science* 15, no. 156 (April 1979).

9. Porras, note 8.

10. Morrison, note 8.

11. Warner Woodworth and Reed Nelson. "Witch Doctors, Messianics, Sorcerers, and OD Consultants: Parallels and Paradigms." *Organizational Dynamics* 8, no. 16, (Autumn 1979).

12. Edward J. Giblin, "Organization Development: Public Sector Theory and Practice." *Public Personnel Management* 5, no. 108 (March 1, 1976).

13. Burke, "Organization Development and Bureaucracies in the 1980s," p. 429.

14. Carl W. Proehl, Jr. *Planned Organizational Change.* Unpublished doctoral dissertation, Appendix A, University of Georgia, 1980.

15. The full bibliography of 574 cases is reported in ibid., and those interested can obtain copies from the senior author.

16. As an exception, Miller isolates 138 applications that are included in the present batch. See Garald J. Miller, *The Laboratory Approach to Planned Change in the Public Sector.* Unpublished doctoral dissertation, University of Georgia, 1979.

17. Arthur Blumberg and Robert T. Golembiewski. *Learning and Change in Groups.* Penguin, London, 1976, pp. 22–35.

18. Ibid., esp. pp. 57–61

19. Proehl, note 14.

20. Jerry I. Porras and Per-Olof Berg. "Evaluation Methodology in Organization Development." *Journal of Applied Behavioral Science* 14, no. 151 (April 1978).

21. Morrison, note 8

22. William N. Dunn and Frederick W. Swierczek. "Planned Organizational Change." *Journal of Applied Behavioral Science* 13, no. 135 (April 1977).

23. Porras, note 20.

24. Newton Margulies, Penny L. Wright, and Richard W. Scholl. "Organization Development Techniques: Their Impact on Change." *Group and Organization Studies* 2, no. 449 (December 1977).

25. A developmental version of guidelines for public sector applications appears in Robert T. Golembiewski, "Managing the Tension between OD Principles and Political Dynamics," pp. 27–46, in W. Warner Burke, ed., *The Cutting Edge: Current Theory and Practice in Organization Development,* University Associates, La Jolla, Calif., 1978. An expanded version will appear in Golembiewski's *Humanizing Public Organizations*(in preparation).

26. David G. Bowers, Jerome L. Franklin, and Patricia A. Pecorella. "Matching Problems, Precursors, and Interventions in OD: A Systematic Approach." *Journal of Applied Behavioral Science* 11, no. 391 (December 1975).

27. Philip H. Mirvis and David N. Berg. eds. *Failures in Organization Development and Change,* John Wiley & Sons, New York, 1977.

II FOUNDATIONS OF ORGANIZATION DEVELOPMENT AND TRANSFORMATION

The field of organization development emerged as advances were made in understanding the nature of change and the nature of organizational dynamics. Organization development uses knowledge from the basic and applied behavioral sciences to design action programs to solve problems, correct deficiencies, and seize opportunities in ongoing organizations. In the broadest and most general sense, the objective of OD programs is to increase short-term and long-term organizational effectiveness.

Operationally this means the client system (organization) must learn to solve current problems and must build the capacity to adapt to changing conditions, demands, and exigencies. Leaders and members of organizations today are required to have problem-solving skills, action-taking skills, and self-renewal skills. The role of the OD practitioner is to help organization members obtain these skills.

At least four kinds of knowledge are required of OD practitioners and leaders who desire to create problem-solving, self-renewing organizations: knowledge of how organizations work; knowledge of how change occurs; knowledge of how to intervene in organizations to produce desired changes; and knowledge of how to diagnose and solve problems.

The knowledge of how organizations work comes mainly from basic behavioral science research and theory. It entails an understanding of the dynamics of individuals, groups, and goal-oriented social systems. Knowledge of how change occurs involves understanding the processes of change and changing. In the case of organization development, gaining this knowledge is difficult because the phenomena are so complex and are themselves changing as they are being studied. Knowledge of how to intervene in organizations relates to change, but goes beyond it to investigate the processes of consultation and "helping." What constitutes effective intervention? What are the ingredients of effective client-consultant relationships? When is help helpful? Other applied disciplines, such as education, psychotherapy, social work, and management, provided insights that are used in OD.

Knowledge of diagnosis and problem solving comes from many sources but culminates in the ability to answer the questions: What is wrong? What made it wrong?

What must be done to correct the situation? Competent problem solving and action taking require being able to do two things: classify problem and opportunity situations accurately, and select appropriate remedies. This competence in turns rests on the prior existence of two bodies of knowledge: valid diagnostic categories (having a good classification scheme for differentiating between different types of problems), and a set of efficacious remedial treatments (having an array of different solutions or actions that will solve different problems). In relatively advanced applied sciences, such as medicine, great progress has been made in refining diagnostic categories and discovering appropriate treatments. Organization development classification schemes are not as advanced as those in medicine, but substantial progress has been made.

It is not possible to explore all the foundations of organization development and transformation in this section. Instead, we will look briefly at the nature of planned change and the nature of organizational dynamics.

The Nature of Planned Change

The action arena of OD is organizations. The name of the game is planned change. Organization improvement programs require an understanding of change processes and knowledge of the nature of organizations.

Kurt Lewin was the great practical theorist whose action and research programs provided much of the early foundation for understanding change processes in social situations.[1] Lewin (1890–1947) was a personality theorist, a social psychologist, and a man who wanted to improve the lot of humankind through behavioral science knowledge and application. To improve things means to change them; to change them requires knowledge of the structure and dynamics of change. Lewin's work had a significant impact on group dynamics, intergroup relations, and applied social psychology. Lewin once said, "If you want to understand a phenomenon, try to change it." And he devoted a considerable part of his career trying to understand processes of change.

Two concepts proposed by Kurt Lewin are especially useful in thinking about change. The first idea suggests that what is occurring at any point in time is the result of a field of opposing forces. Thus, for example, the production level of a manufacturing plant or the level of morale in a work group should be thought of as *equilibrium points* in a field of forces, some forces pushing toward higher and some pushing toward lower levels of production or morale. In order to understand a problematic situation the investigator must know what major forces are operating in that particular instance. A technique called the force field analysis can be used to diagram the field of forces and show how to develop action plans for moving the equilibrium point in one direction or another. This is a useful model for understanding what is going on in complex situations.

The second idea proposed by Lewin analyzes what must occur for permanent change to take place. He conceptualized change as a three-stage process: *unfreezing* the old behavior, *moving* to a new level of behavior, and *freezing* the behavior at the new level. This is a useful model for knowing how to move an equilibrium point to a new, desired level and *keep it there*. These two simple ideas undergird the theories of change of most OD practitioners.

Ronald Lippitt, Jeanne Watson, and Bruce Westley later refined Lewin's three phases into a seven-phase model of the change process as follows:

Phase 1.   The development of a need for change. This phase corresponds to Lewin's *unfreezing* phase.

Phase 2.   The establishment of a change relationship. This is a crucial phase in which a client system in need of help and a "change agent" from outside the system establish a working relationship with each other.

Phase 3.   The clarification or diagnosis of the client system's problem.

Phase 4.   The examination of alternative routes and goals; establishing goals and intentions of action.

Phase 5.   The transformation of intentions into actual change efforts. Phase 3, 4, and 5 correspond to Lewin's *moving* phase.

Phase 6.   The generalization and stabilization of change. This corresponds to Lewin's *freezing* phase.

Phase 7.   Achieving a terminal relationship.[2]

The models of change developed by Lewin and by Lippitt, Watson, and Westley advanced both theory and practice in organization development. They are foundations of the discipline. Causing change in organizations presents additional challenges, however. In an article entitled "Change Does Not Need to Be Haphazard," Kenneth Benne and Max Birnbaum suggest additional principles for effecting organizational change. Their principles are as follows:

1. To change a subsystem or any part of a subsystem, relevant aspects of the environment must also be changed.

2. To change behavior on any one level of a hierarchical organization, it is necessary to achieve complementary and reinforcing changes in organization levels above and below that level.

3. The place to begin change is at those points in the system where some stress and strain exist. Stress may give rise to dissatisfaction with the status quo and thus become a motivating factor for change in the system.

4. If thoroughgoing changes in a hierarchical structure are desirable or necessary, change should ordinarily start with the policy-making body.

5. Both the formal and the informal organization of an institution must be considered in planning any process of change.

6. The effectiveness of a planned change is often directly related to the degree to which members at all levels of an institutional hierarchy take part in the factfinding and the diagnosing of needed changes and in the formulating and reality testing of goals and programs of change.[3]

More recently, authors have focused on the nature of change using the terms *incremental/continuous change* and *radical/discontinuous change*. Incremental change requires modifications, adjustments, and adaptations, but the nature of the organization and its tasks stay relatively the same. Radical or discontinuous change requires massive, systemwide, paradigm-shifting changes in the organization and its tasks.

For example, in Reading 21, Robert A. Zawacki and Carol A. Norman state,

Over the last 50 years, it appears that the nature of organizational change has changed.... Beginning with the 1950s and 1960s, change was incremental; people adapted and were rewarded for their new behaviors. Then, during the 1960s and 1970s change became more rapid and individual contributors responded by working harder and smarter.... The 1980s and 1990s brought even more rapid and random change. Change nowadays seems to lack predictability.

In order to cope with rapid, radical, and unpredictable change, organizations must *transform* themselves. This was a major impetus for developing organization transformation theory and practice. The "self-directed teams" described by Zawacki and Norman represent a fundamental shift in the way people and work are organized and are thus an example of organization transformation.

Warner Burke and George Litwin developed a model to show how *first-order* (incremental, transactional) change and *second-order* (radical, transformational) change occur in organizations.[4] The premise of the Burke-Litwin model is this: OD interventions directed toward organizational structures, management practices, and systems (policies and procedures) will result in first-order change; interventions directed toward the organization's mission and strategy, leadership, and culture will result in second-order change. Thus, if organizations need to be transformed, practitioners and leaders should focus on mission, strategy, leadership philosophy and practice, and culture.

In summary, advances in understanding the nature of change led to improvements in intervention techniques, which resulted in OD programs becoming more effective.

The Nature of Organizational Dynamics

Organization development efforts are directed toward social systems called organizations. Organizations exist to accomplish specific purposes or goals—a mission, task, products, or services. In most organizations the decision to belong is a voluntary choice made by the individual. There is division of labor and responsibility in organizations, with the consequence that a social structure of roles, duties, and offices is created. Individuals perform role behaviors; they are expected to do some things and not others by virtue of the positions they hold. One cannot know how organizations function simply by knowing how individuals function and then summing across individuals, because organizations have unique characteristics of their own.

One characteristic of organizations is that much of the work gets done by teams consisting of bosses and subordinates. Work teams are the basic building blocks of organizations. If teams function well, it is more likely that the organization as a whole will function well. Advances in understanding the dynamics of groups served as a foundation for the development of OD. Insights, theories, and techniques concerning group processes formed a large part of the basic toolkit of early OD practitioners.

Relations between groups in organizations are often problematic and dysfunctional. Another characteristic of organizations is that these relations are very important for organizational performance. As knowledge about intergroup dynamics was developed, it was incorporated into organization development.

A fundamental tenet of OD is that organizations are open systems. Russell Ack-off defines a system as "a set of interrelated elements. Thus a system is an entity which is composed of at least two elements and a relation that holds between each of its elements and at least one other element in the set. Each of a system's elements is connected to every other element, directly or indirectly."[5] Systems (and organizations) must be treated from a holistic point of view, because certain properties derive from the *relationships* between the parts of the system and cannot be discovered from an analysis of the components themselves. In addition, organizations are open systems—they are in interaction with and in exchange with their environments. Organizations are impacted by and have an impact on their environments. As Katz and Kahn state,

> Organizations as a special class of open systems have properties of their own, but they share other properties in common with all open systems. These include the importation of energy from the environment, the throughput or transformation of the imported energy into some product form that is characteristic of the system, the exporting of that product into the environment, and the reenergizing of the system from sources in the environment.[6]

The organization development practitioner must understand the nature of the client systems in which he or she works. That is a basic prerequisite. The selections in this section contribute to that end.

Readings in Part II

The readings in this part are classic statements that improve with age and with each reading.

The first selection is an excerpt from Kurt Lewin's highly influential book, *Field Theory in Social Science.* Lewin's field theory approach postulates that any phenomenon is the resultant in a field of opposing forces—a model that has proved very useful for organizational change. A technique called the force field analysis allows one to map the field of forces and build action plans to change the field of forces. The brief piece by Carl Rogers looks at the dynamics of two-person conflict. He describes four elements that will almost always be found in such situations. Becoming aware of these elements is the first step in resolving interpersonal disputes.

Chris Argyris has made significant contributions to the field of organization development and transformation. This reading is from a very influential book published in 1970. OD practitioners intervene in ongoing organizations to help produce positive results. But the intervention process itself was mainly based on rules of thumb and principles derived from experience until Argyris formulated a systematic statement of intervention theory and method. Argyris sees three primary tasks of the interventionist: to help the client system generate valid information; to help ensure that client system members act on the basis of free and informed choice; and to help ensure internal commitment to the choices made. What is the practitioner trying to do? What theory is available to guide behavior and give overall direction? The reading by Argyris addresses these issues.

Intergroup relations are especially important phenomena in organizations. Just as individuals may be interdependently related on a work team for task accomplishment, entire teams are interdependently related to other teams for task accomplishment. The ways groups work together can either help or hinder organizational performance. The selection by Edgar Schein summarizes much of the literature on cooperation and competition between groups. Schein has packaged a wealth of empirical research, much of it conducted by Muzafer Sherif and Robert Blake and Jane Syrgley Mouton, in such a way that the OD practitioner and the manager alike can gain insights into this important area.

The article on organizational culture is also by Edgar Schein, who has written extensively on the subject. OD practitioners have recognized the importance of culture since the early days of the field, but it was not until the 1980s that serious and systematic attention was given to this important determinant of behavior. The reading by Schein defines organizational culture, shows how to analyze culture, and describes how to think about culture change.

In the final selection, William Fox describes the foundation of sociotechnical systems theory by examining its principles and guidelines. Sociotechnical systems theory (STS) postulates that organizations consist of two interdependently related systems (a social system and a technical system) that must be jointly optimized if the organization is to achieve effective performance. Thus, STS professionals are deeply involved in job design, job redesign, systems design, and organization design programs. Many of the leading ideas for designing high-performance work systems come from STS consultants. Sociotechnical systems theory is an important foundation of both OD and OT.

Endnotes

1. Alfred J. Marrow, *The Practical Theorist: The Life and Work of Kurt Lewin* (New York: Basic Books, 1969).
2. Ronald Lippitt, Jeanne Watson, and Bruce Westley, *The Dynamics of Planned Change* (New York: Harcourt Brace Jovanovich, 1958). See chapter 6 for a discussion.
3. Kenneth D. Benne and Max Birnbaum, "Change Does Not Need to Be Haphazard," *Notebook for Summer Participants*, NTL Institute for Applied Behavioral Science.
4. W. Warner Burke, *Organization Development: A Process of Learning and Changing* (Reading, MA: Addison-Wesley Publishing Company, 1994), chap. 7.
5. Russell L. Ackoff, "Toward a System of Systems Concepts," *Management Science*, July 1971, p. 662.
6. Daniel Katz and Robert L. Kahn, *The Social Psychology of Organizations*, 2nd ed. (New York: John Wiley & Sons, 1978), p. 33.

READING 7
THE FIELD APPROACH: CULTURE AND GROUP LIFE AS QUASI-STATIONARY PROCESSES

Kurt Lewin

This question of planned change or of any "social engineering" is identical with the question: What "conditions" have to be changed to bring about a given result and how can one change these conditions with the means at hand?

One should view the present situation—the status quo—as being maintained by certain conditions or forces. A culture—for instance, the food habits of a certain group at a given time—is not a static affair but a live process like a river which moves but still keeps a recognizable form. In other words, we have to deal, in group life as in individual life, with what is known in physics as "quasi-stationary" processes.[1]

Food habits do not occur in empty space. They are part and parcel of the daily rhythm of being awake and asleep; of being alone and in a group; of earning a living and playing; of being a member of a town, a family, a social class, a religious group, a nation; of living in a hot or a cool climate, in a rural area or a city, in a district with good groceries and restaurants, or in an area of poor and irregular food supply. Somehow all of these factors affect food habits at any given time. They determine the food habits of a group every day anew just as the amount of water supply and the nature of the river bed determine from day to day the flow of the river, its constancy, or its change.[2]

Food habits of a group, as well as such phenomena as the speed of production in a factory, are the result of a multitude of forces. Some forces support each other, some oppose each other. Some are driving forces, others restraining forces. Like the velocity of a river, the actual conduct of a group depends upon the level (for instance, the speed of production) at which these conflicting forces reach a state of equilibrium. To speak of a certain culture pattern—for instance, the food habits of a group—implies that the constellation of these forces remains the same for a period or at least that they find their state of equilibrium at a constant level during that period.

Neither group "habits" nor individual "habits" can be understood sufficiently by a theory which limits its consideration to the processes themselves and conceives of the "habit" as a kind of frozen linkage, an "association" between these processes. Instead, habits will have to be conceived of as a result of forces in the organism *and* its life space, in the group *and* its setting. The structure of the organism, of the group, of the setting, or whatever name the field might have in the given case, has to be represented and the forces in the various parts of the field have to be analyzed if the processes (which might be either constant "habits" or changes) are to be understood scientifically. The process is but the epi-phenomenon, the real object of study is the constellation of forces.

Therefore, to predict which changes in conditions will have what result we have to conceive of the life of the group as a result of specific constellations of forces within a larger setting. In other words, scientific predictions or advice for methods of change should be based on any analysis of the "field as a whole," including both its psychological and nonpsychological aspects.

Endnotes

1. For the general characteristics of quasi-stationary processes see Wolfgang Koehler, *Dynamics in Psychology* (New York: Liveright Publishing, 1940).
2. The type of forces, of course, is different; there is nothing equivalent to "cognitive structure" or "psychological past" or "psychological future" in the field determining the river.

Source: Kurt Lewin, *Field Theory in Social Science* (New York: Harper & Row, 1951), pp. 172–174.

READING 8
TWO-PERSON DISPUTES

Carl Rogers

When persons are in serious discord, whether we are speaking of a discordant marital relationship, friction between an employer and an employee, a formal and icy dispute between two diplomats, or tension growing out of some other base, we tend to find certain very common elements:

1. In such a dispute there is no doubt at all but that I am right and you are wrong. I am on the side of the angels, and you belong with the forces of darkness.

2. There is a breakdown of communication. You do not hear what I say, in any understanding way; and I am unwilling and unable to hear what you are really saying.

3. There are distortions in perception. The evidence which is taken in by my senses—your words, your actions, your responses to my words and actions—is trimmed and shaped by my needs to fit the views of you which I already hold. Evidence which is

clearly and openly contradictory to my rigidly held views is conveniently ignored or made acceptable by being grossly distorted. Thus, a real gesture toward reconciliation on your part can be perceived by me as only another deceitful trick.

4. Implicit in all this is the element of distrust. While whatever *I* do is obviously done with honorable intent, whatever *you* do is equally obviously done with an underlying evil intent, no matter how sweetly reasonable it may appear on the surface. Hence, from the perspective of each opponent, the whole relationship is shot through with suspicion and mistrust.

I believe I am correct in saying that in any serious two-person dispute, these four elements are invariably present and often make the situation appear hopeless. Yet there are knowledge and skill available which can be applied to such a situation. If there is to be progress in reducing this kind of tension, we have learned that the first necessity is a facilitative listener—a person who will listen empathetically and will understand the attitudes of each disputant.

Source: Carl Rogers, "Dealing with Psychological Tensions," in *Journal of Applied Behavioral Science* (1, no. 1) pp. 12–13, copyright © 1965 by NTL Institute for Applied Behavioral Science. Reprinted by permission of Sage Publications, Inc.

READING 9
INTERVENTION THEORY AND METHOD

Chris Argyris

A Definition of Intervention

To intervene is to enter into an ongoing system of relationship, to come between or among persons, groups or objects for the purpose of helping them. There is an important implicit assumption in the definition that should be made explicit: the system exists independently of the intervenor. There are many reasons one might wish to intervene. These reasons may range from helping the clients make their own decisions about the kind of help they need to coercing the clients to do what the intervenor wishes them to do.

Our view acknowledges interdependencies between the intervenor and the client system but focuses on how to maintain, or increase, the client system's autonomy; how to differentiate even more clearly the boundaries between the client system and the intervenor; and how to conceptualize and define the client system's health independently of the intervenor's. This view values the client system as an ongoing, self-responsible unity that has the obligation to be in control over its own destiny. An intervenor, in this view, assists a system to become more effective in problem solving, decision making, and decision implementation in such a way that the system can continue to be increasingly effective in these activities and have a decreasing need for the intervenor.

Basic Requirements for Intervention Activity

Are there any basic or necessary processes that must be fulfilled regardless of the substantive issues involved, if intervention activity is to be helpful with any level of client (individual, group, or organizational)? One condition that seems so basic as

Source: Chris Argyris, *Intervention Theory and Methods: A Behavioral Science View* (Reading, Mass.: Addison-Wesley Publishing, 1970), pp. 15–20. ©1970, Addison-Wesley. Reprinted with permission.

to be defined axiomatic is the generation of *valid information*. Without valid information, it would be difficult for the client to learn and for the interventionist to help.

A second condition almost as basic flows from our assumption that intervention activity, no matter what its substantive interests and objectives, should be so designed and executed that the client system maintains its discreteness and autonomy. Thus, *free, informed choice* is also a necessary process in effective intervention activity.

Finally, if the client system is assumed to be ongoing (that is, existing over time), the clients require strengthening to maintain their autonomy not only vis-à-vis the interventionist but also vis-à-vis other systems. This means that their commitment to learning and change has to be more than temporary. It has to be so strong that it can be transferred to relationships other than those with the interventionist and can do so (eventually) without the help of the interventionist. The third basic process for any intervention activity is therefore the client's *internal commitment* to the choices made.

In summary, valid information, free choice, and internal commitment are considered integral parts of any intervention activity, no matter what the substantive objectives are (for example, developing a management performance evaluation scheme, reducing intergroup rivalries, increasing the degree of trust among individuals, redesigning budgetary systems, or redesigning work). These three processes are called the primary intervention tasks.

Primary Tasks of an Interventionist

Why is it necessary to hypothesize that, in order for an interventionist to behave effectively and in order that the integrity of the client system be maintained, the interventionist has to focus on three primary tasks, regardless of the substantive problems that the client system may be experiencing?

Valid and Useful Information.   First, it has been accepted as axiomatic that valid and useful information is the foundation for effective intervention. Valid information is that which describes the factors, plus their interrelationships, that create the problem for the client system. There are several tests for checking the validity of the information. In increasing degrees of power they are public verifiability, valid prediction, and control over the phenomena. The first is having several independent diagnoses suggest the same picture. Second is generating predictions from the diagnosis that are subsequently confirmed (they occurred under the conditions that were specified). Third is altering the factors systematically and predicting the effects upon the system as a whole. All these tests, if they are to be valid, must be carried out in such a way that the participants cannot, at will, make them come true. This would be a self-fulfilling prophecy and not a confirmation of a prediction. The difficulty with a self-fulfilling prophecy is its indication of more about the degree of power an individual (or subset of individuals) can muster to alter the system than about the nature of the system when the participants are behaving without knowledge of the diagnosis. For example, if an executive learns that the interventionist predicts his subordinates will behave (*a*) if he behaves (*b*), he might alter (*b*) in order not to lead to (*a*). Such an alteration indicates the executive's power but does not test the validity of the diagnosis that if (*a*), then (*b*).

The tests for valid information have important implications for effective intervention activity. First, the interventionist's diagnoses must strive to represent the total client system and not the point of view of any subgroup or individual. Otherwise, the interventionist could not be seen only as being under the control of a particular individual or subgroup, but also his predictions would be based upon inaccurate information and thus might not be confirmed.

This does not mean that an interventionist may not begin with, or may not limit his relationship to,

a subpart of the total system. It is totally possible, for example, for the interventionist to help management, blacks, trade union leaders, etc. With whatever subgroup he works he simply should not agree to limit his diagnosis to its wishes.

It is conceivable that a client system may be helped even though valid information is not generated. Sometimes changes occur in a positive direction without the interventionist having played any important role. These changes, although helpful in that specific instance, lack the attribute of helping the organization to learn to gain control over its problem-solving capability.

The importance of information that the clients can use to control their destiny points up the requirement that the information must not only be valid, it must be useful. Valid information that cannot be used by the clients to alter their system is equivalent to valid information about cancer that cannot be used to cure cancer eventually. An interventionist's diagnosis should include variables that are manipulable by the clients and are complete enough so that if they are manipulated effective change will follow.

Free Choice.   In order to have free choice, the client has to have a cognitive map of what he wishes to do. The objectives of his action are known at the moment of decision. Free choice implies voluntary as opposed to automatic; proactive rather than reactive. The act of selection is rarely accomplished by maximizing or optimizing. Free and informed choice entails what Simon has called "satisficing"; that is, selecting the alternative with the highest probability of succeeding, given some specified cost constraints. Free choice places the locus of decision making in the client system. Free choice makes it possible for the clients to remain responsible for their destiny. Through free choice the clients can maintain the autonomy of their system.

It may be possible that clients prefer to give up their responsibility and their autonomy, especially if they are feeling a sense of failure. They may prefer, as we shall see in several examples, to turn over their free choice to the interventionist. They may insist that he make recommendations and tell them what to do. The interventionist resists these pressures because, if he does not, the clients will lose their free choice and he will lose his own free choice, also. He will be controlled by the anxieties of the clients.

The requirement of free choice is especially important for those helping activities where the processes of help are as important as the actual help. For example, a medical doctor does not require that a patient with a bullet wound participate in the process by defining the kind of help he needs. However, the same doctor may have to pay much more attention to the processes he uses to help patients when he is attempting to diagnose blood pressure or cure a high cholesterol. If the doctor behaves in ways that upset the patient, the latter's blood pressure may well be distorted. Or, the patient can develop a dependent relationship if the doctor cuts down his cholesterol—increasing habits only under constant pressure from the doctor—and the moment the relationship is broken off, the count goes up.

Effective intervention in the human and social sphere requires that the processes of help be congruent with the outcome desired. Free choice is important because there are so many unknowns, and the interventionist wants the client to have as much willingness and motivation as possible to work on the problem. With high client motivation and commitment, several different methods for change can succeed.

A choice is free to the extent the members can make their selection for a course of action with minimal internal defensiveness; can define the path (or paths) by which the intended consequence is to be achieved; can relate the choice to their central needs; and can build into their choices a realistic and challenging level of aspiration. Free choice therefore implies that the members are able to explore as many alternatives as they consider significant and select those that are central to their needs.

Why must the choice be related to the central needs and why must the level of aspiration be realistic and challenging? May people not choose freely unrealistic or unchallenging objectives? Yes,

they may do so in the short run, but not for long if they still want to have free and informed choice. A freely chosen course of action means that the action must be based on an accurate analysis of the situation and not on the biases or defenses of the decision makers. We know, from the level of aspiration studies, that choices which are too high or too low, which are too difficult or not difficult enough will tend to lead to psychological failure. Psychological failure will lead to increased defensiveness, increased failure, and decreased self-acceptance on the part of the members experiencing the failure. These conditions, in turn, will tend to lead to distorted perceptions by the members making the choices. Moreover, the defensive members may unintentionally create a climate where the members of surrounding and interrelated systems will tend to provide carefully censored information. Choices made under these conditions are neither informed nor free.

Turning to the question of centrality of needs, a similar logic applies. The degree of commitment to the processes of generating valid information, scanning, and choosing may significantly vary according to the centrality of the choice to the needs of the clients. The more central the choice, the more the system will strive to do its best in developing valid information and making free and informed choices. If the research from perceptual psychology is valid, the very perception of the clients is altered by the needs involved. Individuals tend to scan more, ask for more information, and be more careful in their choices when they are making decisions that are central to them. High involvement may produce perceptual distortions, as does low involvement. The interventionist, however, may have a greater probability of helping the clients explore possible distortion when the choice they are making is a critical one.

Internal Commitment.   Internal commitment means that course of action or choice that has been internalized by each member so that he experiences a high degree of ownership and has a feeling of responsibility about the choice and its implications. Internal commitment means that the individual has reached the point where he is acting on the choice because it fulfills his own needs and sense of responsibility, as well as those of the system.

The individual who is internally committed is acting primarily under the influence of his own forces and not induced forces. The individual (or any unity) feels a minimal degree of dependence upon others for the action. It implies that he has obtained and processed valid information and that he has made an informed and free choice. Under these conditions, there is a high probability that the individual's commitment will remain strong over time (even with reduction of external rewards) or under stress, or when the course of action is challenged by others. It also implies that the individual is continually open to reexamination of his position because he believes in taking action based upon valid information.

READING 10
INTERGROUP PROBLEMS IN ORGANIZATIONS

Edgar H. Schein

The first major problem of groups in organizations is how to make them effective in fulfilling both organizational goals and the needs of their members. The second major problem is how to establish conditions between groups which will enhance the productivity of each without destroying intergroup relations and coordination. This problem exists because as groups become more committed to their own goals and norms, they are likely to become competitive with one another and seek to undermine their rivals' activities, thereby becoming a liability to the organization as a whole. The overall problem, then, is how to establish collaborative intergroup relations *in those situations where task interdependence or the need for unity makes collaboration a necessary prerequisite for organizational effectiveness.*

Some Consequences of Intergroup Competition

The consequences of intergroup competition were first studied systematically by Sherif in an ingeniously designed setting (Sherif, Harvey, White, Hood, & Sherif, 1961). He organized a boys' camp in such a way that two groups would form and would gradually become competitive. Sherif then studied the effects of the competition and tried various devices for reestablishing collaborative relationships between the groups. Since his original experiments, there have been many replications with adult groups; the phenomena are so constant that it has been possible to make a demonstration exercise out of the experiment (Blake & Mouton, 1961). The effects can be described in terms of the following categories:

A. What happens *within* each competing group?

1. Each group becomes more closely knit and elicits greater loyalty from its members; members close ranks and bury some of their internal differences.

2. The group climate changes from informal, casual, playful to work and task oriented; concern for members' psychological needs declines while concern for task accomplishment increases.

3. Leadership patterns tend to change from more democratic toward more autocratic; the group becomes more willing to tolerate autocratic leadership.

4. Each group becomes more highly structured and organized.

5. Each group demands more loyalty and conformity from its members in order to be able to present a "solid front."

B. What happens *between* competing groups?

1. Each group begins to see the other group as the enemy, rather than merely a neutral object.

2. Each group begins to experience distortions of perception—it tends to perceive only the best parts of itself, denying its weaknesses, and tends to perceive only the worst parts of the other group, denying its strengths; each group is likely to develop a negative stereotype of the other ("they don't play fair like we do").

3. Hostility toward the other group increases while interaction and communication with the other group decreases; thus it becomes easier to maintain the negative stereotype and more difficult to correct perceptual distortions.

Source: Edgar H. Schein, *Organizational Psychology,* 3rd ed., 1980, pp. 172–80. Reprinted by permission of Prentice Hall, Inc., Englewood Cliffs, NJ.

4. If the groups are forced into interaction—for example, if they are forced to listen to representatives please their own and the others' cause in reference to some task—each group is likely to listen more closely to their own representative and not to listen to the representative of the other group, except to find fault with his or her presentation; in other words, group members tend to listen only for that which supports their own position and stereotype.

Thus far, we have listed some consequences of the competition itself, without reference to the consequences if one group actually wins out over the other. Before listing those effects, I would like to draw attention to the generality of the above reactions. Whether one is talking about sports teams, interfraternity competition, labor-management disputes, or interdepartmental competition as between sales and production in an industrial organization—or about international relations and the competition between the Soviet Union and the United States—the same phenomena tend to occur. These responses can be very useful to the group, by making it more highly motivated in task accomplishment, but they also open the door to group thinking. Furthermore, the same factors which improve intragroup effectiveness may have negative consequences for intergroup effectiveness. For example, as we have often seen in labor-management disputes or international conflicts, if the groups perceive themselves as competitors, they find it more difficult to resolve their differences, and eventually both become losers in a long-term strike or even a war.

Let us next look at the consequences of winning and losing, as in a situation where several groups are bidding to have their proposal accepted for a contract or as a solution to some problem. Many intraorganizational situations become win-or-lose affairs, hence it is of particular importance to examine their consequences.

C. What happens to the *winner*?

1. Winner retains its cohesion and may become even more cohesive.

2. Winner tends to release tension, lose its fighting spirit, become complacent, casual, and playful (the condition of being "fat and happy").

3. Winner tends toward high intragroup cooperation and concern for members' needs, and low concern for work and task accomplishment.

4. Winner tends to be complacent and to feel that the positive outcome has confirmed its favorable stereotype of itself and the negative stereotype of the "enemy" group; there is little motivation for reevaluating perceptions or reexamining group operations in order to learn how to improve them, hence the winner does not learn much about itself.

D. What happens to the *loser*?

1. If the outcome is not entirely clear-cut and permits a degree of interpretation (say, if judges have rendered it or if the game was close), there is a strong tendency for the loser to *deny or distort the reality of losing;* instead, the loser will find psychological escapes like "the judges were biased," "the judges didn't really understand our solution," "the rules of the game were not clearly explained to us," "if luck had not been against us at the one key point, we would have won," and so on. In effect, the loser's first response is to say "we didn't really lose!"

2. If the loss is psychologically accepted, the losing group tends to seek someone or something to blame; strong forces toward scapegoating are set up; if no outsider can be blamed, the group turns on itself, splinters, surfaces previously unresolved conflicts, fights within itself, all in the effort to find a cause for the loss.

3. Loser is more tense, ready to work harder, and desperate (the condition of being "lean and hungry").

4. Loser tends toward low intragroup cooperation, low concern for members'

needs, and high concern for recouping by working harder in order to win the next round of the competition.

5. Loser tends to learn a lot about itself as a group because its positive stereotype of itself and its negative stereotype of the other group are disconfirmed by the loss, forcing a reevaluation of perceptions; as a consequence, the loser is likely to reorganize and become more cohesive and effective once the loss has been accepted realistically.

The net effect of the win-lose situation is often that the losers refuse psychologically to accept their loss, and that intergroup tension is higher than before the competition began.

Intergroup problems of the sort we have just described arise not only out of direct competition between clearly defined groups but are, to a degree, intrinsic in any complex society because of the many bases on which a society is stratified. Thus we can have potential intergroup problems between men and women, between older and younger generations, between higher and lower ranking people, between blacks and whites, between people in power and people not in power, and so on (Alderfer, 1977). Any occupational or social group will develop "ingroup" feelings and define itself in terms of members of an "outgroup," toward whom intergroup feelings are likely to arise. Differences between nationalities or ethnic groups are especially strong, particularly if there has been any conflict between the groups in the past.

For intergroup feelings to arise we need not belong to a psychological group. It is enough to feel oneself a member of what has been called a "reference group"; that is, a group with which one identifies and compares oneself or to which one aspires. Thus, aspirants to a higher socioeconomic level take that level as their reference group and attempt to behave according to the values they perceive in that group. Similarly, members of an occupational group uphold the values and standards they perceive that occupation to embody. It is only by positing the existence of reference groups that one can explain how some individuals can con-

tinue to behave in a deviant fashion in a group situation. If such individuals strongly identify with a group that has different norms they will behave in a way that attempts to uphold those norms. For example, in Communist prison camps some soldiers from elite military units resisted their captors much longer than draftees who had weak identification with their military units. In order for the Communists to elicit compliant behavior from these strongly identified prisoners, they had to first weaken the attachment to the elite unit—that is, destroy the reference group—by attacking the group's image or convincing the prisoner that it was not a group worth belonging to (Schein, 1961). Intergroup problems arise wherever there are any status differences and are, therefore, intrinsic to all organizations and to society itself.

Reducing the Negative Consequences of Intergroup Competition

The gains of intergroup competition may, under some conditions, outweigh the negative consequences. It may be desirable to have work groups pitted against one another or to have departments become cohesive loyal units, even if interdepartmental coordination suffers. Often, however, the negative consequences outweigh the gains, and management seeks ways of reducing intergroup tension. Many of the techniques proposed to accomplish this come from the basic researches of Sherif, Blake, Alderfer, and others; they have been tested and found to be successful. The chief stumbling block remains not so much being unable to think of ways for reducing intergroup conflict as being *unable to implement some of the most effective ways.*

Destructive intergroup competition results basically from a conflict of goals and the breakdown of interaction and communication between the groups. This breakdown in turn permits and stimulates perceptual distortion and mutual negative stereotyping. The basic strategy of reducing conflict, therefore, is to locate goals which the competing groups can agree on and to reestablish valid communication between the groups. Each of the tactical devices that follows can be used singly or in combination.

Locating a Common Enemy. For example, the competing teams in a league can compose an all-star team to play another league, or conflicts between sales and production can be reduced if both can harness their efforts to helping their company successfully compete against another company. The conflict here is merely shifted to a higher level.

Bringing Leaders or Subgroups of the Competing Groups into Interaction. An isolated group representative cannot abandon his or her group position, but a powerful leader or a subgroup that has been delegated power not only can permit itself to be influenced by its counterpart negotiation team, but also will have the strength to influence the remainder of its home group if negotiation produces common agreements. This is the basis for "summit meetings" in international relations.

Locating a Superordinate Goal. Such a goal can be a brand-new task which requires the cooperative effort of the previously competing groups, or it can be a task like analyzing and reducing the intergroup conflict itself. For example, the previously competing sales and production departments can be given the task of developing a new product line that will be both cheap to produce and in great customer demand; or, with the help of an outside consultant, the competent groups can be invited to examine their own behavior and reevaluate the gains and losses from competition (Walton, 1969).

Experiential Intergroup Training. The procedure of having the conflicting parties examine their own behavior has been tried by a number of psychologists, notably Blake and Mouton (1962), with considerable success. Assuming the organization recognizes that it has a problem, and assuming it is ready to expose this problem to an outside consultant, the experiential workshop approach to reducing conflict might proceed with the following steps:

1. The competing groups are both brought into a training setting and the common goals are stated to be an exploration of mutual perceptions and mutual relations.

2. The two groups are then separated and each group is invited to discuss and make a list of its perceptions of itself and the other group.

3. In the presence of both groups, representatives publicly share the perceptions of self and others which the groups have generated, while the groups are obligated to remain silent (the objective is simply to report to the other group as accurately as possible the images that each group has developed in private).

4. Before any exchange has taken place, the groups return to private sessions to digest and analyze what they have heard; there is a great likelihood that the representatives' reports have revealed discrepancies to each group between its self-image and the image that the other group holds of it; the private session is partly devoted to an analysis of the reasons for these discrepancies, which forces each group to review its actual behavior toward the other group and the possible consequences of that behavior, regardless of its intentions.

5. In public session, again working through representatives, each group shares with the other what discrepancies it has uncovered and the possible reasons for them, focusing on actual, observable behavior.

6. Following this mutual exposure, a more open exploration is then permitted between the two groups on the *now-shared goal* of identifying further reasons for perceptual distortions.

7. A joint exploration is then conducted of how to manage future relations in such a way as to minimize a recurrence of the conflict.

Interspersed with these steps are short lectures and reading assignments on the psychology of intergroup conflict, the bases for perceptual distortion, psychological defense mechanisms, and so on.

The goal is to bring the psychological dynamics of the solution into conscious awareness and to refocus the groups on the common goal of exploring jointly the problem they share. In order to do this, they must have valid data about each other, which is provided through the artifice of the representative reports.

Blake's model deals with the entire group. Various other approaches begin by breaking down group prejudices on an individual basis. For example, groups A and B, each proposing an alternative product (idea), can be divided into pairs composed of an A and a B member. Each pair can be given the assignment of developing a joint product that combines the best ideas from the A product and the B product. Or, in each pair, members may be asked to argue for the product of the opposing group. It has been shown in a number of experiments that one way of changing attitudes is to ask a person to play the role of an advocate of the new attitude to be learned (Janis & King, 1954). The very act of arguing for another product, even if it is purely an exercise, makes the person aware of some of its virtues which he or she can now no longer deny. A practical application of these points might be to have some members of the sales department spend time in the production department and be asked to represent the production point of view to some third party, or to have some production people join sales teams to learn the sales point of view.

Most of the approaches cited depend on *recognition* of some problem by the organization and a *willingness* on the part of the competing groups to participate in some program to reduce negative consequences. The reality, however, is that most organizations neither recognize the problem nor are willing to invest time and energy in resolving it. Some of the unwillingness also arises from each competing group's recognition that in becoming more cooperative it may lose some of its own identity and integrity as a group. Rather than risk this loss, the group may prefer to continue the competition. This may well be the reason why, in international relations, nations refuse to engage in what

may seem like perfectly simple ways of resolving their differences. They resist partly in order to protect their integrity—that is, save face. For all these reasons, the *implementation* of strategies and tactics for reducing the negative consequences of intergroup competition is often a greater problem than the initial development of such strategies and tactics.

Preventing Intergroup Conflict

Because of the great difficulties of reducing intergroup conflict once it has developed, it may be desirable to prevent its occurrence in the first place. How can this be done? Paradoxically, a strategy of prevention challenges the fundamental premise upon which organization through division of labor rests. Once it has been decided by a superordinate authority to divide up functions among different departments or groups, a bias has already been introduced toward intergroup competition; for in doing its own job well, each group must, to some degree, compete for scarce resources and rewards from the superordinate authority. The very concept of division of labor implies a reduction of communication and interaction between groups, thus making it possible for perceptual distortions to occur.

The organization planner who wishes to avoid intergroup competition need not abandon the concept of division of labor, but should follow some of the steps listed below in creating and handling the different functional groups.

1. Relatively greater *emphasis should be given to total organizational effectiveness* and the role of departments in contributing to it; departments should be measured and rewarded on the basis of their contributions to the total effort, rather than their individual effectiveness.

2. *High interaction and frequent communication* should be stimulated between groups to work on problems of intergroup coordination and help; organization rewards should be given partly on the basis of help rendered to other groups.

3. *Frequent rotation of members* among groups or departments should be encouraged to stimulate a high degree of mutual understanding and empathy for one another's problems.

4. *Win-lose situations should be avoided* and groups should never be put into the position of competing for some scarce organizational reward; emphasis should always be placed on pooling resources to maximize organizational effectiveness; rewards should be shared equally with all the groups or departments.

Most managers find the fourth point particularly difficult to accept because of the strong belief that performance can be improved by pitting people or groups against one another in a competitive situation. This may indeed be true in the short run, and may even on occasion work in the long run, but the negative consequences described above are undeniably the product of the win–lose situation. Thus, if managers wish to prevent such consequences, they must face the possibility that they may have to abandon competitive relationships altogether and seek to substitute intergroup collaboration toward organizational goals. The more *interdependent* the various units are, the more important it is to stimulate collaborative problem solving.

Implementing a preventing strategy is often more difficult, partly because most people are inexperienced in stimulating and managing collaborative relationships. Yet observations of organizations using the Scanlon Plan not only reveal that is possible to establish collaborative relationships, even between labor and management, but also that when this has been done, organizational and group effectiveness have been as high as or higher than under competitive conditions. Training in how to set up collaborative relations may be a prerequisite for any such program to succeed, especially for those managers who have themselves grown up in a highly competitive environment.

References

Alderfer, C. P. (1977). Group and Intergroup Relations. In J. R. Hackman & J. L. Suttle (eds). *Improving Life at Work*. Santa Monica, CA: Goodyear.

Blake, R. R., & Mouton, J. S. (1961). "Reactions to Intergroup Competition under Win-Lose Conditions." *Management Science* 7, 420–35.

Blake, R. R., & Mouton, J. S. (1962). "Headquarters-Field Team Training for Organizational Improvements." *Journal of the American Society of Training Directors* 16.

Janis, I. L., & King, B. T. (1954). The Influence of Role Playing on Opinion Change. *Journal of Abnormal and Social Psychology* 69, 211–18.

Schein, E. H. (1961). Management Development as a Process of Influence. *Industrial Management Review* 2, 59–77.

Sherif, M., & Harvey, O. J., White, B. J., Hood, W. R. and Sherif, C. (1961). *Intergroup Conflict and Cooperation: The Robbers' Cave Experiment*. Norman, OK: University Book Exchange.

Walton, R. E. (1969). *Interpersonal Peacemaking: Confrontations and Third Party Consultation*. Reading, MA: Addison-Wesley.

READING 11
ORGANIZATIONAL CULTURE

Edgar H. Schein

To write a review article about the concept of organizational culture poses a dilemma because there is presently little agreement on what the concept does and should mean, how it should be observed and measured, how it relates to more traditional industrial and organizational psychology theories, and how it should be used in our efforts to help organizations. The popular use of the concept has further muddied the waters by hanging the label of "culture" on everything from common behavioral patterns to espoused new corporate values that senior management wishes to inculcate (e.g., Deal & Kennedy, 1982; Peters & Waterman, 1982).

Serious students of organizational culture point out that each culture researcher develops explicit or implicit paradigms that bias not only the definitions of key concepts but the whole approach to the study of the phenomenon (Barley, Meyer, & Gash, 1988; Martin & Meyerson, 1988; Ott, 1989; Smircich & Calas, 1987; Van Maanen, 1988). One probable reason for this diversity of approaches is that culture, like role, lies at the intersection of several social sciences and reflects some of the biases of each—specifically, those of anthropology, sociology, social psychology, and organizational behavior.

A complete review of the various paradigms and their implications is far beyond the scope of this article. Instead, I will provide a brief historical overview leading to the major approaches currently in use and then describe in greater detail one paradigm, firmly anchored in social psychology and anthropology, that is somewhat integrative in that it allows one to position other paradigms in a common conceptual space.

Source: Edgar H. Schein, "Organizational Culture," *American Psychologist* 45, no. 2 (February 1990), pp. 109–19. Copyright 1990 by the American Psychological Association. Reprinted by permission. Table 1 and Table 2 originally appeared in E. H. Schein's *Organizational Culture and Leadership: A Dynamic View*, pp. 52, 86. Copyright © 1985 by Jossey-Bass, Inc., Publishers. Reprinted by permission.

This line of thinking will push us conceptually into territory left insufficiently explored by such concepts as "climate," "norm," and "attitude." Many of the research methods of industrial/organizational psychology have weaknesses when applied to the concept of culture. If we are to take culture seriously, we must first adopt a more clinical and ethnographic approach to identify clearly the kinds of dimensions and variables that can usefully lend themselves to more precise empirical measurement and hypothesis testing. Though there have been many efforts to be empirically precise about cultural phenomena, there is still insufficient linkage of theory with observed data. We are still operating in the context of discovery and are seeking hypotheses, rather than testing specific theoretical formulations.

A Historical Note

Organizational culture as a concept has a fairly recent origin. Although the concepts of "group norms" and "climate" have been used by psychologists for a long time (e.g., Lewin, Lippitt, & White, 1939), the concept of "culture" has been explicitly used only in the last few decades. Katz and Kahn (1978), in their second edition of *The Social Psychology of Organizations*, referred to roles, norms, and values but presented neither climate nor culture as explicit concepts.

Organizational "climate," by virtue of being a more salient cultural phenomenon, lent itself to direct observation and measurement and thus has had a longer research tradition (Hellriegel & Slocum, 1974; A. P. Jones & James, 1979; Litwin & Stringer, 1968; Schneider, 1975; Schneider & Reichers, 1983; Tagiuri & Litwin, 1968). But climate is only a surface manifestation of culture, and thus research on climate has not enabled us to delve into the deeper casual aspects of how organizations function. We need explanations for variations in climate and norms, and it is this need that ultimately drives us to "deeper" concepts such as culture.

In the late 1940s social psychologists interested in Lewinian "action research" and leadership training freely used the concept of "cultural island" to indicate that the training setting was in some fundamental way different from the trainees' "back home" setting. We knew from the leadership training studies of the 1940s and 1950s that foremen who changed significantly during training would revert to their former attitudes once they were back at work in a different setting (Bradford, Gibb, & Benne, 1964; Fleishman, 1953, 1973; Lewin, 1952; Schein & Bennis, 1965). But the concept of "group norms," heavily documented in the Hawthorne studies of the 1920s, seemed sufficient to explain this phenomenon (Homans, 1950; Roethlisberger & Dickson, 1939).

In the 1950s and 1960s, the field of organizational psychology began to differentiate itself from industrial psychology by focusing on units larger than individuals (Bass, 1965; Schein, 1965). With a growing emphasis on work groups and whole organizations came a greater need for concepts such as "system" that could describe what could be thought of as a *pattern* of norms and attitudes that cut across a whole social unit. The researchers and clinicians at the Tavistock Institute developed the concept of "socio-technical systems" (Jaques, 1951; Rice, 1963; Trist, Higgin, Murray, & Pollock, 1963), and Likert (1961, 1967) developed his "Systems 1 through 4" to describe integrated sets of organizational norms and attitudes. Katz and Kahn (1966) built their entire analysis of organizations around systems theory and systems dynamics, thus laying the most important theoretical foundation for later culture studies.

The field of organizational psychology grew with the growth of business and management schools. As concerns with understanding organizations and interorganizational relationships grew, concepts from sociology and anthropology began to influence the field. Cross-cultural psychology had, of course, existed for a long time (Werner,

1940), but the application of the concept of culture to organizations *within* a given society came only recently as more investigators interested in organizational phenomena found themselves needing the concept to explain (*a*) variations in patterns of organizational behavior, and (*b*) levels of stability in group and organizational behavior that had not previously been highlighted (e.g., Ouchi, 1981).

What has really thrust the concept into the forefront is the recent emphasis on trying to explain why U.S. companies do not perform as well as some of their counterpart companies in other societies, notably Japan. In observing the differences, it has been noted that national culture is not a sufficient explanation (Ouchi, 1981; Pascale & Athos, 1981). One needs concepts that permit one to differentiate between organizations within a society, especially in relation to different levels of effectiveness, and the concept of organizational culture has served this purpose well (e.g., O'Toole, 1979; Pettigrew, 1979; Wilkins & Ouchi, 1983).

As more investigators and theoreticians have begun to examine organizational culture, the normative thrust has been balanced by more descriptive and clinical research (Barley, 1983; Frost, Moore, Louis, Lundberg, & Martin, 1985; Louis, 1981, 1983; Martin, 1982; Martin & Powers, 1983; Martin & Siehl, 1983; Schein, 1985a; Van Maanen & Barley, 1984). We need to find out what is actually going on in organizations before we rush in to tell managers what to do about their culture.

I will summarize this quick historical overview by identifying several different research streams that today influence how we perceive the concept of organizational culture.

Survey Research. From this perspective, culture has been viewed as a property of groups that can be measured by questionnaires leading to Likert-type profiles (Hofstede, 1980; Hofstede & Bond, 1988; Kilmann, 1984; Likert, 1967). The problem with this approach is that it assumes knowledge of the relevant dimensions to be studied. Even if these are statistically derived from large samples of items, it is not clear whether the initial item set is broad enough or relevant enough to capture what may for any given organization be its critical cultural themes. Furthermore, it is not clear whether something as abstract as culture can be measured with survey instruments at all.

Analytical Descriptive. In this type of research, culture is viewed as a concept for which empirical measures must be developed, even if that means breaking down the concept into smaller units so that it can be analyzed and measured (e.g., Harris & Sutton, 1986; Martin & Siehl, 1983; Schall, 1983; Trice & Beyer, 1984; Wilkins, 1983). Thus organizational stories, rituals and rites, symbolic manifestations, and other cultural elements come to be taken as valid surrogates for the cultural whole. The problem with this approach is that it fractionates a concept whose primary theoretical utility is in drawing attention to the holistic aspect of group and organizational phenomena.

Ethnographic. In this approach, concepts and methods developed in sociology and anthropology are applied to the study and organizations in order to illuminate descriptively, and thus provide a richer understanding of certain organizational phenomena that had previously not been documented fully enough (Barley, 1983; Van Maanen, 1988; Van Maanen & Barley, 1984). This approach helps to build better theory but is time consuming and expensive. A great many more cases are needed before generalizations can be made across various types of organizations.

Historical. Though historians have rarely applied the concept of culture in their work, it is clearly viewed as a legitimate aspect of an organization to be analyzed along with other factors (Chandler, 1977; Dyer, 1986; Pettigrew, 1979; Westney, 1987). The weaknesses of the historical method are similar to those pointed out for the ethnographic approach, but these are often offset by the insights that historical and longitudinal analyses can provide.

Clinical Descriptive. With the growth of organizational consulting has come the opportunity to observe in areas from which researchers have

traditionally been barred, such as the higher levels of management where policies originate and where reward and control systems are formulated. When consultants observe organizational phenomena as a byproduct of their services for clients, we can think of this as "clinical" research even though the client is defining the domain of observation (Schein, 1987a). Such work is increasingly being done by consultants with groups and organizations, and it allows consultants to observe some of the systemic effects of interventions over time. This approach has been of how members of the organization react. We can see and feel that one company is much more formal and bureaucratic than another, but that does not tell us anything about why this is so or what meaning it has to the members.

For example, one of the flaws of studying organizational symbols, stories, myths, and other such artifacts is that we may make incorrect inferences from them if we do not know how they connect to underlying assumptions (Pondy, Boland, & Thomas, 1988; Pondy, Frost, Morgan, & Dandridge, 1983; Wilkins, 1983). Organizational stories are especially problematic in this regard because the "lesson" of the story is not clear if one does not understand the underlying assumptions behind it.

Through interviews, questionnaires, or survey instruments one can study a culture's espoused and documented *values*, norms, ideologies, charters, and philosophies. This is comparable to the ethnographer's asking special "informants" why certain observed phenomena happen the way they do. Open-ended interviews can be very useful in getting at this level of how people feel and think; but questionnaires and survey instruments are generally less useful, because they prejudge the dimensions to be studied. There is no way of knowing whether the dimensions one is asking about are relevant or salient in that culture until one has examined the deeper levels of the culture.

Through more intensive observation, through more focused questions, and through involving motivated members of the group in intensive self-analysis, one can seek out and decipher the taken-for-granted, underlying, and usually unconscious *assumptions* that determine perceptions, thought processes, feelings, and behavior. Once one understands some of these assumptions, it becomes much easier to decipher the meanings implicit in the various behavioral and artifactual phenomena one observes. Furthermore, once one understands the underlying taken-for-granted assumptions, one can better understand how cultures can seem to be ambiguous or even self-contradictory (Martin & Meyerson, 1988).

As two case examples I present later will show, it is quite possible for a group to hold conflicting values that manifest themselves in inconsistent behavior while having complete consensus on underlying assumptions. It is equally possible for a group to reach consensus on the level of values and behavior and yet develop serious conflict later because there was no consensus on critical underlying assumptions.

This latter phenomenon is frequently observed in mergers or acquisitions where initial synergy is gradually replaced by conflict, leading ultimately to divestitures. When one analyzes these examples historically, one often finds that there was insufficient agreement on certain basic assumptions, or, in our terms, that the cultures were basically in conflict with each other.

Deeply held assumptions often start out historically as values but, as they stand the test of time, gradually come to be taken for granted and then take on the character of assumptions. They are no longer questioned and they become less and less open to discussion. Such avoidance behavior occurs particularly if the learning was based on traumatic experiences in the organization's history, which leads to the group counterpart of what would be repression in the individual. If one understands culture in this way, it becomes obvious why it is so difficult to change culture.

Deciphering the "Content" of Culture

Culture is ubiquitous. It covers all areas of group life. A simplifying typology is always dangerous because one may not have the right variables in it; but if one distills from small group theory the

dimensions that recur in group studies, one can identify a set of major external and internal tasks that all groups face and with which they must learn to cope (Ancona, 1988; Bales, 1950; Bales & Cohen, 1979; Benne & Sheats, 1948; Bennis & Shepard, 1956; Bion, 1959; Schein, 1988). The group's culture can then be seen as the learned response to each of these tasks (see Table 1).

Another approach to understanding the "content" of a culture is to draw on anthropological typologies of universal issues faced by all societies. Again, there is a danger of overgeneralizing these dimensions (see Table 2), but the comparative studies of Kluckhohn and Strodtbeck (1961) are a reasonable start in this dimension.

If one wants to decipher what is really going on in a particular organization, one has to start more inductively to find out which of these dimensions is the most pertinent on the basis of that organization's history. If one has access to the organization, one will note its *artifacts* readily but will not really know what they mean. Of most value in this process will be noting *anomalies* and things that seem different, upsetting, or difficult to understand.

If one has access to members of the organization, one can interview them about the issues in Table 1 and thereby get a good roadmap of what is going on. Such an interview will begin to reveal *espoused values,* and, as these surface, the investigator will begin to notice inconsistencies between what is claimed and what has been observed. These inconsistencies and the anomalies observed or felt now form the basis for the next layer of investigation.

Pushing past the layer of espoused values into underlying *assumptions* can be done by the ethnographer once trust has been established or by the clinician if the organizational client wishes to be helped. Working with motivated insiders is essential, because only they can bring to the surface their own underlying assumptions and articulate how they basically perceive the world around them.

To summarize, if we combine insider knowledge with outsider questions, assumptions can be brought to the surface; but the process of inquiry has to be interactive, with the outsider continuing to probe

TABLE 1

The external and internal tasks facing all groups

External Adaption Tasks	Internal Integration Tasks
Developing consensus on:	Developing consensus on:
1. The core mission, functions, and primary tasks of the organization vis-à-vis its environments.	1. The common language and conceptual system to be used, including basis concepts of time and space.
2. The specific goals to be pursued by the organization.	2. The group boundaries and criteria for inclusion.
3. The basic means to be used in accomplishing the goals.	3. The criteria for the allocation of status, power, and authority.
4. The criteria to be used for measuring results.	4. The criteria for intimacy, friendship, and love in different work and family settings.
5. The remedial or repair strategies if goals are not achieved.	5. The criteria for the allocation of rewards and punishments.
	6. Concepts for managing the unmanageable—ideology and religion.

Note: Adapted from *Organizational Culture and Leadership* (pp. 52, 56) by E. H. Schein, 1985, San Francisco: Jossey-Bass. Copyright 1985 by Jossey-Bass. Adapted by permission.

until assumptions have really been teased out and have led to a feeling of greater understanding on the part of both the outsider and the insiders.

Two Case Examples

It is not possible to provide complete cultural descriptions in a short article, but some extracts from cases can be summarized to illustrate particularly the distinctions between artifacts, values, and assumptions. The "Action Company" is a rapidly growing high-technology manufacturing concern still managed by its founder roughly 30 years after its founding. Because of its low turnover and intense history, one would expect to find an overall organizational culture as well as functional and geographic subcultures.

A visitor to the company would note the open office landscape architecture; a high degree of informality; frenetic activity all around; a high degree of confrontation, conflict, and fighting in meetings; an obvious lack of status symbols, such as parking spaces or executive dining rooms; and a sense of high energy and emotional involvement of people staying late and expressing excitement about the importance of their work.

If one asks about these various behaviors, one is told that the company is in a rapidly growing high-

technology field where hard work, innovation, and rapid solutions to things are important and where it is essential for everyone to contribute at their maximum capacity. New employees are carefully screened; and when an employee fails, he or she is simply assigned to another task, not fired or punished in any personal way.

If one discusses this further and pushes to the level of assumptions, one elicits a pattern or paradigm such as that shown in Figure 1. Because of the kind of technology the company manufactures, and because of the strongly held beliefs and values of its founder, the company operates on several critical and coordinated assumptions: (*a*) Individuals are assumed to be the source of all innovation and productivity. (*b*) It is assumed that truth can only be determined by pitting fully involved individuals against each other to debate ideas until only one idea survives; and it is further assumed that ideas will not be implemented unless everyone involved in implementation has been convinced through the debate of the validity of the idea. (*c*) Paradoxically, it is also assumed that every individual must think for himself or herself and "do the right thing" even if that means disobeying one's boss or violating a policy. (*d*) What makes it possible for people to live in this high-conflict environment is the assumption that the company

TABLE 2

Some underlying dimensions of organizational culture

Dimension	Questions to Be Answered
1. The organization's relationship to its environment	Does the organization perceive itself to be dominant, submissive, harmonizing, searching out a niche?
2. The nature of human activity	Is the "correct" way for humans to behave to be dominant/pro-active, harmonizing, or passive/fatalistic?
3. The nature of reality and truth	How do we define what is true and what is not true; and how is truth ultimately determined both in the physical and social word? By pragmatic test, reliance on wisdom, or social consensus?
4. The nature of time	What is our basic orientation in terms of past, present, and future, and what kinds of time units are most relevant for the conduct of daily affairs?
5. The nature of human nature	Are humans basically good, neutral, or evil, and is human nature perfectible or fixed?
6. The nature of human relationships	What is the "correct" way for people to relate to each other, to distribute power and affection? Is life competitive or cooperative? Is the best way to organize society on the basis of individualism or groupism? Is the best authority system autocratic/paternalistic or collegial/participative?
7. Homogeneity vs. diversity	Is the group best off if it is highly diverse or if it is highly homogeneous, and should individuals in a group be encouraged to innovate or conform?

Note: Adapted from *Organizational Culture and Leadership* (p. 86) by E. H. Schein, 1985, San Francisco: Jossey-Bass. Copyright 1985 by Jossey-Bass. Adapted by permission.

FIGURE 1

The Action Company paradigm

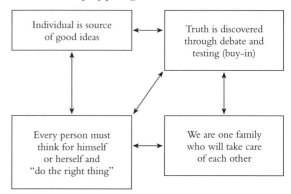

members are one big family who will take care of each other and protect each other even if some members make mistakes or have bad ideas.

Once one understands this paradigm, one can understand all of the different observed artifacts, such as the ability of the organization to tolerate extremely high degrees of conflict without seeming to destroy or even demotivate its employees. The value of the cultural analysis is that it provides insight, understanding, and a roadmap for future action. For example, as this company grows, the decision process may prove to be too slow, the individual autonomy that members are expected to exercise may become destructive and have to be replaced by more disciplined behavior, and the notion of a family may break down because too many people no longer know each other personally. The cultural analysis thus permits one to focus on those areas in which the organization will experience stresses and strains as it continues to grow and in which cultural evolution and change will occur.

By way of contrast, in the "Multi Company," a 100-year-old multidivisional, multinational chemical firm, one finds at the artifact level a high degree of formality; an architecture that puts great emphasis on privacy; a proliferation of status symbols and deference rituals, such as addressing people by their titles; a high degree of politeness in group meetings;

an emphasis on carefully thinking things out and then implementing them firmly through the hierarchy; a formal code of dress; and an emphasis on working hours, punctuality, and so on. One also finds a total absence of cross-divisional or cross-functional meetings and an almost total lack of lateral communication. Memos left in one department by an outside consultant with instructions to be given to others are almost never delivered.

The paradigm that surfaces, if one works with insiders to try to decipher what is going on, can best be depicted by the assumptions shown in Figure 2. The company is science based and has always derived its success from its research and development activities. Whereas "truth" in the Action Company is derived through debate and conflict and employees down the line are expected to think for themselves, in the Multi Company truth is derived from senior, wiser heads and employees are expected to go along like good soldiers once a decision is reached.

The Multi Company also sees itself as a family, but its concept of a family is completely different. Whereas in the Action Company, the family is a kind of safety net and an assurance of membership, in the Multi Company it is an authoritarian/paternalistic system of eliciting loyalty and compliance in exchange for economic security. The paradoxical absence of lateral communication is explained by the deeply held assumption that a job is a person's private turf and that the unsolicited providing of information to that person is an invasion of privacy and a potential threat to his or her self-esteem. Multi Company managers are very much on top of their jobs and pride themselves on that fact. If they ask for information they get it, but it is rarely volunteered by peers.

This cultural analysis highlights what is for the Multi Company a potential problem. Its future success may depend much more on its ability to become effective in marketing and manufacturing, yet it still treats research and development as a sacred cow and assumes that new products will be the key to its future success. Increasingly, the

FIGURE 2

The Multi Company paradigm

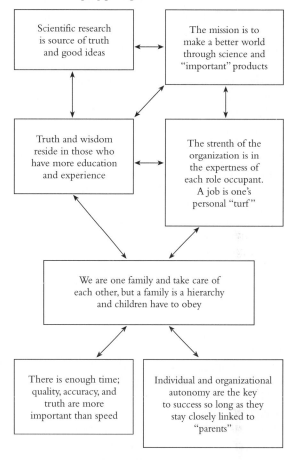

company finds itself in a world that requires rapid decision making, yet its systems and procedures are slow and cumbersome. To be more innovative in marketing it needs to share ideas more, yet it undermines lateral communication.

Both companies reflect the larger cultures within which they exist, in that the Action Company is an American firm whereas the Multi Company is European; but each also is different from its competitors within the same country, thus highlighting the importance of understanding *organizational* culture.

Cultural Dynamics: How Is Culture Created?

Culture is learned; hence learning models should help us to understand culture creation. Unfortunately, there are not many good models of how groups learn—how norms, beliefs, and assumptions are created initially. Once these exist, we can see clearly how leaders and powerful members embed them in group activity, but the process of learning something that becomes shared is still only partially understood.

Norm Formation around Critical Incidents.
One line of analysis comes from the study of training groups (Bennis & Shepard, 1956; Bion, 1959; Schein, 1985a). One can see in such groups how norms and beliefs arise around the way members respond to critical incidents. Something emotionally charged or anxiety producing may happen, such as an attack by a member on the leader. Because everyone witnesses it and because tension is high when the attack occurs, the immediate next set of behaviors tends to create a norm.

Suppose, for example, that the leader counterattacks, that the group members "concur" with silence or approval, and that the offending member indicates with an apology that he or she accepts his or her "mistake." In those few moments a bit of culture has begun to be created—the norm that "we do not attack the leader in this group; authority is sacred." The norm may eventually become a belief and then an assumption if the same pattern recurs. If the leader and the group consistently respond differently to attacks, a different norm will arise. By reconstructing the history of critical incidents in the group and how members dealt with them, one can get a good indication of the important cultural elements in that group.

Identification with Leaders.
A second mechanism of culture creation is the modeling by leader figures that permits group members to identify with them and internalize their values and assumptions. When groups or organizations first form, there are usually dominant figures or "founders" whose own beliefs, values, and assumptions provide a visible and articulated model for how the group should be structured and how it should function

(Schein, 1983). As these beliefs are put into practice, some work out and some do not. The group then learns from its own experience what parts of the "founder's" belief system work for the group as a whole. The joint learning then gradually creates shared assumptions.

Founders and subsequent leaders continue to attempt to embed their own assumptions; but increasingly they find that other parts of the organization have their own experiences to draw on and, thus, cannot be changed. Increasingly the learning process is shared, and the resulting cultural assumptions reflect the total group's experience, not only the leader's initial assumptions. But leaders continue to try to embed their own views of how things should be, and, if they are powerful enough, they will continue to have a dominant effect on the emerging culture.

Primary embedding mechanisms are (*a*) what leaders pay attention to, measure, and control; (*b*) how leaders react to critical incidents and organizational crises; (*c*) deliberate role modeling and coaching; (*d*) operational criteria for the allocation of rewards and status; and (*e*) operational criteria for recruitment, selection, promotion, retirement, and excommunication. *Secondary articulation and reinforcement mechanisms* are (*a*) the organization's design and structure; (*b*) organizational systems and procedures; (*c*) the design of physical space, facades, and buildings; (*d*) stories, legends, myths, and symbols; and (*e*) formal statements of organizational philosophy, creeds, and charters.

One can hypothesize that, as cultures evolve and grow, two processes will occur simultaneously: a process of differentiation into various kinds of subcultures that will create diversity, and a process of integration, or a tendency for the various deeper elements of the culture to become congruent with each other because of the human need for consistency.

Cultural Dynamics: Preservation through Socialization

Culture perpetuates and reproduces itself through the socialization of new members entering the group. The socialization process really begins with recruitment and selection in that the organization is likely to look for new members who already have the "right" set of assumptions, beliefs, and values. If the organization can find such presocialized members, it needs to do less formal socialization. More typically, however, new members do not "know the ropes" well enough to be able to take and enact their organizational roles, and thus they need to be trained and "acculturated" (Feldman, 1988; Ritti & Funkhouser, 1987; Schein, 1968, 1978; Van Maanen, 1976, 1977).

The socialization process has been analyzed from a variety of perspectives and can best be conceptualized in terms of a set of dimensions that highlight variations in how different organizations approach the process (Van Maanen, 1978; Van Maanen & Schein, 1979). Van Maanen identified seven dimensions along which socialization processes can vary:

1. *Group versus individual:* the degree to which the organization processes recruits in batches, as in boot camp, or individually, as in professional offices.

2. *Formal versus informal:* the degree to which the process is formalized, as in set training programs, or is handled informally through apprenticeships, individual coaching by the immediate superior, or the like.

3. *Self-destructive and reconstructing versus self-enhancing:* the degree to which the process destroys aspects of the self and replaces them, as in boot camp, or enhances aspects of the self, as in professional development programs.

4. *Serial versus random:* the degree to which role models are provided, as in apprenticeship or mentoring programs, or are deliberately withheld, as in sink-or-swim kinds of initiations in which the recruit is expected to figure out his or her own solutions.

5. *Sequential versus disjunctive:* the degree to which the process consists of guiding the recruit through a series of discrete steps and roles versus being open-ended and never letting the recruit predict what organizational role will come next.

6. *Fixed versus variable:* the degree to which stages of the training process have fixed timetables for each stage, as in military academies, boot camps, or rotational training programs, or are open-ended, as in typical promotional systems where one is not advanced to the next stage until one is "ready."

7. *Tournament versus contest:* the degree to which each stage is an "elimination tournament" where one is out of the organization if one fails or a "contest" in which one builds up a track record and batting average.

Socialization Consequences. Though the goal of socialization is to perpetuate the culture, it is clear that the process does not have uniform effects. Individuals respond differently to the same treatment, and, even more important, different combinations of socialization tactics can be hypothesized to produce somewhat different outcomes for the organization (Van Maanen & Schein, 1979).

For example, from the point of view of the organization, one can specify three kinds of outcomes: (*a*) a *custodial orientation,* or total conformity to all norms and complete learning of all assumptions; (*b*) *creative individualism,* which implies that the trainee learns all of the central and pivotal assumptions of the culture but rejects all peripheral ones, thus permitting the individual to be creative both with respect to the organization's tasks and in how the organization performs them (role motivation); and (*c*) *rebellion,* or the total rejection of all assumptions. If the rebellious individual is constrained by external circumstances from leaving the organization, he or she will subvert, sabotage, and ultimately foment revolution.

We can hypothesize that the combination of socialization techniques most likely to produce a custodial orientation is (1) formal, (2) self-reconstructing, (3) serial, (4) sequential, (5) variable, and (6) tournament-like. Hence if one wants new members to be more creative in the use of their talents, one should use socialization techniques that are informal, self-enhancing, random, disjunctive, fixed in terms of timetables, and contest-like.

The individual versus group dimension can go in either direction in that group socialization methods can produce loyal custodially oriented cohorts or can produce disloyal rebels if countercultural norms are formed during the socialization process. Similarly, in the individual apprenticeship the direction of socialization will depend on the orientation of the mentor or coach.

Efforts to measure these socialization dimensions have been made, and some preliminary support for the above hypotheses has been forthcoming (Feldman, 1976, 1988; G. R. Jones, 1986). Insofar as cultural evolution is a function of innovative and creative efforts on the part of new members, this line of investigation is especially important.

Cultural Dynamics: Natural Evolution

Every group and organization is an open system that exists in multiple environments. Changes in the environment will produce stresses and strains inside the group, forcing new learning and adaptation. At the same time, new members coming into the group will bring new beliefs and assumptions that will influence currently held assumptions. To some degree, then, there is constant pressure on any given culture to evolve and grow. But just as individuals do not easily give up the elements of their identity or their defense mechanisms, so groups do not easily give up some of their basic underlying assumptions merely because external events or new members disconfirm them.

An illustration of "forced" evolution can be seen in the case of the aerospace company that prided itself on its high level of trust in its employees, which was reflected in flexible working hours, systems of self-monitoring and self-control, and the absence of time clocks. When a number of other companies in the industry were discovered to have overcharged their government clients, the government legislated a system of controls for *all* of its contractors, forcing this company to install time clocks and other control mechanisms that undermined the climate of trust that had been built up over 30 years. It remains to be seen whether the company's basic assumption that people can be trusted will gradually change or whether the company will find a way to discount the effects of an artifact that is in fundamental conflict with one of its basic assumptions.

Differentiation. As organizations grow and evolve they divide the labor and form functional, geographical, and other kinds of units, each of which exists in its own specific environment. Thus organizations begin to build their own subcultures. A natural evolutionary mechanism, therefore, is the differentiation that inevitably occurs with age and size. Once a group has many subcultures, its total culture increasingly becomes a negotiated outcome of the interaction of its subgroups. Organizations then evolve either by special efforts to impose their overall culture or by allowing dominant subcultures that may be better adapted to changing environmental circumstances to become more influential.

Cultural Dynamics: Guided Evolution and Managed Change

One of the major roles of the field of organization development has been to help organizations guide the direction of their evolution; that is, to enhance cultural elements that are viewed as critical to maintaining identity and to promote the "unlearning" of cultural elements that are viewed as increasingly dysfunctional (Argyris, Putnam, & Smith, 1985; Argyris & Schon, 1978; Beckhard & Harris, 1987; Hanna, 1988; Lippitt, 1982; Walton, 1987). This process in organizations is analogous to the process of therapy in individuals although the actual tactics are more complicated when multiple clients are involved and when some of the clients are groups and subsystems.

Leaders of organizations sometimes are able to overcome their own cultural biases and to perceive that elements of an organization's culture are dysfunctional for survival and grown in a changing environment. They may feel either that they do not have the time to let evolution occur naturally or that evolution is heading the organization in the wrong direction. In such a situation one can observe leaders doing a number of different things, usually in combination, to produce the desired cultural changes.

1. Leaders may unfreeze the present system by highlighting the threats to the organization if no change occurs, and, at the same time, encourage the organization to believe that change is possible and desirable.

2. They may articulate a new direction and a new set of assumptions, thus providing a clear and new role model.

3. Key positions in the organization may be filled with new incumbents who hold the new assumptions because they are either hybrids, mutants, or brought in from the outside.

4. Leaders systematically may reward the adoption of new directions and punish adherence to the old direction.

5. Organization members may be seduced or coerced into adopting new behaviors that are more consistent with new assumptions.

6. Visible scandals may be created to discredit sacred cows, to explode myths that preserve dysfunctional traditions, and to destroy symbolically the artifacts associated with them.

7. Leaders may create new emotionally charged rituals and develop new symbols and artifacts around the new assumptions to be embraced, using the embedding mechanisms described earlier.

Such cultural change efforts are generally more characteristic of "midlife" organizations than have become complacent and ill adapted to rapidly changing environmental conditions (Schein, 1985a). The fact that such organizations have strong subcultures aids the change process, in that one can draw the new leaders from those subcultures that most represent the direction in which the organization needs to go.

In cases where organizations become extremely maladapted, one sees more severe change efforts. These may take the form of destroying the group that is the primary cultural carrier and reconstructing it around new people, thereby allowing a new learning process to occur and a new culture to form. When organizations go bankrupt or are turned over to "turnaround managers," one often sees such extreme measures. What is important to note about such cases is that they invariably involve the replacement of large numbers of people, because the members who have grown up in the organization find it difficult to change their basic assumptions.

Mergers and Acquisitions.   One of the most obvious forces toward culture change is the bringing together of two or more cultures. Unfortunately, in many mergers and acquisitions, the culture compatibility issue is not raised until after the deal has been consummated, which leads, in many cases, to cultural "indigestion" and the eventual divestiture of units that cannot become culturally integrated.

To avoid such problems, organizations must either engage in more premerger diagnosis to determine cultural compatibility or conduct training and integration workshops to help the meshing process. Such workshops have to take into account the deeper assumption layers of culture to avoid the trap of reaching consensus at the level of artifacts and values while remaining in conflict at the level of underlying assumptions.

The Role of the Organizational Psychologist

Culture will become an increasingly important concept for organizational psychology. Without such a concept we cannot really understand change or resistance to change. The more we get involved with helping organizations to design their fundamental strategies, particularly in the human resources area, the more important it will be to be able to help organizations decipher their own cultures.

All of the activities that revolve around recruitment, selection, training, socialization, the design of reward systems, the design and description of jobs, and broader issues of organization design require an understanding of how organizational culture influences present functioning. Many organizational change programs that failed probably did so because they ignored cultural forces in the organizations in which they were to be installed.

Inasmuch as culture is a dynamic process within organizations, it is probably studied best by action research methods, that is, methods that get "insiders" involved in the research and that work through attempts to "intervene" (Argyris et al., 1985; French & Bell, 1984; Lewin, 1952; Schein, 1987b). Until we have a better understanding of how culture works, it is probably best to work with qualitative research approaches that combine field work methods from ethnography with interview and observation methods from clinical and consulting work (Schein, 1987a).

I do not see a unique role for the traditional industrial/organizational psychologist, but I see great potential for the psychologist to work as a team member with colleagues who are more ethnographically oriented. The particular skill that will be needed on the part of the psychologist will be knowledge of organizations and of how to work with them, especially in a consulting relationship. Organizational culture is a complex phenomenon, and we should not rush to measure things until we understand better what we are measuring.

References

Ancona, D. G. (1988). "Groups in Organizations: Extending Laboratory Models." In C. Hendrick (ed.), *Annual Review of Personality and Social Psychology: Group and Intergroup Processes.* Beverly Hills, CA: Sage.

Argyris, C.; Putnam, R.; & Smith, D. M. (1985). *Action Science.* San Francisco: Jossey-Bass.

Argyris, C.; & Schon, D. A. (1978). *Organizational Learning: A Theory of Action Perspective.* Reading, MA: Addison-Wesley.

Bales, R. F. (1950). *Interaction Process Analysis.* Chicago, University of Chicago Press.

Bales, R. F.; & Cohen, S.P. (1979). *SYMLOG: A System for the Multiple Level Observation of Groups.* New York: Free Press.

Barley, S. R. (1983). "Semiotics and the Study of Occupational and Organizational Cultures." *Administrative Science Quarterly,* 28, 393–413.

Barley, S. R.; Meyer, C. W.; & Gash, D.C. (1988). "Culture of Cultures: Academics, Practitioners and the Pragmatics of Normative Control." *Administrative Science Quarterly* 33, 24–60.

Bass, B. M. (1965). *Organizational Psychology.* Boston: Allyn & Bacon.

Beckhard, R. (1969). *Organization Development: Strategies and Models.* Reading, MA: Addison-Wesley.

Beckhard, R.; & Harris, R. T. (1977). *Organizational Transitions: Managing Complex Change.* Reading, MA: Addison-Wesley.

Beckhard, R.; & Harris, R. T. (1987). *Organizational Transitions: Managing Complex Change* (2nd ed.). Reading, MA: Addison-Wesley.

Benne, K.; & Sheats, P. (1948). "Functional Roles of Group Members." *Journal of Social Issues* 2, 42–47.

Bennis, W. G. (1966). *Changing Organizations.* New York: McGraw-Hill.

Bennis, W. G. (1969). *Organization Development: Its Nature, Origins and Prospects.* Reading, MA: Addison-Wesley.

Bennis, W. G.; & Shepard, H. A. (1956). "A Theory of Group Development." *Human Relations* 9, 415–37.

Bion, W. R. (1959). *Experiences in Groups.* London: Tavistock.

Bradford, L. P.; Gibb, J. R.; & Benne, K. D. (eds.). (1964). *T-Group Theory and Laboratory Method.* New York: John Wiley & Sons.

Chandler, A.P. (1977). *The Visible Hand.* Cambridge, MA: Harvard University Press.

Deal, T. W.; & Kennedy, A. A. (1982). *Corporate Cultures.* Reading, MA: Addison-Wesley.

Durkin, J. E. (ed.). (1981). *Living Groups: Group Psychotherapy and General Systems Theory.* New York: Brunner/Mazel.

Dyer, W. G., Jr. (1986). *Cultural Change in Family Firms.* San Francisco: Josse-Bass.

Feldman, D. C. (1976). "A Contingency Theory of Socialization." *Administration Science Quarterly* 21, 433–52.

Feldman, D. C. (1988). *Managing Careers in Organizations.* Glenview, IL: Scott, Foresman.

Festinger, L. (1957). *A Theory of Cognitive Dissonance.* New York: Harper & Row.

Fleishman, E. A. (1953). "Leadership Climate, Human Relations Training, and Supervisory Behavior." *Personnel Psychology* 6, 205–22.

Fleishman, E. A. (1973). "Twenty Years of Consideration and Structure." In E. A. Fleishman & J. G. Hunt (eds.), *Current Developments in the Study of Leadership* (pp. 1–39). Carbondale: Southern Illinois University Press.

French, W. L.; & Bell, C. H. (1984). *Organization Development* (3rd ed.). Englewood Cliffs, NJ: Prentice Hall.

Frost, P. J.; Moore, L. F.; Louis, M. R.; Lundberg, C. C.; & Martin, J. (eds.). (1985). *Organizational Culture.* Beverly Hills, CA: Sage.

Hanna, D. P. (1988). *Designing Organizations for High Performance.* Reading, MA: Addison-Wesley.

Harris, S. G.; & Sutton, R. I. (1986). "Functions of Parting Ceremonies in Dying Organizations." *Academy of Management Journal* 29, 5–30.

Hebb, D. (1954). "The Social Significance of Animal Studies." In G. Lindzey (ed.), *Handbook of Social Psychology,* Vol. 2, pp. 532–61. Reading, MA: Addison-Wesley.

Heider, F. (1958). *The Psychology of Interpersonal Relations.* New York: John Wiley & Sons.

Hellriegel, D.; & Slocum, J. W., Jr. (1974). "Organizational Climate: Measures, Research, and Contingencies." *Academy of Management Journal,* 17, 255–80.

Hirschhorn, L. (1987). *The Workplace Within.* Cambridge, MA: MIT Press.

Hofstede, G. (1980). *Culture's Consequences.* Beverly Hills, CA: Sage.

Hofstede, G.; & Bond, M. H. (1988). "The Confucius Connection: From Cultural Roots to Economic Growth." *Organizational Dynamics* 16(4), 4–21.

Homans, G. (1950). *The Human Group.* New York: Harcourt Brace Jovanovich.

Jaques, E. (1951). *The Changing Culture of a Factory.* London: Tavistock.

Jones, A. P.; & James, E. R. (1979). "Psychological Climate: Dimensions and Relationships of Individual and Aggregated Work Environment Perceptions." *Organizational Behavior and Human Performance* 23, 201–50.

Jones, G. R. (1986). "Socialization Tactics, Self-Efficacy, and New-Comers' Adjustments to Organizations." *Academy of Management Journal* 29, 262–79.

Katz, D.; & Kahn, R. L. (1966). *The Social Psychology of Organizations.* New York: John Wiley & Sons.

Katz, D.; & Kahn, R. L. (1978). *The Social Psychology of Organizations* (2nd ed.). New York: John Wiley & Sons.

Kets de Vries, M. F. R.; & Miller, D. (1984). *The Neurotic Organization.* San Francisco: Jossey-Bass.

Kets de Vries, M. F. R.; & Miller, D. (1986). "Personality, Culture, and Organization." *Academy of Management Review* 11, 266–79.

Kilmann, R. H. (1984). *Beyond the Quick Fix.* San Francisco: Jossey-Bass.

Kluckhohn, F. R.; & Strodtbeck, F. L. (1961). *Variations in Value Orientations.* New York: Harper & Row.

Lewin, K. (1952). "Group Decision and Social Change." In G. E. Swanson, T. N. Newcomb, & E. L. Hartley (eds.), *Readings in Social Psychology* (rev. ed., pp. 459–73). New York: Holt, Rinehart & Winston.

Lewin, K; Lippitt, R.; & White, R. K. (1939). "Patterns of Aggressive Behavior in Experimentally Created 'Social Climates.'" *Journal of Social Psychology* 10, 271–99.

Likert, R. (1961). *New Patterns of Management.* New York: McGraw-Hill.

Likert, R. (1967). *The Human Organization.* New York: McGraw-Hill.

Lippitt, G. (1982). *Organizational Renewal* (2nd ed.). Englewood Cliffs, NJ: Prentice Hall.

Litwin, G. H.; & Stringer, R. A. (1968). *Motivation and Organizational Climate.* Boston: Harvard Business School, Division of Research.

Louis, M. R. (1981). "A Cultural Perspective on Organizations." *Human Systems Management* 2, 246–58.

Louis, M. R. (1983). "Organizations as Culture Bearing Milieux." In L. R. Pondy, P. J. Frost, G. Morgan, & T. C. Dandridge (eds.), *Organizational Symbolism* (pp. 39–54). Greenwich, CT: JAI Press.

Martin, J. (1982). "Stories and Scripts in Organizational Settings." In A. Hastorf & A. Isen (eds.), *Cognitive Social Psychology.* New York: Elsevier.

Martin, J.; Feldman, M. S.; Hatch, M. J.; & Sitkin, S. (1983). "The Uniqueness Paradox in Organizational Stories." *Administrative Science Quarterly* 28, 438–54.

Martin, J.; & Meyerson, D. (1988). "Organizational Cultures and the Denial, Channeling, and Acknowledgement of Ambiguity." In L. R. Pondy, R. J. Boland, & H. Thomas (eds.), *Managing Ambiguity and Change.* New York: John Wiley & Sons.

Martin, J.; & Powers, M. E. (1983). "Truth or Corporate Propaganda: The Value of a Good War Story." In L. R. Pondy, P. J. Frost, G. Morgan, & T. C. Dandridge (eds.), *Organizational Symbolism* (pp. 93–108). Greenwich, CT: JAI Press.

Martin, J.; & Siehl, C. (1983). "Organizational Culture and Counter-Culture: An Uneasy Symbiosis." *Organizational Dynamics* 12, 52–64.

Menzies, I. E. P. (1960). "A Case Study in the Functioning of Social Systems as a Defense Against Anxiety." *Human Relations,* 13, 95–121.

O'Toole, J. J. (1979). "Corporate and Managerial Cultures." In C.L. Cooper (ed.), *Behavioral Problems in Organizations.* Englewood Cliffs, NJ: Prentice Hall.

Ott, J. S. (1989). *The Organizational Culture Perspective.* Chicago: Dorsey Press.

Ouchi, W. G. (1981). *Theory Z.* Reading, MA: Addison-Wesley.

Pascale, R. T.; & Athos, A.G. (1981). *The Art of Japanese Management.* New York: Simon & Schuster.

Peters, T. J.; & Waterman, R. H., Jr. (1982). *In Search of Excellence.* New York: Harper & Row.

Pettigrew, A. M. (1979). "On Studying Organizational Cultures." *Administrative Science Quarterly,* 24, 570–81.

Pondy, L. R.; Boland, R. J.; & Thomas, H. (1988). *Managing Ambiguity and Change.* New York: John Wiley & Sons.

Pondy, L. R.; Frost, P. J.; Morgan, G.; & Dandridge, T. C. (eds.). (1983). *Organizational Symbolism.* Greenwich, CT: JAI Press.

Rice, A.K. (1963). *The Enterprise and its Environment.* London: Tavistock.

Ritti, R. R.; & Funkhouser, G. R. (1987). *The Ropes to Skip and the Ropes to Know* (3rd ed.). New York: John Wiley & Sons.

Roethlisberger, F. J.; & Dickson, W. J. (1939). *Management and the Worker.* Cambridge, MA: Harvard University Press.

Schall, M. S. (1983). "A Communication-Rules Approach to Organizational Culture." *Administrative Science Quarterly,* 28, 557–81.

Schein, E. H. (1965). *Organizational Psychology.* Englewood Cliffs, NJ: Prentice Hall.

Schein, E. H. (1968). "Organizational Socialization and the Profession of Management." *Industrial Management Review (MIT)* 9, 1–15.

Schein, E. H. (1969). *Process Consultation.* Reading, MA: Addison-Wesley.

Schein, E. H. (1978). *Career Dynamics.* Reading, MA: Addison-Wesley.

Schein, E. H. (1983). "The Role of the founder in Creating Organizational Culture." *Organizational Dynamics* 12, 13–28.

Schein, E. H. (1985a). *Organizational Culture and Leadership.* San Francisco: Jossey-Bass.

Schein, E. H. (1985b). "Organizational Culture: Skill, Defense Mechanism or Addiction?" In F. R. Brush & J. B. Overmier (eds.), *Affect, Conditioning, and Cognition* (pp. 315–23). Hillsdale, NJ: Erlbaum.

Schein, E. H. (1987a). *The Clinical Perspective in Fieldwork.* Beverly Hills, CA: Sage.

Schein, E. H. (1987b). *Process Consultation* (Vol. 2). Reading, MA: Addison-Wesley.

Schein, E. H. (1988). *Process Consultation* (rev. ed.). Reading, MA: Addison-Wesley.

Schein, E. H.; & Bennis, W. G. (1965). *Personal and Organizational Change through Group Methods.* New York: John Wiley & Sons.

Schneider, B. (1975). "Organizational Climate: An Essay." *Personnel Psychology* 28, 447–79.

Schneider, B.; & Reichers, A. E. (1983). "On the Etiology of Climates." *Personnel Psychology* 36, 19–40.

Smircich, L.; & Calas, M. B. (1987). "Organizational Culture: A Critical Assessment." In F. M. Jablin, L. L. Putnam, K. H. Roberts, & L. W. Porter (eds.), *Handbook of Organizational Communication* (pp. 228–63). Beverly Hills, CA: Sage.

Tagiuri, R.; & Litwin, G. H. (eds.). (1968). *Organizational Climate: Exploration of a Concept.* Boston: Harvard Business School, Division of Research.

Trice, H.; & Beyer, J. (1984). "Studying Organizational Cultures through Rites and Ceremonials." *Academy of Management Review* 9, 653–69.

Trist, E. L.; Higgin, G. W.; Murray, H.; & Pollock, A. B. (1963). *Organizational Choice.* London: Tavistock.

Van Maanen, J. (1976). "Breaking in: Socialization to Work." In R. Dubin (ed.), *Handbook of Work, Organization and Society* (pp. 67–130). Chicago: Rand McNally.

Van Maanen, J. (1977). "Experiencing Organizations." In J. Van Maanen (ed.), *Organizational Careers: Some New Perspectives* (pp. 15–45). New York: John Wiley & Sons.

Van Maanen, J. (1978). "People Processing: Strategies of Organizational Socialization." *Organizational Dynamics,* 7, 18–36.

Van Maanen, J. (1988). *Tales of the Field.* Chicago: University of Chicago Press.

Van Maanen, J. (1984). "Occupational Communities: Culture and Control in Organizations." In B. M. Staw & L. L. Cummings (eds.), *Research in Organizational Behavior* (Vol. 6). Greenwich, CT: JAI Press.

Van Maanen, J.; & Schein, E. H. (1979). "Toward a Theory of Organizational Socializations." In B. M. Staw & L. L. Cummings (eds.), *Research in Organizational Behavior* (Vol. 1, pp. 204–64). Greenwich, CT: JAI Press.

Walton, R. (1987). *Innovating to Compete.* San Francisco: Jossey-Bass.

Werner, H. (1940). *Comparative Psychology of Mental Development.* New York: Follett.

Westney, D. E. (1987). *Imitation and Innovation.* Cambridge, MA: Harvard University Press.

Wilkins, A. L. (1983). "Organizational Stories as Symbols Which Control the Organizations." In L. R. Pondy, P. J. Frost, G. Morgan, & T. C. Dandridge (eds.), *Organizational Symbolism* (pp. 81–91). Greenwich, CT: JAI Press.

Wilkins, A. L.; & Ouchi, W. G. (1983). "Efficient Cultures: Exploring the Relationship between Culture and Organizational Performance." *Administrative Science Quarterly* 28, 468–81.

READING 12
SOCIOTECHNICAL SYSTEM PRINCIPLES AND
GUIDELINES: PAST AND PRESENT

William M. Fox

The sociotechnical systems (STS) approach is devoted to the effective blending of both the technical and social systems of an organization. These two aspects must be considered interdependently, because arrangements that are optimal for one may not be optimal for the other and trade-offs are often required. Thus, for effective organization design, there is need for both dual focus and joint optimization. This article traces the development of STS from the presentation of its first principles by Eric Trist, its leading founder, who was guided by earlier systems thinking, research on participation, and the action research work of Kurt Lewin, to the present, including discussion of adaptations and refinements that have enhanced its applicability to nonmanufacturing organizations. The approach has more relevance today than ever before, as organizational personnel seek more fruitful means of empowerment and as their organizations strive for greater productivity and viability in increasingly turbulent environments.

In 1946, the newly nationalized British coal industry was doing poorly. Productivity had not increased sufficiently to compensate for increases in costly mechanization; labor disputes were frequent and absenteeism was running at about 20%, despite improvements in working conditions.

Ken Bamforth, a postgraduate Tavistock Institute Fellow and former coal miner, gained ready access for himself and one of the Institute's founders, Eric Trist, to observe a highly successful departure from current mining practice: The use of relatively autonomous work groups that interchanged roles and shifts and managed themselves with a minimum of supervision. They found that, in effect, the miners had "rediscovered" a successful, small-group approach that had been used before the advent of mechanization.

Further investigation suggested that most of the industry's problems had resulted from the introduction of significant changes in the technical aspects of production *without* adequate attention to their appropriateness for a particular physical environment or their impact on social structure and needs. Inadvertently, this type of oversight had been encouraged by the post–World War II human relations movement through its emphasis on personal and group development practices that largely shunned the technical aspects of work systems.

These findings provided a revelation for Trist; one that occurs rarely in a lifetime. He suddenly visualized a new paradigm of work: one that would effectively blend the requirements of *both* the technical and social systems. He then set about formulating the sociotechnical systems concept and approach, guided by earlier systems thinking, Lewin's ideas, and his own research. He first presented the new paradigm in 1950 to the British Psychological Society via a paper titled "The Relations of Social and Technical Systems in Coal-Mining" (Trist, 1981; E. L. Trist, personal communication, March 1988).[1]

In addition to Trist's continuing efforts, many others contributed to the subsequent development and refinement of sociotechnical theory and practice. Among them, Trist regards Fred Emery as his most noteworthy co-pioneer. He also cites

Source: William M. Fox, "Sociotechnical System Principles and Guidelines: Past and Present" in *Journal of Applied Behavioral Science* (vol. 31, no. 1) pp. 91–105, copyright © 1995 by NTL Institute for applied Behavioral Science. Reprinted by permission of Sage Publications, Inc.

Louis Davis, Philip Herbst, Cal Pava, A. K. Rice, Gerald Susman, Einar Thorsrud, Hans van Beinum, Richard Walton, and Marvin Weisbord as significant contributors (E. L. Trist, personal communication, March 1988).

Although there is no single, unequivocal set of sociotechnical principles and practices, I will consider those that most knowledgeable researchers and practitioners today agree are highly relevant to the approach. In addition, I will look at various ways in which this approach is being adapted to nonmanufacturing work environments.

Analysis Guidelines

Dual Focus on Two, Interdependent, Open Systems.
The term *sociotechnical systems* (STS) reflects the goal of integrating the social requirements of people doing the work with the technical requirements needed to keep the work systems viable with regard to their environments. These two aspects must be considered interdependently, because arrangements that are optimal for one may not be optimal for the other, and trade-offs are often required. Thus there is a need for both *dual focus* and *joint optimization*.

To the extent that an organization is effective and efficient in creating and distributing products or services, it justifies the human, material, and informational resources that the environment provides. In order for it to survive and develop, the systems involved must remain open to, and interact constructively with, their environments.

The Technological System.
This system comprises the materials, machines, territory, and processes used to convert inputs to outputs. It not only sets limits to what can be done, it creates demands that must be accommodated by the internal organization and by end objectives.

At any time, the technological system may be subject to stresses that arise in the external environment. The extent to which it can tolerate required input and output variations is largely a function of its flexibility. In turn, the quality of this flexibility is an important determiner of the self-regulating properties of the organization (Emery, 1959, pp. 4–5).

Among the important features of the technological system (based on Emery, 1959, pp. 9–15) are the following:

- The characteristics of the material being processed in terms of encouraging or discouraging uncontrollable variation in the labor requirements of the production process.

- The immediate physical work setting in terms of such factors as temperature, light, noise, dust or dirt, and orderliness. Does the setting create over- or understimulation? Are dysfunctional conditions reasonably avoidable?

- The spatio-temporal distribution of machines, workers, and processes. Are operations performed simultaneously or sequentially? On one shift or across several shifts? How are machines and workers physically dispersed? These factors will influence the ease with which interdependent activities can be supplied, informed, coordinated, and maintained.

- The level of mechanization or automation; that is, the contribution made by machines relative to workers in processing inputs into outputs. Changes in this dimension of technology will frequently negate other dimensions or enhance their criticalness.

- The grouping of unit operations (those that transform the material or product) into *production phases* to facilitate the identification of needed changes in coordination and in knowledge and skill demands.

- The identification of necessary as opposed to optional operations and the extent to which these operations demand attention, effort, and/or special skill.

- The nature and placement of repair and maintenance operations that will most economically reduce downtime.

- The nature of supply operations that can maintain planned rates of production in the face of unplanned variations in the transfer of materials from and to the external environment.

The Social System. The social structure—comprising occupational roles—has, to a large extent, been created and institutionalized by the operation of the technological system (Trist & Bamforth, 1951, p. 5).

Among the important features of the social system (based on Emery, 1959, pp. 16, 19–21; Trist, 1971; Trist, 1981, p. 23; Trist & Bamforth, 1951, pp. 14–15) are the following:

- Whether work roles are organized so that workers are cooperative rather than competitive with each other.

- Whether work roles are organized so that workers view an end result as their responsibility or as someone else's responsibility.

- Whether workers are made jointly responsible for how supportive services and implements are delivered or are provided separately and unilaterally to each worker.

- The extent to which *key variances* (those that significantly affect the quantity or quality or operating cost or social cost of production) are imported or exported across the social system boundary rather than being controlled by the workers, supervisors, and managers directly concerned.

- The possibilities for complex and simultaneous interdependencies among the workers to provide for task accomplishment in less time and for continuity in the face of individual failure.

- How each worker's role is experienced; not only in terms of its inherent attractiveness but also in terms of perceptions of dependence, pay equity, subordination, self worth, trust, constraining factors, and isolation with regard to others.

- The extent to which task interdependencies are coordinated in terms of the social relations that are required by the task rather than in terms of social relations that develop for other reasons (such as friendship).

- The presence of personal worker goals and task interdependencies that are threatened by, or are not adequately handled by, formal organizational provisions. The presence of formal overspecification as well as underspecification.

Emery (1987) observes that the critical dimensions of work organization have to do with control and coordination:

> In any work setting, regardless of the technology, the requirements for control and coordination can be determined and then there is, in practically every instance, a choice open to management about how much of that control and coordination is left to the people actually performing the activities....In 1974 we were able to demonstrate in some detail that this same "organizational choice" exists even in the design of maximum security prisons. (p. 4)

With regard to this choice, Emery describes experimentation with an unusual form of worker participation: The owner-manager of a plant in Melbourne, Australia, invited some 40 employees to manage the plant. The workers (for the most part, highly skilled machinists) decided to rotate service on a managing committee by periodically drawing names from a hat, rather than by election. Subsequently, two other Australian plants tried this idea of rotating membership on joint labor-management planning committees through the drawing lots.

Apparently, these three "experiments" were quite successful. Both management and the workers decided that this was the most effective way to sensitize all workers to the problems and dynamics of running the plants (Emery, 1987, p. 6).

As noted by Trist (1981),

> The technical and social systems are *independent* of each other in the sense that the former follows the laws of the natural sciences while the latter follows the laws of the human sciences and is a purposeful system.

Yet they are *correlative* in that one requires the other for the *transformation* of an input into an output, which comprises the functional task of a work system (p. 24)

In some organizations, such as regulative ones, the sociotechnical aspects have secondary instrumentality: They are primarily concerned with instilling, changing, or maintaining values. Those aspects that are primarily sociotechnical are directly dependent on material means for their outputs.

The technical and social systems may spontaneously reorganize to become more or less heterogeneous and complex and achieve a steady state at an operable level. They possess the characteristic of *equi-finality:* the ability to achieve a steady state from different initial conditions and in different ways. This is a concept from systems theory. Typically, these systems grow by processes of internal elaboration. Because both are open systems that interact with external environments, management is confronted with managing both internal systems and external environments (see Bertalanffy, 1950; Emery, 1959, pp. 3, 6; Herbst, 1954; Trist, 1981, pp. 11–12).

Three Levels of Analysis.   Drawing further from systems theory, sociotechnical systems design activity is based on three levels of analysis (Trist, 1981, pp. 6, 11).

The Primary Work System.   This system is associated with a whole and meaningful piece of work; a set of activities that make up a functioning whole in an identifiable and bounded subsystem of an organization. It may comprise one or several face-to-face groups, along with support, specialist, and management-representative personnel and relevant equipment and resources. The system can provide reliable information to the group as to the adequacy of performance.

The most satisfying and efficient primary work system comprises the smallest number of people that can perform a whole task while satisfying the social and psychological needs of system members as well as the performance requirements of the organization (see Hackman & Oldham, 1980, pp. 171–172; Rice, 1958, p. 36; Trist, 1981, p. 24).

The Whole Organization System.   This system comprises plants or equivalent, self-standing workplaces; an entire corporation or public agency.

The Macrosocial System.   This system comprises multiple organizational systems in community and industrial sectors; it could be an institution operating at the overall level of a society.

The target system, and the adjoining systems, should be considered in the context of the organization's *general management system* with regard to the impact of policies or development plans. A key reason for the failure of a primary, new-design work group is lack of support in the surrounding organizational milieu.

At the organization level, the social system is considered in terms of the functions of governing as well as those of production and servicing. Relations among top managers provide the strategic solidarity for the organization.

It is at this level that goals must be set that appropriately reflect organizational capabilities in conjunction with the demands of the external environment. And only at this level do managers have the potential power for aligning the organization's structural arrangements and values.

As a corollary of this, the success of human resources management as an integrating function is dependent on top-management solidarity.

The solidarity of both workers and management is prerequisite to a high level of solidarity in the organization as a whole. The communication of purpose, knowledge, requests, and values among organizational members plays a critical role in the development of shared objectives, norms, and feelings of belonging that underlie loyalty and commitment to common cause (based on Ancona, 1989; O'Reilly & Flatt, 1989; Rice & Trist, 1952; Trist, 1981, p. 35; Tushman, Virany, & Romanelli, 1989; Wilson, 1957).

With regard to the macrosocial system, Trist asserts that a different larger environment has evolved: "The new environment is called *the turbulent field* in which large competing organizations, all acting independently in diverse directions, produce unanticipated and dissonant consequences" (1981, p. 39).

He suggests that organizations can best adapt to this environmental turbulence by identifying shared ideals to guide them in fashioning new objectives and their related goals.

Other Principles and Practices

- The design of a work system should use an *action research* approach, an approach that was contributed to systems theory by Kurt Lewin. It entails collaborative analysis, design, and implementation by those directly concerned—workers, supervisors, and specialists—in seeking the *dual optimization* of the needs of the technological and the social systems (see Trist, 1981, p. 10).

Trist underscores the importance of this never-ending design objective of dual optimization:

> Attempts to optimize for either the technical or social system alone will result in the suboptimization of the socio-technical whole....The distinctive characteristics of each must be respected else their *contradictions* will intrude and their *complementarities* will remain unrealized. (1981, p. 24)

With regard to Trist's concern about contradictions, Campion and Thayer (1985) found that satisfaction of *only* the motivational aspects of the social system (as embodied in the Hackman and Oldham Job Characteristics Theory, 1980) can significantly decrease efficiency and reliability while providing an expected increase in worker satisfaction.

- In designing a work system, comply with the principle of *redundancy of functions* (proliferation of functions within the work group—multiskilling the individual) rather than the traditional principle of *redundancy of parts* (proliferation of individuals performing the same specific function) to provide for flexibility, innovative potential, adaptation to rapid change, and enhanced worker satisfaction (based on Emery, 1967).
- There should be adherence to the principle of minimum critical specifications: Give the

design team for a lower level sociotechnical system only the larger system requirements (boundary conditions) that they must work within, leaving as many design decisions as possible to those closest to the work (based on Herbst, 1974).

- An important consideration is the optimal length of the work cycle (one study suggests a range of 1 to 1 1/2 hours) (see Trist, 1981, p. 31).
- Work roles associated with interdependent tasks should be defined so as to enhance mutual support. The tasks should be so organized or rewarded so as to facilitate the identification of part-tasks with the whole.
- In a stable sociotechnical system, knowledge that is relevant to cooperative performance under varying circumstances should be incorporated in the role system. Then, knowledge of the role system can inform a worker of what to expect of others and of what will be expected of him or her.
- Knowledge of the role system and prevention of harmful misperceptions are facilitated by role rotation, and role rotation is facilitated by the use of a multiskill/skill-based pay system.
- A self-managing group that has some scope for setting standards and ongoing goals, has some responsibility for auxiliary and preparatory tasks, and is characterized by a wide sharing of the skills needed for its tasks is more likely than a traditional group to
  - —provide group members with optimal arousal and feelings of "being in control"
  - —induce group members to set goals and to strive toward group objectives
  - —produce superior results and group-member satisfaction (as the result of more *key variances* being controlled by the group)
  - —adapt well to unexpected conditions and provide a higher degree of continuity in performance (such a group being a learning system that extends its "decision space" as its capabilities increase) (based on Emery, 1959, pp. 24–26, 50; Trist, 1981, p. 34).

In view of the developmental dynamics embodied in the material presented above, the organization must provide opportunities for individual advancement and employment security (so that workers do not perceive that they are being "dead-ended" or that they are being invited to work themselves out of a job). We see, also, that the *sharing of power* is a generic feature of sociotechnical systems.

In this regard, Trist feels that, at some point, *gain-sharing*—sharing the added material fruits made possible by the developing partnership between workers and managers—is necessary to prevent perceptions of inequity on the part of the workers. He regards this as one of the requirements of sound, sociotechnical systems design (E. L. Trist, personal communication, March 1988).

In some installations, an elected team leader who works alongside his or her teammates is given responsibility for facilitating group self-management, training group members, and procuring needed materials, equipment, and support services.

In addition, a coordinator may be appointed by management to assist the group (or groups) and provide liaison with other groups. Based on their field study, Manz and Sims (1987) report that the coordinator's most important contribution to the group resides in encouraging the following: self-reinforcement, self-observation/evaluation, self-expectation, rehearsal, and goal setting (see also Trist, 1981, p. 31; Weisbord, 1987, p. 334).

When only one supervisory position is used, there must be a shift away from traditional management to a greater focus on the management of boundary relationships and the provision of coaching and support to the group toward the enhancement of its self-management.

The following table provides a dramatic contrast of sociotechnical concepts with traditional concepts.

Steps in Data Collection and Analysis

Taylor, Gustavson, and Carter (1986) observe that much of the success of the sociotechnical model is due to its reliance upon a structured process, as outlined below, for analyzing and implementing operational improvements.

Systems Scan. The first phase of a *systems scan* is grounded in the following types of questions: What is the organization's mission (What values does it create and distribute to justify itself)? What managerial philosophy and organizational values underlie this mission? What relationships does the organization have with various stakeholders and the larger environment?

The next phase relates to reconciling agreement about what is and what is likely to be with agreement about what is most desired by organizational stakeholders and at the same time is viable with regard to the outside environment.

The *search conference* provides a useful means for implementing these phases of a systems scan. It was originated by Trist and Emery in 1959 (Weisbord, 1987, p. 282; see also Morley & Trist, 1981). Meaningful mission and philosophy statements are products of this activity.

The next phase of the systems scan has to do with determining existing inputs, outputs, and system boundaries—both physical and technological. The purpose is to identify problems, needs, and opportunities for improvement.

Technical Analysis. Sociotechnical analysis defines technology in terms of inputs and outputs, rather than by tools, processes, or techniques. When input and output boundaries are defined, unit operations can be determined (the output of each unit operation being the physical or informational transformation of input).

This approach assures that technical systems will be analyzed apart from the jobs and work of people, and apart from supervisory systems and other control systems. A *unit-operations flow chart* is a product of this activity, and one of the issues explored is a possible reduction in the number of unit operations.

Next, all product variances—other than those representing human error or breakdowns in the technical process itself—are recorded for each unit operation. The *key variances*—those that have an impact most importantly on quantity, quality, or costs—are identified through the construction of a *key-variance matrix table*.

Then, through the preparation of a *table of variance control,* key variances are examined to determine

TABLE 1

Comparison of the sociotechnical model with the traditional model

Old	*New*
Technology first	Joint optimization of social-technical systems
People as extensions of machines	People as complements to machines
People as expendable spare parts	People as a resource to be developed
Maximum task breakdown, simple, narrow skills	Optimal task grouping, multiple, broad skills
External controls: procedures, supervisors, specialist staffs	Internal controls: self-regulating subsystems
More organization levels, autocratic style: unilateral goal setting, assignment of workers	Fewer levels, participative style: bilateral goal setting, selection of workers
Competitive gamesmanship	Collaboration, collegiality
Organization's purposes only (often with poor understanding/acceptance at lower levels)	Members' and society's purposes also (with good understanding/acceptance at lower levels): shared vision and philosophy
Frequent alienation: "It's only a job"	Commitment: "It's *my* job, group, and organization"
Tendency toward low risk taking, maladaptation	Tendency toward innovation, adaptation
Less individual development opportunity and employment security	More individual development opportunity and employment security

Based on Trist (1981).

the manner in which they are controlled—by whom, through what actions, and with what information. Are they controlled where they arise, by appropriate personnel, and in a timely, effective, and efficient manner?

Social Analysis. A foremost concern of social analysis is called *focal-role analysis*: determination of the role expectations and work-related interactions of those in positions most involved with the control of key variances. This kind of analysis entails mapping patterns of cooperation and coordination among those with focal roles and others within and outside the work process.

Another aspect of social analysis involves examination of the relationships among the work-related interactions of focal persons and four "survival criteria:" sound key-variance control, adaptation to the external environment, integration of in-system people activities, and long-term development.

This examination is aided by construction of a *grid of social relations*. Then, with data from this social grid, focal-role interactions can be mapped in a *focal-role network* that indicates their frequency, direction of contact, and function served.

Quality-of-Working-Life Considerations. Through the use of action research, organizational members and other stakeholders influence design solutions through their participation in the analyses described above about organizational mission, management philosophy, organizational values, and the design (or redesign) of work systems. As far as is feasible, their preferences are accommodated. In addition, the nature and rate of transitional activities to implement a new design reflect both individual and group training and development needs.

Ideally, the sociotechnical systems design process should be iterative or never ending. The question "How can we improve upon the way we operate?" should always remain open. To a large extent, maintenance of this *action-research-based process* is more important than any given design solution.[2]

Limitations and New Directions

The STS concepts presented above have ably guided improvements in the design and redesign of many work systems, both here and abroad. However, most of this successful experience has been with well-defined linear systems rather than with the growing number of ill-defined, nonlinear systems that are characterized by entwined (and often-iterative) multiple-conversion processes.

Well-defined linear systems are characterized by programmed tasks that adhere to a sequential conversion process of "input" to "output." The absence of this property in nonlinear systems makes it difficult to separate different conversion flows into well-bounded entities through the use of such tools as the variance matrix (Pava, 1986, pp. 204–205).

Another property of some nonlinear systems is the absence of an explicit input point. Taylor (1990) describes this aspect with regard to professional work in a nonroutine system: "The throughput is accumulated knowledge and persuasive argument. This throughput has no concrete starting point ... in contrast to other intangible delivery systems, such as service systems, which have requests as inputs" (p. 11).

In addition to this qualification about the use of the matrix, another is presented by Sitter and Hertog (1990). They point out that redesign should not be based on *current* matrix data, but rather upon insight about the quantity and quality of variance in a future approach that takes into account emergent opportunities for improved variance control.

> The designers' goal should be to design an architecture of structure sustaining and reinforcing the development of interactive relationships which support and reinforce each other with respect to all functional requirements such as flexibility, delivery time, throughput time, product quality, innovative capacity, pollution control, quality of work and industrial relations. (p. 8)

On the other hand, Pava (1986, p. 205) discusses how charting independencies in a variance matrix can reveal whether there will be a sufficiently distinct clustering of variances to guide the partitioning of the work system. When used this way, the variance matrix serves as a diagnostic tool for determining the extent of the nonlinear nature of the system.

In addition to Pava (1986), others—such as Sitter and Hertog (1990), and Taylor (1986)—stress the need for increased research to broaden the applicability of STS design concepts. They decry the tendency of some STS consultants who treat the use of self-managing or autonomous groups as a "standard solution" for all occasions rather than as a carefully arrived at design choice based on an organization's special characteristics.

In addressing this standard solution mistake, Pava (1986) notes:

> Many professionals doing nonroutine tasks are extensively trained specialists.... all their expectations about work activities, career advancement, and reward emphasize individual contributions.... Because specialization is extreme and not highly transferable, shared skills are less likely to be a source of cohesion, making autonomous work groups an impractical solution (pp. 205–206).

New Approaches to Technical/Social Analysis. For complex, nonlinear situations, Pava (1986, pp. 206–208) suggests an additional type of analysis: determination of the quality of interpersonal and group "deliberations" (encounters, meetings, personal reflections) about problematic issues facing the organization. He conceptualizes "discretionary coalitions" of people associated with the various deliberations, and the determination of a "role network" of persons for each issue. Such analysis includes determining the incidence and locus of informed trade-offs—as well as barriers to such trade-offs—and the absence of ritual posturing and arbitrary battles.

Pava sees the technique of "blockmodeling" as a promising analytical tool for guiding these determinations (see 1986, pp. 206–208). He points out that such analysis can set the stage for change agents to

> acknowledge and charter major deliberations . . . delineate responsibility within each coalition . . . and identify technical enhancements . . . that assist discretionary coalitions engaged in major deliberations. . . . In linear work systems, this emergent configuration has been designated the autonomous work group organization. In nonlinear work systems, this new template is a *recticular organization,* which is characterized by a fluid distribution of information and authority that shifts as required (Pava, 1986, pp. 208–209).

Another innovation, the integration of *cause maps* and *social network analysis* to produce a *juxtaposition matrix,* has been developed by Nelson and

Mathews (1991). They point out that the former two are useful for operationalizing the concepts of organizational complexity and structure in a concrete, practical manner and that the latter matrix can identify where we may expect interdependence in an organization to be highest. Also, they point out that the matrix should be useful for estimating new-design effects.

To increase efficiency and effectiveness, Sitter and Hertog (1990) discuss the design strategy of *reducing required variation* (while increasing options for process variations through such means as flexible automation, integrated tasks, and multiskilled personnel). As a means for doing this, they propose *deconcentrating structure* by a first step they call *parallelization*: splitting the production system into subsystems. This causes an exponential reduction in the input complexity of a system and thus a reduction in the amplifying effects of variations in the system.

The next step they propose is the selective clustering of performance operations in these parallel flows or subsystems into segments with a minimum of interfaces, to reduce internal variation further. They call this step *segmentation*. The performance functions to be clustered are those with a maximum of mutual interdependence.

As the above measures reduce variety, they reduce the need for control, because it is variety that creates this need. This is why the design of production structures should precede the design of control structures and should be done top down, and the allocation of control activity should be done bottom up. In summary, "debureaucratization" involves moving from complex structures comprising simple tasks to simple structures comprising complex tasks (Sitter & Hertog, 1990, pp. 12–16, 19).

Last, in their report on contemporary STS design modeling in the Netherlands, van Eijnatten, Hoevenaars, and Rutte (1992) discuss a multilevel method of integrating task design and organization design.

Current Research Sites. Research on the adaptation and further development of STS concepts and practices is being pursued by various organizations and research centers. Among the organizations in North America are Alcan, the American Productivity Center in Houston, AT&T, Best Foods, Clark Equipment, Cummins Engine, Digital Equipment Company, Exxon, Ford, General Foods, General Motors, Harman International, Hewlett Packard, Inland Steel, LTV Steel, Mead Paper, Proctor and Gamble, Shell Oil, Sherwin-Williams, Tektronix, TRW, Weyerhauser, the Work in America Institute in New York, Xerox, Zilog, and various U.S. and Canadian government agencies, such as the Total Quality Management program of the U.S. Defense Department.

Among the organizations abroad that are conducting research are the Dutch Maastricht Economic Research Institute on Innovation and Technology (MERIT), the more than 100 companies and public institutions that are involved in the Swedish Work Environment Fund's LOM program, and the Work Research Institute in Oslo, Norway.

Campus researchers are now active at Case Western Reserve University, Cornell, the Fielding Institute, and the University of Toronto, as well as Pennsylvania State University's Harrisburg campus Center for Managing Technology and Organizational Change, Sonoma State University's Center for Studies on Human Dignity in Organizations, Texas Technological University's Center for Productivity and QWL, the University of California at Los Angeles's Center for Quality of Working Life, the University of Indiana's Center for Quality and Productivity Improvement, the University of Michigan's National Quality of Work Center, and the University of Southern California's Center for Effective Organizations (Cummings & Huse, 1989, pp. 264–270; Engelstad, 1990, p. 8; Sitter & Hertog, 1990, p. 5; Taylor, 1990, pp. 4–12; J. C. Taylor, personal communication, November 1990).

Conclusion

Initially, sociotechnical principles and practices were developed for, and were applied to, routine, linear work systems. Consequently, they were less useful for dealing with the nonroutine office work of managers and professionals.

For example, the absence of an explicit input point, and/or the absence of a clear-cut input to output conversion system, makes it difficult to separate different conversion flows into well-bounded entities through the use of the *variance matrix*. However, as Pava points out, the matrix can still be a useful diagnostic tool for determining the nonlinear nature of the system.

In addition, Pava (1986, pp. 205–206) qualifies the use of the sociotech principle of redundancy of functions (the multiskilling of individuals). He points out that it is less applicable to professional personnel in that their in-depth areas of specialization are not readily diffused in a group. In fact, at times the traditional principle of redundancy of parts (proliferation of individuals) may be preferable as a means of enhancing an organization's innovative potential.

Also, the creation of a recticular organization (characterized by a fluid distribution of information and authority that changes as required) may be more appropriate than the use of the STS autonomous work group in some nonlinear work systems. Still, Cohen and Ledford (1994) and Teram (1991) report that self-managing groups are more effective than traditionally managed groups in a variety of nonmanufacturing work settings.

Clearly, a major revolution is not required to broaden the applicability of STS principles. Pava (1986) observes that

> modifying the practices employed in STS design to include nonlinear work systems is consistent with the essential precepts of STS design: open systems analysis, a best match of social and technical subsystems, redundant function over redundant parts, systemic interrelationships between design factors, self-design, and minimum critical specifications. (p. 211)

In fact, such broadening has already occurred. Taylor (1990, pp. 10, 13) reports more than 28 currently operative STS designs or redesigns in the United States for noncontinuous process technologies such as dimensional manufacturing work, transaction processing work, service work, nonroutine work, and professional work.

Today, as organizational personnel seek more fruitful means of empowerment and their organizations strive for greater productivity and viability

in increasingly turbulent environments, we may well conclude that the STS movement—given its fundamental strengths and demonstrated adaptability—has more relevance than ever before.

Endnotes

1. As a matter of interest, the validity of STS principles for coal mining was reaffirmed by Winterton (1994).
2. This whole section on data collection and analysis has drawn heavily upon the presentation by Taylor, Gustavson, and Carter (1986, pp. 158–163).

References

Ancona, D. G. (1989, August 13–16). *Top management teams: Preparing for the revolution*. Paper presented at the annual meetings of the Academy of Management, Washington, DC.

Bertalanffy, L. (1950). The theory of open systems in physics and biology. *Science, 3*, 23–29.

Campion, M. A., & Thayer, P. W. (1985). Development and field evaluation of an interdisciplinary measure of job design. *Journal of Applied Psychology, 70*, 29–43.

Cohen, S. G., & Ledford, G. E., Jr. (1994). The effectiveness of self-managing teams: A quasi-experiment. *Human Relations, 47*, 13–43.

Cummings, T. G., & Huse, E. F. (1989). *Organizational development and change*. New York: West.

Emery, F. E. (1959). *Characteristics of socio-technical systems* (Document No. 527). London: Tavistock Institute of Human Relations.

Emery, F. E. (1967). The next thirty years: Concepts, methods and anticipations. *Human Relations, 20*, 199–237.

Emery, F. E. (1987, June 15–19). *Paper No. 24*. Paper presented at Einar Thorsrud memorial symposium and workshop: Strategies for work and learning—1999. Work Research Institute, Oslo, Norway.

Engelstad, P. H. (1990, August 12–15). *The evolution of network strategies in action research supported sociotechnical redesign programs in Scandinavia*. Symposium presentation at Academy of Management meetings, San Francisco.

Hackman, J. R. & Oldham, G. R. (1980). *Work redesign*. Menlo Park, CA: Addison-Wesley.

Herbst, P. G. (1954). The analyses of social flow systems. *Human Relations, 7,* 327–336.

Herbst, P. G. (1974). *Socio-technical design.* London: Tavistock Institute of Human Relations.

Manz, C. C., & Sims, H. P. (1987). Leading workers to lead themselves: The external leadership of self-managing work teams. *Administrative Science Quarterly, 32,* 106–128.

Morley, D., & Trist, E. (1981). *Children: Our number one resource, a report on the Saskatchewan search conference on day care.* Unpublished manuscript, York University, Faculty of Environmental Studies, Toronto.

Nelson, R. E., & Mathews, K. M. (1991). Cause maps and social network analysis in organizational diagnosis. *Journal of Applied Behavioral Science, 27,* 379–397.

O'Reilly, C. A., & Flatt S. (1989, August 13–16). *Executive team demography, organizational innovation, and firm performance.* Paper presented at the annual meetings of the Academy of Management, Washington, DC.

Pava, C. (1986). Redesigning sociotechnical systems design: Concepts and methods for the 1990s. *Journal of Applied Behavioral Science, 22,* 201–221.

Rice, A. K. (1958). *Productivity and social organization: The Ahmedabad experiment.* London: Tavistock Institute of Human Relations.

Rice, A. K., & Trist, E. L. (1952). Institutional and sub-institutional determinants of change in labour turnover. *Human Relations, 5,* 347–372.

Sitter, L. U. de, & Hertog, J. F. de. (1990, August 12–15). *Simple organizations, complex jobs: The Dutch sociotechnical approach.* Paper presented at the annual meetings of the Academy of Management, San Francisco.

Taylor, J. C. (1986). Long-term sociotechnical systems change in a computer operations department. *Journal of Applied Behavioral Science, 22,* 303–313.

Taylor, J. C. (1990, August 12–15). *Two decades of sociotechnical systems in North America.* Symposium paper presented at the annual meetings of the Academy of Management, San Francisco.

Taylor, J. C., Gustavson, P., & Carter, W. (1986). Integrating the social and technical systems of organizations. In D. D. Davis and Associates (Eds)., *Managing technological innovation* (pp. 154–186). San Francisco: Jossey-Bass.

Teram, E. (1991). Interdisciplinary teams and the control of clients: A sociotechnical perspective. *Human Relations, 44,* 343–356.

Trist, E. L. (1971). Critique of scientific management in terms of socio-technical theory. *Prakseologia, 39–40,* 159–174.

Trist, E. L. (1981). *The evolution of soci-technical systems: A conceptual framework and action research program* (Occasional paper No. 2). Ontario, Canada: Ontario Quality of Working Life Centre.

Trist, E. L. & Bamforth, K. (1951). Social and psychological consequences of longwall coal mining. *Human Relations, 4,* 3–38.

Tushman, M. L., Virany, B., & Romanelli, E. (1989, August 13–16). *Effects of CEO and executive team succession on subsequent organization performance.* Paper presented at the annual meetings of the Academy of Management, Washington, DC.

van Eijnatten, F. M., Hoevenaars, A. M., & Rutte, C. G. (1992). Holistic and participative (re)design: Contemporary STSD modeling in the Netherlands. In Dian M. Hosking & N. Anderson (Eds.), *Organizational change and innovation: Psychological perspectives and practices in Europe* (pp. 187–207). London: Routledge.

Weisbord, M. R. (1987). *Productive workplaces: Organizing for dignity, meaning, and community.* San Francisco: Jossey-Bass.

Wilson, A. T. (1957). *General management and the personnel function: Research report to Unilever, Ltd.* London: Tavistock Institute of Human Relations.

Winterton, J. (1994). Social and technological characteristics of coal face work: A temporal and spatial analysis. *Human Relations, 47,* 89–118.

III   FUNDAMENTAL INTERVENTIONS

Part III is central to this volume because it includes fairly detailed descriptions of many interventions that tend to be widely used in contemporary OD practice. Techniques for use in team building, intergroup activities, survey feedback, and other interventions are described. Although diagnostics activities underlie all of these interventions, diagnosis is so fundamental that additional attention is paid to it.

The introduction to Part III first defines intervention, then looks at different ways of classifying interventions, and then looks at diagnosis as a special, but pervasive, kind of intervention on OD. A brief comment on each of the essays then follows.

A Definition of *Intervention*

Argyris defines *intervention* as follows: "To intervene is to enter into an on-going system of relationships, to come between or among persons, groups, or objects for the purpose of helping them."[1] More specifically related to OD, the term OD *interventions* refers to the range of planned, programmatic activities clients and consultants participate in during the course of an organization development program. Largely these are diagnostic and problem-solving activities that ordinarily occur with the assistance of a consultant who is not a regular member of the particular system or subsystem culture. However, many of the activities typically become absorbed by the client system as the process unfolds.

Classifications of OD Interventions

There are a number of ways of classifying OD interventions, depending on the dimensions one wishes to emphasize.[2] Several classification methods are based on the *type of causal mechanism* hypothesized to underlie the particular technique used. For example, feedback, which refers to receiving new data about oneself, others, or group dynamics, is assumed to have potential for constructive change if it is not too threatening. Techniques for providing more *awareness of changing organizational norms* are assumed to result in modification of behavior, attitudes, and values. *Increased interaction* and communication may effect changes in attitudes and behavior. Homans, for example, suggests that increased interaction leads to positive sentiments,[3] and Murphy refers to "tunnel vision" or "autism," which develops in individuals and groups in isolation.[4] *Confrontation*, a surfacing and addressing of differences in perceptions, values, attitudes, feelings, or norms, is assumed to help remove obstacles to effective interaction if handled in constructive ways. *Education* is designed to upgrade (1) knowledge and concepts, (2) out-moded beliefs and attitudes, or (3) skills and has long been accepted as a change mechanism.

Depth of intervention is another useful dimension for classifying interventions. In an essay by Roger Harrison that appears in Part V, interventions can be distinguished in terms of the accessibility of the data and the degree of individuality or self-exposure involved. For example, we see a family T-group involving a work group and formal leader ("family" group) as a deeper intervention than a task-oriented team-building (problem-solving) workshop with such a group. The use of collages describing where team members see their unit going may be a deeper intervention than an interview that includes general questions about how things are going in the unit.

A different approach to classifying OD interventions is provided by Robert Blake and Jane Mouton when they list the major interventions in terms of their underlying cause and mechanisms.[5] They describe the following kinds of interventions: (1) a *discrepancy intervention*, which calls attention to a contradiction in action or attitudes that then leads to exploration; (2) a *theory intervention*, in which behavioral science knowledge and theory are used to explain present behavior and assumptions underlying the behavior; (3) a *procedural intervention*, which represents a critiquing of how something is being done to determine whether the best methods are being used; (4) a *relationship intervention*, which focuses attention on interpersonal relations (particularly ones where there are strong negative feelings) and surfaces the issues for exploration and possible resolution; (5) an *experimentation intervention*, in which two different action plans are tested for their consequences before final decision on one is made; (6) a *dilemma intervention*, in which an imposed or emergent dilemma is used to force close examination of the possible choices involved and the assumptions underlying them; (7) a *perspective intervention*, which draws attention away from immediate actions and demands and allows a look at historical background, context, and future objectives in order to assess whether or not the actions are still on target; (8) an *organization structure intervention,* which calls for examination and evaluation of structural causes for organizational ineffectiveness; and (9) a *cultural intervention*, which examines traditions, precedents, and practices—the fabric of the organization's culture—in a direct, focused approach. These are largely process consultation interventions, and they tend to occur within the context of a broader intervention, such as team building or in intergroup activities.

The *time and comprehensiveness* involved in the intervention can be another way of distinguishing between interventions. Some interventions, such as the use of a simple questionnaire, may take only minutes; others, such as the role analysis process (called "Operation KPE" in the Dayal and Thomas article) may take two hours relative to one job incumbent. Team building of different varieties may be an intervention taking place over one to three or more days and will include within it a variety of brief interventions. It should be added that successful interventions will probably always have a broader context; even the simplest of interventions needs to occur in the setting of some prework, which serve to make the intervention acceptable to the client, and needs follow-up to maximize the odds of success.

Another way of classifying OD interventions might be in terms of the emphasis on *task* versus *process*. Some team-building activities, for example, may have a high focus on interpersonal and group processes, such as the quality of communications or the dynamics of informal leadership and influence processes occurring in the group. Other activities might have a more task-related orientation, such as goal setting or the reallocating of responsibilities. This dichotomy of task and process can be somewhat misleading, however, because they are highly interrelated.

Finally, another way of classifying OD interventions is in terms of the *size and complexity of the client group*. For example, the client group may consist of *(a) individuals, (b) dyads or triads, (c) a self-managed team, (d) an intact work team,* including the formal leader, *(e) intergroup configurations* (two or more interfacing units), *(f) all of the managers of an organization,* or *(g) everybody in the total organization.* As we move from interventions with individuals, to dyads, to group, to intergroups and then to the total organization, the interdependencies and the number of dimensions to be concerned about obviously increases. For example, an intervention that is successful in dealing with two groups in conflict must also successfully deal with the intragroup communications problems and conflict that become manifest. That is one reason it is usually a wise step to help teams deal with internal problems and increase their interpersonal and group skills before undertaking intergroup activities.

A simple classification scheme based on the size and complexity of the client group is shown in Figure 1. Some interventions appear in more than one category because they have utility with more than one type of client group. What the figure does not show are the many mini-interventions used by OD consultants within the context of broader interventions like team building or even within techniques used in team building (e.g., the rose analysis technique)—that is, there are interventions within interventions within interventions. For example, this typology says nothing about the consultant's ability to point out a discrepancy, to provide support, to clarify, to use subgroups, or to have data made visible on newsprint, or, for that matter, to know when to use various interventions. (A number of these professional skills are discussed in Part V.)

This classification scheme generally underlies the organization of Part III. The first several essays are largely on team interventions. Part III then moves to intergroup interventions and then to more comprehensive interventions, such as the use of the collateral organization and survey feedback.

FIGURE 1

Typology of interventions based on the size and complexity of the client group

Client Group	Types of Interventions
Interventions designed to improve the effectiveness of *individuals* (although most are conducted in group settings).	Life and career-planning activities. Role analysis technique. Coaching and counseling. T-group (sensitivity training). Training to increase technical skills, relationship skills, group process skills, or decision-making, problem-solving, planning, goal-setting skills. Grid OD phase 1.★ Transactional analysis. Behavior modeling.
Interventions designed to improve the effectiveness of *dyads/triads*.	Process consultation. Third-party peacemaking. Transactional analysis.
Interventions designed to improve the effectiveness of *teams and groups*.	Interviews or questionnaires. Team building. Responsibility charting. Survey feedback. Process consultation. Appreciations and concerns exercise. Role negotiation. Role analysis technique. Collages. Gestolt OD. "Start-up" team-building activities. Training in decision making, problem solving, planning, goal setting in group settings. Grid OD phase 2. Appreciative inquiry. Visioning.
Interventions designed to improve the effectiveness of *intergroup relations*.	Interviews or questionnaires. Intergroup activities. Organizational mirroring (three or more groups). Process consultation. Third-party peacemaking at group level. Grid OD phase 3. Survey feedback.
Interventions designed to improve the effectiveness of the *total organization*.	Interviews or questionnaires. Sensing. "Confrontation" meetings (Beckhard). Team building at all levels. Appreciative inquiry. Strategic planning activities. Grid OD phases 4, 5, 6. Survey feedback. OD strategy planning. Quality of work life programs. Total quality management programs.

★For a discussion of the Managerial Grid® approach to OD, see Robert R. Blake and Jane Srygley Mouton, *Consultation* (Reading, MA: Addison-Wesley Publishing, 1976), chap. 27.

Source: Modified from Wendell L. French and Cecil H. Bell, Jr., *Organization Development: Behavioral Science Interventions for Organization Improvement*, 6th ed. (Englewood Cliffs, NJ: Prentice Hall, 1998, chap. 8.)

Notes on Diagnosis

As will be evident in the essays that follow, diagnostic activities are pervasive aspects of the participant action research model that underlies most organization development interventions. Basically, to diagnose is to identify the underlying forces or conditions giving rise to the present state of affairs. Diagnosis may pertain broadly to the present state of a system, including the many positive forces giving rise to desirable outcomes; or it may be narrower in the sense of focusing on the dysfunctional forces that are producing undesirable outcomes, or it may focus on changes in the state of the system over time.

Three Types of Theories

As Ronald Lippitt has stated, "Every consultant has a cluster of ideas, or a set of concepts, which guide his perception of 'what exists' and 'what is going on' when he or she comes in contact with a particular group or organization." This *descriptive-analytic theory*, to whatever degree of refinement, assists the consultant in understanding and interpreting the complexities of group or organization functioning. Lippitt goes on to say that every consultant has, in addition, some form of *diagnostic theory* that assists in identifying symptoms of disturbances in the system and what some of the probable causes might be. A diagnostic theory, to Lippitt then, is a set of notions that relate more to the dysfunctional or anomalous aspects of organizational life than does descriptive analytic theory.[6] We might add that OD consultants also need some form of *change theory* that assists in understanding the consequences of the interaction of various forces over time. This would be congruent with Lippitt's ides. Thus organizational diagnosis stems from some theoretical base, however partially or completely formulated.

An illustration of a descriptive analytic theory (perhaps combined with a diagnostic theory) is the theory underlying the "Survey of Organizations" questionnaire developed by the Institute for Social Research at the University of Michigan. The survey is based, as Taylor and Bowers describe, on a "metatheory of organizational system functioning" as presented by Rensis Likert and others in various writings. Part of the theory is represented by a model, which includes the notions of causal variables, intervening variables, and end-result variables. Questionnaire categories and items are related to these broader concepts and to the underlying theory.[7]

Dimensions to Consider in Diagnosis

In addition to the importance of the consultant having descriptive, analytic, and diagnostic theories, a number of other dimensions of diagnosis are important for the consultant to consider. A description of seven such dimensions follows.

Timing of the diagnostic activities is a significant dimension. For example, it is one thing to collect and analyze organizational climate data and then to develop a strategy for how to use it, but quite another to gather data about the perceived usefulness and timeliness of doing a climate survey in the first place. Much time, and therefore many resources, can be wasted if organizational participants are not prepared to work with the data.

Extent of participation is a key aspect of diagnosis. Who, in a preliminary way, decided that diagnosis should take place? Who decided how it should be done? Which people were systematically involved in supplying data, and further in analyzing and describing the dynamics revealed by the data? One person? Two people? The top team? The top team plus others? One or more people in conjunction with a consultant? All of the members of the system or subsystem? Customers of the system? One of the underlying assumptions in OD is the efficacy of participative problem identification and diagnosis in contrast to unilateral problem identification and diagnosis.

The dimension of *confidentiality*, or individual-anonymous versus group surfacing of data, has important facets. In the early stages of an OD effort, when trust between group members may be low and their feedback skills inadequate, the situation may call for individual interviews, with responses kept anonymous and only reported to the group in terms of themes. As trust is earned and grows, people can become more open in terms of surfacing attitudes, feelings, and perceptions about organizational dynamics in group settings.

The degree to which there *was preselection of variables versus an emergent selection of variables* to be considered is another important dimension. The University of Michigan version of survey feedback utilizes the Survey of Organizations questionnaire, which taps some 19 dimensions subsumed under three broad categories: leadership, organizational climate, and satisfaction. Another approach, Grid OD, depends heavily in early phases on an analysis of leadership style using a questionnaire called the "Managerial Grid." This analysis focuses on two dimensions: concern for people and concern for production. On the other hand, data gathering can be more emergent with less structuring of questions. Some OD consultants will use interviews that are structured only to the extent that two or three general questions are asked at the outset, such as: What things are going well in the organization? What problems do you see? Follow-up probes are then used to pursue important issues uncovered. Positive and problem themes are then distilled from this data.

The extent to which data gathering and analysis are isolated events in contrast to being part of a long-range strategy is also important. One usual assumption in OD efforts is that diagnostic activities should be part of an overall plan. Diagnostic activities lead to action programs that in turn call for diagnostic activities—this is the action research model. Diagnostic activities that are not part of any such plan or that are prompted by someone's whim to know "what they are thinking" may produce resentment and resistance and can seriously hinder attempts to get valid data from system members.

The nature of the target population in both preliminary and later systematic data gathering and analysis is also a key dimension. The size and nature of the target group can affect the acceptability of the diagnostic process, what kinds of inter-dependencies can be examined, and what kinds of issues can be worked successfully. The data-providing group can be different from the data-analyzing group, of course, but in OD, suppliers of the information usually work with their own data in intact work teams.

And finally, *the type of technique used* obviously has a number of important ramifications. By type we mean questionnaire-versus-interview techniques, individual-versus-group surfacing of data, or other categories of techniques that can be differentiated in major ways. We have already discussed how the type of instrument, such as the Survey of Organizations, can structure the responses. As another example of the importance of technique selection, an interview can be used for trust building as well as collecting data; a face-to-face conversation is a better vehicle for building a relationship than sending someone a questionnaire. Concerns can be expressed and responded to, questions can be answered, assurances can be provided as to how the data will be used, and so on. As another example of the importance of the type of technique selected, giving diagnostic assignments to subgroups in a workshop setting can be a powerful diagnostic technique. But the way these groups are constituted—for example, heterogeneous versus homogeneous in terms of rank, position, or aggressiveness-reticence—can be crucial to the amount and candor of the data generated.

Readings in Part III

The readings in this part describe widely used basic OD and OT interventions. The interventions vary from methods of finding out what is going on to more complex interventions such as team-building in collateral organizations.

Jack Fordyce and Raymond Weil's "Methods for Finding out What's Going On" presents seven methods for collecting information in order of their degree of confrontation. The second, interviewing, is probably the most fundamental intervention in OD. Each method is discussed in terms of uses, benefits, limitations, and operating hints.

Ishwar Dayal and John Thomas's "Operation KPE" describes an intervention that we call role analysis technique or role analysis process,[8] in which a job incumbent listens to what extent colleague expectations are being met relative to the incumbent's performance and is provided an opportunity to respond.

The selection of Richard Beckard and Reuben Harris entitled "Planning Procedures/Managing Interface/Charting Responsibility" describes a technique for allocating work responsibilities. This occurs in a series of "responsibility charting conferences."

In "When Power Conflicts Trigger Team Spirit," Roger Harrison describes a role negotiation technique that can be used in small or large groups, although he recommends that groups of over 8 or 10 be subdivided. Underlying the technique is the assumption that "most people prefer a fair negotiated settlement to a state of unresolved conflict." Harrison states that he has used the technique with such diverse groups as top management teams and husband and wife pairs.

Robert Blake, Herbert Shepard, and Jane Mouton's "Strategies for Improving Headquarters-Field Relations" is an early, classic essay describing a process for managing intergroup confrontation and conflict resolution. Personal correspondence with Blake and Mouton reveals that they saw no fundamental improvements in the design over a 25-year span after its invention.

Richard Beckhard's "Confrontation Meeting" describes an intervention design that allows the total management group "to take a quick reading on its own health, and—*within a matter of hours*—to set action plans for improving it."

Dale Zand's "Collateral Organization" features an intervention design creating a "supplemental organization coexisting with the usual, formal organization." A case study is presented that describes a fairly structured process that unfolds over an 18-month period.

The essay "Survey-Guided Development" by David Bowers and Jerome Franklin describes the nature of and rationale for a powerful intervention strategy that includes the administration of a comprehensive questionnaire; feedback of the results to intact work groups, including the formal leader, problem solving based on the data; and planning for feedback to successively lower levels of the organization. The questionnaire design and the survey feedback process are based on many years of research.

Endnotes

1. Chris Argyris, *Intervention Theory and Method: A Behavioral Science View* (Reading, MA: Addison-Wesley Publishing, 1970), p. 15.
2. For a more detailed discussion of several of these dimensions, see Wendell French and Cecil Bell, *Organization Development: Behavioral Science Interventions for Organization Improvement*, 6th ed. (Englewood Cliffs, NJ: Prentice Hall, 1998), chap. 8.
3. George C. Homans, *The Human Group* (New York: Harcourt Brace Jovanovich, 1950).
4. G. Murphy, "The Freeing of Intelligence," *Psychological Bulletin* 42 (1945), pp. 1–19.
5. Robert R. Blake and Jane Srygley Mouton, *The Managerial Grid* (Houston: Gulf Publishing, 1964), pp. 282–83.
6. Ronald Lippitt, "Dimensions of the Consultant's Job," in *The Planning of Change*, 1st ed., ed. Warren G. Bennis, Kenneth D. Benne, and Robert Chin (New York: Holt, Rinehart & Winston, 1961), p. 157.
7. James C. Taylor and David G. Bowers, *Survey of Organizations* (Ann Arbor: Institute for Social Research, University of Michigan, 1972), pp. 1–6.
8. Wendell L. French and Cecil H. Bell, Jr. *Organization Development: Behavioral Science Interventions for Organization Improvement*, 5th ed. (Englewood Cliffs, NJ: Prentice Hall, 1995), p. 181.

Jack K. Fordyce
Raymond Weil

This section contains seven basic methods for collecting information. They include:

- Questionnaires and Instruments.
- Interviewing.
- Sensing.
- Polling.
- Collages.
- Drawings.
- Physical Representation of Organizations.

The methods are ranked in order of degree of confrontation. Thus Questionnaires are generally relatively impersonal because the source of the information is not publicly revealed, while Physical Representations (in which, for example, participants literally position themselves according to degree of influence) are highly confronting.

As a rule of thumb, the more confronting the method, the richer the response and the stronger the impulse to change. But groups vary considerably in their readiness to work with intimate methods.

Another important method for collecting information is Subgrouping. However, Subgrouping has more general uses and consequently it is described in the section on Methods for Better Meetings.

1. Questionnaires and Instruments

Questionnaires are an old standby for detecting opinion and sentiment. We send out questionnaires to customers, production workers, the professional staff, constituents, television and movie viewers, lower levels of management, people who sojourn at motels and ride in planes, and others.

Unfortunately, traditional questionnaires have often been disappointing as a means of bringing about significant change within organizations. They do not create the kind of personal involvement and discussion that is so valuable in changing hearts and minds. The information garnered by questionnaires tends to be canned, anonymous, ambiguous, and detached—cool data rather than hot. The replies may be interesting but they lack punch. It is too easy to hold them at arm's length, put them off until another day, or take token action. And the questionnaire asks the person only what *we* want to know, not what he or she thinks we should know. You might say a filled-out questionnaire amounts to half a conversation. The employee opinion questionnaire is regarded by many as a device that some managements use to avoid coming to grips with strong opinions and sentiments.

Nevertheless, to our mind the questionnaire can be useful when it is developed jointly by the manager and representatives of the population to be canvassed.

The *instrument* as used in organization development is similar to the questionnaire, with the important addition that it is constructed around a theory of management in such manner as to help the respondent understand the theory and rate himself or herself or the organization in terms of that theory. Thus in "Grid Organization Development," the manager answers questions which help to place himself or herself in the grid model of management styles. Others in the group rate the manager, too. In this manner, instruments are a means by which a group can collect information from itself about itself. This information then provides the starting point for feedback and confrontation within the group.

Source: Jack K. Fordyce and Raymond Weil, *Managing with People*, 2nd ed., (pp. 143–158). © 1979 Jack K. Fordyce and Raymond Weil. Reprinted by permission of Addison Wesley Longman.

Uses.

As a primary vehicle for learning in one complete system of organization development (Grid Organization Development).

To collect information as part of a specific, planned strategy of change, preferably jointly managed.

Instruments may be used by a group to collect information quickly about itself, as part of a diagnostic or team-building meeting. In this use, the instrument is the same as Polling except that the instrument is predesigned and may incorporate criteria for evaluation.

Benefits.

Questionnaire and instruments are economical means for gathering information from a large population.

They lend themselves readily to legitimate statistical use.

Instruments are valuable for self-confrontation, for learning, and as stepping stones to interpersonal confrontations.

You can more readily afford to spend time and money or the quality of the questionnaires or instruments because the unit cost is low.

There is wide acceptance of these methods.

They reduce reliance on expert third parties.

Anonymity may bring to light previously undisclosed strong sentiment.

Limitations.

Questionnaires and instruments produce findings which seem canned, a quality which is mitigated if they are used, as in Grid Organization Development, as a stepping stone to confrontation. The hazard is that the parties involved may merely imitate the motions of engaging with one another—shadowbox, so to speak.

One becomes too readily dependent on the questionnaire, pressing upon it (and thrusting away from oneself) a load it can't carry: direct human communication.

Operating Hints.

Unless the objective is purely personal learning, be sure the questionnaire or instrument leads to real engagement among people. Make sure that those involved are really hearing one another well enough—both heart-to-heart and head-to-head—so that their communication may have consequences in construction action.

2. Interviewing

Before a team-building or similar meeting, it is common practice to interview the participants. The interviewer is generally a third party. The purpose of the interview is to explore ways in which the group can be more effective. The interviews uncover both positive and negative opinions and sentiments about a wide range of subjects—for example, clarity of individual and group goals, impact of the manager's style, and personal concerns that have never been aired.

The question should help the interviewee to express whatever is on his or her mind about life in the organization. Examples of general opening questions:

"How are things going around here?"

"What changes would you like to see?'

"How do you think this organization could be more effective? What do you feel it does best? Does poorly?"

The interviewer may also ask about management:

"How would you describe the management style of X? How do you think he or she could be more effective?"

Questions may also be asked about relationships within the organization:

"Whom do you like to work with most? Least?"

"Who is most influential in your organization?"

"Are you kept informed of what goes on?"

And about relationships with other organizations:

"When there are problems with other organizations, what can you do about them?"

"Can you give examples of unresolved issues with other organizations?"

"Do you think you could give them advice that would help them do a better job?"

Information from the interviews is fed back to the total group, usually at the beginning of the meeting.

Uses.   Interviewing is a way to get private views and feeling on the table. The information collected often furnishes the principal basis for the meeting agenda.

Benefits.   The interview is an excellent way to probe for the problems and opportunities of the organization. Interviewing has the virtue of facilitating private expression. A sensitive interviewer can also invite ideas and emotions that the subject has not previously formulated in any conscious way. Interviewing also furnishes an occasion to develop trust between the third party and members of the organization; such trust in valuable in later work.

Limitations.

A good interview often takes one to two hours. For a large organization, interviewing can therefore consume a lot of time.

Skillful interviewing runs the risk of turning up more information of a personal and perhaps threatening nature than the group is ready to deal with. When confronted with the interview findings, the group may close up, reject the information, and attack the interviewers.

If the interviewer is clumsy or is not trusted as impartial, interviewing may worsen matters. Under these circumstances, it is best to gather information by open group process. (See methods 3–7 in this section.)

Operating Hints.

There should be an understanding between the interviewer, the manager, and members of the team as to how the information will be used, especially with respect to protecting the privacy of sources. Normally, interviewees are promised that the information will be presented anonymously. The interviewer must keep that promise. The information can be presented verbatim or thematically. The former has greater impact but does not protect privacy as well, and some data may be too hot for the group to handle. Thematically presented material has the opposite virtues: it's cooler, protects privacy better, has a softer impact. It is usually easily summarized, and hence easier to grasp.

One variation in reporting is to present themes and to back them up with supporting verbatim quotes.

If the findings are highly critical of the manager or another member of the group, it is advisable for the interviewer to disclose enough of the information to the manager in advance of the group meeting so that he or she will not feel ambushed.

Interviews may be carried out on an individual or subgroup basis, the latter having the obvious advantage of saving time. Interviewing of subgroups does not confer the same advantages of privacy and sensitivity, but the information disclosed tends to be of a character that the group is ready and willing to deal with. Moreover, the person who volunteers data in a subgroup interview normally feels committed to confirm it in a larger meeting. A way to disseminate the interview findings is to type and distribute copies to all members of the group. Summary statements and corroborative information can then be posted on chart pads.

3. Sensing

Sensing is an organized method by which a manager can learn about the issues, concerns, needs, and resources of persons in any suborganization with which he or she has limited personal contact. It takes the form of an unstructured group interview and is usually tape-recorded. The recording may be then used to educate others.

Example. The general manager of an organization which employs 2,000 wants to make an annual report to employees highly pertinent to their interests. To discover what subjects most concern them, the personnel manager schedules a series of meetings with a sampling of employees.

The personnel manager schedules four meetings, each two hours in length and each with a different group of 12 employees. To help the general manager get a "feel" for people in all parts of the organization, the personnel manager selects the attendees as follows:

Group I—Nonsupervisory, shop and service, and technical and office employees.

Group II—Professional employees and staff specialists.

Group III—Supervisors.

Group IV—A diagonal cross section (i.e., one person from each organizational level; no one of the persons selected reports to any other).

Before scheduling the meetings, the personnel manager contacts the supervisor of each prospective participant. He or she explains the purpose of the meeting and the intention that no direct actions will ensue which might affect the supervisor or people who report to the supervisor.

Each meeting begins with a statement from the personnel manager who says that the general manager will arrive in half an hour. The personnel manager explains the general manager's purpose for the meeting and the hope that the conversation will be open and informal. The personnel manager suggests: "Suppose you board an airplane to Europe and you happen to find yourself sitting next to the general manager. What would you say?" The personnel manager also tells the group that, unless they object, to ease the burden of notetaking, the meeting will be tape-recorded. The general manager may also later use the tape as an aid to memory or to present illustrative excerpts to the division's top staff. If any member of the group prefers, the recorder will be promptly turned off now or at any time during the conversation.

During the meeting, the general manager spends most of the time listening, sometimes asking clarifying questions. The general manager also expresses his or her own thoughts and intentions regarding the various topics introduced.

Another Example. A manager has been hearing from outsiders that recently hired engineers in the organization are dissatisfied. To better understand the nature of their complaints, the manager asks the personnel manager to rearrange sensing sessions with several groups of engineers and a group of engineering supervisors.

Another Example. A third party uses the sensing procedure to make a quick assessment of the health of a company. He or she meets with four representative small groups from different parts of the organization, asking each group to discuss what is going well in the company and what needs to be changed. To avoid inhibiting the discussion, the third party does not record it but periodically stops the conversation and, in front of the group, dictates into the tape recorder a digest of what they have said. Then, with the recorder still running, he or she asks if they have been heard correctly and records their response. In a day's time, a 15-minute tape can summarize the four discussions. This tape is given to the top-management group of the company.

If the consultant were collecting information for a team-building meeting, he or she might use a different question, such as: "The general manager and the division directors are going to hold an off-site meeting to work on improving their performance as a management team. What issues do you think they should take up?"

Uses.

To collect information as part of a general diagnosis of the organization.

To learn the desires and agonies of a group that seems to be dissatisfied.

To learn how organization objectives are understood by diverse people within an organization.

To test a proposed course of action for its effect on various groups of people.

To collect information for a team-building meeting.

Benefits.

The interaction of the group often produces rich information and ideas.

More economical than individual interviews.

May provide a quick glimpse of what's going on.

Allows for communication of impressions and feelings as well as opinions and ideas.

Provides a check on conventional and more formal communication channels.

Admits the rumble of humanity into the ivory tower.

Tapes from sensing sessions communicate more vividly to later listeners than second-hand transmission, written reports, or questionnaires.

Limitations.

Won't work well unless the relations at various levels in the organization are basically trusting.

Is not as statistically rigorous or as economical as a questionnaire.

May be suspected as "snooping."

Success of the meeting is highly dependent on the manager's ability to listen effectively and on a willingness to engage with the members of the group in a personal way.

The meeting may fail to get at the attendees' real concerns because for one reason or another they are not willing to reveal them.

Operating Hints.

Make sure that all intermediate supervisors understand the objectives and possible outcomes of the meeting so that they will not feel "spied on." Be clear and explicit about the objectives of the meeting and what is to become of the information.

Notetaking may interfere with easy, informal discussion while the tape recorder is less likely to. But tape-record the session only if the group is willing. Be explicit about how the tape will be used and make a commitment to control its use.

Don't try to use sensing as a substitute for maintaining effective communication channels

throughout the organization, or to "get the boss's message across," or to reprimand or judge.

Allow about two hours (enough time for a comfortable discussion).

Provide some warm-up time with a third party, especially for people who have never seen the big boss.

Convene the session in a comfortable setting and one that is not strange or intimidating to the group. (Don't meet in the boss's office.)

Establish a single and limited objective for a given sensing session. Don't try to cover too much at once. Start the meeting in an open-ended way. This will permit individuals to express their view points (e.g., "How does it feel to work around here?" or "I'm interested in how things are going," rather than, "Do you like the company benefits plan?").

If the manager doing the sensing is a poor listener, include a third party who, by prearrangement, can intervene if the manager seems to be blocking the group's efforts to express itself.

Don't do a lot of sensing unless the groups sensed can see positive results coming from it. Overuse of sensing can be as bad as overuse of questionnaires. Sensing may be conducted by persons other than a key manager; for example, by a third party or someone from the personnel department.

4. Polling

Sometimes a group becomes uneasy with itself. The members may feel anxious, bored, or in some way out of tune with one another. Such conduct is a common symptom of a buried issue. The way out is to move the discussion to the unspoken agenda item. Polling is a way to reveal it. Or, in a more positive way, a group may wish to evaluate its current state as a prelude to action.

One approach is to poll the group on a question that calls attention to its present condition. The third party might float a tentative question and, with the help of the group, modify the question so that it becomes one that the group wants to deal with. The participants must also decide upon the procedure for conducting the poll.

Example. The group has been planning goals for improvement. At this time, the discussion is agreeable but lethargic. The third party suggests polling the group members on their optimism about whether they can agree upon and later achieve a goal involving significant change. The group consents. He or she suggests a procedure and draws on the chalkboard a scale of optimism:

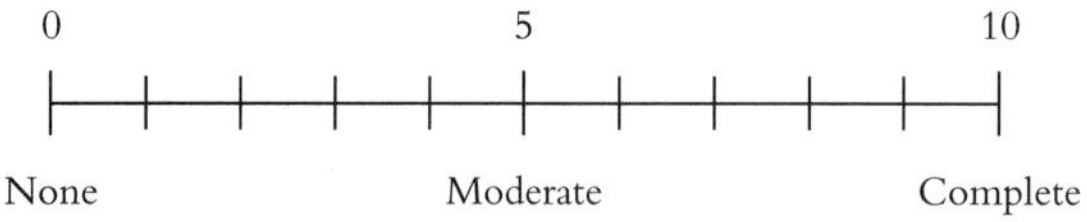

Each member is asked to assign a number to his or her degree of optimism. The third party will mark each response on the scale.

The responses cluster around 2½. Now the group members begin to comment on their pessimism, on their history of past failures at meeting their goals. They begin to analyze weaknesses in their methods of planning and execution of change. More than one member acknowledges a feeling of guilt at not having been able to subscribe to the manager's wishes, having done instead what seemed fitting and necessary.

The truth begins to sink in. As a group, they have a way to travel before they can plan realistic goals to which they will feel strongly committed.

Another Example. One person remarks that participation in the meeting has been uneven. Some have said little or nothing. Others have made important comments to which there was no response; perhaps they have not been heard. One or two have dominated the conversation.

The group determines to poll itself on this concern. The members will score one another (from 1 to 5) on two questions:

- Amount of participation?
- Quality of participation?

Each member writes a self-rating and a rating of the others with respect to the two questions. The results are presented to the group on grids, one grid for each question (see Figure 1). Following the poll, the group members agree on the need to police themselves better. They also decide to rotate the responsibility for calling attention to weaknesses in future meetings.

Another Example. One member wonders aloud how effective the group is a team. The third party suggests that the members first decide upon the attributes of an effective team (in their situation) and then rate themselves on each attribute. The group now *develops its own* questionnaire, which is posted. Each member now marks his or her ratings (see Figure 2). Now the group members reflect on why the ratings came out as they did. They become specific about what they do well and what they do poorly as a team.

Another Example. The third party asks on what questions would the members like to know the position of the others. The group arrives at a set of questions:

- Should we do something about our relationship with organization X?
- Am I able to influence what goes on in this organization?
- Do I plan to leave this organization in the next two years?

FIGURE 1

Subjects \ *Raters*	John	Betty	Ted	Sam	Frances	Fred
John	②	1	1	1	2	1
Betty	5	⑤	5	5	5	5
Ted	4	5	③	4	4	5
Sam	2	1	2	①	2	2
Frances	1	2	1	1	③	1
Fred	1	1	1	1	1	②

Circled numbers are self-ratings

FIGURE 2

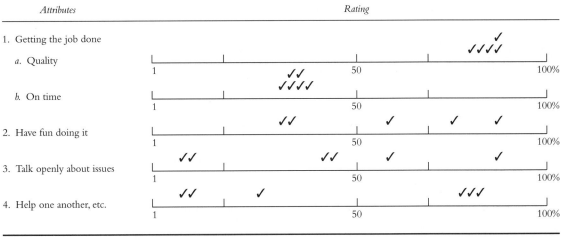

Attributes	Rating
1. Getting the job done	
a. Quality	
b. On time	
2. Have fun doing it	
3. Talk openly about issues	
4. Help one another, etc.	

Each members jots down a yes or no reply to each question, and then predicts the number of yes and no answers for the total group. The results are tabulated and posted on the wall (see Figure 3). The range of the *predictions* is an indicator of common understanding. The *actual count* starts the group working on some real problems.

Another Example. After an effort lasting some period of time, the group has reached a fairly high level of trust and mutual helpfulness. However, one member is troubled by certain relationships among members, and feels the group has been avoiding the subject.

The third party invites each group member to pursue two questions:

- Which two persons in the group do I *like* working with the *most*?
- Which two persons in the group do I *like* working with the *least*?

The responses are collected on signed slips of paper and tabulated on a grid (see Figure 4). In the ensuing discussion, the group deals with the intensity of the choices, the reasons for them, and perhaps what sort of conduct can improve the relationships.

Uses. Polling is a quick way of bringing buried issues to light. Such issues may be of two types:

- Those which are interfering with the progress of a meeting.
- Chronic problems in the organization.

Benefits.

Polling is fast, interesting, and simple.

Anyone can devise his or her own questions and polling procedure.

The whole group takes part in the process and feels greater commitment to the results. It is an easy way to get issues out into the open, and a good way to move from general, inconclusive discussions to specifics that can be dealt with. It is a highly flexible method that can be improvised to suit the needs of the moment.

Limitations. The questions aren't as carefully thought out as those on professionally developed questionnaires, and they don't lend themselves to large groups. They are most useful in groups of 5 to 30.

FIGURE 3

	Actual Count		Predicted Count (range)	
Question	*Yes*	*No*	*Yes*	*No*
1. Organization X	5	5	3–8	2–7
2. Influence	3	7	1–4	6–9
3. Leaving, etc.	4	6	2–5	5–8

FIGURE 4

Choosers (columns); *Chosen* (rows)

	Jane	Frank	Nan	Mary	Ken	Mark
Jane		✔		✘	✘	✘
Frank	✔		✔			✔
Nan	✔	✔		✔	✔	✔
Mary	✘		✔		✔	
Ken		✘	✘	✔		✘
Mark	✘	✘	✘	✘	✘	

✔ = Most ✘ = Least

Operating Hints.

Don't rush into polling at your next meeting to suit *your* interests. The questions and the procedure must make sense to the group. If not, the responses won't be very useful, and other members will start wondering about *you*.

Group involvement is important for another reason. As the examples show, polls can touch people where they are quite sensitive. The group's OK to go ahead is the only evidence that they feel up to it.

If sensitive relationships are to be taken up, it's wise to have a competent third party present.

Be cautious about secretive methods of collecting information. An occasional secret ballot may be all right, but beware of raising issues which the group is unwilling to confront openly.

Once the questions have been answered, move the discussion to specifics as soon as possible. General discussions leave a lot of fog in the atmosphere.

5. Collages

Individuals, subgroups, or groups may be asked to prepare collages around a theme (e.g.,"How do you feel about this team?", "How do you feel about yourself in this organization, and this organization in the company?", "What is happening to this organization and the team?"). Materials for the collage include large sheets of paper, magazines from which pictures and words may be clipped, crayons, felt pens, glue, scissors, and so on. Each finished collage is then described for the total group by the individual or subgroup preparing it. If a single, large collage is prepared by the total group, it becomes the focal point for a total group discussion.

Uses. As an instrument for tracing the cultural and emotional topography of a group. The collage allows the members to express themselves to one another on a fairly deep, personal leave. Common themes from collages tend to find their way onto group agendas.

Benefits.

Collages can be quite effective in breaking the ice. Afterward, the group may be more willing to deal with personal and interpersonal issues. Besides, they are fun to do.

When the group produces a large single collage, the members are apt to be proud of their accomplishment. The experience is unifying.

Limitations.

Groups that are formal in behavior may resist what first appears to be a children's game.

As noted, collages are highly expressive. On the other hand, they may reveal little that is hard and specific.

Operating Hints.

Lead boldly into the assignment to help the group overcome its resistance to this "child's play."

If they want, let the participants suggest the theme for the collage. Provide plenty of magazines and ample space, and be prepared to wind up with a cluttered room. Suggest to the participants that they cut out any pictures or words which "ring a bell" without giving much thought to why they do so.

The time for preparing the collages should be approximately one-half hour to an hour and a half. Judge the time by whether the participants seem productively employed, but apply deadline pressure to discourage excessive deliberation.

Don't let the responses to the presentation turn into a game of interpretation. The object is to understand the presenter without putting words into his or her mouth and without awakening defensiveness.

The boss's collage should be presented last so as not to set the tone for others.

6. Drawings

One member of the group (or some, or all members) is asked to make a drawing about an aspect of the individual's life, or something about the nature of the organization. The drawings are made on large sheets of paper posted on the walls. The authors are then asked to discuss their drawings in the presence of the group. Members of the group may ask questions to clarify the author's intent. Common themes and problems, or significant differences of opinion, are then culled from the drawings and posted on chart pads. Here is an example of an instruction given to all members of a group:

> Draw a circle for each person in the group, including your boss and your boss's boss. Make the circle proportionately larger for those individuals who seem to have greater influence over the way the group does its work.

> Place the circles near or far apart, depending on how closely you feel those individuals must work together to get their job done. Label the circles with the names of the people.

> With a blue line, connect those people who are personally close to one another. Connect with a red line those people who are far apart (i.e.,

individuals who communicate very little with one another or between whom you feel there is friction).

Other Examples.

Draw a picture of how it feels to be in your organization.

Draw a picture of your organization today and another picture of what you would like it to be in five years.

The drawings may vary in style from conventional organizational charts to imaginative symbolic representations.

Uses.

Drawings of the sort suggested can be a powerful way of unearthing for the group issues that have been buried alive—for example, the presence of cliques, inappropriate competition, or personal influence contrary to organizational goals. While they may be used to describe a current situation, drawings can also display what people want and hope for in place of what they have now.

Drawings can be used for building an agenda for team-building or similar meetings.

Benefits.   Pictures are often rich compressions of meaning. Moreover, they are inherently stimulating to work with. Drawings may also afford an easy entry into discussion of tender subjects.

Limitations.   Drawings are an expressive medium. But they are difficult for some to enter into unless the directions are quite literal and easy to follow.

Operating Hints.

Don't attempt to cover too many subjects in a single drawing or it will become difficult to understand.

Spend enough time on the instructions so that the members understand the *objectives* of the activity. Don't discourage people from departing from your rules; they may do better in their own fashion.

When a person presents a drawing to the group, encourage clarifying questions. *Discourage* general discussion, debate, or clever interpretation of the drawing by other members of the group.

Keep in readiness large sheets of paper, colored markers, and tape.

Some groups need more guidance than others. A group that is esthetically inclined is apt to respond swiftly to the assignment. Others may want more specific instruction.

7. Physical Representation of Organization

Members of a group are asked to arrange themselves physically in the room according to some group characteristic they are troubled about. For example, if the participants are apparently concerned about cliques, they may be asked to position themselves in the room so that each stands nearest to those he or she feels warmest about and farthest from those he or she feels coolest about. Or, if inappropriate influence is an issue, they may be asked to arrange themselves closer or farther from the boss according to the amount of influence they feel they have. Usually, the manager takes a position in the middle of the room as a starting point. Members are asked to call attention to any aspect of the deployment which they believe to be inaccurate. Usually no further instructions are given. Discussion normally occurs spontaneously.

Uses.   For bringing into the open relationship issues which are bothering the group. These may include cliques, feelings about being "in" or "out" of the group, influence, competitiveness, communication channels, and the like.

Benefits.

A good, rapid, and dramatic diagnostic tool for disclosing interpersonal issues that are hindering a group.

Creates strong motivation to improve the situation.

Limitations.   Many groups find this sort of thing too "far out," so the method isn't useful to them and may do more harm than good.

Operating Hints.   You will need a qualified third party.

Reading 14
Operation KPE:
Developing a New Organization

Ishwar Dayal
John M. Thomas

It was . . . decided that analysis of each role in the organization might be facilitated if, as a group, we could strive for an atmosphere in these sessions where individuals could express disagreement with the manner in which a particular role was being defined or currently being performed by the focal role incumbent, particularly in terms of how this performance either failed to meet expectations from others or convey obligations to others. Analysis of the role system could best be accomplished alongside some critical analysis of current role performance, with a view toward helping individuals understand how they might alter their characteristic styles of working with others. Our hope here was to be able to assist the group in developing a climate where it could begin to undertake analysis of the interpersonal sphere in conjunction with analysis of its task interdependencies: in other words, how the group might begin to share and work together on these concerns about interpersonal needs discussed with us in individual counseling sessions. In addition to ideas of one's own role, it would be valuable for each other member of the group to think about the role under discussion in terms of its specific linkages with his role.

As a model for role analysis in the group we attempted to integrate the Glacier formulations of *prescribed* and *discretionary* components of roles (Brown, 1960) with that of Kahn, et al. (1964). This included discussion of the following:

1. Analysis of why a particular role is needed and what purpose in the organization it

would serve. This point has relevance to the expressed individual problem of identity.

2. The expectations and obligations of related roles in relation to a focal role (Kahn, et al., 1964).

Thus each role analysis consisted of three parts: discussion of purpose of the role, its prescribed and discretionary components, and its linkages with other roles.

Beginning with the GM as the first focal role, the phase aimed at developing what we have termed interdependence was launched. To date, each member of the management group has taken sessions in which he has been a focal role under discussion. The live format evolved for these discussions came to include the following steps:

The focal role individual initiates discussion and the group begins an analysis of the purpose of the role in the organization, how it fits into the overall objectives of the company, and its rationale.

The focal role individual lists on the blackboard the activities which he feels constitute his role; other members discuss this and ask for clarification; additions and subtractions are often made to this list. The group agrees upon the prescribed elements of the role and helps the role incumbent analyze its discretionary elements. Often this enables the individual to clarify the responsibility he must take on himself for decisions, the choices open to him for alternative courses of action, and new competencies he must develop in his assigned role. For example, during discussion of the role of the sales manager, he thought that the GM should initiate contact with major customers because he was more likely to influence them by virtue of his social contacts with top management in those

Source: Ishwar Dayal and John M. Thomas, "Operation KPE: Developing a New Organization," in *The Journal of Applied Behavioral Science* (vol. 4, no. 4) pp. 443–505, copyright © 1968 by NTL Institute for Applied Behavioral Science. Reprinted by permission of Sage Publications, Inc.

companies. In contrast, the consultants suggested that the sales manager might, for various reasons, be taking "flight" from this responsibility and wondered whether he had any feelings about this matter that he could explore with the group. This led to an intensive, useful clarification of the relationship of the general manager with customers and with the sales manager. Similar issues came to center stage while discussing the roles of the purchasing and personnel officers. These discussions also helped the GM and the members of the management team visualize what kind of support they would have to give to one another in this activity. For example, the sales and purchasing role incumbents discussed the development of a formal system for effective exchange of information about customers and suppliers.

The focal role individual then lists his expectations from each of those other roles in the group which he feels most directly affect his own role performance. Often a lively dialogue ensues at this point between the focal role incumbent and the role sender under discussion. They may disagree over expectations and obligations. Other group members enter in to help clarify by adding their own perceptions of that role relationship. In the end a workable formula is evolved describing mutual expectations and obligations.

Each role sender then presents his list of expectations from the focal role. This consists of their views of his obligations to them in role performance, and much the same process as in the previous step is repeated.

Upon concluding an individual role analysis, the focal role incumbent is held responsible for writing up the major points evolved during the group discussion. This consists of *(a)* a set of activities classified as to the prescribed and discretionary elements of the role, *(b)* the obligations of the role to each role in its set, and *(c)* the expectations of this role from others in its set. Viewed in toto, this provides a comprehensive understanding of each individual's "role space." In addition, note is made of procedures and suggestions which may have been brought out as to how the role incumbent might more effectively implement his role activities. This write-up is done with the aid of the consultants and is circulated to all group members.

Briefly, at the next meeting, before another focal role is taken up, the previous role write-up is discussed and points are clarified. This statement is then accepted as a picture of the responsibilities and activities of that position in the organization. Unlike the traditional job description, however, this statement has been evolved live and entirely in the context of the *interaction* of that role with others. It expresses the group's views of how that role fits into the internal structure of the organization.

References

Argyris, C. *Interpersonal Competence and Organizational Effectiveness.* Homewood, IL: Irwin-Dorsey, 1962.

Bamforth, K. "Some Experiences of the Use of T-Groups and Structured Groups with a Company." *Working paper no. 3.* University of Leeds, U.K.: Industrial Management Division, 1963.

Benne, K. "Deliberate Changing as the Facilitation of Growth." In Bennis, W. G., Benne, K., & Chin, R., eds. *The Planning of Change.* New York: Holt, Rinehart & Winston, 1961.

Bennis, W. G. *Changing Organizations.* New York: McGraw-Hill, 1966.

Brown, W. *Explorations in Management.* London: Heinemann, 1960.

Burns, T., & Stalker, G. *The Management of Innovation.* London: Tavistock, 1961.

Dayal, I. "Organization of Work." In Baumgartel, H., Bennis, W., & De, N., eds. *Readings in Group Development for Managers and Trainers.* Bombay: Asia Publishing House, 1967.

Deutsch, M. "Cooperation and Trust: Some Theoretical Notes." In Bennis, W., Schein, E., Berlew, D., & Steele, F., eds. *Interpersonal Dynamics.* Homewood, IL: Dorsey Press, 1964.

Jaques, E., & Brown, W. *The Glacier Project Papers.* London: Heinemann, 1965.

Kahn, R., & Rosenthal, R. *Organizational Stress,* New York: John Wiley & Sons, 1964.

Lorsch, J., & Lawrence, P. "Organizing for Product Innovations." *Harvard Business Review* 43, no. 1 (1965) pp. 109–22.

Rogers, C., & Roethlisberger, F.J. "Barriers and Gateways to Communication." *Harvard Business Review* 30, no. 4 (1952), pp. 46–52.

Schultz, W. *FIRO—B.* New York: Holt, Rinehart & Winston, 1958.

Selznick, P. *Leadership in Administration.* New York: Harper & Row, 1957.

Shepard, H., & Blake, R. "Changing Behavior through Cognitive Change." *Human Organization* 21, no. 2 (1962), pp. 88–96.

Walker, C. *Modern Civilization and Technology.* New York: McGraw-Hill, 1958.

Reading 15
Planning Procedures/Managing Interfaces/Charting Responsibility

Richard Beckhard
Reuben T. Harris

From new structures, multiple roles, and new reporting relationships emerge problems of job definitions, reporting lines, accountability, and performance review. In managing a change effort in a large system, the point of pressure for change will probably occur at some organizational interface. Significant changes occur when: (1) the task relationships between, say, market research and market development are reorganized; (2) it is necessary to superimpose programs on top of functional organizations; or (3) there are mergers of different organizations with different backgrounds or cultures. Such reorganizations tend to have some characteristics of a matrix organization—increased ambiguity, role confusion, problems with decision making, and communications problems.

The typical ways of resolving these dilemmas are to:

1. Try to get clearer job descriptions of each job or position involved.
2. Use a mediating mode (e.g., upper management defines the responsibilities of the various roles).
3. Utilize intergroup development activities designed to clarify responsibilities, authority, and rewards.

Most of these efforts do not succeed too well, however, because they are focused on improving the decision making *or* the communications *or* the power. They are not focused directly on *optimizing work,* although they may appear to.

Source: Richard Beckhard and Reuben T. Harris, *Organizational Transitions: Managing Complex Change,* (pp. 76–82). © 1987, 1977 Addison Wesley Longman, Inc. Reprinted by permission of Addison Wesley Longman.

Responsibility Charting

In recent years a new technique has emerged which does focus on allocating work responsibilities; this technique is called *responsibility charting.* The first step is to construct a grid; the types of decisions and classes of actions that need to be taken in the total area of work under discussion are listed along the left-hand side of the grid, and the actors who might play some part in decision making on those issues are identified across the top of the grid (see Figure 1).

The process, then, is one of assigning a behavior to each of the actors opposite each of the issues. There are four classes of behavior:

1. *Responsibility (R)*—the responsibility to initiate action to ensure that the decision is carried out. For example, it would be a department head's responsibility (R) to initiate the departmental budget.
2. *Approval required, or the right to veto (A–V)*—the particular item must be reviewed by the particular role occupant, and this person has the option of either vetoing or approving it.
3. *Support (S)*—providing logistical support and resources for the particular item.
4. *Inform (I)*—*must be* informed and, by inference, cannot influence.

Each item is considered and responsibility (R) assigned. A very important aspect of the technique is that there can be only *one* R on any one horizontal line. Therefore, a consensus must be reached or an authoritarian decision made on who has the responsibility. If the group is unable to agree about where the R should go, there are three options:

174

FIGURE 1

Responsibility chart

CODE:	R–	Responsibility (initiates)													
	A–V	Approval (right to veto)													
	S–	Support (put resources against)													
	I–	Inform (to be informed)													

Actors →
Decisions
↓

1. Break the problem out—always the most desirable alternative. For example, the R for a large capital expenditure might be different from the R for small capital expenditure.
2. Move the R up one level in the organization hierarchy. For example, if the marketing manager and production manager cannot agree which one of them should have the R for defining monthly production targets, move the R up to their boss, the division general manager.
3. Move the *decision about assigning the* R up one level. In the previous example, the division general manager would assign the

R for setting production targets rather than define the targets themselves.

Once the R has been assigned, the next step is to take a new item and assign a behavior for the various actors. In addition to R–A–S–I alternatives, it is possible that an actor has no assigned behavior opposite a particular type of activity, and this situation should be indicated by a dash (—).

Completion of the horizontal line gives one a de facto modus operandi for handling that particular class of task and its associated roles. Completion of a responsibility chart for all of the tasks relevant to the interfaces between departments or organizations and reading down a column vertically reveals the consensus role description of a particular actor on all those matters in which he or she is interdependent with other roles.

Some Further Guidelines in the Process

1. If an item has several As—for example, one R, six As, one S, and one I—undoubtedly it will be very difficult to accomplish that task. For example, one organization decided to increase its benefits plan for management. The plan was agreed to by all levels of the organization; the board approved it, and the compensation people were told to install the plan. Nine months later, the plan was still not in. A responsibility-charting exercise indicated that each of the major profit centers had defined itself as having an A because it was an independent profit center with a budget commitment to the center. Because this new program required investment of funds not budgeted, each profit center's manager felt it was his or her choice to decide whether or not to institute the program this year or next year. It did not take long for the managing director to indicate, and for the profit center managers to see, that S rather than A was the appropriate symbol to describe the profit center's role. Then the program got instituted very quickly.

2. Depending on who is filling out the chart, one might find a skewing of As under the senior executive. Subordinate managers tend to give their bosses more As than in fact the bosses want. It is desirable to try to minimize the number of As for any task if one wishes to facilitate the accomplishment of the task.

3. The decision about who can allocate a letter to a role can be tricky. In one situation, for example, the management group decided that first-line supervisors in the production organization should be held accountable for weekly scrap losses and various other things and should have timely information about their progress toward their objectives and organization standards. However, the controller's department, which was part of the general headquarters, refused to develop and introduce a new cost-accounting system. The department's requirements for accounting systems were focused primarily on the needs of the top of the organization, the tax people, and the like, and another system would have to be added in order to provide this new type of information. The department felt that as the top financial resource, it should have responsibility for deciding whether or not such a system, with the attendant costs, would be introduced.

At a responsibility-charting session, it became clear that the department had defined itself as having an A, whereas others lower in the organization felt strongly that the department should have an S—that it should be required to produce the system. At the meeting, the general manager supported those who were arguing for the S on the basis that the task required it. This changed the basis for making decisions from hierarchy position to task accomplishment.

Some Applications

Illustration One: A Change in Structure. A large consumer company identified with a particular product orientation decided to "go to market" in a different way. Previously the company had sold its product, which was used in interior decorating, through specialty stores. Instead of being known as a single-product company, the company now wanted to be known as a decorating company. This meant changing the products in the stores, changing the relationship of the franchised stores to the corporation, differentiating the various types of buyers—housewives, contractors, and so on—and providing outlets for customers' different needs.

The prechange organization was a marketing-sales-functional organization. All selling was done in the geographic regions under the direction of division and, ultimately, regional sales managers. Plants made products on demand from the different regions. The technical-service organization made the special blends of products required by the sales organization.

The company's top management felt that, given the new marketing plan and corporate image, a new organizational structure was needed. Accordingly, the sales organization was maintained, but purely as a selling organization. Product managers were created within the marketing organization and were given worldwide responsibility for sales in their particular product or market area. Also created were product-technical mangers, who came from the technical organization but also had a product or business orientation. People in the new technical-service role would now receive all of their instructions from the product-technical director, rather than from the sales organization.

Everyone in the organization, with the exception of the production and finance organizations, now had a new role, a new set of task responsibilities, and new relationships. Much confusion could be expected.

The strategy for dealing with the confusion was to conduct a series of *responsibility-charting conferences*. The first two-day conference focused on the new roles—the product managers from marketing, the technical-product managers, and the top of the organization (i.e., the directors of marketing, manufacturing, technical and finance, and the group vice president). After opening remarks by the group vice president, the participants proceeded to do a responsibility-charting exercise. They identified areas of decision and activities that needed to be done, made a list of the actors, and then assigned behaviors to these actors. Because the top of the organization was also present, the assigned behavior could be "reality-tested" right then. The output of the two days was a "map" of the general modus operandi as seen by the top management and the occupants of the new roles.

Next, the two sets of roles in marketing—sales and product management—and the two sets of technical roles—product management and technical service—met to work through responsibilities and to assign behaviors for their roles in the new setup. Difficulties arising with the earlier models and maps were resolved by the top-management group that had attended the first workshops. The results were then distributed to everybody and became the basis for work.

The change, a massive one involving several thousand managers, was in effect. People were operating in their new roles within six weeks of the announcement of the change. The process of having all of the key people sit down together and develop the new modus operandi was credited by most as having a significant effect on the efficiency of the change.

WHEN POWER CONFLICTS TRIGGER TEAM SPIRIT

Roger Harrison

Getting people to work together in harmony is no easy task. Modern management techniques abound with new approaches to improving the working relationship between employees. In the United States, sensitivity training has had quite a vogue, and various techniques such as the T-group or the managerial grid have been brought forth to encourage managers to abandon their competitiveness and to create mutual trust and egalitarian approaches to decision making.

Or managers have been urged to change their motivations from reliance upon monetary reward or punishment to more internal motivation based on intrinsic interest in the job and personal commitment to meeting work objectives: for example, in Management by Objectives and programs of job enrichment. Still other practitioners have developed purely rational approaches to group problem solving: for example, Kepner Tregoe in the United States, and Coverdale in Britain.

Running through these approaches is the tendency to ignore or explain away competition, conflict and the struggle for power and influence. They assume people will be cooperative and productive if they are taught how, or if the barriers to their so being are removed. These approaches may be called *tender minded,* in that they see power struggles as a symptom of a managerial *mistake,* rather than a basic and ubiquitous process in organizations.

The problem of organizational change is seen as one of *releasing* human potential for collaboration and productivity, rather than as one of controlling or checking competition for advantage and position.

However, consider the case of the production and engineering managers of a plant who had frequent disagreements over the work that was done by the latter for the former. The production manager

Source: Roger Harrison, *European Business,* Spring 1972, pp. 57–65.

complained that the engineering manager set maintenance priorities to meet his own convenience and reduce his own costs, rather than to make sure production targets were met. The engineering manager maintained that the production manager gave insufficient notice of jobs which could be anticipated, and the production operators caused unnecessary breakdowns by failure to carry out preventive maintenance procedures faithfully. The two men aired their dissatisfaction with one another's performance from time to time; but, according to both parties, no significant change has occurred.

Or take the case of the scientist in a development department, who complains of overly close supervision by his section manager. According to the scientist, the manager intervenes to change the priorities he assigns to work, or to interfere with his development of promising lines of enquiry, and to check up with insulting frequency to see whether the scientist is carrying out the manager's instructions.

The scientist is actively trying to get a transfer to another section, because he feels he cannot do a proper job with so much hampering interference from above.

On the other hand, the section manager says the scientist does competent work but is secretive and unwilling to heed advice. He fails to let the manager know what he is doing and deviates without discussion from agreements the manager thought they had reached about how the work should be carried out. The manager feels he has to spend far too much time checking up on the scientist and is beginning to wonder whether his otherwise good work is worth the trouble required to manage him.

In both of these examples, the men are concerned with either gaining increased control over the actions of the other, reducing control by the other or both. And they know it. A consultant talking to them about communication problems or target setting would no doubt be listened to politely, but in their hearts, these men would still feel it was a question of who was going to have the final say, who was going to be boss.

And, in a way, they are more intuitively right than any outside consultant could be. They know where the power and influence lie, whether people are on their side or against them. They are aware of those with whom they can be open and honest and those who will use information against them. And these concerns are much more accurate and real than an outsider's suggestions for openness and collaboration.

Knowing Where the Power and Coercion Lie

Does this mean that most behavioral science approaches to business are too optimistic? What is certain is that they fail to take into account the forces of power, competitiveness, and coercion. In this article, I shall propose a method that does work directly with these issues, a method that gets tough with the team spirit.

This program is based on role negotiation. This technique describes the process that involves changing through *negotiation* with other interested parties the *role* that an individual or group performs in the organization. By an individual's or a group's *role,* I mean what activities he is supposed to perform, what decisions he can make, to whom he reports and about what and how often, who can legitimately tell him what to do and under what circumstances, and so on. Some people would say that a man's *job* is the same as what I have called his *role,* and I would partially agree with this. But what I mean by *role* includes not only the formal job description but also all the informal understandings, agreements, expectations, and arrangements with others which determine the way one person's or group's work affects or fits in with another's.

Role negotiation intervenes directly in the relationships of power, authority, and influence within the group. The change effort is directed at the work relationships among members. It avoids probing into the likes and dislikes of members for one another. In this it is more consonant with the task-oriented norms of business than are most other behavioral approaches.

The Fear of Touchy Emotional Confrontations

When I first developed the technique, I tried it out on a client group which was proving particularly hard to work with. They were suspicious and mistrustful of me and of each other, and said quite openly that talking about their relationships was both "irrelevant to our work problems" and "dangerous—it could split the group apart." When I introduced them to role negotiation, they saw ways they could deal with issues that were bothering them without getting into touchy emotional confrontations they could not handle. They dropped their resistance dramatically and turned to work with a will that surprised and delighted me.

I have used role negotiation successfully with top management groups, project teams, even between husbands and wives. The technique can be used with very small or quite large groups—although groups of over 8 or 10 should be broken down.

The technique makes one basic assumption: *most people prefer a fair negotiated settlement to a state of unresolved conflict,* and they are willing to invest some time and make some concessions in order to achieve a solution. To operate the program a modest but significant risk is called for from the participants: they must be open about the changes in behavior, authority, responsibility, and so on they wish to obtain from others in the situation.

If the participants are willing to specify concretely the changes they desire from others, then significant changes in work effectiveness can usually be obtained.

How does this program work in reality? First of all, the consultant must have the participants' sufficient confidence in his motives and competence so that they are willing at his behest to try something new and a bit strange. It also stands to reason that the consultant should know enough about the people, their work system, and their relationship problems to satisfy himself that the members of the group are ready to make a real effort towards improvement. No technique will work if the clients don't trust the consultant enough to give it a fair try or if the members of the group (particularly the high-influence members) devote most of their effort to maintaining the status quo. In the description that follows I am assuming that this confidence and readiness to work have been established. Although this is a rather large assumption, these problems are universal in consulting and not peculiar to role negotiation. If anything, I have found that role negotiation requires somewhat less preparation than other team development techniques I have used.

Let us say we are working with a group of five to seven people, including a manager and his subordinates, two levels in the formal organization. Once basic assumptions of trust are established, I try to get at least a day with the group away from the job location to start the role negotiation process going. A two-day session with a commitment to follow up in three to four weeks is best. If the group is not felt to be quite prepared to undertake serious work, the session may be made longer with some trust building and diagnostic activities in the beginning, working into the role negotiation when and if the group is ready for it.

No Probing into People's Feelings

The first step in the actual role negotiation is *contract setting*. Its purpose is to make it clear between the group and the consultant what each may expect from the other. This is a critical step in the change process. It controls and channels everything that happens afterwards.

My contract is usually based on the following provisions, which should be written down, if only as a first practice step in the formal way of working which I try to establish.

It is not legitimate for the consultant to press or probe anyone's *feelings*. We are concerned about work: who does what, how, and with whom. How people *feel* about their work or about others in the

group is their own business, to be introduced or not according to their own judgment and desire. The expression or nonexpression of feelings is not part of the contract.

Openness and honesty about behavior are expected and essential for achieving results. The consultant will insist that people be specific and concrete in expressing their expectations and demands for the behavior of others. Each team member is expected to be open and specific about what he wants others to do *more* or *do better* or *do less* or *maintain unchanged*.

No expectation or demand is adequately communicated until it has been *written down* and is clearly understood by both sender and receiver, nor will any change process be engaged in until this has been done.

The full sharing of expectations and demands does not constitute a completed change process. It is only the precondition for change to be agreed through negotiation. It is unreasonable for anyone in the group, manager or subordinate, to expect that any change will take place merely as a result of communicating a demand or expectation. Unless a team member is willing to change his own behavior in order to get what he wants from the other(s), he is likely to waste his and the group's time talking about the issue. When a member makes a request or demand for changed behavior on the part of another, the consultant will always ask what quid pro quo (something for something) he is willing to give in order to get what he wants. This goes for the manager as well as for the subordinates. If the former can get what he wants simply by issuing orders or clarifying expectations from his position of authority, he probably does not need a consultant or a change process.

The change process is essentially one of bargaining and negotiation in which two or more members each agree to change behavior in exchange for some desired change on the part of the other. This process is not complete until the agreement can be *written down* in terms which include the agreed changes in behavior and make clear what each party is expected to give in return.

Threats and pressures are neither illegitimate nor excluded from the negotiation process. However, group members should realize that overreliance on threats and punishment usually results in defensiveness, concealment, decreased communication and retaliation, and may lead to breakdown of the negotiation. The consultant will do his best to help members accomplish their aims with positive incentives wherever possible.

The Secret Game of Influence Bargaining

Each member has power and influence in the group, both positively to reward and collaborate with others, and negatively to resist, block or punish. Each uses his power and influence to create a desirable and satisfying work situation for himself. Most of the time this process is gone about secretly. People use a lot of time and energy trying to figure out how to influence another person's behavior covertly; but since they rarely are aware of others' wants and needs, their attempts fail.

Although in stable organizations, employees can learn what works on others just through trial and error over long periods of time, nowadays the fast personnel turnover makes this primitive process obsolete.

Role negotiation tries to replace this old process with a more efficient one. If one person knows because it has been made public what another's wants or intentions are, he is bound to be more effective in trying to influence that person. In addition, when someone tries to influence him, the quid pro quo put forward is more likely to be one he really wants or needs. I try to show my clients that, by sharing the information about desires and attempts, *role negotiation increases the total amount of influence group members have on one another.*

The next stage is *issue diagnosis.* Each member spends some time thinking about the way business is conducted between himself and the others in the group. What would he change if he could? What would he like to keep as is? Who and what would have to change in order to improve things? I ask the participants to focus especially on the things

which might be changed to improve their *own effectiveness,* since these are the items to be discussed and negotiated.

After he has spent 20 minutes or so thinking about these matters and perhaps making a few notes, each member fills out one Issue Diagnosis Form (like the one in Figure 1) for each other member, listing those things he would like to see the other person:

1. Do more or do better.

2. Do less or stop doing.

3. Keep on doing, maintain unchanged.

All of these messages are based on the sender's increasing his own effectiveness in his job.

These lists are exchanged so that each person has all the lists pertaining to his work behavior. Each member makes a master list for himself on a large piece of paper itemizing the behavior which each other person desires him to do *more* or *better, less,* or *continue unchanged* (Figure 2). These are posted so that the entire group can peruse and refer to each list. Each member is allowed to question the others who have sent messages about his behavior, querying the what, why, and how of their requests; *but no one is allowed a rebuttal, defense or even a yes or no reply to the messages he has received.* The consultant must assure that only clarification is taking place; argument, discussion, and decision making about issues must be engaged in at a later stage.

Defensiveness Just to Save Face

The purpose of the consultant's rather rigid and formal control on communication is to prevent the group from having a negative problem-solving experience, and members from becoming polarized on issues or taking up extreme positions which they will feel impelled to defend just to save face. Communication is controlled to prevent escalation of actual or potential conflicts. Channeling the energy released by the sharing of demands and expectations into successful problem solving and mutual influence is behind this strategy of control.

FIGURE 1

Issue Diagnosis Form

Messages from _____ Jim Farrell _____

to _____ David Sills _____

1. If you were to do the following things <u>more</u> or <u>better</u>, it would help me to increase my own effectiveness:

    —Being more receptive to improvement suggestions from the process engineers.
    —Give help on cost control (see 2).
    —Fight harder with the G.M. to get our plans improved.

2. If you were to do the following things <u>less</u>, or were to <u>stop</u> doing them, it would help me to increase my own effectiveness:

    —Acting as judge and jury on cost control.
    —Checking up frequently on small details of the work.
    —Asking for so many detailed progress reports.

3. The following things which you have been doing help to increase my own effectiveness, and I hope you will continue to do them:

    —Passing on full information in our weekly meetings.
    —Being available when I need to talk to you.

The consultant intervenes to inhibit hostile and destructive expression at this point and later to facilitate constructive bargaining and negotiation of mutually beneficial agreements.

This initial sharing of desires and change goals among group members leads to a point at which the team development process is most vulnerable. If sufficient anger and defensiveness are generated by the problem sharing, the consultant will not be able to hold the negative processes in check long enough for the development of the positive problem-solving spiral on which the process depends for its effectiveness. It is true that such an uncon-trollable breakthrough of hostility has not yet occurred in my experience with the method. Nevertheless, concern over the negative possibilities is in part responsible for my slow, deliberate, and rather formal development of the confrontation of issues within the group.

The Influence Trade

After each member had had an opportunity to clarify the messages he has received, the group selects the issues for negotiation. The consultant begins this phase by reemphasizing that, unless a quid pro quo can be offered in return for a desired behavior change, there is little point in having a discussion about it: *unless behavior changes on both sides the most likely prediction is that the status quo will continue.*

If behavior changes merely as the result of an exchange of views between men of good will, all the better. However, one cannot count on it.

Each participant is asked to choose one or more issues on which he particularly wants to get some changes on the part of another. He is also asked to select one or more issues on which he feels it may be possible for him to move in the direction desired by others. He does this by marking his own flip chart and those of the other members. In effect, *each person indicates the issues upon which he most wants to exert influence and those on which he is most willing to accept influence.* With the help of the consultant, the group then goes through the list to select the most negotiable issues, those where there is a combination of a high desire for change on the part of an initiator and a willingness to negotiate on the part of the person whose behavior is the target of the change attempt. The consultant asks for a group of two or more persons who are involved in one such issue to volunteer for a negotiation demonstration before the rest of the group.

The negotiation process consists of the parties making contingent offers to one another such as "If you do X, I will do Y." The negotiation ends when all parties are satisfied that they will receive a reasonable return for whatever they are agreeing to

FIGURE 2

Summary of messages to James Farrell from other group members

MORE OR BETTER:	LESS OR STOP:	CONTINUE AS NOW:
Give information on project progress (completion date slippage)—Bill, Tony, David.	Let people go to other good job opportunities— stop hanging on to your good engineers—Tony, Bill.	Training operators on preventive maintenance— Henry.
Send progress reports on Sortair project—Bill.	Missing weekly planning meetings frequently—Jack, Henry, David.	Good suggestions in meetings—Tony, Henry.
Make engineers more readily available when help needed— Jack, Henry.	Ignoring memos and reports re cost control—David.	Asking the difficult and awkward questions—Tony, Jack.
Keep better informed re plans and activities—David.	Setting aside my priorities on engineering work—Henry, Jack.	Willingness to help on design problems—Bill, Jack.
Enforce safety rules on engineers when in production area—Henry.	Charging time on Sortair to other accounts—David.	Good quality project work— Bill, Henry, David, Jack.
Push harder on the Sensiter project—David, Henry, Tony, Jack.	Overrunning agreed project budget without discussing beforehand—David.	

give. The consultant asks that the agreement be formalized by writing down specifically and concretely what each party is going to give and receive in the bargain (Figure 3). He also asks the participants to discuss openly what sanctions can be applied in the case of nonfulfillment of the bargain by one or another party. Often this involves no more than reversion of the status quo, but it may involve the application of pressures and penalties as well.

After the negotiation demonstration, the members are asked to select other issues they wish to work on. A number of negotiations may go on simultaneously, the consultant being involved at the request of any party to any negotiation. All agreements are published to the entire group, however, and questioned by the consultant and the other members to test the good faith and reality orientation of the parties in making them. Where agreement proves impossible, the consultant and other group members try to help the parties find further

incentives (positive or, less desirably, coercive) which they may bring to bear to encourage agreement.

This process is, of course, not as simple as it sounds. All kinds of difficulties can occur, from bargaining in bad faith, to refusal to bargain at all, to escalation of conflict. In my experience, however, group members tend to be rather wise about the issues they can and cannot deal with, and I refrain from pushing them to negotiate issues they feel are unresolvable. My aim is to light the sparks of team development with a successful experience which group members can look on as a fruitful way of improving their effectiveness and satisfaction.

The Consultant Withers Away

The cycle ends here. Each group must then try living with their agreements. There is always, of course, the occasion to meet later with the consultant to work out new agreements or renegotiate old ones.

FIGURE 3

Final agreement between James Farrell and David Sills

Jim agrees to let David know as soon as agreed completion dates and cost projections look as though they won't be met, and also to discuss each project's progress fully with David on a bi-weekly basis.

In return, David agrees not to raise questions about cost details and completion dates, pending a trial of this agreement to see if it provides sufficient information soon enough to deal with questions from above.

Ideally, the group should learn this process so thoroughly that the consultant's role withers away. To do this, though, they must be so fully aware of the dangers and pitfalls involved in the negotiation process that a third party's arbitration is no longer needed.

So far this has not occurred in my experience. The positive results are expressed mostly in terms of less backsliding between visits than has occurred in groups where I have applied more interpersonal behavior-change methods. Role negotiation agreements have more teeth in them.

What are the advantages of role negotiation? First of all, participants seem more at home with problems of power and influence than other interpersonal issues. They feel more competent and less dependent on the consultant in dealing with the problems and so they are ready to work sooner and harder.

Furthermore, the consultant's or referee's amount of skill and professional training which is required to conduct role negotiation is less than for more sensitive approaches.

That does not mean that role negotiation poses no threat to organization members. The consultant asks participants to be open about matters that are often kept secret in everyday life. This requires more than the normal amount of trust and confidence. If not, these matters would have been talked about before the group ever got to the role negotiation.

There also seems to be some additional discomfort involved in *writing down* the changes one

would like to see another make in his work behavior. Several times participants have questioned the necessity of doing this, because one feels so *exposed* when his concerns are written out for all to see, and there is the fear that others will think them silly, childish or odd (though this never seems to happen). If the matter comes up, I point out that one need not write down *all* the concerns he has, but only those he would like to work on with others at this time.

Of course, role negotiation, like any other process that changes relationships, does pose a threat to the participants. The members are never sure they will personally be better off after the change than before. In the case of role negotiation, most of these fears arise around losing power and influence, or losing freedom and becoming more controlled by others. Particular resistance to talking openly about issues occurs when someone is trying to manipulate another person to his own advantage, or when he feels that he might want to do this in the future. I think this is the main reason participants in role negotiation so often try to avoid the step of writing down their agreements. If things aren't down in black and white, they feel, it will be easier to ignore the agreement later on if it becomes inconvenient. Also, writing down agreements seems to dispel the aura of trust and good fellowship which some groups like to create on the surface and below which they engage in quite a lot of cutthroat competition.

Role negotiation is of course no panacea for power problems in groups and between people. People may bargain in bad faith; agreements once reached may be broken; circumstances and personnel may change so that the work done becomes irrelevant. Of course, these problems can exist in any group or organization. What role negotiation *does* is try to deal with the problems directly and to identify and use constructively those areas of *mutual* advantage where both sides can benefit from discussion and agreement. These areas are almost always larger than people think they are, and when they find that they can achieve something *for* themselves by open negotiation which they could not achieve by covert competition, then the more constructive process can begin to grow.

Avoiding the Consultant's High Fees

One other likely advantage of role negotiation is the ease and economy with which it can be introduced into the firm.

One disadvantage of most behavioral approaches to team development is that the consultant's level of skill and experience must be very high indeed. Managers themselves are not confident in dealing with these issues, and because they feel uneasy in this area they reasonably want to have as much safety and skill as money can buy. This demand for skilled consultants on interpersonal and group processes has created a shortage and a meteoric rise in consulting fees. It seems unlikely that the supply will soon catch up with the demand.

The shortage of highly skilled workers in team development argues for deskilling the requirements for effective consultant performance. I see role negotiation as a way of reducing the skill requirements for team development consultation. Preliminary results by internal consultants using the approach have been promising.

For example, one management development manager teamed up with a colleague to conduct a successful role negotiation with his own top management. He reported that his main problem was getting up enough confidence to take on the job. The team development session itself went smoothly. Although I cannot say whether this experience was typical (I suspect it was not), it does lead me to hope that role negotiation will prove to be practical for use by internal consultants without professional training in the behavioral sciences.

What then are the main points about role negotiation? First, role negotiation focuses on work relationships: what people do, and how they facilitate and inhibit one another in the performance of their jobs. It encourages participants to work with problems using words and concepts they are used to using in business. It avoids probing to the deeper levels of their feelings about one another unless this comes out naturally in the process.

Second, it deals directly with problems of power and influence which may be neglected by other behavioral approaches. It does not attempt to dethrone the authority in the group, but other members are helped to explore realistically the sources of power and influence available to them.

Also, unlike some other behavioral approaches to team development, role negotiation is highly action-oriented. Its aim is not just the exposing and understanding of issues as such, but achieving changed ways of working through mutually negotiated agreements. Changes brought about through role negotiation thus tend to be more stable and lasting than where such negotiated commitments are lacking.

In addition, all the procedures of role negotiation are clear and simple if a bit mechanical, and can be described to participants in advance so they know what they are getting into. There is nothing mysterious about the technique, and this reduces participants' feelings of dependency upon the special skill of the consultant.

Furthermore, role negotiation actually requires less skill from the consultant than some other behavioral approaches. Internal consultants can suitably use the technique without lengthy special training in the behavioral sciences. It can therefore be a moderate cost approach to organization change.

It's important to understand that role negotiation does not necessarily replace other "soft" behavioral approaches to organization change. Work groups can be effective and achievement-oriented and at the same time allow open and deeply satisfying interpersonal relationships.

However, resolving conflict successfully at the interpersonal level can only be done by first attacking the ever-present issues of power and influence among members. Role negotiation does this and provides a sound and effective base on which to build more satisfying relationships.

If role negotiation is an effective first or "basic" approach to team development, it goes without saying that employee growth means moving beyond this stage into a deeper exploration of integrating work and relationships.

READING 17
STRATEGIES FOR IMPROVING HEADQUARTERS-FIELD RELATIONS

Robert Blake
Herbert A. Shepard
Jane S. Mouton

Organizations whose operations extend over great distances encounter complex problems in maintaining effective integration between the headquarters facility and field installations.[1] Geographical distance makes communications difficult. Differences in regional experience are hard for the person at a distance to comprehend. Psychological distance develops to enhance the mechanical difficulties created by geography.

In all other parts of an organization, subordinate groups are joined to subordinate groups by a common member (i.e., the leader of a subordinate group is himself a subordinate in the group consisting of himself, his peers, and his boss).[2] The linkpin between groups of unequal power, while more responsive to those above than below, nonetheless has a powerful mediating effect. He is placed in personal conflict and stress if the two groups in which he has membership are in conflict. The stresses on the foreman are so great that in many organizations he loses membership in both groups; that is, he has little influence up or down. Clearly, there is no linkpin between union and management, and, through unionization and legislative supports, union and management are approximately equal in power.

Most headquarters-field relationships lack this cement, and it is not uncommon for negative attitudes to develop between the parties. In formal theory, field units are subordinate to headquarters, but field units can acquire great informal power. This is particularly true if one field organization is very much larger than other field divisions and accounts for a majority, or at least a large portion,

of the company's business. In such cases, the head of the field division may be given formal membership in the top corporate group, thus providing the missing cement. But if, as is more often the case, there are several large or many small field units, headquarters maintains its power by placing them in competition with one another. Building good relations and a good record with headquarters can lead to promotion for key executives in a field unit and to a favored position when headquarters contemplates new investment.

Field groups can develop resentment toward headquarters for many reasons. For example, each field unit is, in most companies, treated as a profit center. However, the profitability of the whole corporation may sometimes require that a given field unit do something which reduces its own profitability. Similarly, new investment by headquarters in one field unit can arouse feelings of injustice in others.

Such problems were causing severe deterioration of relationships between headquarters and a large division in the Tennex Corporation. The following pages describe the problem-solving procedures employed to bring about adequate working relationships. The design was, of course, adapted to the particular set of problems being experienced by Tennex. A different design would be used, for example, if the object were to build better team relations among several field units, and between them and headquarters.

The Scofield Case

The following example illustrates an approach to the improvement of working relationships between headquarters and field. The Scofield Division is one

Source: Robert Blake, Herbert A. Shepard, and Jane S. Mouton, *Managing Intergroup Conflict in Industry* (Houston: Gulf Publishing, 1964), pp. 114–21.

of several subsidiaries of the Tennex Corporation. The Tennex Corporation is a highly diversified organization, moderately decentralized.

Since World War II, Tennex has grown quite rapidly, partly by acquisition. Corporate efforts to develop strategies in marketing and production which took advantage of its diverse resources brought many changes which affected Scofield, one of the divisions. Over a period of years, a number of points of friction had developed between the division's management and the top corporate management.

Headquarters personnel felt the division managers were "secretive" and "unresponsive." The division was looked upon as unwilling to provide information that headquarters felt it needed. In turn, Scofield Division management saw the headquarters management as "prying" and "arbitrary." For example, headquarters was critical of the labor relations practices of the division. The division management resented the criticism, regarding it as prejudiced and ill-informed. Again, headquarters felt that Scofield managers had been "dragging their feet" in implementing corporate marketing policies. Scofield felt that headquarters' demands in the area were unrealistic and that the corporate marketing group was behaving "unilaterally," and so on.

The behavioral science consultants called in to help first acquainted themselves with key management in both locations and were exposed to the patterns of action and reaction, frustration, and negative stereotypes, which characterize a deteriorating intergroup working relationship. Some of the headquarters executives were considering replacing certain Scofield managers. The latter, in their turn, were attempting to influence other top corporate officers in Scofield's behalf.

Gaining Perspective on Intergroup and Intragroup Dynamics.

In separate three-day conferences with each group, the consultants provided intragroup (or "team") and intergroup training experiences and theory. The intergroup training had two effects. First, managers were able to see the

headquarters-field problem in sufficient perspective to analyze the destructive consequences of the win-lose trap which had been dictating their actions. Second, an intergroup experiment and its analysis created a degree of openness within each group of managers that enable them to review their own intragroup relationships and to develop greater mutual understanding and acceptance. This team-work training is an important prelude to intergroup confrontation, because friction, "politics," or inability to level within each team clouds and confuses intergroup communication when the two groups are brought together.

The Headquarters-Field Laboratory.

As a next step after the separate three-day conferences, the two teams met together, again for a three-day period. It will be convenient to describe their work as a sequence of phases.

Phase I: Listing Issues Requiring Joint Problem Solving.   The laboratory opened with a joint session in which members discussed those issues they felt the group should debate. These were then listed in order of priority to provide an overview of the work to be accomplished over the three-day period.

Phase II: Preparation of Group Self-Images and Images of the Other Group.   Each group met separately to prepare a description of itself as viewed by its members. The issues listed in Phase I provided a basis for elaborating and giving substance to the self-image descriptions.

Next, each group constructed a verbal image *of the other group*. Scofield's "secretiveness" as experienced by headquarters and headquarters' "prying" as experienced by Scofield could thus be brought into open communication.

Finally, each group built a description of the relationship between Tennex headquarters and the Scofield Division.

These images were developed to provide a background statement of existing attitudes, feelings, and difficulties which needed to be examined, understood, and overcome.

Phase III: Exchange of Images.   During this phase, each group in turn exposed its own image of itself, and in turn listened to the image as perceived by the other group. The process of bringing these images into the open created a background of understanding and brought a new atmosphere of mutual acceptance into the discussion.

Finally, a review was undertaken of relationship problems with respect to the issues that had been listed at the beginning of the conference. Since most of these were related to specific functions and activities, they provided the basis for moving to the subgroup meetings of Phase IV.

Phase IV: Subgroup Meetings Based on Similarity of Function in Field and Headquarters. During Phase IV, members from the headquarters staff with functional responsibilities at the corporate level met with Scofield managers who had responsibility for the corresponding function in the plant.

The purpose of these discussions was akin to the "team development" of the earlier three-day conferences: to explore relationship problems between individuals whose responsibilities make them interdependent. Once interpersonal relationship issues had been explored and sources of difficulty had been cleared out of the way, it was possible to discuss functional problems in a climate conducive to understanding and collaboration.

The latter part of Phase III and beginning of Phase IV brought out dramatically how confused and inadequate communication between Scofield and headquarters had been in many areas. The headquarters group seized on the relationship-image exchange as an excellent opportunity to "explain" to Scofield things that they believed Scofield did not understand. As the discussion proceeded, however, the tables were turned. When the field group presented its view of the relationship it began to "get through" to headquarters. By the end of Phase IV, headquarters staff members were *really* able to understand operational difficulties from a field point of view. They were also able to see more clearly how they might serve as consultants in the field, rather than as persons who attempt to "control" field operations.

Phase V: Review and Planning.   In this phase the two groups met to prepare an overall summary of problems that had been identified and defined. This led to a joint discussion of the kinds of changes required to bring about improvements. Some of the problems implied changes in the behavior of only one of the groups, but most required joint implementation by functional subgroups.

The most significant product of this phase was that it provided a new concept of the way to bring about change and innovation. For instance, prior to the headquarters-field conference, it was accepted that "headquarters formulates policy; the field implements it." The inappropriateness of this concept for policies which had long been in force was evident to both parties. Reports from the field told headquarters whether the policy was being implemented adequately and enabled the headquarters to take special action where departures from policy were detected.

Conference discussions clearly disclosed that this control was woefully inadequate during a period of policy changing, policymaking, or during implementation of new or changed policies. Communication distortions and breakdowns, areas of mutual frustration with the accompanying charges of "foot-dragging" and "arbitrariness," were seen to be the result of those methods which had been used in developing and implementing new policies.

Both sides came to see clearly that making and implementing new or changed policy is a complex process requiring continuous feedback among those involved. Efforts to implement a change are experiments, the results of which need to be quickly available to the organization. They are reality tests which may lead to policy modification, and they are explorations to find sufficient methods of implementation. The policy-making-and-implementing process was thus seen as an innovation phase requiring open communication and collaboration among members of the leadership groups.

Phase VI: Followup. By the end of Phase V, much had been accomplished in the areas of mutual trust, respect, and understanding. Moreover, the groups had made a number of commitments to new ways of working and had reached a number of agreements in defining certain problems and the courses of action to be taken in solving them.

Realizing that planning is insufficient to bring about desired results, the groups established some means for operational follow-up. The groups also agreed to reconvene for review and evaluation after a period of implementation. The purpose of this meeting would be to insure that they could find ways to handle possible difficulties in carrying out the plans of Phase V, and in "checking on the health" of the relationship. Thus, if new sources of friction were to arise for which no problem-solving procedure was available, they could be dealt with appropriately.

Summary

The normal day-by-day arrangements between the headquarters facilities and field units often generate many problem areas. Some of the problems tend to become chronic. As a rule, formal communication and decision-making arrangements are insufficient for correcting these chronic difficulties.

Headquarters-field training situations as described in this article are useful devices for exploring and improving organizational interrelationships, including: headquarters interrelations and operations, field interrelations and operations, problems at the general level between headquarters and the field, and functional and concrete operational difficulties within those segments of the organization which are responsible for smooth working arrangements between headquarters and field.

Appendix: Postscript for "Strategies for Improving Headquarters-Field Relations"

This article represented one of the series of spin-off applications of the basic intergroup confrontation and resolution design that we pioneered in the mid-50s. We see no revisions, based on our experience with it over 25 years, that constitute fundamental improvements. However, consultants using this design implement it in short-cut ways that may fail to solve problems underlying headquarters-field tensions. Limitations such as this in using the design are most likely to derive from the consultant's failure to sense the depth of intergroup tensions, and therefore to prompt premature informality in a way that is not present in the design itself. This is likely to lead to mutual accusations and defensive retaliations, rather than to constructive efforts to resolve the underlying problems.[3]

Endnotes

1. R. R. Blake and J. S. Mouton, "Headquarters-Field Team Training for Organizational Improvement." *ASTD J.* 16, no. 3 (1962), pp. 3–11.
2. R. R. Blake and J. S. Mouton, *The Managerial Grid* (Houston: Gulf Publishing, 1964); and R. Likert, *New Patterns of Management* (New York: McGraw-Hill, 1961).
3. Robert Blake and Jane Mouton, personal correspondence.

READING 18
THE CONFRONTATION MEETING

Richard Beckhard

One of the continuing problems facing the top-management team of any organization in times of stress or major change is how to assess accurately the state of the organization's health. How are people reacting to the change? How committed are subordinate managers to the new conditions? Where are the most pressing organization problems?

In the period following a major change—such as that brought about by a change in leadership or organization structure, a merger, or the introduction of a new technology—there tends to be much confusion and an expenditure of dysfunctional energy that negatively affects both productivity and morale.

At such times, the top-management group usually spends many hours together working on the business problems and finding ways of coping with the new conditions. Frequently, the process of working together under this pressure also has the effect of making the top team more cohesive.

Concurrently, these same managers tend to spend less and less time with their subordinates and with the rest of the organization. Communications decrease between the top and middle levels of management. People at the lower levels often complain that they are less in touch with what is going on than they were before the change. They feel left out. They report having less influence than before, being more unsure of their own decision-making authority, and feeling less sense of ownership in the organization. As a result of this, they tend to make fewer decisions, take few risks, and wait until the "smoke clears."

When this unrest comes to the attention of top management, the response is usually to take some action such as:

Having each member of the top team hold team meetings with his subordinates to communicate the state of affairs, and following this procedure down through the organization.

Holding some general communication improvement meetings.

Conducting an attitude survey to determine priority problems.

Any of these actions will probably be helpful, but each requires a considerable investment of time, which is competitive with the time needed to work on the change problem itself.

Action Plans

Recently I have experimented with an activity that allows a total management group, drawn from all levels of the organization, to take a quick reading on its own health, and—*within a matter of hours*—to set action plans for improving it. I call this a "confrontation meeting."

The activity is based on my previous experience with an action-oriented method of planned change in which information on problems and attitudes is collected and fed back to those who produced it, and steps are taken to start action plans for improvement of the condition.

Sometimes, following situations of organizational stress, the elapsed time in moving from identification of the problem to collaborative action planning must be extremely brief. The confrontation meeting can be carried out in 4½ to 5 hours' working time, and it is designed to include the entire management of a large system in a joint action planning program.

I have found this approach to be particularly practical in organization situations where there are large numbers in the management group and/or where it is difficult to take the entire group off the job for any length of time. The activity has been conducted several times with one evening and one morning session—taking only 2½ hours out of a regular working day.

The confrontation meeting discussed in this article has been used in a number of different organization situations. Experience shows that it is appropriate where:

> There is a need for the total management group to examine its own workings.
>
> Very limited time is available for the activity.
>
> Top management wishes to improve the conditions quickly.
>
> There is enough cohesion in the top team to ensure follow-up.
>
> There is real commitment to resolving the issues on the part of top management.
>
> The organization is experiencing, or has recently experienced, some major change.

In order to show how this technique can speed the process of getting the information and acting on it, let us first look at three actual company situations where this approach has been successfully applied. Then we will examine both the positive results and the possible problems that could occur through the use and misuse of this technique. Finally, after a brief summary there are appendixes for the reader interested in a more elaborate description of the phasing and scheduling of such a meeting.

Case Example A. The initial application of the confrontation meeting technique occurred in 1965 in a large food products company. Into this long-time family-owned and closely controlled company, there was introduced for the first time a nonfamily professional general manager. He had been promoted from the ranks of the group that had previously reported to the family-member general manager.

This change in the "management culture," which had been carefully and thoroughly prepared by the family executives, was carried out

with a minimum number of problems. The new general manager and his operating heads spent many hours together and developed a quite open problem-solving climate and an effective, cohesive team. Day-to-day operations were left pretty much in the hands of their immediate subordinates, while the top group focused on planning.

A few months after the change, however, the general manager began getting some information that indicated all was not well further down in the organization. On investigation, he discovered that many middle-level mangers were feeling isolated from what was going on. Many were unclear about the authority and functions of the "management committee" (his top team); some were finding it very difficult to see and consult with their bosses (his operating heads); others were not being informed of decisions made at his management committee meetings; still others were apprehensive that a new power elite was developing which in many ways was much worse than the former family managers.

In discussing this feedback information with his operating heads, the general manager found one or two who felt these issues required immediate management committee attention. But most of the members of the top team tended to minimize the information as "the usual griping," or "people needing too many decisions made for them," or "everybody always wanting to be in on everything."

The general manager than began searching for some way to:

> Bring the whole matter into the open.
>
> Determine the magnitude and potency of the total problem.
>
> Give his management committee and himself a true picture of the state of the organization's attitudes and concerns.
>
> Collect information on employee needs, problems, and frustrations in some organized way so that corrective actions could be taken in priority order.
>
> Get his management committee members in better tune with their subordinates' feelings

and attitudes, and put some pressure on the team members for continued two-way communication within their own special areas.

Make clear to the total organization that he—the top manager—was personally concerned.

Set up mechanisms by which all members of the total management group could feel that their individual needs were noticed.

Provide additional mechanisms for supervisors to influence the whole organization.

The confrontation meeting was created to satisfy these objectives and to minimize the time in which a large number of people would have to be away from the job.

Some 70 managers, representing the total management group, were brought together for a confrontation meeting starting at 9:00 in the morning and ending at 4:30 in the afternoon. The specific "design" for the day, which is broken down into a more detailed description in Appendix A, had the following components:

1. Climate setting—establishing willingness to participate.
2. Information collecting—getting the attitudes and feelings out in the open.
3. Information sharing—making total information available to all.
4. Priority setting and group action planning—holding work-unit sessions to set priority actions and to make timetable commitments.
5. Organization action planning—getting commitment by top management to the working of these priorities.
6. Immediate follow-up by the top management committee—planning first actions and commitments.

During the daylong affair, the group identified some 80 problems that were of concern to people throughout the organization; they selected priorities from among them; they began working on these priority issues in functional work units, and

each unit produced action recommendations with timetables and targets; and they got a commitment from top management of actions on priorities that would be attended to. The top-management team met immediately after the confrontation meeting to pin down the action steps and commitments.

(In subsequent applications of the confrontation meeting approach, a seventh component—a progress review—has been added, since experience has shown that it is important to reconvene the total group four to six weeks later for a progress review both from the functional units and from the top-management team.)

Case Example B. A small company which makes products for the military had been operating at a stable sales volume of $3 million to $4 million. The invention of a new process and the advent of the war in Vietnam suddenly produced an explosion of business. Volume rose to the level of $6 million within six months and promised to redouble within another year.

Top management was desperately trying to (a) keep raw materials flowing through the line, (b) get material processed, (c) find people to hire, (d) discover quicker ways of job training, and (e) maintain quality under the enormously increased pressure.

There was constant interaction among the five members of the top-management team. They were aware of the tension and fatigue that existed on the production line, but they were only vaguely aware of the unrest, fatigue, concern, and loneliness of the middle manager and foreman groups. However, enough signals *had* filtered up to the top team to cause concern and a decision that something needed to be done right away. But, because of the pressures of work, finding the time to tackle the problems was as difficult as the issues themselves.

The entire management group agreed to give up one night and one morning; the confrontation meeting was conducted according to the six component phases described earlier, with phases 1, 2, and 3 being held in the evening and phases 4, 5, and 6 taking place the following morning.

Case Example C. A management organization took over the operation of a hotel, which was in a sorry state of affairs. Under previous absentee ownership, the property had been allowed to run down; individual departments were independent empires; many people in management positions were non-professional hotel people (i.e., friends of the owners); and there was very low competence in the top management team.

The general manager saw as his priority missions the need to:

Stop the downhill trend.

Overcome a poor public image.

Clean up the property,

Weed out the low-potential (old friends) management.

Bring in professional managers in key spots.

Build a management team.

Build effective operating teams, with the members of the top-management team as links.

He followed his plan with considerable success. In a period of one year he had significantly cleaned up the property, improved the service, built a new dining room, produced an enviable food quality, and begun to build confidence in key buyers, such as convention managers. He had acquired and developed a very fine, professional, young management team that was both competent and highly motivated. This group had been working as a cohesive team on all the hotel's improvement goals; differences between them and their areas seemed to have been largely worked through.

At the level below the top group, the department and section heads, many of whom were also new, had been working under tremendous pressure for over a year to bring about improvements in the property and in the hotel's services. They felt very unappreciated by the top managers, who were described as "always being in meetings and unavailable," or "never rewarding us for good work," or "requiring approval on all decisions but we can't get to see them," or "developing a fine top-

management club but keeping the pressure on us and we're doing the work."

The problem finally was brought to the attention of the top managers by some of the department heads. Immediate action was indicated, and a confrontation meeting was decided on. It took place in two periods, an afternoon and the following morning. There was an immediate follow-up by the top-management team in which many of the issues between departments and functions were identified as stemming back to the modus operandi of the top team. These issues were openly discussed and were worked through. Also in this application, a follow-up report and review session was scheduled for five weeks after the confrontation meeting.

Positive Results

The experience of the foregoing case examples, as well as that of other organizations in which the confrontation meeting technique has been applied, demonstrates that positive results—particularly, improved operational procedures and improved organization health—frequently occur.

Operational Advantages. One of the outstanding plus factors is that procedures which have been confused are clarified. In addition, practices which have been nonexistent are initiated. Typical of these kinds of operational improvement, for example, are the reporting of financial information of operating units, the handling of the reservation system at a hotel, and the inspection procedures and responsibilities in a changing manufacturing process.

Another advantage is that task forces, and/or temporary systems, are set up as needed. These may be in the form of special teams to study the overlap in responsibilities between two departments and to write new statements and descriptions, or to work out a new system for handling order processing from sales to production planning, or to examine the kinds of information that should flow regularly from the management committee to middle management.

Still another improvement is in providing guidance to top management as to specific areas needing priority attention. For example, "the overtime policy set under other conditions is really impeding the achievement of organization requirements," or "the food in the employee's cafeteria is really creating morale problems," or "the lack of understanding of where the organization is going and what top management's goals are is producing apathy," or "what goes on in top management meetings does not get communicated to the middle managers."

Organization Health.   In reviewing the experiences of companies where the confrontation meeting approach has been instituted, I have perceived a number of positive results in the area of organization health:

> A high degree of open communication between various departments and organization levels is achieved very quickly. Because people are assigned to functional units and produce data together, it is possible to express the real feeling of one level or group toward another, particularly if the middle echelon believes the top wants to hear it.
>
> The information collected is current, correct, and "checkable."
>
> A real dialogue can exist between the top management team and the rest of the management organization, which personalizes the top manager to the total group.
>
> Larger numbers of people get "ownership" of the problem, since everyone has some influence through his unit's guidance to the top-management team; thus people feel they have made a real contribution. Even more, the requirement that each functional unit take personal responsibility for resolving some of the issues broadens the base of ownership.
>
> Collaborative goal setting at several levels is demonstrated and practiced. The mechanism provides requirements for joint goal setting within each functional unit and between top and middle managers. People report that this helps them to understand "management by objectives" more clearly than before.
>
> The top team can take corrective actions based on valid information. By making real commitments and establishing check or review points, there is a quick

building of trust in management's intentions on the part of lower level managers.

> There tends to be an increase in trust and confidence both toward the top-management team and toward colleagues. A frequently appearing agenda item is the "need for better understanding of the job problems of other departments," and the output of these meetings is often the commitment to some "mechanism for systematic interdepartmental communication." People also report a change in their stereotypes of people in other areas.
>
> This activity tends to be a "success experience" and thus increases total morale. The process itself, which requires interaction, contribution, and joint work on the problems and which rewards constructive criticism, tends to produce a high degree of enthusiasm and commitment. Because of this, the follow-up activities are crucial in ensuring continuation of this enthusiasm.

Potential Problems

The confrontation meeting technique produces, in a very short time, a great deal of commitment and desire for results on the part of a lot of people. Feelings tend to be more intense than in some other settings because of the concentration of time and manpower. As a result, problems can develop through misuse of the techniques.

If the top-management team does not really use the information from its subordinates, or if there are great promises and little follow-up action, more harm can be caused to the organization's health than if the events were never held.

If the confrontation meeting is used as a manipulative device to give people the "feeling of participation," the act can boomerang. They will soon figure out management's intentions, and the reaction can be severe.

Another possible difficulty is that the functional units, full of enthusiasm at the meeting, set unrealistic or impractical goals and commitments. The behavior of the keyman in each unit—usually a department manager or division head—is crucial in keeping suggestions in balance.

One more possible problem may appear when the functional units select a few priority issues to report out. While these issues may be the most *urgent,* they are not necessarily the most *important.* Mechanisms for working *all* of the information need to be developed within each functional unit. In one of the case examples cited earlier, the groups worked the few problems they identified very thoroughly and never touched the others. This necessitated a "replay" six months later.

In Summary

In periods of stress following major organization changes, there tends to be much confusion and energy expended that negatively affects productivity and organization health.

The top-management team needs quick, efficient ways of sensing the state of the organization's attitudes and feelings in order to plan appropriate actions and to devote its energy to the most important problems.

The usual methods of attitude surveys, extended staff meetings, and so forth demand extensive time and require a delay between getting the information and acting on it.

A short micromechanism called a "confrontation meeting" can provide the total management group with:

An accurate reading on the organization's health.

The opportunity for work units to set priorities for improvement.

The opportunity for top management to make appropriate action decisions based on appropriate information from the organization.

An increased involvement in the organization's goals.

A real commitment to action on the part of subgroups.

A basis for determining other mechanisms for communication between levels and groups, appropriate location of decisions, problem solving within subunits, as well as the machinery for upward influence.

Appendix A: Confrontation Meeting

Here is a detailed description of the seven components which make up the specific "design" for the day-long confrontation meeting.

Phase 1. Climate Setting (45 minutes to one hour).   At the outset, the top manager needs to communicate to the total management group his goals for the meeting, and his concern for and interest in free discussion and issue facing. He also has to assure his people that there is no punishment for open confrontation.

It is also helpful to have some form of information session or lecture by the top manager or a consultant. Appropriate subjects might deal with the problems of communication, the need for understanding, the assumptions and the goals of the total organization, the concept of shared responsibility for the future of the organization, and the opportunity for and responsibility of influencing the organization.

Phase 2. Information collecting (one hour). The total group is divided into small heterogeneous units of seven or eight people. If there is a top-management team that has been holding sessions regularly, it meets as a separate unit. The rest of the participants are assigned to units with a "diagonal slice" of the organization used as a basis for composition—that is, no boss and subordinate are together, and each unit contains members from every functional area.

The assignment given to each of these units is along these lines:

Think of yourself as an individual with needs and goals. Also think as a person concerned about the total organization. What are the obstacles, "demotivators," poor procedures or policies, unclear goals, or poor attitudes that exist today? What different conditions, if any, would make the organization more effective and make life in the organization better?

Each unit is instructed to select a reporter to present its results at a general information-collecting session to be held one hour later.

Phase 3. Information Sharing (one hour). Each reporter writes his unit's complete findings on newsprint, which is tacked up around the room.

The meeting leader suggests some categories under which all the data from all the sheets can be located. In other words, if there are 75 items, the likelihood is that these can be grouped into six or seven major categories—say, by type of problem, such as "communications difficulties"; or by type of relationship, such as "problems with top management"; or by type of area involved, such as "problems in the mechanical department."

Then the meeting breaks, either for lunch or, if it happens to be an evening session, until the next morning.

During the break all the data sheets are duplicated for general distribution.

Phase 4. Priority Setting and Group Action Planning (one hour and 15 minutes). The total group reconvenes for a 15-minute general session. With the meeting leader, they go through the raw data on the duplicated sheets and put category numbers by each piece of data.

People are now assigned to their functional, natural work units for a one-hour session. Manufacturing people at all levels go to one unit, everybody in sales to another, and so forth. These units are headed by a department manager or division head of that function. This means that some units may have as few as 3 people and some as many as 25. Each unit is charged to perform three specific tasks:

1. Discuss the problems and issues which affect its area. Decide on the priorities and early actions to which the group is prepared to commit itself. (They should be prepared to share this commitment with their colleagues at the general session.)
2. Identify the issues and/or problems to which the top-management team should give its priority attention.
3. Decide how to communicate the results of the session to their subordinates.

Phase 5. Organization Action Planning (one to two hours). The total management group reconvenes in a general session, where:

1. Each functional unit reports its commitment and plans to the total group.
2. Each unit reports and lists the items that its members believe the management team should deal with first.
3. The top manager reacts to this list and makes commitments (through setting targets or assigning task forces or timetables, and so on) for action where required.
4. Each unit shares briefly its plans for communicating the results of the confrontation meeting to all subordinates.

Phase 6. Immediate Follow-Up by Top Team (one to three hours). The top-management team meets immediately after the confrontation meeting ends to plan first follow-up actions, which should then be reported back to the total management group within a few days.

Phase 7. Progress Review (two hours). Follow-up with total management group four to six weeks later.

Appendix B: Sample Schedule

9:00 A.M. Opening Remarks, by general manager.

Background, goals, outcomes.

Norms of openness and "leveling."

Personal commitment to follow-up.

9:10 General Session.

Communications Problems in Organizations, by general manager (or consultant).

The communications process.

Communications breakdowns in organizations and individuals.

Dilemmas to be resolved.

Conditions for more openness.

10:00 Coffee.

10:15 Data Production Unit Session.

  Sharing feelings and attitudes.

  Identifying problems and concerns.

  Collecting data.

11:15 General Session.

  Sharing findings from each unit (on newsprint).

  Developing categories on problem issues.

12:15 P.M. Lunch.

2:00 General Session.

  Reviewing list of items in categories.

  Instructing functional units.

2:15 functional Unit Session.

  Listing priority actions to be taken.

  Preparing recommendations for top team.

  Planning for presentation of results at general meeting.

3:15 General Session.

  Sharing recommendations of functional units.

  Listing priorities for top team action.

  Planning for communicating results of meeting to others.

4:15 Closing Remarks, by general manager.

4:30 Adjournment.

READING 19
COLLATERAL ORGANIZATION:
A NEW CHANGE STRATEGY

Dale E. Zand

Part One: Concepts

Many organization development specialists who emphasize behavioral rather than structural or technical change contend that free-form organizations, participative leadership, and humanistic values should—indeed, will—displace hierarchical organizations, directive leadership, and mechanistic values (Argyris, 1970; Bennis, 1965, 1966; Golembiewski, 1972; Likert, 1961, 1967; McGregor, 1960; Marguilies & Raia, 1972; Slater & Bennis, 1964; Tannenbaum & Davis, 1969). It is their view that knowledge rather than level of authority should (or will) determine decisions, and that environmental complexity and turbulence should (or will) cause one-man decision making to give way to group decision making.

These assertions have merit and are especially attractive to social scientists, but they are controversial to managers. Indeed, the idea of totally displacing existing systems may well have diverted managers into choosing sides, and thereby seriously interfered with their learning to improve their organization's adaptability and effectiveness. There is increasing evidence of a need for flexibility in structure and leadership style across different tasks and individuals; the superiority of any one approach above all others cannot be defended (Fiedler, 1967; Lawrence & Lorsch, 1967). The key issue is: How can OD specialists help managers design creative, problem-solving organizations and use them flexibly?

This article seeks to clarify and extend our concepts of organizational form and behavior by introducing the strategy of *collateral organization*[1] as a means of increasing flexibility. I shall present supporting theory and research; describe two field cases which illustrate methods of introducing collateral modes of organization; contrast collateral organizations with task forces, temporary systems, and matrix organizations; and finally, discuss their impact on the use of groups for solving problems and on the role of middle managers.

Collateral Mode Defined. Research into the relation between the structure of a problem and the effectiveness of different organizations suggests that a work group benefits from using more than one mode of organization. To state it simply: authority/production-centered organizations work best with "well-structured" problems; knowledge/problem-centered organizations work best with "ill-structured" problems. These organizational modes and problem structures will be described in great detail later; the important point is that, since problems vary in structure, managers can and should operate in more than one organizational mode.

The concept of a secondary mode of working will be called a collateral organization. Hence, a collateral organization is a supplemental organization coexisting with the usual, formal organization.[2] Of course a manager may develop more than one collateral organization, but to keep matters simple we will talk of only one collateral mode in the remainder of this article.

Typically, a group has a chain of command and a division or responsibilities designed primarily for coping with well-defined, repetitive problems.

Source: Dale E. Zand, *Journal of Applied Behavioral Science* (vol. 10, no. 1) pp. 63–69, copyright © 1974 by NTL Institute of Applied Behavioral Science. Reprinted by permission of Sage Publications Inc.

Continued changes in consumers' desires, competitors' tactics, and product technology introduce unforeseen, ill-defined problems and opportunities. The hierarchical organizational structure is not designed to discover and solve these "ill-structured" problems. Managers, regardless of organizational level, therefore need collateral modes.

But managers hesitate to depart from the formal hierarchy to use a collateral mode because they are rarely given concepts explaining and legitimizing such departures. Traditional organization theory, for example, offers only the vague concept of "informal organization" (Pfiffner & Sherwood, 1960). Moreover, managers are advised to avoid and suppress informal organization because it is unsanctioned, unplanned, and unpredictable (Delbecq, 1968).

The manager's confusion is sometimes compounded by laboratory-method organizational development programs. Sensitivity training, grid laboratories, and variations of group methods focus on improving the manager's skill in individual and group behavior, but rarely introduce relevant organization theory. When a manager applies his new knowledge to his formal organization, he usually encourages open questioning of goals and methods, which blurs formal boundaries between jobs. Other managers interpret his actions as undermining authority and disrupting the formal organization, so they resist and discard his changes. The manager is in a theoretical limbo; without concepts, he cannot explain to other managers what he is doing in terms they can understand.

The concept of collateral organization is offered to aid managerial understanding and use of organizational development efforts. To explain and illustrate it, I shall first discuss the relationship between organizational problems and organizational structures, and the characteristics of a collateral organization.

Matching Problems and Modes.   A problem is a dilemma and an organization is an instrument. It is useful to think of a problem and an organization as a set which is poorly or well matched. If the manager is to choose the right instrument for the job,

it is important to understand when a problem and an organization are matched.

A problem can be classified as either well structured or ill structured. Some problems of course will have characteristics found in both categories, but analysis of the pure types will contribute most to understanding the matching process.

A well-structured problem—for example, preparing a customer's bill from a list of items and prices or putting values into a computer program which calculates the present worth of a capital investment—has the characteristics of physical or routine mental work.

In contrast, an ill-structured problem—for example, determining what new products should be added to a line over the next three years, preparing a schedule of prices for products that do not exist in any market, or projecting the long-range organizational, financial, and employment effects of a new marketing strategy—has the characteristics of complex, nonroutinized mental work. The elements of well- and ill-structured problems are outlined in Figure 1.

Usually a manager assumes that he has only one organization, which he must use for all problems. That is like a carpenter who uses a hammer for all jobs. A more effective manager first classifies a problem and then chooses an instrument best suited for it.

An organization (work group) can be classified as *(a)* authority/production centered or *(b)* knowledge/problem centered. Of course, some organizations will cross both categories, but again we learn the most from studying the two pure types. The authority/production form is concerned with mobilizing people and equipment to maximize output of a finished product. The knowledge/problem form is concerned with processing or inventing knowledge to solve problems. Elements of the two organizational forms are compared in Figure 2.

Research Findings.   Experimental research with small groups suggests that some combinations of organizations and problems are more productive

FIGURE 1

Characteristics of well-structured and ill-structured problems

Element	Well-Structured Problems	Ill-Structured Problems
Variation of output with hours of work	Known. Proportional.	Unknown. Nonproportional.
Variation of output with number of people	Known. Proportional.	Unknown. Nonproportional.
Characteristics of input and output	Countable. Quality accurately measurable. Errors detected quickly, precisely.	Not countable. Quality difficult to measure. Errors difficult to detect.
Information available	Relevant. Accurate. Complete.	Uncertain. Inaccurate. Incomplete.
Solutions	Few are feasible. All are known. Best one determined easily.	Many are feasible. Few are known. Best one difficult to determine.
Experts	Past solution of similar problems is a reliable indication of expertise.	Many claim to be expert, but past experience is an unreliable guide to expertise.
Methods of control	External standards such as output targets, hours allowed, cost goals can effectively control performance.	External standards are inapplicable and misleading.
Feedback about results	Occurs shortly after action. Can be attributed to the action.	Occurs long after the action. Cannot be attributed only to the action.

than others. Communication network studies are especially relevant because they simulate many of the properties of the two types of organizations described in Figure 2, and the problems used fit well into one or the other of the two classes of problems described above. Transfer of results from experimental settings to operating organizations requires caution; so the findings summarized here can be viewed only as suggestive. They are presented in condensed form for purposes of theory development, with some of the complex differences in morale and other factors set aside.

For well-structured problems, it appears that groups in the authority/production mode produce more output, more rapidly, than groups in the knowledge/problem mode (Bavelas, 1950; Christie, Luce, & May, Jr., 1952; Leavitt, 1951). And when groups organized in the knowledge/problem mode are given a series of well-structured problems and are allowed to reorganize, they shift toward the authority/production mode. They install a hierarchy, divide labor, and cut unused communication links (Guetzkow & Dill, 1957; Guetzkow & Simon, 1955).

For ill-structured problems, however, groups in the knowledge/problem mode devise solutions of better quality, more rapidly, than do groups in the authority/production mode (Shaw, Rothchild, & Strickland, 1957). The hierarchy, the division of labor, and the rules that make the authority/production mode effective for well-structured problems seem to interfere with the group's ability to devise quality solutions to ill-structured problems.

Another characteristic of the authority/production mode makes it unsuitable for ill-structured problems; it tends to reject unsolicited innovation. In this mode managers view an uninvited proposal for improvement as a distraction that will reduce output. In contrast, the knowledge/problem group tends to accept and use unsolicited innovations to improve productivity (Bavelas, 1950).

There are no experimental data on whether authority/production groups, given ill-structured problems, shift to a knowledge/problem mode. Observation of authority/production organizations suggests that when they are confronted with an ill-structured problem, such as entering a

FIGURE 2

Types of organizations

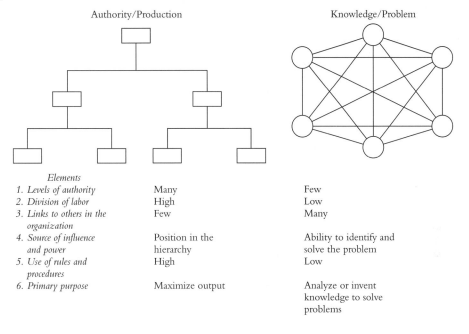

Elements	Authority/Production	Knowledge/Problem
1. Levels of authority	Many	Few
2. Division of labor	High	Low
3. Links to others in the organization	Few	Many
4. Source of influence and power	Position in the hierarchy	Ability to identify and solve the problem
5. Use of rules and procedures	High	Low
6. Primary purpose	Maximize output	Analyze or invent knowledge to solve problems

volatile market undergoing rapid technical change, managers do not shift to another mode but try to redefine the problem, forcing it to fit the existing hierarchy and division of labor. Burns and Stalker (1961) found that companies unable to shift to a knowledge/problem mode were unsuccessful in the new environment.

The most effective combinations (see Figure 3) are well-structured problems with authority/production organization (Quadrant I), and ill-structured problems with knowledge/problem organization (Quadrant III). The other combinations (II and IV) are not so well matched.

Displacement Trap.   Contrary to the "displacement belief," there is little likelihood that the authority/production mode, which is characteristic of most business organizations, will vanish. It works for well-structured problems and minimally disrupts the organization. There is, however, a limit to how far it can be stretched; and when a problem keeps recurring, that limit has by definition been

exceeded. The challenge is: Can a manager and his group shift to a secondary mode before their primary mode becomes ineffective?

Many managers who make the shift to a new mode of organization are led to believe by poorly conceptualized OD efforts that they and their subordinates never again need directive behavior, specialized assignments, and limited communication. Such expectations prove unrealistic. Upon "regressing" to the authority/production mode, managers feel guilty and disappointed. Subordinates are frustrated and dissatisfied at relinquishing their newly found influence. Managers and subordinates frequently conclude that organizational development is a sham.

There may be a similar lack of realism about shifting even when the primary mode is knowledge/problem centered. For example, research units and educational institutions resist using the authority/production mode when it is needed, fearing that the primary, participative mode would not only be displaced but would be unrecoverable.

FIGURE 3

Relationship between type of problem and type of organization

Type of Problem	Type of Organization	
	Authority/Production	*Knowledge/Problem*
Well-Structured	**I** High output. Rapid processing. Small number of errors in output. Members low in authority report low satisfaction. Tends to reject unsolicited innovations.	**II** Lower output. Slower processing. More errors in output. More satisfying. Accepts unsolicited innovations.
Ill-Structured	**IV** Lower output. Slower processing. Low-quality solutions. Low in creativity. Orderly, but not functional.	**III** High output. Rapid processing. High-quality solutions. High creativity. Appears disorderly but is functional.

An understanding of collateral organization can help managers integrate needed changes while maintaining the primary organization.

Relation of Collateral Organization to Formal Organization. In the remainder of this paper, for discussion purposes, I shall assume that the formal organization is in the authority/production mode. The collateral organization will be in the knowledge/problem mode. (This state of affairs may of course be reversed in some organizations; e.g., research units and educational organizations.)[3]

In Tandem. A collateral organization is distinguishable from and linked to the formal organization as follows:

1. The purpose of the collateral organization is to identify and solve problems not solved by the formal (primary) organization.

2. A collateral organization creatively complements the formal organization. It allows new combinations of people, new channels of communication, and new ways of seeing old ideas.

3. A collateral organization operates in parallel or in tandem with the formal organization. Both the collateral and the formal organizations are available; a manager chooses one or the other, depending on the problem. A collateral organization does not displace the formal organization.

4. A collateral organization consists of the same people who work in the formal organization. There are no new people.

5. The outputs of the collateral organization are inputs to the formal organization. The ultimate value of a collateral organization depends on successfully linking it to the formal organization, so its outputs are used.

6. A collateral organization operates with norms (that is, expectations of how people will behave) that are different from the norms in the formal organization. The different norms facilitate new ideas and new approaches to obstacles.

Characteristics. A collateral organization has the following characteristics:

1. All channels are open and connected. Managers and specialists are free to communicate without being restricted to formal channels in the hierarchy.
2. There is a rapid and complete exchange of relevant information.
3. Norms encourage careful questioning and analysis of goals, assumptions, methods, alternatives, and criteria for evaluation.
4. A manager can approach and enlist others in the organization to help solve a problem, without being restricted to his formal subordinates.

Part Two: Applications

The two cases that follow illustrate different social technologies for introducing collateral organization. They are brief descriptions of change efforts in the field. They do not have the benefit of control groups or the statistical data characteristic of rigorous experimental research, though information is presented about end results—ill-structured problems identified and solved, and productivity. The cases do not dwell on the interpersonal dynamics of group-based change efforts, which are described in other studies (e.g., Argyris, 1970; Golembiewski, 1972).

Silver City Bank. In August of 1968, Ralph Brady, vice president of Silver City Bank,[4] was concerned about future strategy for the international banking department. He wanted to improve the department's ability to compete with well-established competitors in a changing, worldwide market. At this stage in his thinking he felt the issues, problems, and opportunities were ill structured. He discussed his concern, in general terms, with his superiors, who encouraged him to recommend changes in strategy.

His work group functioned primarily in an authority/production mode. He and his subordinates were amiable and cooperative and deeply involved in getting work out. Although there was the glamour of international travel and negotiating loans of large dollar value, most of the situations were well structured.

Mr. Brady discussed strategy with several key subordinates but felt he and they were not able to dig into issues in any depth. Each could focus only on short-term obstacles close to his own group's productivity. The ill-structured problems of analyzing long-term strategy seemed to elude the problem-solving capability of his group. Finally, Mr. Brady consulted an OD specialist (the author) who had been working with another department in the bank.

Preparation for Introduction of Collateral Mode. The specialist interviewed Mr. Brady and his division managers. He observed that their daily work required many immediate decisions and was extremely demanding. They could not be away from a telephone. He concluded they would have great difficulty establishing the relationships needed to identify and solve the ill-structured issues of strategy. Although the managers were competent problem solvers with extensive knowledge of international banking, they could not direct their skills toward analyzing strategy. Somehow, they would have to depart from the norms of their intensive authority/production-centered work.

The OD specialist explained the need for a collateral organization to Mr. Brady and his group. He proposed an initial three-day meeting, at which strategy and operating issues would be discussed, analyzed, and if possible, resolved. (The men were so busy they insisted it be from Friday afternoon to Sunday evening.) Aware that collateral organizations frequently fail because managers may have unrealistic expectations and cannot foresee the difficulties of a mode, the specialist stressed setting limited, attainable goals. He suggested that the group try to identify key issues but discuss only two or three priority issues in detail. Since there would be many unanswered questions after the meeting, they would also have to approve some structure which could be used to work on finding answers after they returned to work. Finally they should discuss how they could organize to solve ill-structured problems more effectively in the future.

Ten days before the meeting, the OD specialist interviewed each manager, gathering information for the meeting and answering questions about format. Each manager described the issues he most wanted discussed, the outcomes that would make him feel the meeting was worthwhile, and the difficulties that might interfere with managers' being reasonably open about important issues. The interview process itself stimulated managers to think about norms that departed from those of the primary mode.

Learning the Collateral Mode.   At the start of the meeting, the specialist made the following statements to clarify the norms of the collateral mode and to assure its proper connection to the primary mode.

> The power differences in the formal organization would still exist when the managers returned to work.
>
> Mr. Brady, the vice president, was the group's superior, and this was his meeting, not the consultant's.
>
> The group or its members could make recommendations, but Mr. Brady would have to approve any proposal before it could be implemented.
>
> Regardless of formal position, managers usually have valuable insights and proposals that cut across many different areas. It would be the responsibility of the higher managers to facilitate expression and use of these views.
>
> The OD specialist would suggest procedures and ask questions to help the group's problem solving.

The OD specialist then reported a summary of the issues managers wanted to discuss. At first, the group operated in an authority/production mode. Managers frequently proposed solutions before a problem had been clearly defined. The specialist made process observations to alter these norms. Discussion was brought back to managers whose views had not been heard adequately. There was regular testing to ensure that any problem was understood by all before solutions were discussed in depth. Regardless of status, managers began contributing important information and insights. This helped the senior managers see how the open channels of the collateral mode improved problem solving.

On the second day, the managers agreed to experiment with a collateral mode after they returned to work. They would set aside "unstructured" time (multichannels, free questioning, and so on) to study several ill-structured problems. Based on their new experience, they also adopted a special norm for their collateral mode: incomplete ideas, although not thoroughly reasoned and defendable, were welcomed. This was a deliberate and significant departure from behavior in their primary organization. It was intended to stimulate search and creativity. They reiterated, however, that in the hierarchical (primary) organization, a recommendation would still have to be supported by thorough reasoning and documentation. They had grasped the distinction between primary and collateral modes without falling into the trap of insisting that one had to displace the other.

Connecting to the Hierarchical Organization.   After returning to work at the bank, Mr. Brady and his group used their collateral mode to analyze ill-structured problems one morning each week for the first six weeks. This helped stabilize the collateral mode and increase cohesion. They worked out a long-term agenda, which they used to enlarge their collateral organization with several task forces for specific problems. The daytime meetings were conflicting with work, so they reviewed their needs and shifted to one evening a month. They also convened three-day, off-site, collateral meetings at five-month intervals to review progress and react to task force reports. The task forces made proposals to Mr. Brady and the full group during the year; gradually a comprehensive international banking strategy was formulated.

There were differences of opinion within the task forces, and sometimes there were conflicting responses to reports from the task forces. The process had its difficulties, and in two instances Mr. Brady encouraged and arranged for the transfer of two individuals who were personally dissatisfied by and unable to contribute to the collateral mode. In general, the managers at this level were bright and aggressive and enjoyed the opportunity to do a better job of planning their department's future. At their daily work, the nature of their activities, however, impelled them toward an authority/production mode. (Incidentally, this did not mean that they were not caring, friendly, and thoughtful of one another and their subordinates.)

In any case, the primary and the collateral mode remained quite distinct. Managers were well aware of the distinct properties of the two modes and when one or the other was in use. The department was relatively autonomous and top management stayed out of its internal activities, so the use of the collateral mode caused no problems and raised no outside concerns.

Results.   The original stimulus for the collateral organization was the need to develop a strategy for international banking. No before-after measures were taken of attitudes, perceptions, share in influence, or other intervening variables. At the time of the intervention, gathering data about casual variables was secondary to the change effort. Nevertheless, in terms of the criterion measure—quality of the strategy—the decisions made in 1969 are impressive, in view of the political and economic developments in Latin America, the Far East, and Europe in the early 1970s. The group decided to expand in Latin America and the Orient, where competition was thin, demand was growing, and the bank could effectively use its existing relationships to tap an expected increase in U.S. trade with countries in those areas. In Europe, where competition was heavy for the existing large

market, a strategy of affiliating with strong foreign banks, and selectively establishing a few home office branches was instituted. To support the new strategy, relations between international banking officers and domestic banking officers who served U.S. companies with large overseas affiliates or subsidiaries were reviewed and significantly improved. Procedures in the bank's main European office were also substantially changed, facilitating more accurate and rapid responses to customers. The department's formal structure was changed to fit the new strategies. Several divisions were eliminated, others were combined. Finally, a manpower development plan which systematically rotated upcoming managers to selected world areas and headquarters assignments was instituted. Since 1968, top management has rated the international banking department's performance as outstanding each year. Mr. Brady was promoted to senior vice president and a subordinate moved into his job.

Of course, without control groups we cannot assert that an equally good strategy would not have developed without a collateral mode. Using Mr. Brady's group as its own control, however, we recall that it had repeatedly tried to formulate strategy while working in its primary mode but had been dissatisfied with the results.

Another interesting result is that the collateral organization concept spread during the three years following its initial use by Mr. Brady. Each of his five division managers developed collateral organizations with their own subordinates.

Ajax Corporation.   Now we turn to the introduction of a complex multistage collateral organization. Again our purpose is to illustrate the usefulness of the collateral organization concept and to outline some social technology for introducing one. We do not intend to delve deeply into the interpersonal or social dynamics of the development process.

Fred Anderson, manager of the Maintenance and Laboratory Service Division of Ajax Corporation, a large research and development company, was concerned about the cost effectiveness of his unit. His division had been performing more work with the same budget, and although objective standards were difficult to establish, he felt improvement was possible. Since the Service Division employed 300 of the 3,000 people in Ajax, it was a major expense.

The Service Division had been formed two years earlier by consolidating into one unit activities that had previously been performed by small groups in each of the major research and engineering divisions of Ajax. After consolidation, the foreman's job changed from supervising only craftsmen in one specialty (such as machinists or electricians) to supervising a team which could completely build and repair complex laboratory facilities. Thus, at the level of the foremen and below, the organization took on some properties of a *matrix*. Specialized craftsmen were assigned to different projects as needed, and they usually worked on several projects with groups of varying size and membership. In addition, for the first time, foremen and craftsmen were rotated between the company's two locations, 20 miles apart.

Middle managers advised Mr. Anderson that the foremen were at the crux of the division's difficulties and would be the key to any improvement effort. They described the foremen as unwilling to stress high output, reluctant to discipline workers, resistant to cost reduction and work changes, and tending to promise work dates that frequently were not met.

Mr. Anderson consulted organization development specialists, who observed that foremen were affected by the behavior and attitudes of their managers and that the problems Mr. Anderson was trying to solve were complex, ill defined, and substantially different from the well-structured routines of daily manager-foreman relations.[5] The consultants proposed, and management accepted, a sequence of collateral organizations involving both managers and foremen (Figure 4).

Collateral Phase 1. All 16 managers in the division met for three days away from the plant in order to (1) identify and solve work problems of concern to managers and foremen and (2) learn a collateral mode of problem solving.

To help introduce the collateral mode, the OD specialists constrained the managers to work on one element of problem solving at a time, in a method called "staged problem solving." They also facilitated information flow, wider use of resources, and norms that encouraged questioning and creativity by placing managers in different groups with varying membership.

First, the managers developed an inventory of problems while working in three "diagonal slice" groups (no manager and immediate subordinate in the same group). Then, in a plenary meeting of all 16 managers, the groups discussed their problem inventories and consolidated them. At first the small groups were "stiff" and concerns were stated indirectly. However, with the aid of process observations by the OD specialists, role-playing, small-group exercises, and the discipline of discussing each group's product in plenary session, this stiffness disappeared.

Next each group diagnosed causes of a subset of problems. A written summary of each diagnosis was immediately duplicated and distributed to all the managers. The managers met again in plenary session and each group explained and discussed its diagnosis. By this time the managers were deeply involved in the effort. Highly relevant problems had been identified, and causes were being discussed without disguising names or incidents. The managers were stimulated by the open exchange of views and the increasing probability that several important problems might be solved.

On the second day of the meeting, the OD team arranged for the managers to meet in three peer groups. The groups were given the following tasks: (1) assign priorities to problems, (2) nominate managers to task forces that would recommend solutions to Mr. Anderson at the meeting, and (3) nominate managers to a steering committee that would take control of the remainder of the meeting and also guide the collateral organization after returning to the plant and the hierarchical (primary) organization.

Linking to the Formal Organization. To assure that the collateral organization would tie into the formal one, the managers were asked to use the following criteria for nominating candidates to a task force: *(a)* at least one manager should have formal authority to act on the problem; *(b)* several should be technical and procedural experts on the problem; *(c)* at least one should know and represent the views of people who would be affected by a solution.

The managers elected a five-man steering committee and asked the division manager to serve as chairman. Thus they connected the collateral organization's steering committee to the highest authority in their formal organization.

The steering committee formed task forces for the high-priority problems and assigned every manager (including themselves) to a task force. The task forces rediagnosed their assigned problems and developed solutions.

Then, in plenary session, each task force presented and discussed its progress. All managers freely questioned, commented, and provided additional inputs. The task forces absorbed the new inputs and met again to refine their proposals. By this stage, involvement was intense. Groups worked late into the night to prepare their recommendations for the next day. The norms in these groups very closely followed the knowledge/problem-centered mode: A manager's position was secondary to his contribution.

During the last half day, each task force presented its recommendations in plenary session. To clarify that the organization was shifting back to its primary mode, the OD team explicitly stated that the division manager, Mr. Anderson, could respond in any of the following ways: (1) He could accept the task force recommendation, designate a manager to implement it, specify a completion date, and state how a report of progress would be given to all the managers. (2) He could suggest modifications, discuss them, and approve a modified recommendation. (3) He could withhold a decision, pending additional information or alternatives, and authorize the task force to continue its work back at the plant. (4) He could withhold a decision if in his judgment the proposal was not

appropriate now but might be at a later date. (5) He could reject the recommendation and not give any reasons.

There was a good deal of excitement and joking as Mr. Anderson stood at the front of the room waiting to hear each group's statement of the problem, review of causes, and recommended solutions. During the presentations, managers freely called from the floor for clarification or elaborated a point when they felt it was misunderstood. The cohesiveness of the managers was noticeably higher than before the three-day meeting.

By this time much information that had been known only in isolated pockets of the formal hierarchy had been exchanged across the organization. Managers had demonstrated their trust in one another through the openness of their discussions during the preceding two and one-half days. With this background, solutions that were not feasible or not integrative were readily discarded in the task forces. As a result, the final recommendations were appropriate and well thought out. Mr. Anderson neither rejected nor withheld a decision on any of the recommendations.

Results: Collateral Phase 1. A new information system for managers was instituted. A new strategy for recruiting engineering and scientific specialists was approved. Middle managers were delegated additional decision powers. A task force was established to redesign the division's organizational structure.

The managers also made plans to follow up in the hierarchical organization problems they had identified but did not have time to solve during the three-day meeting. Finally, they agreed they would join the foremen in a collateral organization if the foremen invited them. They discussed how they might work with the foremen in a collateral mode.

Collateral Phase 2. One week after the managers' collateral organization experience, all 18 foremen met for three days at the off-site location. The OD specialists had decided to separate managers from foremen to prevent tension and distorted communication between levels from interfering

FIGURE 4

Multiphase collateral organization

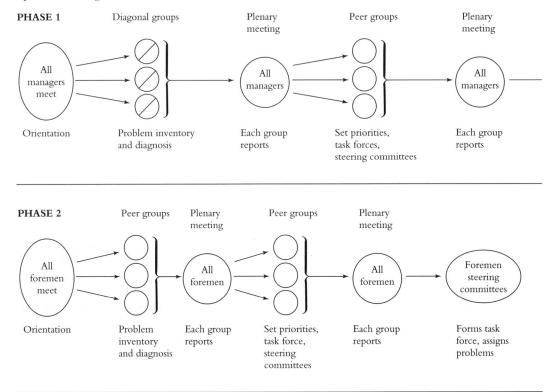

PHASE 1

Diagonal groups — Plenary meeting — Peer groups — Plenary meeting

All managers meet / Orientation

Problem inventory and diagnosis

All managers / Each group reports

Set priorities, task forces, steering committees

All managers / Each group reports

PHASE 2

Peer groups — Plenary meeting — Peer groups — Plenary meeting

All foremen meet / Orientation

Problem inventory and diagnosis

All foremen / Each group reports

Set priorities, task force, steering committees

All foremen / Each group reports

Foremen steering committees / Forms task force, assigns problems

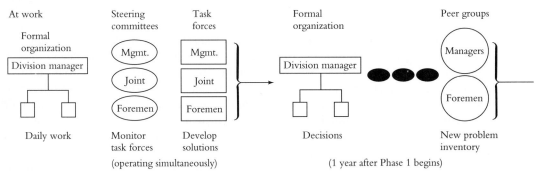

PHASE 3

At work — Steering committees — Task forces — Formal organization — Peer groups

Formal organization / Division manager / Daily work

Mgmt. / Joint / Foremen / Monitor task forces

Mgmt. / Joint / Foremen / Develop solutions

(operating simultaneously)

Division manager / Decisions

Managers / Foremen / New problem inventory

(1 year after Phase 1 begins)

FIGURE 4

(concluded)

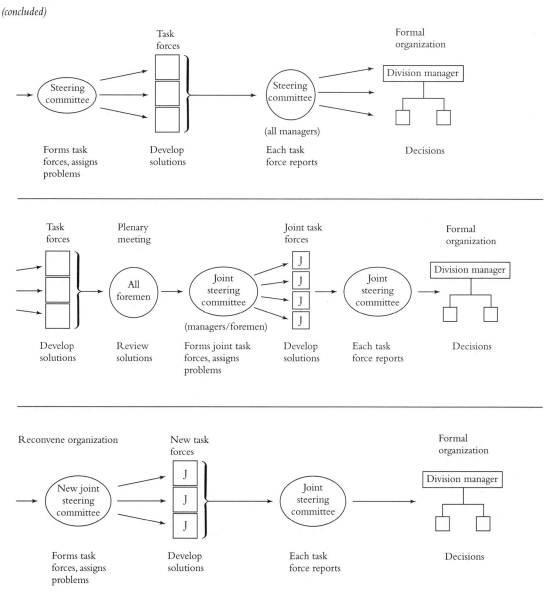

with learning to work in a collateral mode. The managers' collateral organization was developed first so they could decide from personal experience whether to approve a collateral organization for foremen.

The procedure and activities in the foremen's meeting were similar to the managers' meeting. Some minilectures and demonstration exercises were eliminated to save time, but in all other ways the foremen's collateral organization used the same "staged problem solving," small-group discussions, and plenary sessions.

The foremen, like the managers, developed their own inventory of problems, diagnosed causes, set priorities, and elected their own steering committee to take control of their meeting. The steering committee established foremen task forces, which began work at the meeting. At first, like the managers, the foremen were resistant and indirect. Again with the aid of process observations from the OD specialists, exercises, and the regimen of having to present their groups' deliberations to all other foremen, the norms of the groups changed toward those in a knowledge/problem mode.

Linking Two Collateral Organizations. Anticipating the need to link the managers' collateral organization to the foremen's collateral organization for work on common problems, management had agreed to the OD specialists' recommendation that foremen be permitted to invite managers to join them the last day and a half. The foremen (contrary to management's stereotype of foremen as insensitive) did not wish to offend any manager by not inviting him and negotiated with management to have all managers join them, except for five who were left to run the division.

A joint steering committee of foremen and managers assigned both foremen and managers to joint task forces. Comprehensive, ill-structured issues had been identified for work. Sample items which both managers and foremen agreed were adversely affecting the performance of foremen included: confusion about foremen's authority to work crews overtime, purchase inexpensive materials which were delaying completion of a job, or

grant workers time off; misunderstandings about the scope of the foreman's job; need for a better system for screening and assigning priorities to incoming jobs; inadequate engineering services on complex, technical jobs; inadequate pay differentials between foremen and craftsmen; conflict about the merit pay system; need for a better manpower assignment system; conflict about training of foremen and craftsmen. There was tension within the joint task forces as managers and foremen who knew each other by name but had never worked closely together before prepared to discuss problems that had been suppressed, distorted, or circumvented in the formal organization. Some foremen became guarded when a manager tried to dominate, but the issues and the withheld information that had been constraining the organization were nevertheless introduced via the "impersonal" written task force reports.

During the last half day, the joint task forces presented their recommendations to Mr. Anderson (format as before), who immediately made several important decisions. Procedures for working on unsolved problems after returning to the plant were also established.

Results: Collateral Phase 2. The recommendations approved by Mr. Anderson included the following: Foremen were given wider latitude in authorizing overtime to complete a job without their supervisor's approval; they could authorize workers' time off without pay; they could purchase parts that were delaying job completion up to $200 per job without going through time-consuming formal purchasing procedures. These measures cut costs and sped completion of jobs.

Mr. Anderson also decided that task forces concerned with the responsibilities of foremen, the training of foremen, the merit and performance review system, providing proper engineering support, and reviewing pay differentials between foremen and workers were to continue their investigation after they returned to the plant and the hierarchical organization.

Much misinformation about foremen attitudes and behavior had been dispelled, and managers had tested some of their stereotyped reactions to foremen and found them inappropriate. The outcome was a concerted effort on the part of both groups to provide the conditions that would enable foremen to be effective, rather than to blame them for inadequacies not under their control.

Thirty important problems had been identified, nine had been assigned to task forces, three had been resolved. Completion and review dates had been established for the others, and procedures had been developed for following through on the remaining problems. An attitude survey showed that managers and foremen felt they had learned much about one another and about problem solving. They were enthusiastic about the collateral organization.

Collateral Phase 3.   After returning to the plant and the hierarchical organization, task forces of managers, foremen, and joint membership continued their work. Progress was slower than expected because of daily work pressures.

There also was testing of the authority/ production mode. Some foremen task forces, impressed with their new influence potential, attempted to circumvent middle managers and moved directly to the joint steering committee or the division manager with short-term work issues. Senior foremen quickly sensed the resentment this was arousing among middle managers and redirected the foremen task forces to the issues they had been assigned. Managers of other divisions in the laboratory were skeptical about allowing foremen on task forces. They were also concerned that foremen might usurp higher management's authority. Mr. Anderson was able to reassure the other divisions that this dual mode of operation need not spread to other divisions unless they wanted it. He was also able to convince them on the basis of preliminary results that the performance of the Maintenance Division would improve over the long run.

Based on the measure of identifying and solving ill-structured problems, the collateral mode contributed to the organization's effectiveness.

After nine months, six of the nine original high-priority and five secondary problems were solved. All but three task forces had completed their assignments and were dissolved. Work was to begin on 12 less-critical problems.

The collateral organization was self-operating; no OD specialists were used. One year after the first meetings, a new division manager (promoted from within the division) continued the collateral organization with the aid of the joint steering committee. Using small groups, a new inventory of problems was developed, three new task forces were formed, and progress was reviewed with the steering committee until the new problems were solved.

To obtain information about attitudes toward the collateral mode, interviews were conducted 18 months after the start of the project. Five managers and five foremen representing all levels of management, every task force, and both steering committees were interviewed. Each respondent felt strongly that the collateral mode was extremely useful and strongly supported its continuation.

Additional Issues.   These two cases, one relatively simple, the other more complexly structured, illustrate strategies for using collateral organization. Using the case material as reference, some additional issues deserve discussion: the distinction between collateral organization and related concepts such as "matrix organization" and "temporary systems," and some problems which may arise in the use of collateral organization.

Relation to Matrix Organization.   Managers may sometimes confuse a matrix organization with a collateral mode. A matrix organization is intended to provide a project manager with easier access to functional specialists. Nevertheless it may operate primarily in an authority/production mode, as in the Ajax case. Internal competition for resources and conflicts among functional managers and project managers are heightened in a matrix organization (Galbraith, 1971). These conditions stimulate managers to overstate needs, to hoard resources, to withhold information, and to block others from access to needed manpower, in short, to behave in an authority/production mode with high conflict. Thus a matrix organization may itself need a collateral problem-solving mode. Much of the organizational development activity at TRW Systems can be interpreted as an effort to build collateral modes to complement its matrix (primary) organization (Davis, 1967).

Relation to Task Forces.   In both Silver City and Ajax, each collateral organization created task forces as part of its structure. This can be confusing, because a manager may assume he can install a collateral organization simply by forming a task force. The important question is: Does the task force operate with norms different from those in the hierarchical (primary) organization? Many task forces, spun off by conventional hierarchies, operate in the same authority/production mode as the primary organization. Individuals project their provincial interests and minimally question values, assumptions, methods, and criteria of evaluation. Such a task force contributes to restricted flow of information, legitimizes restricted use of resources, and adds little creativity to the hierarchical organization. The task forces in both Silver City Bank and Ajax worked in a collateral mode. They had learned the foundation for this mode in their initial off-site meeting. If they had not, it is doubtful that they would have contributed so creatively to the development of strategy. Indeed, a task force which operates under the authority/production norms prevailing in its primary organization will need a collateral mode for itself.

Relation to Temporary Systems.   The relationship between collateral organization and a temporary system (Miles, 1964) also merits clarification. A temporary system is brought into existence with the understanding it will have limited duration. Its dissolution may be linked to (1) time (a two-day conference), (2) the occurrence of an event (the completion of a report), or (3) the attainment of a condition or level of functioning (a marketing unit solves its sales training problems without further

aid from headquarters staff). A collateral organization is likely to terminate for one of two reasons. First, the ill-structured problems it is intended to solve are solved and there are no more. Second, the permanent, primary organization has internalized the norms and the competence of the collateral organization. In the second instance, the primary organization has attained a new level of functioning, thereby making the collateral mode redundant.

A collateral organization will be useful so long as it performs two functions: *(a)* it compensates for a deficiency in the primary system; *(b)* it is a vehicle for introducing needed changes in the primary system. In Silver City Bank, for example, the collateral mode was used intensively for strategy problems for about a year and a half. Then it was used to examine problems of implementation for about a year, but much less intensively. After that, it was used at semiannual intervals to take stock of unresolved, ill-structured problems, with the understanding that its shift to more intensive use would be made if the problems warranted it.

Operating Problems.   Collateral organization tends to increase the use of groups, at least initially, puts more stress on middle managers, and surfaces problems of individual tolerance and flexibility.

Need for Groups. A manager may be concerned that introducing a collateral organization will increase the number of problems going to groups for solution. This may happen initially for two reasons. First, there appears to be a temporary increase in the number of problems, because a collateral organization identifies problems that were previously diffused or unshared. Second, collateral organizations concentrate on high-priority, organizationwide problems, which are usually solved better by a group than by one person working alone. After an initial surge, the need for groups rapidly decreases, because the collateral mode diligently separates problems that should go to one manager (or a pair of managers) from those that should go to a larger group.

Stress on Middle Managers. When a collateral organization permits lower and higher managers to interact directly, the stress on middle managers increases. Higher managers may discover that middle managers have been distorting and editing the upward flow of information. Lower managers may discover they can influence higher management decisions more easily than they thought possible. Both higher and lower managers discover they need less time to identify and solve complex problems. Management may be promoted to redesign the hierarchical organization and redefine the role of middle managers.

In the Silver City Bank, after working in a collateral mode, managers discovered they could expand operations more rapidly than planned because an anticipated shortage of managers could be met by freeing several middle managers for other assignments. In the Ajax case, managers in the collateral mode concluded that several middle-management positions were redundant but should be kept for back-up purposes and for training.

Individual Flexibility. Some subordinates have a strong need for structure and a relationship with their superior that does not change. They are comfortable only when working in one mode all the time—either authority/production or knowledge/problem solving. The important element for them is stability and consistency (Adorno, Frenkel-Brunswick, Levinson, & Sanford, 1950; Vroom, 1959). Even though problems may change and require organizational versatility, they find shifting from one mode to another confusing. Most subordinates, however, can be productive in more than one organizational mode provided they understand the purposes of a collateral mode, know which mode they are in, and know when it will end.

Sometimes a superior may not have the flexibility to work in more than one mode. If this is the case, attempts to use a collateral organization will meet strong resistance. The majority of managers, however, seem to have enough flexibility to use collateral organizations. The achievements in the two cases described above were heavily dependent on the flexibility of Mr. Brady and Mr. Anderson.

Too often, a manager's skepticism toward attempts to displace one organizational mode with another have been misconstrued as a sign of deep-seated personal rigidity. This "rigidity" usually fades when the manager understands the concept of collateral organization. When he sees how it can productively complement the hierarchical organization without displacing or destroying it, he can be remarkably flexible. As a matter of fact, after a manager experiences his first successful collateral organization, the problem is usually not one of rigidity but of overoptimism. He feels he and his group have broken through to a new form of relationship and productivity, and he easily develops overly optimistic expectations of future accomplishment. The demands of daily work, however, quickly intrude, as they must, making continued use of the collateral mode an infrequent, disjointed activity. Some ill-structured problems are solved, but, because of interruptions, solutions take longer to implement than he planned. New ill-structured problems that are identified take much greater effort to solve than he expected. He discovers that time for the collateral mode must be fought for and taken from the primary mode.

After using a collateral mode, the manager and his subordinates learn that the hierarchical organization can continue. Disorder does not take over. Directive behavior can still be used, but there is better understanding of how to integrate participation and group effort with the formal organization through use of a collateral mode. Perhaps most important, organization members learn concepts and methods which enable them to freely invent and use new modes for solving ill-structured problems.

Endnotes

1. I shall use the word *organization* to mean the communication channels, relationships, and the inner workings of a group composed of a superior and his subordinates, and the working relationships between such groups—rather than the distinct major divisions of a company.

2. *Collateral,* when used as a noun, denotes assets pledged as security for a loan. It is used here as an adjective, meaning to exist at the same time and level as, hence in association with, another organization.

3. When the knowledge/problem mode is primary, the organization requires and attracts individuals who value

individual contribution, creativity, self-motivation, and low interdependence. Going from a knowledge/problem mode to an authority/production mode introduces complex problems of coordination, reduction of individual freedom, group operation, and conflicts with personal values. It is not simply the reverse of going from the authority/production mode to the knowledge/problem mode.

4. Names in this case and the one that follows are fictitious.

5. I acknowledge my gratitude to Matthew B. Miles and William O. Lytle, Jr., who were the OD team with me. This case is based upon Enlarging Organization Choice through Use of a Temporary Problem-Solving System, by D. E. Zand, M. B. Miles, and W. O. Lytle, Jr. (mimeo, available from author).

References

Adorno, T. W.; Frenkel-Brunswick, E.; Levinson, D. J.; and Sanford, R. N. *The Authoritarian Personality.* New York: Harper & Row, 1950.

Argyris, C. *Intervention Theory and Method.* Reading, MA: Addison-Wesley Publishing, 1970.

Bavelas, A. "Communication Patterns in Task-Oriented Groups." *Journal of Acoustical Society of America* 22, (1950), pp. 725–30.

Bennis, W. G. "Beyond Bureaucracy." *Trans-Action,* July–August 1965.

Bennis, W. G. *Changing Organizations.* New York: McGraw-Hill, 1966.

Burns, T.; & Stalker. G. M. *Management of Innovation.* London: Tavistock, 1961.

Christie, L. S.; Luce, R. D.; & May, J., Jr. "Communications and Learning in Task-Oriented Groups." Cambridge, MA: Research Laboratory Electronics, 1952.

Davis, S. A. "An Organic Problem-Solving Method of Organizational Change." *Journal of Applied Behavioral Science* 3 (1967), pp. 3–21.

Delbecq, A. L. "How 'Informal' Organization Evolves: Interpersonal Choice and Subgroup Formation." *Business Perspectives,* 1968, IV (3), 17–21.

Fiedler, F. E. *A Theory of Leadership Effectiveness.* New York: McGraw-Hill, 1967.

Galbraith, J. R. "Matrix Organization Designs." *Business Horizons,* February 1971, pp. 24–40.

Golembiewski, R. T. *Renewing Organizations: The Laboratory Approach to Planned Change.* Itasca, IL: Peacock, 1972.

Guetzkow, H.; & Dill, W. R. "Factors in the Organizational Development of Task-Oriented Groups." *Sociometry* 20 (1957), pp. 175–204.

Guetzkow, H.; & Simon, H. A. "The Impact of Certain Communication Nets upon Organization and Performance in Task-Oriented Groups." *Management Science* 1 (1955), pp. 233–50.

Lawrence, P. R.; & Lorsch, J. W. "New Management Job: The Integrator." *Harvard Business Review,* November–December 1967, p. 142.

Leavitt, H. J. "Some Effects of Certain Communication Patterns on Group Performance." *Journal of Abnormal and Social Psychology,* 46 (1951), pp. 38–50.

Likert, R. *New Patterns of Management.* New York: McGraw-Hill, 1961.

Likert, R. *The Human Organization.* New York: McGraw-Hill, 1967.

McGregor, D. *The Human Side of Enterprise.* New York: McGraw-Hill, 1960.

Margulies, N.; & Raia, A. P. *Organizational Development.* New York: McGraw-Hill, 1972.

Miles, M. B. "On Temporary Systems." In M.B. Miles, ed., *Innovation in Education.* New York: Columbia University Press, 1964, pp. 437–92.

Pfiffner, J. M.; & Sherwood, F. P. *Administrative Organization.* Englewood Cliffs, NJ: Prentice Hall, 1960, pp. 16–32.

Shaw, M. E.; Rothchild, G. H.; & Strickland, J. F. "Decision Process in Communication Nets." *Journal of Abnormal and Social Psychology* 54 (1957) pp. 323–30.

Slater, P. E.; & Bennis, W. G. "Democracy is Inevitable." *Harvard Business Review,* March–April 1964, p. 51.

Tannenbaum, R.; & Davis, S. A. "Values, Men, and Organizations." *Industrial Management Review,* Winter 1969, pp. 67–83.

Vroom, V. H. "Some Personality Determinants of the Effects of Participation." *Journal of Abnormal and Social Psychology* 59 (1959), pp. 322–27.

READING 20
SURVEY-GUIDED DEVELOPMENT: USING HUMAN RESOURCES MEASUREMENT IN ORGANIZATIONAL CHANGE

David G. Bowers
Jerome L. Franklin

As it exists today, organizational development (OD) in various forms and practices includes many common values and goals. However, there is also a considerable degree of difference in the various concepts, procedures, and assumptions that are identified within this field. The common elements reflect to some extent the fact that those engaged in the field share some aspects of their backgrounds. The differences reflect different evolutionary streams from which the practice of OD has emerged. Much of what is currently considered within the realm of OD can be traced to the fields of adult education, personnel training, industrial consultation, and clinical psychology. Organizational development now represents a crystallization of the experiences of practitioners from these fields. Examples of the techniques and procedures that have evolved in this way include sensitivity training, human relations training, team development training, process consultation, and role-playing.

Some portion of what presently may be considered organizational development came into existence through a different route, which is perhaps best described as a concern for the utilization of scientific knowledge. This data-based type of development and, specifically, the survey feedback technique, originated not from the search by practitioners for more effective helping tools, but from the concern of organizational management researchers for better ways of moving new scientific findings from the producers (researchers) to the consumers (organizational managers).

Source: David G. Bowers and Jerome L. Franklin, "Survey-Guided Development: Using Human Resources Measurement in Organizational Change," *Journal of Contemporary Business* 1, no. 3 (Summer 1972), pp. 43–55. School of Business Administration, University of Washington, DJ-10, Seattle. Reprinted with permission.

This view is clearly spelled out in the prospectus which launched the organizational behavior research program at the Institute for Social Research over 25 years ago:

> The general objective of this research program will be to discover the underlying principles applicable to the problems of organizing and managing human activity. *A second important objective of the project will be to discover how to train persons to understand and skillfully use these principles* [9, p. 2].

> The major emphasis during the last four years of the project will be on the experimental verification of the results and *especially on learning how to make effective use of them in everyday situations. . . .* Each experiment will be analyzed in terms of measures made before and after the experiment, and often a series of measures will be made during the experiment [9, p. 10].

> The entire process of our society depends upon our skill in organizing our activity. Insofar as we can achieve efficiently through systematic research new understandings and skills instead of relying on trial and error behavior, we can speed the development of a society capable of using constructively the resources of an atomic age. Unless we achieve this understanding rapidly and intelligently, we may destroy ourselves in trial and error bungling. Understanding individual behavior is not enough, nor is an understanding of the principles governing the behavior of men in small groups. We need generalizations and principles which will point the way to organizing human activity on the scale now required [9, p. 12].

This same prospectus also stated that the basic measurement tool to be used in the proposed studies would be the sample survey, employing procedures that the proposers had developed during their years with the Program Surveys Division of the Department of Agriculture. It was also stated

215

that the study design would be generally like that employed by Rensis Likert in the Agency Management Study [7].

Thus the stage was set for an organizational development emphasis that first engaged in scientific search for principles of organizational management, and then, once such principles were established, set forth to identify effective implementation strategies for them. This plan was provided impetus by real-life circumstances. Researchers rapidly discovered that the generation of sound findings regarding organizational management was one thing and their implementation quite another. Two factors seriously diminished the effective use of early findings. First, although survey items referred to work-world events, there was often no readily accepted "map" tying what was measured to operating realities in ways that were readily understood. Second, because there was a lack of implementation procedures geared to the data, presentation of findings normally involved a narrative report. As a result of both these factors, there was a great propensity either to file the report away, to pass it along to lower levels accompanied by vague directives to "use it," or simply to seize selectively upon bits which reinforced managers' existing biases [3].

The Nature of Survey Feedback

In an effort to solve this problem, Floyd Mann and his colleagues at the Institute for Social Research developed the *survey feedback* procedure as an implementation tool. No authoritative volume has as yet been written about this development tool. Partially as a result of this absence of detailed description, many persons mistakenly believe that survey feedback consists of a rather superficial handing back of tabulated numbers and percentages, but little else. On the contrary, where the survey feedback is employed with skill and experience, it becomes a sophisticated tool for using the data as a springboard to development. Data are typically tabulated for each and every work group in an organization, as well as for each combination of groups that represents an area of responsibility, including the total organization.

Each supervisor and manager receives a tabulation of this sort, containing data based on the responses of *his own* immediate subordinates, together with documents describing their interpretation and use. A resource person, sometimes from an outside (consulting) agency and at other times from the client system's own staff, usually counsels privately with the supervisor-recipient about the contents of the package and then arranges a suitable time when the supervisor can meet with his subordinates to discuss the findings and their implications. The resource person attends that meeting to provide help to the participants, both in the technical aspects of the tabulations and in the process aspects of the discussion.

Procedures by which the feedback process progresses through an organization may vary from site to site. In certain instances a "waterfall" pattern is adhered to, in which the process substantially is completed at high-level groups before moving down to subordinate groups. In other instances, feedback is more or less simultaneous to all groups and echelons.

By whichever route it takes, an effective survey feedback operation depicts the organization's groups as moving, by a discussion process, from the tabulated perceptions, through a cataloging of their implications, to commitment for solutions to the problems that the discussion has identified and defined.

The Necessity of Differential Diagnosis

From these general and specific concerns there has emerged a viewpoint, largely identified with persons associated with the Institute for Social Research, that constructive change is measurement-centered, beginning with a quantitative reading of the state of the organization and direction of movement. Even more than this, change is, throughout, a rational process that makes use of information, pilot demonstrations, and the persuasive power of evidence and hard fact.

A successful change effort begins with rigorous measurement of the way in which the organization presently is functioning. These measurements provide the material for a diagnosis, and the diagnosis forms the basis for the design of a program of change activities. Likert has stated this quite pointedly in an early publication:

> One approach that can be used to apply the findings of human relations research to your own operation can be described briefly. Your medical departments did not order all of your supervisors nor all of your employees to take penicillin when it became available, even though it is a very effective antibiotic. They have, however, administered it to many of your employees. But note the process of deciding when it should be administered. The individual was given certain tests and measurements obtained—temperature, blood analysis, etc. The results of these measurements were compared with known facts about diseases, infections, etc., and the penicillin was prescribed when the condition was one that was known or believed to be one that would respond to this antibiotic.
>
> We believe the same approach should be used in dealing with the human problems of any organization. This suggests that human relations supervisory training programs should not automatically be prescribed for all supervisory and management personnel. Nor should other good remedies or methods for improvement be applied on a blanket basis to an entire organization hoping it will yield improved results [5, p. 35].

One of the reasons for the importance of the diagnostic step early in the life of a change program is stated explicitly in the preceding quotation: it will increase the probability of focusing upon the right, not the wrong, problems, and it will add to the likelihood of the right, not the wrong, course of treatments being prescribed. A clear statement of the problems, courses of action, and change objectives, based on sound measurements allied to the best possible conceptualization

from research and theory, will maximize the likelihood that true causal conditions, rather than mere symptoms, will be dealt with [2].

The Rationale for Survey-Guided Development

The preceding sections have pointed to the existence of two somewhat different approaches to organization development. One, growing out of applied practice, is identified more obviously with the laboratory approach to education. It uses the *immediate* behavior (verbal and nonverbal) of the participants as the source material around which development forms. It focuses much more on the "here-and-now" than on the "there-and-then" and emphasizes experience-based learnings. It focuses more sharply on issues related to interpersonal processes than those less observable issues of role and structure.

The other approach, which we propose to elaborate on in greater detail, is related more obviously to an information-systems approach to adaptation. This approach uses participants' summarized perceptions of behavior and situation as the source material around which development is focused. It focuses on the there-and-then at least as much as on the here-and-now, attaches considerably more importance to cognitive understanding than does the other approach, and is concerned with such issues as role and structure, at least as much as with those of interpersonal process.

These brief identifications are more descriptive than explanatory. A true understanding of the survey-guided approach requires that we look more closely at the assumptions which it appears to make and the operating propositions which it derives from those assumptions.

Like most organization development techniques, survey feedback is only one aspect of a measurement-guided approach to change. As a tool or procedure, it emerged as a response to a practical need to see research findings implemented. It did not emerge as the logical conclusion of a formal body of scientific thought, and it remains for us presently to search, after the fact, for a rationale about how and why it works.

In this vein, two bodies of scientific thought seem relevant. One comes from the research done in the area of perception and involves the fundamental concept that a difference between perceptions is motivating—an idea originally and most clearly stated by Peak [8]. This is perhaps illustrated by the following example: if I perceive, on the one hand, that I cannot complete a particular piece of work by the end of the normal workday and perceive, on the other hand, that that work must be complete by the start of office hours in the morning, I am motivated to work late or to take home a work-loaded briefcase.

According to this view, the perceptions must be associated (i.e., they must be seen as belonging to the same "domain"). I may perceive that I do not play the piano as well as Arthur Rubenstein, but his discrepancy is hardly motivating, because I do not consider myself to be a professional concert pianist. Although associated, the perceptions must be different, yet not so different as to destroy their association. The perceptions may be related to emotion-laden or "feelings" issues, or they may consist of different perceptions of conditions in the external world. Peak illustrates the process by drawing an analogy:

> Think of a thermostat. Here there are two events. One is the temperature setting (an expected state if you will). The other event or term in the system is the height of the mercury in the tube, representing the present state of affairs (room temperature). These are analogous then to the two events in our motive construct, and disparity exists between them when there is a difference in the setting and in the temperature reading. Now, the second feature of our motive construct, which is called contact or association, is provided by the structure of the thermostat and is not modifiable in this system as it is in the motive system. In other words, the two terms (or events) remain in association. Only disparity can vary, and when there is disparity there is "motivation" and action; i.e., the furnace starts to run. The results of this action are fed back to produce change in one of the terms of the disparity relation (the mercury level). When the disparity disappears through rise in temperature or resetting of the thermostat, action ceases. . . . But since the thermostat lacks the capacity to stop action through isolation, and in the simple design we have described, cannot select different actions, the model must be regarded merely as illustrative . . . [8, pp. 172–73].

Another closely related set of ideas comes from engineering psychology and begins with the observation that human behavior is goal-seeking or goal-oriented. As such, behavior is characterized by a search for processes by which the human being controls his environment (i.e., means by which he reshapes it toward more constructive or productive ends).

Oversimplifying the control process greatly, at least four elements are involved: (1) a model, (2) a goal, (3) an activity, and (4) feedback. The *model* is a mental picture of the surrounding world, including not only structural properties, but cause-and-effect relations. It is built by the person(s) from past accumulations of information, stored in memory. From the workings of the model and from the modeling process which he employs, alternative possible future states are generated, of which one is selected as a *goal*. At this point what is called the "goal selection system" ends and that is known as the "control system" per se begins. *Activities* are initiated to attain the goal, and *feedback*, which comes by some route from the person's environment, is used to compare, confirm, adjust, and correct responses by signaling departures from what was expected.

The process as just described is beguilingly simple. However, in actual life it is often extremely complex. The thermostat example, although embodied in a marvelous and valuable piece of equipment, is basically a simple instance of an adaptive system. Others are much more complicated, such as that contained in the role of a Mississippi river boat pilot. The shifting character of currents and channels make this adaptive task quite complex. Therefore the difficulty in this as in other complex systems stems from not having learned how to predict system performance under various conditions. As one of the foremost human factors writers has described it, "The ability to predict system performance is in major respects the same as the ability to control the system" [4, p. 42].

The human organization reflects the same type of a complex, difficult control system, in part for these same reasons. Activity is only as good as the model which leads to it, yet human organizations are often managed according to grossly imperfect models (models which ignore much of what is known from research about organizational structure and functioning). Predictability is enhanced, in human systems as elsewhere, by quantification, yet many of the relationships are often not quantified, if, indeed, they are recognized at all.

In the absence of a sound model, what is expected varies with immediate experience. It is for this reason that objective feedback on organizational functioning is absolutely essential in organizational development. In its absence, true deviations are unknown because expectations constantly adjust to incurred performance.

From this very condensed discussion, it is apparent that, when organizational change is viewed as a problem in optimal control or adaptation (which it inherently is) several things are required:

1. An adequate model—one which is a valid representation of that external reality known as "the organization," including both structural properties, knowledge of cause-effect relations, and predictive capability.

2. A goal—a preferred potential future state, generated by the model.

3. An activity—selected as instrumental to attaining that goal.

4. Objective feedback—about deviations from what the model would lead us to expect.

These two sets of concepts—the one drawn from basic work in the area of perception, the other taken from the human factors work of engineering psychology—provide jointly a plausible rationale for survey-guided development. As in the human factors area, feedback of information about the actual state of functioning provides key input to selecting development goals and making midcourse corrections. It tells the developing system what needs to be done. The power source, which in human factors descriptions is shown as an external input, is in survey-guided development provided by the sort of discrepancy described by Peak. Survey feedback, by pointing to the existence of differences between what is actually going on and what the model indicates one wants and needs, provides the energy (motivation) to undertake change activities.

In detail, as in general, organizational development (as the survey-guided approach envisions) may be seen as an analog of adaptation as described by human factors theorists. What they have termed the "goal selection system" is, in survey-based development, the *diagnostic* process. What they have referred to as the "control system" is the *therapeutic* process.

To serve its function within the diagnostic process, the work group draws inputs from the same sorts of areas drawn upon by all adaptive systems:

From higher-level systems: from the larger organization, its top management, and from society in general in the form of performance trends, top-management evaluations, labor relations trends, changes in laws or regulations, and so on.

From its own information about the model which they have thus far accepted, as well as information concerning past experiences and results.

From a reading of how things actually are: from the survey; through what we have described as survey feedback, which deals largely with intragroup behavior, attitudes, and relationships; and from a more formal *diagnosis* (an analytic report prepared by persons skilled in the survey data area), which deals with intergroup and systemic properties.

From the environment: in many forms, but particularly from the "change agent," the organizational development scientist-consultant who helps to catalyze the overall change process.

Each of these input sources has potential impact by virtue of its presence or comparative absence, its kind, and its quality. For example, the higher-level system inputs ordinarily create some degree of felt urgency. Often, discrepancy generated by this input motivates the initial search and culminates in serious consideration of organizational development as a possible course of action. The extent to which these inputs encourage the development efforts of the client entity is also critical. Many of the development failures occur in instances in which higher-level system inputs are either lacking, which indicates acquiescence, or instead, are signaling outright disapproval of organizational development. A general example of such an instance might involve a supervisor who verbally acquiesces to an organizational development effort for his subordinates but behaves and rewards his subordinates for behaving in ways which are incongruent with the values, assumptions, and goals that are emphasized in organizational development. Efforts that proceed in the face of such higher-level system inputs run a great risk of death by neglect.

From the group's own information storage comes the model of organizational functioning already held by group members. This includes information regarding past organizational practices (behaviors, interaction patterns, managerial styles) as well as outcomes at various levels of finality (absenteeism, turnover, profit, production efficiency, growth, et cetera).

The survey provides a means by which multiple perceptions of behaviors and organizational conditions related to effectiveness can be gathered, compiled, and compared. As has been indicated above, one must consider not one, but two, separate input streams from the survey. One of these input streams consists of the survey feedback process itself, in which tabulations of the group's *own data*, especially concerning its internal functioning, is used as a springboard to the identification, understanding, and solving of problems. The other consists of a more formal diagnosis, prepared by persons skilled in multivariate analysis, and

focuses on those problem streams which occur in the system as a whole and which can be seen only by careful comparison of the tabulated data of many groups.

The Change Agent's Role

The change agent, as an adjunct person, seems to have no exact counterpart in *manual* control problems. The reason for his presence in organizational development is that a model of organizational functioning and human behavior is not as simple or programmable as that involved in manual control. Reading and digesting survey data are not the same as reading a gauge. Accomplishing an organizational "correction" is much more complicated than pushing a button or turning a wheel a certain number of degrees. In most instances the controller in organizational change—the client group—must be shown what the "gauge" says and how to read it, and must be guided through the operations of making the desired changes. The survey discrepancy, properly digested with the aid of the change agent, both builds the *motivation* to make the change and indicates *what* changes in functioning must occur. However, the change agent helps the client group learn *how* to make the necessary changes.

The primary role of the change agent in survey-guided development is that of a transducer (i.e., an energy link between scientific knowledge regarding principles of organizational functioning and the particular organization or group with which he is working). As such, the change agent enters into both the diagnostic and therapeutic phases of the development effort. During the diagnostic phase, the model that the change agent presents must be reasonably complete, predictive, and adequate to provide the client with useful information. If the model lacks any of these characteristics, the change agent will be supplying the system with little more than noise.

In addition to having these characteristics, the model must be presented to the members of the group or organization accurately and adequately. The issue of acceptance is critical: the best model loses its value unless it is understood in useful ways by members of the system. The model and evidence in its support must be presented in such a manner that acceptance is based upon rational evaluations of the evidence as well as the experiences and insights of those involved in the organization. During this activity, the change agent must have the model clearly in mind, must be able to present the model and its evidence clearly, and must also be able to call upon his group process and related skills to facilitate understanding and acceptance.

As in any other situation in which the talents and knowledge of one man are to be made available to assist another, the manner in which that occurs is, of course, important. In the area of human organizational development, of all places, it is important that the knowledge be made available in a supportive, not a demeaning, fashion; it is not to be "laid on," ordered into place, or delivered as some form of speech from a pretentious throne. Skill in patient explanation, in aiding understanding, and in helping the client entities themselves to come to grips with reality—in short, the whole array of interpersonal skills—are extremely important. But the change agent must have the knowledge of what must be explained, the grasp of what must be understood, and the comprehension of what that reality is.

In this vein, the change agent facilitates the understanding and digesting of diagnostically useful information. In the survey-guided approach, this role involves helping members of the system to understand better the survey feedback information. It also may involve a range of activities, from a detailed explanation of the meaning and relevance of certain content areas to helping group members understand information from the survey in terms of the here-and-now of the feedback meeting process. In addition, he aids the client group members in setting goals and formulating action plans for the development effort. In this activity, as in the others, the change agent may serve both as a source of information (e.g., suggesting potential actions to be undertaken or considered) and as a facilitator who focuses upon the group's processes.

The change agent also serves as a transducer in the therapeutic phase of survey-guided organizational development. Once a diagnosis has pointed to problem areas in organizational functioning, the change agent provides a link between scientific knowledge regarding effective methods of correcting specific problems and the problems exhibited in the immediate situation. A variety of activities may be undertaken during this phase. Each has, as its ultimate goal, movement toward the model of organizational functioning held (after its initial establishment) by both change agent and clients.

In part, the specific type of activity undertaken depends on the stage in the therapeutic phase. In the early stages, the change agent is likely to be involved largely with supplying informational inputs regarding specific possible activities, helping organizational members cope with attitudinal shifts, and handling defensive reactions. The motivation to change created by a discrepancy between the ideal model and the actual state of the organization is alone not sufficient to produce change. Methods of actually accomplishing the change must also be evident to organizational members. In this respect, the change agent in part fulfills his transducer role by informing members of the client system of the available alternatives.

In later stages, the change agent is often involved with skill acquisition and perfection by group members. The range and variety of potentially necessary skills is large. Problem solving, giving and receiving personal feedback, listening, general leadership, goal-setting, resolving conflict, and diagnosing group processes are but a few of those which might be cited. The change agent must not only know which skills are needed but also must be competent in guiding their acquisition. It is a result of this acquisition and perfection of skill that organizational members come to rely less on the change agent and more on themselves in movement toward the goal.

In addition to the emphasis on skills, the change agent provides and facilitates informal intermediate-phase feedback during the therapeutic phase. For example, he may provide the group with feedback in the form of process comments inserted during or after key intragroup interactions. He may also facilitate attempts by the members themselves to gather and understand information regarding their progress toward accepted goals.

A Recapitulation

As the preceding pages have indicated, the survey-guided approach suggests several general propositions regarding: (1) certain basic assumptions of organizational development; (2) change processes; and (3) the change agent's role.

Basic Assumptions of OD.   There are systemic properties (i.e., characteristics of the organization as a total system) not definable by the simple sum of individual and/or group behaviors.

A *model* of organizational functioning, which includes these systemic properties, reflecting available evidence and testable by quantifiable and scientific means, should be used as a basis for development efforts.

Systemic properties in particular can improve only as a result of *carefully sequenced planned interventions.*

Valid information about the state of group and organizational functioning (objectives and useful reflections of reality) is best obtained from summarized, quantified longitudinal perceptions. (There-and-then data are at least as useful as here-and-now data.)

A *diagnosis* based upon a quantitative comparison with the model and prepared by competent professionals should be used to evaluate the organization on both intragroup and systemic levels.

Prescription of intervention activities should be *diagnostically based.*

Change Processes.   *Motivation* is created by the realization that the actual state differs from the accepted model (i.e., a discrepancy exists between that which is desired and that which exists).

The discrepancies exist in terms of both *intragroup* and *systemic* processes and properties.

Change involves a *sequence of events,* including: informational inputs; formation of a model; selection of a goal; assessment of the situation; formation of a diagnosis, feedback; adjustment; and reevaluation.

Change Agent's Role and Activities.   The change agent acts as *transducer* between scientific knowledge regarding organizational functioning and change processes, on the one hand, and the particular situation, on the other.

He has a *model* of organizational functioning and *works toward* its realization.

Except in those rare instances which require a nondirective stance, the change agent is an *active advocate of goal-oriented behavior.* He evaluates and helps the client group to *evaluate progress toward the goals,* but he is not punitive.

He must have a *wide range of knowledge and skills* and not be bound to one or two particular techniques.

These general propositions of survey-guided development are illustrated as a flow of events in Figure 1.

Perspective and Prologue

We conclude by offering an apology to the reader who anticipated a less-labored description. What has been written has been, in many ways, a rather technical document. It reflects our strong belief that organizational development rightfully is becoming more a science than an art. This view was expressed several years ago by one of the authors:

> By science I mean discernible in replicable terms—objective, understandable (rather than "mystique"), verifiable, and predictive. Should these conditions for organizational development fail to be met, it will go the way of the Great Auk and the "Group Talking Technique." In short, organizational development will die, having been remembered as one more fad.
>
> Organizational development cannot survive on the goodwill of top management persons who are already sold on its potential and effectiveness. It can survive only if it proves its method and its contribution beyond reasonable doubt to the hardheaded skeptics. Organizational development must prove

FIGURE 1

Survey-guided development

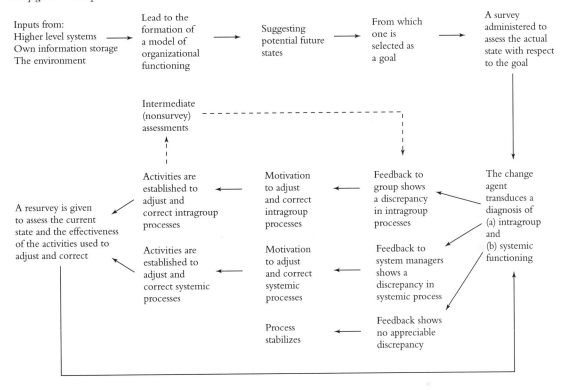

with hard, rigorous evidence that it can beneficially affect: *(a)* the volume of work done by the organization, *(b)* the cost per unit of doing the organization's work, and *(c)* the quality of work done [1, p. 62].

The same article described barriers which, up to that time, had impeded the progress of organizational development as a science:

The lack of a "critical mass" of knowledge in the field.

The tendency for organizational development to take the form of a single general practitioner, operating on an isolated island.

The absence of an adequate measuring instrument, geared to an adequate model of organizational functioning, for use in organizational development efforts.

Within the last decade, considerable progress has been made on each of these fronts. Books and articles, describing and integrating findings in this field, have appeared in increasing numbers and richness. This present journal issue is a case in point.

To the extent that our own experience is typical, opportunities for researchers and change agents to collaborate in multifaceted, large system development efforts have emerged.

Efforts have similarly been undertaken by a number of persons to develop procedures and instruments for rigorous description of change agent interventions and their immediate effects.

Finally, we feel that survey-guided development has pressed, from its own necessity, the construction of reliable, valid, standardized instruments for assessing organizational functioning.

The availability of such instruments, together with the accumulating critical mass of knowledge, leads us to considerable optimism concerning the future of organizational development in general and concerning the survey-guided approach, in particular.

References

1. Bowers, D. G. "The Scientific Data-Based Approach to Organization Development," Part 2, in A.L. Hite, ed. *Organizational Development: The State of the Art.* Ann Arbor, MI: Foundation for Research on Human Behavior, 1971.

2. Bowers, D. G. *System 4: The Ideas of Rensis Likert.* New York: Basic Books, 1972.

3. Katz, Daniel, and Kahn, Robert L. *The Social Psychology of Organizations.* New York: John Wiley & Sons, 1966.

4. Kelly, C. R. *Manual and Automatic Control.* New York: John Wiley & Sons, 1968.

5. Likert, R. "Findings on Research on Management and Leadership." *Proceedings*, 43, Pacific Coast Gas Assn., 1952.

6. Likert, R. *The Human Organization.* New York: McGraw-Hill, 1967.

7. Likert, R., and Willets, J.M. *Morale and Agency Management.* Hartford, CT: Life Insurance Agency Management Association, 1940, 4 vols.

8. Peak, H. "Attitude and Motivation," in M.R. Jones, ed., *Nebraska Symposium on Motivation.* Lincoln, NE: University of Nebraska Press, 1955.

9. Survey Research Center. *A Program of Research on the Fundamental Problems of Organizing Human Behavior.* Ann Arbor: University of Michigan, 1947.

10. Taylor, J. C., and Bowers, D. G. *The Survey of Organizations: A Machine-Scored, Standardized Questionnaire Instrument.* Ann Arbor: Institute for Social Research, 1972.

IV CUTTING-EDGE CHANGE STRATEGIES

This part includes seven articles that address what we call cutting-edge strategies because they describe organization development and transformation (OD&T) interventions that are relatively new or are in the process of development and refinement. All have a strong foundation of "systems" thinking. Some are relatively abstract and difficult to explain, for example, "appreciative inquiry" and "the learning organization," but all can be translated into specific interventions. All are difficult to implement successively.

Because some of these interventions are nontraditional and may not be easily recognized as organization development and transformation, it might be useful to review what kind of intervention we include in a book on OD & T. Figure 1 attempts to summarize the characteristics of intervention strategies we call OD & T and, conversely, what characteristics would suggest that a particular intervention or set of interventions falls outside that domain. Reengineering, for example, is not included because most descriptions of reengineering pay little attention to the social system or human-social-psychological processes of organizations.

The article by Robert A. Zawacki and Carol A. Norman, "Successful Self-Directed Teams and Planned Change: A Lot in Common," begins with an overview of the transition from first-generation planned change (OD) to second-generation planned change (OT). They then go on to assert that self-directed teams (SDTs) are part of this second-generation OT and are rapidly growing in popularity. They go on to say that the utilization of SDTs has resulted in significant increases in productivity when implemented effectively. They also discuss the law as it relates to SDTs and end their essay with guidelines for successful implementation.

Rita Williams's article, "Survey Guided Appreciative Inquiry: A Case Study," presents a description of an appreciative inquiry intervention that was blended with a survey feedback process. The site was an $11 billion regional commercial banking institution. According to Williams, the appreciative inquiry phase started with "hopes, dreams and visions" rather than a "mirror of what is," and thus became a vehicle for "what might be." Although appreciative inquiry is evolving as an OD &

FIGURE 1

Organizational improvement strategies

	Organization Development (OD)	Non-OD (examples)
Target of intervention	Work-related groups.	Individuals, or noninterdependent persons in a group or audience setting.
Consultant model used	Collaborative equal power (change agent model)	Expert or "purchase" model.
Task or structure versus process orientation	Focuses largely on processes such as group interaction, norms, leadership, decision making; outcomes may be task/structural changes.	Focuses largely on changing tasks or structure.
Depth of culture managed	Attempt to manage culture in depth; both formal aspects and informal (e.g., cognizance of attitudes, perceptions, feelings).	Primary focus on one selected aspect of formal system (e.g., structure, technology, tasks, or goals).
Time perspective	Two to three years and beyond.	Ad hoc, short-range orientation.
Systems perspective	High systems orientation (i.e., high cognizance of interdependencies).	Narrow attention to functional organizational subsystem or problem.

T intervention, basically the central interventions are interviews with organizational members and then discussions in small work groups or organizationwide meetings focusing on such questions as,

1. What have been the peak moments in the life of this organization—"when people felt most alive, most energized, most committed, and most fulfilled . . . ?"
2. What do organizational members value most "about themselves, their tasks, and the organization as a whole?"
3. "What have been the organizational factors that most fostered realization of excellence?"
4. What are the "most significant embryonic possibilities . . ." that indicate "realistic possibilities for an even better organization[1]?"

Marvin Weisbord's essay, "Inventing the Future: Search Strategies for Whole Systems Improvement," is a chapter from his book *Productive Workplaces.* In this chapter Weisbord describes a future search conference that "brings together thirty to sixty people for two or three days. Together they do a series of structured tasks, looking at the organization's past, present, and preferred future." Weisbord describes the evolution of such conferences in terms of both theory and practice and in terms of the historical figures who were key to that evolution. Some of the pioneers to whom Weisbord refers were Fred Emery, Eric Trist, Ronald Lippitt, and Edward Lindaman.

Gary Jusela's essay, "Meeting the Global Competitive Challenge: Building Systems That Learn on a Large Scale," was written especially for an earlier edition of this book.

Building on Weisbord's work and that of many of the theorists and practitioners cited by Weisbord, Jusela describes "getting the whole system in the room," an intervention used successfully at the Ford Motor Company and at Boeing Aerospace and Electronics Division. The total process at Boeing included three major phases. Phase I was a two-day working session with the Aerospace and Electronics Division manager and 15 of the top executives. Phase II was expanded to include the top 170 managers of the division who met for three days and then two more days 13 weeks later. Phase III, a series of three-day sessions, brought a total of some 3,000 managers into the strategic planning process in groups of 180 to 330 managers per session.

In "Centers of Excellence," Steven Lyle and Robert A. Zawacki describe a form of organization that has these characteristics: "a logical grouping of related skills or disciplines," "an administrative entity focused on the well-being and development of people," and "a place where individuals learn skills and share knowledge across functional boundaries." The COE is headed by a "coach" who has responsibilities in training and development, mentoring, "facilitating and enabling the exchange and sharing of ideas and information," recruitment and assignment of individuals, and salary administration and administrative support. COE members are sourced out to vertically organized project teams across the organization.

David Garvin, in his essay "Building a Learning Organization," adds some clarity to the concept of the "learning organization" or the "knowledge-creating companies," a topic that he says "in large part remains murky, confused, and difficult to penetrate." His definition: *"A learning organization is an organization skilled at creating, acquiring, and transferring knowledge, and at modifying its behavior to reflect new knowledge and insights."* He cites Honda, Corning, and General Electric as passing this definitional test and gives illustrations from Xerox, Chaparral Steel, General Food's Topeka plant, GM's Saturn Division, and the Copeland Corporation. At Xerox, for example, employees are trained in "family groups" and learn a six-step process for problem solving and such skills as brainstorming, interviewing, and surveying.

In "Teaching Smart People How to Learn," Chris Argyris describes "single loop" and "double loop" learning and discusses how highly skilled professionals can be trapped into patterns of defensive reasoning. He goes on to describe how people can be taught to identify the inconsistencies between their espoused and actual theories of action and to reason productively. One technique Argyris uses is to have workshop participants write a case study of an actual business problem and dissect it, including examining the underlying assumptions being made.

Endnotes

1. Based on or inferred from Frank J. Barrett and David L. Cooperrider, "Generative Metaphor Intervention: A New Approach for Working with Systems Divided by Conflict and Caught in Deceptive Perception," *Journal of Applied Behavioral Science* 26, no. 2 (1990), pp. 219–239.

Reading 21
Successful Self-Directed Teams and Planned Change: A Lot in Common

Robert A. Zawacki
Carol A. Norman

Over the last 50 years, it appears that the nature of organizational change has changed. In the past, change flowed along a reasonably predictable course and individual contributors in the organization adjusted by working harder and smarter to stay ahead of the changes (Morland, 1984). Recently, however, organizations are facing high-speed change that is frequently transforming the direction and behavior of individual contributors.

This notion of rapid and random change is further discussed in Argyris (1991). He claims that the very behavior that has been reinforced by yesterday's performance can become a liability in the organization of the future. A brief example illustrates this point. The computer giant, IBM, built its success delivering mainframe computers. However, when the pace of change quickened, this computer giant was not flexible enough to perform effectively. In fact, the very behaviors that made it successful in the first few decades have now become a handicap.

Figure 1 illustrates this shift. Beginning with the 1950s and 1960s, change was incremental; people adapted and were rewarded for their new behaviors. Then, during the 1960s and 1970s change became more rapid and individual contributors responded by working harder and smarter. Leaders and managers in organizations helped people stay ahead of the increasing rate of change by introducing more and improved technologies such as personal computers and networks, and demonstrated some general movement toward empowering employees. The 1980s and 1990s brought even

more rapid and random change. Change nowadays seems to lack predictability.

Interestingly, it was during the early decades of adaptive change that Organization Development as a response was born. The first generation of change agents, the OD practitioners, helped organizations respond to change over the long term. Numerous change initiatives were planned and delivered over a period of several years.

Now, however, as we move increasingly toward rapid and random change, business leaders do not have the luxury of time. It is out of this extreme need for more timely change that a second generation of OD is being born. Some in the profession call it Organization Transformation (OT), with its experimental feel and self-designing emphasis (Porras & Silvers, 1991). Whatever you call it, there is a shift in the approach organizations and OD practitioners are taking to respond to random change, and that is the use of teams. Organizations no longer rely on individual contributors to wade their way through change. Self-directed teams (SDTs), total quality circles, and employee empowerment are just a few of the team-oriented technologies designed to cope with fast-paced, random change.

The purpose of this article is to help organizations of the future improve their ability to adapt to random change, yet maintain some degree of order, stability, and internal equity through the successful use of self-directed teams.

The History of Self-Directed Teams

The concept of self-directed teams came from the early research of Kurt Lewin at the Research Center for Group Dynamics and of the Tavistock Institute of Human Relations, whose members

Source: Reprinted by permission of the Organization Development Network, 71 Valley Street, Suite 301, South Orange, NJ 07079-2825. (973) 763-7337—voice, (973) 763-7488—fax, http://www.odnet.org.

The changing nature of organizational change

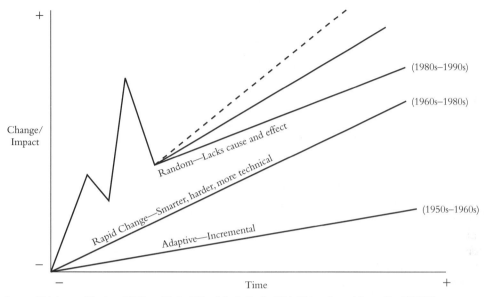

+

(1980s–1990s)

(1960s–1980s)

Change/
Impact

Random—Lacks cause and effect

Rapid Change—Smarter, harder, more technical

(1950s–1960s)

Adaptive—Incremental

−

−   Time   +

Source: This is a modification of D. Verne Morland, "Lear's Fool: Coping With Change Beyond Future Shock" (1984).

conceptualized sociotechnical systems theory as an approach to designing organizations (Lewin, 1951).

The Research Center at MIT (the initial group dynamics effort founded in 1945 under Lewin's direction, which later evolved into the National Training Laboratory in Group Development) introduced the idea of feedback to group members and the effect of feedback on individual and group behavior (French & Bell, 1984). At about the same time, the Tavistock group began to look at the interdependence between technology and people. "A concrete outcome of this theoretical perspective was the development of self-regulating work groups," according to Cummings (1978). Various authors have named these groups: autonomous, self-managed, self-regulating, composite, self-directed, or work teams. Yet the common denominator across the initiatives was the goal of transferring the control of work process over time from the manager to members in the work unit.

It is our experience that many managers, coaches, and OD consultants view SDTs as binary: You either have them or you don't. However, recent research indicates that the key to successful SDTs is that the transfer of control must be planned and implemented over time with managers who have the ability to make the transition into coaches.

In fact, successful SDTs evolve through five stages. Figure 2 depicts the evolution from a control model to a self-directed model and the corresponding organizational structure. Stage 1 reflects the typical hierarchical organization; Stage 2 introduces the group manager whose role is to make the transition into team coordinator/coach; in Stage 3 the group manager provides a structure for the necessary training for SDT members to take on more leadership tasks; in Stage 4 the team assumes most of the duties of the previous manager, who now becomes a boundary interface; and finally, in Stage 5, the manager is a resource for the SDT. A typical organization will have SDTs in all five stages at various times. Furthermore, any SDT can revert back to an earlier stage as team members of the SDT leave or new members enter the group.

FIGURE 2

The evolution of a self-directed team

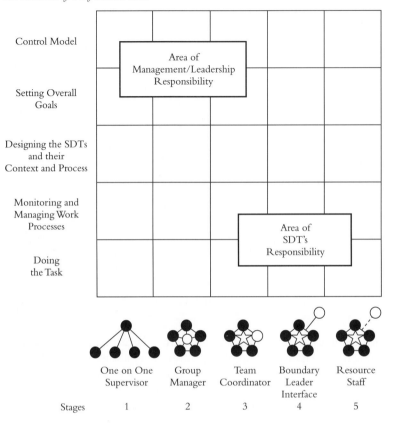

Cummings (1978) adds to our understanding of SDTs. He states, ". . . the design of self-regulating work groups depends on at least three conditions that enhance technically required cooperation and employees' capacity to control variances from goal attainment: task differentiation, boundary control, and task control."

Task differentiation refers to the autonomous nature of the teams' work. This permits the SDT to develop an identity whereby technical specialists emerge within the team to solve technical problems.

Boundary control is defined as the ability of the team members to control quality decisions, staffing and performance appraisal issues rather than relying on outside resources. Also, a well-defined work area increases the boundary control of the SDT.

Task control is the degree of control that the team members have over how they change inputs into a completed product or service.

Based on our research and experience with successful SDTs, we will add a fourth condition to Cummings's list. The fourth condition is the ability of the control manager to make the transition into a coach.

Why SDTs Succeed or Fail

For the last six years we have experimented with SDTs in organizations from small manufacturing firms to large service companies. Our experience is that SDTs can succeed or fail, regardless of the core technology, for several reasons.

Many organizations that profess to having SDTs in fact do not. A further examination of their teams reveals that they typically violated one or usually all four of the conditions mentioned above. Thus, what some organizations claim are SDTs are really only people going to staff meetings. Many organizations are chasing the quick fix and do not plan properly or even understand the dimensions of successful SDTs.

Additionally, only about 50 percent of managers can make the transition from controller to coach because of the need to unlearn old behaviors and learn new helping, negotiation, and conflict resolution skills.

Combined with this lack of understanding of the dimensions of successful SDTs is the impatience of top management. Top management is generally looking for the next quick fix because they usually are rewarded on a quarterly basis and are willing to "stay the course" for a long-term planned change program such as SDTs.

The key is to have people who believe they are valued and empowered, managers who can make the transition into coaches over time, and a well-designed plan. Cummings recognized the need to plan for SDTs and implement them over time. He refers to this process as "developmental system design," which came out of the early Tavistock research.

Development System Design

There are a group of leadership competencies that must be performed within an SDT; the key to becoming a successful SDT is to transfer these competencies from leader to team members with a plan over time. Although rare to find, there are managers who have the ability to sense the timing and training required before team members share in some of the leadership tasks. Figure 3 illustrates this transfer of competencies.

The critical activities are transferred from the leader to the team members over a period of 30 months, which our experience suggests is an optimum goal. OD consultants should experiment with reducing this time even more if they are to be perceived in the 1990s as adding value to the organization. With a good plan and checklist you can load the experiment for success!

Establish a Steering Committee. The first activity we recommend is to establish a steering committee to help the SDT, the primary purpose of which is to demonstrate top-level support but also to provide linkages to other parts of the organization. The steering committee should be a 12-member team consisting of senior executives, middle managers, technical people, and the individual contributors who report directly to the president or CEO. Their primary activity is to meet every three to six months with the SDT to check progress and provide needed support. In some organizations, the steering committee even becomes an SDT because it functions as a role model for the rest of the organization.

Provide Training for the SDT. Although each activity on the checklist is extremely important, training is critical to successful SDTs and will be discussed briefly. Many leaders of technical organizations attempt to save money by not committing to sufficient training before and during the evolution of SDTs. One leader, who attempted to save money up front, stated later, "If only I would have listened to you and approved of the training before we started SDTs. Now we are playing 'catch up' as the team grew without any planned way to deal with conflict."

At the outset. After the formation of an SDT, the first skill set needed by the group is a course on problem solving, since decision making in the group becomes the primary function. Additionally, the SDT will need training in team building, followed by courses on *facilitating meetings* and *making presentations.*

After 12 months. As the group matures, interviewing and hiring decisions transfer from the leader to the SDT. However, the transfer must not happen until the team members have been trained in *interviewing skills, performance appraisal,* and *giving constructive feedback.*

FIGURE 3

The transfer of competencies to SDTs

Activity	Before Design/ Implementation	Months					
		3	6	12	18	24	30
1. Steering committee	X	X	X	X	X	X	X
2. Leadership's/coach's responsibilities	X						
3. Team members' responsibilities	X						
4. Goals	X						
5. Assumptions (about SDTs and people)	X						
6a. Technical and quality training		X					
6b. People skills training:							
Problem solving		X					
Team building			X	X	X	X	X
Conducting meetings			X				
Presentation skills			X				
Conflict resolution				X			
Change skills				X			X
6c. Management skills training							
Interviewing				X			
Feedback and coaching				X			
Performance appraisal					X		
Group rewards		X			X		
Budgets							X
7a. Internal measurement		X	X	X	X		
7b. Customer service measurement				X		X	
8. Feedback—Team and other SDTs		X	X	X	X	X	X

After 18 months. In most traditional hierarchical organizations, managers tend to resist performance appraisal and are usually late doing the performance appraisals of their subordinates. One typically hears employees report that they do not receive sufficient feedback. Norman & Zawacki (1991) describe the process for a peer evaluation system within SDTs. Our early findings indicate that although the leader/coach may be threatened or at best hesitant to turn this process over to the team, once the new process is in place, the leader/coach becomes a strong advocate because it relieves him/her of a burden—getting those performance appraisals into personnel on time. However, transferring the performance appraisal process from the leader/coach to the team members should occur only after adequate training has taken place.

Tracking SDT Performance.   Internal and external measures of performance are critical to the success of SDTs. Those things that get measured get done! If the leaders of an organization support a pilot SDT, invariably someone will ask for measures of effectiveness or value added. There are many good measures of customer service that should be administered every six months. Furthermore, the measures should be simple and quick so the customer is not burdened with bureaucracy. Internal measures of team satisfaction usually are administered every week during the early stages of the SDT. As the SDT matures, the team should measure and feed back the results to the team every two weeks. After the sixth month, the SDT can move back to a three- or four-month cycle.

Teams and the Law

On December 16, 1992 the National Labor Relations Board issued a decision in Electromation, Inc., 309 NLRB No. 163 (1992), which raised the issue of whether employee committees are labor organizations as defined in the 1935 National Labor Relations Act. The decision of the NLRB was that Electromation violated the 1935 act against setting up a company union by establishing and dominating five employee representation committees. Unfortunately, the NLRB's decision is a setback for organizations looking to teams to increase motivation and productivity. However, the decision will continue to be challenged in the courts or addressed by Congress because the NLRB's decision ". . . was narrowly focused on the particular facts of the case, which was a disappointment to many who had hoped the Board would provide general guidelines for lawfully creating and maintaining employee involvement committees" (Frum, 1993).

The problem is that the National Labor Relations Act of 1935 is a statute ". . . largely written in the days of wrenches and blast furnaces, [and] can be read as outlawing these groups" (Frum, 1993). OD consultants should continue to help organizations design SDTs; however, they must be aware of this outdated law and use every opportunity to communicate with their representatives in Congress the need for a change in it.

Our advice to change agents is to watch the OD and human resource journals for further comment on this extremely serious development regarding teams. For example, the NLRB is likely to rule on a similar case at DuPont.

Guidelines for Implementing Successful SDTs

Successful SDTs have a lot in common with processes firmly rooted in the realm of OD. For example, both have elements of the definition of OD by French and Bell (1984), such as long-range effort, top management support, improved problem-solving, emphasis on teams, the assistance of a facilitator, and the use of theory to guide change agents.

To stack your SDT for success requires:

- Setting up a steering committee with top management support and planning a long-range effort with a pilot SDT.

- Making certain that the pilot SDT is congruent with organizational values and goals. Recognize that designing and implementing SDTs is a Theory Y philosophy and this may be a cultural shift for the organization.

- Selecting a natural work group whose members are committed to employee empowerment and are involved in a technology/product/service with task interdependencies.

- Establishing base-line customer measures of internal team satisfaction and customer service to inform all members of the organization on the progress of the pilot and future SDTs. Consider having SDT members brief top leaders on their progress. Feedback permits the program to adjust, grow, and remain viable over time (Goodman & Dean, 1981).

- Visiting other organizations with SDTs to determine "best practices."

- Recognizing that many managers are threatened by the mere mention of SDTs. No longer the expert, managers must now become coaches and problem solvers or facilitators. It is our experience that only about one-half of existing managers can make the transition even after training in the new competencies. Organization leaders need to clearly state expectations up front that good managers who cannot make the transition to coaches will be retrained as individual contributors as long as they add value to the bottom line.

- Revamping the reward system to allow for greater employee participation in reward decisions and designing gain-sharing plans or profit-sharing schemes that encourage cross-functional cooperation. At about the 18-month point, consider changing the reward from individual to part group/individual. Consider a bonus for the volunteers in the first pilot SDT.

- Being patient. There is an actual drop in productivity during the early stages of an SDT because the team members are learning new skills, conducting staff meetings, and so on. But as the team grows and as the individual members feel they are truly empowered, the gains are greater productivity, lower costs, higher quality products, greater customer service, and more adaptability. It may be 18-24 months before the organization begins to see the positive results of the change program.

References

Argyris, C. (1991). "Teaching Smart People How to Learn," *Harvard Business Review,* May–June: 99–109.

Cummings, G. T. (1978). "Self-Regulating Work Groups: A Socio-Technical Synthesis," *Academy of Management Review,* No. 3, July: 625–634.

French, W. L. and Bell, C. H. Jr. (1984). "A History of Organization Development," in *Organization Development: Behavioral Science Interventions for Organization Development,* 3rd ed. Englewood Cliffs, NJ: Prentice Hall.

Frum, D. (1993). "Electromation Appeals NLRB Ruling," *Human Resources Management,* No. 293, January 20:9.

Goodman, P. S. and Dean, J. W. Jr. (1981). "Why Productivity Efforts Fail." Paper presented at the American Psychological Association, August 1981.

Morland, D. V. (1984). "Lear's Fool: Coping with Change Beyond Future Shock," *New Management,* 2(2).

Norman, C. A. and Zawacki, R. A. (1991). "Team Appraisals-Team Approach," *Personnel Journal,* September: 101–104.

Overman, S. (1993). "NLRB Ruling on Teams Fails to End Dispute," *HR News,* January, p. A3. See also "Manager's Newsfront," *Personnel Journal,* February 1993:20.

Porras, J. I. and Silvers, R. C. (1991). "Organization Development and Transformation," *Annual Review of Psychology,* 42: 51–78.

Trist, E. L. and Bamforth, K. W. (1951). "Some Social and Psychological Consequences of the Longwall Method of Coal Getting," *Human Relations,* 4:3–38.

READING 22
SURVEY GUIDED APPRECIATIVE INQUIRY:
A CASE STUDY

Rita F. Williams

The purpose of this article is to explore Appreciative Inquiry (AI) as a powerful example of one of the most often used Organizational Development (OD) methods, survey guided development. To date, survey guided development has been wedded almost exclusively to a problem-solving view of OD. However, Wendell French and Cecil H. Bell, Jr., in *Organizational Development* (1995) describe second generation OD methods which includes nontraditional interventions.

> The context for the application of OD approaches has changed to a more turbulent environment. While there is still a major reliance on OD basics, considerable attention is being given to new concepts, interventions, and areas of application. Second generation OD includes interest in organizational transformation, organizational culture, the learning organization, teams and their various configurations, total quality management, visioning, and "getting the whole system in the room" (page 61).

This article proposes a radical rethinking of the survey guided method from the perspective of AI. Appreciative Inquiry is a form of organizational analysis first developed by Dr. David Cooperrider of Case Western Reserve University. The purpose of survey guided AI is to invite whole system exploration into an organization's highest human values. Instead of problem diagnosis, there is inquiry into hopes, dreams and visions. Instead of the survey itself being a "mirror of what is" it is an intervention into what "might be" (see Table 1).

Source: Reprinted by permission of the Organization Development Network, 71 Valley Street, Suite 301, South Orange, NJ 07079-2825. (973) 763-7337—voice, (973) 763-7488—fax, http://www.odnet.org.

I. Background

The Appreciative Inquiry process was successfully used as an intervention in an organization that was in a serious crisis. It served as a catalyst for change and as a vehicle for focusing an entire organization on a collective vision of the future. The site was an $11 billion regional commercial banking institution located in the Midwest which will be referred to as First Peoples Bank (FPB).

The organization evolved from a rich history that consistently reflected dedication to serving its customers and their communities. The company's roots go back to 1893, when the bank was founded. In the decades that followed, the company established its strength in the industry through financial stability, asset growth, and product development. It was one of the few institutions to guarantee funds to its customers following the stock market crash of 1929 and to remain open throughout the Great Depression. Key highlights include:

- 1950s . . . the branch banking network grew
- 1960s . . . the addition of a new building, and new automation for operations
- 1970s . . . among the first banks in the Midwest to introduce automated teller equipment and cards; the company name changed reflecting a constantly broadening position
- 1980s . . . gained a presence in 11 states with significant operations in Ohio, Indiana, Michigan and Texas

After deregulation went into effect in the late 1980s, the banking industry became unstable. Crisis and change had become a way of life as

235

TABLE 1

Notes on appreciative inquiry

Problem Solving	Appreciative Inquiry
"Felt Need" Analysis of Causes	Appreciating Valuing the Best of "What Is"
↓	↓
Analysis of Causes	Envisioning "What Might Be"
↓	↓
Analysis of Possible Solutions	Dialoguing "What Will Be"
↓	↓
Action Planning (Treatment)	Envisioning "What Will Be"

Source: From Cooperrider and Srivastva (1987) "Appreciative Inquiry into Organizational Life" in *Research in Organizational Change and Development.* Pasmore and Woodman (eds) JAI Press.

acquisitions, mergers, and problems with foreign loan portfolios created an unstable environment. In the late 1980s, FPB was beginning to feel the strain. An organization that had previously set an aggressive course for the future with confidence and without hesitation, suddenly had an air of uncertainty about its future business strategies. The leaders feared that the wrong decision would have long term negative consequences. In the early 1990s the organization began to experience even more difficulty. Some of the Strategic Business Units (SBUs) at FPB were very profitable while others lost money and became a drain on profits. There was a hostile takeover attempt, major loss in profits for the year, all occurring within two consecutive years of record earnings. Loan losses from a risky foreign loan portfolio were balanced by drastic cost cutting measures including a corporate-wide downsizing, which involved laying off over 850 of FPB's 8,000 employees.

As Vice President of the organization, I was the project manager on the cost-cutting program. The project deliverables involved the development and implementation of a detailed plan for downsizing, including a resource guide and training method for the management team. Aggressive employee relation plans and programs were needed to stabilize the organization. Outplacement assistance was put in place for laid off staff along with comprehensive communication strategies to keep everyone informed. Uncertainty surrounding the downsizing created concern about retaining the high quality staff needed to move the organization forward.

Because managers were affected by the downsizing, a vision and statement of values was created by the organizations' leaders and reviewed with each staff member. A more sincere effort was deemed necessary by managers because of the seriousness of the situation. There was a growing consensus about the need for a powerful intervention which would identify the organization's values and commit the staff to a vision of the future.

The process of Appreciative Inquiry (AI) could help in the identification of a common vision and values. However, there was concern that most of the previous AI applications had included healthy and/or growth oriented organizations. There were many unanswered questions about the potential impact of engaging an organization that was experiencing difficulty in the AI process.

The corporate human resources communication plan called for an aggressive employee relations campaign. The major focus of the campaign was on the construction of a common vision of the future around which employees and managers could align their efforts. It was critical that the vision statement be based on the values and ideals contributed by staff and that an opportunity for employees be available at all levels to develop an agreement and buy-in to this vision. Despite the risk, it appeared that Appreciative Inquiry was the best tool for accomplishing this goal. In the initial stages of this intervention, it was difficult to predict how far the process would go. The typical AI process included five phases (see Table 2). At FPB, a pilot was developed that involved one-on-one interviews with 250 randomly selected employees.

TABLE 2

Key phases of the process

An Overview

Phase 1.   Affirmation Topic Choice *(Definition)*

Phase 2.   Inquiry into the "Life-Giving Properties" *(Data Collection and Discovery)*

Phase 3.   Articulation of Possibility Propositions *(Visioning the Ideal—Dreaming)*

Phase 4.   Consensual Validation/Agreement *(Design through Dialogue)*

Phase 5.   Co-Construction of the Preferred Future *(Destination)*

Source: From Cooperrider, Workbook on Appreciative Inquiry.

TABLE 3

Sample interview protocol

1. **What attracted you to FPB?**
   - What were your initial excitements and impressions when you joined the company?

2. **Without being humble, what do you value most about yourself, the organization, your work?**
   - What is the single most important thing the company has contributed to your life?

3. **Looking at your entire experience, can you recall a time when you felt most alive, most involved or most excited about working at FPB?**
   - What made it an exciting experience?
   - Who were the most significant others?
   - Why were they significant?

II. Appreciative Inquiry Intervention

Phase I: Affirmative Topic Choice. An interview protocol was created by using primarily open-ended questions which were designed to help people identify the best of "what is" and to allow the topics to emerge. Unlike traditional surveys that focus on participants' opinions, AI focused on the participants' experiences and observations and promoted storytelling of positive and significant events during their careers. An example of an interview protocol is shown in Table 3.

Phase 2: Inquiry into "Life-Giving Properties." The data collection and discovery phase was handled by 20 of FPB's senior human resources staff who, altogether, interviewed 250 bank employees. Each interview was designed to inquire into the life giving properties of the organization as perceived by these employees. The interviewees represented a cross section of staff across the corporation at all levels in the organization. The HR interviewers received training on theory, practice, and application of AI through workshops and practice sessions. The 250 interviews took approximately three weeks to complete. Overall responses were extremely positive, and they generated powerful stories and examples of situations when the organization was functioning at its best:

- "We have a billing clerk that has taken ownership of her job. She says, 'We can make it better if we do things differently.' She is not afraid to initiate. And she gets recognized. She is a change agent. To be an owner is to be in the business of making continuous improvements."

- "Throughout my career here I have had the fortune to work with people who were for me. I've been given every opportunity imaginable. There were times when I was given opportunities that were such a stretch that I didn't even know if I was capable. I have worked for people who could somehow see things in me I couldn't even see in myself. Without that confidence, I don't think my career would have unfolded as it has."

Comments from employees interviewed about the AI process included:

- "We need to do this throughout the organization."

- "This is the perfect time for us to be working towards generating a common focus."

- "I feel better just being interviewed. The questions were hard, but they made me think, and showed me why I stay here and why I want to be a part of FPB's future."

Phase 3: Articulation of Possibility Propositions/Emerging Themes. The collected data was analyzed and summarized into a report that identified ten emerging values. The values were fashioned from the interviewee's actual experience and reflected the culture of FPB as they understood it from an appreciation of its proven strengths. They also represented a bold extension of those strengths—a focused vision to which people said they aspire as an organization.

The major themes were stated as provocative propositions which bridged the best of "what is" with the understanding of "what might be." They were provocative because they stretched the realm of the status quo, and helped suggest a course of action for the future. Because of this, the values reported were stated in the present tense, not because they had been totally attained, but because people were saying this was their present "ideal" based on experiences when the organization was at its best. In the report, each proposition was supported by actual employee quotes that detailed specific events and/or experiences (Table 4 briefly describes the ten themes).

A summary of the report was reviewed with FPB's CEO and President. They were surprised by the depth and breadth of the employees' responses. One commented that it was exciting to know that among tellers, clerks and managers there were common values and collective commitment to the future.

The information was so compelling that they felt the entire executive management team should review it. A two day off-site planning conference was held to present the findings and to develop a plan to move the process forward.

Phase 4: Consensual Validation Agreement. The senior management team decided that all employees in the organization should participate in the process and have an opportunity to give their input. The call for action included a plan to administer a written survey to all 8,000 employees over a 30 day period. Unlike traditional "off the shelf documents" this survey was internally developed, reflecting the emerging themes identified in the

pilot and exploring values, ideals and practices of the organization. The questionnaires allowed all employees to: (1) have a voice in identifying what is important to the company and to them as individuals; (2) evaluate how well they practice those ideals today; and (3) indicate how much they have experienced their values in their career.

Employees were asked to think about times when they were really excited about FPB, where they thought it was going, what it was doing and what they were doing at the time that made it exciting (see Table 5). This vitality was the life and strength of the organization; it was the proven strengths that they would build upon. That inspection was important to all.

The data was collected so that a statistical analysis could be performed to review it for the organization as a whole and by SBU. The following coding system aided in the development of reports, feedback and action planning:

- Exempt or Non-exempt Status
- Years of Service
- Location (City and State)
- Strategic Business Unit (SBU)

The fixed response questionnaire made it easy to conduct a quantitative analysis in a short period of time. In addition to the fixed responses, the survey included a section with blank space that asked for additional comments and posed the following open-ended question: *If you could develop or transform FPB in any way what would you do to heighten its vitality and overall health?*

The data collection phase of the process was conducted in orientation meetings with employees in each SBU, kicked off by the senior executive. A video tape, featuring a message from the Chairman and President, described the goals of the project, and the steps of the "Call for Action" initiative. Participation was voluntary and each employee was encouraged to give his/her input.

Approximately 6,500 of the 8,000 employees participated in the survey. This was an exceptional response. Even more surprising was the response

TABLE 4

Core values emerging themes

We Value People
The company flourishes because each individual is valued as a precious resource.

Service and Caring
"To serve others"—our unifying purpose. We provide excellent and innovative products that add value and exceed the expectations of those we serve.

Honesty
Integrity is expected. It is a way of life. And it begins and ends with example, not proclamations.

Being a Significant Corporation—Rock Solid
FPB's rock solid stability is a core value that gives life to the organization. People stay because of the stability. Customers stay because FPB has been steady. Steady, Sturdy and Stable.

Being in Full Voice
When FPB is in full voice, three things occur: (1) new ideas are given full consideration; (2) information is openly shared and (3) participation in decision making is pushed to the lowest possible level.

Responsive Performance
FPB is a corporation made up of people who take pride in their work, and who consider responsive performance as modus operandi.

Unifying Structures
The formal structure is clearly understood but not constraining. FPB supports the use of networks, project teams, and task forces to manage issues that cross formal boundaries.

Ownership
Employees act as Owners. Owners do things that hired hands will not see.

Community
FPB's image in the community is precious. The involvement and commitment has been consistent. It is one of the most important legacies we have inherited.

Servant Leadership
Leadership at FPB is a process of serving others. It involves seeing potential in people in ways that they cannot even see themselves. It involves removing obstacles, coordinating, educating, listening, and coaching.

---

to the open-ended questions that asked for their ideas and comments. Of the 6,500 surveys, 4,000 contained extensive responses. Many wrote suggestions and comments, some as long as two and three pages. It seemed that a safety valve had been opened to release constructive energy and thoughtful responses creating a collective hope and vision for the future. A team of HR professionals analyzed the data and prepared detailed reports for the entire organization and SBU.

The data was fed to the management team and employees through meetings across the organization. Of the ten themes included in the survey, the following topics emerged as values and strengths:

• Rock Solid Business Practice
• Exceptional Customer Service
• Honesty

In the thematic analysis of the open-ended comments of the survey the value of teamwork emerged as a strength.

Phase 5: Construction of the Preferred Future. Team leaders were trained to facilitate brainstorming sessions with focus groups of employees throughout the organization. The goal of these sessions was to identify ways to build on the identified strengths and to take action in their work group to improve productivity and performance. These brainstorming sessions provided an opportunity for ongoing dialogue, action and commitment to change. A workbook was developed so that the data was uniformly collected and reported to Corporate Human Resources. Opportunities identified included both organizational and SBU specific initiatives (see Table 6 for using the theme exceptional customer service).

III. Impact of AI Process on FPB

The AI process powerfully impacted the nature of the conversations in the organization, causing a fundamental shift in the daily dialogue. Employees

TABLE 5

Examples of consensus validation survey

Employee Survey—Confidential

BUILDING ON OUR PROVEN STRENGTHS

Instructions: What follows is a series of statements about the way our organization should work, works, or has worked. For each statement, consider these three ratings:

- **Important to me as an IDEAL.** How important on a scale of 1–7, do you think the statement should be an ideal for FPB to pursue?
- **Practiced NOW in the Present.** Using the scale of 1–7, how well do you think FPB lives the statement today?
- **To what extent have you EXPERIENCED THIS IN YOUR CAREER AT FPB?** Again using the scale.

1. FPB has been recognized as progressive—even ahead of its times—in the treatment of people.

	very little					very great	
• Important to me as an ideal	1	2	3	4	5	6	7
• Practiced now	1	2	3	4	5	6	7
• Experienced in my career	1	2	3	4	5	6	7

2. We have high expectations of ourselves. We deliver the best.

	very little					very great	
• Important to me as an ideal	1	2	3	4	5	6	7
• Practiced now	1	2	3	4	5	6	7
• Experienced in my career	1	2	3	4	5	6	7

3. Employees at all levels are aware of our customers' needs and are committed to responding with first-class service. We put ourselves in our customers' shoes and remember that—from the phone calls we answer to the paperwork we process—the way we do our jobs and work together significantly affects our customers' lives.

	very little					very great	
• Important to me as an ideal	1	2	3	4	5	6	7
• Practiced now	1	2	3	4	5	6	7
• Experienced in my career	1	2	3	4	5	6	7

4. FPB has a reputation as being a rock solid, secure and prestigious financial institution. FPB maintains its reputation through good business decisions and sound business practices.

	very little					very great	
• Important to me as an ideal	1	2	3	4	5	6	7
• Practiced now	1	2	3	4	5	6	7
• Experienced in my career	1	2	3	4	5	6	7

5. We recognize the value of each employee's contribution and eliminate the obstacles to get the job done.

	very little					very great	
• Important to me as an ideal	1	2	3	4	5	6	7
• Practiced now	1	2	3	4	5	6	7
• Experienced in my career	1	2	3	4	5	6	7

began to view problems as opportunities and the optimism inherent in the conversations led to feelings of empowerment; employees were ready to take action in the face of possibility rather than staying frozen in the face of problems and circumstances.

The exceptional response of the staff reinforced the fact that an intervention like AI can breathe life, strength and a proactive response to a crisis. A consensus and shared vision allowed the organization's leaders to move forward aggressively to stabilize the situation. Within one year of the AI interviews, the organization merged with another bank forming a large national holding company. It appeared that understanding its strengths made it easier for the organizations to honor those things that should be preserved. Part of the merger negotiation included selling a group of branch offices to another bank. The management of the new bank commented on the positive and productive outlook of the FPB staff. They felt that their attitudes made the transition easy and that they were more receptive than their own staff members. The FPB case is a true example of the positive impact AI can have in the most negative situations.

TABLE 6

Putting our valued commitments to work

Discussion Workbook for Focus Groups

Customer Service

FPB provides first-class customer service.
- We go the extra mile to provide excellent service
- We provide caring, responsive service
- We exceed customer expectations
- We have high expectations of ourselves
- We work together
- We deliver the best

Team Discussion

A. ***What we do best and should keep doing.*** What do we have in place that shows great customer service? ("Customers" can be fellow employees, too.) Why does it work well?

B. ***What we should begin or start doing.*** What new things should we introduce to improve customer service?

C. ***What we should change or stop doing.*** What are we currently doing that we should question, change, or stop doing?

Conclusion

The AI process in FPB served both as a catalyst and invitation. This was an invitation to participate in an organization-wide process where everyone at each location had the opportunity to think strategically and imaginatively about the future of the organization. As a catalyst, the report provided inspiring snapshots of the future. The information revealed the many strengths of the organization when it was working at its best. There, it must be acknowledged, is an undeniably positive quality about AI. Some of this stems from the nature of the questions that are asked and the responses that are collected. Equally important, much of this quality comes from tapping into the real sense of optimism people feel about the company and its prospects for the future.

In retrospect, several distinguishing features make this case unique. First, the AI intervention was spontaneously initiated by the HR department without the customary rigmarole of top management clearances. The self-sustaining enthusiasm of the employees generated a momentum of its own resulting in over 8,000 employees being surveyed in thirty days.

Second, the AI process collapsed the customary distinctions between leader and follower or between manager and employee by providing everyone in the organization with a meaningful sense of engagement in the organizational renewal process during a prior acute crisis.

Third, the case is an eloquent testimony to the power of AI as a transformative force; the survey questions generated powerful stories that unleashed the collective imagination of the workforce generating boundless optimism that stabilized the situation. AI, in the ultimate analysis, provided a powerful paradigm shift that led employees to view their current situation through a completely interpretive lens wherein problems were viewed as possibilities and the best of "what is" stimulated imagination of "what can be." It provided a new mode of consciousness akin to what Einstein alluded to when he said, "No problem can be solved from the same level of consciousness that created it."

READING 23
INVENTING THE FUTURE: SEARCH STRATEGIES FOR WHOLE SYSTEMS IMPROVEMENT

Marvin R. Weisbord

On the way to the moon the Apollo astronauts made tiny "mid-course corrections" that enabled them to land at an exact predetermined spot. The corrections were small, but because the moon was far away they made a big difference. It is like that with us. Some of the changes we make in society, in our lives, or in our organizations seem insignificant, but over the years they can have major impact.

Edward B. Lindaman and Ronald Lippitt,
Choosing the Future You Prefer, 1979, p. 4

Planner Russell L. Ackoff (1977), of the University of Pennsylvania, once observed that corporate planning was like rain dancing: whether or not it brought rain, it made the dancers feel better. Ackoff's point was that extending past trends to predict the future is an exercise in futility. Economists can't do it, politicians can't do it, scientists can't do it, nor, alas, can you and I.

The Future Search Conference

What are corporate alternatives to rain dancing on the crest of the third wave? In this chapter I want to describe an extremely promising method for getting whole systems in one room and focusing on the future—the search conference. Like so many workplace innovations, its origins are traceable to creative extensions of Kurt Lewin's insight that you steer a ship by feedback from outside, not by how the rudder, engines, or crew are behaving. Innovators in both Europe and the United States began extending Lewin's work to larger systems many years ago, responding to the psychological stresses of accelerating change.

In the late 1950s in Great Britain, for example, a forced merger led to a serious market crisis in the

Bristol/Siddeley aircraft engine company. Eric Trist and Fred Emery were asked to help. The pair had recently begun work on the managerial dilemmas of increasingly turbulent environments (see Chapter Eight). To the firm's top managers, suffering, in Trist's words, from "stiff upper-lip paralysis," they proposed a week-long collaborative inquiry. The group of managers undertook an intense marathon dialogue on changes in the world, their industry, and their own company—to search for new possibilities. The managers later made crucial strategic choices, including a new product line integrating the capabilities of the merged companies. In that historic conference Emery and Trist (1960) invented a new group orientation to help people integrate economics and technology—the whole open system—in a fast-changing environment, and turned around a serious crisis.

From this experience evolved the "environmental scan"—an integral step in sociotechnical work design in which people describe the network of outside pressures on their organization. More, Emery, collaborating with his wife Merrelyn, began an extraordinary conceptual and practical expansion of the methodology, teaching it to aspiring conference managers on several continents (Emery, 1982). The procedure has been used repeatedly to create common visions among disparate stakeholders within corporations, cities, towns, industries, unions, and trade associations. More than 300 search conferences have been held in Australia, and dozens more in Africa, Britain, Canada, India, and Scandinavia.

The Emerys' conference typically lasts two or three days. They begin by mapping the networks of people and external pressures linked to the institution under study, what they call the "extended social field." They end with action planning for the future. In between they draw on a flexible menu—history, desirable and undesirable features, constraints on change, values to be carried forward, desirable futures—based on data produced and analyzed solely by the participants. Many adaptations have been made, from downsizing business firms (Hirschhorn and Associates, 1983) to refocusing social service agencies (Clarkson, 1981).

Ludwig von Bertalanffy, author of general systems theory, once observed that the same ideas spring up in parallel in diverse fields (see Chapter Seven). From the late 1940s on Ronald Lippitt, Lewin's American colleague and a founder of NTL Institute, had sought, like Emery and Trist, to extend group dynamics learning to large organizations, networks, and communities. Lippitt too had moved from small-group problem solving to future-oriented conferences for huge networks. What started Lippitt down this road were tape recordings he secured (some with Douglas McGregor's help) of thirty planning groups in action.

Lippitt was appalled as he heard people build long problem lists, set priorities, generate solutions—a direct extension of his own pioneer work in group dynamics. He was struck most by how voices grew more depressed as people attributed problems to causes beyond their control. They used words like "hopeless" and "frustrating." Action steps tended to be short-term, designed to deal with symptoms and reduce anxiety. The motivation, noted Lippitt (1983), was to escape the pain induced in part by the method itself: the piecemeal listing of problems, the solution of any one of which might create still more problems.

In the 1950s Ronald Fox, Lippitt, and Eva Schindler-Rainman (1973) began speaking of "images of potential"—envisioning what could be instead of lamenting what was. In the 1970s Lippitt teamed with the late futurist Edward Lindaman, who had directed planning for the Apollo moon shot. Lindaman believed that the future was created by our present ways of confronting "events, trends and developments" in the environment. The "preferred future"—an image of aspiration—could be a powerful guidance mechanism for making far-reaching course corrections. Lindaman and Lippitt (1979) found that when people plan present actions by working backward from what is really desired, they develop energy, enthusiasm, optimism, and high commitment.

So "futuring" focused awareness away from interpersonal relationships and toward the experiences and values affecting everybody. Lippitt adapted that insight to national voluntary organizations like the YMCA, and to conferences for more than eighty cities, towns, and states (Schindler-Rainman and Lippitt, 1980). Diverse interest groups could jointly envision desirable futures, for example, the PTA, manufacturers' association, doctors, community activists, juvenile authorities, chamber of commerce, and school board all at once. Searching together gave organizations more dependable anchor points for their own planning. It tied everybody to reality through taking joint snapshots, and became the basis for a more truthful movie based on mutual interest.

People learned to think of the future as a condition created intentionally out of values, visions, and what's technically and socially feasible. Such purposeful action greatly increased the probability of making the desired future come alive. Repeating the process over and over again with relevant others, what Ackoff (1974) calls "interactive planning" could become a way of life for corporate planners if they could bring the whole system into the room.

Lippitt and Lindaman typically used one-day conferences to trigger systemwide planning that might then continue indefinitely. They too devised a menu of activities geared to the past, present, and future: a history, a list of events, trends and developments shaping the future, "prouds and sorries" of present operations, and detailed ideal future scenarios. Eric Trist (1987 memo to author) notes the recent emergence of several new search models, for example, Michel Chevalier's search position conferences in Canada for executives who can't be away more than a day a month, and Russell Ackoff's idealized design sessions.

A Conference Model

The model I will describe is another example of this evolution. For several years my colleagues and I have experimented with a future search conference that integrates ideas from both developmental streams. From Lippitt and Lindaman we learned the importance of going "back to the future." From the Emerys we learned concepts and processes for managing conferences consistent with democratic values. We have used variations in steel, textile, and financial services industries, medical education, service organizations, schools, colleges, and an agricultural co-op in Sweden. We have managed search conferences lasting as little as half a day (unsatisfying) and up to three days (very exciting). We have witnessed little or no followup, and extensive activities carried forward for a year or more. We have worked with as few as a dozen people (too few) and as many as a hundred (hard and doable). We have found that within forty-eight hours people often generate important new learnings that influence their organization's future course for years.

Search conferences excite, engage, produce new insights, and build a sense of common values and purpose. They have been especially attractive to organizations faced with significant change: markets, mergers, reorganizations, new technologies, new leadership, the wish for a coherent culture and corporate philosophy. We have used the conference to set the stage for work design. We also have used it at turning points when people knew they had to do something new and were not sure what.

We base the future search on three assumptions:

1. Change is so rapid that we need *more*, not less, face-to-face discussion to make intelligent strategic decisions. Teleconfer-

encing won't do. As John Naisbitt wrote in *Megatrends,* "Talking with people via television cannot begin to substitute for the high touch of a meeting, no matter how rational it is in saving fuel and overhead" (1982, p. 46).

2. Successful strategies—for quality goods and services, lower costs, more satisfying ways of working—come from *envisioning preferred futures.* Problem solving old dilemmas doesn't work under fast-changing conditions. Each narrow solution begets two new problems.

3. People will commit to plans they have helped to develop. Lewin and anthropologist Margaret Mead showed that during World War II when they found that housewives were more likely to change their food habits through discussion than exhortation by nutritionists. The principle has never been improved upon.

A forty-eight-hour investment in a search conference may reduce misunderstanding and raise commitment way beyond previous levels. It may also uncover new possibilities that can't be born in any other forum. The typical conference brings together thirty to sixty people for two to three days. Together they do a series of structured tasks, looking at the organization's past, present, and preferred future. Tasks are cumulative. Each session builds on previous ones. The last event involves everybody in action planning for the future.

Getting Organized.   Below I describe one typical version. My goal is not to "cookbook" the conference but to indicate its ingredients as evolved within the firm I know best and I encourage you to make up your own menu. The conference fully embodies third-wave managing and consulting—getting the whole system in the room, focusing on the future, having people do the work themselves.

How?   You can't wing it. You have to spend a day or more in planning, and another day preparing materials. The search is best planned by the conference managers (consultants) and a voluntary

What's Good for the Goose . . .

In 1983 the late Ronald Lippitt helped Block-Petrella-Weisbord organize a future search with client managers from AT&T, Bethlehem Steel, McNeil Consumer Products, Smith Kline & French, Soabar Corporation, Warner Cosmetics, and consulting colleagues from the United States and Sweden. Together we looked at the future of the work world, and the meaning for clients and consultants alike.

Our decision to open a private meeting to clients and friends was triggered by a startling statement in *Megatrends* (Naisbitt, 1982). Producers fear losing control if they invite consumers into strategy and policy discussions. "Too many corporations that should know better are terrified

of this whole idea," Naisbitt wrote. "I do not think it an oversimplification to state that producers can only become more successful by learning how better to satisfy consumers" (1982, p. 178).

In our conference we compared notes on major trends reshaping business firms. All noted the need for constant retraining, the emergence of a world marketplace, a smaller gap between blue-collar and white-collar work, fewer jobs at the middle and top. The ways in which our company's future scenario must take account of these trends became plainer to us. My confidence in participative work design and reorganizations was greatly strengthened by manager comments in this conference.

---

committee of four to six potential participants. They decide participant-selection method, place, schedule, meals and breaks, group tasks, and goal focus, for example "Designing XYZ Corporation for 1995." Each task is structured to support the overall focus. Worksheets are provided so that small groups can organize their tasks without special facilitators.

Who?   We seek to involve *only* people who have a stake in the sponsoring organization's future. They must be active participants. Any group important to implementation should be there. Top management always participates, with people from as many functions and levels as feasible. The guideline is diversity, the whole system to the extent possible. Business firms, for example, should consider customers, suppliers, union leaders, all dimensions of sex, age, racial, and ethnic backgrounds of employees, and all functions and levels of management.

We prefer groups of fifty or sixty people, which permit great diversity of views, knowledge, and experience, a higher potential for creative solutions, more likelihood of follow-through, more

linkages with outside. For logistical reasons an organization may run a series of conferences. A few volunteers from each meet afterward to sort through the data and ideas and prepare a combined scenario or discussion paper.

Schedule.   I like Merrelyn Emery's idea (1982) that the conference start with dinner on a Wednesday evening, followed by the first work session. This makes use of the Zeigarnik effect (see Chapter Three)—the tendency to recall unfinished tasks—and ensures a fast startup next morning. It's desirable to end a future search on a Friday afternoon. That gives people a weekend to collect their thoughts, review key events, and digest important ideas rather than plunge into paperwork at the office.

People are invited to bring newspaper and magazine clippings describing events and trends they believe are shaping their organization's future. These clippings will be displayed on a bulletin board and used in the discussion. Sometimes a planning group will request artifacts and mementos from the past—old ads, news clips, uniforms, photographs, awards, brochures, posters, trophies—that symbolize and embody history. People display and discuss these materials, making them a foundation for imagining desirable futures.

Startup.   People usually sit at tables of six to eight, each with its own easel, colored markers, and tape. Who sits where depends on the conference's purpose. During the two days, we will have no more than three groupings—one by function or common interest, another with maximum diversity of levels, functions, ages, and so on, perhaps a third of self-selected volunteers—in addition to the total group.

A few ground rules are discussed at the start. One, this is *not* a problem-solving conference. It's an exercise in learning, awareness, understanding, and mutual support. Two, every idea and comment are valid. People need not agree. Every contribution is written on flip charts in words as close to the speaker's as possible. Three, it's a task-focused meeting. Every task has output, and all output is recorded and discussed. Four, we stick to time. Groups are responsible for completing tasks on schedule. Five, the consultants manage time and structure tasks. Participants generate and analyze information, derive meanings, propose action steps, take responsibility for output. Consultants may add their two cents, but only as another contribution to the discussion. There are no lectures.

Steps in the Process.   There are four or five major segments, lasting up to half a day each. Each one requires that people (a) build a data base, (b) look at it together, (c) interpret what they find, and (d) draw conclusions for action. The last task includes action proposals and a structure—task forces, assignments—for carrying them out. A successful search conference always uncovers important shared values and leads to congruent action plans. All this is discussed at the start.

Past.   The first activity focuses on history. People examine their collective past from three perspectives: self, company (or industry, or town), and society.

Task: Alone, make notes on significant events, milestones, highlights, or activities you recall during each decade. When ready, take a magic marker and transfer your memories to the appropriate sheets on the wall.

This task gets everybody participating and quickly experiencing success. There is no way to do it wrong. It takes about thirty minutes for everybody to write on flip charts scattered around the room. With two sheets for each topic in each of three decades, eighteen people can write at once. See "Looking at the Past" for the clip chart array. Simple contributions make a potent whole. As the data go up, reluctance turns to interest, then surprise, as people rediscover and interpret how much change they have lived through together and how much this influences the present. The activity is a powerful community builder. People see that for a long time they have been in the same boat. Younger members learn much they never knew about the past, older members about youthful values and commitments.

Each table analyzes one theme across three decades—one table looks at all the items under "myself," another "company," a third "society"—for patterns and meanings. As tables report, a consultant notes emerging trends. The whole group then interprets good and bad trends and the direction of movement of each, a way of discovering important values. Those who brought mementos say a few words about them, adding to the sense of continuity, anchor points in the sea of change.

Present, from Outside and Inside.   The present is examined from two perspectives. One is a list of external events, trends, and developments shaping the future right now. This analysis is helped along by the news clippings and articles. We ask all participants to tell their table group why their clipping is important. A recorder notes each person's remarks. Then people select priorities from the group list. A poll of priorities reveals several common themes shared by all tables. Pooling these creates a map much like what Emery calls "the extended social field," the relevant outside network

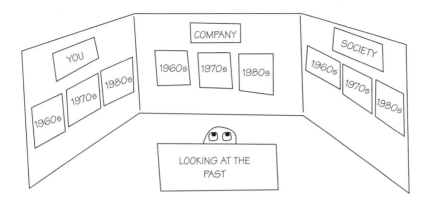

of forces and institutions demanding attention. Group analysis reveals what these trends and forces mean to us, and what we believe will happen in the future that cannot be ignored now. See "Mapping the Environment" for an example.

We also look at the present from a second, internal perspective, using a simple Lippitt exercise that surfaces values. People are asked to generate lists of "prouds" and "sorries," the things going on right now within their organization about which they feel good and bad. This leads to a shared appreciation of present strengths, needs, and hopes. It also results in a mutual owning up to mistakes and shortcomings and builds commitment to do something about them.

People cast votes for their "proudest prouds" and "sorriest sorries." These are toted up, displayed, and discussed. This step often leads to a productive dialogue across levels, and the sharing of a good deal of new information in the total group. Conference managers actively probe, summarize, and note key statements on flip charts during the dialogue.

Future.   Now it is time to generate future images. People either form new voluntary groups based on their own needs or work in groups set by the steering committee. They are given one to two hours to create a rough-draft "preferred future" scenario. They are asked to imagine the most desirable, attainable future five years out. (Futurists consider five years short term, twenty or thirty years as long. The important thing is to disconnect people from the present so that dreams and ideals take over.)

The more imaginative the method, the better the scenarios. People have ridden magic carpets or rocket ships into the future, floated on clouds, written newspaper stories or TV documentaries. Plenty of media—crayons, colored paper, scissors, tape—stimulate new ideas. Background music helps. One conference ran a county fair, with each group building a booth to display the future. Others have put on segments of "60 Minutes" or written a cover story for *Time*.

As a final step people are asked to reflect on what they have learned and to make three lists: suggested actions for themselves, their function, and the whole organization. Suggestions are reviewed and discussed over a two-hour lunch break on the last day. People keep "action steps for myself" for personal use. Departments sit together, review members' functional proposals, and decide on next steps. Meanwhile the steering committee or top manager group engages in an intense work session, recording "action proposals for the organization"—policy or systems matters that cut across departmental lines and cannot be handled within one group. They are compiled, discussed, and prioritized, and an action plan is prepared. In the final large group meeting, the functions and the steering group present and discuss their action plans.

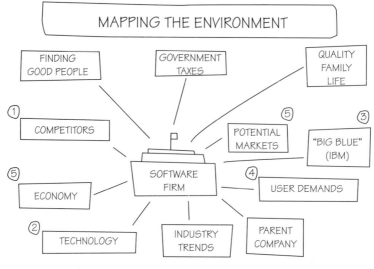

MAPPING THE ENVIRONMENT

NUMBERS=PRIORITY

Before closing, volunteers are recruited to document the meeting, communicate to others, and carry forward next steps. In one search a dozen task forces were organized to search out new markets and explore new technologies. In another, a group undertook to merge future scenarios into a philosophy and an action plan for an entire company.

Search Conferences Build Community

One way to appreciate the future search is to compare it with traditional business conferences. Some organizations, for example, organize three to five days of guest speakers as a way of stimulating top executives. Speakers are picked for charisma, ability to entertain, or reputation as authors of best-selling books. Guest-speaker audiences like to be amused and stimulated. They do not expect to do any work, and might resent it if asked without warning to become active. They enjoy watching the dance and do not expect rain.

Or consider the statistical business review, a two-hour slide show of budgets, costs, product lines, and variances. Data, of course, help meet people's needs for feedback and information. In a "data dump," though, there are too many numbers and too little time to digest them. People become overloaded, their circuits clogged. Rarely is time given to discussing ways to make the numbers come up differently.

Neither expert input nor data dump takes advantage of the significant resources present in the room. Neither accesses the thoughts, ideas, perceptions, attitudes, and reactions of the audience. If future action is desirable, there are better ways to use the time and energy of those fifty people.

Search conference participants receive advance briefing on their involvement. They know that they are actors and audience both. True, the work is paradoxical and seems confusing at first. But as people sort out the past and present, they become more focused and purposeful. By devising whole future scenarios, they create a new perspective on optimistic, value-based action. Traditional meeting formats subtly reinforce dependency and passivity. The search conference promotes dignity, meaning, and community.

A few years ago I organized a search as part of an NTL laboratory in Bethel, Maine. Townspeople, lab participants, and NTL staff joined in looking at their mutual interests—from the standpoint of stores, restaurants, churches, schools, medical facilities, hotels, banks. NTL's summer labs provide local income and jobs, and the local community offers important support services. Among the problems noted was a culture gap between lab participants and service people in stores and restaurants, leading to misunderstanding and mutual irritation.

Several good ideas were proposed, not just for reducing the tension but for creative steps that would benefit everybody. One central insight was that townspeople had lived for years with persistent rumors that NTL planned to pull out. NTL leaders realized that this chronic headache could be cured only by a committed policy. NTL took a public stand on remaining in Bethel, and has since invested in improving its conference facilities—a key ingredient in community building. Townspeople took over the writing of the summer participant guide to services. A joint committee of townspeople and NTL staff has continued to build a productive community of interest. Only in a face-to-face discussion of the future by many stakeholders could this new spirit be infused into an old relationship.

The future search fits any organization and strategic situation: manufacturing, sales, voluntary, retail, government, health care, education, staff or line. It doesn't matter whether people see each other once a day, once a year, or have never met. Given a few simple tools and instructions, they are able to search out desirable futures together. The governing board of a prestigious medical specialty, for example, meets only once a year. Using a day and a half of their annual meeting for a future search, they established policies that unified curriculum development efforts in many medical schools. Two years later members continued to build on the work done in that conference.

The search has proved to be a powerful tool of productive workplaces. Far from requiring conformity in thought and action, it provides a forum and norms that respect individual differences. Personal attitudes, thoughts, feelings, and styles are honored. People sometimes fear past disagreements

will intrude and prove disruptive. Under the guidance of experienced conference managers working with a committed steering group, this does not happen. A major strength of the search conference is its unifying effect on people even when they fear divisiveness. It is a sort of town meeting structured toward output and productivity.

The conference is not personally threatening. It does not focus on how people feel about each other but rather how they feel about the future. It tends to bring people closer together in their goals and attitudes, rather then heighten their differences. Instead of gazing inward, or being problem centered, the search links strong personal feelings to external realities—the events, trends, and developments shaping the world. Problem solving, as Lippitt's research showed, depresses. A future search energizes. It creates hope and optimism. Many people have reported this pleasant surprise.

Projecting a "big picture" into the future also gets people thinking about product end use. My partner Tony Petrella witnessed a dramatic consequence when one company, after futuring, decided to reduce its manufacture of silicone breast implants, a product employees were ashamed of, in favor of brain shunts—a life saving device based on the same technology. Another time I saw biodegradability of disposable products escalate from a minor technical matter to a central strategic issue in a manufacturing firm as several groups (unexpectedly) flagged the issue. It wasn't "just an R&D problem." It became the core of one scenario in a proposed reorganization.

Each of us is a repository of experience, skill, knowledge, gossip, new developments, old techniques, war stories, legends, myths, colorful characters. More, we all have visions and aspirations, sometimes only half-formed, for what we want most. These fertilize productive workplaces. In traditional conferences this sense of community often comes alive only in the bar after hours. That's why people say social time is the best part of business meetings. Only over drinks or dinner do we become fully ourselves with one another. That is because typical conferences do not call on us to work and learn together, only to listen and react. No wonder the "real work" happens afterward.

In my enthusiasm for this mode I don't want to imply that one conference transforms forever, or that no further hard work is needed. I do believe that anyone who has attended one of these events remembers it for a lifetime. The search conference links values and action in real time. It promotes productive workplaces by using more of each person's reality. It joins people who need one another, yet rarely interact, in a new kind of relationship. It stimulates creativity and innovative thinking. It offers a unique third-wave springboard for planning and goal setting. In the last half of the twentieth century few media exist as powerful as this one for raising awareness of who we are, what we are up against, what we want, and how we might work together to get it.

READING 24
MEETING THE GLOBAL COMPETITIVE CHALLENGE:
BUILDING SYSTEMS THAT LEARN ON A LARGE SCALE

Gary E. Jusela

Introduction

Global competition, corporate downsizing, industrial renaissance, economic dislocation, these are the new watchwords of American business. Through the Cold War era the American public viewed the principal external threat to the United States as the military and political force of the Soviet Union and its allies. With the dissolution of the former Soviet Union and the Eastern Bloc this threat has nearly evaporated, while an economic threat from Japan has emerged as the more serious perceived challenge to the future of the United States.[1] Postman (1985, as cited in Mitroff, 1987) argues that the United States is organized to fight the wrong enemy, specifically the Soviet Union, when the more serious enemy, the root of our non-competitiveness, is contained within our own borders.[2]

While we have shored up our military strength, our economic vitality has atrophied at an alarming rate. The United States world market share has dropped more than 50 percent in 20 years in 20 major industries.[3] Where in 1972 9 of the 10 largest banks in the world, as ranked by total assets, were American, today the top 8 and 15 of the top 25 belong to Japan.[4] Our standard of living has declined significantly in the last two decades; our rate of productivity growth from 1950 to 1985 (2.5 percent) lags far behind that of Japan (8.4 percent), Germany (5.5 percent), Italy (5.5 percent), and France (5.3 percent); and economists estimate that as many as 30 million people within the United States have been dislocated in their working careers by the "restructuring" in manufacturing during the

Source: Written especially for this volume.

last decade.[5] So what has happened, and what is industrial America to do about it?

This paper will examine some of the organizing assumptions and models that have contributed to the competitive decline within U.S. industry and explore one approach to addressing this decline that has been applied within the Ford Motor Company beginning in 1981 and within the Boeing Company beginning in 1988. The approach is called "large-scale systems change" and represents an evolutionary application of many elements of planned change and team development. The large-scale systems change methodology will be described as it has been applied in cultural change and in strategic planning efforts. The paper will further explore some of the outcomes of the large-scale process, internal political prerequisites for applying the methodology, and how the approach may be expected to evolve further.

Organizing Paradigms

While recognizing that industrial competitiveness is rooted in an array of factors broader than within-firm behavior (see, for example, Porter, 1990), the present discussion will be kept principally at the intrafirm level, with some attention given to changes in market expectations and external competitive conditions. The premise of this exploration, and of the intervention work on which it is based, is that many aspects of competitiveness can be addressed and resolved by rethinking and reorienting internal management practices. The chairman of Toyota Motors has been quoted as saying that "competitiveness is a microeconomic issue."[6] While this may be viewed by many as an oversimplification, there are beginning to be enough examples of individual firms turning around declining fortunes to assert that microeconomic factors are, at a minimum, an important dimension of competitive success.[7]

Peters (1988) argues that what is required are new models of industrial organization. Ackoff (1981) has laid out two contrasting organizing paradigms, the machine bureaucracy and the organization as system, that reflect respectively the dominant model for industrial organization for the past hundred years and the evolving model being adopted by the world's most successful firms. The large-scale systems change methodology is aimed at enabling large complex enterprises built around the machine model to adapt to changing external circumstances and move toward the systems model of organization. Before exploring the methodology, we will look first at these contrasting views of the organization.

The Machine Bureaucracy. The machine bureaucracy model of organization evolved out of early industrial engineering and scientific management concepts and Weberian concepts of hierarchical control (see Figure 1).[8] As described by Ackoff (1981), the machine model is based on analysis and reductionism. The underlying assumption is that, for the organization as a whole to work most effectively, each of its parts must be designed and honed to achieve a local optimum of performance. Within the machine bureaucracy, problems are solved by breaking them into their component parts, fixing the parts, and then reaggregating the whole. Authority is clearly defined by organizational level and work is neatly subdivided between functions. As the machine bureaucracy evolves (or devolves), the boundaries between levels and functions may become very severely drawn, limiting local coordination and the flow of people, of ideas, and of resources between units and placing a large responsibility for regulation and control on senior levels of management. In this case the organization may be characterized as "over-bounded" or "arthritic" (see Alderfer, 1976; Dannemiller, 1985). Under conditions in which the owner of the firm has enormous power over his or her employees, the skill requirements of jobs and educational level of employees is

low, and the external environment of the organization is relatively stable, this model of industrial organization may be extraordinarily effective. In fact, the rise of the U.S. economy through the first seven decades of this century bears witness to the success of this dominant paradigm.

The Systems Model. Where the machine model is founded on analysis or taking things apart, systems thinking is built on synthesis or putting things together (Ackoff, 1981). Ackoff defines a system as a set of two or more elements that satisfies the following three conditions:

1. The behavior of each element has an effect on the behavior of the whole.
2. The behavior of the elements and their effects on the whole are interdependent.
3. However subgroups of the elements are formed, each has an effect on the behavior of the whole and none has an independent effect on it (p.15).

Ackoff describes further that:

> The essential properties of a system taken as a whole derive from the interactions of its parts, not their actions taken separately. Therefore, when a system is taken apart it loses its essential properties. Because of this—and this is the critical point—a system is a whole that cannot be understood by analysis (p. 16).

Under the systems way of thinking, problems are solved not by taking things apart but rather by (1) identifying the larger whole containing the element to be explained, (2) explaining the behavior or properties of the containing whole, and then (3) explaining the behavior or characteristics of the element in question in terms of the role or function it serves within the larger context. Perhaps the most significant implication of this paradigm for organizational effectiveness is that, to the extent each part of the system is considered independently and is made to operate as efficiently as possible, the system as a whole will not operate to its potential. The logic of this paradigm suggests that the optimal performance of the system as a whole requires suboptimization at the unit level.

FIGURE 1

The machine bureaucracy

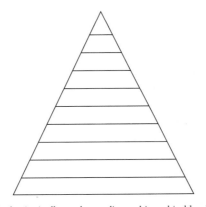

Authority is allocated according to hierarchical level.

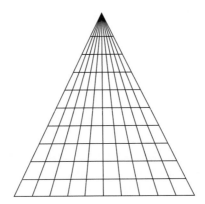

Responsibilities are delineated by clear divisions between functional groups (e.g., engineering, manufacturing, finance, sales, and human resources).

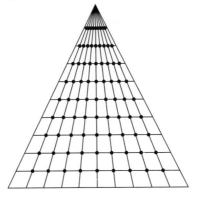

Over time, and with increasing specificity of rules, procedures, and organization charters, the organization becomes overbounded or "arthritic" in its joints and information flow and coordination across subunit boundaries is impeded.

For an organization to function effectively as a whole system, boundary permeability between an organization and its environment and among sub-units within the organization must be maintained at an optimal level (Alderfer, 1976). Under conditions of either overboundedness or underboundedness, effective internal regulation or adaptation to a changing external environment breaks down. The extreme form of the machine bureaucracy, where boundaries are hardened to near impermeable states, may be considered, in these terms, a highly overbounded system.

The contrast between the machine and the system paradigms parallels Mitroff's (1987) characterization of old organizing assumptions and new organizing assumptions in the design of jobs and organizations (based on Mills and Lovell, 1985) and Imai's (1986) comparison of Western innovation-oriented management with the Japanese kaizen or continuous improvement philosophy. Two of the core concepts that appear repeatedly in recent discussions of new organizing paradigms are an emphasis on continual learning and the involvement of everyone in the continuous improvement of the system as a whole (see, for example, Hayes, Wheelwright and Clark, 1988; Imai, 1986, Keichel, 1990; Mitroff, 1987; and Stata, 1989). In fact, one of the common targeted objectives of the new paradigm models is that of creating organizations that learn within the context of dynamic boundary relations internally and externally.

Given the objective of moving large complex bureaucracies from old organizing paradigms to new systems perspectives, what are the implications for the practice of organization development and planned change? The answer to this can be found in tracing the roots of organization development and integrating historical group or team-oriented practice with systems-level thinking.

Beyond Teambuilding: Large-Scale Systems Change as a Vehicle for Shifting Culture

Teambuilding. The practice of organization development has grown in large part out of the early research on group dynamics by Lewin, Lippitt, Brad-ford, and Benne and the experiential learning processes pioneered by the National Training Laboratories beginning in 1947.[9] This origin is reflected in a predominant focus on group behavior and team development by organization development practitioners. Describing characteristics of successful organization development efforts, Beckhard (1969) suggests that they entail a planned program involving the whole system, and that they usually rely on some form of experience-based learning activities. Yet he says they also work primarily with groups. In practice, this has tended to mean relatively small groups.

Today throughout much of industry, one finds cadres of internal facilitators providing consultative support to quality circles and problem-solving teams with 8 to 10 members. Teambuilding has probably been the most common intervention of organization development practitioners in the past 30 years. While the core tenets of early T-group theory parallel systems thinking, the field of organization development seemed to lock onto small-group technology. Teambuilding can have many positive contributions to an organization's vitality or effectiveness. Teams and the individuals within them can develop process skills for handling conflict, making decisions, and setting direction. Yet, when teambuilding is conducted at a subunit level within a complex organization, large system level phenomena, if addressed at all, are typically addressed in only an oblique way (see Figure 2).

Teambuilding, as a vehicle for organization development, can be an instrument for reinforcing the machine bureaucracy and for tightening, rather than opening, the boundaries between groups. Within-group cohesion may be increased at the expense of between-group or systemic integration. Each group being built separately is likely to work with its own unique dataset and shape its objectives in a way that optimizes sub-unit performance, rather than the performance of the system as a whole. This is a natural consequence not simply of an inherent bias toward self interest but of the fact that the whole system is not present or represented in the room. In the absence of relevant stakeholders influencing the discussion, groups will tend to focus on their own parochial needs.

FIGURE 2

Teambuilding

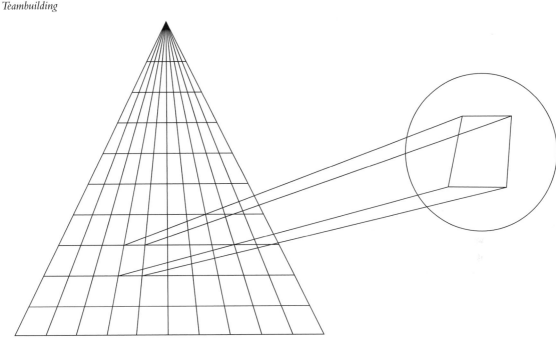

Teambuilding is typically conducted by extracting a single subunit from the larger system, developing the group's skills and capabilities, and then returning the subunit to the larger system, the elements of which often exert pressure to return to the original status quo.

Getting the Whole System in the Room. Weisbord (1987a) describes an evolution in the practice of management consulting and organization development starting in the early 1900s with Frederick Taylor's scientific management up to the present. The evolution process begins with experts solving problems for others. The second stage, which Weisbord dates from the 1950s to the middle 1960s, has everyone getting involved in the problem-solving process. Stage three is characterized by experts working to improve whole systems. The final stage, which Weisbord sees as the next evolution in organization development, entails getting everyone involved in improving whole systems.

Drawing on the community development and futuring the research and practice of Lippitt and Schindler-Rainman (1980), Weisbord (1987a, 1987b) describes four useful practices he feels characterize this next or "third wave" of managing and consulting. The first is an assessment of the potential for action by determining the presence of three prerequisite conditions: committed leadership, a good business opportunity (i.e., a critical business need that must be addressed, such as merger, acquisition, reorganization, business strategy planning, overhead crises, or new technologies), and energized people. Before proceeding, Weisbord advocates a thorough "should we/shouldn't we" discussion with the key stakeholders. The second useful practice is to "get the whole system in the room." The third is to focus on the future, and the fourth is to structure tasks that people can do for themselves. Weisbord's description of these four practices as the next phase of organization development practice matches closely with the large-scale systems change methodology that was initiated within the Ford Motor Company in 1982 and which is the subject of the present discussion.

Large-Scale Systems Change at Ford Motor Company. Ford Motor Company in 1981 was in the depths of a competitive crisis. The economy was in a cyclical downturn, new and stronger competitors were challenging the market, and customer expectations about automotive quality and performance were shifting dramatically. The company lost nearly 10 percentage points of U.S. market share, and, between 1980 and 1983, recorded losses of $3.3 billion and a North American workforce reduction of approximately 100,000 employees. Chrysler had recently gone to the U.S. government for a bailout, and Ford appeared to be not far behind. With the company hemorrhaging in the newly competitive global environment, in what Peter Vaill (1986) calls the "permanent whitewater" of present day environmental turbulence, small-scale quick fixes aimed at repairing the boxes of the organization would not produce the required cultural and competitive adjustment or the capacity for continual renewal. Out of these circumstances was born the earliest iteration of the large-scale systems change methodology applied within a large corporate setting.

Ford Motor Company and the United Auto Workers signed an agreement on Employee Involvement as part of their contract negotiations in 1979. This agreement resulted in the initiation of extensive problem solving and quality circle group activities at the shop floor level of the company. As a result of these activities, the company culture in the manufacturing plants began to shift from the highly authoritarian model of the past to a more participative model that engaged the employees' minds as well as their hands. By 1980, as business performance was beginning to collapse severely, the senior management of the company began a process of personal study and education on quality improvement under the tutelage of Dr. W. Edwards Deming. At this time, Ford launched its "Quality is Job #1" campaign, internally as well as externally. The pressure for change within Ford was becoming enormous as the company's competitive position continued to slip, and with these new initiatives, Employee Involvement and "Quality is Job #1," change was beginning nearly simultaneously at the bottom and at the top.

By 1981, the pressure for change had become particularly acute within the Diversified Products Operations (DPO) of the Ford Motor Company. This unit consisted of approximately 70,000 employees within 10 operating divisions, most of which supplied component parts or materials for the automotive business (e.g., steel, castings, climate control, electronics, glass, plastics, paint, and vinyl). These divisions were under especially acute pressure, given that alternative sources for many or most of their products were available outside the company. Their customer divisions were beginning to demand that they meet or beat the external competition in quality, cost, and delivery. This provided the impetus for Tom Page, then executive vice president in charge of DPO, to seek a means to bring about a cultural change rapidly within his entire 70,000 person organization.

Page could see the beginning of positive momentum at the top with the new focus on quality and at the bottom with the emphasis on Employee Involvement. These initiatives, however, left a large gap in the middle, that vast domain containing the roughly 20 layers of hierarchy between his office and the shop floor. Not only had this large bulk of employees not been brought into the fold of the new quality and employee involvement initiatives, but they had been schooled in and continued to practice the best of the old paradigm, machine bureaucracy model of management. Authorities and perquisites were carefully allocated among the vertical layers, and functions were tightly segmented into what were referred to as the "chimneys" (including such organizations as engineering, finance, labor relations, manufacturing, research, and sales). Small-scale initiatives, such as training or teambuilding with groups of 20 to 25, would not reach a critical mass of people quickly enough, nor would they get at the root of the organizational arthritis that had crept into the organization latticework.

To address the competitive crisis and the necessity for large-scale change, a group of external consultants was invited to collaborate with Page and his management team.[10] The consultants came from Ann Arbor, Michigan, where several of them had each been influenced by the research and practice of Ron Lippitt. Page asked the group to develop a strategy to shift the mass of his organization from an old authoritarian management style to the participative management style he was seeking. The external consultants collaborated with Page's manager for employee involvement and training to develop a methodology they believed could accomplish the needed magnitude and speed of change.[11] What they proposed to Tom Page in 1981 is precisely what Weisbord (1987a, 1987b) describes as the next phase of organization development. The consultants came back to Page with a proposal to work with each of his 10 divisions by developing and conducting what would be division-specific participative management seminars using a large-scale systems change methodology.

The proposed seminars were to be conducted with the division general manager and his top five layers of management as an intact group, which included anywhere from 60 to 150 people (see Figure 3). The intent of the sessions was to create a highly interactive learning environment where participative management would be the medium and a real-time, real-life case analysis of the division's business conducted by the program participants would be the content. Participants were to work together in a series of small group and large group configurations that would bring people together across the hierarchical and functional barriers that had traditionally kept them apart. What the seminar proposed to do, consistent with Weisbord's prescription, was to get the whole system into the room, to focus on the future (and also on the past and present), and to design tasks that people could do for themselves. The participants would provide the vast majority of the content within a context that was designed to promote interactive individual, group, and organizational learning across the whole system. Tom Page was eager to bring about a rapid transformation and saw no better alternative for getting there. Therefore, in an act reflecting what Kanter (1983) describes as the paradox of initiation, Page decreed that each of his general managers should launch the large-scale participative management seminar process within their respective divisions.

The participative management seminar was designed as a five-day event, beginning with an initial three-day meeting followed six to eight weeks later with a two-day follow-up. The sessions were held off-site and brought the top five layers of division management together into what might be called an "organization quality circle." In many cases, this was the first time the entire management group had been in one room at the same time. The seminar was intended to both build participative skills in the management team and to help managers find new ways of working together vertically and horizontally within the system. Managers worked in different teams during the five days; they were grouped variously in maximum-mix teams (microcosm groups consisting of multiple levels and functions), functional teams, natural work teams, Myers-Briggs-personality-type teams, and, finally, as a team of the whole, planning, voting, and coming to consensus around a shared vision for the future.

Within each of the 10 divisions, the seminars were designed using a five-step process:

1. The creation of a consultant/client division collaborative design team to plan the event.
2. The collection of data from key stakeholders within the system.
3. The development of a clear statement of purpose.
4. The development of a detailed process plan for the flow of each day in the five-day design.
5. The continual evaluation of the plan against the purpose and the data and the evaluation of the events themselves at the end of each day.

Using this approach, each seminar could be customtailored to meet the unique and specific requirements of a given division. The design process itself became a vehicle for learning, renewal, and the building of ownership for the large-scale methodology by the microcosm group participating in the planning.

Part of the internal architecture for the seminar was provided by the Gleicher formula for

FIGURE 3

Large-scale systems change

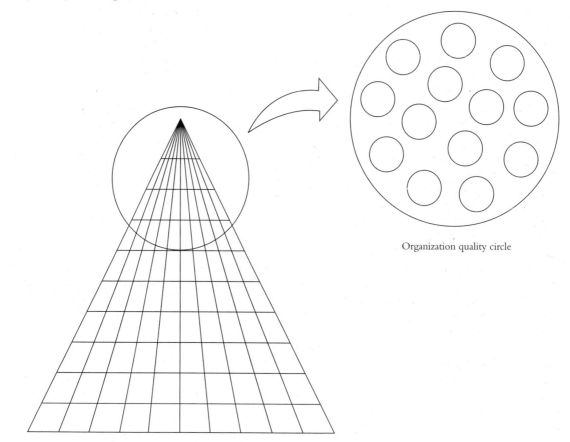

Organization quality circle

The large-scale systems change methodology employed in the Ford participative management seminars took the top five layers of an operating division off-site as an intact group. Participants worked in a variety of small group and large group configurations, beginning with maximum-mix teams that mixed people by level and function into microcosms of the whole.

organizational change described by Beckhard and Harris (1977). The formula was adapted for mnemonic purposes as follows:

$$C = D \times V \times F > R$$
$$C = \text{Change}$$
$$D = \text{Dissatisfaction with the status quo}$$
$$V = \text{Vision of the future}$$
$$F = \text{First steps}$$
$$R = \text{Resistance to change}$$

This equation suggests that in order to bring about change in a large system there must be a sufficient degree of dissatisfaction with the status quo (D), a vision of the future that is clear, compelling, and different from the present (V), and practical first steps to move toward the vision (F). Multiplied together these three variables must be greater than the resistance to change, which is assumed to always have a value greater than zero. If any of the three variables D, V, or F is equal to zero the total product will be equal to zero, and resistance to change will win out.

Building from this change formula, the participative management seminar was designed in its various division specific iterations to build a shared systemwide understanding (a common database) of D, V, and F. the participants were invited to identify (through a series of interactive processes working with self-facilitated table teams) what was working and not working within the division and in the division's relationship with key external stakeholders. Second, they were asked to build preferred future visions for the whole system and for their natural work teams. Finally, they were given the opportunity to work together both cross-functionally and in natural teams to begin to develop the first steps and action plans that would move the division toward the shared vision.

One of the significant outcomes of the participative management seminars was that the participants left the sessions better connected with one another across system boundaries (functional and hierarchical) that had historically kept them apart. They left with more understanding of the interdependencies that would determine the future success of the enterprise. The seminars not only addressed Page's concerns about creating the right environment for participative management and quality improvement but, by breaking people out of narrow arthritic boxes, helped move each division from the machine model into the systems age.

While the large-scale change process in each division was initiated with the top five management layers, there was soon demand to diffuse the process through the rest of the organization in order to expand and accelerate the change process through all of the layers. Diffusion seminars were created to accommodate this need. These diffusion seminars were built in a similar fashion to the original participative management seminar, with the difference that those who were at the lowest levels in the initial event became the senior levels of the next event and so on through the system. This linking pin and cascading process provided an opportunity for many layers of management to demonstrate their leadership capabilities and for the system as a whole to build a broad and shared understanding around the key elements of the change formula. The sense of shared understanding and participation in creating a new vision for

quality, participation, and teamwork became refined and enriched by each level as the process moved down through the entirety of the Diversified Products divisions.

The process of large-scale systems change came to be viewed positively within the leadership hierarchy at Ford as a vehicle for effecting cultural change and organization learning. The Diversified Products divisions were able, for the most part, to make significant quantifiable gains in their quality performance and were able to hold onto their business base in a highly competitive environment. The internal manager of employee involvement and training within DPO, with the support of Tom Page and then Ford chairman Donald Petersen, was promoted and given responsibility to create the Ford Executive Development Center for the top managers in the company worldwide. The methodology employed in the large-scale systems change process was integrated as a part of the core technology in the new executive university.

This large-scale change methodology was developed initially to address the need to change management style and build new skills in a management team that was fighting for its competitive life. Thus the initial application was designed to address two (style and skills) of what Pascale and Athos (1980) refer to as the "soft S's" in their seven S model of organization effectiveness. Next we will look at how the large-scale approach has been applied to one of the "hard S's," strategy, within a different context, the Boeing Company in Seattle, Washington.[12]

Large-Scale Strategic Planning

A Vehicle for Building Alignment.   Getting the whole system in the room helps to build an internal community within the organization and to break down barriers between individuals, between groups, and between different functions and hierarchical levels. One potential advantage that was not clearly anticipated at the outset was that of gaining organization alignment around a common strategic direction. In the box-by-box teambuilding approach to organization development there is the opportunity to help subteams within the organization establish clarity of mission, goals, and objectives. Unfortunately this is often conducted without a systems view, and the various subunits aim themselves in different and incompatible directions. Some groups head off to the northeast, while others decide a westerly direction makes more sense. This leads to a lack of coordination internally, confusion for external stakeholders (including customers), and a diminished capacity for a rapid and effective response to a changing business environment. The large-scale systems change process provides a methodology for getting all of the functions and multiple layers of management aligned in one direction simultaneously.

A story from Waterman (1987) based on a consulting project with the Sanwa Bank in Japan illustrates this point nicely. Waterman describes how the broad involvement of multiple layers and functions within the bank led to the successful turnaround of market share losses in record time.

The application of the large-scale systems change methodology to the strategic planning process is a vehicle for creating the type of simultaneity in planning and implementation that Waterman describes. Designed properly, the process of planning can have at least as much influence on organizational outcomes as the specifics of the plan itself.[13] Large-scale strategic planning was launched within Boeing Computer Services in March of 1989 and within Boeing Aerospace and Electronics in September of 1989. The present discussion of the process will focus on the work with the Aerospace and Electronics Division, since this represents the most advanced evolution of the approach. The discussion of outcomes, however, will address observations from each of these Boeing Company divisions.

Boeing Aerospace and Electronics. The circumstances under which large-scale strategic planning was launched at Boeing Aerospace and Electronics Division were not as dire as those confronting the Diversified Products Operations of Ford Motor Company in 1981. However, early warning signs were apparent to the senior division

leadership that the organization was headed for trouble. The division was on its way to its first-ever net loss year, with several key programs running behind schedule and over cost and a number of historically loyal customers beginning to question the division's capabilities. The impetus for initiating the process came from Art Hitsman, the executive vice president responsible for the 27,000 person Boeing Aerospace and Electronics Division.[14] In his new role, Hitsman was seeking to both build bridges among the many units making up his division and to establish a strategic alignment from top to bottom.

One of Hitsman's customer divisions within Boeing had begun experimenting with the Japanese concept of hoshin planning, modeled after Hewlett-Packard's application of the same concept. Under this hoshin planning philosophy, the organization as a whole established clear measurable goals for the year and communicated these to all employees. Each successive layer of the organization from the top on down was responsible for taking the division goals and translating those into unit specific actions that would enable the division to achieve its annual targets. Hitsman was impressed with what he saw in the other division. In his own division, Hitsman hoped to both break down the traditional barriers among functions and hierarchical levels and to achieve a strategic flowdown that would enable each employee to understand how he or she fit into the larger picture. A joint consultant/client design team was created to develop a process that would address the needs for both cultural change and strategic alignment.

The Strategic Planning Model.   Following a development process consistent with that used in creating the participative management seminars at Ford, the design team began its work by conducting diagnostic interviews with key members of the division management team. The data from the interviews were shared openly in the design sessions, as were the views of the design team members on the state of the organization. These data and a simple model for strategic planning (see Figure 4) were used to shape the purpose and process for the intervention.

FIGURE 4

Strategic planning model

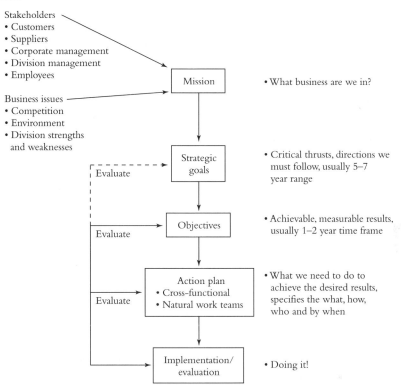

Applying Ackoff's (1981) concept of systems thinking, the strategic planning model starts by looking at the larger containing whole within which the focal subsystem (in this case Boeing Aerospace and Electronics Division) is contained. Before agreeing on the division level strategic focus, the organization members first develop a clear understanding of their key stakeholders and trends within their industry. Therefore, step one in the strategic planning process is to create the means for bringing the relevant data about the operating environment into the room. This includes information about customers, industry trends, and corporate management expectations, as well as internal management and employee perceptions of organizational performance and the quality of work life. The next step is to take that understanding of the environment and come to an agreement on the specific business mission of the organization. In this case, "mission" is understood to mean the definition of the division's business or reason for being.

Next, based on the agreed statement of mission, and the opportunities and challenges identified in the environmental assessment, strategic goals are established. Strategic goals are defined as the critical thrusts or directions the organization should pursue or on which it should focus its energies in the next five to seven years if it is to be successful in achieving its mission.[15] By looking five to seven years out, the participants in the process have the opportunity to define a preferred future for the organization; they can create a picture of what they want to see happen, rather than simply planning from where they are and extending themselves inchbug style into the future. In this model, the strategic goals are not developed by building best case and worst case scenarios. Rather, they are built in a manner consistent with what Ackoff (1981) describes as interactive planning. Ackoff's interactive planning begins with what he calls the "formulation of the mess"—that is understanding the system's threats and opportunities. From that understanding, Ackoff's model moves to the definition of the desirable future state or what he calls "ends planning." The goal planning stage identified in Figure 4 is analogous to this idea of ends planning or to what Lindeman and Lippitt (1979) describe as preferred futuring. Rather than predicting the future and then planning according to the prediction (what Ackoff calls "preactive planning"), the preferred futuring approach works from the premise that the organization members can define a realistic and desirable future state for themselves and then build their plans accordingly. Lippitt (1983), moreover, finds that groups working on preferred futures, as contrasted with those addressing past or present problems, have higher energy and greater ownership for the plans they develop and that their solutions are more creative.

This longer-term goal formation step in the planning process also addresses another common organization dilemma, the activity bias. Often, out of a keen bias for action, organizations, groups, or individuals will jump directly from an environmental squeaky wheel directly to an action to stop the squeak. While this may be effective for addressing near-term problems, this approach can be highly destructive in the long run. In the absence of a coherent set of strategic goals, organization members are left to respond to whatever squeaky wheels they may happen to see and hear, and, as a result, the organization strategy becomes a random assortment of independent actions. These actions over time can work at cross purposes and lead to the dissipation of the organization's energy. This is an example of the optimization of parts of the system at the expense of the whole. In contrast, the strategic planning process organizes a myriad of internal and external squeaky wheels, first into a coherent environmental analysis, and second, into a clear statement of mission and a preferred set of priority goals. This strategic planning process then can reduce the tyranny of

a reactive management style and bring alignment and discipline to near-term actions.

While the strategic goals provide a general sense of direction, the objectives specify achievable and measurable results that must be realized within one or two years if the organization is to make progress toward its desired future state. The objectives are developed with the idea of moving from the abstract to the concrete. The objectives begin to translate the vision implied in the goals to the practical first steps the organization must take to achieve them. The process gets even more specific in the action planning stage. In this phase, action plans—identifying what needs to happen, who needs to be involved, and by when—are developed for each of the organization objectives. This type of action planning is done both on a cross-functional total organization basis and at the natural work team level.

The final element of the strategic planning model is the implementation and continual monitoring and evaluation of the plans. This entails both doing what was planned and the evaluation of what was done. Evaluation of the actions in this case should be done not only in relation to the action plans (did we do what we said we were going to do?) but in relation to the objectives (by doing what we agreed to do, did we achieve the results we expected?) and in relation to the goals (by doing what we agreed to and achieving or not achieving the results we expected, did we move ourselves any closer toward the destination we agreed was desirable?). This model, together with the Gleicher formula for organization change, provided the framework for the strategic planning process.

Involving the Organization in Three Phases. Using a top-down and bottom-up approach, the strategic planning process was designed in three phases, each phase building towards and being enriched by the next (see Figure 5). Phase I was designed as a two-day working session for the division general manager and 14 of his top executives representing the major functional organizations and the four major product units (Electronics Systems, Missile Systems, Space Systems, and the Huntsville Division) which make up the division. Following the path laid out in the strategic planning model,

FIGURE 5

Involving the organization in three phases
Boeing Aerospace and Electronics

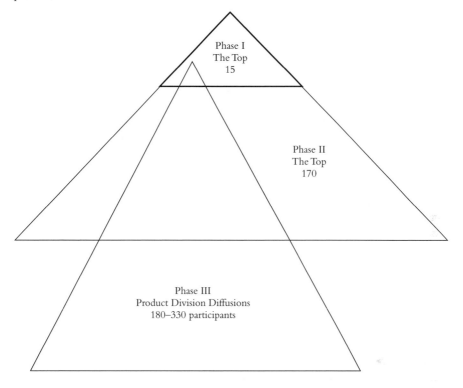

this executive group spent most of the first day building a common understanding of the corporation's mission, goals, and objectives, and of how the Aerospace and Electronics Division was viewed by several key stakeholders, including senior corporate management, customers, suppliers, and employees. The group also analyzed the strengths and weaknesses of their key competitors, assessed the existing business environment within the defense and space industry, and evaluated the current capabilities of their organization by examining each of their respective organizations against the Malcom Baldrige National Quality Award criteria.

This environmental analysis provided the basis for the top-management group to develop a first-draft statement of mission, goals, and objectives for the Aerospace and Electronics Division. The objective of this two-day session was to both strengthen

the division leadership group (they were referred to as the Division Quality Council) as a team and to develop a preliminary strategic plan that could be used as the basis for further evolution in phase II.

Phase II occurred four weeks after phase I. This phase expanded the planning circle from the top 15 to the top 170 managers in the division. Phase II was designed as a five-day intervention, with the first three days separated from the last two days by a 13-week interim period (see Figure 6). The phase II event began in a similar way to phase I, starting with an assessment of the key stakeholders, several of whom participated in the meeting, and of the existing business environment.

Once they had the opportunity to build a border understanding of the business environment, the 155 participants below the top 15 were asked to critique and recommend changes to the draft

FIGURE 6

Boeing Aerospace and Electronics
Large-scale systems change, phase II, October 23–25, 1989, and January 16–17, 1990

Purpose: To come together as leaders of Boeing Aerospace and Electronics to:

- Build a shared understanding of our business environment.
- Agree on our BA&E Mission, Goals, and Objectives.
- Identify what we need to do individually and together to lead BA&E successfully into the future with a sense of urgency and strategic intent.

Agenda

Day 1

7:30	Continental Breakfast
8:00	Opening and Welcome—Art Hitsman
8:10	Purpose, Agenda, and Norms
8:30	Telling Your Story
9:15	Break
9:30	View from the Corporate Bridge—Frank Shrontz, Boeing Company Chairman and CEO
10:30	View from the BA&E Bridge—Dan Pinick, President, Boeing Defense and Space Group, and Art Hitsman, Executive Vice President, Boeing Aerospace and Electronics
12:10	Lunch
1:10	Celebrating Diversity (Myers-Briggs)
3:20	Organization Diagnosis: Glads and Sads
4:50	Evaluation
5:00	Adjourn

Day 2

7:30	Continental Breakfast
8:00	Feedback on Evaluations and Agenda for the Day
8:10	Industry Assessment
9:45	Break
10:00	Voice of the Customer
11:40	Lunch
12:30	Interorganization Conflict
3:20	Break
3:35	Revisit Mission, Strategic Goals, and Objectives
3:55	Critique of Mission, Strategic Goals, and Objective
4:40	Feedback to Quality Council
5:10	Evaluation of the Day
5:15	Adjourn
5:20	Quality Council (Leadership Team) and Design Team remain to read evaluations and integrate feedback to achieve new consensus on Mission, Strategic Goals, and Objectives

Day 3

7:30	Continental Breakfast
8:00	Feedback on Evaluations and Agenda for the Day
8:10	Quality Council Response to Critique of Mission, Strategic Goals, and Objectives
9:15	Participants Self-select to Work on Objectives
9:25	BA&E Objective Strategy Groups
	• Preferred Futuring on Objectives
	• Systemwide Action Recommendations

FIGURE 6

(concluded)

12:00	Lunch
1:00	BA&E Objective Strategy Groups (continued)
1:30	Roomwide Post, Read, and Vote
2:00	Quality Council Summarizes and Reports Voting Results
2:30	Break
2:45	Back Home Groups: Planning for the Interim
3:45	Headline Reports
4:15	Quality Council Commitments for the Interim
4:30	Wrap-up and Next Steps
4:45	Evaluation of the Three Days
5:00	Social Hour

A 13-week interim period separated days three and four.

Day 4

7:30	Continental Breakfast
8:00	Welcome—Art Hitsman
8:10	Purpose, Agenda, and Logistics
8:20	Look Back: Learnings from the Interim
9:50	Break
10:05	Introductions in New Maximum-mix Teams
10:10	Executive Vice President's Commentary on Reports from the Interim
10:15	Motorola Story: What Motorola Learned from Pursuing the Malcolm Baldrige National Quality Award—William Smith, Corporate Senior Executive for Quality, Motorola
11:45	Lunch
12:30	Assessment of BA&E Against the Malcolm Baldrige Criteria
2:45	Break
3:00	View from the BA&E Leadership Bridge—Programs in the News
4:55	Evaluation of the Day
5:00	Adjourn

Day 5

7:30	Continental Breakfast
8:00	Feedback on Evaluations and Agenda for the Day
8:10	Global View—Dr. William J. Taylor, Vice President, International Security Programs, Center for Strategic International Studies
9:45	Strategic Objective Analysis—Assessment of Progress on Objectives Plans Since Day 3 and Identification of Show Stoppers
11:45	Lunch—Show-stopper lists posted in main room for reading and voting for show-stoppers with the most leverage under each objective
1:00	Show-stopper Action Planning
2:45	Break
3:00	Show-stopper Reports
3:35	Back Home Planning
4:35	Headline Reports
5:05	Closing Comments—Art Hitsman
5:15	Evaluation of the Two Days
5:20	Social Hour

mission, goals, and objectives proposed by the leadership team. The output from phase I thus became input for phase II. The leadership group took all of the feedback from the 155 on the evening of day two and, working late into the night, integrated their comments into a final statement of mission, goals, and objectives. This was reviewed with the 155 the next morning and became the basis for subsequent systemwide and work unit level action planning on day three and in the postinterim session on days four and five. With the overnight turnaround on recommendations for changes to the mission, goals, and objectives, the ownership for the strategy underwent a major shift from the top 15 to the entire group of 170. Many saw their specific words and concerns incorporated and reflected in the revised document.

Phase III was designed as a series of three-day diffusion events to bring the other 3,000 managers within the division into the strategic planning process. These meetings involved between 180 and 330 managers at a time and each was organized with a focus on one of the four product units. These sessions began with the Corporate and Aerospace and Electronics Division mission, goals, and objectives as givens. The product unit manager and his top leadership team (approximately 15 people in each case) were the principal clients for each of these events. They played the same role that the division general manager and his leadership team had in the phase II events.

As in the phase II process, the product unit leadership team developed a draft statement of mission, goals, and objectives for its organization before the session began. This draft strategy then became the material for debate, critique, and modification by the next tiers of the hierarchy across the functional spectrum in the phase III events. The product units were large organizations in their own right, ranging from 2,000 to 8,000 employees each.

In the product program events, the overall product unit strategy was taken as a given. The results of these sessions included stronger bonds among the participants and an agreed-to set of action priorities and plans at the program level. These priorities and plans were targeted at serving the identified needs of both external and internal customers and at supporting the overall strategic direction of the product unit, the Aerospace and Electronics Division, and ultimately the corporation as a whole.

Phase III was a vehicle for greatly broadening the involvement base in the planning process and for knitting together, through a series of overlapping and interlocking events, the many management layers, functional organizations, product units, and program groups that made up the division. Subsequently, the involvement and teambuilding process was cascaded through the nonmanagement ranks of the organization.

Systems Theory in the Context of Planning. Ackoff (1981) outlines three operating principles for carrying out his model of interactive planning: the participative principle, the holistic principle, and the principle of continuity. The participative principle, as Ackoff describes, implies that:

> no one can plan effectively for someone else. It is better to plan for oneself, no matter how badly, than to be planned for by others, no matter how well. The reason for this derives from the meaning of development: an increase in one's desire and ability to satisfy one's own desires and those of others. This ability and desire are not increased by being planned for by others, but by planning for oneself (p. 66).

The three phases of planning outlined here were not designed to simply inform the 3,000 members of management what their leaders had decided, but to involve them actively and simultaneously in both strategy formulation and implementation.

The holistic principle applies Ackoff's systems model of the organization within the planning context and argues for the criticality of building coordination and integration into the process:

> Problems, no matter where they appear, should be attacked simultaneously and cooperatively from as many points of view as possible (p. 73).

and:

> planning done independently at any level of a system cannot be as effective as planning carried out interdependently at all levels (p. 73).

Combining these concepts of coordination and integration, Ackoff maintains that:

> the more parts of a system and levels of it that plan simultaneously and interdependently the better. This concept of all-over-at-once planning stands in opposition to sequential planning, either top-down or bottom-up (p. 74).

In his principle of continuity, Ackoff simply cautions that planning should not be done as a discontinuous or static process, but rather should be continuous and dynamic. In the process of moving toward a destination, new information is gained. Plans therefore need to have the flexibility built in to accommodate new data and to allow the setting of new and more appropriate courses.

The process outlined in the present discussion is an attempt to address in particular Ackoff's principles of participation and holism. The effective application of these two principles is likely to build within the organization the adaptive and renewing capabilities addressed by the principle of continuity. While many have argued for the need to address broad participation and holistic thinking in the planning process, little has been written on how to effectively bring this about. What seems to have been missing is a process model for working with large groups. It is in this domain that the work at Ford and Boeing has provided an especially unique opportunity for learning.

Getting the Whole System in the Room Sounds Good in Theory, but What Do You Do When They Actually Show Up?

Conceptually, getting the whole system in the room—what Weisbord (1987) describes as the next phase in the evolution of organization development—makes sense. For all the reasons stated above, about the limitations of the machine model in contrast to the systems perspective, we need to find ways to plan and manage organizations as a whole and not simply on a box by box basis. But in reality, how do you do it? What do you do when the whole system decides to show up?

Large-Scale Application of Small Group Principles.   What I have learned, first as a participant observer of the large-scale methodology and subsequently as a process designer, is that the same principles that hold true for managing process effectively at the small group level also apply when larger numbers are brought into the room. Schutz (1984) identifies inclusion, control, and openness as critical elements of effectiveness in a small group's life. When one brings into the room 30 groups of eight people each, the same principles apply. Issues of inclusion, control, and openness must be addressed at the table group level and at the level of the whole room.

In the large-scale systems change methodology, inclusion mechanisms range from the simple—such as having name tags and clear table assignments when people arrive (participants are assigned to cross-level, cross-functional microcosm groups called "maximum-mix teams")—to the more substantial, such as having each participant share his or her personal story about life in the organization with the others at his or her table. Throughout the process of a multiday large group event, the design encourages a maximum of individual involvement and a minimum of passive one-way listening. In each of the series of structured subgroup activities that make up the three days of a phase III event, the subteams are asked to designate members of their group to serve as group facilitator, flipchart recorder, and group spokesperson. Guidelines and coaching for effective performance in these roles are provided by the conference facilitation team. The groups are expected to rotate these roles among their members in successive rounds. This approach is inclusive and places responsibility for control squarely in the groups' hands. In other parts of the design, individuals are given the opportunity to use post-it notes to generate ideas on a roomwide basis under specific strategic issues or to vote with stick-on dots (green for "go for it," red for "don't even think of it") on action plans generated by their own and other subteams. Each element of the design is attentive to both the adult learning principle of active engagement and the individual level needs for inclusion.

Issues of control are also addressed throughout the process, with the objective of keeping the locus of control internal to the participants to the maximum extent possible. Starting with the involvement of the multilevel, cross-functional client/consultant team in the design of each event, participants are involved in shaping the process. The consultants provide an organizing framework for the process, including such concepts as the change formula, the strategic planning model, and the principles of effective group process. The client representatives on the design team and the session participants during the evens identify the issues that must be addressed and bring the content specifics to the mission, goals, objectives, and action plans. Both before and during the events, the participants are kept informed of the purpose, agenda, and the underlying theoretical models. Selective prereadings are assigned to prepare the participants to contribute effectively.

Assessment of the process is sought systemically at the end of each day through written participant evaluations. The design team gathers after each session to read the participant evaluations and, based on the feedback, to make any required changes in the subsequent day's agenda. The evaluations are also summarized in extensive detail overnight and fed back to the group as a whole the next morning. The evaluation feedback helps to create a common database of perception on the process and allows the participants to self-correct their behaviors. In this way, the entire process is managed as an open system, with real-time ongoing feedback and adjustment of the design in accordance with the needs of the participants.

Openness is fostered in several ways. Through much of the design, participants are seated in microcosm groups that, by design, exclude their immediate bosses and their direct subordinates. The sessions themselves are conducted in off-site settings and the participants are asked to dress in casual attire. The elements of the design invite the subgroups to diagnose aspects of system performance that under normal circumstances might be considered undiscussable (Argyris, 1986). However, given that the diagnosis is allowed to be carried out and reported as a group product, no individual is

required to risk his or her career or reputation in raising difficult questions or in identifying troublesome problems. Diagnostic data, images of the future, and action plans are generated in teams and shared openly across the room through table team reports, either verbal or written. The sessions are designed to both (1) build a common understanding among the participants of how their management peers view the organization and (2) model an environment of openness that may be continued back in the workplace. The transfer of openness back to the work setting may be expected to be enhanced (when contrasted with learning designs involving only a few individuals or a single unit within the organization) by the fact that a large mass of the system is sharing in the opening process simultaneously.

Designing Simultaneously for the Individual, Group, Intergroup, and the Whole System.
The Tavistock model (Bion, 1961; Miller and Rice, 1967) views organization life simultaneously through multiple windows, analyzing behavior at the levels of the individual, the group, intergroup relations, and the organization as a whole system. Similarly, the large-scale systems change methodology is designed to address all four of these levels of behavior.

At the individual level, participants in the large-scale process have the opportunity to simply be students of their own organization and of the organization's stakeholders. The top leader of the subject organization will usually gain insights into how he or she is perceived by others in the system. Each of the participants has the opportunity to gain insights into each's behavioral and leadership style through a self-assessment and group discussion with like-type peers applying the Myers-Briggs Type Indicator. Each participant is also encouraged throughout to take the learnings from the broad view and apply them to his or her product or functional perspective.

Group level phenomena are addressed in a variety of configurations. During the three days of a phase III event, participants work in several team formats: maximum-mix, Myers-Briggs type, functional, self-select around strategic issues, and back home work group. Many of these are artificially created temporary task teams with a life span limited to a portion of the conference. For the participants, however, these temporary task teams provide opportunities to try out and practice new group roles (e.g., leader, follower, arbitrator, facilitator, recorder, or spokesperson) and to make connections and form relationships with counterparts from other work units. Some of the temporary task teams continue to meet back in the workplace. Natural or back home work teams provide the most obvious transfer device for learnings from the session back into the organization. In some sessions, opportunity is provided for natural work teams to meet for the purpose of assessing, discussing, and improving how they work together. In all of the sessions, the natural work teams serve as the focal points for taking systemwide strategies and action plans and translating them into specific follow-up actions with clear timelines and accountability. The probability of effective follow up is enhanced by virtue of the fact that the entire natural work team experiences the process together.

Intergroup relations are addressed most directly through a process called "organizational valentines."[16] For this activity, participants are seated in functional groups and are asked to work as a team to prepare and send valentines to every other functional group. In this case, a valentine is a response to the statement "these are the things you do as a part of your job that make it more difficult for us to get our job done." Each team receives a blank valentine to send to each of the other functional teams and is asked to work quickly to generate intergroup feedback that is as behaviorally specific as possible. The teams are also asked to sign each valentine with the name of their function. At the conclusion of the writing period, all of the valentines are posted in the main meeting room under headers with the different function names. Again, operating as an open system process, all of the participants are invited to read as many of the valentines as they wish in the time allowed. In this way, individuals can compare the feedback to their own groups with that sent to others.

The functional teams are then sent back to breakout rooms with their valentines and asked to go through a four-step assignment: (1) react and ventilate, (2) listen to and understand what the data are saying, (3) summarize the major themes, and (4) prepare a nondefensive response to the feedback. At the conclusion, the teams return to the main room to report their summaries and responses. All of the participants are asked to hiss softly if they detect defensiveness in a given report. The hissing, humorously and gently, provides feedback on how a group's response to conflict data is perceived by the others in the room. The valentines process not only helps to create part of the database for effective planning but identifies many specific issues on which the functional teams can follow up.

Intergroup relations are also addressed subtly through the relationship building in various subteam configurations and explicitly in the back home action planning where teams are invited to make requests for assistance from other teams.

Systemwide considerations are built into every facet of the design at a large-scale systems change meeting. The organizational valentines process expands intergroup conflict resolution to a whole system level. Each maximum-mix working team provides its members the opportunity to view the organization from other functional or hierarchical perspectives. The mission, goals, and objectives are the product of hundreds of inputs from the many points of view represented; and action planning is designed with at least two phases—a cross-functional systemwide look and the view from within natural back home work teams. By bringing five layers and all of the functions of the organization together at one time, the large-scale systems change methodology provides the opportunity for creating new circuits of connection within the system as a whole. Systems thinking is at the core of the process.

A Dynamic Environment for Learning. Meetings within Boeing (and many other organizational environments) have historically been designed as a process in which one or a few presenters share information in a show-and-tell format. These sessions usually make use of overhead projectors and are managed in a way that minimizes interaction among members of the audience. The interactions that occur are usually limited to questions or commentary from individuals in the audience to the presenters. In this way, the complexity of group interaction is kept to a minimum, control of meetings is relatively easily maintained, and the audience has relatively little input to the shaping of ideas or decisions and little accountability for follow-on action. Meetings, in many cases, have been conducted in a manner analogous to read only memory in a computer, as a one-way information sharing exercise. This has been a virtually absolute norm for meetings with over 20 participants and fairly typical even of much smaller gatherings.

The large-scale systems change approach represents a major departure from the historical meeting paradigm. At one level, what we are attempting to accomplish is to teach the participants a new process model. We have designed a way of coming together with other organizational members, whether in small groups or large, that encourages openness, dialogue, participation, and complex multilayer and multifunctional communication. By giving the table groups guidelines on facilitation and recording and asking them to select and rotate members to serve in these roles, we are both setting an expectation of and providing practice in effective meeting management. In instances where the agenda calls for presentations by key stakeholders, such as customers, suppliers, senior management, or industry experts, we give the presenters very specific guidelines on the issues we want them to address. Further, we ask that they limit their remarks to a narrow prescribed time, and that they use no slides or viewgraphs. We have found that this approach minimizes audience passivity and maximizes the energy and spontaneity in the presenter's delivery. Such presentations are then immediately followed by time for table discussions, where the participants are asked to share with each other what they heard and their reactions and to generate, as a group, the questions of clarification or understanding they need to ask of the given stake-

holder to better comprehend the stakeholder's point of view. The question-generation process then leads to an extended open forum give and take, where table groups are called on to ask their questions of the presenter. In this way, the participants are given the opportunity to shape the agenda with each stakeholder, and important information is shared through a dynamic exchange. Both the presenters and the session participants have responded enthusiastically to this process.

The other elements of the design, as described earlier, involve even more audience participation as subteams are call on to diagnose the effectiveness of existing management systems and practices, critique the draft mission, goals, and objectives, and develop the action plan to move the organization toward the desired future state. So, when the whole system actually does arrive in the room, what we do is provide a framework, including a statement of purpose and process design, that allows the participants maximum opportunity to create their own database, their own vision for the future, and their own plan to get there. The framework, designed effectively, allows a complex array of inputs to be organized into a coherent plan that is both understood and owned by the people responsible for implementation.

Outcomes

Improved organizational performance is the most significant outcome sought through the large-scale systems change methodology. The precise causal linkage between the large-systems approach and performance factors, such as quality, profitability, and customer and employee satisfaction, is difficult to establish, because, in the circumstances in which the methodology has been applied, other management and organization development initiatives have been underway simultaneously. Within the Ford Motor Company, the large-scale systems change methodology was used in concert with a major joint effort between the union and the company to promote employee involvement and an extensive companywide focus on quality improvement and cost-cutting. Each of these interventions is likely to have contributed to the major improvements the company realized in product quality, profitability, and employee satisfaction between the early 1980s and late 1980s. However, one indication of the perceived value of large-scale change process at Ford was the fact that several of the division general managers instituted the methodology as a regular part of their annual business planning activity—bringing together their top 160 managers each year to create a systemwide business plan. Feedback from program participants as well as qualitative assessments within the organization suggested that many of the intervention objectives (e.g., promotion of cross-functional teamwork, increased awareness of the business environment and the need for change, and a shift toward participative management) were achieved. Thompson (1989) documents both business and cultural outcomes associated with the large-scale change applications at Ford.

At Boeing, the large-scale strategic planning methodology was implemented both within the Aerospace and Electronics Division and Boeing Computer Services. Common observations of the organization leaders, as well as other stakeholders, pertain to increased teamwork across functional boundaries and with suppliers and customers, accelerated implementation of major systems and programs, a broader awareness of the needs of customers both internal and external, and much more extensive understanding of business goals and objectives within the organizations. The president of Boeing Computer Services, when asked by the company chairman for his assessment of the process, identified two significant changes. First, he noted that his calendar was much more open than before, because people below him were assuming greater responsibility for running the business, thus freeing him to devote more time to customer relations and strategic issues. Second, he felt his division had achieved unprecedented penetration of awareness even to the nonmanagement ranks regarding the organization's mission, goals, and objectives. One manager within the division

remarked that he had accomplished the implementation of an interorganizational network system within six months, which previously would have taken two to three years, given the history of turf battles among the organizations involved. An outside computing hardware vendor noted a significant improvement in internal communications that increased both the efficiency and the effectiveness of his work with the division.

In other cases, organizations within Boeing Computer Services became much more proactive in forming teaming relationships with their customers. Several have created their own large-scale systems change meetings with the customer to focus on their working relationship. In one such meeting, where the historical customer-supplier relationship had been fractious, the principals from the two interfacing organizations enacted their historical conflict by simultaneously dousing one another with lemon meringue pies. As they did so, over 100 of their respective subordinates cheered them on and celebrated the cathartic parody of their past. Then they got down to work and forged a new partnership.

Employees and managers who have participated in the events (both within Boeing Computer Services and Boeing Aerospace and Electronics) have responded in an overwhelmingly positive manner to the experience, based on the data from postsession evaluations and later anecdotal evidence. Several have indicated that the meetings were the most productive they had seen in their careers with the company. Others have been observed explaining, to skeptical nonparticipants from other organizations, the power of seeing their own words incorporated into the substance of the division strategic plan.

In both of the Boeing divisions engaging in this process, significant initiatives were launched to address the strategic goals and objectives developed through the large-scale meetings. However, not all of the goals or objectives received equal attention nor was every subunit within the two organizations equally vigilant in pursuing their actions plans. The long-term impact and implementation depends, as with most organizational initiatives, on the quality of the strategy and plan that is developed as well as on individual responsibility, on division and subunit leadership, on the ongoing measurement and tracking of performance, and on the linkage of performance to pay and other incentives. The preliminary qualitative evidence of positive impact within Boeing is encouraging. The ultimate measure will be based on how much more effectively the organizations are able to serve the needs of their customers as well as their own employees.

Next Steps

Participation in an initial round of large-scale strategic planning does not deliver an organization wholesale from the machine model into the systems age. The intent of the intervention approach described here is to launch and accelerate the cultural transformation process. Much more remains to be done. Most immediately will be a continuation of the large-scale meeting process to encompass the managers and nonmanagers alike who have not yet been involved. At the same time, the development of internal consulting resources to support the substantial demand for follow-on activity within and between subunits is a practical necessity. Some of the internal resources have been developed already through participation in large-scale system change design and implementation teams. Yet, further skill building for these and other resources will be important to equip the organization to extend the process independently. For the leadership teams that have been through one or two rounds of the process, periodic large-scale sessions will help prevent the reinstitution of organizational arthritis and maintain a whole system perspective.

In the longer term, career development philosophies, information systems, and organization structures will need to be adapted to develop and reinforce systemic thinking and behavior. Increased cross-functional career rotation could go a long way toward bridging the differences among disciplines. Information systems designed with broad

access can shorten the communication paths among hierarchical layers and among functional organizations. Finally, new organization structures (e.g., Ackoff's, 1981, 1989 circular organization) can bring different organization elements into closer proximity and easier and more fluid relationships. All of these approaches will need to be pursued in assisting old-line corporate hierarchies in the evolution toward whole system integration.

Getting Started: Internal Political Considerations

The approach to cultural and systems change described represents a substantial investment of both financial and human resources. Such an approach can only be undertaken in an environment where the senior leadership is convinced of the necessity for change and has confidence that the large-scale systems change methodology can help. The divisions within Ford and within Boeing where the process was launched were the parts of the respective systems experiencing the most pressure for change. This pressure, coupled in each case with a top leader willing to take a risk, made the large-scale systems change interventions possible. Without a compelling need to change, the intervention would probably appear too complex or too expensive, or both. Without the willingness to take a risk, the leaders would most likely settle for a more conservative and perhaps less demanding approach. The willingness to trust the process at Ford was based both on the criticality of the presenting crisis and pure faith that the consultants were competent. By the time the process was proposed at Boeing, there were already six years of experience with the approach at Ford on which to draw.

I was hired into Boeing in September of 1987 as corporate manager for organization development, with the explicit objective of initiating the type of cultural change approach with which I had been involved at Ford. My position was announced broadly in the organization and came with a good amount of corporate endorsement. The impact of this endorsement and the early footing it provided should not be underestimated. At a minimum, this positioning opened the door to several of what Weisbord (1987) calls "should we/shouldn't we" conversations about the large-scale systems change methodology. Moreover, it may have given the respective leaders confidence that the methodology itself had the blessing and support of corporate management and was thus less of a political risk than it might otherwise have been.

Beyond these considerations, the respective leaders also needed to be convinced purely on their own terms that the approach had merit. In the first year of my tenure with Boeing, I made numerous presentations on the evolution of organization theory from the machine bureaucracy to the systems model and on the experience with large-scale systems change at Ford. The presentations became the basis for planting seeds that might lead to further in-depth conversations with key organization leaders.

In both of the divisions within Boeing, as well as in the Diversified Products Operations within Ford where the process was begun, the senior leader made a decision to proceed with the approach with minimal or no input from his staff. While the approach was greeted initially by the staffs with skepticism, as they became involved their skepticism tended to fade. Symbolically, the large-scale events have sent a message of a willingness to open the company's systems and processes for broad scrutiny. The method has proved valuable for engaging a wide range of employees in the process of change and for taking the first steps toward organizational alignment.

There are also many organizations within Boeing that so far have not been involved. The process is best expanded on a pull basis, drawing on the internal motivation of organization leaders to select themselves for involvement in the approach. Further diffusion of the methodology into Boeing may be easier, because of growing awareness in the organization of the approach and the potential it represents. On the other hand, further diffusion may be more difficult. Other organizations may not experience as much urgency for change as those

that went first; or, because of a not-invented-here bias, a general skepticism about the methodology, or an intracompany rivalry, these organizations may opt out.

At the moment, considerable energy and a raft of folklore have been unleashed as a result of the large-scale interventions. How the process continues to unfold within the company as a whole cannot be easily predicted. Boeing has embarked on a significant cultural shift. The large-scale systems change methodology is one vehicle for effecting the shift.

Reprise on Global Competitiveness

The large-scale systems change methodology was developed as a vehicle to accelerate change within overbounded, arthritic corporate hierarchies buffeted by global competition. Building new organizations with effective practices from the ground up certainly presents many unique challenges. Undoing the past and beginning anew with an existing workforce and infrastructure presents quite another set of dilemmas. The large-scale approach was created within this latter context. Neither of the companies described have the luxury of simply shutting down and building afresh with a new workforce and an entirely new set of resources. The challenges they face are not dissimilar to the challenge faced by many other corporations across the United States and throughout the world: that of building their capacity for learning and for adaptation in an increasingly competitive environment.

De Geus (1988) suggests that the only sustainable competitive advantage any firm enjoys is the ability to learn faster than its competitors. Whether one started with a new or an existing workforce, the necessity to build in a continuous learning capability would be the same. None of our large industrial enterprises can afford for long to close themselves off from new learning or to self-righteously cling to a comfortable status quo. There is much renewal to be done in the enterprises that make up our economy, and for many the time available to accomplish this before succumbing to outside competition is growing frightfully short (Dertouzos, Lester, and Solow, 1989; Grayson and O'Dell, 1988). If we are to be successful in turning around our large enterprises and the millions of people they employ, we must find new models of management and people involvement strategies that will greatly accelerate the rate at which these new models are learned and absorbed into the fiber of the organization. Preliminary evidence indicates that the large-scale systems change methodology represents a promising avenue for both accelerated learning and the accelerated involvement of the workforce in the process of change.

Endnotes

1. "Rethinking Japan." *Business Week*, August 7, 1989, pp. 44–52.
2. Postman argues that the seeds of our national decline may be found in the trivialization of issues and the neutering of substantive debate brought about through the medium of television. While this is not my contention in this paper, I am in agreement with Postman that much of the explanation for our relative decline can be found in factors internal to our society. However, rather than focusing on causality at the macrosocietal level, I will restrict my focus to the firm level.
3. *United Nations International Trade Statistics Yearbook.* New York: United Nations Publications, 1989. The assessment of market share loss was conducted by Colin Fox, managing director, Deltapoint Corporation, Bellevue, WA.
4. "The 100 Largest Commercial Banking Companies." *Fortune,* August 24, 1992, pp. 213–14. Grayson, C. J., and O'Dell, C. *American Business: A Two Minute Warning.* New York: Free Press, 1988. The 1972 banking statistic was provided by Colin Fox, managing director, Deltapoint Corporation, Bellevue, WA
5. Peters, T. *Thriving on Chaos.* New York: Alfred A. Knopf, 1987, pp. 4–5.
6. Peters, T. "Restoring American Competitiveness: Looking for New Models of Organizations." *Academy of Management Executive,* May 1988, pp. 103–09.

7. The United States business landscape is dotted with companies having made significant turnarounds in quality, profitability, and customer and employee satisfaction. Some of those most commonly referenced include Ford Motor Company, Harley Davidson, Hewlett-Packard, Milliken, Motorola, and Xerox.
8. Kathleen Dannemiller provided the original illustration of the arthritic organization. See Jusela, G. E.; Ball, R. A.; Tyson, C. E.; and Dannemiller, D. K. "Work Innovations at Ford Motor." In Shetty, Y. K., and Buehler, V. M. *Quality, Productivity and Innovation.* New York: Elsevier, 1987.
9. See Chin, R., and Benne, K. D. "General Strategies for Effecting Changes in Human Systems." In Bennis, W. G.; Benne, K. D.; and Chin, R. *The Planning of Change.* 2nd ed. New York: Holt, Rinehart & Winston, 1969.
10. The consultants included Kathleen Dannemiller, Alan Davenport, Bruce Gibb, Chuck Tyson, and Jeff Walsh, each of whom had been working independently until they were called together to collaborate on this project.
11. The consulting team was managed and coordinated by Nancy Badore, manager of employee involvement and training for DPO. I joined Ford as an internal organization development consultant in June of 1983 and began to collaborate with the Ann Arbor consultants on further iterations of the large-scale systems change methodology over the next few years.
12. I left the Ford Motor Company in August 1987 to assume the position of corporate manager for organization development with the Boeing Company.
13. See De Geus, A. P. "Planning as Learning." *Harvard Business Review,* March–April 1988, pp. 70–74. See also Stata, R. "Organizational Learning—The Key to Management Innovation." *Sloan Management Review,* Spring 1989, pp. 63–74.
14. The Boeing Electronics Division and its 5,000 employees were subsequently merged with the Aerospace Division, and Hitsman was given responsibility for the entire combined division.
15. The time frame for the look at strategic goals is influenced both by the size of the organization and the magnitude of change required. A smaller organization than Boeing Aerospace and Electronics seeking less substantial changes might use a narrower time horizon.
16. The organizational valentines process was developed by the original large-scale design team at Ford Motor Company as an element of the participative management seminar.

References

Ackoff, R. L. *Creating the Corporate Future.* New York: John Wiley & Sons, 1981.

Ackoff, R. L. "The Circular Organization: An Update." *Academy of Management Executive,* February 1989, pp. 11–16.

Alderfer, C. P. "Boundary Relations in Organizational Diagnosis." In H. Meltzer, and F. R. Wicker, (eds.), *Humanizing Organizational Behavior* Springfield, IL: Thomas, 1976.

Argyris, C. "Skilled Incompetence." *Harvard Business Review,* September–October 1986, pp. 74–79.

Beckhard, R. *Organization Development: Strategies and Models.* Reading, MA: Addison-Wesley, 1969.

Beckhard, R., and Harris, R. T. *Organizational Transitions.* Reading, MA: Addison-Wesley, 1977.

Bion, W. R. *Experiences in Groups.* London: Turistock, 1961.

Dannemiller, K. D. "Teambuilding at a Macro Level or Ben Gay for Arthritic Organizations." Arlington, VA: NTL Publications, 1985.

De Geus, A. P. "Planning as Learning." *Harvard Business Review,* March–April 1988, pp. 70–74.

Dertouzos, M. L.; Lester, R. K.; and Solow, R. M. *Made in America: Regaining the Productive Edge.* Cambridge, MA: MIT Press, 1989.

Grayson, C. J., Jr., and O'Dell, C. *American Business: A Two-Minute Warning.* New York: Free Press, 1988.

Hayes, R. H.; Wheelwright, S. C.; and Clark, R. B. *Dynamic Manufacturing: Creating the Learning Organization.* New York: Free Press, 1988.

Imai, M. *Kaizen: The Key to Japan's Competitive Success.* New York: Random House, 1986.

Kanter, R. M. *The Change Masters.* New York: Simon & Schuster, 1983.

Keichel, W., III. "The Organization That Learns." *Fortune,* March 12, 1990, pp. 133–36.

Lindaman, E. B., and Lippitt, R. O. *Choosing the Future You Prefer.* Washington, DC: Development Publications, 1979.

Lippitt, R. "Future before You Plan." In *NTL Managers' Handbook.* Arlington, VA: NTL Institute, 1982.

Miller, E. J., and Rice, A. K. *Systems of Organization.* London: Tavistock, 1967.

Mills, D. Q., and Lovell, M. R., Jr. "Enhancing Competitiveness: The Contribution of Employee Relations." In B. R. Scott and G. C. Lodge (eds.), *U.S. Competitiveness in the World Economy.* Boston: Harvard Business School Press, 1985, pp. 455–78.

Mitroff, I. I. *Business Not as Usual.* San Francisco: Jossey-Bass Publishers, 1987.

Pascale, R., and Athos, A. *The Art of Japanese Management.* New York: Simon & Schuster, 1980.

Peters, T. *Thriving on Chaos.* New York: Alfred A. Knopf, 1987.

Peters, T. "Restoring American Competitiveness: Looking for New Models of Organizations." *Academy of Management Executive,* May 1988, pp. 103–9.

Porter, M. E. "The Competitive Advantage of Nations." *Harvard Business Review,* March–April, 1990, pp. 73–93.

Postman, N. *Amusing Ourselves to Death: Public Discourse in the Age of Show Business.* New York: Viking Penguin, 1985.

"Rethinking Japan." *Business Week,* August 7, 1989, pp. 44–52.

Schindler-Rainman, E., and Lippitt, R. O. *Collaborative Community: Mobilizing Citizens for Action.* Riverside: University of California, 1980.

Schutz, W. *The Truth Option.* Berkeley, CA: Ten Speed Press, 1984.

Stata, R. "Organizational Learning—The Key to Management Innovation." *Sloan Management Review,* Spring 1989, pp. 63–74.

Thompson, G. "Large-System Change at the Executive Level in a Traditional Maufacturing Industry." Pepperdine University, unpublished master's thesis, 1989.

United Nations International Trade Statistics Yearbook. New York: United Nations Publication, 1989.

Vaill, P. B. "Seven Process Frontiers for Organization Development." George Washington University, 1986, prepublication draft.

Waterman, R. H., Jr. *The Renewal Factor.* Toronto: Bantam Books, 1987.

Weisbord, M. R. *Productive Workplaces.* San Francisco: Jossey-Bass, 1987a.

Weisbord, M. R. "Toward Third-Wave Managing and Consulting." *Organizational Dynamics,* Winter 1987b, pp. 4–24.

READING 25
CENTERS OF EXCELLENCE:
EMPOWERING PEOPLE TO MANAGE CHANGE

Steven W. Lyle
Robert A. Zawacki

Problems Addressed

Historically, organizations have bounced from centralized organizational structures to decentralized structures and back again. The cycle of restructuring has been endless; only the specific forms of redesign have changed.

Against this backdrop, today's information technology (IT) managers attempt to add value to the bottom line of their business units. While facing reductions in staff, they are challenged to maintain or even increase customer satisfaction and productivity.

IT managers look to structural change as the answer to the multiple challenges they face. The efforts of many managers to apply the latest quick-fix or management tenets often fail, however, because they aim to implement changes designed for the organizations of the 1950s, not the 1990s.

In the past, change flowed along a reasonably predictable course. Individual contributors in the IT organization adjusted to change by working harder and smarter, and by introducing technology that helped them stay ahead of change. Today's organizations, however, are facing high-speed random change that affects the direction, focus, strategy, and behaviors of the organization and its members.[1]

Several similar organizational structures have been designed to facilitate random change: the learning organization, the horizontal organization, the shamrock organization, the STAR (i.e., strategic goals in a constant state of transition and renewal) organization, and the high-velocity organization. One additional, evolving design is the

Source: Reprinted by permission from *Information Management: Strategy, Systems, and Technologies* (1-03-35), pp. 1–7, 1996. Copyright CRC Press, Boca Raton, Florida.

center of excellence (COE). This article describes the center of excellence and reports on Texas Instruments' experience with it.

Conceptual Model of the Center of Excellence

Organizational design and restructuring have traditionally involved the transfer of control—the control of people. Yet organizational redesign is not about controlling people. It is about providing a strategy and structure that facilitates the growth of people by giving them the opportunity to do their best work. True organizational restructuring enables people to use their unique talents and abilities to the best interest of the business or institution—in other words, it empowers them.

The concept of a center of excellence is designed to prevent businesses from repeating past mistakes and stop the constant transfer of control over people. However, effective implementation of a center of excellence can only be accomplished by change agents who have abandoned the mindset of the 1950s.

The COE model concentrates on the acquisition and development of the skill sets that foster the distinctive competencies the organization needs to remain competitive. Two mutually dependent imperatives are key to the success of today's organization:

1. An organizational structure must be implemented that ensures fast mobilization and development of intellectual property (i.e., time-based competition).

2. The organization must engage and keep the customer's attention (i.e., customer satisfaction).

Most organizations have focused more on the second imperative than on the first—that is, they focus on the execution of projects (i.e., engagement of customers) rather than on investing in the development of their people. This pattern is not the result of a lack of desire to invest in people or poor management per se; rather, it stems from a lack of focus. Organizational leaders and managers are human, and they can only focus their attention on a limited number of tasks.

Lack of focus on the development of people has caused many organizations to perform poorly in their ability to engage customers. The end result is that they not only lose customers, they lose their people too. Many companies never recover from this costly spiral.

Characteristics of a Center of Excellence

The COE model provides a framework for creating an environment that allows organizations to address the imperatives for success in the 1990s and gain competitive advantage. The mission of a COE is to place people resources where they are needed most by the business and to ensure that people are trained appropriately and have the necessary experiences and background to succeed on projects.

A COE is defined by the following characteristics:

- It is a logical grouping of related skills or disciplines.
- It is an administrative entity focused on the well-being and development of people.
- It is a place where individuals learn skills and share knowledge across functional boundaries.
- It is a physical organizational unit in which members are all together or a virtual unit that is only a learning and communications vehicle.
- It matches resources to demand.

Appropriate placement, training, and development of human resources necessitates that the COE be staffed with a forward-thinking coach who is able to stay ahead of the need curve. To ensure that there is an equal emphasis on the two organizational imperatives to success—time-based competition and user satisfaction—the responsibilities of the coach must be separate from those of the organization leader or project leader. Separating the coach's responsibilities not only helps achieve this equality of emphasis, it promotes the cultural change process by sending a clear signal to the organization that management is serious about valuing its people resources. When people feel valued, they add value to the customer. The COE is about valuing people.

IT Transformation at Texas Instruments

Like many IT organizations around the world, the IT organization at Dallas-based Texas Instruments is faced with increased pressure to perform and deliver at greatly reduced cycle times. To meet the challenge, the IT organization commissioned a project to reengineer information technology at Texas Instruments. The project is known by the acronym RITTI.

The IT leadership team recognized that a transformation of the IT environment requires a concurrent engineering approach involving several elements:

- Organization.
- People.
- Business processes.
- Technology.

The team realized that each of these elements alone would not guarantee successful business leadership for the IT organization or its customers. Considering these elements together, however, could achieve major improvements.

Three major strategies address the elements:

1. A process strategy necessitates that the team map, understand, and address entire business processes versus piecemeal patch work.
2. An architecture strategy based on Texas Instruments' component-based applications

development methodology and object-modeling techniques separates the presentation level, the data level, and the logic (i.e., business rules) level. The methodology is facilitated by Composer and Arranger, two business products of Texas Instruments Software, as well as by repository technology currently being jointly developed by Texas Instruments Software and Microsoft Corp.

3. An organization and people strategy promotes the ability to develop, deploy, and retain the critical skills needed to compete.

Texas Instruments has successfully implemented the center of excellence concept to achieve an equality of focus between the development of human resources and the engagement of customers and to allow the IT team to develop the talent needed to refine and execute the three transformation strategies. Unlike many organizational leadership bodies whose members assert that people are their most valued resource, the leadership team at Texas Instruments wanted to back its words with actions.

Horizontal Skills-Centered Units

Texas Instruments' IT organization went from a vertical functional-department structure to a horizontal skills-centered COE structure that sources people to vertical project teams across the organization. The COE structure separates the traditional elements of control between two distinct roles: a COE coach and a project or organization leader.

To ensure that everyone understands the roles and the accountability within the COE structure, the IT organization rewrote organizational processes to reflect the new roles. The processes were published and then explained during open discussion meetings. Some of the major processes rewritten for the IT organization at Texas Instruments include:

- The performance-evaluation process.
- The development planning process.

- The compensation planning process.
- The staffing and assignment process.
- The knowledge-capture process.
- The cost-management and labor-tracking process.

Originally published in October 1994 by an implementation team, the processes were refined in June 1995. Each process is currently owned by a COE coach who is responsible for leading any further refinement activity. Both the coach and project or organization leader work with COE members to ensure that each individual understands—from both a project standpoint and a self-development standpoint—the requirements of success within the organization and the market.

Responsibilities of the COE Coach. The COE coach has no responsibilities outside the center of excellence. The responsibilities of the coach include:

- Training, developing, and assessing COE members in support of projects.
- Mentoring COE members in their areas of expertise or discipline.
- Facilitating and enabling the exchange and sharing of ideas and information.
- Recruiting and facilitating the assignment of individuals to projects.
- Managing the base salaries of COE members.
- Providing administrative support to COE members.
- Managing costs within the COE.

Responsibilities of the Project or Organization Leader. The project or organization leader/manager has the following responsibilities:

- Attaining performance objectives for all project milestones.
- Forecasting time-phased and skills-based resource requirements.
- Providing technical project direction and setting task-level priorities.

- Validating COE core competencies and future skills development.
- Providing coaches with feedback from team members' performance evaluations in support of the performance-evaluation feedback process and the promotion and base-salary adjustment process.
- Initiating and participating in the corrective-action process regarding performance issues.
- Managing and distributing variable compensation to project members.

Human Resource and Other Support Programs.

The center of excellence at Texas Instruments is supported by three human-resource-related processes that are of great importance to the individual and the organization. These are:

- The staffing and assignment process.
- The performance-evaluation process.
- The compensation planning process.

The following sections summarize the significant characteristics of these processes.

The Staffing and Assignment Process.

Under the staffing and assignment process, administrative responsibilities for individuals resides with only one COE. Individuals are encouraged to remain with their project assignment until completion of a major phase or milestone. They are also encouraged to participate in a wide range of assignments that provide exposure across the IT environment.

An open process for communication of assignment opportunities helps individuals achieve maximum exposure across the organization. Assignment changes are discussed with all involved parties (i.e., the individual, the project or organization leader, and the coach) before they occur.

The Performance-Evaluation Process.

Performance review sessions are held with the coach when individuals change assignments, or at least annually. They are initiated by individuals and based on feedback the coach obtains from various project or organization leaders. In addition, individuals are expected to collect 360-degree feedback throughout the year. As much as possible, performance review sessions are separate from the compensation review process.

The Compensation Planning Process.

COE coaches manage the base pay (i.e., salary) of COE members. Base pay is determined according to the individual's competency level within the skill set/discipline, customer results, skills acquisition, teamwork, and knowledge sharing. Project and organization leaders manage variable compensation based on superb execution of tasks that map back to a key customer or organizational success criterion. All leaders are compensated based on attainment of performance objectives and staff development, not organization size.

Recommended Course of Action

Many IT organizations are limited in their ability to enable the type of business change required by their customers. These organizations must take care not to repeat the historical change pattern of centralization and decentralization.

Random change warrants implementation of a learning organization that is based on the center of excellence model. Successful implementation of a center of excellence depends on several factors.

CSFs for Implementing a Center of Excellence.

A successful implementation has the following:

- Leaders who are visibly committed to the change in focus.
- A clearly articulated vision.
- Benchmarking activity that facilitates learning.
- Clear communication of the reason for and benefits of the change.
- Involvement of as many organizational members as possible.

- Thorough communications planning throughout the transition.

A center of excellence implemented along these lines provides the flexibility organizations need to meet the two imperatives of success:

- It engages the customer.
- It provides continuity to an individual's career and development while adding value to the bottom line of the customer in a timely fashion.

Organizations should not waste their and their peoples' time with repeated reorganizations. An organizational design that is flexible, responsive to random change, and customer-focused will outlive the next technology wave. The center of excellence model offers a fix, not another management fad.

Endnotes

1. R. A. Zawacki et al; *Transforming the Mature Information Technology Organization* (Colorado Springs CO: EagleStar Publishing, 1995), pp. 22–23.

READING 26
BUILDING A LEARNING ORGANIZATION

David A. Garvin

Continuous improvement programs are sprouting up all over as organizations strive to better themselves and gain an edge. The topic list is long and varied, and sometimes it seems as though a program a month is needed just to keep up. Unfortunately, failed programs far outnumber successes, and improvement rates remain distressingly low. Why? Because most companies have failed to grasp a basic truth. Continuous improvement requires a commitment to learning.

How, after all, can an organization improve without first learning something new? Solving a problem, introducing a product, and reengineering a process all require seeing the world in a new light and acting accordingly. In the absence of learning, companies—and individuals—simply repeat old practices. Change remains cosmetic, and improvements are either fortuitous or short-lived.

A few farsighted executives—Ray Stata of Analog Devices, Gordon Forward of Chaparral Steel, Paul Allaire of Xerox—have recognized the link between learning and continuous improvement and have begun to refocus their companies around it. Scholars too have jumped on the bandwagon, beating the drum for "learning organizations" and "knowledge-creating companies." In rapidly changing businesses like semiconductors and consumer electronics, these ideas are fast taking hold. Yet despite the encouraging signs, the topic in large part remains murky, confused, and difficult to penetrate.

Meaning, Management, and Measurement

Scholars are partly to blame. Their discussions of learning organizations have often been reverential and utopian, filled with near mystical terminology.

Paradise, they would have you believe, is just around the corner. Peter Senge, who popularized learning organizations in his book *The Fifth Discipline,* described them as places "where people continually expand their capacity to create the results they truly desire, where new and expansive patterns of thinking are nurtured, where collective aspiration is set free, and where people are continually learning how to learn together."[1] To achieve these ends, Senge suggested the use of five "component technologies": systems thinking, personal mastery, mental models, shared vision, and team learning. In a similar spirit, Ikujiro Nonaka characterized knowledge-creating companies as places where "inventing new knowledge is not a specialized activity . . . it is a way of behaving, indeed, a way of being, in which everyone is a knowledge worker."[2] Nonaka suggested that companies use metaphors and organizational redundancy to focus thinking, encourage dialogue, and make tacit, instinctively understood ideas explicit.

Sound idyllic? Absolutely. Desirable? Without question. But does it provide a framework for action? Hardly. The recommendations are far too abstract, and too many questions remain unanswered. How, for example, will managers know when their companies have become learning organizations? What concrete changes in behavior are required? What policies and programs must be in place? How do you get from here to there?

Most discussions of learning organizations finesse these issues. Their focus is high philosophy and grand themes, sweeping metaphors rather than the gritty details of practice. Three critical issues are left unresolved; yet each is essential for effective implementation. First is the question of *meaning.* We need a plausible, well-grounded definition of learning organizations; it must be actionable and easy to apply. Second is the question of *management.* We need clearer guidelines for practice, filled with operational advice rather than high aspirations. And third is the question of *measurement*. We need better tools for assessing an organization's rate and level of learning to ensure that gains have in fact been made.

Once these "three Ms" are addressed, managers will have a firmer foundation for launching learning organizations. Without this groundwork, progress is unlikely, and for the simplest of reasons. For learning to become a meaningful corporate goal, it must first be understood.

What Is a Learning Organization?

Surprisingly, a clear definition of learning has proved to be elusive over the years. Organizational theorists have studied learning for a long time; the accompanying quotations suggest that there is still considerable disagreement (see the insert "Definitions of Organizational Learning"). Most scholars view organizational learning as a process that unfolds over time and link it with knowledge acquisition and improved performance. But they differ on other important matters.

Some, for example, believe that behavioral change is required for learning; others insist that new ways of thinking are enough. Some cite information processing as the mechanism through which learning takes place; others propose shared insights, organizational routines, even memory. And some think that organizational learning is common, while others believe that flawed, self-serving interpretations are the norm.

How can we discern among this cacophony of voices yet build on earlier insights? As a first step, consider the following definition:

> A learning organization is an organization skilled at creating, acquiring, and transferring knowledge, and at modifying its behavior to reflect new knowledge and insights.

This definition begins with a simple truth: new ideas are essential if learning is to take place. Sometimes they are created de novo, through flashes of insight or creativity; at other times they arrive from outside the organization or are communicated by knowledgeable insiders. Whatever their source, these ideas are the trigger for organizational improvement. But they cannot by themselves create a learning organization. *Without accompanying changes in the way that work gets done, only the potential for improvement exists.*

This is a surprisingly stringent test for it rules out a number of obvious candidates for learning organizations. Many universities fail to qualify, as do many consulting firms. Even General Motors, despite its recent efforts to improve performance, is found wanting. All of these organizations have been effective at creating or acquiring new knowledge but notably less successful in applying that knowledge to their own activities. Total quality management, for example, is now taught at many business schools, yet the number using it to guide their own decision making is very small. Organizational consultants advise clients on social dynamics and small-group behavior but are notorious for their own infighting and factionalism. And GM, with a few exceptions (like Saturn and NUMMI), has had little success in revamping its manufacturing practices, even though its managers are experts on lean manufacturing, JIT production, and the requirements for improved quality of work life.

Organizations that do pass the definitional test—Honda, Corning, and General Electric come quickly to mind—have, by contrast, become adept at translating new knowledge into new ways of behaving. These companies actively manage the learning process to ensure that it occurs by design rather than by chance. Distinctive policies and practices are responsible for their success; they form the building blocks of learning organizations.

Building Blocks

Learning organizations are skilled at five main activities: systematic problem solving, experimentation with new approaches, learning from their own experience and past history, learning from the experiences and best practices of others, and transferring

Definitions of Organizational Learning

Scholars have proposed a variety of definitions of organizational learning. Here is a small sample:

Organizational learning means the process of improving actions through better knowledge and understanding.
C. Marlene Fiol and Marjorie A. Lyles, "Organizational Learning," *Academy of Management Review,* October 1985.

An entity learns if, through its processing of information, the range of its potential behaviors is changed.
George P. Huber, "Organizational Learning: The Contributing Processes and the Literatures," *Organization Science,* February 1991.

Organizations are seen as learning by encoding inferences from history into routines that guide behavior.
Barbara Levitt and James G. March, "Organizational Learning," *American Review of Sociology,* Vol. 14, 1988.

Organizational learning is a process of detecting and correcting error.
Chris Argyris, "Double Loop Learning in Organizations," *Harvard Business Review,* September– October 1977.

Organizational learning occurs through shared insights, knowledge, and mental models . . . [and] builds on past knowledge and experience—that is, on memory.
Ray Stata, "Organizational Learning—The Key to Management Innovation," *Sloan Management Review,* Spring 1989.

knowledge quickly and efficiently throughout the organization. Each is accompanied by a distinctive mind-set, tool kit, and pattern of behavior. Many companies practice these activities to some degree. But few are consistently successful because they rely largely on happenstance and isolated examples. By creating systems and processes that support these activities and integrate them into the fabric of daily operations, companies can manage their learning more effectively.

1. Systematic problem solving. This first activity rests heavily on the philosophy and methods of the quality movement. Its underlying ideas, now widely accepted, include:

- Relying on the scientific method, rather than guesswork, for diagnosing problems (what Deming calls the "Plan, Do, Check, Act"

cycle, and others refer to as "hypothesis-generating, hypothesis-testing" techniques).

- Insisting on data, rather than assumptions, as background for decision making (what quality practitioners call "fact-based management").

- Using simple statistical tools (histograms, Pareto charts, correlations, cause-and-effect diagrams) to organize data and draw inferences.

Most training programs focus primarily on problem-solving techniques, using exercises and practical examples. These tools are relatively straightforward and easily communicated; the necessary mind-set, however, is more difficult to establish. Accuracy and precision are essential for learning. Employees must therefore become more disciplined in their thinking and more attentive to

Xerox's problem-solving process

Step	Question to Be Answered	Expansion/ Divergence	Contraction/ Convergence	What's Needed to Go to the Next Step
1. Identify and select problem	What do we want to change?	Lots of problems for consideration	One problem statement, one "desired state" agreed upon	Identification of the gap "Desired state" described in observable terms
2. Analyze problem	What's preventing us from reaching the "desired state"?	Lots of potential causes identified	Key cause(s) identified and verified	Key cause(s) documented and ranked
3. Generate potential solutions	How *could* we make the change?	Lots of ideas on how to solve the problem	Potential solutions clarified	Solution list
4. Select and plan the solution	What's the *best* way to do it?	Lots of criteria for evaluating potential solutions Lots of ideas on how to implement and evaluate the selection solution	Criteria to use for evaluating solution agreed upon Implementation and evaluation plans agreed upon	Plan for making and monitoring the change Measurement criteria to evaluate solution effectiveness
5. Implement the solution	Are we following the plan?		Implementation of agreed-on contingency plans (if necessary)	Solution in place
6. Evaluate the solution	How well did it work?		Effectiveness of solution agreed upon Continuing problems (if any) identified	Verification that the problem is solved, or Agreement to address continuing problems

details. They must continually ask, "How do we know that's true?", recognizing that close enough is not good enough if real learning is to take place. They must push beyond obvious symptoms to assess underlying causes, often collecting evidence when conventional wisdom says it is unnecessary. Otherwise, the organization will remain a prisoner of "gut facts" and sloppy reasoning, and learning will be stifled.

Xerox has mastered this approach on a companywide scale. In 1983, senior managers launch the company's Leadership Through Quality initiative; since then, all employees have been trained in small-group activities and problem-solving techniques. Today a six-step process is used for virtually all decisions (see the insert "Xerox's Problem-Solving Process"). Employees are provided with tools in

four areas: generating ideas and collecting information (brainstorming, interviewing, surveying); reaching consensus (list reduction, rating forms, weighted voting); analyzing and displaying data (cause-and-effect diagrams, force-field analysis); and planning actions (flow charts, Gantt charts). They then practice these tools during training sessions that last several days. Training is presented in "family groups," members of the same department or business-unit team, and the tools are applied to real problems facing the group. The result of this process has been a common vocabulary and a consistent, companywide approach to problem solving. Once employees have been trained, they are expected to use the techniques at all meetings, and no topic is off-limits. When a high-level group was formed to review Xerox's organizational structure and suggest alternatives, it employed the very same process and tools.[3]

2. Experimentation. This activity involves the systematic searching for and testing of new knowledge. Using the scientific method is essential, and there are obvious parallels to systematic problem solving. But unlike problem solving, experimentation is usually motivated by opportunity and expanding horizons, not by current difficulties. It takes two main forms: ongoing programs and one-of-a-kind demonstration projects.

Ongoing programs normally involve a continuing series of small experiments, designed to produce incremental gains in knowledge. They are the mainstay of most continuous improvement programs and are especially common on the shop floor. Corning, for example, experiments continually with diverse raw materials and new formulations to increase yields and provide better grades of glass. Allegheny Ludlum, a specialty steelmaker, regularly examines new rolling methods and improved technologies to raise productivity and reduce costs.

Successful ongoing programs share several characteristics. First, they work hard to ensure a steady flow of new ideas, even if they must be imported from outside the organization. Chaparral Steel sends its first-line supervisors on sabbaticals around the globe, where they visit academic and industry leaders, develop an understanding of new work practices and technologies, then bring what they've learned back to the company and apply it to daily operations. In large part as a result of these initiatives, Chaparral is one of the five lowest cost steel plants in the world. GE's Impact Program originally sent manufacturing managers to Japan to study factory innovations, such as quality circles and kanban cards, and then apply them in their own organizations; today Europe is the destination, and productivity improvement practices the target. The program is one reason GE has recorded productivity gains averaging nearly 5 percent over the last four years.

Successful ongoing programs also require an incentive system that favors risk taking. Employees must feel that the benefits of experimentation exceed the costs; otherwise, they will not participate. This creates a difficult challenge for managers, who are trapped between two perilous extremes. They must maintain accountability and control over experiments without stifling creativity by unduly penalizing employees for failures. Allegheny Ludlum has perfected this juggling act: it keeps expensive, high-impact experiments off the scorecard used to evaluate managers but requires prior approvals from four senior vice presidents. The result has been a history of productivity improvements annually averaging 7 percent to 8 percent.

Finally, ongoing programs need managers and employees who are trained in the skills required to perform and evaluate experiments. These skills are seldom intuitive and must usually be learned. They cover a broad sweep: statistical methods, like design of experiments, that efficiently compare a large number of alternatives; graphical techniques, like process analysis, that are essential for redesigning work flows; and creativity techniques, like storyboarding and role playing that keep novel ideas flowing. The most effective training programs are tightly focused and feature a small set of techniques tailored to employees' needs. Training in design of experiments, for example, is useful for manufacturing engineers, while creativity techniques are well suited to development groups.

Demonstration projects are usually larger and more complex than ongoing experiments. They involve holistic, systemwide changes, introduced at a single site, and are often undertaken with the goal of developing new organizational capabilities. Because these projects represent a sharp break from the past, they are usually designed from scratch, using a "clean slate" approach. General Foods's Topeka plant, one of the first high-commitment work systems in this country, was a pioneering demonstration project initiated to introduce the idea of self-managing teams and high levels of worker autonomy; a more recent example, designed to rethink small-car development, manufacturing, and sales, is GM's Saturn Division.

Demonstration projects share a number of distinctive characteristics:

- They are usually the first projects to embody principles and approaches that the organization hopes to adopt later on a larger scale. For this reason, they are more transitional efforts than endpoints and involve considerable "learning by doing." Mid-course corrections are common.

- They implicitly establish policy guidelines and decision rules for later projects. Managers must therefore be sensitive to the precedents they are setting and must send strong signals if they expect to establish new norms.

- They often encounter severe tests of commitment from employees who wish to see whether the rules have, in fact, changed.

- They are normally developed by strong multifunctional teams reporting directly to senior management. (For projects targeting employee involvement or quality of work life, teams should be multilevel as well.)

- They tend to have only limited impact on the rest of the organization if they are not accompanied by explicit strategies for transferring learning.

All of these characteristics appeared in a demonstration project launched by Copeland Corporation, a highly successful compressor manufacturer, in the mid-1970s. Matt Diggs, then the new CEO, wanted to transform the company's approach to manufacturing. Previously, Copeland had machined and assembled all products in a single facility. Costs were high, and quality was marginal. The problem, Diggs felt, was too much complexity.

At the outset, Diggs assigned a small, multifunctional team the task of designing a "focused factory" dedicated to a narrow, newly developed product line. The team reported directly to Diggs and took three years to complete its work. Initially, the project budget was $10 million to $12 million; that figure was repeatedly revised as the team found, through experience and with Diggs's prodding, that it could achieve dramatic improvements. The final investment, a total of $30 million, yielded unanticipated breakthroughs in reliability testing,

automatic tool adjustment, and programmable control. All were achieved through learning by doing.

The team set additional precedents during the plant's start-up and early operations. To dramatize the importance of quality, for example, the quality manager was appointed second-in-command, a significant move upward. The same reporting relationship was used at all subsequent plants. In addition, Diggs urged the plant manager to ramp up slowly to full production and resist all efforts to proliferate products. These instructions were unusual at Copeland, where the marketing department normally ruled. Both directives were quickly tested; management held firm, and the implications were felt throughout the organization. Manufacturing's stature improved, and the company as a whole recognized its competitive contribution. One observer commented, "Marketing had always run the company, so they couldn't believe it. The change was visible at the highest levels, and it went down hard."

Once the first focused factory was running smoothly—it seized 25 percent of the market in two years and held its edge in reliability for over a decade—Copeland built four more factories in quick succession. Diggs assigned members of the initial project to each factory's design team to ensure that early learnings were not lost; these people later rotated into operating assignments. Today focused factories remain the cornerstone of Copeland's manufacturing strategy and a continuing source of its cost and quality advantages.

Whether they are demonstration projects like Copeland's or ongoing programs like Allegheny Ludlum's, all forms of experimentation seek the same end: moving from superficial knowledge to deep understanding. At its simplest, the distinction is between knowing how things are done and knowing why they occur. Knowing how is partial knowledge; it is rooted in norms of behavior, standards of practice, and settings of equipment. Knowing why is more fundamental: it captures underlying cause-and-effect relationships and accommodates exceptions, adaptations, and unforeseen events. The ability to control temperatures and pressures to align grains of silicon and form silicon

Stages of Knowledge

Scholars have suggested that production and operating knowledge can be classified systematically by level or stage of understanding. At the lowest levels of manufacturing knowledge, little is known other than the characteristics of a good product. Production remains an art, and there are few clearly articulated standards or rules. An example would be Stradivarius violins. Experts agree that they produce vastly superior sound, but no one can specify precisely how they were manufactured because skilled artisans were responsible. By contrast, at the highest levels of manufacturing knowledge, all aspects of production are known and understood. All materials and processing variations are articulated and accounted for, with rules and procedures for every contingency. Here an example would be a "lights out," fully automated factory that operates for many hours without any human intervention.

In total, this framework specifies eight stages of knowledge. From lowest to highest, they are:

1. Recognizing prototypes (what is a good product?).
2. Recognizing attributes within prototypes (ability to define some conditions under which process gives good output).

3. Discriminating among attributes (which attributes are important? Experts may differ about relevance of patterns; new operators are often trained through apprenticeships).
4. Measuring attributes (some key attributes are measured; measures may be qualitative and relative).
5. Locally controlling attributes (repeatable performance; process designed by expert, but technicians can perform it).
6. Recognizing and discriminating between contingencies (production process can be mechanized and monitored manually).
7. Controlling contingencies (process can be automated).
8. Understanding procedures and controlling contingencies (process is completely understood).

Source: Adapted from work by Ramchandran Jaikumar and Roger Bohn, "The Development of Intelligent Systems for Industrial Use: A Conceptual Framework," *Research on Technological Innovation, Management and Policy,* Vol. 3 (1986), pp. 182–188.

steel is an example of knowing how; understanding the chemical and physical process that produces the alignment is knowing why.

Further distinctions are possible, as the insert "Stages of Knowledge" suggests. Operating knowledge can be arrayed in a hierarchy, moving from limited understanding and the ability to make few distinctions to more complete understanding in which all contingencies are anticipated and controlled. In this context, experimentation and problem solving foster learning by pushing organizations up the hierarchy, from lower to higher stages of knowledge.

3. Learning from past experience. Companies must review their successes and failures, assess them systematically, and record the lessons in a form that employees find open and accessible. One expert has called this process the "Santayana Review," citing the famous philosopher George Santayana, who coined the phrase "Those who cannot remember the past are condemned to repeat it." Unfortunately, too many managers today are indifferent, even hostile, to the past, and by failing to reflect on it, they let valuable knowledge escape.

A study of more than 150 new products concluded that "the knowledge gained from failures

[is] often instrumental in achieving subsequent successes. . . . In the simplest terms, failure is the ultimate teacher."[4] IBM's 360 computer series, for example, one of the most popular and profitable ever built, was based on the technology of the failed Stretch computer that preceded it. In this case, as in many others, learning occurred by chance rather than by careful planning. A few companies, however, have established processes that require their managers to periodically think about the past and learn from their mistakes.

Boeing did so immediately after its difficulties with the 737 and 747 plane programs. Both planes were introduced with much fanfare and also with serious problems. To ensure that the problems were not repeated, senior managers commissioned a high-level employee group, called Project Homework, to compare the development processes of the 737 and 747 with those of the 707 and 727, two of the company's most profitable planes. The group was asked to develop a set of "lessons learned" that could be used on future projects. After working for three years, they produced hundreds of recommendations and an inch-thick booklet. Several members of the team were then transferred to the 757 and 767 start-ups, and guided by experience, they produced the most successful, error-free launches in Boeing's history.

Other companies have used a similar retrospective approach. Like Boeing, Xerox studied its product development process, examining three troubled products in an effort to understand why the company's new business initiatives failed so often. Arthur D. Little, the consulting company, focused on its past successes. Senior management invited ADL consultants from around the world to a two-day "jamboree," featuring booths and presentations documenting a wide range of the company's most successful practices, publications, and techniques. British Petroleum went even further and established the post-project appraisal unit to review major investment projects, write up case studies, and derive lessons for planners that were then incorporated into revisions of the company's planning guidelines. A five-person unit reported to the

board of directors and reviewed six projects annually. The bulk of the time was spent in the field interviewing managers.[5] This type of review is now conducted regularly at the project level.

At the heart of this approach, one expert has observed, "is a mind-set that...enables companies to recognize the value of productive failure as contrasted with unproductive success. A productive failure is one that leads to insight, understanding, and thus an addition to the commonly held wisdom of the organization. An unproductive success occurs when something goes well, but nobody knows how or why."[6] IBM's legendary founder, Thomas Watson, Sr., apparently understood the distinction well. Company lore has it that a young manager, after losing $10 million in a risky venture, was called into Watson's office. The young man, thoroughly intimidated, began by saying, "I guess you want my resignation." Watson replied, "You can't be serious. We just spent $10 million educating you."

Fortunately, the learning process need not be so expensive. Case studies and post-project reviews like those of Xerox and British Petroleum can be performed with little cost other than managers' time. Companies can also enlist the help of faculty and students at local colleges or universities; they bring fresh perspectives and view internships and case studies as opportunities to gain experience and increase their own learning. A few companies have established computerized data banks to speed up the learning process. At Paul Revere Life Insurance, management requires all problem-solving teams to complete short registration forms describing their proposed projects if they hope to qualify for the company's award program. The company then enters the forms into its computer system and can immediately retrieve a listing of other groups of people who have worked or are working on the topic, along with a contact person. Relevant experience is then just a telephone call away.

4. Learning from others. Of course, not all learning comes from reflection and self-analysis. Sometimes the most powerful insights come from looking outside one's immediate environment to gain a new perspective. Enlightened managers

know that even companies in completely different businesses can be fertile sources of ideas and catalysts for creative thinking. At these organizations, enthusiastic borrowing is replacing the "not invented here" syndrome. Milliken calls the process SIS, for "Steal Ideas Shamelessly"; the broader term for it is benchmarking.

According to one expert, "benchmarking is an ongoing investigation and learning experience that ensures that best industry practices are uncovered, analyzed, adopted, and implemented."[7] The greatest benefits come from studying *practices,* the way that work gets done, rather than results, and from involving line managers in the process. Almost anything can be benchmarked. Xerox, the concept's creator, has applied it to billing, warehousing, and automated manufacturing. Milliken has been even more creative: in an inspired moment, it benchmarked Xerox's approach to benchmarking.

Unfortunately, there is still considerable confusion about the requirements for successful benchmarking. Benchmarking is not "industrial tourism," a series of ad hoc visits to companies that have received favorable publicity or won quality awards. Rather, it is a disciplined process that begins with a thorough search to identify best-practice organizations, continues with careful study of one's own practices and performance, progresses through systematic site visits and interviews, and concludes with an analysis of results, development of recommendations, and implementation. While time-consuming, the process need not be terribly expensive. AT&T's Benchmarking Group estimates that a moderate-sized project takes four to six months and incurs out-of-pocket costs of $20,000 (when personnel costs are included, the figure is three to four times higher).

Benchmarking is one way of gaining an outside perspective; another, equally fertile source of ideas is customers. Conversations with customers invariably stimulate learning; they are, after all, experts in what they do. Customers can provide up-to-date product information, competitive comparisons, insights into changing preferences, and immediate feedback about service and patterns of use. And companies need these insights at all levels, from the executive suite to the shop floor. At Motorola, members of the Operating and Policy Committee, including the CEO, meet personally and on a regular basis with customers. At Worthington Steel, all machine operators make periodic, unescorted trips to customers' factories to discuss their needs.

Sometimes customers can't articulate their needs or remember even the most recent problems they have had with a product or service. If that's the case, managers must observe them in action. Xerox employs a number of anthropologists at its Palo Alto Research Center to observe users of new document products in their offices. Digital Equipment has developed an interactive process called "contextual inquiry" that is used by software engineers to observe users of new technologies as they go about their work. Milliken has created "first-delivery teams" that accompany the first shipment of all products; team members follow the product through the customer's production process to see how it is used and then develop ideas for further improvement.

Whatever the source of outside ideas, learning will only occur in a receptive environment. Managers can't be defensive and must be open to criticism or bad news. This is a difficult challenge, but it is essential for success. Companies that approach customers assuming that "we must be right, they have to be wrong" or visit other organizations certain that "they can't teach us anything" seldom learn very much. Learning organizations, by contrast, cultivate the art of open, attentive listening.

5. Transferring knowledge. For learning to be more than a local affair, knowledge must be spread quickly and efficiently throughout the organization. Ideas carry maximum impact when they are shared broadly rather than held in a few hands. A variety of mechanisms spur this process, including written, oral, and visual reports, site visits and tours, personnel rotation programs, education and training programs, and standardization programs. Each has distinctive strengths and weaknesses.

Reports and tours are by far the most popular mediums. Reports serve many purposes: they summarize findings, provide checklists of dos and don'ts, and describe important processes and events. They cover a multitude of topics, from benchmarking studies to accounting conventions to newly discovered marketing techniques. Today written reports are often supplemented by videotapes, which offer greater immediacy and fidelity.

Tours are an equally popular means of transferring knowledge, especially for large, multidivisional organizations with multiple sites. The most effective tours are tailored to different audiences and needs. To introduce its managers to the distinctive manufacturing practices of New United Motor Manufacturing Inc. (NUMMI), its joint venture with Toyota, General Motors developed a series of specialized tours. Some were geared to upper and middle managers, while others were aimed at lower ranks. Each tour described the policies, practices, and systems that were most relevant to that level of management.

Despite their popularity, reports and tours are relatively cumbersome ways of transferring knowledge. The gritty details that lie behind complex management concepts are difficult to communicate secondhand. Absorbing facts by reading them or seeing them demonstrated is one thing; experiencing them personally is quite another. As a leading cognitive scientist has observed, "It is very difficult to become knowledgeable in a passive way. Actively experiencing something is considerably more valuable than having it described."[8] For this reason, personnel rotation programs are one of the most powerful methods of transferring knowledge.

In many organizations, expertise is held locally: in a particularly skilled computer technician, perhaps, a savvy global brand manager, or a division head with a track record of successful joint ventures. Those in daily contact with these experts benefit enormously from their skills, but their field of influence is relatively narrow. Transferring them to different parts of the organization helps share the wealth. Transfers may be from division to division, department to department, or facility to facility; they may involve senior, middle, or first-level managers. A supervisor experienced in just-in-time

production, for example, might move to another factory to apply the methods there, or a successful division manager might transfer to a lagging division to invigorate it with already proven ideas. The CEO of Time Life used the latter approach when he shifted the president of the company's music division, who had orchestrated several years of rapid growth and high profits through innovative marketing, to the presidency of the book division, where profits were flat because of continued reliance on traditional marketing concepts.

Line to staff transfers are another option. These are most effective when they allow experienced managers to distill what they have learned and diffuse it across the company in the form of new standards, policies, or training programs. Consider how PPG used just such a transfer to advance its human resource practices around the concept of high-commitment work systems. In 1986, PPG constructed a new float-glass plant in Chehalis, Washington; it employed a radically new technology as well as innovations in human resource management that were developed by the plant manager and his staff. All workers were organized into small, self-managing teams with responsibility for work assignments, scheduling, problem solving and improvement, and peer review. After several years running the factory, the plant manager was promoted to director of human resources for the entire glass group. Drawing on his experiences at Chehalis, he developed a training program geared toward first-level supervisors that taught the behaviors needed to manage employees in a participative, self-managing environment.

As the PPG example suggests, education and training programs are powerful tools for transferring knowledge. But for maximum effectiveness, they must be linked explicitly to implementation. All too often, trainers assume that new knowledge will be applied without taking concrete steps to ensure that trainees actually follow through. Seldom do trainers provide opportunities for practice, and few programs consciously promote the application of their teachings after employees have returned to their jobs.

Xerox and GTE are exceptions. As noted earlier, when Xerox introduced problem-solving techniques to its employees in the 1980s, everyone, from the top to the bottom of the organization, was taught in small departmental or divisional groups led by their immediate superior. After an introduction to concepts and techniques, each group applied what they learned to a real-life work problem. In a similar spirit, GTE's Quality: The Competitive Edge program was offered to teams of business-unit presidents and the managers reporting to them. At the beginning of the 3-day course, each team received a request from a company officer to prepare a complete quality plan for their unit, based on the course concepts, within 60 days. Discussion periods of two to three hours were set aside during the program so that teams could begin working on their plans. After the teams submitted their reports, the company officers studied them, and then the teams implemented them. This GTE program produced dramatic improvements in quality, including a recent semifinalist spot in the Baldrige Awards.

The GTE example suggests another important guideline: knowledge is more likely to be transferred effectively when the right incentives are in place. If employees know that their plans will be evaluated and implemented—in other words, that their learning will be applied—progress is far more likely. At most companies, the status quo is well entrenched; only if managers and employees see new ideas as being in their own best interest will they accept them gracefully. AT&T has developed a creative approach that combines strong incentives with information sharing. Called The Chairman's Quality Award (CQA), it is an internal quality competition modeled on the Baldrige prize but with an important twist: awards are given not only for absolute performance (using the same 1,000-point scoring system as Baldrige) but also for improvements in scoring from the previous year. Gold, silver, and bronze Improvement Awards are given to units that have improved their scores 200, 150, and 100 points, respectively. These awards provide the incentive for change. An accompanying Pockets of Excellence program simplifies knowledge transfer. Every year, it identifies every unit within the company that has scored at least 60 percent of the possible points in each award category and then publicizes the names of these units using written reports and electronic mail.

Measuring Learning

Managers have long known that "if you can't measure it, you can't manage it." This maxim is as true of learning as it is of any other corporate objective. Traditionally, the solution has been "learning curves" and "manufacturing process functions." Both concepts date back to the discovery, during the 1920s and 1930s, that the costs of airframe manufacturing fell predictably with increases in cumulative volume. These increases were viewed as proxies for greater manufacturing knowledge, and most early studies examined their impact on the costs of direct labor. Later studies expanded the focus, looking at total manufacturing costs and the impact of experience in other industries, including shipbuilding, oil refining, and consumer electronics. Typically, learning rates were in the 80 percent to 85 percent range (meaning that with a doubling of cumulative production, costs fell to 80 percent to 85 percent of their previous level), although there was wide variation.

Firms like the Boston Consulting Group raised these ideas to a higher level in the 1970s. Drawing on the logic of learning curves, they argued that industries as a whole faced "experience curves," costs and prices that fell by predictable amounts as industries grew and their total production increased. With this observation, consultants suggested, came an iron law of competition. To enjoy the benefits of experience, companies would have to rapidly increase their production ahead of competitors to lower prices and gain market share.

Both learning and experience curves are still widely used, especially in the aerospace, defense, and electronics industries. Boeing, for instance, has established learning curves for every work station in its assembly plant; they assist in monitoring productivity, determining work flows and staffing levels, and setting prices and profit margins on new airplanes. Experience curves are common in semiconductors and consumer electronics, where they are used to forecast industry costs and prices.

For companies hoping to become learning organizations, however, these measures are incomplete. They focus on only a single measure of output (cost or price) and ignore learning that affects other competitive variables, like quality, delivery, or new product introductions. They suggest only one possible learning driver (total production volumes) and ignore both the possibility of learning in mature industries, where output is flat, and the possibility that learning might be driven by other sources, such as new technology or the challenge posed by competing products. Perhaps most important, they tell us little about the sources of learning or the levers of change.

Another measure has emerged in response to these concerns. Called the "half-life" curve, it was originally developed by Analog Devices, a leading semiconductor manufacturer, as a way of comparing internal improvement rates. A half-life curve measures the time it takes to achieve a 50 percent improvement in a specified performance measure. When represented graphically, the performance measure (defect rates, on-time delivery, time to market) is plotted on the vertical axis, using a logarithmic scale, and the time scale (days, months, years) is plotted horizontally. Steeper slopes then represent faster learning (see the insert "The Half-Life Curve" for an illustration).

The logic is straightforward. Companies, division, or departments that take less time to improve must be learning faster than their peers. In the long run, their short learning cycles will translate into superior performance. The 50 percent target is a measure of convenience; it was derived empirically from studies of successful improvement processes at a wide range of companies. Half-life curves are also flexible. Unlike learning and experience curves, they work on any output measure, and they are not confined to costs or prices. In addition, they are easy to operationalize, they provide a simple measuring stick, and they allow for ready comparison among groups.

Yet even half-life curves have an important weakness: they focus solely on results. Some types of knowledge take years to digest, with few visible changes in performance for long periods. Creating a total quality culture, for instance, or developing new approaches to product development are difficult systemic changes. Because of their long gestation periods, half-life curves or any other measures focused solely on results are unlikely to capture any short-run learning that has occurred. A more comprehensive framework is needed to track progress.

Organizational learning can usually be traced through three overlapping stages. The first step is cognitive. Members of the organization are exposed to new ideas, expand their knowledge, and begin to think differently. The second step is behavioral. Employees begin to internalize new insights and alter their behavior. And the third step is performance improvement, with changes in behavior leading to measurable improvements in results: superior quality, better delivery, increased market share, or other tangible gains. Because cognitive and behavioral changes typically precede improvements in performance, a complete learning audit must include all three.

Surveys, questionnaires, and interviews are useful for this purpose. At the cognitive level, they would focus on attitudes and depth of understanding. Have employees truly understood the meaning of self-direction and teamwork, or are the terms still unclear? At PPG, a team of human resource experts periodically audits every manufacturing plant, including extensive interviews with shop-floor employees, to ensure that the concepts are well understood. Have new approaches to customer service been fully accepted? At its 1989 Worldwide Marketing Managers' Meeting, Ford presented participants with a series of hypothetical situations in which customer complaints were in conflict with short-term dealer or company profit goals and asked how they would respond. Surveys like these are the first step toward identifying changed attitudes and new ways of thinking.

The Half-Life Curve

Analog Devices has used half-life curves to compare the performance of its divisions. Here monthly data on customer service are graphed for seven divisions. Division C is the clear winner: even though it started with a high proportion of late deliveries, its rapid learning rate led eventually to the best absolute performance. Divisions D, E, and G have been far less successful, with little or no improvement in on-time service over the period.

On-Time Customer Service Performance—Monthly Data (August 1987–July 1988)

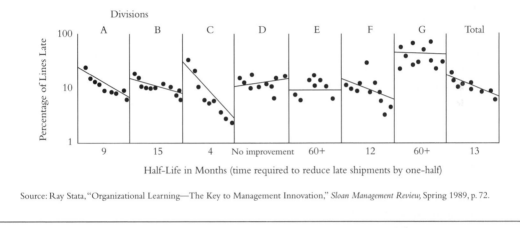

Half-Life in Months (time required to reduce late shipments by one-half)

Source: Ray Stata, "Organizational Learning—The Key to Management Innovation," *Sloan Management Review,* Spring 1989, p. 72.

To assess behavioral changes, surveys and questionnaires must be supplemented by direct observation. Here the proof is in the doing, and there is no substitute for seeing employees in action. Domino's Pizza uses "mystery shoppers" to assess managers' commitment to customer service at its individual stores; L.L. Bean places telephone orders with its own operators to assess service levels. Other companies invite outside consultants to visit, attend meetings, observe employees in action, and then report what they have learned. In many ways, this approach mirrors that of examiners for the Baldrige Award, who make several-day site visits to semifinalists to see whether the companies' deeds match the words on their applications.

Finally, a comprehensive learning audit also measures performance. Half-life curves or other performance measures are essential for ensuring that cognitive and behavioral changes have actually produced results. Without them, companies would lack a rationale for investing in learning and the assurance that learning was serving the organization's ends.

First Steps

Learning organizations are not built overnight. Most successful examples are the products of carefully cultivated attitudes, commitments, and management processes that have accrued slowly and steadily over time. Still, some changes can be made immediately. Any company that wishes to become a learning organization can begin by taking a few simple steps.

The first step is to foster an environment that is conducive to learning. There must be time for reflection and analysis, to think about strategic plans, dissect customer needs, assess current work systems, and invent new products. Learning is difficult when employees are harried or rushed; it tends to be driven out by the pressures of the moment. Only if top management explicitly frees up employees' time for the purpose does learning occur with any frequency. That time will be doubly productive if employees possess the skills to use it wisely. Training in brainstorming, problem solving, evaluating experiments, and other core learning skills is therefore essential.

Another powerful lever is to open up boundaries and stimulate the exchange of ideas. Boundaries inhibit the flow of information; they keep individuals and groups isolated and reinforce preconceptions. Opening up boundaries, with conferences, meetings, and project teams, which either cross organizational levels or link the company and its customers and suppliers, ensures a fresh flow of ideas and the chance to consider competing perspectives. General Electric CEO Jack Welch considers this to be such a powerful stimulant of change that he has made "boundarylessness" a cornerstone of the company's strategy for the 1990s.

Once managers have established a more supportive, open environment, they can create learning forums. These are programs or events designed with explicit learning goals in mind, and they can take a variety of forms: strategic reviews, which examine the changing competitive environment and the company's product portfolio, technology, and market positioning; systems audits, which review the health of large, cross-functional processes and delivery systems; internal benchmarking reports, which identify and compare best-in-class activities within the organization; study missions, which are dispatched to leading organizations around the world to better understand their performance and distinctive skills; and jamborees or symposiums, which bring together customers, suppliers, outside experts, or internal

groups to share ideas and learn from one another. Each of these activities fosters learning by requiring employees to wrestle with new knowledge and consider its implications. Each can also be tailored to business needs. A consumer goods company, for example, might sponsor a study mission to Europe to learn more about distribution methods within the newly unified Common Market, while a high-technology company might launch a systems audit to review its new product development process.

Together these efforts help to eliminate barriers that impede learning and begin to move learning higher on the organizational agenda. They also suggest a subtle shift in focus, away from continuous improvement and toward a commitment to learning. Coupled with a better understanding of the "three Ms," the meaning, management, and measurement of learning, this shift provides a solid foundation for building learning organizations.

Endnotes

1. Peter M. Senge, *The Fifth Discipline* (New York: Doubleday, 1990), p. 1.
2. Ikujiro Nonaka, "The Knowledge-Creating Company," *Harvard Business Review,* November-December 1991, p. 97.
3. Robert Howard, "The CEO as Organizational Architect: An Interview with Xerox's Paul Allaire," *Harvard Business Review,* September-October 1992, p. 106.
4. Modesto A. Maidique and Billie Jo Zirger, "The New Product Learning Cycle," *Research Policy,* Vol. 14, No. 6 (1985), pp. 299, 309.
5. Frank R. Gulliver, "Post-Project Appraisals Pay," *Harvard Business Review,* March-April 1987, p. 128.
6. David Nadler, "Even Failures Can Be Productive," *New York Times,* April 23, 1989, Sec. 3, p. 3.
7. Robert C. Camp, *Benchmarking: The Search for Industry Best Practices That Lead to Superior Performance* (Milwaukee: ASQC Quality Press, 1989), p. 12.
8. Roger Schank, with Peter Childers, *The Creative Attitude* (New York: Macmillan, 1988), p. 9.

READING 27
TEACHING SMART PEOPLE HOW TO LEARN

Chris Argyris

Any company that aspires to succeed in the tougher business environment of the 1990s must first resolve a basic dilemma: success in the marketplace increasingly depends on learning, yet most people don't know how to learn. What's more, those members of the organization that many assume to be the best at learning are, in fact, not very good at it. I am talking about the well-educated, high-powered, high-commitment professionals who occupy key leadership positions in the modern corporation.

Most companies not only have tremendous difficulty addressing this learning dilemma; they aren't even aware that it exists. The reason: they misunderstand what learning is and how to bring it about. As a result, they tend to make two mistakes in their efforts to become a learning organization.

First, most people define learning too narrowly as mere "problem solving," so they focus on identifying and correcting errors in the external environment. Solving problems is important. But if learning is to persist, managers and employees must also look inward. They need to reflect critically on their own behavior, identify the ways they often inadvertently contribute to the organization's problems, and then change how they act. In particular, they must learn how the very way they go about defining and solving problems can be a source of problems in its own right.

I have coined the terms *single loop* and *double loop* learning to capture this crucial distinction. To give a simple analogy: a thermostat that automatically turns on the heat whenever the temperature in a room drops below 68 degrees is a good example of single-loop learning. A thermostat that could ask, "Why am I set at 68 degrees?" and then explore whether or not some other temperature might more economically achieve the goal of heating the room would be engaging in double-loop learning.

Highly skilled professionals are frequently very good at single-loop learning. After all, they have spent much of their lives acquiring academic credentials, mastering one or a number of intellectual disciplines, and applying those disciplines to solve real-world problems. But ironically, this very fact helps explain why professionals are often so bad at double-loop learning.

Put simply, because many professionals are almost always successful at what they do, they rarely experience failure. And because they have rarely failed, they have never learned how to learn from failure. So whenever their single-loop learning strategies go wrong, they become defensive, screen out criticism, and put the "blame" on anyone and everyone but themselves. In short, their ability to learn shuts down precisely at the moment they need it the most.

The propensity among professionals to behave defensively helps shed light on the second mistake that companies make about learning. The common assumption is that getting people to learn is largely a matter of motivation. When people have the right attitudes and commitment, learning automatically follows. So companies focus on creating new organizational structures—compensation programs, performance reviews, corporate cultures, and the like—that are designed to create motivated and committed employees.

But effective double-loop learning is not simply a function of how people feel. It is a reflection of how they think—that is, the cognitive rules or reasoning they use to design and implement their actions. Think of these rules as a kind of "master program" stored in the brain, governing all behavior. Defensive reasoning can block learning even when the individual commitment to it is high, just as a computer program with hidden bugs can produce results exactly the opposite of what its designers had planned.

Companies can learn how to resolve the learning dilemma. What it takes is to make the ways managers and employees reason about their behavior a focus of organizational learning and continuous improvement programs. Teaching people how to reason about their behavior in new and more effective ways breaks down the defenses that block learning.

All of the examples that follow involve a particular kind of professional: fast-track consultants at major management consulting companies. But the implications of my argument go far beyond this specific occupational group. The fact is, more and more jobs—no matter what the title—are taking on the contours of "knowledge work." People at all levels of the organization must combine the mastery of some highly specialized technical expertise with the ability to work effectively in teams, form productive relationships with clients and customers, and critically reflect on and then change their own organizational practices. And the nuts and bolts of management—whether of high-powered consultants or service representatives, senior managers or factory technician—increasingly consists of guiding and integrating the autonomous but interconnected work of highly skilled people.

How Professionals Avoid Learning

For 15 years, I have been conducting in-depth studies of management consultants. I decided to study consultants for a few simple reasons. First, they are the epitome of the highly educated professionals who play an increasingly central role in all organizations. Almost all of the consultants I've studied have MBAs from the top three or four U.S. business schools. They are also highly committed to their work. For instance, at one company, more

than 90 percent of the consultants responded in a survey that they were "highly satisfied" with their jobs and with the company.

I also assumed that such professional consultants would be good at learning. After all, the essence of their job is to teach others how to do things differently. I found, however, that these consultants embodied the learning dilemma. The most enthusiastic about continuous improvement in their own organizations, they were also often the biggest obstacle to its complete success.

As long as efforts at learning and change focused on external organizational factors—job redesign, compensation programs, performance reviews, and leadership training—the professionals were enthusiastic participants. Indeed, creating new systems and structures was precisely the kind of challenge that well-educated, highly motivated professionals thrived on.

And yet the moment the quest for continuous improvement turned to the professionals' *own* performance, something went wrong. It wasn't a matter of bad attitude. The professionals' commitment to excellence was genuine, and the vision of the company was clear. Nevertheless, continuous improvement did not persist. And the longer the continuous improvement efforts continued, the greater the likelihood that they would produce ever-diminishing returns.

What happened? The professionals began to feel embarrassed. They were threatened by the prospect of critically examining their own role in the organization. Indeed, because they were so well paid and generally believed that their employers were supportive and fair, the idea that their performance might not be at its best made them feel guilty.

Far from being a catalyst for real change, such feelings caused most to react defensively. They projected the blame for any problems away from themselves and onto what they said were unclear goals, insensitive and unfair leaders, and stupid clients.

Consider this example. At a premier management consulting company, the manager of a case team called a meeting to examine the team's performance on a recent consulting project. The client was largely satisfied and had given the team relatively high marks, but the manager believed the team had not created the value added that it was capable of and that the consulting company had promised. In the spirit of continuous improvement, he felt that the team could do better. Indeed, so did some of the team members.

The manager knew how difficult it was for people to reflect critically on their own work performance, especially in the presence of their manager, so he took a number of steps to make possible a frank and open discussion. He invited to the meeting an outside consultant whom team members knew and trusted—"just to keep me honest," he said. He also agreed to have the entire meeting tape-recorded. That way, any subsequent confusions or disagreements about what went on at the meeting could be checked against the transcript. Finally, the manager opened the meeting by emphasizing that no subject was off limits—including his own behavior.

"I realize that you may believe you cannot confront me," the manager said. "But I encourage you to challenge me. You have a responsibility to tell me where you think the leadership made mistakes, just as I have the responsibility to identify any I believe you made. And all of us must acknowledge our own mistakes. If we do not have an open dialogue, we will not learn."

The professionals took the manager up on the first half of his invitation but quietly ignored the second. When asked to pinpoint the key problems in the experience with the client, they looked entirely outside themselves. The clients were uncooperative and arrogant. "They didn't think we could help them." The team's own managers were unavailable and poorly prepared. "At times, our managers were not up to speed before they walked into the client meetings." In effect, the professionals asserted that they were helpless to act differently—not because of any limitations of their own but because of the limitations of others.

The manager listened carefully to the team members and tried to respond to their criticisms. He talked about the mistakes that he had made during the consulting process. For example, one professional objected to the way the manager had run the project meetings. "I see that the way I asked questions closed down discussions," responded the manager. "I didn't mean to do that, but I can see how you might have believed that I had already made up my mind." Another team member complained that the manager had caved in to pressure from his superior to produce the project report far too quickly, considering the team's heavy work load. "I think that it was my responsibility to have said no," admitted the manager. "It was clear that we all had an immense amount of work."

Finally, after some three hours of discussion about his own behavior, the manager began to ask the team members if there were any errors *they* might have made. "After all," he said, "this client was not different from many others. How can we be more effective in the future?"

The professionals repeated that it was really the clients' and their own managers' fault. As one put it, "They have to be open to change and want to learn." The more the manager tried to get the team to examine its own responsibility for the outcome, the more the professionals bypassed his concerns. The best one team member could suggest was for the case team to "promise less"—implying that there was really no way for the group to improve its performance.

The case team members were reacting defensively to protect themselves, even though their manager was not acting in ways that an outsider would consider threatening. Even if there were some truth to their charges—the clients may well have been arrogant and closed, their own managers distant—the *way* they presented these claims was guaranteed to stop learning. With few exceptions, the professionals made attributions about the behavior of the clients and the managers but never publicly tested their claims. For instance, they said that the clients weren't motivated to learn but never really presented any evidence supporting that assertion. When their lack of concrete evidence was pointed out to them, they simply repeated their criticisms more vehemently.

If the professionals had felt so strongly about these issues, why had they never mentioned them during the project? According to the professionals, even this was the fault of others. "We didn't want to alienate the client," argued one. "We didn't want to be seen as whining," said another.

The professionals were using their criticisms of others to protect themselves from the potential embarrassment of having to admit that perhaps they, too, had contributed to the team's less-than-perfect performance. What's more, the fact that they kept repeating their defensive actions in the face of the manager's efforts to turn the group's attention to its own role shows that this defensiveness had become a reflexive routine. From the professionals' perspective, they weren't resisting; they were focusing on the "real" causes. Indeed, they were to be respected, if not congratulated, for working as well as they did under such difficult conditions.

The end result was an unproductive parallel conversation. Both the manager and the professionals were candid: they expressed their views forcefully. But they talked past each other, never finding a common language to describe what had happened with the client. The professionals kept insisting that the fault lay with others. The manager kept trying, unsuccessfully, to get the professionals to see how they contributed to the state of affairs they were criticizing. The dialogue of this parallel conversation looks like this:

> *Professionals:* "The clients have to be open. They must want to change."
> *Manager:* "It's our task to help them see that change is in their interest."
> *Professionals:* "But the clients didn't agree with our analyses."
> *Manager:* "If they didn't think our ideas were right, how might we have convinced them?"
> *Professionals:* "Maybe we need to have more meetings with the client."
> *Manager:* "If we aren't adequately prepared and if the clients don't think we're credible, how will more meetings help?"

> *Professionals:* "There should be better communication between case team members and management."
> *Manager:* "I agree. But professionals should take the initiative to educate the manager about the problems they are experiencing."
> *Professionals:* "Our leaders are unavailable and distant."
> *Manager:* "How do you expect us to know that if you don't tell us?"

Conversations such as this one dramatically illustrate the learning dilemma. The problem with the professionals' claims is not that they are wrong but that they aren't useful. By constantly turning the focus away from their own behavior to that of others, the professionals bring learning to a grinding halt. The manager understands the trap but does not know how to get out of it. To learn how to do that requires going deeper into the dynamics of defensive reasoning—and into the special causes that make professionals so prone to it.

Defensive Reasoning and the Doom Loop

What explains the professionals' defensiveness? Not their attitudes about change or commitment to continuous improvement; they really wanted to work more effectively. Rather, the key factor is the way they reasoned about their behavior and that of others.

It is impossible to reason anew in every situation. If we had to think through all the possible responses every time someone asked, "How are you?" the world would pass us by. Therefore everyone develops a theory of action—a set of rules that individuals use to design and implement their own behavior as well as to understand the behavior of others. Usually, these theories of actions become so taken for granted that people don't even realize they are using them.

One of the paradoxes of human behavior, however, is that the master program people actually use is rarely the one they think they use. Ask people in an interview or questionnaire to articulate the rules they use to govern their actions, and they will give you what I call their "espoused" theory of action. But observe these same people's behavior, and you will quickly see that this espoused theory has very little to do with how they actually behave. For example, the professionals on the case team said they believed in continuous improvement, and yet they consistently acted in ways that made improvement impossible.

When you observe people's behavior and try to come up with rules that would make sense of it, you discover a very different theory of action—what I call the individual's "theory-in-use." Put simply, people consistently act inconsistently, unaware of the contradiction between their espoused theory and their theory-in-use, between the way they think they are acting and the way they really act.

What's more, most theories-in-use rest on the same set of governing values. There seems to be a universal human tendency to design one's actions consistently, according to four basic values:

1. To remain in unilateral control.
2. To maximize "winning" and minimize "losing."
3. To suppress negative feelings.
4. To be as "rational" as possible—by which people mean defining clear objectives and evaluating their behavior in terms of whether or not they have achieved them.

The purpose of all these values is to avoid embarrassment or threat, feeling vulnerable or incompetent. In this respect, the master program that most people use is profoundly defensive. Defensive reasoning encourages individuals to keep private the premises, inferences, and conclusions that shape their behavior and to avoid testing them in a truly independent, objective fashion.

Because the attributions that go into defensive reasoning are never really tested, it is a closed loop, remarkably impervious to conflicting points of view. The inevitable response to the observation that somebody is reasoning defensively is yet more defensive reasoning. With the case team, for example, whenever anyone pointed out the professionals' defensive behavior to them, their initial reaction was to look for the cause in somebody else—clients who were so sensitive that they would have been alienated if the consultants had criticized them or a manager so weak that he couldn't have taken it had the consultants raised their concerns with him. In other words, the case team members once again denied their own responsibility by externalizing the problem and putting it on someone else.

In such situations, the simple act of encouraging more open inquiry is often attacked by others as "intimidating." Those who do the attacking deal with their feelings about possibly being wrong by blaming the more open individual for arousing these feelings and upsetting them.

Needless to say, such a master program inevitably short-circuits learning. And for a number of reasons unique to their psychology, well-educated professionals are especially susceptible to this.

Nearly all the consultants I have studied have stellar academic records. Ironically, their very success at education helps explain the problems they have with learning. Before they enter the world of work, their lives are primarily full of successes, so they have rarely experienced the embarrassment and sense of threat that comes with failure. As a result, their defensive reasoning has rarely been activated. People who rarely experience failure, however, end up not knowing how to deal with it effectively. And this serves to reinforce the normal human tendency to reason defensively.

In a survey of several hundred young consultants at the organizations I have been studying, these professionals describe themselves as driven internally by an unrealistically high ideal of performance: "Pressure on the job is self-imposed." "I must not only do a good job; I must also be the best." "People around here are very bright and hardworking; they are highly motivated to do an outstanding job." "Most of us want not only to succeed but also to do so at maximum speed."

These consultants are always comparing themselves with the best around them and constantly trying to better their own performance. And yet they do not appreciate being required to compete openly with each other. They feel it is somehow inhumane. They prefer to be the individual contributor—what might be termed a "productive loner."

Behind this high aspiration for success is an equally high fear of failure and a propensity to feel shame and guilt when they do fail to meet their high standards. "You must avoid mistakes," said one. "I hate making them. Many of us fear failure, whether we admit it or not."

To the extent that these consultants have experienced success in their lives, they have not had to be concerned about failure and the attendant feelings of shame and guilt. But to exactly the same extent they also have never developed the tolerance for feelings of failure or the skills to deal with these feelings. This in turn has led them not only to fear failure but also to fear the fear of failure itself. For they know that they will not cope with it superlatively—their usual level of aspiration.

The consultants use two intriguing metaphors to describe this phenomenon. They talk about the "doom loop" and "doom zoom." Often, consultants will perform well on the case team, but, because they don't do the jobs perfectly or receive accolades from their managers, they go into a doom loop of despair. And they don't ease into the doom loop, they zoom into it.

As a result, many professionals have extremely "brittle" personalities. When suddenly faced with a situation they cannot immediately handle, they tend to fall apart. They cover up their distress in front of the client. They talk about it constantly with their fellow case team members. Interestingly, these conversations commonly take the form of bad-mouthing clients.

Such brittleness leads to an inappropriately high sense of despondency or even despair when people don't achieve the high levels of performance they aspire to. Such despondency is rarely psychologically devastating, but, when combined with defensive reasoning, it can result in a formidable predisposition against learning.

There is no better example of how this brittleness can disrupt an organization than performance evaluations. Because it represents the one moment when a professional must measure his or her own behavior against some formal standard, a performance evaluation is almost tailor-made to push a professional into the doom loop. Indeed, a poor evaluation can reverberate far beyond the particular individual involved to spark defensive reasoning throughout an entire organization.

At one consulting company, management established a new performance-evaluation process that was designed to make evaluations both more objective and more useful to those being evaluated. The consultants participated in the design of the new system and, in general, were enthusiastic because it corresponded to their espoused values of objectivity and fairness. A brief two years into the new process, however, it had become the object of dissatisfaction. The catalyst for this about-face was the first unsatisfactory rating.

Senior managers had identified six consultants whose performance they considered below standard. In keeping with the new evaluation process, they did all they could to communicate their concerns to the six and to help them improve. Managers met with each individual separately for as long and as often as the professional requested to explain the reasons behind the rating and to discuss what needed to be done to improve—but to no avail. Performance continued at the same low level and, eventually, the six were let go.

When word of the dismissal spread through the company, people responded with confusion and anxiety. After about a dozen consultants angrily complained to management, the CEO held two lengthy meetings where employees could air their concerns.

At the meetings, the professionals made a variety of claims. Some said the performance-evaluation process was unfair because judgments were subjective and biased and the criteria for minimum performance unclear. Others suspected that the real cause for the dismissals was economic and that the performance-evaluation procedure was just a fig leaf to hide the fact that the company was in trouble. Still others argued that the evaluation process was antilearning. If the company were truly a learning organization, as it claimed, then people performing below the minimum standard should be taught how to reach it. As one professional put it: "We were told that the company did not have an up-or-out policy. Up-or-out is inconsistent with learning. You misled us."

The CEO tried to explain the logic behind management's decision by grounding it in the facts of the case and by asking the professionals for any evidence that might contradict these facts.

Is there subjectivity and bias in the evaluation process? Yes, responded the CEO, but "we strive hard to reduce them. We are constantly trying to improve the process. If you have any ideas, please tell us. If you know of someone treated unfairly, please bring it up. If any of you feel that you have been treated unfairly, let's discuss it now or, if you wish, privately."

Is the level of minimum competence too vague? "We are working to define minimum competence more clearly," he answered. "In the case of the six, however, their performance was so poor that it wasn't difficult to reach a decision." Most of the six had received timely feedback about their problems. And in the two cases where people had not, the reason was that they had never taken the responsibility to seek out evaluations—and, indeed, had actively avoided them. "If you have any data to the contrary," the CEO added, "let's talk about it."

Were the six asked to leave for economic reasons? No, said the CEO. "We have more work than we can do, and letting professionals go is extremely costly for us. Do any of you have any information to the contrary?"

As to the company being antilearning, in fact, the entire evaluation process was designed to encourage learning. When a professional is performing below the minimum level, the CEO explained, "we jointly design remedial experiences with the individual. Then we look for signs of improvement. In these cases, either the professionals were reluctant to take on such assignments or they repeatedly failed when they did. Again, if you

have information or evidence to the contrary, I'd like to hear about it."

The CEO concluded: "It's regrettable, but sometimes we make mistakes and hire the wrong people. If individuals don't produce and repeatedly prove themselves unable to improve, we don't know what else to do except dismiss them. It's just not fair to keep poorly performing individuals in the company. They earn an unfair share of the financial rewards."

Instead of responding with data of their own, the professionals simply repeated their accusations but in ways that consistently contradicted their claims. They said that a genuinely fair evaluation process would contain clear and documentable data about performance—but they were unable to provide firsthand examples of the unfairness that they implied colored the evaluation of the six dismissed employees. They argued that people shouldn't be judged by inferences unconnected to their actual performance—but they judged management in precisely this way. They insisted that management define clear, objective, and unambiguous performance standards—but they argued that any humane system would take into account that the performance of a professional cannot be precisely measured. Finally, they presented themselves as champions of learning—but they never proposed any criteria for assessing whether an individual might be unable to learn.

In short, the professionals seemed to hold management to a different level of performance than they held themselves. In their conversation at the meetings, they used many of the features of ineffective evaluation that they condemned—the absence of concrete data, for example, and the dependence on a circular logic of "heads we win, tails you lose." It is as if they were saying, "Here are the features of a fair performance-evaluation system. You should abide by them. But we don't have to when we are evaluating you."

Indeed, if we were to explain the professionals' behavior by articulating rules that would have to be in their heads in order for them to act the way they did, the rules would look something like this:

1. When criticizing the company, state your criticism in ways that you believe are valid—but also in ways that prevent others from deciding for themselves whether your claim to validity is correct.

2. When asked to illustrate your criticisms, don't include any data that others could use to decide for themselves whether the illustrations are valid.

3. State your conclusions in ways that disguise their logical implications. If others point out those implications to you, deny them.

Of course, when such rules were described to the professionals, they found them abhorrent. It was inconceivable that these rules might explain their actions. And yet, in defending themselves against this observation, they almost always inadvertently confirmed the rules.

Learning How to Reason Productively

If defensive reasoning is as widespread as I believe, then focusing on an individual's attitudes or commitment is never enough to produce real change. And as the previous example illustrates, neither is creating new organizational structures or systems. The problem is that, even when people are genuinely committed to improving their performance and management has changed its structures in order to encourage the "right" kind of behavior, people still remain locked in defensive reasoning. Either they remain unaware of this fact, or, if they do become aware of it, they blame others.

There is, however, reason to believe that organizations can break out of this vicious circle. Despite the strength of defensive reasoning, people genuinely strive to produce what they intend. They value acting competently. Their self-esteem is intimately tied up with behaving consistently and performing effectively. Companies can use these universal human tendencies to teach people how to reason in a new way—in effect, to change the master programs in their heads and thus reshape their behavior.

People can be taught how to recognize the reasoning they use when they design and implement their actions. They can begin to identify the inconsistencies between their espoused and actual theories of action. They can face up to the fact that they unconsciously design and implement actions that they do not intend. Finally, people can learn how to identify what individuals and groups do to create organizational defenses and how these defenses contribute to an organization's problems.

Once companies embark on this learning process, they will discover that the kind of reasoning necessary to reduce and overcome organizational defenses is the same kind of "tough reasoning" that underlies the effective use of ideas in strategy, finance, marketing, manufacturing, and other management disciplines. Any sophisticated strategic analysis, for example, depends on collecting valid data, analyzing it carefully, and constantly testing the inferences drawn from the data. The toughest tests are reserved for the conclusions. Good strategies make sure that their conclusions can withstand all kinds of critical questioning.

So, too, with productive reasoning about human behavior. The standard of analysis is just as high. Human resource programs no longer need to be based on "soft" reasoning but should be as analytical and as data-driven as any other management discipline.

Of course, that is not the kind of reasoning the consultants used when they encountered problems that were embarrassing or threatening. The data they collected was hardly objective. The inferences they made rarely became explicit. The conclusions they reached were largely self-serving, impossible for others to test, and as a result, "self-sealing," impervious to change.

How can an organization begin to turn this situation around, to teach its members how to reason productively? The first step is for managers at the top to examine critically and change their own theories-in-use. Until senior managers become aware of how they reason defensively and the counterproductive consequences that result, there will be little real progress. Any change activity is likely to be just a fad.

Change has to start at the top, because otherwise defensive senior managers are likely to disown any transformation in reasoning patterns coming from below. If professionals or middle managers begin to change the way they reason and act, such changes are likely to appear strange—if not actually dangerous—to those at the top. The result is an unstable situation where senior managers still believe that it is a sign of caring and sensitivity to bypass and cover up difficult issues, while their subordinates see the very same actions as defensive.

The key to any educational experience designed to teach senior managers how to reason productively is to connect the program to real business problems. The best demonstration of the usefulness of productive reasoning is for busy managers to see how it can make a direct difference in their own performance and in that of the organization. This will not happen overnight. Managers need plenty of opportunity to practice the new skills. But once they grasp the powerful impact that productive reasoning can have on actual performance, they will have a strong incentive to reason productively not just in a training session but in all their work relationships.

One simple approach I have used to get this process started is to have participants produce a kind of rudimentary case study. The subject is a real business problem that the manager either wants to deal with or has tried unsuccessfully to address in the past. Writing the actual case usually takes less than an hour. But then the case becomes the focal point of an extended analysis.

For example, a CEO at a large organizational-development consulting company was preoccupied with the problems caused by the intense competition among the various business functions represented by his four direct reports. Not only was he tired of having the problems dumped in his lap, but he was also worried about the impact the interfunctional conflicts were having on the organization's flexibility. He had even calculated that the money being spent to iron out disagreements amounted to hundreds of thousands of dollars every year. And the more fights there were, the more defensive people became, which only increased the costs to the organization.

In a paragraph or so, the CEO described a meeting he intended to have with his direct reports to address the problem. Next, he divided the paper in half, and on the right-hand side of the page, he wrote a scenario for the meeting—much like the script for a movie or play—describing what he would say and how his subordinates would likely respond. On the left-hand side of the page, he wrote down any thoughts and feelings that he would be likely to have during the meeting but that he wouldn't express for fear they would derail the discussion.

But instead of holding the meeting, the CEO analyzed this scenario *with* his direct reports. The case became the catalyst for a discussion in which the CEO learned several things about the way he acted with his management team.

He discovered that his four direct reports often perceived his conversations as counterproductive. In the guise of being "diplomatic," he would pretend that a consensus about the problem existed, when in fact none existed. The unintended result: instead of feeling reassured, his subordinates felt wary and tried to figure out 'what is he *really* getting at."

The CEO also realized that the way he dealt with the competitiveness among department heads was completely contradictory. On the one hand, he kept urging them to "think of the organization as a whole." On the other, he kept calling for actions—department budget cuts, for example—that placed them directly in competition with each other.

Finally, the CEO discovered that many of the tacit evaluations and attributions he had listed turned out to be wrong. Since he had never expressed these assumptions, he had never found out just how wrong they were. What's more, he learned that much of what he thought he was hiding came through to his subordinates anyway—but with the added message that the boss was covering up.

The CEO's colleagues also learned about their own ineffective behavior. They learned by examining their own behavior as they tried to help the

CEO analyze his case. They also learned by writing and analyzing cases of their own. They began to see that they, too, tended to bypass and cover up the real issues and that the CEO was often aware of it but did not say so. They, too, made inaccurate attributions and evaluations that they did not express. Moreover, the belief that they had to hide important ideas and feelings from the CEO and from each other in order not to upset anyone turned out to be mistaken. In the context of the case discussions, the entire senior management team was quite willing to discuss what had always been undiscussable.

In effect, the case study exercise legitimizes talking about issues that people have never been able to address before. Such a discussion can be emotional—even painful. But for managers with the courage to persist, the payoff is great: management teams and entire organizations work more openly and more effectively and have greater options for behaving flexibly and adapting to particular situations.

When senior managers are trained in new reasoning skills, they can have a big impact on the performance of the entire organization—even when other employees are still reasoning defensively. The CEO who led the meetings on the performance-evaluation procedure was able to defuse dissatisfaction because he didn't respond to professionals' criticism in kind but, instead, gave a clear presentation of relevant data. Indeed, most participants took the CEO's behavior to be a sign that the company really acted on the values of participation and employee involvement that it espoused.

Of course, the ideal is for all the members of an organization to learn how to reason productively. This has happened at the company where the case team meeting took place. Consultants and their managers are now able to confront some of the most difficult issues of the consultant-client relationship. To get a sense of the difference productive reasoning can make, imagine how the original conversation between the manager and case team might have gone had everyone engaged in effective reasoning. (The following dialogue is based on

actual sessions I have attended with other case teams at the same company since the training has been completed.)

First, the consultants would have demonstrated their commitment to continuous improvement by being willing to examine their own role in the difficulties that arose during the consulting project. No doubt they would have identified their managers and the clients as part of the problem, but they would have gone on to admit that they had contributed to it as well. More important, they would have agreed with the manager that as they explored the various roles of clients, managers, and professionals, they would make sure to test any evaluations or attributions they might make against the data. Each individual would have encouraged the others to question his or her reasoning. Indeed, they would have insisted on it. And in turn, everyone would have understood that act of questioning not as a sign of mistrust or an invasion of privacy but as a valuable opportunity for learning.

The conversation about the manager's unwillingness to say no might look something like this:

Professional #1: "One of the biggest problems I had with the way you managed this case was that you seemed to be unable to say no when either the client or your superior made unfair demands." (Gives an example.)

Professional #2: "I have another example to add. (Describes a second example.) But I'd also like to say that we never really told you how we felt about this. Behind your back we were bad-mouthing you—you know, 'he's being such a wimp'—but we never came right out and said it."

Manager: "It certainly would have been helpful if you had said something. Was there anything I said or did that gave you the idea that you had better not raise this with me?"

Professional #3: "Not really. I think we didn't want to sound like we were whining."

Manager: "Well, I certainly don't think you sound like you're whining. But two thoughts come to mind. If I understand you correctly, you *were* complaining, but the complaining about me and my inability to say no was covered up. Second, if we had discussed this, I might have gotten the data I needed to be able to say no."

Notice, that, when the second professional describes how the consultants had covered up their complaints, the manager doesn't criticize her. Rather, he rewards her for being open by responding in kind. He focuses on the ways that he, too, may have contributed to the cover-up. Reflecting undefensively about his own role in the problem then makes it possible for the professionals to talk about their fears of appearing to be whining. The manager then agrees with the professionals that they shouldn't become complainers. At the same time, he points out the counterproductive consequences of covering up their complaints. Another unresolved issue in the case team meeting concerned the supposed arrogance of the clients. A more productive conversation about that problem might go like this:

> *Manager:* "You said that the clients were arrogant and uncooperative. What did they say and do?"
> *Professional #1:* "One asked me if I had ever met a payroll. Another asked how long I've been out of school."
> *Professional #2:* "One even asked me how old I was!"
> *Professional #3:* "That's nothing. The worst is when they say that all we do is interview people, write a report based on what they tell us, and then collect our fees."
> *Manager:* "The fact that we tend to be so young is a real problem for many of our clients. They get very defensive about it. But I'd like to explore whether there is a way for them to freely express their views without our getting defensive.

> "What troubled me about your original responses was that you assumed you were right in calling the clients stupid. One thing I've noticed about consultants—in this company and others—is that we tend to defend ourselves by bad-mouthing the client."
> *Professional #1:* "Right. After all, if they are genuinely stupid, then it's obviously not our fault that they aren't getting it!"
> *Professional #2:* "Of course, that stance is antilearning and overprotective. By assuming that they can't learn, we absolve ourselves from having to."
> *Professional #3:* "And the more we all go along with the bad-mouthing, the more we reinforce each other's defensiveness."
> *Manager:* "So what's the alternative? How can we encourage our clients to express their defensiveness and at the same time constructively build on it?"
> *Professional #1:* "We all know that the real issue isn't our age; it's whether or not we are able to add value to the client's organization. They should judge us by what we produce. And if we aren't adding value, they should get rid of us—no matter how young or old we happen to be."
> *Manager:* "Perhaps that is exactly what we should tell them."

In both these examples, the consultants and their manager are doing real work. They are learning about their own group dynamics and addressing some generic problems in client-consultant relationships. The insights they gain will allow them to act more effectively in the future—both as individuals and as a team. They are not just solving problems but developing a far deeper and more textured understanding of their role as members of the organization. They are laying the groundwork for continuous improvement that is truly continuous. They are learning how to learn.

V   IMPLEMENTATION GUIDELINES AND ISSUES

Successful OD and OT programs depend on many things: sound theory regarding the nature of change and the nature of organizations, solid and robust interventions appropriately chosen for the tasks at hand, and effective implementation and execution. This section examines guidelines and issues for effective implementation.

A sizable body of knowledge exists to guide leaders' and practitioners' implementation efforts. One aspect of implementation relates to the overall flow of events, what Warner Burke calls the *phases* of OD programs.[1] These are:

1. Entry
2. Contracting
3. Diagnosis
4. Feedback
5. Planning change
6. Intervention
7. Evaluation

Entry represents the initial contact between consultant and client; this includes exploring the situation that led the client to seek a consultant and determining whether there is a good match between the client, the consultant, and the problematic situation. *Contracting* involves establishing mutual expectations; reaching agreement on expenditures of time, money, and resources; and generally clarifying what each party expects to get and give to the other. *Diagnosis* is the fact-finding phase, which produces a picture of the situation through interviews, observations, questionnaires, examination of organization documents, and the like. This phase has two steps: collecting information and analyzing it. *Feedback* represents returning the analyzed information to the client system. In this phase, the clients explore the information for understanding, clarification, and accuracy; they own the data as their picture of the situation and their problems and opportunities. *Planning change* involves the clients' deciding what actions to take on the basis of information they have just learned. Alternatives are explored and critiqued; action plans are selected and developed. *Intervention* involves implementing sets of actions designed to correct the problems or seize the opportunities. *Evaluation* represents assessing the effects of the program: What changes occurred? Are we satisfied with the results?

One very important aspect of this sequence of steps is that each phase builds the foundation for subsequent phases; therefore, each phase must be executed with care and precision. For example, if expectations are not clear in the contracting phase, this mismatch will surface later in unmet expectations and dissatisfaction. Or, if the analysis of the data during the diagnostic phase is incorrect, interventions may not be appropriate. Thus, understanding the phases and attending to the details of each phase are critical for success.

Cummings and Worley also explore implementation issues.[2] They identify five sets of activities required for effective management of OD and OT programs: (1) motivating change, (2) creating a vision, (3) developing political support, (4) managing the transition, and (5) sustaining momentum. These activities include specific steps for the consultant to take to ensure effective implementation. For example, *motivating change* involves creating readiness for change and overcoming resistance to change. *Creating a vision* involves providing a picture of the future and showing how individuals and groups will fit into that future, as well as providing a road map and interim goals. *Developing political support* involves obtaining the support of key individuals and groups and influencing key stakeholders to move the change effort forward. *Managing the transition* means planning the needed transition activities, getting commitments of people and resources, and creating necessary structures and milestones to help people locomote from "where we are" to "where we want to be." *Sustaining momentum* involves providing resources for the change effort, helping people develop new competencies and skills, and reinforcing the desired new behaviors. These are the details consultants and leaders must attend to when implementing organization development and transformation programs.

There are other issues as well, such as trust, the consultant's expertise, making competent diagnoses, choosing appropriate interventions, dealing with power and politics, treating confidential information with integrity, and the like. Learning the craft of facilitating organizational change involves both art and science.

Readings in Part V

The articles in this section cover a range of topics related to managing OD and OT programs for success. The first selection, by Gareth Jones and Jennifer George, is a theoretical discourse on trust in organizations—how it is established, how it is dissolved, how it impacts cooperation and teamwork. The concept of trust is very important in organization development because most practitioners view trust as a necessary condition for interpersonal and organizational effectiveness.

The article by Achilles Armenakis, Stanley Harris, and Kevin Mossholder deals with the issue of creating readiness for change. This is a practical piece written by change agents for change agents. A major ingredient of success in change programs is creating readiness for change in the client system. The authors present good insights and sound advice for leaders and practitioners alike.

Larry Greiner and Virginia Schein's selection deals with power, a troublesome topic for many OD practitioners. The authors evaluate three models of how organizations work and argue for the validity and usefulness of a "pluralistic/political" model. The pluralistic/political model assumes that organizations contain self-interested groups seeking their own goals. This selection is from their book *Power and Organization Development: Mobilizing Power to Implement Change,* a must read for organization development practitioners.

The next selection goes all the way back to the early days of the T-group movement. It deals with leadership and group (team) effectiveness. Kenneth Benne and Paul Sheats identify important group member roles that increase group effectiveness, along with a number of individual roles that can block effective group functioning. In later years, OD consultants and T-group trainers have been more likely to refer to these roles as behaviors. Training group members to be effective in the use of these behaviors can be very important to constructive team building and other organization development and transformation activities.

Roger Harrison looks at OD interventions in terms of their impact and intrusiveness on individuals, and asks the question, How deeply should we be intruding into people's private lives? Or, put another way, What is the appropriate depth of OD interventions?

This is clearly an important issue for practitioners and laypersons. Harrison suggests two criteria to answer these questions: *"first, to intervene at a level no deeper than that required to produce enduring solutions to the problems at hand;* and second, *to intervene at a level no deeper than that at which the energy and resources of the client can be committed to problem solving and to change."* Practitioners need to think seriously about these issues.

The next selection, by Herbert Shepard, is a classic, insightful essay that presents some rules of thumb for intervening in organizations. Issues of survival, initial entry, and building support are examined. Shepard uses a model of organizational change that includes notions about complexity and interdependency in organizations, about the use of power, and about helping relationships (i.e., the need for empathy, participation, and patience).

The final selection, by Paul Nutt and Robert Backoff, introduces propositions and problems associated with organization transformations. Transformations are difficult, complicated, and costly; they attempt to cause radical change. "Visioning," "issue tensions," and "win-win" concepts are examined in this theoretical analysis of the critical elements involved in transforming organizations.

Endnotes

1. W. Warner Burke, *Organization Development: A Process of Learning and Changing* (Reading, MA: Addison Wesley Longman, Inc., 1994), chap. 4.
2. T. G. Cummings and C. G. Worley, *Organization Development and Change* (St. Paul, MN: West Publishing Company, 1993), chap. 8.

READING 28
THE EXPERIENCE AND EVOLUTION OF TRUST:
IMPLICATIONS FOR COOPERATION AND TEAMWORK

Gareth R. Jones
Jennifer M. George

Scholars have widely acknowledge that trust can lead to cooperative behavior among individuals, groups, and organizations (e.g., Axelrod, 1984; Gambetta, 1988; Good, 1988; Mayer, Davis, & Schoorman, 1995; McAllister, 1995). Today, in an era when organizations are searching for new ways to promote cooperation between people and groups to enhance the value they create, it is not surprising that interest in the concept of trust and, in particular, how to promote or actualize it is increasing (Kramer & Tyler, 1996). For example, many organizations have sought to increase cooperation between people and groups by reengineering their structures into flatter, more team-based forms, in which authority is decentralized to "empowered" lower-level employees. Empowerment is only likely to enhance cooperation and, ultimately, organizational performance, however, if trust exists in an organization. In order to promote trust between two or more parties, managers must understand how an individual experiences trust in another person, group, or organization and how trust evolves between people or groups over time. In other words, it is necessary to understand how trust in others is experienced psychologically before its impact on behavioral expectations and outcomes, such as the level of cooperation between people in an organization, can be adequately analyzed. In this article we explore these issues.

We greatly appreciate the many insightful comments from Special Issue Editor Sim Sitkin and the anonymous reviewers, who have helped us to develop the ideas in this article.

Source: Republished with permission of Academy of Management, PO Box 3020, Briar Cliff Manor, NY, 10510-8020. "The Experience and Evoloution of Trust: Implications for Cooperation," Gareth R. Jones and Jennifer M. George, *Academy of Management Review*, 1998, Vol. 23, No. 3. Reproduced by permission of publisher via Copyright Clearance Center, Inc.

Using a theoretical framework based on values, attitudes, and moods and emotions, we analyze how people experience trust in a psychological sense, as well as the feelings, beliefs, and meanings that underlie it. Then, based on this framework, we provide an account of the evolution of trust. We examine how trust spreads among people and is sustained or strengthened, or, conversely, how it comes to be weakened, broken, or dissolved. We also distinguish between two different states or forms of trust: conditional trust and unconditional trust. To illustrate the potential performance benefits to be derived from actualizing and unconditional trust, we focus on a construct that is increasingly being used to explain differences in competitive advantage and performance between organizations: interpersonal cooperation and teamwork.

The Experience of Trust

Researchers have devoted considerable attention to clarifying the meaning of trust in different social contexts and the conditions or determinants of trust. Commonly, they view trust as an expression of confidence between the parties in an exchange of some kind—confidence that they will not be harmed or put at risk by the actions of the other party (Axelrod, 1984; Bateson, 1988; Zucker, 1987) or confidence that no party to the exchange will exploit the other's vulnerability (Sabel, 1993). Mayer et al. recently developed a model of trust in which several characteristics of the trustor and trustee (such as the trustee's benevolence and integrity) lead to trust in the trustee, trust being defined as "the willingness of a party to be vulnerable to the actions of another party based on the expectation that the other will perform a particular action important to the trustor, irrespective of the ability to monitor or control that other party" (1995: 712). From this perspective, trust leads to a set of behavioral expectations among people, allowing them to manage the uncertainty or risk associated with their interactions so that they can jointly optimize the gains that will result from cooperative behavior.

In discussing how expectations underlying trust affect subsequent behavior, several researchers have alluded to the fact that trust is a multidimensional construct. For example, Driscoll (1978) and Scott (1980) distinguish between the generalized or global aspects of trust and the situationally specific aspects of trust. Butler (1991) identifies different conditions under which trust may occur. Barber (1983) argues that trust encompasses moral, cognitive, and emotional elements.

Despite an overall consensus that trust is a complex multidimensional construct, scholars have little discussed how the moral, cognitive, and emotional elements of trust interact to determine subsequent expectations and behavior. In particular, both the analysis of the different possible forms or states of trust that can emerge from these interactions and the role of emotion or affect in creating trust are relatively unexplored issues. In order to explore these issues, we propose that trust is a psychological construct, the experience of which is the outcome of the interaction of people's values, attitudes, and moods and emotions. We discuss the role of values, attitudes, and moods and emotions in the experience of trust below.

Values.   Values are general standards or principles that are considered intrinsically desirable ends, such as loyalty, helpfulness, fairness, predictability, reliability, honesty, responsibility, integrity, competence, consistency, and openness (Olson & Zanna, 1993; Rokeach, 1973). Typically, people incorporate values into their value system and prioritize them in terms of their relative importance as guiding principles (Rokeach, 1973). A person's value system, thus, guides behavior and the interpretation of experience by furnishing criteria that a person can use to evaluate and make sense of events and

actions in the surrounding world. That value system determines which types of behaviors, events, situations, or people are desirable or undesirable.

Researchers have shown that what people view as desirable or ideal—that is, their internalized values—conditions the experience of trust and is upheld as a standard to strive for in the future (e.g., Butler, 1991; Butler & Cantrell, 1984; Gabarro, 1978; Jennings, 1967, 1971). An individual whose value system emphasizes loyalty and honesty, for example, will strive to achieve loyalty and honesty in his or her relationships with others. Values contribute to the generalized experience of trust and can even create a propensity to trust (Mayer et al., 1995) that surpasses specific situations and relationships.

These assertions are consistent with the larger body of literature on trust. For example, Barber (1983) suggests that trust serves to maintain and express the shared values that trust originates from and, also, that shared values help create relationships characterized by trust. Another example, consistent with the research of Rotter (e.g., Rotter, 1980), comes from Good (1988), who suggests that people who are trustworthy (or endorse such values as honesty) tend to view others as trustworthy (or as endorsing similar values underlying trust). As a final example, existing theory and research on the stable underpinnings of trust inherent in the trustor, such as Mayer et al.'s (1995) notion of the propensity to trust, Rotter's (1980) notion of a general tendency to trust others, and Stack's (1978) research on trust as a somewhat stable disposition, suggest that trust is based in enduring and relatively stable characteristics of individuals.

Attitudes.   We can view attitudes as (1) the knowledge structures containing the specific thoughts and feelings people have about other people, groups, or organizations and (2) the means through which they define and structure their interactions with others (Anderson & Armstrong, 1989; Kruglanski, 1989; Olson & Zanna, 1993). In addition to experiencing trust in a stable and general manner through values, individuals also experience trust in a more specific mode (Butler, 1991)—that is, as part of an attitude toward another entity based on knowledge, beliefs, and feelings about the nature of that entity (e.g., McAllister, 1995; Robinson, 1996).

The attitudes that people form toward each other in an organizational context are likely to contain information concerning the other party's trustworthiness. There are three reasons for this. First, most interactions in organizations entail uncertainty, and when there is uncertainty, there must be some element of trust. Even when another party provides guarantees that something will occur, uncertainty about the exact outcome remains; for example, a supervisor may make promises to a subordinate about an upcoming promotion, but the promotion may, nonetheless, be uncertain because of organizational initiatives beyond the supervisor's control. Hence, in forming attitudes about others in an organizational context, individuals are likely to include assessments of trustworthiness. Second, interdependence is an essential feature of organizational life (Thompson, 1967). Since individuals have to depend upon one another as do groups and organizations as a whole, attitudes toward interdependent entities are likely to include feelings, beliefs, and knowledge about the entities' trustworthiness. Third, given that social interaction is built on expectations that are partially cognitive and based on past experience, it is likely that people's attitudes toward others contain beliefs about the trustworthiness of these others based on past experience, knowledge, and interactions (Rempel, Holmes, & Zanna, 1985).[1]

Given that the specific attitudes individuals form toward other people and toward groups and organizations as a whole are likely to contain knowledge concerning the trustworthiness of the party in question, these individuals' attitudes will be an important aspect of the experience of trust—serving to define and structure social interactions and the experience of trust in ongoing relationships. As Lewis and Weigert (1985) suggest, trust develops from cognitive evaluations of the trustworthiness of other people and groups. Moreover, and as we mentioned previously, whereas trust is

experienced at a general level through values, attitudes are a means through which trust is experienced at a specific level (Butler, 1991; Driscoll, 1978; Scott, 1980), since attitudes are, by definition, object specific and responsive to ongoing experiences with the attitude object. Hence, attitudes structure the experience of trust in specific ongoing relationships.

Note that attitudes and values interact and can affect one another over time (George & Jones, 1997). Attitudes are evaluative in nature, and values are a key determinant of how people come to evaluate other people and organizations. Conversely, changes in attitudes can precipitate a change in values over time so that, for example, repeated exposure to episodes of unethical behavior can change the degree to which a person believes that "honesty is the best policy."

Moods and Emotions.   Moods and emotions capture how people feel as they go about their daily activities, including interacting with other people; they are affective states or feelings that provide people with information about their ongoing experiences and their general state of being (Jacobsen, 1957; Morris, 1989, Nowlis, 1970; Pribam, 1970). The intensity of the affective state is a primary distinguishing feature between moods and emotions. Emotions are intense affective states that interrupt ongoing cognitive processes and behaviors and are tied to particular events or circumstances (Simon, 1982), whereas moods are less intense, pervasive, and generalized affective states that are not explicitly linked to particular events or circumstances. Moods capture more of the day-to-day feelings that people experience—not interrupting ongoing activities but affecting them in more subtle, but also significant, ways (Clare & Isen, 1982; Thayer, 1989).

A well-accepted way of describing moods and emotions is in terms of the extent to which they entail positive or negative affect (Meyer & Shack, 1989; Watson & Pennebaker, 1989; Watson & Tellegen, 1985). Moods and emotions entailing high levels of positive affect can be described by such terms as "excited," "enthusiastic," "active," "elated," "peppy," and "strong," whereas moods and emotions entailing high levels of negative affect can be described by such terms as "distressed," "hostile," "jittery," "nervous," "scornful," and "fearful" (Tellegen, 1985; Watson, Clark, & Tellegen, 1988; Watson & Tellegen, 1985).

Emotions and moods are fundamental aspects of the experience of trust for at least three reasons. First, the experience of trust embodies affect, whether it be in terms of strong or intense feelings (emotions) or more subtle feelings (moods). People often decide if they can initially trust someone by examining the feelings they have toward that person. For example, if, when meeting a stranger, a person experiences high negative affect (e.g., feels jittery, nervous, or even afraid), he or she may initially distrust that person. However, in the presence of a trusted party, a person may experience positive affect and be excited and enthusiastic. The affectively charged nature of trust is also revealed in situations where people feel they have been taken advantage of or betrayed by others; in these situations, emotions become the means used to express feelings of distrust. Moreover, these feelings are transmitted to and recognized by other people so that one person's positive or negative emotions and moods can influence others.

Second, one's current affective state may color one's experience of trust and, thus, the way a person forms opinions and makes judgments about the trustworthiness of others (Schwartz, 1990; Schwartz & Clore, 1988). Suppose, for instance, that a supervisor is in a negative mood when interacting with a subordinate. In trying to assess the trustworthiness of the subordinate in carrying out an important assignment, the supervisor may question the reliability and capabilities of the subordinate, based on his or her negative mood. Similarly, suppose a manager is engaged in negotiations with a supplier while in a particularly good mood. The manager may infer, based on the positive feelings surrounding the interaction, that the supplier is to be trusted.

Experiencing positive moods or emotions may cause one to have more positive perceptions of others and see the world though "rose-colored glasses," resulting in a heightened experience of trust in another person. Conversely, negative moods and emotions may add a negative tone to interactions and may result in an individual perceiving others as less trustworthy than they actually are. Consistent with this reasoning, researchers have shown positive moods to heighten liking for others and to cause people to have more positive beliefs about human nature (Gouaux, 1971; Veitch & Griffitt, 1976), to increase helping and generosity (Isen, 1970; Isen & Levin, 1972), and to promote more integrative as opposed to contentious bargaining in negotiations (Carnevale & Isen, 1986).

Third, trust is built on expectations that are, in part, emotional. When these expectations are broken, an individual often experiences strong emotions, which signal the individual about the violation of trust and the need to attend to the relationship (Barber, 1983; Frijda, 1988). Since they are concerned with current feelings or affective states, moods and emotions—much more so than values or attitudes—contribute to the ongoing experience of trust, providing people with signals concerning the changing nature of their ongoing experience of trust with other people or in particular situations (Frijda, 1988; Schwartz & Clore, 1988).

More so than values and attitudes, moods and emotions fluctuate over time to signal changes in the experience of trust. Also, in contrast to values, which are general in focus, and attitudes, which are object specific, moods and emotions are both general and specific. They are general in that the same kind of mood or emotion may be experienced across a variety of situations and relationships—for example, fear or joy—and they are specific in that certain people, situations, or relationships may be associated with certain kinds of feelings. For example, a person may feel scornful in the presence of a conniving colleague or enthusiastic in the presence of a highly capable collaborator. The feelings are specific to the person, interaction, or relationship but are general in the sense that the same kind of feeling will be experienced again, across people and situations (George & Jones, 1997).

Moods and emotions interact with values and attitudes to determine the experience of trust. Negative feelings arise from witnessing behaviors or activities that are inconsistent with one's values; attitudes affect how people feel, so a very positive attitude toward another can lead to a person feeling good or being in a positive mood. Conversely, if a person experiences a negative mood over a prolonged period of time, his or her attitude can become more negative, which can induce changes in values over time.

In sum, based on the preceding arguments, we propose that, psychologically, the multidimensional experience of trust evolves from the interactions among people's values, attitudes, and moods and emotions. Values provide standards of trust that people strive to achieve in their relationships with others, attitudes provide knowledge of another person's trustworthiness, and current moods and emotions are signals or indicators of the presence and quality of trust in a relationship. We now examine how trust evolves, over time, through the interactions of values, attitudes, and moods and emotions in an organizational setting.

A Model of the Evolution of Trust

When examining the evolution of trust, we believe it useful to model trust from a symbolic interactionist perspective (Blumer, 1962; Mead, 1934). Symbolic interactionism is based on two main assumptions that are pertinent to an analysis of trust: (1) people act in social situations based on the meanings that they have learned to associate with them, and (2) these meanings are acquired by interactions with other people so that a definition of the social situation is created over time. More specifically, in any particular encounter two (or more) parties mutually develop and negotiate a definition of the social situation.

This joint creation of the definition of a social situation involves each party trying to understand the other party's expectations, needs, and goals. As Mead (1934) puts it, a person takes the perspective or role of the other in order to call out the same response in the self. What one party says or does affects the other; the parties then adjust communication and behavior patterns to fit the unfolding,

mutually determined definition of the social situation. In this way the parties develop new definitions of the social situation and the basis of social action changes.

In the context of the evolution of trust, two or more parties are involved in creating a joint definition of the social situation. Each party brings its own set of interpretive schemes to the social situation. To the extent that they use or develop similar interpretive schemes to define the social situation, the parties will tend to agree on their perceptions of the level of trust present in the social situation, so adjustment to each other takes place. The likely nature of this adjustment depends on the degree of congruence or similarity between the values, attitudes, and moods and emotions of the two parties.

The Creation of Conditional and Unconditional Trust. At the beginning of a social encounter, each person does not simply assume that the other is trustworthy; rather, each suspends belief that the other's values may be different from their own—that the other may not be trustworthy. This does not mean that the individual is gullible—a gullible person is one who, in the absence of any information of any kind, takes the other's trustworthiness on faith and assumes the risk of being exploited. The actor in our model simply suspends belief that the other is not trustworthy and behaves as if the other has similar values and can be trusted.

This paradoxical beginning to the experience of trust is likely because, as Luhmann (1980) suggests, trusting another and assuming the other shares one's own values is often preferred to initial distrust, since trust is the easier option; for this reason, there is a strong incentive to begin a relationship with trust. An enormous amount of time and energy would be taken up in discovering the true nature of the other's value system, leading to a major advantage associated with suspending belief that another person has sinister motives (Deutsch, 1958, 1960).

This is not to say that people do not use their own values to decide whether or not to trust another. Perceptions of value incongruence can quickly lead to distrust (Sitkin & Roth, 1993). In meeting a stranger, a person uses his or her value system to decide if the stranger is fit to transact with. In other words, people use their values to decide if others fall within the "zone of their indifference" (Barnard, 1938) and to decide whether their values do not appear to be so divergent that they make themselves vulnerable to the other party. This does not mean, however, that each person's values need to be the same for trust to emerge in a relationship. Rather, we propose that people approach interactions based on their own orienting values, and, if they have no obvious sense that some form of value incongruence exists, they suspend their beliefs that the other party is not to be trusted.

Assuming, then, that distrust is not the outcome of the initial encounter, the experience of future trust will be determined by the content of the behavioral exchanges between the parties— exchanges experienced psychologically, through the evolving attitude developed toward the other party. If trust is to build over time, both parties must be able to take the role of the other and exchange and share the feelings and thoughts that structure the exchange relationship—literally, to develop attitudes toward the other reflecting the other as a trustworthy party. As noted earlier, attitudes have this specific focus and provide the engine of the evolution of trust, capturing the meaning of the behavioral exchanges that lead to the development of trust.

What is the role of moods and emotions in the evolution of trust? As we discussed, the ongoing evolution of trust depends on the development of favorable attitudes and expectations through behavioral exchanges. At every exchange point— from the initial encounter on—moods and emotions affect the ongoing experience and meaning of the relationship. The extent to which one or both parties experience positive moods and emotions in the context of the relationship (1) affects their immediate perceptions and judgments that the other party can be trusted, and will not harm or exploit them, and (2) enhances the likelihood that the parties will develop shared interpretive schemes. Successful behavioral exchanges are accompanied by positive moods and emotions, which help to cement the experience of trust and set the scene for the continuing exchange and building of greater trust. In contrast, negative moods and emotions accompany unfavorable evaluations of the other party, signaling a lack of trust.

Especially important is the role played by moods and emotions, as the mechanisms by which both parties continually evaluate the ongoing quality of the trust experience. More specifically, to the extent that both parties succeed in developing a common frame of reference and can successfully take the role of the other, they promote positive moods. At significant points in the ongoing relationship, such as the achievement of significant preestablished benchmarks, both parties will experience positive emotions. These positive emotions will provide a powerful signal to them that they have succeeded in building trust and that they do, in fact, share the same attitudes and values. At this stage in the experience of trust, the parties' decisions to suspend belief transform into the desire to trust each other, because both feel secure that they will not be harmed or put at risk by the actions of the other and that the other is, in fact, trustworthy.

The point at which the parties to an exchange (1) have strong confidence in each other's values and trustworthiness, (2) have favorable attitudes toward each other, and (3) experience positive affect in the context of the relationship is crucial in the evolution of trust. In order to distinguish between the experience of trust before and after this point, we find it useful to make a distinction between the states of conditional and unconditional trust. *Conditional trust* is a state of trust in which both parties are willing to transact with each other, as long as each behaves appropriately, uses a similar interpretive scheme to define the situation, and can take the role of the other. In conditional trust attitudes of one party toward the other are favorable enough to support future interactions; sufficient positive affect and a relative lack of negative affect reinforce these attitudes.

Conditional trust usually is sufficient to facilitate a wide range of social and economic exchanges; it is consistent with the idea that one of the bases for trust is knowledge (e.g., Lewicki & Bunker, 1996; Shapiro, Sheppard, & Cheraskin, 1992; Sheppard & Tuchinsky, 1996) or positive expectations of the other (Sitkin & Roth, 1993). Indeed, the most common form of trust existing in organizational settings is probably conditional trust.

Unconditional trust, however, characterizes an experience of trust that starts when individuals abandon the "pretense" of suspending belief, because shared values now structure the social situation and become the primary vehicle through which those individuals experience trust. With unconditional trust each party's trustworthiness is now assured, based on confidence in the other's values that is backed up by empirical evidence derived from repeated behavioral interactions—knowledge of which is contained in each individual's attitude toward the other (Butler, 1983). Also, positive affect increases as positive moods and emotions strengthen the affective bonds between parties and bolster the experience of trust. Thus, when unconditional trust is present, relationships become significant and often involve a sense of mutual identification (Lewicki & Bunker, 1996; Shapiro et al., 1992). For this reason, unconditional trust is something to strive for in important social situations.

In our interactionist model, therefore, we propose that there are three distinct states or forms of the trust experience: (1) distrust, (2) conditional trust, and (3) unconditional trust. Note that this model differs from other models of trust found in the literature in two significant ways. First, in this model we conceptualize distrust, conditional trust, and unconditional trust as three different states of the same construct—the trust experience—rather than different constructs. Thus, although our interactionist model shares with that of Sitkin and Roth (1993) and of Fox (1974) the proposition that shared values and expectations help determine the experience of trust, it differs from these models, for they conceptualize trust and distrust as separate constructs, each of which has a different set of determinants. For example, Sitkin and Roth (1993) see the level of trust as determined by met expectations,

whereas distrust is engendered by value incongruence. In our model of trust, the interaction of values, attitudes, and moods and emotions is the mechanism by which both trust and distrust are engendered. It is the interactions among values, attitudes, and moods and emotions that determine whether or not trust exists and what state trust takes—that is, conditional or unconditional.

Second, our interactionist model of trust differs from those developed by Shapiro et al. (1992) and Lewicki and Bunker (1996), who propose that different types of trust are brought about by different kinds of determinants. For example, Shapiro et al. (1992) propose that there are three types of trust: (1) deterrence-based trust, sustained by threat of sanctions; (2) knowledge-based trust, sustained by the ability to predict the behavior of others; and (3) identification-based trust, sustained by a complete empathy with the other party's desires and needs. Each type is quite different or may even be sequential, in a Maslovian, need fulfillment way (Lewicki & Bunker, 1996). As we noted earlier, however, few people have the time or resources to engage in the extensive information processing necessary to monitor the other party's behavior in order to apply appropriate sanctions—or to do so in a way that allows one to predict their future behavior or intentions. Furthermore, ultimately, people are "unknowable," and it is, therefore, impossible to have complete empathy with their often hidden or inexpressible desires and needs. In our model the important state of conditional trust streamlines information processing and allows people to economize on their cognitive and emotional energy while forging ongoing relationships that can lead to unconditional trust but that might also end in distrust.

Thus, rather than asserting that different determinants lead to different types of trust, our interactionist model conceptualizes trust as a changing or evolving experience, in which values, attitudes, and moods and emotions operate simultaneously to produce an overall state of trust or distrust. Hence, we view trust as a more dynamic kind of experience—one that can shift or change, sometimes quickly, among trust states. Indeed, one important implication of the analysis is that conditional trust can change into unconditional trust, but it is also possible for unconditional trust to change into conditional trust or even distrust.

The Dissolution of Trust.   Researchers have given the ways in which trust can dissolve or disappear over time considerable attention. For example, Butler (1983) found that when one party signals positive expectations or favorable attitudes to another and the other reciprocates those expectations, trust spirals upwards; when expectations are not reciprocated, trust spirals downwards. The symbolic interactionist model of trust sheds additional light on the process by which trust spirals down or dissolves because it conceptualizes trust as a construct that has three principal states and because it focuses on the interactions among values, attitudes, and moods and emotions as determinants of which state currently exists.

At the beginning of a relationship, for example, if experiencing trust between the parties appears impossible because obvious value differences preclude the ability of each to take the role of the other, trust will not develop; distrust will be engendered if obvious value incongruence exists (Sitkin, 1995; Sitkin & Roth, 1993). Assuming that trust evolves into conditional trust, any subsequent discrepant behavioral exchanges or violations of mutually agreed upon expectations will cause trust to be reduced (Sitkin & Roth, 1993), thus putting the trust relationship in jeopardy. In terms of the present model, what were once favorable attitudes toward the other become increasingly unfavorable, positive affect disappears, and negative affect is experienced. In this scenario conditional trust can quickly spiral downward and dissolve, and distrust will appear at the point where the ability to suspend belief that the other is not trustworthy is lost.

If trust has become unconditional, however, the dissolution process becomes more complex. When unconditional trust exists, the exchange relationship is infused with meaning and positive affect derived from value sharing. Now, short-term behavioral lapses by one party are likely to be forgiven by the other, because shared values orient the parties to the future and condition the prospective exchange relationship. Behavioral lapses, thus, may not dissolve the trust bond, but emotional outbursts will be likely since they are the means by which parties signal the experience of broken trust and its accompanying negative affect. The wronged party's negative emotions signal to him or her that the relationship is in need of attention (Frijda, 1988), and the expression of these feelings via emotional outbursts signals to the other party that a lapse in trust has occurred.

In this case emotion is the signal that triggers a reappraisal of the relationship; it brings to consciousness again the question of whether or not one party might be put at risk by the actions of the other. Responses of both parties to this signal, therefore, can quickly change the quality of the experience of trust, and potentially destroy it. Emotional outbursts may cause unconditional trust to shift to conditional trust, but under certain circumstances, they can also cause unconditional trust to shift to distrust.

The strength of the perceived violation that puts trust to the test is the key contingency in determining whether unconditional trust shifts to conditional trust or distrust. Sometimes, the magnitude of the discrepant behavior can be so enormous that is precipitates an immediate collapse of trust: the injured party is assured that discrepant values exist, attitudes become unfavorable, and negative emotions signal the end of the trust experience. For example, a small business owner who discovers that a trusted employee has been embezzling funds may experience an immediate breakdown in trust. In this case the business owner's strong negative emotions (Lewicki & Bunker, 1996) are accompanied by a realization of value incongruence and the development of a very negative attitude toward the other party; distrust is immediately engendered (Sitkin & Roth, 1993).

In other situations an individual may perceive repeated lapses to be minor enough to be forgiven in the context of shared values and favorable attitudes. Indeed, one of the purposes of an individual's emotional outburst—and, thus, a key role affect plays in the model—is to signal strongly to the other party the need to change specific behaviors in order to maintain the experience of unconditional trust. Over time, if such changes in behavior do not occur, negative moods and emotions begin to pervade the relationship, and attitudes evolve to be more and more unfavorable, in line with observed behavioral lapses.

When the change in attitudes, accompanied by negative affect, alters an individual's perceptions of shared values, the interactions among these constructs precipitate a downward spiral, and unconditional trust turns into conditional trust. Finally, if trust continues to deteriorate, a party can no longer take the role of the other and believe in the other's trustworthiness, which results in conditional trust shifting to distrust. Common expressions, such as "that was the last straw," capture how a wronged party, who has sought to recreate or perpetuate a trust relationship through successive behavioral lapses, eventually finds it impossible to keep taking the role of the other. At this point distrust appears, as parties feel they have reason to believe they might be exploited by the other in the future.

Trust cannot be reestablished until either both parties willingly renegotiate the relationship or the injured party willingly reconciles him- or herself to the violation(s) and is able to restore the former positive attitude toward the other. Our interactionist model thus differs from others because all three factors—values, attitudes, and moods and emotions—are needed to analyze the transformation of trust among the conditional trust, unconditional trust, and distrust states.

Trust and Cooperation in Organizations

In the 1990s scholars have given considerable attention to the importance of increasing the level of interpersonal cooperation and teamwork in organizations. The increased use of self-managed work teams in organizations, combined with the elimination of middle management positions as a result of organizational restructuring, has highlighted the importance of interpersonal cooperation and teamwork for organizational effectiveness (Cohen, Ledford, & Spreitzer, 1996; Dunphy & Bryant, 1996). In addition, many researchers have argued that extra-role behavior and organizational citizenship behavior can be promoted by raising the level of cooperation (e.g., Katz, 1964; Organ, 1988; Organ & Ryan, 1995; Van Dyne, Cummings, & Parks, 1995). Others have argued further that the organizational capabilities that can give an organization a sustainable competitive advantage are embedded in the skills and knowledge of organizational members (Amit & Schoemaker, 1993) and in the interactions among them—particularly in groups and teams.

As we noted earlier, scholars have widely acknowledged that trust can lead to cooperative behavior in organizations (Axelrod, 1984; Mayer et al., 1995; McAllister, 1995). Using the model of trust described above, we can examine how the substantive differences between conditional and unconditional trust have different implications for the level of cooperative behavior and associated performance benefits in group and organizational settings. As a case in point, we focus here on an important kind of cooperative behavior in organizations: interpersonal cooperation and teamwork. Although both conditional and unconditional trust may result in interpersonal cooperation and teamwork, we propose that the nature of organizational cooperation will be fundamentally different under these two forms of trust.

As we stated previously conditional trust—in which developing attitudes are favorable enough to support future interactions—is sufficient to facilitate many kinds of exchanges between coworkers in organizational settings or between business acquaintances. When unconditional trust exists—in which shared values create a common bond—a different scenario occurs; people begin to feel that they are not mere coworkers or business acquaintances but colleagues, friends, or team members. In other words, although the presence of conditional trust allows a group to work toward a common goal, the existence of unconditional trust can fundamentally change the quality of the exchange relationship and convert a group into a team. With teamwork what one person does is determined by what all others are doing, and the parties must be constantly alert to the ways others are behaving in order to be able to respond appropriately.

In terms of the model of trust described above, if only conditional trust exists and attitudes primarily govern the exchange process, parties to an exchange are likely to cooperate to maintain their own good standing in the eyes of others. However, because they lack the same stake or investment in the relationship that is present when unconditional trust exists, parties are less likely to cooperate in ways that entail considerable personal costs or self-sacrifice; the assurance of shared values that orient the parties to the future is absent, and positive affect is less likely to infuse relationships.

In contrast, if unconditional trust exists, parties' shared values determine their behavioral expectations as they invest in their relationship and look more to the future than the present when deciding how to behave (Dasgupta, 1988). Shared values and positive moods and emotions are manifested in interpersonal cooperation and teamwork and the strong desires of team members to contribute to the common good. Cooperative acts themselves often make people feel good and stimulate others to act in a similar fashion, reinforcing shared values and positive attitudes and affect.

Additionally, researchers have found that positive affective states promote social interaction and creativity (e.g., Isen & Baron, 1991; Isen, Daubman, & Nowicki, 1987)—two important contributors to the development of synergistic team relationships. Shared values result in strong desires to cooperate, even at personal expense, which overcomes problems of shirking and free riding.

Although unconditional trust has direct effects on interpersonal cooperation and teamwork, it can have indirect effects as well. This is because the sharing of values characteristic of unconditional trust also promotes seven kinds of social processes that can lead to the development of synergistic

team relationships in an organizational setting, which, in turn, can lead to superior performance. These include (1) broad role definitions, (2) communal relationships, (3) high confidence in others, (4) help-seeking behavior, (5) free exchange of knowledge and information, (6) subjugation of personal needs and ego for the greater common good, and (7) high involvement (e.g., Anderson & Williams, 1996; Clark, Ouellette, Powell, & Milberg, 1987; Morrison, 1994). We consider each of these social processes in turn (Figure 1).

Broad Role Definitions.   How broadly or narrowly individuals define their work roles has been shown to influence cooperative behaviors (Morrison, 1994). When conditional trust exists, individuals define their roles in accordance with expected job behaviors and assigned duties. When unconditional trust exists, the interactions among values, attitudes, and moods and emotions are likely to lead individuals to define their roles more broadly.

For example, shared values and expressions of positive affect typically result in individuals wanting to cooperate and to do whatever they can for the common good; hence, they will define their roles broadly to include whatever acts they are capable of performing that contribute to common goals and raise performance and competitive advantage. Thus, organizational citizenship behavior improves in a climate of unconditional trust.

Communal Relationships.   Many exchange relationships in organizations are driven by a quid pro quo orientation, in which individuals cooperate and help each other to compensate for past help received or in anticipation of future help needed. Cooperation driven by conditional trust is likely to involve such a calculative mentality, and, as long as behavioral expectations are realized, attitudes sustain the cooperative behavior.

Researchers have contrasted these kinds of exchange relationships with communal relationships, in which people not only feel obligated to help each other and cooperate but also want to and feel responsible for doing so, thus leading to

FIGURE 1

Proposed effects of unconditional trust on interpersonal cooperation and teamwork

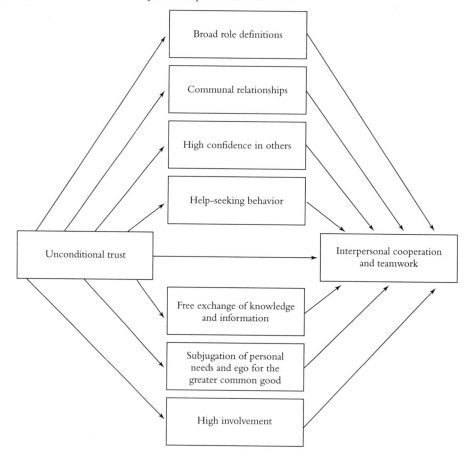

increased helping and cooperation (Clark & Mills, 1979; Clark et al., 1987). The shared values underlying unconditional trust guide people to strive for communal relationships characterized by helpfulness and responsibility, and to contribute to the development of such relationships. Communal relationships, in turn, are likely to promote interpersonal cooperation and teamwork.

High Confidence in Others.   Positive attitudes characteristic of conditional trust may provide an individual with a certain degree of confidence in others, but this confidence is guarded, in that the individual can never be sure about the others' real intentions or ultimate goals (Dasgupta, 1988). In contrast, the shared values that underlie unconditional trust provide individuals with the high degree of confidence in each other necessary for synergistic team relationships to emerge. The sharing of values promotes high confidence in others, because one can be assured of others' ultimate intentions and objectives (Bateson, 1988); moreover, consequent displays of positive affect promote social bonding. Hence, people are more likely to engage in synergistic social behaviors and make organizational-specific investments.

Help-Seeking Behavior.   Whether or not cooperation and teamwork occur depends upon group members being aware of opportunities for them. When members of a group actively seek help, this increases other members' awareness of opportunities for cooperative behavior (Anderson & Williams, 1996). However, there are sometimes powerful constraints against help seeking. For example, when conditional trust exists, people may refrain from seeking help because they do not want others to think they are inadequate, they do not want to be indebted to another person, or they do not want to feel threatened by being dependent upon another person (e.g., Brehm, 1966; Greenberg, 1980; Nadler, 1991; Walster, Walster, & Berscheid, 1978).

Unconditional trust is likely to remove these constraints against help seeking. When trust is unconditional, feelings of indebtedness are irrelevant, as shared values and reciprocated feelings underlie cooperation and make people want to cooperate. Seeking help is not threatening under unconditional trust because interdependence is seen as a positive force—not something to be avoided—and shared values and positive attitudes ensure against attributions of inadequacy. Hence, we propose that individuals will be much more likely to seek help under condition of unconditional, as opposed to conditional, trust. Also, help seeking contributes to cooperative interpersonal behavior and teamwork and their consequent benefits (Anderson & Williams, 1996).

Free   Exchange   of   Knowledge   and Information.   Knowledge and information are not likely to be exchanged freely when one party cannot be sure about the moral basis of another party's actions or the values that are prospectively guiding that party's behavior. Positive attitudes characteristic of conditional trust will promote the sharing of knowledge to accomplish ongoing tasks, but little more (Williamson, 1985). When people are unsure of others' values, they will refrain from freely exchanging knowledge and information because of their uncertainty about how the others will use this information (e.g., for their own benefit) and because

possessing that knowledge (particularly if it is hard to come by) is a source of power (Fama & Jensen, 1983a, b). Under conditions of unconditional trust, however, shared values underlying trust provide individuals with the assurance that knowledge and information will be used for the greater good and that one need not exercise power to protect one's own interests.

Subjugation of Personal Needs and Ego. Individuals are unlikely to subjugate their own needs and egos to pursue a common goal when only conditional trust exists, because they cannot be sure if others will be doing the same. There is always the potential that some individuals will passively shirk or free ride on the efforts of others (Holmstrom, 1979) or that individuals seek their own gain at the expense of the greater good (e.g., Alchian & Demsetz, 1972; Hill, 1990). The "sucker effect" (e.g., Jackson & Harkins, 1985; Kerr, 1983) suggests that, in such circumstances, people will subjugate their needs and egos so as not to be taken advantage by others.

However, the shared values underlying unconditional trust provide individuals with greater assurance that others will act in good faith and will be guided by the same prospective standards as oneself. Hence, unconditional trust is more likely to lead people to subjugate their own needs and egos for the greater good because of the greater assurance that others are doing the same.

High Involvement.   Interpersonal cooperation and teamwork necessitate a high degree of involvement on the part of individuals. Each individual must not only contribute fully but also must be highly involved in the activities of others; high involvement requires members of a team to commit fully to the team endeavor. Conditional trust is unlikely to promote high involvement because, although positive attitudes may facilitate communication and the sharing of information, uncertainty about others' ultimate intentions [is] likely to cause an individual to refrain from getting too highly involved.

The sharing of values characteristic of unconditional trust provides individuals with the assurance they need to become fully involved in a team endeavor. As Mead notes, "The sense of teamwork is found when all are working towards a common end and everyone has a sense of the common end interpenetrating the particular function which he (she) is carrying on" (1934: 276); unconditional trust can produce this feeling of high involvement.

In sum, we propose that when unconditional trust is present in relationships, organizational members are more likely to cooperate and develop synergistic team relationships. In turn, these synergistic team relations lead to superior performance benefits, such as the development of unique organizational capabilities and extra-role behaviors that can give an organization a competitive advantage.

Implications and Conclusions

We can use the theoretical distinction between conditional and unconditional trust, rooted in the interactions among values, attitudes, and moods and emotions, to explain why organizational cooperation does and does not occur, as well as why different kinds and degrees of cooperation develop. Conditional trust promotes those cooperative behaviors not entailing significant personal costs or self-sacrifice. However, when an organization needs employees to perform cooperative behaviors that are arduous and time consuming and that entail considerable self-sacrifice and no tangible reward, conditional trust may not be enough.

We propose that in these cases unconditional trust is key; when it exists people want to perform these acts. The psychological experience of unconditional trust, accompanied by the positive feelings that flow from its actualization, is its own reward. At the organizational level the performance benefits deriving from unconditional trust include the competitive advantage that accrues from an organization's ability to reap the value added produced by teamwork, synergy, and the development of valuable organizational capabilities.

Indeed, many researchers have argued that one of the sources of an organization's competitive advantage is its organizational capabilities producing tacit knowledge—the unspoken, implicit knowledge embedded in the interactions among people in teams that contributes to superior performance (Amit & Schoemaker, 1993; Prahalad & Hamel, 1990). One of the central characteristics of organizational capabilities that contributes to their value is the extent to which they are unique and cannot be imitated. To the degree that other organizations can copy or mimic a focal organization's capabilities, these capabilities will not be a long-term source of competitive advantage. Hence, researchers have focused on identifying the "isolating mechanisms" that make it difficult or impossible for competitors to imitate organizational capabilities (Rumelt, 1984). One of these isolating mechanisms is trust (Barney & Hansen, 1994).

Based on our analysis of trust, we propose that the development of the unique capabilities that lead to tacit knowledge depends on the existence of unconditional, rather than conditional, trust between people. Conditional trust develops as people exchange information and develop positive attitudes toward each other, allowing them to take the role of the other. Through conditional trust people develop stable expectations of each other that routinize their interactions and make them predictable and reliable. Yet, the emergence of these stable, routine interactions is a necessary but not sufficient condition for the emergence of tacit knowledge, because such routine interactions can be systematized into sets of rules and procedures, which, by definition, can be copied and imitated by other organizations (Granovetter, 1985; Mahoney, 1996).

We propose that in order for organizations to have the capability for real synergy among their members, leading to the development of tacit knowledge that cannot be translated into rules or routines, individuals must develop unconditional trust. This is because only unconditional trust promotes the kind of intense interpersonal cooperation and synergistic relationships discussed above. The tacit knowledge that results from real synergy is often taken for granted by organizational members (Itami, 1987; Ployani, 1962). But it is difficult and extremely time consuming to translate into standards or procedures or to explain to people who are not involved in the interactions themselves. The intense interactions in teams, facilitated by unconditional trust, are both the generators and actualizers of tacit knowledge. Hence, a real source of competitive advantage deriving from organizational capabilities is an organization's ability to create the conditions that allow its members to experience unconditional trust.

However, the development of trust (conditional or unconditional) is a function of an organization's ability to create the setting within which trust can develop over time. Does the work environment and context promote positive attitudes and positive moods and emotions? Does the organizational culture endorse and encourage the expression of the values underlying trust (Fiol, 1991)? Are individuals given the opportunity to explore shared values? Does the organization's structure provide the appropriate set of task and reporting relationships that facilitates the development of positive attitudes and moods?

We need to make an important distinction between organizations that strive to create unconditional trust versus those that are content simply to operate with a predominance of relationships built on conditional trust. Although significant advantages may accrue from the state of unconditional trust—heightened cooperative behavior leading to synergistic team relationships, for one—unconditional trust does not come without costs (Jones, 1983). It takes time, effort, and considerable resources to build and maintain unconditional trust. For example, a relationship of unconditional trust between a supervisor and a subordinate necessitates that the supervisor be supportive of the subordinate and look out for the subordinate's well-being (Eisenberger, Fasolo, & Davis-La Mastro, 1990).

Some organizations may not be willing to make investments in their employees or to provide the kinds of organizational support that will promote the development of unconditional trust. Other organizations may want or need the flexibility to lay off employees as economic conditions warrant. Within these kinds of organizations, unconditional trust is not a viable option, and conditional trust will remain the more common state of trust. But, for organizations that can choose to encourage the development of unconditional trust among their employees, the benefits can be many, especially in terms of cooperation and teamwork that promote high performance and competitive advantage.

Endnotes

1. Beliefs are a more general concept than attitudes, since they embrace both attitudes and values. For example, Sproull (1981) distinguishes between three types of beliefs: (1) descriptive beliefs, which are quasi-objective statements of fact about a person or situation (the way things are around here); (2) causal beliefs, which explain why certain events happen (things are the way they are because of . . .); and (3) normative beliefs, which specify a preference or preferred way for what should happen (things should be this way because . . .). Thus, normative beliefs are akin to values, whereas the other two are dimensions of attitudes and have a more specific focus. In this article we view attitudes as object specific and values as more general orienting factors.

References

Alchian, A. A., & Demsetz, H. 1972. Production, information costs, and economic performance. *American Economic Review,* 62: 777–795.

Amit, R., & Schoemaker, P. J. H. 1993. Strategic assets as organizational rent. *Strategic Management Journal,* 14: 33–46.

Anderson, N. H., & Armstrong, N. A. 1989. Cognitive theory and methodology for studying marital interaction. In D. Brindberg & D. Jaccard (Eds.), *Dyadic decision making:* 3–49. New York: Springer-Verlag.

Anderson, S. E., & Williams, L. J. 1996. Interpersonal, job, and individual factors related to helping processes at work. *Journal of Applied Psychology,* 81: 282–296.

Axelrod, R. 1984. *The evolution of cooperation.* New York: Basic Books.

Barnard, C. I. 1938. *The functions of the executive.* Cambridge, MA: Harvard University Press.

Barney, J. B., & Hansen, M. H. 1994. Trustworthiness as a source of competitive advantage. *Strategic Management Journal.* 15: 175–190.

Barber, B. 1983. *The logic and limits of trust.* New Brunswick, NJ: Rutgers University Press.

Bateson, P. 1988. The biological evolution of cooperation and trust. In D. Gambetta (Ed.), *Trust: Making and breaking cooperative relations:* 14–30. New York: Basil Blackwell.

Blumer, H. 1962. Society as symbolic interactionism. In A. Rose (Ed.), *Human behavior and social processes.* London: Routledge and Kegan Paul.

Brehm, J. W. 1966. *A theory of psychological reactance.* New York: Academic Press.

Butler, J. K. 1983. Reciprocity of trust between professionals and their secretaries. *Psychological Reports.* 53: 411–416.

Butler, J. K. 1991. Toward understanding and measuring conditions of trust: Evolution of a conditions of trust inventory. *Journal of Management,* 17: 643–663.

Carnevale, P. J. D., & Isen, A. M. 1986. The influence of positive affect and visual access on the discovery of integrative solutions in bilateral negotiation. *Organizational Behavior and Human Decision Processes.* 37: 1–13.

Clark, M. S., & Isen, A. M. 1982. Towards understanding the relationship between feeling states and social behavior. In A. H. Hastorf & A. M. Isen (Eds.), *Cognitive social psychology:* 73–108. New York: Elsevier Science Publications.

Clark, M. S., & Mills, J. 1979. Interpersonal attraction in exchange and communal relationships. *Journal of Personality and Social Psychology,* 37: 12–24.

Clark, M. S., & Ouellette, R., Powell, M. C., & Milberg, S. 1987. Recipient's mood, relationship type, and helping. *Journal of Personality and Social Psychology,* 53: 94–103.

Cohen, S. G., Ledford, G. E., & Spreitzer, G. M. 1996. A predictive model of self-managing work team effectiveness. *Human Relations,* 49: 643–676.

Dasgupta, P. 1988. Trust as a commodity. In D. G. Gambetta (Ed.), *Trust:* 49–72. New York: Basil Blackwell.

Deutsch, M. 1958. Trust and suspicion. *Journal of Conflict Resolution,* 2: 265–279.

Deutsch, M. 1960. The effect of motivational orientation upon trust and suspicion. *Human Relations.* 13: 123–140.

Driscoll, J. W. 1978. Trust and participation in organizational decision making as predictors of satisfaction. *Academy of Management Journal,* 21: 44–56.

Dunphy, D., & Bryant, B. 1996. Teams: Panaceas or prescriptions for improved performance? *Human Relations.* 49: 677–699.

Eisenberger, R., Fasolo, P., & Davis-La Mastro, V. 1990. Perceived organizational support and employee diligence, commitment, and innovation. *Journal of Applied Psychology,* 75: 51–59.

Fama, E. F., & Jensen, M. C. 1983a. Agency problems and residual claims. *Journal of Law and Economics,* 26: 327–349.

Fama, E. F., & Jensen, M. C. 1983b. Separation of ownership and contract. *Journal of Law and Economics,* 26: 301–325.

Fiol, C. M. 1991. Managing culture as a competitive resource: An identity based view of sustainable competitive advantage. *Journal of Management,* 17: 191–211.

Fox, A. 1974. *Beyond contract: Work power and trust relations.* London: Faber and Faber.

Frijda, N. H. 1988. The laws of emotion. *American Psychologist,* 43: 349–358.

Gabarro, J. 1978. The development of trust, influence, and expectations. In A. G. Athos & J. J. Gabarro (Eds.), *Interpersonal behavior: Communication and understanding in relationships:* 290–303. Englewood Cliffs, NJ: Prentice-Hall.

Gambetta, D. G. (Ed.). 1988. Can we trust trust? In D. G. Gambetta (Ed.), *Trust:* 213–237. New York: Basil Blackwell.

George, J. M., & Jones, G. R. 1997. Experiencing work: Values, attitudes, and moods. *Human Relations,* 30: 393–416.

Good, D. 1988. Individuals, interpersonal relations, and trust. In D. G. Gambetta (Ed.), *Trust:* 131–185. New York: Basil Blackwell.

Gouaux, C. 1971. Induced affective states and interpersonal attraction. *Journal of Personality and Social Psychology,* 20: 37–43.

Granovetter, M. 1985. Economic action and social structure: The problems of embeddedness. *American Journal of Sociology,* 91: 481–510.

Greenberg, M. S. 1980. A theory of indebtedness. In K. J. Gergen, M. S. Greenberg, & R. H. Willis (Eds.), *Social exchange: Advances in theory and research:* 190–210. New York: Plenum.

Hill, C. W. L. 1990. Cooperation, opportunism, and the invisible hand: Implications for transaction cost theory. *Academy of Management Review,* 15: 500–513.

Holmstrom, B. 1979: Moral hazard and observability. *Bell Journal of Economics,* 10: 74–91.

Isen, A. M. 1970. Success, failure, attention, and reactions to others: The warm glow of success. *Journal of Personality and Social Psychology,* 15: 294–301.

Isen, A. M., & Baron, R. A. 1991. Positive affect as a factor in organizational behavior. In B. M. Staw & L. L. Cummings (Eds.). *Research in organizational behavior,* vol. 13: 1–54. Greenwich, CT: JAI Press.

Isen, A. M., Daubman, K. A., & Nowicki, G. P. 1987. Positive affect facilitates creative problem solving. *Journal of Personality and Social Psychology,* 52: 1122–1131.

Isen, A. M., & Levin, A. F. 1972. Effects of feeling good on helping: Cookies and kindness. *Journal of Personality and Social Psychology,* 21: 384–388.

Itami, H. 1987. Mobilizing invisible assets. Boston: Harvard University Press.

Jackson, J. M., & Harkins, S. G. 1985. Equity in effort: An explanation of the social loafing effect. *Journal of Personality and Social Psychology,* 49: 1199–1206.

Jacobsen, E. 1957. Normal and pathological moods: Their nature and functions. In R. S. Eisler, A. F. Freud, H. Harman, & E. Kris (Eds.), *The psychoanalytic study of the child.* 731–13. New York: International University Press.

Jennings, E. E. 1967. *The mobile manager.* Ann Arbor, MI: University of Michigan.

Jennings, E. E. 1971. *Routes to the executive suite.* New York: McGraw-Hill.

Jones, G. R. 1983. Transaction costs, property rights, and organizational culture: An exchange perspective. *Administrative Science Quarterly,* 28: 454–467.

Katz, D. 1964. The motivational basis or organizational behavior. *Behavioral Science,* 9: 131–146.

Kerr, N. L. 1982. Motivation losses in small groups: A social dilemma analysis. *Journal of Personality and Social Psychology,* 45: 819–828.

Kramer, R. M., & Tyler, T. R. (Eds.). 1996. *Trust in organizations.* Thousand Oaks, CA: Sage.

Kruglanski, A. W. 1989. *Lay epistemics and human knowledge: Cognitive and motivational bases.* New York: Plenum.

Lewicki, R. J., & Bunker, B. B. 1996. Developing and maintaining trust in work relationships. In R. M. Kramer & T. R. Tyler (Eds.), *Trust in organizations:* 114–139. Thousand Oaks, CA: Sage.

Lewis, J., & Weigert, A. 1985. Trust as a social reality. *Social Forces,* 63: 967–985.

Luhmann, N. 1980. *Trust and power.* New York: Wiley.

Mahoney, J. T. 1996. *The management of resources and the resource of management.* Working paper, University of Illinois at Urbana-Champaign.

Mayer, R. C., Davis, J. H., & Schoorman, F. D. 1995. An integrative model of organizatoinal trust. *Academy of Management Review,* 20: 709–734.

McAllister, D. J. 1995. Affect- and cognition-based trust as foundations for interpersonal cooperation in organizations. *Academy of Management Journal,* 38: 24–59.

Mead, G. H. 1934. *Mind, self, and society.* Chicago: University of Chicago Press.

Meyer, G. J. & Shack, J. R. 1989. Structural convergence of mood and personality: Evidence for old and new directions. *Journal of Personality and Social Psychology,* 57: 691–706.

Morris, W. N. 1989. *Mood: The frame of mind.* New York: Springer-Verlag.

Morrison, E. W. 1994. Role definitions and organizational citizenship behavior: The importance of the employee's perspective. *Academy of Management Journal,* 37: 1543–1567.

Nadler, A. 1991. Help-seeking behavior: Psychological costs and instrumental benefits. In M. S. Clark (Ed.), *Prosocial behavior: Review of personality and social psychology:* 290–311. New York: Academic Press.

Nowlis, V. 1970. Mood: Behavior and experience. In M. Arnold (Ed.), *Feelings and emotions:* 261–277. New York: Academic Press.

Olson, J. M., & Zanna, M. P. 1993. Attitudes and attitude change. *Annual Review of Psychology,* 44: 117–154.

Organ, D. W. 1988. *Organizational citizenship behavior: The good soldier syndrome.* Lexington, MA: Lexington Books.

Organ, D. W., & Ryan, K. 1995. A meta-analytic review of attitudinal and dispositional predictors of organizational citizenship behavior. *Personnel Psychology,* 48: 775–802.

Polyani, M. 1962. *Personal knowledge.* Chicago: University of Chicago Press.

Prahalad, C. K., & Hamel, G. 1990. The core competence of the corporation. *Harvard Business Review,* 90(3): 79–91.

Pribam, K. H. 1970. Feelings as monitors. In M. Arnold (Ed.), *Feelings and emotions:* 41–53. New York: Academic Press.

Rempel, J. K., Holmes, J. G., & Zanna, M. P. 1985. Trust in close relationships. *Journal of Personality and Social Psychology,* 49: 95–112.

Robinson, S. L. 1996. Trust and breach of the psychological contract. *Administrative Science Quarterly,* 41: 574–599.

Rokeach, M. 1973. *The nature of human values.* New York: Free Press.

Rotter, J. B. 1980. Interpersonal trust, trustworthiness, and gullibility. *American Psychologist,* 35: 1–7.

Rumelt, R. P. 1984. Towards a strategic theory of the firm. In R. B. Lamb (Ed.), *Competitive strategic management:* 556–570. Englewood Cliffs, NJ: Prentice-Hall.

Sabel, C. F. 1993. Studied trust: Building new forms of cooperation in a volatile economy. *Human Relations,* 46: 1133–1170.

Schwartz, N. 1990. Feelings as information. In E. T. Higgins & R. M. Sorrentino (Eds.), *Handbook of motivation and cognition: Foundations of social behavior,* vol. 2: 527–561. New York: Guilford Press.

Schwartz, N., & Clore, G. L. 1988. How do I feel about it? The informative function of affective states. In K. Fiedler & J. Forgas (Eds.), *Affect, cognition and social behavior:* 44–62. Lewiston, NY: Hogrefe.

Scott, C. L. III. 1980. Interpersonal trust: A comparison of attitudinal and situational factors. *Human Relations,* 33: 805–812.

Shapiro, D. L., Sheppard, B. H., & Cheraskin, L. 1992. Business on a handshake. *Negotiation Journal,* 8(4): 365–377.

Sheppard, B. H., & Tuchinsky, M. 1996. Micro-OB and the network organization. In R. M. Kramer & T. R. Tyler (Eds.), *Trust in organizations:* 140–165. Thousand Oaks, CA: Sage.

Simon, H. A. 1982. Comments. In M. S. Clark & S. T. Fiske (Eds.), *Affect and cognition:* 333–342. Hillsdale, NJ: Lawrence Erlbaum Associates.

Sitkin, S. B. 1995. On the positive effect of legalization on trust. In R. J. Bies, R. J. Lewicki, & B. H. Sheppard (Eds.), *Research in negotiations in organizations,* vol. 5: 185–217. Greenwich, CT: JAI Press.

Sitkin, S. B., & Roth, N. L. 1993. Explaining the limited effectiveness of legalistic "remedies" for trust/distrust. *Organization Science,* 4: 367–392.

Sproull, L. 1981. Beliefs in organizations. In P. C. Nystrom & W. H. Starbuck (Eds.), *Handbook of organizational designs:* 203–224. Oxford, England: Oxford University Press.

Stack, L. 1978. Trust. In H. London & J. E. Exner, Jr. (eds.), *Dimensions of personality:* 561–599. New York: Wiley.

Tellegen, A. 1985. Structures of mood and personality and their relevance to assessing anxiety, with an emphasis on self-report. In A. H. Tuma & J. D. Maser (Eds.), *Anxiety and the anxiety disorders:* 681–706. Hillsdale, NJ: Lawrence Erlbaum Associates.

Thayer, R. E. 1989. *The biopsychology of mood and arousal.* New York: Oxford University Press.

Thompson, J. D. 1967. Organizations in action. New York: McGraw-Hill.

Van Dyne, L., Cummings, L. L., & Parks, J. M. 1995. Extra-role behaviors: In pursuit of construct and definitional clarity. In B. M. Staw & L. L. Cummings (Eds.), *Research in organizational behavior,* vol. 17: 215–285. Greenwich, CT: JAI Press.

Veitch, R., & Griffitt, W. 1976. Good news-bad news: Affective and interpersonal effects. *Journal of Applied Social Psychology,* 6: 69–75.

Walster, E., Walster, G. W., & Berscheid, E. 1978. *Equity: Theory and Research.* Boston: Allyn and Bacon.

Watson, D., Clark, L. A., & Tellegen, A. 1988. Development and validation of brief measures of positive and negative affect: The PANAS scales. *Journal of Personality and Social Psychology,* 54: 1063–1070.

Watson, D., & Pennebaker, J. W. 1989. Health complaints, stress, and distress: Exploring the central role of negative affectivity. *Psychological Review,* 96: 234–254.

Watson, D., & Tellegen, A. 1985. Toward a consensual structure of mood. *Psychological Bulletin,* 98: 219–235.

Williamson, O. E. 1985. The economic institutions of capitalism. New York: Free Press.

Zucker, L. G. 1987. Institutional theories of organization. *Annual Review of Sociology,* 13: 443–464.

READING 29
CREATING READINESS FOR ORGANIZATIONAL CHANGE

Achilles A. Armenakis
Stanley G. Harris
Kevin W. Mossholder

Introduction

Because of increasingly dynamic environments, organizations are continually confronted with the need to implement changes in strategy, structure, process, and culture. Many factors contribute to the effectiveness with which such organizational changes are implemented. One such factor is readiness for change. Readiness, which is similar to Lewin's (1951) concept of unfreezing, is reflected in organizational members' beliefs, attitudes, and intentions regarding the extent to which changes are needed and the organization's capacity to successfully make those changes. Readiness is the *cognitive* precursor to the *behaviors of* either resistance to, or support for, a change effort. Schein (1979) has argued "the reason so many change efforts run into resistance or outright failure is usually directly traceable to their not providing for an effective unfreezing process before attempting a change induction" (p. 144). Although some researchers have discussed the importance of readiness (cf. Beckhard & Harris, 1987; Beer & Walton, 1987; Turner, 1982), it has seldom been recognized as being distinct from resistance (cf. Coch & French, 1948; Kotter & Schlesinger, 1979; Lawrence, 1954). Specifically, creating readiness has been most often explained in conjunction with prescriptions for reducing resistance. For example, Kotter and Schlesinger (1979) discuss several strategies in dealing with resistance (e.g., education and communication, participation and involvement, facilitation and support, negotiation and agreement). Such prescriptions are effective in reducing resistance to

the extent that they first create readiness. In essence, readiness for change may act to preempt the likelihood of resistance to change, increasing the potential for change efforts to be more effective.

Making an explicit distinction between readiness and resistance helps refine discussions of the implementation of change efforts and captures the spirit of the proactive change agent (cf. Armenakis, Mossholder, & Harris, 1990; Kanter, 1983; Kissler, 1991). Framing a change project in terms of readiness seems more congruent with the image of proactive managers who play the roles of coaches and champions of change, rather than those whose role is to reactively monitor the workplace for signs of resistance.

The purpose of this article is to clarify the readiness concept and examine how change agents can influence organizational members' readiness for change. Because the energy, inspiration, and support necessary to create readiness must come from within the organization, this article focuses primarily on the activities of internal change agents (i.e., organizational leaders, managers, etc.). Clearly, external change agents can also benefit from a heightened sensitivity to the creation of readiness. In addition to playing a role in providing information important to readiness creation, external change agents are often in a position to educate internal change agents regarding the importance of readiness.

As a means of fulfilling the article's purpose, the theoretical underpinnings of the readiness concept and the strategies used in creating readiness will be described and an integrative model offered. To enrich this discussion, the actual efforts of one organization to create readiness for a large-scale change are highlighted.

Source: Achilles A. Armenakis, Stanley G. Harris, and Kevin W. Mossholder, "Creating Readiness for Organizational Change," *Human Relations,* vol. 46, no. 6, pp. 681–703. Reprinted by permission of Plenum Publishing Corporation.

A Readiness Model

Theoretical Basis.   A classic study by Coch and French (1948), traditionally described as an experiment in reducing resistance to change, demonstrated the value of allowing organization members to participate in change efforts. Four research groups were formed to represent varying degrees of participation including no participation (the comparison group), participation via representation, and total participation. The researchers found that the productivity of the experimental groups exceeded that of the comparison group and concluded that participation reduced resistance to organizational change. Interestingly, Bartlem and Locke (1981) and Gardner (1977) have subsequently identified differing readiness-creating procedures used by Coch and French with the four groups as an overlooked factor in the original research design. The comparison group was told that competitive conditions required a higher productivity standard. The new standard was explained and questions were answered. In contrast, for each of the experimental groups, a meeting was called during which the need for the change was presented in stark fashion. For example, as part of this presentation, the presence of fierce price competition was dramatized by showing two identical garments produced in the factory. One was produced in 1946 and had sold for 100 percent more than its match, produced in 1947. When asked to do so, the group could not identify the cheaper garment. This dramatization effectively communicated that cost reduction was a very real necessity (Coch & French, 1948).

As exemplified in the Coch and French experiment, creating readiness involves proactive attempts by a change agent to influence the beliefs, attitudes, intentions, and ultimately the behavior of a change target. As its core, the creation of readiness for change involves changing individual cognition's across a set of employees. The dynamics concerned with bringing about such changes in individuals has been explored at length in the cognitive change literature (see, e.g., Bandura, 1982; Fishbein & Azjen, 1975). It is important to note, however, that the creation of readiness for organizational change must extend beyond individual cognitions since it involves social phenomena as well. As social-information processing models suggest (cf. Griffin, 1987), any individual's readiness may also be shaped by the readiness of others. Factors relevant in creating readiness for change are summarized in Figure 1. Drawing on the individual-level cognitive change, collective behavior, social-information processing, mass communications, and organizational change literature's, each aspect of this model is addressed in more detail below.

The Message.   The primary mechanism for creating readiness for change among members of an organization is the message for change. In general, the readiness message should incorporate two issues: (*a*) the need for change, that is, the discrepancy between the desired end-state (which must be appropriate for the organization) and the present state; and, (*b*) the individual and collective efficacy (i.e., the perceived ability to change) of parties affected by the change effort.

Discrepancy. The discrepancy aspect of the message communicates information about the need for change and should be consistent with relevant contextual factors (e.g., increased competition, changes in governmental regulations, depressed economic conditions). Creating the belief that change is needed requires showing how the current performance of the organization differs from some desired end-state (Katz & Kahn, 1978). Pettigrew (1987) emphasizes the importance of changes in external contextual factors (namely, social, economic, political, and competitive environments) in justifying the need for organizational change. He argues that the legitimacy for organizational change can be established by interpreting the effect of external contextual factors on an organization's performance. In the Coch and French experiment, the pricing discrepancy between the garments implied that the productivity standard was too low (relative to the competition) and that the challenge was to increase productivity to facilitate competitive pricing.

FIGURE 1

Creating readiness for change

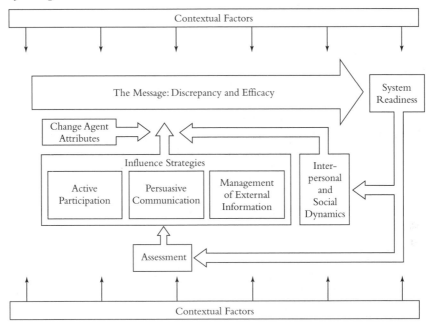

Others have discussed the importance of creating the awareness of a discrepancy concept, using different phraseology. For example, Nadler and Tushman (1989) refer to creating intellectual pain, the realization that something is awry. Spector (1989) advocates diffusing dissatisfaction throughout the organization to make appropriate discrepancies self-evident. Bandura (1982) frames this in terms of unfavorable personal consequences, the organizational analog of which would be the threat of a complete failure of the organization. In essence, intellectual pain, diffused dissatisfaction, and organizational failure may be used to suggest aspects of a discrepancy between the present state and some apparent or implied desired end-state.

While the appropriateness of certain end-states, such as survival, is rarely questioned, the appropriateness of others may be. For example, successfully convincing members of an organization that changes are necessary to become *No. 1* in the industry on some measure rests on their acceptance of being *No. 1* as an appropriate end-state. Much of the recent literature on leadership vision emphasizes the importance of clarifying and gaining commitment to the end-state against which the organization is judging its present condition and justifying the need for change (ef. Bennis & Nanus, 1985). Therefore, the discrepancy message involves communicating where the organization is currently, where it wants to be, and why that end-state is appropriate.

Efficacy. While the realization that a discrepancy exists can be a powerful motivator for change, other reactions are also possible. For example, Nadler and Tushman (1989) discuss the possibility that awareness of discrepancy can result in counterproductive energy. They warn that negative information can result in defensive reactions, like denial, flight, or withdrawal.

To minimize the possibility of a counterproductive reaction, a change agent should build the target's confidence that it has the capability to correct the discrepancy. This confidence has been referred to as efficacy (Bandura, 1982, 1986) and may be viewed as the perceived capability to overcome the discrepancy. Efficacy has been consistently found to influence thought patterns, actions, and emotional arousal. Bandura (1982) reports that individuals will avoid activities believed to exceed their coping capabilities, but will undertake and perform those which they judge themselves to be capable of. Thus, in creating readiness, one must not only communicate a salient discrepancy, but must also bolster the efficacy of organizational members regarding the proposed changes to reduce the discrepancy.

Interpersonal and Social Dynamics.   Because a readiness effort involves convincing a collection of socially-interacting individuals to change their beliefs, attitudes, and intentions in accordance with the discrepancy and efficacy aspects of the message, a change agent must understand the distinction between individual and collective readiness, as well as what influences the collective interpretation of the readiness message. This understanding can be facilitated by an integration of the literature on collective behavior (cf. Smelser, 1963), social information processing (cf. Griffin, 1987), and mass communications (cf. DeFleur & Ball-Rokeach, 1989).

Interventions to create readiness for change are attempts to mobilize collective support by building and shaping awareness across organizational members regarding the existence of, the sources of, and solutions to the organization's problems (cf. Smelser, 1963). Through the dynamics of social information processing, an organization's collective readiness is constantly being influenced by the readiness of the individuals comprising it. System members look to one another for clues regarding the meaning of events and circumstances facing the organization. Any readiness-building activities must take this social exchange into account. It is important to consider that the change agent is not the sole source of discrepancy and efficacy information. The impact of any message generated by the change agent will be shaped by the *social* interpretation of that message.

From the mass communications literature, three theories offer insight into various social dynamics that could operate in readiness interventions—the individual differences, social differentiation, and social relationships theories (DeFleur & Ball-Rokeach, 1989).

Individual differences theory argues that the response of one individual may diverge from that of another because of differing cognitive structures. One example of this can be found in research by Kirton (1980) on the different reactions of individuals characterized as innovators or adaptors. Kirton's findings suggest that innovators are likely to respond favorably to readiness programs designed to prepare the target for fundamental change (i.e., change that requires job incumbents to use different mental processes and to develop new skills) while adaptors are more likely to respond favorably to readiness programs designed to prepare the target for incremental change (i.e., change that requires incumbents to make minor modifications in thought patterns and to fine tune existing skills). In sum, individual difference theory serves as a reminder that specific individuals may react differently to the same message.

Social differentiation theory argues that the response to influence attempts will be determined by the target's cultural or subcultural membership. Such cultural memberships may polarize the beliefs, attitudes, and intentions of members. Hierarchical differentiation (i.e., executives, managers, supervisors, and workers) or other differentiates (e.g., union/non-union, engineers/non-engineers) shape group membership and result in psychological boundaries that may affect the beliefs, attitudes, intentions, and behaviors of members (cf. Van Maanen & Barley, 1985; Bushe, 1988). These psychological boundaries affect the ease with which readiness is evenly created across the subcultures within the organization.

Finally, social relationships theory suggests that responses to an influence attempt will hinge on the network of relationships individuals have. In particular, the influence of opinion leaders on others' sentiments can be powerful in affecting those others' readiness for change. Identifying and recognizing the influence of opinion leaders in the organization may enable the change agent to more effectively design them into the readiness intervention. Building readiness in these opinion leaders first could allow them to provide social cues for others in the organization and, in effect, act as informal change agents in disseminating the logic of the readiness program. As a result, a social information processing-based *snowball effect* might be generated.

Influence Strategies. Given the above conceptualization of readiness dynamics, how might a change agent intervene in the natural flow of social information processing occurring among organizational members to increase their readiness for change? Two strategies offered by Bandura (1977) and Fishbein and Azjen (1975) for influencing individual cognitions are appropriate for creating readiness for organizational change: persuasive communication (both oral and written) and active participation. A third strategy consists of the management of external sources of information. These three strategies have certain advantages and disadvantages (e.g., timeliness and manageability). The skillful change agent will capitalize on opportunities and the strengths of each strategy and utilize them in concert to influence readiness. Each of these strategies offers a lever for conveying discrepancy and efficacy information.

Persuasive Communication. Persuasive communication is primarily a source of explicit information regarding discrepancy and efficacy. However, the form of persuasive communication employed also sends symbolic information regarding the commitment to, prioritization of, and urgency for the change effort. For example, a CEO who travels to all corporate locations to discuss the need for change sends the message explicitly communicated in his/her comments and the symbolic message that the issues are important enough to take the time and resources necessary to communicate them directly. Oral persuasive communication consists of in-person speeches, either live (e.g., speaking in person or through teleconferencing

technology) or recorded (e.g., audio/videotape). Written persuasive communication consists of documents prepared by the organization (e.g., newsletters, annual reports, memos).

Lengel and Daft (1988) have assessed communication media in terms of *richness,* a composite dimension comprising the extent of simultaneous multiple information cues, personal focus, and timeliness of feedback. In-person is the richest medium because it establishes a personal focus and permits multiple information cues and immediate feedback. Written media (e.g., annual reports, newsletters) are considered lean, being impersonal and providing for few information cues, and no direct feedback opportunities. Between these two extremes are other media like audio/videotape and electronic mail. For nonroutine communications (i.e., ones that are emotional and difficult to express) more richness is required. Messages that are simple, straightforward, rational, and logical can be communicated via lean media.

Oral persuasive communication involves direct, explicit message transmission through meetings, speeches, and other forms of personal presentation. Live in-person presentations would be rated high in richness, according to Lengel and Daft's criteria. If this form of presentation is not feasible, a videotape of the presentation may be appropriate. For example, Eden and Kinnar (1991) recently employed both verbal persuasion and videotape presentation to boost self-efficacy and increase volunteering for a special-forces service. Elsewhere, Barrett and Cammann (1984) describe a case in which the CEO of National Steel Company conducted a series of personal meetings and prepared a videotape that would be available to all employees. The main objective was to communicate that the ongoing downturn in the steel industry (a contextual factor) was not simply a cyclical one. Thus, this CEO was creating readiness using live and video-recorded presentations.

Management of External Information. Sources outside the organization can be used to bolster messages sent by the change agent. For example, a diagnostic report prepared by a consulting firm may be used to add credibility to a message sent by the change agent. Generally, a message generated by more than one source, particularly if external to the organization, is given a greater air of believability and confirmation (Gist, 1987).

The news media is one form of external source that can play an important role in creating readiness for change. Employee knowledge about issues influencing their readiness can be affected through mass media channels like radio and television broadcasts, magazines, and newspapers. Information provided by such sources tends to have an air of objectivity and is therefore often persuasive with regard to creating readiness for change. However, while such information is persuasive, it is not easily managed by the change agent.

There are two ways in which a change agent may attempt to manage such information. First, information can be provided to the external press. Organizations often use press releases in this manner. Warren (1984) described a case involving the president of Antioch College who supplied the press (e.g., *The New York Times, Newsweek,* and the local newspaper) with information regarding the college's fiscal difficulties (i.e., discrepancy) and a plan (i.e., efficacy) to restore Antioch to fiscal stability. A second way a change agent can manage such media information is by making change-relevant information available by disseminating copies of selected articles, books, or film clips to organizational members. For example, many organizations distribute copies of business books which highlight particular desired messages.

Active Participation. Persuasive communication and the management of external information both emphasize the direct communication of readiness messages. Change agents can also manage opportunities for organizational members to learn through their own activities, and thereby send readiness messages indirectly. The message generated by active participation is essentially self-discovered (Fishbein & Azjen, 1975). This source of information is advantageous since individuals tend to place greater trust in information discovered by

themselves. It is important to note that while a change agent may manage opportunities for organizational members to be exposed to information which influences readiness, the message is generated through the activity and is therefore outside of the explicit control of the change agent.

One form of active participation is directly involving individuals in activities which are rich in information pertaining to potential discrepancy and efficacy messages. For example, participating in formalized strategic planning activities can lead to self-discovery of discrepancies facing the organization. Answering customer complaints can lead to a similar self-discovery. Furthermore, experiential learning exercises have been recognized as effective in providing change relevant insights in training programs. For example, Kirton's (1980) work suggests that experiential learning exercises may be used to teach *adaptive* style individuals the appropriateness of a more *innovative* style.

Another form of active participation is vicarious learning. For example, a vicarious learning experience can be designed to bolster confidence that new production techniques, not only offer competitive advantages, but can be implemented in their own work environment. Gist, Schwoerre, and Rosen (1989) successfully applied vicarious learning in getting workers to being using computer software. The act of observing others applying new productive techniques enhances one's confidence in adopting the innovation.

A third form active participation can take is enactive mastery. Enactive mastery can be used to prepare a target for change by taking small incremental steps. Success from the small-scale efforts can generate efficacy with regard to the challenge of implementing changes necessary for large-scale change. This logic has been discussed by Schaffer (1981) and Thompson (1981) in terms of getting clients to buy into, initiate, and sustain needed changes.

Change Agent Attributes.   The effectiveness of the influence strategies is dependent upon the change agent wielding them. Attributes, such as credibility, trustworthiness, sincerity, and expertise of the change agent are gleaned from what people know about the agent and/or the agent's general reputation. Clearly, readiness-creating messages will have more influence if the change agent generating those messages has a good reputation in these domains (Gist, 1987). Conversely, when these attributes are unfavorable, the change agent's ability to create readiness for change will be hampered.

Readiness Assessment. To guide readiness building efforts, it is beneficial to assess the system's readiness. Assessments of the perceived discrepancy and efficacy of the target would be performed in gauging the state of readiness. Pond, Armenakis, and Green (1984) and Fox, Ellison, and Keith (1988) provide evidence that readiness can be assessed through survey research methodology. As described in the evaluation literature (cf. Armenakis, Field, & Holley, 1976) assessment methodologies can include the use of questionnaire, interview, and observation methods.

Whatever methods are used in sensing readiness, the change agent must respect the importance of reliability and validity issues (cf. Sackett & Larson, 1990). However, this respect should be tempered by the realization that readiness assessments may be for the purpose of discovery as much as for the purpose of confirmation. Thus, as McCall and Bobko (1990) note, a broader perspective on what is acceptable in the way of methodology may be required by the context in which the assessment is conducted. Qualitative techniques become more necessary in fluid, dynamic contexts. For example, polling opinion leaders or identifying and tracking rumors may help clarify trends that appear in survey data. Domain or taxonomic analyses, which are directed at understanding semantics, symbolic structures, and underlying perceptions of employees (McCall & Bobko, 1990), are other examples of procedures that may be useful in an attempt to determine the collective readiness of the organization. Naturally, the typical constraints of availability of time, funds, and expertise, and the importance placed on the

assessment will influence the design. If properly conducted, such assessments can reveal the need to intensify efforts, use additional strategies to create readiness, and offer insights into how readiness messages might be modified.

A Typology of Readiness Programs

The purpose of the preceding discussion was to describe the major components of a program for creating employee readiness for change. However, decisions about leveraging each of the components into a readiness program should be guided by two considerations, the *extent to which employees are ready* (as determined through an assessment) and the *urgency of the change* (the amount of time available before changes must be implemented).

As described, employee readiness is influenced by the message transmitted via the strategies, the change agent attributes, and the interpersonal and social dynamics of organizational members. In addition to these planned efforts, however, employee readiness may be influenced by at least three other factors, *viz.*, unplanned media information, existing organizational conditions, and significance of the change effort. Information disseminated through the media (e.g., industry layoffs, increasing foreign competition, economic conditions) may affect employee readiness for change, heightening awareness of changing external contextual factors. Furthermore, existing organizational conditions affect employee loyalty, commitment, or other feelings toward an organization and its leaders, consequently influencing readiness. Indeed, Fox et al. (1988) found that effective management practices (e.g., planning, delegating, communicating) influenced employee cooperation and perceived equity and were associated with higher employee readiness for implementing improvements in procedures and problem solving. In contrast, ineffective practices were associated with lower readiness.

In addition, some changes are more intense and potentially more threatening. Fundamental change, such as changing from a functional form to a strategic business unit organization or from an assembly line to an autonomous workgroup arrangement, requires different mental processes and the development of new skills. In contrast, incremental change, such as rearranging work stations to capitalize on a more efficient plant layout (without re-engineering jobs), requires lesser modifications of thought processes and a simple fine-tuning of job skills. Thus, employees may be less ready for fundamental than for incremental change.

Sometimes organizational changes are urgently needed and require rapid implementation. In such cases, a readiness program will have to be implemented which utilizes the most effective and efficient strategies. Thus, a change agent may only utilize a persuasive communication strategy. In other situations, needed changes may not be so urgent, permitting the implementation of a readiness effort broader in scope and more thorough in detail. Such a program may involve persuasive communication as well as active participation (e.g., vicarious learning) and the management of external information (e.g., press releases).

By combining readiness and urgency, various combinations of change conditions can be hypothesized. Hypothetical programs appropriate for four generic urgency and readiness conditions are summarized in Table 1. Although readiness and urgency are both continuous dimensions, for the sake of clarity, programs consistent with the combinations of the extreme conditions of readiness and urgency will be described.

Low Readiness/Low Urgency. An *aggressive program* is appropriate when employees are not ready for organizational change yet there is ample time for creating that readiness. A comprehensive readiness program leveraging all components is appropriate for this set of conditions. A variety of rich and lean persuasive communication methods (i.e., in-person presentations, video/audiotapes, newsletters) is suitable. Active participation experiences (e.g., visits to model manufacturing facilities) can be employed. If the organizational changes include introducing new technology (e.g., computerized

TABLE 1

Hypothetical readiness programs for various combinations of system readiness and urgency

Conditions	Program Nomenclature	Salient Characteristics
Low readiness/ low urgency	Aggressive	Persuasive communication. Active participation. External information. Change agent attributes.
Low readiness/ high urgency	Crisis	Persuasive communication. Change agent attributes.
High readiness/ low urgency	Maintenance	Persuasive communication. Active participation. External information.
High readiness/ high urgency	Quick response	Persuasive communication.

systems as part of a change to autonomous workgroups) some form of enactive mastery could be appropriate. Furthermore, external information sources (e.g., press releases, speeches by recognized experts) can be incorporated into the program. Some attempt to build the credibility of the change agent may also be fruitful. For example, a CEO or other internal key figure in the change effort may participate in magazine and newspaper interviews describing previous experiences or recent awards so that credibility can be enhanced. When external change agents are involved, organizational leaders will want to select those with established reputations so their involvement will lend credibility to the anticipated changes. These actions will be expected to favorably influence opinion leaders, thus marshalling their support among other members of the change target.

Low Readiness/High Urgency. A *crisis program* may be appropriate when employees are not ready and there is great urgency in implementing needed organizational changes. The organization is in a crisis situation and must react immediately or face severe consequences. Obviously, this is an undesirable situation and requires drastic measures. The system needs to be *jolted,* which may include replacing the current change agent or augmenting this position with key personnel. Any personnel changes may be necessary in order to add credibility, trustworthiness, sincerity, and expertise. In addition, persuasive communication (e.g., in-person presentations) is required. Given time constraints, managing external information and active participation are likely to be infeasible.

High Readiness/Low Urgency. A *maintenance program* may be appropriate when employees are ready for change but there is little urgency in implementing needed organizational changes. The threat in this situation is that readiness may wane before changes are implemented. Therefore, the emphasis should be on maintaining readiness. Efforts should focus on keeping the discrepancy and efficacy messages current and visible. Lean persuasive communication methods (e.g., newsletters) and managed external information (e.g., magazine and newspaper press releases) may suffice as information sources. Active participation is not as critical to this program as in the aggressive program, but may still be appropriate.

High Readiness/High Urgency. A *quick response* program may be appropriate when employees are ready and the time available for implementing needed change is short. Thus, organizational changes can be implemented almost immediately. The challenge here is to maintain readiness energy as the change begins to unfold. Once again, persuasive communication, particularly rich persuasive communication is appropriate. Because of the urgency of the needed changes and the high readiness state, active participation and management of external information may not be suited for this program.

The brief descriptions of these four generic readiness programs provide the salient characteristics for the extremes of the readiness and urgency conditions. For whatever reason, a change agent may elect to vary from the programs described. Attempts to leverage any combination of the components contained in the readiness model would be a matter of whether the conditions are conducive to their use. To provide a detailed comprehensive example of the readiness model, the readiness creating efforts of the Whirlpool Corporation, the world's largest

manufacturer of major home appliances, are described. In terms of Table 1, Whirlpool's program can be classified as an aggressive readiness program.

An Integrative Example of Readiness Interventions

Whirlpool's leaders, Jack Sparks in 1983, succeeded by David Whitwam in 1987, began a long-term program designed to improve the company's competitiveness by fundamentally altering the organization to become more aggressive, responsive, innovative, and market-oriented. In the following discussion, a summary of the external contextual factors and the readiness-building activities of Sparks and Whitwam are reviewed.

Contextual Factors.   During the 1960s and 1970s, the fierce competition within the appliance industry resulted in the consolidation of numerous companies into relatively few players, namely, Whirlpool, General Electric, Electrolux, and Maytag. The strategy adopted by Whirlpool Corporation leaders was to emphasize cost control and operational efficiency rather than market aggressiveness, growth, and globalization. While the supply of appliances in the U.S. had been largely domestically based, foreign competitors began entering the already competitive market in the 1980s. These increasingly competitive pressures were compounded when the U.S. demand for appliances leveled off. The opportunities for expansion abroad, however, were growing (Stewart, 1990).

The Message.   The content of the message Sparks and Whitwam communicated to build readiness for change included discrepancy and efficacy aspects. The discrepancy part of the message was that competitive pressures were mounting and that to remain competitive, Whirlpool would have to become more aggressive, more sensitive to the marketplace, more *lean and mean,* and a global player. To enhance efficacy, Whirlpool employees were sent to observe model manufacturing operations (in Japan and Korea), were reminded of other companies that had successfully implemented changes resulting in classic turnaround examples, and were assured that Whirlpool could make the fundamental changes needed to prosper in the emerging environment.

Active Participation.   Three active participation interventions that were implemented to create readiness are particularly noteworthy—formalized strategic planning efforts, the Global Awareness Program, and the 75th Anniversary Celebration and Show.

Formalized Strategic Planning. One of the first actions Sparks initiated in 1983 was a formalized strategic planning process to augment the organization's traditional profit planning activities. This strategic planning activity required managers in all major operational units and functions to identify their strengths and weaknesses and for corporate managers to analyze competitors' strengths and weaknesses, industry trends, and merge the operational plans. Involvement in such activities had the effect of participants discovering the discrepancy (need for change) as well as enhancing efficacy through developing the plans necessary to capitalize on the opportunities available in the marketplace.

The Global Awareness Program. To further emphasize the increased competitiveness facing the company, the Global Awareness Program was conceived. This program, initiated in 1986, involved sending groups of employees drawn from various levels and functions to visit companies operating in Japan and Korea. The program was designed to allow employees to observe first-hand the nature of the competition they faced as well as build confidence that Whirlpool could implement the same processes. It was hoped that the experience would lead them to conclude that the changes being advocated by Whirlpool leaders were indeed appropriate. Furthermore, the fact that their competitors were operating in this manner was intended to transmit the message "if they can do it, so can we."

In addition to offering an opportunity for active participation by a subgroup of employees, the Global Awareness Program was implemented on the assumption that the participants would return

and share their discoveries with their peers. Though an appreciation for the potential of social synergy was evident in several of Whirlpool's readiness interventions, this is perhaps best illustrated with the Global Awareness Program. First, specially selected subgroups (from the lowest to the highest levels in the hierarchy) were formed to participate. Then, these participants were expected to exercise their personal influence and create readiness for change. For example, discussion groups involving participants and nonparticipating co-workers were established. Furthermore, videotape technology was used to expose as many employees as possible to the program. The 13-minute videotape describing the program and capturing the thoughts of participants (Global Awareness Program, 1986) could be viewed not only by those who were absent at the live presentations, but could be viewed in peer groups without supervisors being present.

The 75th Anniversary Celebration and Show. To celebrate the company's 75th anniversary in 1986, an elaborate Broadway-style stage production was developed. The show traveled to company locations throughout the U.S. and played to packed houses of employees. In addition to celebrating the company's history, the show had an implicit efficacy message for all employees. Throughout the production, several points bearing on readiness for change were emphasized: (1) Whirlpool has, and can in the future, succeed against the odds, (2) change and aggressiveness were the bedrock of the company's early history, and (3) Whirlpool cares about its people and will take care of them. While these messages were not explicitly stated, they were under the surface awaiting self-discovery and self-insight by the members of the audience.

Management of External Information Sources.   External sources of information used by Whirlpool to help mold readiness consisted of increased coverage of the company's operations in business periodicals and a diagnostic analysis by a well-known consulting firm.

Business Periodical Publicity. In contrast to the traditional low-key approach taken at Whirlpool,

Sparks and Whitwam made an effort to increase company coverage in the business media. This visibility effort coupled with the degree of change and increase in competitive activities by Whirlpool resulted in increased coverage and exposure. For example, during the period 1983–1990, the number of magazine articles (not including *The Wall Street Journal)* mentioning Whirlpool increased almost threefold from the average of the previous 10 years. *Business Week* and *Fortune* published articles about the company's change efforts. In addition to this coverage, Whirlpool employees were constantly exposed to media bearing on issues of readiness. For example, articles regarding the company's activities and broader industry trends were routinely copied and distributed among managers.

The McKinsey and Company Structures Study. In 1987, after Whitwam's move to CEO, the consulting firm of McKinsey and Company analyzed Whirlpool's structure. Several observations were offered about the inadequacies of the current structure, and resulted in a recommended major reorganization. The details of this study remained unannounced until presented by Whitwam in the New Structure Speech described below. When released, the report served to provide an important message regarding the need for change.

Persuasive Communication.   In addition to the sharing of knowledge about their overseas experiences by Global Awareness Program participants described above, several other internally generated persuasive communication efforts are notable. The majority of these efforts involved instrumental, high-profile speeches and spoken and written statements of vision.

The New Vision Speech. Probably the most visible example of persuasive communication was the New Vision Speech personally delivered in 1986, 29 times in 13 different locations to approximately 5,500 employees. A 52-minute videotape (New Vision Speech, 1986) of the speech was also made so that all employees could view it as desired. The New Vision Speech was compelling for two reasons: it was the most comprehensive statement of the

need for change, plan for change, and encouragement for change, yet offered, and the organization's leaders had expended a great deal of time and effort to share it as widely and personally as possible.

Simply stated, the focus of the new vision message was the need for change at Whirlpool with references to other successful large-scale change efforts. Two significant external contextual factors were cited to support the need for change. First, the increase in foreign competition was described. It was noted that imports in the appliance industry had increased 400 percent from 1982–1986. Second, it was noted that the consolidation among domestic appliance manufacturers had resulted in four fierce competitors, namely, Whirlpool, Maytag, GE, and Electrolux.

Part of the message devoted to efficacy was a brief history of how Whirlpool had successfully experienced change in the past by evolving from one product (a washing machine in 1911) to the multiple product company of 1986. Furthermore, the much celebrated Chrysler Corporation turnaround was used as an example to build efficacy.

The New Structure Speech. At the February 1988, Corporate Quarterly Review (which was attended by most officers, directors, and managers), Whitwam (New Structure Speech, 1988) stressed that the old structure was not permitting Whirlpool to be competitive. Although he did not explicitly report the company's performance, his audience was aware that 1987 company performance was below projections (Zellner, 1988). Whitwam referred to the diagnostic analysis conducted by McKinsey, thus providing additional support for the impending reorganization.

Whitwam explained the company was to reorganize around the strategic business unit concept. The intended result of this reorganization was to increase accountability and stimulate a sense of ownership throughout the company, push decision making closer to the marketplace, and to improve operating effectiveness and efficiency. After describing the benefits of the new structure, he challenged Whirlpool employees telling them the company needed their patience, support, and cooperation. His determination to succeed was reflected in his exclamation that Whirlpool would not fail in the bitterly contested marketplace.

Readiness Assessment.   An important part of Whirlpool's change efforts has been an attempt to track the progress of change and assess the degree of readiness and resistance to change. Specifically, Sparks and Whitwam commissioned assessments of the attitudes of the company's leadership regarding these issues. These assessments were conducted by a team of university-based researchers who surveyed the opinions of the top four levels of management throughout the organization. These assessments were used to guide the interventions designed to create readiness for large-scale change. For example, the 1986 assessment suggested that not very many employees, even in the leadership cadre, fully understood the company's vision. This finding helped in the refinement of the influence strategies used to create readiness, including the New Vision Speech.

Epilogue.   In March 1988, Whirlpool began the implementation of the SBU reorganization. In addition, in August 1988, Whirlpool completed the negotiations for a new joint venture with N. V. Philips Gloeilampenfabricken of the Netherlands to produce and market appliances in Europe, thus becoming the world's largest global competitor in the home appliance industry. Although the home appliance industry has been sluggish, due to the nationwide downturn in housing construction, Whirlpool has been described several times in the business media as a company aggressively positioning itself to meet the challenges of a slowed domestic economy and to take advantage of the economic unification of Europe (e.g., Woodruff & Kapner, 1991).

Conclusion

This article has emphasized the importance of creating readiness as a precursor to organizational change and examined the influence strategies available to help generate readiness. Some further implications for, and contributions to, the management of organizational change are summarized below.

First, the readiness concept complements previous contributions made by Lawrence (1954), Kotter and Schlesinger (1979), and others regarding resistance to change. The potential causes of resistance should be appreciated in designing the discrepancy and efficacy content of the readiness message and in selecting the strategies for creating readiness. The findings from mass communications research are useful in understanding that individual and cultural differences are influential in the response of the target group to readiness efforts. This information can be coupled with the traditional causes of resistance (e.g., lack of trust) in designing readiness programs to address the pertinent issues in eliciting the necessary support to accomplish successful change.

Second, the readiness model suggests the importance of building readiness within the context facing the organization. For example, Whirlpool's readiness efforts, begun in 1983, were not a response to an immediate crisis but rather to anticipated challenges. Beer and Walton (1987) and Pettigrew (1987) emphasize the role of contextual factors in bringing about change. It is apparent from the Whirlpool experience that company leaders were very deliberate in incorporating the appropriate contextual factors in the message to communicate discrepancy and efficacy information.

Third, decisions about implementing readiness programs should be guided by the urgency of the change and the extent to which employees are ready for the needed change. By conceptualizing high and low urgency to implement needed organizational change in combination with high and low readiness for change, four generic readiness programs (i.e., aggressive, crisis, maintenance, and quick response) were described. This typology of readiness programs is useful because it describes various scenarios faced by change agents. Within the constraints imposed by time limitations and the readiness challenge, a change agent can understand the practicalities of readiness creation.

Fourth, the detailed description of Whirlpool's aggressive readiness program demonstrated the full complement of strategies available to change agents. A change agent can use this program as a basis from which to extract ideas and tailor a readiness program for another organization.

Fifth, this article argues for the active creation of readiness. Recognizing the importance of readiness, some authors have argued that change agents may direct their initial efforts to areas where organization members are ready (cf. Beer & Walton, 1987; Pond et al., 1984). The framework presented in this article makes a case for identifying where change is needed then designing a readiness program to influence the appropriate beliefs, attitudes, and intentions so that changes can be successfully implemented. Instruments designed to assess readiness can then be administered to determine the effectiveness of readiness activities. New strategies can be implemented and messages transmitted through existing strategies can be modified to achieve the readiness intended. The creation of readiness is not necessarily a pre-change concern only. Readiness must be maintained throughout the process of large-scale change particularly since such change is composed of smaller changes which are ongoing. A single initial creation-of-readiness effort may not be adequate to maintain the required levels of readiness throughout the duration of the change process. Thus, employees need to be made ready and readiness efforts should be conducted as needed throughout the change effort.

Finally, the concepts presented in this article can be extended to include other change applications. For example, readiness can be aimed at the individual level, taking on more of the appearances of coaching and counseling. That is, a primary change agent, such as a CEO or some key officer, may need to ready other top officers so that they can become effective change agents for the organization as a whole.

The topic of readiness represents a rudimentary issue in the management of change, and as presented here illustrates the need for further refinement in the planned change process. The implications of overlooking the importance of readiness may very well be that an appropriate intervention may not produce the intended organization changes because organization members are simply not ready (cf. Pasmore & Fagans, 1992). It is hoped that this article will stimulate change agents to consciously think about and plan readiness interventions. Furthermore, urgency and readiness are concepts whose values were discussed in relative terms. Currently, the relativity of these concepts must be determined by the change agent. However, more research under conditions permitting experimental control may provide useful findings and needed guidance for the design and implementation of readiness programs.

Acknowledgments

We would like to thank David Whitwam, Chairman and Chief Executive Officer and E. R. Dunn, Corporate Vice President of Human Resources for allowing us to observe and report on Whirlpool Corporation's change activities. In addition, we gratefully acknowledge the constructive comments offered by Art Bedeian, Alan Glassman, Bernie Keys, Bob Pond, Alan Randolph, and John Slocum. An earlier version of this article was presented at the 51st Annual Academy of Management Meeting.

References

Armenakis, A., Field, H., & Holley, W. Guidelines for overcoming empirically identified evaluation problems of organizational development change agents. *Human Relations*, 1976, *129*, 1147–1161.

Armenakis, A., Mossholder, K., & Harris, S. Diagnostic bias in organizational consultation. *Omega: The International Journal of Management Science*, 1990, *18*(6), 161–179.

Bandura, A. Self-efficacy: Toward a unifying theory of behavioral change. *Psychological Review*, 1977, *84*, 194–215.

Bandura, A. Self-efficacy mechanism in human agency. *American Psychologist*, 1982, *37*(2). 122–147.

Bandura, A. *Social foundations of thought and action: A social-cognitive view.* Englewood Cliffs, NJ: Prentice Hall, 1986.

Barrett, A., & Cammann, C. Transitioning to change: Lessons from NSC. In J. R. Kimberly and R. E. Quinn (Eds.), *Managing organizational transitions.* Homewood, IL.: Richard D. Irwin, 1984, pp. 218–239.

Bartlem, C., & Locke, E. The Coch and French study: a critique and reinterpretation. *Human Relations,* 1981, *34*(7), 555–566.

Beckhard, R., & Harris, R. *Organizational transitions: Managing complex change.* Reading, MA: Addison-Wesley Publishing Company, 1987.

Beer, M., & Walton, A. Organization change and development. *Annual Review of Psychology,* 1987, *38,* 339–367.

Bennis, W., & Nanus, B. Leaders: The strategies for taking charge. New York: Harper & Row, 1985.

Bushe, G. Developing cooperative labor–management relations in unionized factories: A multiple case study of quality circles and parallel organizations within joint quality of work life projects. *Journal of Applied Behavioral Science,* 1988, *24*(2), 129–150.

Coch, L. & French, J. Overcoming resistance to change. *Human Relations,* 1948, *1*(4). 512–532.

DeFluer, M., & Ball-Rokeach, S. *Theories of mass communication,* New York: Longman, 1989.

Eden, D., & Kinnar, J. Modeling Galatea: Boosting self-efficacy to increase volunteering. *Journal of Applied Psychology,* 1991, *76,* 770–780.

Fishbein, M., & Azjen, I. *Belief, attitude, intention, and behavior: An introduction to theory and research.* Reading, MA: Addison-Wesley Publishing Company, 1975.

Fox, D., Ellison, R., & Keith, K. Human resource management: An index and its relationship to readiness for change. *Public Personnel Management,* 1988, *17*(3), 297–302.

Gardner, G. Workers' participation: A critical evaluation of Coch and French. *Human Relations,* 1977, *30*(12), 1071–1078.

Gist, M., Self-efficacy: Implications for organizational behavior and human resource management. *Academy of Management Review,* 1987, *12*(3). 472–485.

Gist, M., Schwoerer, C., & Rosen, B. Effects of alternative training methods on self-efficacy and performance in computer software training. *Journal of Applied Psychology,* 1989, *74*(6), 884–891.

Global Awareness Program (Videotape). Benton Harbor, MI: Whirlpool Corporation, 1986.

Griffin, R. Toward an integrated theory of task design. In L. L. Cummings and B. M. Staw (Eds.), *Research in organizational behavior* (Vol. 9). Greenwich, CT: JAI Press, 1987, pp. 79–120.

Kanter, R. *The change masters.* New York: Simon and Schuster, 1983.

Katz, D., & Kahn, R. *The social psychology of organization.* New York: John Wiley, 1978.

Kirton, M. Adaptors and innovators in organizations. *Human Relations,* 1980, *3,* 213–224.

Kissler, G. The change riders. Reading, MA: Addison-Wesley Publishing Company, 1991.

Kotter, J., & Schlesinger, L. Choosing strategies for change. *Harvard Business Review,* 1979, *57*(2), 106–114.

Lawrence, P. How to deal with resistance to change. *Harvard Business Review,* 1954, *32*(3), 49–57.

Lengel, R., & Daft, R. The selection of communication media as an executive skill. *Academy of Management Executive.* 1988, *2*(3), 225–232.

Lewin, K. Field theory in social science. New York: Harper and Row, 1951.

McCall, M., & Bobko, P. Research methods in the service of discovery. In M. Dunnette and L. Hough (Eds.), *Handbook of industrial and organizational psychology* (Vol. 1). Palo Alto, CA: Consulting Psychologists Press, 1990, pp. 381–418.

Nadler, D., & Tushman, M. Organizational frame bending: Principles for managing reorientation. *Academy of Management Executive,* 1989, *3*(3), 194–204.

New Structure Speech (Videotape). Benton Harbor, MI: Whirlpool Corporation, 1986.

New Vision Speech (Videotape). Benton Harbor, MI: Whirlpool Corporation, 1988.

Pasmore, W., & Fagans, M. Participation, individual development, and organizational change: A review and synthesis. *Journal of Management,* 1992, *18,* 375–397.

Pettigrew, A. Context and action in transforming the firm. *Journal of Management Studies,* 1987, *24*(6), 649–670.

Pond, S., Armenakis, A., & Green, S. The importance of employee expectations in organizational diagnosis. *Journal of Applied Behavioral Science,* 1984, *20,* 167–180.

Sackett, P., & Larson, J. Research strategies and tactics in industrial and organizational psychology. In M. Dunnette & L. Hough (Eds.), *Handbook of industrial and organizational psychology* (Vol. 1). Palo Alto, CA: Consulting Psychologists Press, 1990, pp. 419–490.

Schaffer, R. Productivity improvement strategy: Make success the building block. *Management Review,* 1981, *70,* 46–52.

Schein, E. Personal change through interpersonal relationships. In W. Bennis, J. Van Maanen, E. Schein, and F. Steele (Eds.), *Essays in interpersonal dynamics.* Homewood, IL: The Dorsey Press, 1979, pp. 129–162.

Smelser, N. Theory of collective behavior. New York: Free Press, 1963.

Spector, B. From bogged down to fired up: Inspiring organizational change. *Sloan Management Review,* Summer, 1989, 29–34.

Stewart, T. A. Heartland industry takes on the world. *Fortune,* 1990, *121*(6), 110–112.

Thompson, H. Consulting for results. *Business Horizons,* 1981, *24*(6), 62–65.

Turner, A. Consulting is more than giving advice. *Harvard Business Review,* 1982, *60*(5), 120–129.

Van Maanen, J., & Barley, S. Cultural organization: Fragments of a theory. In P. J. Frost, L. F. Moore, M. R. Louis, C. C. Lundberg, and J. Martin (Eds.), *Organizational culture.* Beverly Hills, CA: Sage, 1985, pp. 31–54.

Warren, D. Managing in crisis: Nine principles for successful transition. In J. R. Kimberly and R. E. Quinn (Eds.), *Managing organizational transitions.* Homewood, IL: Richard D. Irwin, 1984, pp. 85–106.

Woodruff, D., & Kapner, F. Whirlpool goes on a world tour. *Business Week,* June 3, 1991, 99–100.

Zellner, W. A. Tough market has Whirlpool in a spin. *Business Week,* May 2, 1988, 121–122.

READING 30
DEFINING A POLITICAL MODEL OF ORGANIZATIONS

Larry E. Greiner
Virginia E. Schein

The most commonly considered expression of power in organization research and practice is *downward* power, which is the influence of a superior over a subordinate. This kind of influence in the form of one having power over another is a central focus in much of our traditional leadership research and training, such as Theory X versus Theory Y or task oriented versus people oriented styles.

Upward power refers to attempts by subordinates to influence their superiors. Until recently, subordinates were considered relatively powerless. But a small and growing body of research indicates that subordinates can and do influence their superiors in subtle ways. Studies by Kipnis, Schmidt, and Wilkinson (1980) and Schlilit and Locke (1982) have identified subordinate influence strategies such as persistence, logical presentation of ideas, coalition formation, and ingratiation. And Gabarro and Kotter (1980) have argued that the leadership challenge for most subordinates is to learn how to manage one's boss.

A third direction, *sideways* power, refers to influence attempts directed at those people who are neither subordinates nor superiors in one's immediate reporting chain of authority. *Horizontal power, interdepartmental power, external relationships,* and *lateral relationships* are all terms that reflect expressions of sideways power. Various researchers have called attention to this increasingly important expression of power in organizations—Mintzberg, 1973; Strauss, 1962, at the individual level and Hickson et al., 1971; Pfeffer and Salancik, 1974, at the subunit level.

Interestingly, the net result of these research studies has been to show that sideways power—the

Source: L. Greiner and V. Schein, *Power and Organizational Development,* (pp. 14–24). © 1988 Addison-Wesley Publishing Company, Inc. Reprinted by permission of Addison Wesley Longman, Inc.

predominant form of power expression outside the formal boss–subordinate relationship—is absolutely essential if managers are to get their jobs done. Downward power—getting work done through subordinates—represents a much smaller portion of a manager's time and effort than heretofore considered. The bulk of a manager's efforts is often spent outside the work unit, dealing with other department heads, divisions, or subsidiaries, over whom he or she has no formal control.

Developing, using, and maintaining multiple sources of power other than formal position becomes essential for today's managers in complex organizations. When managers move outside clean-cut authority relationships to get things done, dependence on others is greater than the formal power and control given to people to do these jobs. According to Kotter (1979), "Power dynamics, under these circumstances, are inevitable and are needed to make organizations function well."

Models of Organization

How we view power directions is often a function of the conceptual model that we use to understand behavior in organizations. All of us utilize our mental maps to determine how organizations actually and ideally should function. Sometimes we use these models as tools for diagnosis and other times we use them as idealized versions of how life should be in organizations. It is not unusual for us to confuse our idealized model with how organizations actually do function.

Our concern in this book is with deciding on a model that comes closer to representing organizational reality, even if it departs from our idealized models. It is this reality that OD consultants have to work with before they attempt to move an organization to some other "reality." Two authors have prepared several models. Baldridge (1971) describes three organizational archetypes—bureaucratic, collegial, and political. Pfeffer (1981) suggests four organizational decision models—rational, bureaucratic, organized anarchy, and political. Distilling from these various alternatives, we present three organizational models of our own and relate them to the power directions discussed in the previous section. As we shall see, our three models treat power directions differently, and thereby affect which types of power we attend to, ignore, or, possibly, try to eliminate.

Rational/Bureaucratic Model.   The Rational/Bureaucratic model is most likely to be espoused by traditional management scholars, and one that most of us know well. It emphasizes rationally structured systems, built on division of labor and job specialization in a functional structure. Authority is top down, and utilizes formal communication channels, usually vertical, and well-defined policies and procedures. Organizational goals are clearly specified to direct efforts of employees toward greater efficiency. Formal systems and policies are used to provide control, predictability, and stability.

If we as OD practitioners use or even prefer this model, how are we likely to view power in organization? First, power is seen as hierarchial and so gaining formal approval from top management becomes the sine qua non of successful organizational change. The focus of change is directed toward improving the way superiors use power to manage subordinates. Managerial effectiveness is equated with subordinate performance, and it is achieved through what is known as humanistic management. The leader acts with greater sensitivity to soften the impact of downward power. Although the humanistic leadership labels have changed over the years, Theory Y Management, the Considerate Leader, and the Situational Leader are all concepts that are conditioned by a concern with the exercise and effects of downward power.

Upward power in the Rational/Bureaucratic model is generally seen as disruptive and non-

legitimate. Under limited circumstances, it may be tolerated or even encouraged if its expression is narrowly controlled, such as in the use of Management by Objectives or Quality Circles. Sideways power receives virtually no consideration in this model, since vertical authority is the prescribed decision-making channel; integration occurs only at the apex of the pyramid.

Collegial/Consensus Model.   The Collegial/Consensus model places emphasis on interpersonal and small group behavior in organizations (Argyris, 1962). Rules, policies, and procedures are relaxed, or even disbanded, in order to enhance interaction and participation in decision making. In contrast to the Rational/Bureaucratic model, formal authority relationships are minimized in the Collegial/Consensus model. The need for direction and control is replaced by teamwork in the spirit of "all for one, one for all." Individual contributions are highly valued, within a focus on collaboration and integration.

The view here is that human involvement and participation are good for both the organization and the individual. Equalizing the distribution of authority is assumed to lead to better decision making and fuller commitment to decisions.

Upward power is seen as legitimate and encouraged in this model. All forms of power redistribution are part of the organizational "should's," such as an Employee Bill of Rights, profit-sharing, worker councils, and employee representation on the board of directors. A flat organizational structure, appropriate to a professional group, reflects the high priority given to upward power.

In the Collegial/Consensus model, downward power is barely tolerated, and then only in limited situations in which peer pressure proves ineffective, such as in firing a troublesome employee. Sideways power proves unnecessary because consensus and collaboration are the accepted norms.

Pluralistic/Political Model.   The Pluralistic/Political Model sees organizations as composed of differing interest groups. Each party pursues its own goals, sometimes on selfish grounds but often for well-intended reasons based on its view of what is best for the organization as a whole. Conflict is viewed as inevitable and a normal part of the way things get done. Political behavior results when an attempt at influence is countered by another interested party or group.

According to Cyert and March (1964) (among the first to espouse a political theory of organizations), the objectives of the firm are arrived at through a process of bargaining among and between coalitions as they respond to environmental changes. Basic to the idea of a coalition is the expectation that those with similar interests will band together to influence the direction of the organization toward goals attributed to it by the coalition. Power becomes the intervening variable between desired outcomes and actual results.

Kotter (1977, 1985) sees power and political behavior arising naturally out of the inherent interdependency in most managerial jobs. Power and political behavior are dependent on a wide range of people outside the formal authority chain to get decisions made and work accomplished—for example, in dealing with suppliers, government officials, bankers, and technical experts. Lacking formal authority over these people, the use of power and influence becomes essential for effective managerial functioning.

The Pluralistic/Political Model allows for all forms of power expression. Power is truly everywhere and naturally used by those desiring to fulfill their work-related objectives. The arena of work activity expands beyond the traditional superior–subordinate relationship to include the entire organization. For example, a product manager in the marketing department may discover that one plant in manufacturing is producing defective products. The product manager may go directly to the VP of manufacturing (sideways and upwards power) and convince him to fix things. This VP will then have to influence his subordinates to correct the problems (downward power). The product manager may even have to involve his boss (upward power) to bring about the change.

Sideways power is recognized as a necessary and frequently exercised component of managerial effectiveness. Groups across the organization must compete for scarce resources, and they are horizontally dependent on one another to perform their jobs on schedule. Similarly, upward power takes on importance as individuals lower on the organization chart attempt to exercise influence over senior managers with greater control over needed resources.

Downward power is important, too, to assure that the needs of the overall organization, as perceived by the powerholders at the top, are being considered in decision making at lower levels. Sometimes downward power is required to force a solution on conflicting parties. However, downward power can lose its potency when lower level units also possess significant power, such as found in conflicts with a labor union or with a group of prima donna research scientists.

Organizational Realities

Which of the three models, or archetypes, comes closer to matching organizational reality? We agree with Cyert and March (1964), Baldridge (1971), and Pfeffer (1981), among other organizational theorists, who advance the Pluralistic/Political Model as a more accurate representation of how organizations and managers really function. It is not because people in organizations are greedy or corrupt, but simply because people are different and resources are scattered and limited. A compromise must be reached if the organization is to continue to function.

Moreover, Kotter (1985, 1986) contends that today's organizations possess even greater diversity and interdependence than companies of a few years ago. Technologies have proliferated, economic resources have become constrained, and competition has intensified, Unfortunately, according to Kotter, "The recentness of these changes is one of the key reasons why many people are only partially aware of the realities" of the Pluralistic/Political model.

The Pluralistic/Political model is, in our opinion, a less idealized model than the other two models. These other models may be worth striving for in certain situations, because research evidence suggests that the Rational/Bureaucratic model may be more effective in dealing with simple technologies and stable environments, while the Collegial/Consensus model fits better with more complex and uncertain environments (Lawrence and Lorsch, 1967).

However, these two "desirable" models for unique situations often work out differently in practice (Greiner and Schein, 1981; Schein and Greiner, 1977). The Rational/Bureaucratic model can produce overly restrictive formal systems that stifle initiative and reduce responsiveness to change. And the Collegial/Consensus model can create anarchic behavior at lower levels that undermines teamwork and, ultimately, the firm. We also know from research on human personality that not all people want to work in teams; some people prefer greater structure (Lorsch and Morse, 1974). The point is that both models, even in their most perfect states, will always contain strong threads of the Pluralistic/Political perspective.

Therefore, the key to understanding power in organizations is to acknowledge the pervasive reality of political behavior across and throughout all organizational forms. It means accepting power as natural and necessary to decision making regardless of formal structure. By using a Pluralistic/Political model, we can diagnose the many and varied expressions of power in a broader and more unbiased way. Adhering to either the Rational/Bureaucratic or Collegial/Consensus models may blind us to many aspects of power-oriented behavior.

•   •   •   •

Implications for OD

Warren Bennis, in his book, *Organization Development* (1969), predicts what can happen to OD if it does not acknowledge the reality of the Pluralistic/Political model. "The organization development consultant tends to use the truth–love model when it may not be appropriate and has no alternative model to guide his practice under conditions of distrust . . . and conflict. . . . This means that in pluralistic power situations . . . organization

development may not reach its desired goal. . . . This may explain why OD has been reasonably successful where power is relatively centralized . . . organization development has not met with success in diffuse power structures."

Understanding the realities of power with one's blinders off is essential for the healthy survival of the OD field. We have listed three directional expressions of power and their relationship to three models in use so that we can reexamine our own ways of diagnosing organizations, as well as question our own attitudes toward various expressions of power in them.

Few would deny that OD's model in use has for many years been dominated by the Collegial/Consensus model. OD has focused mainly on upward power within formal work groups, thereby ignoring or denying other expressions of power. If OD categorizes other forms of power as neurotic, selfish, or even unnecessary, it fails to recognize that work-related power is expressed naturally in a variety of ways across the entire work environment. The Pluralistic/Political model, in contrast, assumes that the expression of power is essential in reaching a trade-off between vested interests and organizational goals.

For OD to let go of the Collegial/Consensus model as a primary model for understanding and influencing behavior in organizations does not mean abandoning OD's traditional values of trust, openness, and collaboration or its techniques of team building and interpersonal feedback. Instead, these values and techniques must be treated as limited expressions of power to be supplemented by many other forms of influence that are selectively applied in a particular political context.

References

Argyris, C. 1962. *Interpersonal Competence and Organizational Effectiveness.* Homewood, IL: Irwin-Dorsey.

Baldridge, J. V. 1971. *Power and Conflict in the University.* New York: John Wiley.

Bennis, Warren. 1969. *Organization Development.* Reading, MA: Addison-Wesley.

Cyert, Richard M., and James G. March. 1964. *A Behavioral Theory of the Firm*. Englewood Cliffs, NJ: Prentice Hall.

Gabarro, John I., and John P. Kotter. 1980. "Managing Your Boss." *Harvard Business Review*, January–Febuary, 92–100.

Greiner, Larry E., and Virginia E. Schein. 1981. "The Paradox of Managing a Project-Oriented Matrix: Establishing Coherence within Chaos." *Sloan Management Review*, Winter, 17–22.

Hickson, D. J., C. A. Lee, R. E. Schneck, and J. M. Pennings. 1971. "A Strategic Contingency Theory of Intraorganizational Power." *Administrative Science Quarterly*, 16, 216–229.

Kipnis, D., S. M. Schmidt, and I. Wilkinson. 1980. "Intraorganizational Influence Tactics: Exploration in Getting One's Way." *Journal of Applied Psychology*, 65, 440–452.

Kotter, John P. 1986. "Why Power and Influence Issues Are at the Very Core of Executive Work." In *Executive Power*, ed. by S. Srivastva Assoc. San Francisco: Jossey-Bass, 20–32.

Kotter, John P. 1985. *Power and Influence*. New York: Free Press.

Kotter, John P. 1979. *Power in Management*. New York: Amacom.

Kotter, John P. 1977. "Power, Dependence and Effective Management." *Harvard Business Review*, July–August, 125–136.

Lawrence, Paul, and Jay Lorsch. 1967. *Organization and Environment*. Boston: Division of Research, Harvard Business School.

Lorsch, Jay, and John Morse. 1974. *Organizations and Their Members: A Contingency Approach*. New York: Harper and Row.

Pfeffer, J. *Power in Organizations*. Marshfield, MA: Pitman.

Pfeffer, J. and G. R. Salancik. 1974. "Organizational Decision Making as a Political Process." *Administrative Science Quarterly*, 19, 135–151.

Mintzberg, Henry. 1973. *The Nature of Managerial Work*. New York: Harper and Row.

Schein, V. E., and L. E. Greiner. 1977. "Can Organization Development Be Fine-Tuned to Bureaucracies?" *Organizational Dynamics*, Winter, 48–61.

Schlilit, W. K., and E. A. Locke. 1982. "A Study of Upward Influence." *Administrative Science Quarterly*, 27, 304–316.

Strauss, G. 1962. "Tactics of Lateral Relationships: The Purchasing Agent." *Administrative Science Quarterly*, 7, 161–186.

READING 31
FUNCTIONAL ROLES OF GROUP MEMBERS

Kenneth D. Benne
Paul Sheats

The Relative Neglect of Member Roles in Group Training

Efforts to improve group functioning through training have traditionally emphasized the training of group leadership. And frequently this training has been directed toward the improvement of the skills of the leader in transmitting information and in manipulating groups. Little direct attention seems to have been given to the training of group members in the membership roles required for effective group growth and production. The present discussion is based on the conviction that both effective group training and adequate research into the effectiveness of group training methods must give attention to the identification, analysis, and practice of leader *and* member roles, seen as co-relative aspects of over-all group growth and production.

Certain assumptions have undergirded the tendency to isolate the leadership role from membership roles and to neglect the latter in processes of group training. (1) "Leadership" has been identified with traits and qualities inherent within the "leader" personality. Such traits and qualities can be developed, it is assumed, in isolation from the functioning of members in a group setting. The present treatment sees the leadership role in terms of functions to be performed within a group in helping that group to grow and to work productively. No sharp distinction can be made between leadership and membership functions, between leader and member roles. Groups may operate with various degrees of diffusion of "leadership" functions among group members or of concentration of such functions in one member or a few

members. Ideally, of course, the concept of leadership emphasized here is that of a multilaterally shared responsibility. In any event, effectiveness in the leader role is a matter of leader-member relationship. And one side of a relationship cannot be effectively trained in isolation from the retraining of the other side of that relationship. (2) It has been assumed that the "leader" is uniquely responsible for the quality and amount of production by the group. The "leader" must see to it that the "right" group goals are set, that the group jobs get done, that members are "motivated" to participate. On this view, membership roles are of secondary importance. "Membership" is tacitly identified with "followership." The present discussion assumes that the quality and amount of group production is the "responsibility" of the group. The setting of goals and the marshalling of resources to move toward these goals is a group responsibility in which all members of a mature group come variously to share. The functions to be performed both in building and maintaining group-centered activity and in effective production by the group are primarily member roles. Leadership functions can be defined in terms of facilitating identification, acceptance, development, and allocation of these group-required roles by the group. (3) There has frequently been a confusion between the roles which members enact within a group and the individual personalities of the group members. That there are relationships between the personality structures and needs of group members and the range and quality of group membership roles which members can learn to perform is not denied. On the contrary, the importance of studies designed to describe and explain and to increase our control of these relationships is affirmed. But,

Source: Kenneth D. Benne and Paul Sheats. Reprinted with permission of *The Journal of Social Issues,* Spring 1948, pp. 41–49.

347

at the level of group functioning, member roles, relevant to group growth and accomplishment, must be clearly distinguished from the use of the group environment by individuals to satisfy individual and group-irrelevant needs, if clear diagnosis of member-roles are to be advanced. Neglect of this distinction has been associated traditionally with the neglect of the analysis of member roles in group growth and production.

A Classification of Member Roles

The following analysis of functional member roles was developed in connection with the First National Training Laboratory in Group Development, 1947. It follows closely the analysis of participation functions used in coding the content of group records for research purposes. A similar analysis operated in faculty efforts to train group members in their functional roles during the course of the laboratory.[1]

The member-roles identified in this analysis are classified into three broad groupings.

1. Group task roles. Participant roles here are related to the task which the group is deciding to undertake or has undertaken. Their purpose is to facilitate and coordinate group effort in the selection and definition of a common problem and in the solution of that problem.

2. Group building and maintenance roles. The roles in this category are oriented toward the functioning of the group as a group. They are designed to alter or maintain the group way of working, to strengthen, regulate, and perpetuate the group as a group.

3. Individual roles. This category does not classify member-roles as such, since the "participations" denoted here are directed toward the satisfaction of the "participant's" individual needs. Their purpose is some individual goal which is not relevant either to the group task or to the functioning of the group as a group. Such participants are, of course, highly relevant to the problem of group training, insofar as such training is directed toward improving group maturity or group task efficiency.

Group Task Roles

The following analysis assumes that the task of the discussion group is to select, define, and solve common problems. The roles are identified in relation to functions of facilitation and coordination of group problem-solving activities. Each member may of course enact more than one role in any given unit of participation and a wide range of roles in successive participations. Any or all of these roles may be played at times by the group "leader" as well as by various members.

a. The *initiator-contributor* suggests or proposes to the group new ideas or a changed way of regarding the group problem or goal. The novelty proposed may take the form of suggestions of a new group goal or a new definition of the problem. It may take the form of a suggested solution or some way of handling a difficulty that the group has encountered. Or it may take the form of a proposed new procedure for the group, a new way of organizing the group for the task ahead.

b. The *information seeker* asks for clarification of suggestions made in terms of their actual adequacy, for authoritative information and facts pertinent to the problem being discussed.

c. The *opinion seeker* asks not primarily for the facts of the case but for a clarification of the values pertinent to what the group is undertaking or of values involved in a suggestion made or in alternative suggestions.

d. The *information giver* offers facts or generalizations which are "authoritative" or relates his own experience pertinently to the group problem.

e. The *opinion giver* states his belief or opinion pertinently to a suggestion made or to alternative suggestions. The emphasis is on his proposal of what should become the group's view of pertinent values, not primarily upon relevant facts or information.

f. The *elaborator* spells out suggestions in terms of examples or developed meanings, offers a rationale for suggestions previously made, and tries to deduce how an idea or suggestion would work out if adopted by the group.

g. The *coordinator* shows or clarifies the relationships among various ideas and suggestions, tries to pull ideas and suggestions together, or tries to coordinate the activities of various members or subgroups.

h. The *orienter* defines the position of the group with respect to its goals by summarizing what has occurred, points to departures from agreed-upon directions or goals, or raises questions about the direction which the group discussion is taking.

i. The *evaluator-critic* subjects the accomplishment of the group to some standard or set of standards of group-functioning in the context of the group task. Thus he may evaluate or question the "practicality," the "logic," the "facts," or the "procedure" of a suggestion or of some unit of group discussion.

j. The *energizer* prods the group to action or decision, attempts to stimulate or arouse the group to "greater" or "higher quality" activity.

k. The *procedural technician* expedites group movement by doing things for the group—performing routine tasks (e.g., distributing materials) or manipulating objects for the group (e.g., rearranging the seating or running the recording machine, etc.)

l. The *recorder* writes down suggestions, makes a record of group decisions, or writes down the product of discussion. The recorder role is the "group memory."

Group Building and Maintenance Roles

Here the analysis of member-functions is oriented to those participations which have for their purpose the building of group-centered attitudes and orientation among the members of a group or the maintenance and perpetuation of such group-centered behavior. A given contribution may involve several roles and a member of the "leader" may perform various roles in successive contributions.

a. The *encourager* praises, agrees with, and accepts the contribution of others. He indicates warmth and solidarity in his attitude toward other group members, offers commendation and praise, and in various ways indicates understanding and acceptance of other points of view, ideas, and suggestions.

b. The *harmonizer* mediates the differences between other members, attempts to reconcile disagreements, relieves tension in conflict situations through jesting or pouring oil on the troubled waters, etc.

c. The *compromiser* operates from within a conflict in which his idea or position is involved. He may offer compromise by yielding status, admitting his error, by disciplining himself to maintain group harmony, or by "coming half-way" in moving along with the group.

d. The *gate-keeper and expediter* attempts to keep communication channels open by encouraging or facilitating the participation of others ("We haven't got the ideas of Mr. X yet," etc.) or by proposing regulation of the flow of communication ("Why don't we limit the length of our contributions so that everyone will have a chance to contribute?", etc.)

e. The *standard setter* or *ego ideal* expresses standards for the group to attempt to achieve in its functioning or applies standards in evaluating the quality of group processes.

f. The *group-observer* and *commentator* keeps records of various aspects of group process and feeds such data with proposed interpretations into the group's evaluation of its own procedures.

g. The *follower* goes along with the movement of the group, more or less passively accepting the ideas of others, serving as an audience in group discussion and decision.

"Individual" Roles

Attempts by "members" of a group to satisfy individual needs which are irrelevant to the group task and which are nonoriented or negatively oriented to group building and maintenance set problems of group and member training. A high incidence of "individual-centered" as opposed to "group-centered" participation in a group always calls for self-diagnosis of the group. The diagnosis may reveal one or several of a number of conditions—low level of skill-training among members, including the group leader; the prevalence of "authoritarian" and "laissez faire" points of view toward group functioning in the group; a low level of group maturity, discipline, and morale; and inappropriately chosen and inadequately defined group task, etc. Whatever the diagnosis, it is in this setting that the training needs of the group are to be discovered and group training efforts to meet these needs are to be defined. The outright "suppression" of "individual roles" will deprive the group of data needed for really adequate self-diagnosis and therapy.

a. The *aggressor* may work in many ways—deflating the status of others, expressing disapproval of the values, acts, or feelings of others, attacking the group or the problem it is working on, joking aggressively, showing envy toward another's contribution by trying to take credit for it, etc.

b. The *blocker* tends to be negativistic and stubbornly resistant, disagreeing and opposing without or beyond "reason" and attempting to maintain or bring back an issue after the group has rejected or bypassed it.

c. The *recognition-seeker* works in various ways to call attention to himself, whether through boasting, reporting on personal achievements, acting in unusual ways, struggling to prevent his being placed in an "inferior" position, etc.

d. The *self-confessor* uses the audience opportunity which the group setting provides to express personal, nongroup-oriented, "feeling," "insight," "idealogy," etc.

e. The *playboy* makes a display of his lack of involvement in the group's processes. This may take the form of cynicism, nonchalance, horseplay, and other more or less studied forms of "out of field" behavior.

f. The *dominator* tries to assert authority or superiority in manipulating the group or certain members of the group. This domination may take the form of flattery, of asserting a superior status or right to attention, giving directions authoritatively, interrupting the contribution of others, etc.

g. The *help-seeker* attempts to call forth "sympathy" response from other group members or from the whole group, whether through expressions of insecurity, personal confusion or depreciation of himself beyond "reason."

h. The *special interest pleader* speaks for the "small business man," the "grass roots" community, the "housewife," "labor," and so forth, usually cloaking his own prejudices or biases in the stereotype which best fits his individual need.

The Problem of Member Role Requiredness

Identification of group task roles and of group building and maintenance roles which do actually function in processes of group discussion raises but does not answer the further question of what roles are required for "optimum" group growth and productivity. Certainly the discovery and validation of answers to this question have a high priority in any advancing science of group training and development. No attempt will be made here to review the bearing of the analyzed data from the First National Training Laboratory in Group Development on this point.

It may be useful in this discussion, however, to comment on two conditions which effective work on the problem of role-requiredness must meet. First, an answer to the problem of optimum task role requirements must be projected against a scheme of the process of group production. Groups in different stages of an act of problem selection and solution will have different role requirements. For example, a group early in the stages of problem selection which is attempting to lay out a range of possible problems to be worked on, will probably have relatively less need for the roles of "evaluator-critic," "energizer," and "coordinator" than a group which has selected and discussed its problem and is shaping a decision. The combination and balance of task role requirements is a function of the group's stage of progress with respect to its task. Second, the group building role requirements of a group are a function of its stage of development—its level of group maturity. For example, a "young" group will probably require less of the role of the "standard setter" than a more mature group. Too high a level of aspiration may frustrate a "young" group where a more mature group will be able to take the same level of aspiration in its stride. Again, the role of "group observer and commentator" must be carefully adapted to the level of maturity of the group. Probably the distinction between "group" and "individual" roles can be drawn much more sharply in a relatively mature than in a "young" group.

Meanwhile, group trainers cannot wait for a fully developed science of group training before they undertake to diagnose the role requirements of the groups with which they work and to help these groups to share in such diagnosis. Each group which is attempting to improve the quality of its functioning as a group must be helped to diagnose its role requirements and must attempt to train members to fill the required roles effectively. This describes one of the principal objectives of training of group members.

The Problem of Role Flexibility

The previous group experience of members, where this experience has included little conscious attention to the variety of roles involved in effective group production and development, has frequently stereotyped the member into a limited range of roles. These he plays in all group discussions whether or not the group situation requires them. Some members see themselves primarily as "evaluator-critics" and play this role in and out of season. Others may play the roles of "encourager" or of "energizer" or of "information giver" with only small sensitivity to the role requirements of a given group situation. The development of skill and insight in diagnosing role requirements has already been mentioned as an objective of group member training. An equally important objective is the development of role flexibility, of skill and security in a wide range of member roles, on the part of all group members.

A science of group training, as it develops, must be concerned with the relationships between the personality structures of group members and the character and range of member roles which various personality structures support and permit. A science of group training must seek to discover and accept the limitations which group training per se

encounters in altering personality structures in the service of greater role flexibility on the part of all members of a group. Even though we recognize the importance of this caution, the objective of developing role flexibility remains an important objective of group member training.

Methods of Group Member Training

The objectives in training group members have been identified. Some of the kinds of resistances encountered in training group members to diagnose the role requirements of a group situation and to acquire skill in a variety of member roles have been suggested. Before analyzing briefly the methods used for group member training in the First National Training Laboratory, a few additional comments on resistances to member training may be useful. The problem of group training is actually a problem of retraining. Members of a training group have had other group experiences. They bring to the training experience attitudes toward group work, more or less conscious skills for dealing with leaders and other members, and a more or less highly developed rationale of group processes. These may or may not support processes of democratic operation in the training group. Where they do not, they function as resistances to retraining. Again, trainees are inclined to make little or no distinction between the roles they perform in a group and their personalities. Criticism of the role a group member plays is perceived as criticism of "himself." Methods must be found to reduce ego-defensiveness toward criticism of member roles. Finally, training groups must be helped to make a distinction between group feeling and group productivity. Groups which attain a state of good group feeling often perceive attempts to diagnose and criticize their level of productivity as threats to this feeling of group warmth and solidarity.

1. Each Basic Skill Training group in the Laboratory used self-observation and diagnosis of its own growth and development as a primary means of member training.

a. Sensitization to the variety of roles involved in and required by group functioning began during the introduction of members to the group. In one BST group, this early sensitization to member role variety and role requiredness began with the "leader's" summarizing, as part of his introduction of himself to the group, certain of the member roles in which he was usually cast by groups and other roles which he found it difficult to play, even when needed by the group. He asked the group's help in criticizing and improving his skill in those roles where he felt weakest. Other members followed suit. Various members showed widely different degrees of sensitivity to the operation of member roles in groups and to the degree of their own proficiency in different roles. This introduction procedure gave the group a partial listing of member roles for later use and supplementation, initial self-assessments of member strengths and weaknesses, and diagnostic material concerning the degree of group self-sophistication among the members. The training job had come to be seen by most members as a retraining job.

b. A description of the use of training observers in group self-evaluation sessions is given in the next paper in this issue (David H. Jenkins, "Feedback and Group Self-Evaluation"). At this point, only the central importance which self-evaluation sessions played in member training needs to be stressed. Research observers fed observational data concerning group functioning into periodic discussions by the group of its strengths and weaknesses as a group. Much of these data concerned role requirements for the job the group had been attempting, which roles had been present, which roles had probably been needed. "Individual" roles were identified and interpreted in an objective and non-blaming manner. Out of these discussions, group members came to identify various kinds of member roles, to relate role requiredness to stages in group production and in group growth, and to assess the range of roles each was able to play well when required. Out of these discussions came group decisions concerning the supplying of needed roles in the next session. Member commitments concerning behavior in future sessions also came out of these evaluations. These took the form both of silent commitments and of public commitments in which the help of the group was requested.

c. Recordings of segments of the group's discussion were used by most Basic Skill Training groups. Groups listened to themselves, diagnosed the member and leader functions involved, and assessed the adequacy of these.

2. Role-played sessions in each group, although they were pointed content-wise to the skills of the change agent, offered important material for the diagnosis of member roles and of role-requiredness. These sessions offered an important supplement to group self-diagnosis and evaluation. It is easier for members to get perspective on their participation in a role-played episode of group process than it is on their own participation in a "real" group. The former is not perceived as "real." The role is more easily disengaged for purposes of analysis and evaluation from the person playing the role. Ego-defensiveness toward the role as enacted is reduced. Role-playing sessions also provided practice opportunity to members in a variety of roles.

3. Practice by group members of the role of *observer-commentator* is especially valuable in developing skill in diagnosing member roles and in assessing the role requirements of a group situation. In several groups, each member in turn served as observer, supplementing the work of the research observers in evaluation sessions. Such members worked more or less closely with the anecdotal observer for the group on skill-problems encountered. Practice opportunity in the *observer-commentator* role was also provided in clinic group meetings in the afternoon.

Summary

Training in group membership roles requires the identification and analysis of various member roles actually enacted in group processes. It involves further the analysis of group situations in terms of roles required in relation both to a schema of group production and to a conception of group growth and development. A group's self-observation and self-evaluation of its own processes provides useful content and practice opportunity in member training. Practice in enacting a wider range of required roles and in role flexibility can come out of member commitment to such practice with help from the group in evaluating and improving the required skills. Member training is typically retraining and resistances to retraining can be reduced by creating a nonblaming and objective atmosphere in group self-evaluation and by using role-playing of group processes for diagnosis and practice. The training objectives of developing skill in the diagnosis of group role requirements and developing role flexibility among members also indicate important research areas for a science of group training.

Endnotes

1. A somewhat different analysis of member-participations, in terms of categories used by interaction observers in observation of group processes in the First National Training Laboratory, is described in the *Preliminary Report* of the laboratory, pages 122–32. The number of categories used by interaction observers was "directed primarily by limitations of observer load."

READING 32
CHOOSING THE DEPTH OF ORGANIZATIONAL INTERVENTION

Roger Harrison

Since World War II there has been a great prolifer-ation of behavioral science-based methods by which consultants seeks to facilitate growth and change in individuals, groups, and organizations. The methods range from operations analysis and manipulation of the organization chart, through the use of Grid laboratories, T-groups, and non-verbal techniques. As was true in the development of clinical psychology and psychotherapy, the early stages of this developmental process tend to be accompanied by considerable competition, criti-cism, and argument about the relative merits of various approaches. It is my conviction that con-troversy over the relative goodness or badness, effectiveness or ineffectiveness, of various change strategies really accomplishes very little in the way of increased knowledge or unification of behav-ioral science. As long as we are arguing about what method is better than another, we tend to learn very little about how various approaches fit together or complement one another, and we cer-tainly make more difficult and ambiguous the task of bringing these competing points of view within one overarching system of knowledge about human processes.

As our knowledge increases, it begins to be apparent that these competing change strategies are not really different ways of doing the same thing—some more effective and some less effective—but rather that they are different ways of doing *differ-ent* things. They touch the individual, the group, or the organization in different aspects of their func-tioning. They require differing kinds and amounts of commitment on the part of the client for them to be successful, and they demand different vari-eties and levels of skills and abilities on the part of the practitioner.

I believe that there is a real need for conceptual models which differentiate intervention strategies from one another in a way which permits rational matching of strategies to organizational change problems. The purpose of this paper is to present a modest beginning which I have made toward a conceptualization of strategies, and to derive from this conceptualization some criteria for choosing appropriate methods of intervention in particular applications.

The point of view of this paper is that the depth of individual emotional involvement in the change process can be a central concept for differentiating change strategies. In focusing on this dimension, we are concerned with the extent to which core areas of the personality or self are the focus of the change attempt. Strategies which touch the more deep, personal, private, and central aspects of the indi-vidual or his relationships with others fall toward the deeper end of this continuum. Strategies which deal with more external aspects of the individual and which focus on the more formal and public aspects of role behavior tend to fall toward the sur-face end of the depth dimension. This dimension has the advantage that it is relatively easy to rank change strategies upon it and to get fairly close consensus as to the ranking. It is a widely discussed dimension of difference which has meaning and relevance to practitioners and their clients. I hope in this paper to promote greater flexibility and rationality in choosing appropriate depths of inter-vention. I shall approach this task by examining the effects of interventions at various depths. I shall also

Source: Roger Harrison, "Choosing the Depth of Organizational Intervention" in *Journal of Applied Behavioral Science* (6, no.2) pp. 182–202, copyright © 1970 by NTL Institute of Applied Behavoiral Science. Reprinted by permission of Sage Publications, Inc.

explore the ways in which two important organizational processes tend to make demands and to set limits upon the depth of intervention which can produce effective change in organizational functioning. These two processes are the autonomy of organization members and their own perception of their needs for help.

Before illustrating the concept by ranking five common intervention strategies along the dimension of depth, I should like to define the dimension somewhat more precisely. We are concerned essentially with how private, individual, and hidden are the issues and processes about which the consultant attempts directly to obtain information and which he seeks to influence. If the consultant seeks information about relatively public and observable aspects of behavior and relationships, if he tries to influence directly only these relatively surface characteristics and processes, we would then categorize his intervention strategy as being closer to the surface. If, on the other hand, the consultant seeks information about very deep and private perceptions, attitudes, or feelings, and if he intervenes in a way which directly affects these processes, then we would classify his intervention strategy as one of considerable depth. To illustrate the surface end of the dimension let us look first at operations research or operations analysis. This strategy is concerned with the roles and functions to be performed within the organization, generally with little regard to the individual characteristics of persons occupying the roles. The change strategy is to manipulate role relationships; in other words, to redistribute the tasks, the resources, and the relative power attached to various roles in the organization. This is essentially a process of rational analysis in which the tasks which need to be performed are determined and specified and then sliced up into role definitions for persons and groups in the organization. The operations analyst does not ordinarily need to know much about particular people. Indeed, his function is to design the organization in such a way that its successful operation does not depend too heavily upon any uniquely individual skills, abilities, values, or attitudes of persons in various roles. He may

perform this function adequately without knowing in advance who the people are who will fill these slots. Persons are assumed to be moderately interchangeable, and in order to make this approach work it is necessary to design the organization so that the capacities, needs, and values of the individual which are relevant to role performance are relatively public and observable, and are possessed by a fairly large proportion of the population from which organization members are drawn. The approach is certainly one of very modest depth.

Somewhat deeper are those strategies which are based upon evaluating individual performance and attempting to manipulate it directly. Included in this approach is much of the industrial psychologist's work in selection, placement, appraisal, and counseling of employees. The intervener is concerned with what the individual is able and likely to do and achieve, rather than with processes internal to the individual. Direct attempts to influence performance may be made through the application of rewards and punishments, such as promotions, salary increases, or transfers within the organization. An excellent illustration of this focus on end results is the practice of management by objectives. The intervention process is focused on establishing mutually agreed-upon goals for performance between the individual and his supervisor. The practice is considered to be particularly advantageous because it permits the supervisor to avoid a focus on personal characteristics of the subordinate, particularly those deeper, more central characteristics which managers generally have difficulty in discussing with those who work under their supervision. The process is designed to limit information exchange to that which is public and observable, such as the setting of performance goals and the success or failure of the individual in attaining them.

Because of its focus on end results, rather than on the process by which those results are achieved, management by objectives must be considered less deep than the broad area of concern with work style which I shall term instrumental process analysis. We are concerned here not only with performance but with the processes by which that performance is achieved. However, we are primarily concerned with styles and processes of work rather than with the processes of interpersonal relationships which I would classify as being deeper on the basic dimension.

In instrumental process analysis we are concerned with how a person likes to organize and conduct his work and with the impact which this style of work has on others in the organization. Principally, we are concerned with how a person perceives his role, what he values and disvalues in it, and what he works hard on and what he chooses to ignore. We are also interested in the instrumental acts which the individual directs toward others: delegating authority or reserving decisions to himself, communicating or withholding information, collaborating or competing with others on work-related issues. The focus on instrumentality means that we are interested in the person primarily as a doer of work or as a performer of functions related to the goals of the organization. We are interested in what facilitates or inhibits his effective task performance.

We are not interested per se whether his relationships with others are happy or unhappy, whether they perceive him as too warm or too cold, too authoritarian or too laissez-faire, or any other of the many interpersonal relationships which arise as people associate in organizations. However, I do not mean to imply that the line between instrumental relationships and interpersonal ones is an easy one to draw in action and practice, or even that it is desirable that this be done.

Depth Gauges: Level of Tasks and Feelings

What I am saying is that an intervention strategy can focus on instrumentality or it can focus on interpersonal relationships, and that there are important consequences of this difference in depth of intervention.

When we intervene at the level of instrumentality, it is to change work behavior and working relationships. Frequently this involves the process of

bargaining or negotiation between groups and individuals. Diagnoses are made of the satisfactions or dissatisfactions of organization members with one another's work behavior. Reciprocal adjustments, bargains, and trade-offs can then be arranged in which each party gets some modification in the behavior of the other at the cost to him of some reciprocal accommodation. Much of the intervention strategy which has been developed around Blake's concept of the Managerial Grid is at this level and involves bargaining and negotiation of role behavior as an important change process.

At the deeper level of interpersonal relationships the focus is on feelings, attitudes, and perceptions which organization members have about others. At this level we are concerned with the quality of human relationships within the organization, with warmth and coldness of members to one another, and with the experiences of acceptance and rejection, love and hate, trust and suspicion among groups and individuals. At this level the consultant probes for normally hidden feelings, attitudes, and perceptions. He works to create relationships of openness about feelings and to help members to develop mutual understanding of one another as persons. Interventions are directed toward helping organization members to be more comfortable in being authentically themselves with one another, and the degree of mutual caring and concern is expected to increase. Sensitivity training using T-groups is a basic intervention strategy at this level. T-group educators emphasize increased personalization of relationships, the development of trust and openness, and the exchange of feelings. Interventions at this level deal directly and intensively with interpersonal emotionality. This is the first intervention strategy we have examined which is at a depth where the feelings of organization members about one another as persons are a direct focus of the intervention strategy. At the other levels, such feelings certainly exist and may be expressed, but they are not a direct concern of the intervention. The transition from the task orientation of instrumental process analysis to the feeling orientation of interpersonal process analysis seems, as I shall suggest later, to be a critical one for many organization members.

The deepest level of intervention which will be considered in this paper is that of intrapersonal analysis. Here the consultant uses a variety of methods to reveal the individual's deeper attitudes, values, and conflicts regarding his own functioning, identity, and existence. The focus is generally on increasing the range of experiences which the individual can bring into awareness and cope with. The material may be dealt with at the fantasy or symbolic level, and the intervention strategies include many which are non-interpersonal and nonverbal. Some examples of this approach are the use of marathon T-group sessions, the creative risk-taking laboratory approach of Byrd (1967), and some aspects of the task group therapy approach of Clark (1966). These approaches all tend to bring into focus very deep and intense feelings about one's own identity and one's relationships with significant others.

Although I have characterized deeper interventions as dealing increasingly with the individual's affective life, I do not imply that issues at less deep levels may not be emotionally charged. Issues of role differentiation, reward distribution, ability and performance evaluation, for example, are frequently invested with strong feelings. The concept of depth is concerned more with the *accessibility* and *individuality* of attitudes, values, and perceptions than it is with their strength. This narrowing of the common usage of the term *depth* is necessary to avoid the contradictions which occur when strength and inaccessibility are confused. For instance, passionate value confrontation and bitter conflict have frequently occurred between labor and management over economic issues which are surely toward the surface end of my concept of depth.

In order to understand the importance of the concept of depth for choosing interventions in organizations, let us consider the effects upon organization members of working at different levels.

The first of the important concomitants of depth is the degree of dependence of the client on the special competence of the change agent. At the surface end of the depth dimension, the methods of intervention are easily communicated and made public. The client may reasonably expect to learn something of the change agent's skills to improve his own practice. At the deeper levels, such as interpersonal and intrapersonal process analyses, it is more difficult for the client to understand the methods of intervention. The change agent is more likely to be seen as a person of special and unusual powers not found in ordinary men. Skills of intervention and change are less frequently learned by organization members, and the change process may tend to become personalized around the change agent as leader. Programs of change which are so dependent upon personal relationships and individual expertise are difficult to institutionalize. When the change agent leaves the system, he may not only take his expertise with him but the entire change process as well.

A second aspect of the change process which varies with depth is the extent to which the benefits of an intervention are transferable to members of the organization not originally participating in the change process. At surface levels of operations analysis and performance evaluation, the effects are institutionalized in the form of procedures, policies, and practices of the organization which may have considerable permanence beyond the tenure of individuals. At the level of instrumental behavior, the continuing effects of intervention are more likely to reside in the informal norms of groups within the organization regarding such matters as delegation, communication, decision making, competition and collaboration, and conflict resolution.

At the deepest levels of intervention, the target of change is the individual's inner life; and if the intervention is successful, the permanence of individual change should be greatest. There are indeed dramatic reports of cases in which persons have changed their careers and life goals as a result of such interventions, and the persistence of such change appears to be relatively high.

One consequence, then, of the level of intervention is that with greater depth of focus the individual increasingly becomes both the target and the carrier of change. In the light of this analysis, it is not surprising to observe that deeper levels of intervention are increasingly being used at higher organizational levels and in scientific and service organizations where the contribution of the individual has greatest impact.

An important concomitant of depth is that, as the level of intervention becomes deeper, the information needed to intervene effectively becomes less available. At the less personal level of operations analysis, the information is often a matter of record. At the level of performance evaluation, it is a matter of observation. On the other hand, reactions of others to a person's work style are less likely to be discussed freely, and the more personal responses to his interpersonal style are even less likely to be readily given. At the deepest levels, important information may not be available to the individual himself. Thus as we go deeper the consultant must use more of his time and skill uncovering information which is ordinarily private and hidden. This is one reason for the greater costs of interventions at deeper levels of focus.

Another aspect of the change process which varies with the depth of intervention is the personal risk and unpredictability of outcome for the individual. At deeper levels we deal with aspects of the individual's view of himself and his relationships with others which are relatively untested by exposure to the evaluations and emotional reactions of others. If in the change process the individual's self-perceptions are strongly disconfirmed, the resulting imbalance in internal forces may produce sudden changes in behavior, attitudes, and personality integration.

Because of the private and hidden nature of the processes into which we intervene at deeper levels, it is difficult to predict the individual impact of the change process in advance. The need for clinical sensitivity and skill on the part of the practitioner thus increases, since he must be prepared to diagnose and deal with developing situations involving considerable stress upon individuals.

The foregoing analysis suggests a criterion by which to match intervention strategies to particular organizational problems. It is *to intervene at a level* *no deeper than that required to produce enduring solutions to the problems at hand.* This criterion derives directly from the observations above. The cost, skill demands, client dependency, and variability of outcome all increase with depth of intervention. Further, as the depth of intervention increases, the effects tend to locate more in the individual and less in the organization. The danger of losing the organization's investment in the change with the departure of the individual becomes a significant consideration.

Autonomy Increases Depth of Intervention

While this general criterion is simple and straightforward, its application is not. In particular, although the criterion should operate in the direction of less depth of intervention, there is a general trend in modern organizational life tends to push the intervention level ever deeper. This trend is toward increased self-direction of organization members and increased independence of external pressures and incentives. I believe that there is a direct relationship between the autonomy of individuals and the depth of intervention needed to effect organizational change.

Before going on to discuss this relationship, I shall acknowledge freely that I cannot prove the existence of a trend toward a general increase in freedom of individuals within organizations. I intend only to assert the great importance of the degree of individual autonomy in determining the level of intervention which will be effective.

In order to understand the relationship between autonomy and depth of intervention, it is necessary to conceptualize a dimension which parallels and is implied by the depth dimension we have been discussing. This is the dimension of predictability and variability among persons in their responses to the different kinds of incentives which may be used to influence behavior in the organization. The key assumption in this analysis that the more unpredictable and unique is the individual's response to the particular kinds of controls and incentives one can bring to bear upon him, the more one must know about that person in order to influence his behavior.

Most predictable and least individual is the response of the person to economic and bureaucratic controls when his needs for economic income and security are high. It is not necessary to delve very deeply into a person's inner processes in order to influence his behavior if we know that he badly needs his income and his position and if we are in a position to control his access to these rewards. Responses to economic and bureaucratic controls tend to be relatively simple and on the surface.

Independence of Economic Incentive.   If for any reason organization members become relatively uninfluenceable through the manipulation of their income and economic security, the management of performance becomes strikingly more complex; and the need for more personal information about the individual increases. Except very generally, we do not know automatically or in advance what styles of instrumental or interpersonal interaction will be responded to as negative or positive incentives by the individual. One person may appreciate close supervision and direction; another may value independence of direction. One may prefer to work alone; another may function best when he is in close communication with others. One may thrive in close, intimate, personal interaction; while others are made uncomfortable by any but cool and distant relationships with colleagues.

What I am saying is that, when bureaucratic and economic incentives lose their force for whatever reason, the improvement of performance *must* involve linking organizational goals to the individual's attempts to meet his own needs for satisfying instrumental activities and interpersonal relationships. It is for this reason that I make the assertion that increases in personal autonomy dictate change interventions at deeper and more personal levels. In order to obtain the information necessary to link organizational needs to individual goals, one must probe fairly deeply into the attitudes, values, and emotions of the organization members.

If the need for deeper personal information becomes great when we intervene at the instrumental and interpersonal levels, it becomes even greater when one is dealing with organization members who are motivated less through their transactions with the environment and more in response to internal values and standards. An example is the researcher, engineer, or technical specialist whose work behavior may be influenced more by his own values and standards of creativity or professional excellence than by his relationships with others. The deepest organizational interventions at the intrapersonal level may be required in order to effect change when working with persons who are highly self-directed.

Let me summarize my position about the relationship among autonomy, influence, and level of intervention. As the individual becomes less subject to economic and bureaucratic pressures, he tends to seek more intangible rewards in the organization which come from both the instrumental and interpersonal aspects of the system. I view this as a shift from greater external to more internal control and as an increase in autonomy. Further shifts in this direction may involve increased independence of rewards and punishments mediated by others, in favor of operation in accordance with internal values and standards.

I view organizations as systems of reciprocal influence. Achievement of organization goals is facilitated when individuals can seek their own satisfactions through activity which promotes the goals of the organization. As the satisfactions which are of most value to the individual change, so must the reciprocal influence systems, if the organization goals are to continue to be met.

If the individual changes are in the direction of increased independence of external incentives, then the influence systems must change to provide opportunities for individuals to achieve more intangible, self-determined satisfactions in their work. However, people are more differentiated, complex, and unique in their intangible goals and values than in their economic needs. In order to create systems which offer a wide variety of intangible satisfactions, much more private information about individuals is needed than is required to create and maintain systems based chiefly on economic and bureaucratic controls. For this reason, deeper interventions are called for when the system which they would attempt to change contains a high proportion of relatively autonomous individuals.

There a number of factors promoting autonomy, all tending to free the individual from dependence upon economic and bureaucratic controls, which I have observed in my work with organizations. Wherever a number of these factors obtain, it is probably an indication that deeper levels of intervention are required to effect lasting improvements in organizational functioning. I shall simply list these indicators briefly in categories to show what kinds of things might signify to the practitioner that deeper levels of intervention may be appropriate.

The first category includes anything which makes the evaluation of individual performance difficult:

A long time span between the individual's actions and the results by which effectiveness of performance is to be judged.

Nonrepetitive, unique tasks which cannot be evaluated by reference to the performance of others on similar tasks.

Specialized skills and abilities possessed by an individual which cannot be evaluated by a supervisor who does not possess the skills or knowledge himself.

The second category concerns economic conditions:

Arrangements which secure the job tenure and/or income to the individual.

A marketing permitting easy transfer from one organization to another (e.g., engineers in the United States aerospace industry).

Unique skills and knowledge of the individual which make him difficult to replace.

The third category includes characteristics of the system or its environment which lead to independence of the parts of the organization and decentralization of authority such as:

An organization which works on a project basis instead of producing a standard line of products.

An organization in which subparts must be given latitude to deal rapidly and flexibly with frequent environmental change.

I should like to conclude the discussion of this criterion for depth of intervention with a brief reference to the ethics of intervention, a problem which merits considerably more thorough treatment than I can give it here.

The Ethics of Delving Deeper.   There is considerable concern in the United States about invasion of privacy by behavioral scientists. I would agree that such invasion of privacy is an actual as well as a fantasized concomitant of the use of organizational change strategies of greater depth. The recourse by organizations to such strategies has been widely viewed as an indication of greater organizational control over the most personal and private aspects of the lives of the members. The present analysis suggests, however, that recourse to these deeper interventions actually reflects the greater *freedom* of organization members from traditionally crude and impersonal means of organizational control. There is no reason to be concerned about man's attitudes or values or interpersonal relationships when his job performance can be controlled by brute force, by economic coercion, or by bureaucratic rules and regulations. The "invasion of privacy" becomes worth the cost, bother, and uncertainty of outcome only when the individual has achieved relative independence from control by other means. Put another way, it makes organizational sense to try to get a man to *want* to do something only if you cannot *make* him do it. And regardless of what intervention strategy is used, the individual still retains considerably greater control over his own behavior than he had when he could be manipulated more crudely. As long as we can maintain a high degree of voluntarism regarding the nature and extent of an individual's participation in the deeper organizational change strategies, these strategies can work toward adapting the organization to the individual quite as much as they work the other way around. Only when an individual's participation in one of the deeper change strategies is coerced by economic or bureaucratic pressures, do I feel that the ethics of the intervention clearly run counter to the values of a democratic society.

Role of Client Norms and Values in Determining Depth

So far our attention to the choice of level of intervention has focused upon locating the depth at which the information exists which must be exchanged to facilitate system improvement. Unfortunately, the choice of an intervention strategy cannot practically be made with reference to this criterion alone. Even if a correct diagnosis is made of the level at which the relevant information lies, we may not be able to work effectively at the desired depth because of client norms, values, resistances, and fears.

In an attempt to develop a second criterion for depth of intervention which takes such dispositions on the part of the client into account, I have considered two approaches which represent polarized orientations to the problem. One approach is based upon analyzing and overcoming client resistance; the other is based upon discovering and joining forces with the self-articulated wants or "felt needs" of the client.

There are several ways of characterizing these approaches. To me, the simplest is to point out that when the change agent is resistance-oriented he tends to lead or influence the client to work at a depth greater than that at which the latter feels comfortable. When resistance-oriented, the change agent tends to mistrust the client's statement of his problems and of the areas where he wants help. He suspects the client's presentation of being a smoke screen or defense against admission of his "real" problems and needs. The consultant works to expose the underlying processes and concerns and to influence the client to work at a deeper level. The resistance-oriented approach grows out of the work of clinicians and psychotherapists, and it characterizes much of the work of organizational consultants who specialize in sensitivity training and deeper intervention strategies.

On the other hand, change agents may be oriented to the self-articulated needs of clients. When so oriented, the consultant tends more to follow and facilitate the client in working at whatever level the latter sets for himself. He may assist the client in defining problems and needs and in working on solutions, but he is inclined to try to anchor his work in the norms, values, and accepted standards of behavior of the organization.

I believe that there is a tendency for change agents working at the interpersonal and deeper levels to adopt a rather consistent resistance-oriented approach. Consultants so oriented seem to take a certain quixotic pride in dramatically and self-consciously violating organizational norms. Various techniques have been developed for pressuring or seducing organizations members into departing from organizational norms in the service of change. The "marathon" T-group is a case in point, where the increased irritability and fatigue of prolonged contact and lack of sleep move participants to deal with one another more emotionally, personally, and spontaneously than they would normally be willing to do.

I suspect that unless such norm-violating intervention efforts actually succeed in changing organizational norms, their effects are relatively short-lived, because the social structures and interpersonal linkages have not been created which can utilize for day-to-day problem solving the deeper information produced by the intervention. It is true that the consultant may succeed in producing information, but he is less likely to succeed in creating social structures which can continue to work in his absence. The problem is directly analogous to that of the community developer who succeeds by virtue of his personal influence in getting villagers to build a school or a community center which falls into disuse as soon as he leaves because of the lack of any integration of these achievements into the social structure and day-to-day needs and desires of the community. Community developers have had to learn through bitter failure and frustration that ignoring or subverting the standards and norms of a social system often results in temporary success followed by a reactionary increase in resistance to the influence of the change agent. On the other hand, felt needs embody those problems, issues, and difficulties which have a high conscious priority on the part of community or organization members. We can expect individuals and groups to be ready to invest time, energy, and resources in dealing with their felt needs, while they will be relatively passive or even resistant toward those who attempt to help them with externally defined needs. Community developers have found that attempts to help with felt needs are met with greater receptivity, support, and integration within the structure and life of the community than are intervention attempts which rely primarily upon the developer's value system for setting need priorities.

The emphasis of many organizational change agents on confronting and working through resistances was developed originally in the practice of individual psychoanalysis and psychotherapy, and it is also a central concept in the conduct of therapy groups and sensitivity training laboratories. In all of these situations, the change agent has a high degree of environmental control and is at least temporarily in a high status position with respect to the client. To a degree that is frequently underestimated by practitioners, we manage to create a situation in which it is more unpleasant for the client to leave than it is to stay and submit to the pressure to confront and work through resistances. I believe that the tendency is for behavioral scientists to overplay their hands when they move from the clinical and training situations where they have environmental control to the organizational consulting situation where their control is sharply attenuated.

This attenuation derives only partially from the relative ease with which the client can terminate the relationship. Even if this most drastic step is not taken, the consultant can be tolerated, misled, and deceived in ways which are relatively difficult in the therapeutic or human relations training situations. He can also be openly defied and blocked if he runs afoul of strongly shared group norms; whereas when the consultant is dealing with a group of strangers, he can often utilize differences among the members to overcome this kind of resistance. I suspect that, in general, behavioral

scientists underestimate their power in working with individuals and groups of strangers, and overestimate it when working with individuals and groups in organizations. I emphasize this point because I believe that a good many potentially fruitful and mutually satisfying consulting relationships are terminated early because of the consultant's taking the role of overcomer of resistance to change, rather than that of collaborator in the client's attempts at solving his problems. It is these considerations which lead me to suggest my second criterion for the choice of organization intervention strategy: *to intervene at a level no deeper than that at which the energy and resources of the client can be committed to problem solving and to change.* These energies and resources can be mobilized through obtaining legitimation for the intervention in the forms of the organization and through devising intervention strategies which have clear relevance to consciously felt needs on the part of the organization members.

The Consultant's Dilemma:
Felt Needs versus Deeper Levels

Unfortunately, it is doubtless true that the forces which influence the conditions we desire to change often exist at deeper levels than can be dealt with by adhering to the criterion of working within organization norms and meeting felt needs. The level at which an individual or group is willing and ready to invest energy and resources is probably always determined partly by a realistic assessment of the problems and partly by a defensive need to avoid confrontation and significant change. It is thus not likely that our two criteria for selection of intervention depth will result in the same decisions when practically applied. It is not the same to intervene at the level where behavior-determining forces are most potent as it is to work on felt needs as they are articulated by the client. This, it seems to me, is the consultant's dilemma. It always has been. We are continually faced with the choice between leading the client into areas which are threatening, unfamiliar, and dependency-provoking for him (and where our own expertise shows up to best advantage) or, on the other hand, being guided by the client's own understanding of his problems and his willingness to invest resources in particular kinds of relatively familiar and nonthreatening strategies.

When time permits, this dilemma is ideally dealt with by intervening first at a level where there is good support from the norms, power structure, and felt needs of organizational members. The consultant can then, over a period of time, develop trust, sophistication, and support within the organization to explore deeper levels at which particularly important forces may be operating. This would probably be agreed to, at least in principle, by most organizational consultants. The point at which I feel I differ from a significant number of workers in this field is that I would advocate that interventions should *always* be limited to the depth of the client's felt needs and readiness to legitimize intervention. I believe we should always avoid moving deeper at a pace which outstrips a client system's willingness to subject itself to exposure, dependence, and threat. What I am saying is that, if the dominant response of organization members indicates that an intervention violates system norms regarding exposure, privacy, and confrontation, then one has intervened too deeply and should pull back to a level at which organization members are more ready to invest their own energy in the change process. This point of view is thus in opposition to that which sees negative reactions primarily as indications of resistances which are to be brought out into the open, confronted, and worked through as a central part of the intervention process. I believe that behavioral scientists acting as organizational consultants have tended to place overmuch emphasis on the overcoming of resistance to change and have underemphasized the importance of enlisting in the service of change the energies and resources which the client can consciously direct and willingly devote to problem solving.

What is advocated here is that we in general accept the client's felt needs or the problems he presents as real and that we work on them at a level at which he can serve as a competent and willing collaborator. This position is in opposition to one which sees the presenting problem as more or less a smoke screen or barrier. I am not advocating this point of view because I value the right to privacy of organization members more highly than I value their growth and development or the solution of organization problems. (This is an issue which concerns me, but it is enormously more complex than the ones with which I am dealing in this paper.) Rather, I place first priority on collaboration with the client, because I do not think we are frequently successful consultants without it.

In my own practice I have observed that the change in client response is frequently quite striking when I move from a resistance-oriented approach to an acceptance of the client's norms and definitions of his own needs. With quite a few organizational clients in the United States, the line of legitimacy seems to lie somewhere between interventions at the instrumental level and those focused on interpersonal relationships. Members who exhibit hostility, passivity, and dependence when I initiate intervention at the interpersonal level may become dramatically more active, collaborative, and involved when I shift the focus to the instrumental level.

If I intervene directly at the level of interpersonal relationships, I can be sure that at least some members, and often the whole group, will react with anxiety, passive resistance, and low or negative commitment to the change process. Furthermore, they express their resistance in terms of norms and values regarding the appropriateness or legitimacy of dealing at this level. They say things like, "It isn't right to force people's feelings about one another out into the open"; "I don't see what this has to do with improving organizational effectiveness"; "People are being encouraged to say things which are better left unsaid."

If I then switch to a strategy which focuses on decision making, delegation of authority, information exchange, and other instrumental questions, these complaints about illegitimacy and the inappropriateness of the intervention are usually sharply reduced. This does not mean that the clients are necessarily comfortable or free from anxiety in the discussions, nor does it mean that strong feelings may not be expressed about one another's behavior. What is different is that the clients are more likely to *work with* instead of *against* me, to feel and express some sense of ownership in the change process, and to see many more possibilities for carrying it on among themselves in the absence of the consultant.

What I have found is that, when I am resistance-oriented in my approach to the client, I am apt to feel rather uncomfortable in "letting sleeping dogs lie." When, on the other hand, I orient myself to the client's own assessment of his needs, I am uncomfortable when I feel I am leading or pushing the client to operate very far outside the shared norms of the organization. I have tried to indicate why I believe the latter orientation is more appropriate. I realize of course that many highly sophisticated and talented practitioners will not agree with me.

In summary, I have tried to show in this paper that the dimension of depth should be central to the conceptualization of intervention strategies. I have presented what I believe are the major consequences of intervening at greater or lesser depths; and from these consequences I have suggested two criteria for choosing the appropriate depth of intervention: first, *to intervene at a level no deeper than that required to produce enduring solutions to the problems at hand;* and second, *to intervene at a level no deeper than that at which the energy and resources of the client can be committed to problem solving and to change.*

I have analyzed the tendency for increases in individual autonomy in organizations to push the appropriate level of intervention deeper when the first criterion is followed. Opposed to this is the countervailing influence of the second criterion to work closer to the surface in order to enlist the energy and support of organization members in the change process. Arguments have been presented for resolving this dilemma in favor of the second, more conservative, criterion. The dilemma remains, of course, the continuing tension under which the change agent works is between the desire to lead and push, or to collaborate and follow. The middle ground is never very stable, and I suspect we show our values and preferences by which criterion we choose to maximize when we are under the stress of difficult and ambiguous client-consultant relationships.

References

Byrd, R. E. "Training in a Nongroup." *Journal of Humanistic Psychology* 7, no. 1 (167), pp. 18–27.

Clark, J. V. "Task Group Therapy." Unpublished manuscript, University of California, Los Angeles, 1966.

READING 33
RULES OF THUMB FOR CHANGE AGENTS

Herbert A. Shepard

The following aphorisms are not so much bits of advice (although they are stated that way) as things to think about when you are being a change agent, a consultant, an organization, or a community development practitioner—or when you are just being yourself trying to bring about something that involves other people.

Rule I: Stay Alive

This rule counsels against self-sacrifice on behalf of a cause that you do not wish to be your last.

Two exceptionally talented doctoral students came to the conclusion that the routines they had to go through to get their degrees were absurd, and decided they would be untrue to themselves to conform to an absurd system. That sort of reasoning is almost always self-destructive. Besides, their noble gesture in quitting would be unlikely to have any impact whatever on the system they were taking a stand against.

This is not to say that one should never take a stand, or a survival risk. But such risks should be taken as part of a purposeful strategy of change, and appropriately timed and targeted. When they are taken under such circumstances, one is very much alive.

But Rule I is much more than a survival rule. The rule means that you should let your whole being be involved in the undertaking. Since most of us have never been in touch with our whole beings, it means a lot of putting together of parts that have been divided, of using internal communications channels that have been closed or were never opened.

Source: Herbert A. Shepard, "Rules of Thumb for Change Agents," *Organization Development Practitioner,* November 1975, pp. 1–5. (Publication of the National Organization Development Network, P.O. Box 69329, Portland, OR 97201.)

Staying alive means loving yourself. Self-disparagement leads to the suppression of potentials, to a win-lose formulation of the world, and to wasting life in defensive maneuvering.

Staying alive means staying in touch with your purpose. It means using your skills, your emotions, your labels and positions, rather than being used by them. It means not being trapped in other people's games. It means turning yourself on and off, rather than being dependent on the situation. It means choosing with a view to the consequences as well as the impulse. It means going with the flow even while swimming against it. It means living in several worlds without being swallowed up in any. It means seeing dilemmas as opportunities for creativity. It means greeting absurdity with laughter while trying to unscramble it. It means capturing the moment in the light of the future. It means seeing the environment through the eyes of your purpose.

Rule II: Start Where the System Is

This is such ancient wisdom that one might expect its meaning had been fully explored and apprehended. Yet in practice, the rule—and the system—are often violated.

The rule implies that one should begin by diagnosing the system. But systems do not necessarily *like* being diagnosed. Even the term *diagnosis* may be offensive. And the system may be even less ready for someone who calls himself or herself a change agent. It is easy for the practitioner to forget that the use of jargon, which prevents laymen from understanding the professional mysteries, is a hostile act.

Starting where the system is can be called the Empathy Rule. To communicate effectively, to obtain a basis for building sound strategy, the change agent needs to understand how the client sees himself and his situation, and needs to understand the culture of the system. Establishing the required rapport does not mean that the change agent who wants to work in a traditional industrial setting should refrain from growing a beard. It does mean that, if he has a beard, the beard is likely to determine where the client is when they first meet, and the client's curiosity needs to be dealt with. Similarly, the rule does not mean that a female change agent in a male organization should try to act like one of the boys, or that a young change agent should try to act like a senior executive. One thing it does mean is that sometimes where the client is, is wondering where the change agent is.

Rarely is the client in any one place at any one time. That is, she or he may be ready to pursue any of several paths. The task is to walk together on the most promising path.

Even unwitting or accidental violations of that Empathy Rule can destroy the situation. I lost a client through two violations in one morning. The client group spent a consulting day at my home. They arrived early in the morning, before I had my empathy on. The senior member, seeing a picture of my son in the living room, said, "What do you do with boys with long hair?" I replied thoughtlessly, "I think he's handsome that way." The small chasm thus created between my client and me was widened and deepened later that morning when one of the family tortoises walked through the butter dish.

Sometimes starting where the client is, which sounds both ethically and technically virtuous, can lead to some ethically puzzling situations. Robert Frost[1] described a situation in which a consultant was so empathic with a king who was unfit to rule that the king discovered his own unfitness and had himself shot, whereupon the consultant became king.

Empathy permits the development of a mutual attachment between client and consultant. The resulting relationship may be one in which their creativities are joined, a mutual growth relationship. But it can also become one in which the client becomes dependent and is manipulated by the consultant. The ethical issues are not associated with starting where the system is, but with how one moves with it.

Rule III: Never Work Uphill

This is a comprehensive rule, and a number of other rules are corollaries or examples of it. It is an appeal for an organic, rather than a mechanistic approach to change, for a collaborative approach to change, for building strength and building on strength. It has a number of implications that bear on the choices the change agent makes about how to use him/herself, and it says something about life.

Corollary 1: Don't Build Hills as You Go. This corollary cautions against working in a way that builds resistance to movement in the direction you have chosen as desirable. For example, a program which has a favorable effect on one portion of a population may have the opposite effect on other portions of the population. Perhaps the commonest error of this kind has been in the employment of T-group training in organizations: turning on the participants and turning off the people who didn't attend, in one easy lesson.

Corollary 2: Work in the Most Promising Arena. The physician-patient relationship is often regarded as analogous to the consultant-client relationship. The results for system change of this analogy can be unfortunate. For example, the organization development consultant is likely to be greeted with delight by executives who see in his specialty the solution to a hopeless situation in an outlying plant. Some organization development consultants have disappeared for years because of the irresistibility of such challenges. Others have whiled away their time trying to counteract the Peter Principle by shoring up incompetent managers.

Corollary 3: Build Resources. Don't do anything alone that could be accomplished more easily or more certainly by a team. Don Quixote is not the only change agent whose effectiveness was handicapped by ignoring this rule. The change agent's task is an heroic one, but the need to be a hero does not facilitate team building. As a result, many change agents lose effectiveness by becoming spread too thin. Effectiveness can be enhanced by investing in the development of partners.

Corollary 4: Don't Overorganize. The democratic ideology and theories of participative management that many change agents possess can sometimes interfere with common sense. A year or two ago I offered a course, to be taught by graduate students. The course was oversubscribed. It seemed that a data-based process for deciding whom to admit would be desirable, and that participation of the graduate students in the decision would also be desirable. So I sought data from the candidates about themselves, and xeroxed their responses for the graduate students. Then the graduate students and I held a series of meetings. Then the candidates were informed of the decision. In this way we wasted a great deal of time and everyone felt a little worse than if we had used an arbitrary decision rule.

Corollary 5: Don't Argue If You Can't Win. Win-lose strategies are to be avoided because they deepen conflict instead of resolving it. But the change agent should build her or his support constituency as large and deep and strong as possible so that she or he can continue to risk.

Corollary 6: Play God a Little. If the change agent doesn't make the critical value decisions, someone else will be happy to do so. Will a given situation contribute to your fulfillment? Are you creating a better world for yourself and others, or are you keeping a system in operation that should be allowed to die? For example, the public education system is a mess. Does that mean that the change agent is morally obligated to try to improve it, destroy it, or develop a substitute for it? No, not even if he or she knows how. But the change agent does need a value perspective for making choices like that.

Rule IV: Innovation Requires a Good Idea, Initiative, and a Few Friends

Little can be accomplished alone, and the effects of social and cultural forces on individual perception are so distorting that the change agent needs a partner, if only to maintain perspective and purpose.

The quality of the partner is as important as the quality of the idea. Like the change agent, partners must be relatively autonomous people. Persons who are authority-oriented—who need to rebel or need to submit—are not reliable partners: the rebels take the wrong risks and the good soldiers don't take any. And rarely do they command the respect and trust from others that is needed if an innovation is to be supported.

The partners need not be numerous. For example, the engineering staff of a chemical company designed a new process plant using edge-of-the-art technology. The design departed radically from the experience of top management, and they were about to reject it. The engineering chief suggested that the design be reviewed by a distinguished engineering professor. The principal designers were in fact former students of the professor. For this reason he accepted the assignment, charged the company a large fee for reviewing the design (which he did not trouble to examine), and told the management that it was brilliantly conceived and executed. By this means the engineers not only implemented their innovations but also grew in the esteem of their management.

A change agent experienced in the Washington environment reports that he knows of only one case of successful interdepartmental collaboration in mutually designing, funding, and managing a joint project. It was accomplished through the collaboration of himself and three similarly minded young men, one from each of four agencies. They were friends and met weekly for lunch. They conceived the project and planned strategies for implementing it. Each person undertook to interest and influence the relevant key people in his own agency. The four served one another as consultants and helpers in influencing opinion and bringing the decision makers together.

An alternative statement of Rule IV is as follows: Find the people who are ready and able to work, introduce them to one another, and work with them. Perhaps because many change agents have been trained in the helping professions, perhaps because we have all been trained to think bureaucratically, concepts like organization position, representatives, or need are likely to guide the change agent's selection of those he or she works with.

A more powerful beginning can sometimes be made by finding those persons in the system whose values are congruent with those of the change agent, who possess vitality and imagination, who are willing to work overtime, and who are eager to learn. Such people are usually glad to have someone like the change agent join in getting something important accomplished, and a careful search is likely to turn up quite a few. In fact, there may be enough of them to accomplish general system change, if they can team up in appropriate ways.

In building such teamwork the change agent's abilities will be fully challenged, as he joins them in establishing conditions for trust and creativity; dealing with their anxieties about being seen as subversive; enhancing their leadership, consulting, problem solving, diagnosing, and innovating skills; and developing appropriate group norms and policies.

Rule V: Load Experiments for Success

This sounds like counsel to avoid risk taking. But the decision to experiment always entails risk. After that decision has been made, take all precautions.

The rule also sounds scientifically immoral. But whether an experiment produces the expected results depends upon the experimenter's depth of insight into the conditions and processes involved. Of course, what is experimental is what is new to the system; it may or may not be new to the change agent.

Build an umbrella over the experiment. A chemical process plant, which was to be shut down because of the inefficiency of its operations, undertook a union-management cooperation project to improve efficiency, which involved a modified form of profit sharing. Such plans were contrary to company policy, but the regional vice president was interested in the experiment and successfully concealed it from his associates. The experiment was successful; the plant became profitable. But in this case, the umbrella turned out not to be big enough. The plant was shut down, anyway.

Use the Hawthorne effect. Even poorly conceived experiments are often made to succeed

when the participants feel ownership. And conversely, one of the obstacles to the spread of useful innovations is that the groups to which they are offered do not feel ownership of them.

For example, if the change agent hopes to use experience-based learning as part of his or her strategy, the first persons to be invited should be those who consistently turn all their experiences into constructive learning. Similarly, in introducing team development processes into a system, begin with the best-functioning team.

Maintain voluntarism. This is not easy to do in systems where invitations are understood to be commands; but nothing vital can be built on such motives as duty, obedience, security seeking, or responsiveness to social pressure.

Rule VI: Light Many Fires

Not only does a large, monolithic development or change program have high visibility and other qualities of a good target, it also tends to prevent subsystems from feeling ownership of and consequent commitment to the program.

The meaning of this rule is more orderly than the random prescription—light many fires—suggests. And part of a system is the way it is partly because of the way the rest of the system is. To work toward change in one subsystem is to become one more determinant of its performance. Not only is the change agent working uphill but, as soon as he turns his back, other forces in the system will press the subsystem back toward its previous performance mode.

If many interdependent subsystems are catalyzed and the change agent brings them together to facilitate one another's efforts, the entire system can begin to move.

Understanding patterns of interdependency among subsystems can lead to a strategy of firesetting. For example, in public school systems it requires collaboration among politicians, administrators, teachers, parents, and students to bring about significant innovation, and active opposition on the part of only one of these groups to prevent it. In parochial school systems, on the other hand, collaboration between the administration and the church can provide a powerful impetus for change in the other groups.

Rule VII: Keep an Optimistic Bias

Our society grinds along with much polarization and cruelty, and even the helping professions compose their world of grim problems to be "worked through." The change agent is usually flooded with the destructive aspects of the situations he or she enters. People in most systems are impressed by one another's weaknesses, and stereotype each other with such incompetencies as they can discover.

This rule does not advise ignoring destructive forces. But its positive prescription is that the change agent be especially alert to the constructive forces, which are often masked and suppressed in a problem-oriented, envious culture.

People have as great an innate capacity for joy as for resentment, but resentment causes them to overlook opportunities for joy. In a workshop for married couples, a husband and wife were discussing their sexual problem and how hard they were working to solve it. They were not making much progress, since they didn't realize that sex is not a problem but an opportunity.

Individuals and groups locked in destructive kinds of conflict focus on their differences. The change agent's job is to help them discover and build on their commonalities, so that they will have a foundation of respect and trust which will permit them to use their differences as a source of creativity. The unhappy patterns focus on past hurts and continue to destroy the present and future with them. The change agent's job is to help them change the present so that they will have a new past on which to create a better future.

Rule VIII: Capture the Moment

A good sense of relevance and timing is often treated as though it were a "gift" or "intuition," rather than something that can be learned, something spontaneous, rather than something planned.

The opposite is nearer the truth. One is more likely to "capture the moment" when everything one has learned is readily available.

Some years ago my wife and I were having a very destructive fight. Our nine-year-old daughter decided to intervene. She put her arms around her mother and asked: "What does Daddy do that bugs you?" She was an attentive audience for the next few minutes while my wife told her, ending in tears. She then put her arms around me: "What does Mommy do that bugs you?" and listened attentively to my response, which also ended in tears. She then went to the record player and put on a favorite love song ("If Ever I Should Leave You") and left us alone to make up.

The elements of my daughter's intervention had all been learned. They were available to her, and she combined them in a way that could make the moment better.

Perhaps it's our training in linear cause-and-effect thinking and the neglect of our capacities for imagery that makes us so often unable to see the multiple potential of the moment. Entering the situation "blank" is not the answer. One needs to have as many frameworks for seeing and strategies for acting available as possible. But it's not enough to involve only one's head in the situation: one's heart has to get involved, too. Cornelia Otis Skinner once said that the first law of the stage is to love your audience. You can love your audience only if you love yourself. If you have relatively full access to your organized experience, to yourself, and to the situation, you will capture the moment more often.

Endnotes

1. Robert Frost, "How Hard It Is to Keep from Being King When It's in You and in the Situation," *In The Clearing* (New York: Holt, Rinehart & Winston, 1962), pp. 74–84.

READING 34
FACILITATING TRANSFORMATIONAL CHANGE

Paul C. Nutt
Robert W. Backoff

Transformation has become a key survival tool for organizations coping with the turbulence that characterizes today's environment. This article offers leaders a process to help them fashion the radical change required to transform an organization. We show how radical change, with transformational possibilities, stems from a vision (Nanus, 1989; Wheatley, 1992). For example, Carlzon (1987) used "50,000 moments of trust" to describe how services were to be delivered to the customers of Scandinavian airlines. Leaders seeking a transformation draw on such a vision and fashion actions to help it become a reality. However, there is little agreement about what leaders should do to uncover these radical change ideas. Key activities meriting clarification include the role of vision in a transformation and uncovering barriers to making radical change. To cope with these barriers, leaders must find a way to identify key obstacles, fashion responses, and find synergy in a set of actions that can sustain the transformation.

In this article, we offer propositions that increase the prospect of realizing a transformation designed to improve organizational performance. These propositions identify elements of an action theory similar to the prescriptive science found in the engineering and medicine literatures (e.g., Argyris, 1982; Simon, 1969). Because of their prescriptive nature, the propositions have a "producer-product" logic that identifies the necessary but not sufficient conditions to produce a desired outcome (Ackoff, 1981).

Progressive coherence provides the basis for our action theory recommendations. Progressive coherence calls for fitting the results of process steps

Source: Paul C. Nutt and Robert W. Backoff, "Facilitating Transformational Change" in *Journal of Applied Behavioral Science* (33, no.4) pp. 490–508, copyright © 1997 NTL Institute of Applied Behavioral Science. Reprinted by permission of Sage Publications, Inc.

together so that one result flows from the other. We begin with the notion of vision. The vision identifies the first move to make in a radical change. Next, we explore obstacles to the vision by uncovering issue tensions. We show how a bundle of interrelated tensions can imply win–win actions with synergistic features. Aligning these actions provides a plan with the synergy needed to realize a radical change. To transform their organizations, leaders must find these actions (formulation) and carry them out (implementation). This coherent spiraling outward to broader and broader considerations is a central argument in our action theory. A coherence criterion, as a test of truthfulness, also undergirds much contemporary philosophical thinking. Coherency has much more explanatory power than does consistency.

Even though we do not consider several important questions, such as steps to unfreeze and communicate during change, we believe that our propositions will be useful in prompting a much needed discussion of how to craft radical change ideas. The article shows leaders how to move through the transformation stages that call for visioning, make assessments with issue tensions, finding win–win actions to a core tension, and fashioning a circle of change. We discuss these stages and illustrate key steps in our procedure with examples.

Visioning

The need for a transformation stems from environmental turbulence that can render current organizational practices valueless. To respond, leaders must transform their organizations. A transformation creates a jump to a new level of organized complexity that provides added value for all organizational stakeholders. After a transformation in a private organization, products are designed to fit the emerging lifestyles of current and future customers. The transformed public organization can serve a greater variety of clients in new and different ways. These new practices have synergistic qualities that add to and complement the organization's core competencies. The movement to a new level of organized complexity calls for a new way of doing things, often described as vision (e.g., Block, 1991; Tichy & Devanna, 1992).

A vision outlines a strategic and lofty action plan. The strategic aspects suggest important actions such as how to serve customers/users. To be lofty, the vision must be sufficiently imaginative to be engaging and inspiring. Illustrations of strategic and lofty visions include Monet's European economic community; AT&T's universal phone service, where everyone can "reach out and touch" everyone else; and CBS's Paley, who saw radio as a broadcast and not just a sending medium. Note how these visions show key aspects of a move to a higher level of organized complexity. The notion of an unrealized vision provides energy to make a transformational jump.

Proposition 1: Vision provides a triggering event essential to realize a successful transformation.

Transformation calls for leaders who have discretion and a vision. It is important to meet both tests. A leader must have sufficient discretion to call for radical change. Vision calls for insight into possibilities. To initiate a transformation, a leader must offer an idea that makes fundamental changes in an organization.

The comprehensiveness of a transformation depends on the comprehensiveness of the triggering vision. The most basic stems from a vision that a leader has developed or adapted (called Vision 1). More comprehensive transformations seek a broader range of possibilities. The first move is to incorporate the ideas of key insiders (Vision 2). Drawing on the ideas of both insiders and outsiders broadens the vision by incorporating the interests of an even more diverse set of stakeholders, which makes the

vision more comprehensive (Vision 3). The comprehensiveness of the vision increases as it includes more levels of organizational complexity. As complexity increases, the resulting vision integrates and differentiates in new ways to provide added value for all stakeholders (Ackoff, 1981). Each broader vision provides an appreciation of possibilities and circumstances that are entirely new and were previously hidden from the leader when formulating the last vision (Bateson & Bateson, 1987).

Proposition 2: A vision that incorporates the views of many stakeholders with dissimilar interests and ideas increases the prospect of a successful transformation.

A vision provides a way for stakeholders to enter into a "possibility space" that describes new ideas for an enterprise (Block, 1991). So people can find a way to become involved, the best visions are inspirational, value adding, significant for key people, challenging but reachable, and energy releasing. Visions inspire by drawing people to them, suggesting what it would be like at a point in time in the future to live in this new possibility space. A vision has attractive power if it challenges and inspires, with the prospect of adding value, and releases obstacles that keep people form being creative. For example, Mary Kay Ash's vision of women as entrepreneurs selling products that improved their image gave impetus to her cosmetics company. Kodak's one-hour processing solidified its position as the world leader in amateur photography. Visions such as JFK's "military strength with moral purpose" and Gorbachev's Glasnost and Perestroika transformed public policy. However, visions do not guarantee success, as Coca-Cola's new formula and People Express' no frills air travel illustrate.

Proposition 3: Visions that are challenging, inspirational, value adding, and energy releasing have the best chance of prompting a transformation.

Assessments Using Issue Tensions

A vision can provoke uncertainty that leads people to resist it. It is hard to live in a new space that is largely undefined. People may resist a radical change when it exposes their weaknesses or makes them invest time, energy, and resources without a likely payoff in sight. To cope with resistance to change, a leader initiates the change process by calling on a developmental team to uncover barriers that can block the vision. These obstacles are treated as issue tensions and presented as an issue agenda. When the leader offers a broader vision (Vision 2 or 3), issue tensions change in character to reveal new obstacles. These broader visions bring out a new set of issue tensions that move closer to the core difficulties that have been holding the organization back. By implementing these broader visions, leaders can gradually penetrate the mystery surrounding actions required to make a sweeping transformational change.

The transformation process is initiated by having a developmental team look for issue tensions that reveal obstacles to realizing a current vision (typically, Vision 1 or 2). The issue tensions capture concerns that are pulling in opposite directions, creating barriers to realizing transformation. Because these issue tensions express core values of key stakeholders in an organization, no two organizations, no matter how similar, are apt to have the same set of issue tensions. Because of their personal views and commitments, stakeholders in an organization see some issue tensions but not others. Facilitators need tools to draw out these hidden concerns and form them as tensions.

The Nature of Issue Tensions.   Issue tensions capture competing concerns, highlighting conflicting interests and values (Nutt 7 Backoff, 1993). Such concerns can arise within the organization or between the organization and its environment, producing forces that push an organization in several directions at the same time (Mason & Mitroff, 1981; Quinn & Cameron, 1988). The opposing pull of a tension prompts strong claims and counterclaims. Strategic leaders who deal with one of the concerns that made up a pull and neglect the other are less apt to be successful (Cameron, 1986; Van de Ven & Poole, 1987). For example, a mental health center may have to deal with an increase in court-specified clients and budget reductions at the same time. If these concerns are not managed as tensions,

the mental health agency can be whipsawed by powerful people in oversight bodies such as legislatures and the courts. Pascale (1990), Johnson (1992), and Hampden-Turner (199) found that dealing with the opposing concerns in a tension leads to superior results.

Examining issues as conflicting concerns prompts divergent thinking, which is essential for creativity. Contending with opposing concerns simultaneously is more apt to produce a breakthrough than dealing with the same concerns one at a time. Rothenberg (1979) found that breakthroughs in the work of 54 creative scientists and artists resulted from accepting opposing concerns as equally valid and accurate. The tension that resulted from these seeming incompatibilities produced a springboard from which creative insights emerged that overcame both of the opposing concerns. Examples include musicians who thought of dissonance and harmony in constructing a musical chord and artists who painted dissonance and harmony in the same scene. An issue posed as a tension does not identify a problem to be solved but a paradox to be understood and then transcended. A win-win solution is more apt to emerge with a simultaneous consideration of the concerns that create the tension.

Proposition 4: Forming issues as tension increases the prospect of a successful transformation.

Uncovering Strategic Issues.   Organizational stakeholders form beliefs that are important to understand before attempting radical change (Hampden-Turner, 1990; Mason & Mitroff, 1981). To understand and appreciate these beliefs, we build an issue agenda by eliciting the concerns of stakeholders. To construct an issue agenda, we call on leaders to appoint a facilitator, find or form an interdisciplinary team made up of key stakeholders, and select a group process such as the nominal group technique (NGT) to manage the team's efforts (Delbecq, Van de Ven, & Gustafson, 1986; Nutt, 1992).

The development team leads the change process. The team is formed by the organization's chief executive with members drawn from a top management team, such as an executive committee, with a few additional members that provide expertise and represent key power centers. The chief executive charges the team to search for radical change ideas. The team either facilitates this process itself or trains a top manager to carry it out. The efforts of the developmental team are coordinated with the work of other teams and projects by using retreats and similar forums.

The facilitator asks the team to identify anticipated or actual concerns that, if continued, will influence the organization's ability to reach a desired future, expressed by the vision. Issue tensions emerge by asking team members to examine the concerns on their list and then find the most significant concern that is pulling in the opposite direction. For instance, in one of our facilitation efforts, a family medicine department's loss of a subsidy from a state legislature was paired with increased demands to serve low-income patients in a state-subsidized clinic. After a voting step by the team, it is possible to identify a prioritized list of issue tensions.

Testing the Issue Agenda.   Organizations have dominant values that draw their members toward certain types of concerns such as human relationships or efficiency. Often, some of the concerns are suppressed. Uncovering suppressed concerns improves the change for success (Quinn, 1996). To search for suppressed concerns, an initial list of issue tensions is sorted into issue tension types. To identify issue types, we developed a framework by extending the ideas of Quinn (1988) and Morgan (1988). They found that particular types of concerns arise from stakeholders who prefer to scan for signals by looking inward or outward with either an open/flexible or a control posture. This causes a leader to see and highlight equity, preservation, productivity, or transition concerns; as shown in Table 1. The table also illustrates how equity, preservation, productivity, and transition concerns can arise during a radical change attempt. Combinations of equity, preservation, productivity, and transition concerns identify 10 generic types of tensions, as shown in Table 2.

To find missing tension types, the facilitator examines the initial issue agenda and classifies the issue tensions as one of the 10 types in Table 2. The development team carries out additional searches to uncover hidden concerns, which helps to identify missing issue tensions. At least one in each category should be uncovered, so the issue agenda reveals and portrays all 10 types of issue tensions.

> Proposition 5: An issue agenda that includes all 10 types of issue tensions is more apt to produce a transformation.

Issue Tension Priorities.   Issue tensions identify difficulties that tend to be interrelated. These relationships indicate where to start, as well as the crucial interdependencies among issue tensions considered in any radical change attempt. Techniques such as cognitive mapping can be used to capture the relationships among issue tensions seen by a development team (Eden & Radford, 1990; Nutt & Backoff, 1992; Warfield, 1990; Weick, 1979). The facilitator draws maps that capture the team's view of precedence (which issue tension must be managed first) and producer-product (which issue tensions are more likely to produce or result from the other) to find core tensions and related tensions. A core tension will tend to precede the others and be a producer, not a product. Related tensions have interdependent precedence and producer-product relationships that connect them to each other and to the core tension, giving the related tensions synergistic properties. To deal with this synergy, mutually reinforcing action must be uncovered (Senge, 1990).

> Proposition 6: Finding actions for related tensions that support actions developed for the core issues tension, and for each other, makes it more likely that a transformation vision will be realized.

Finding Win-Win Actions

Responses to a core tension can take shape as lose-lose, win-lose, compromise, or win-win. The lose-lose alternative suggests what can happen when no action is taken to deal with the concerns that make up a core issue tension. Win-lose describes action designed to respond to one of the concerns that make up the core issue tension. Compromise actions stem from negotiations among people supporting each of the win-lose actions to find what

TABLE 1

Scanning approach and types of concerns

Scanning Approach	Concern Identified[*]	Illustration
Inwardly directed scanning that is flexible	Human resource needs that suggest *equity* concerns	Scanning is drawn to the network of relationships that run an organization to determine if people (staff/customers) are being treated fairly. For insiders, fairness concerns often involve growth and development (e.g., training). For outsiders, interpretations are made of their demands (e.g., increased staffing to provide products/services) by insiders.
Control-oriented scanning that is directed inwardly	The need to maintain tradition provokes *preservation* concerns	Stakeholders call for a return to a previous status quo or to maintain a current one (e.g., preserving a culture, practice, or implicit treaty)
Flexible scanning directed externally	*Transition concerns* in which change is proposed to respond to opportunities and/or environmental flux	The transition suggests how the organization can change to respond to environmental flux or take advantage of an opportunity (e.g., new products or services)
Externally directed scanning with a control perspective	Adaptations that can cope with *productivity* concerns	Developments posed in productivity terms, seeking the optimum output level (e.g., process modification that improves efficiency or effectiveness)

[*]Developments become concerns when thought to influence a particular organization's capacity to reach a desired future.

others will accept. An agreement typically calls for both parties to relinquish something. The notion of a win-win solution draws on ideas found in conflict management (Thomas, 1976), integrated negotiation (Lewicki & Litterer, 1985), and leadership (Covey, 1989). In our treatment, a win-win must satisfy both of the concerns that make up a core issue tension. The win-win solution shifts form the destructive competitive urges that lie behind most organizational tensions toward a cooperative culture (Pascale, 1990). Win-win actions create something of value for each interest group calling for a win-lose action.

The negotiation literature (e.g., Fisher & Ury, 1981; Lewicki & Litterer, 1985) provides several useful ideas that help to move a developmental team from distributive (compromise) to integrated (win-win) bargaining. Two key ideas call for separating people from problems and focusing on *interests* instead of the position held by key stakeholders. Exploring perceptions, emotions, and communication with active listening and other techniques helps to depersonalize the situation. The shift from reconciling positions to reconciling interest reaches for outcomes that can serve all stakeholders and helps to deal with people engaging in power and hidden agenda games. These ideas are well known and need not be repeated. We attempt to build on them by showing how to clarify interests using tensions and valued outcomes and by offering ways to uncover synergistic win-win actions.

Issue Tensions and Win-Win Actions.   An analysis of Ford's transformation in the 1980s shows how issue tensions link to win-win actions (Pascale, 1990). The Ford Motor Company in the 1970s found itself in decline with a critical leadership succession decision to make. A visionary, Don

TABLE 2

Types of issue tensions

Type	Often Signaled by	Illustration
Equity-equity	Whose interest will be served	Clashes among customers and key staff people with different interests
Transition-transition	Several plans for change	Each plan calls for a different set of actions that appear to benefit a different set of stakeholders
Productivity-productivity	Disputes over diagnostics	Several different measures of performance that suggest different actions are being used by stakeholders
Preservation-preservation	Groping for core values	Allocating resources among strategic business units (SBUs) serving different market niches, some with traditional products, others with innovative products
Equity-transition	Who gets what during change	Disputes over anticipated utility surpluses in which new products/services or internal operations are being claimed by upwardly mobile executives
Transition-productivity	Meeting demands during change	Organization facing a budget cutback or a short-fall in cash flow that is attempting to mount new programs
Preservation-productivity	Squeezing a stressed system wedded to tradition	Organization with a critical need to increase output proposes change that is resisted by people who argue that the new norms violate important organizational traditions
Preservation-equity	When fairness clashes with tradition	When Congress instituted performance-based compensation for civil servants, implementation was stalled by rules that called for compensation based on seniority
Preservation-transition	Dealing with inertia during change	Inertia causes organizations to get sucked into a degrading cycle with no apparent way to break out
Productivity-equity	Reconciling cost cutting with human commitments	Organizations forced to cut costs but must do so in accordance with union contracts and commitments to key people

Peterson, and a rational manager, Red Poling, were contending for the top position. Their incompatible styles signaled the prospect of an internecine battle to industry observers ("'Wrong road?'" 1986). Instead, Ford engaged in one of the most remarkable transformations of the decade.

Concerns identified by Pascale (1990) that prompted the crisis at Ford are presented in the left column of Table 3. Note how each concern identified by Peterson and his top management team can be fashioned as an issue tension (Table 3, middle column). The win-win actions devised by Ford are below the tension in the middle column. In each case, Ford's top management was able to find ways to manage the tension by fashioning win-win actions.

In the last column of Table 3, we classify the issue tensions considered by Ford using the issue tension framework. This assessment suggests that Ford's transformation may be incomplete because equity-preservation, equity-transition, and productivity-preservation tensions were overlooked. Equity-preservation tensions could arise at Ford when the traditional maxims of customer, quality, cost, and service produce an equity conflict among stakeholders such as dealers and stockholders. For instance, it can be difficult to pay good dividends and invest in quality during the slow growth predicted for the next decade. Equity-transition tensions can stem from perceptions about who got what during the Peterson era. Key middle managers may attempt to block further change that

TABLE 3

Issue tensions and win-win action at Ford

Concerns (recognized by top management)	The Issue Tension (win-win action)	Classifying the Tension
Product designs stifle new ideas	*Planned development-opportunism:* Change new ideas to fit evolving circumstance using planning skills	Productivity-transition
Demands for increased productivity	*High productivity-evolving excellence:* Continuous learning about what creates productivity	
Managerial change	*Systematization-change:* Built top management team with both control and transformational skills	
Little cross-functional cooperation	*Elitist-pluralist:* Insist that process with teams be used to work things out; reward cooperation and good team players	Preservation-transition
Emphasis on control	*Mandatory-discretionary:* Good decisions valued in addition to goals and budget; quality improvement allowed to buck rules and procedures	
Silo mentality	*Individuality-collegiality:* Promote team building by physically integrating work space, executive reeducation, staff and line job rotation	
Reputation as a bad place to work	*Results-human relations:* Productivity sought by making people the company's most important resource	Productivity-equity

seems desirable if they have smoldering grievances or if they were ignored during past changes. Productivity-preservation tensions can emerge if slow sales lead to cost reductions that squeeze tradition-ridden work units. This suggests that further transformation at Ford may hinge on addressing these overlooked tensions (Nutt & Backoff, 1993).

Finding Win-Win Actions. A development team, made up of key stakeholders, creates a win-win action. A facilitator begins by helping the team identify lose-lose, or what can happen if the core tension is not managed. This step motivates action. The next move has the team create a win-lose action for each concern found in the pulls of a core tension to work out the interests of its stakeholders in concrete terms. Next, the facilitator has the team look for a compromise to promote the notion of working together. To sanction searching for a win-win, the facilitator asks the team if it is willing to invest more time to look for a better solution—one that increases the net payoff to all stakeholders. The prospect of increasing net payoff justifies additional effort.

A picture or a map such as that suggested by Hampden-Turner (1990) demonstrates these steps. Each axis of the map represents one of the concerns producing the pulls found in the core issue tension, as shown in Figure 1. The solution space is filled with lose-lose (down the diagonal), win-lose (at each axis), compromise (at the midpoint), and win-win (up the diagonal, upper right). To use the map, a facilitator makes a series of moves that work toward a win-win.

An example, drawn from the Ford Motor Company, illustrates these moves (Figure 1). After Ford had revitalized its top management, the company experienced a drop in sales stemming from the slow economic growth that plagued the world economy in the early 1990s. This created an issue tension between the company's need to cut costs and the job stress experienced by middle management left out of the management retraining in the 1980s (Spreitzer & Quinn, 1996). The lose-lose outcome for this issue tension can lead to increased job stress and declines in cost cutting that amplify the stress, creating a vicious cycle that leads to more cost problems. A win-lose action for job stress could be a reduction in the job demands for middle managers (e.g., more staff leading to more company costs). A win–lose action for cost cutting could be an incentive program that leads to more middle management job stress. Note how win–lose actions help one party by hurting the other. A compromise action could add staff funded by middle manager pay cuts or deferred pay increases.

Ford, however, fashioned a win–win by investing in human capital (Spreitzer & Quinn, 1996). Ford began a training program for its middle managers to help them become more effective change agents. The training program had the middle managers find projects to work on that had cost reduction potential. This led to a number of searches for ways to reduce costs. The empowered managers found new energy to make much needed process improvements. The company benefited from these improvements, and middle managers benefited from the empowerment and training that created more meaningful and less stressful jobs. Note how the net payoff at Ford increased by assuming an abundance mentality.

A Procedure to Craft Win–Wins. To devise win–win actions, the facilitator shows the development team how to move up the diagonal (Figure 1) by broadening the scope of search to create more possibilities, carrying out context reversal, and guiding the search for win–win actions using creativity techniques. We discuss the steps required to make these moves.

Move up the Diagonal. Moving too quickly up the diagonal in Figure 1 can cause a developmental team to "get stuck." The concerns of one power center seem favored, and interest groups square off—one to protect further erosion of its interests, the other to get more consideration. Using the Ford example, as shown in Figure 1, an emphasis on the concerns of middle managers could have created actions that sacrificed company welfare, potentially threatening the company's viability. Stressing Ford's welfare would ignore large numbers of alienated middle managers who hear the

company's message as "just do more with less." To avoid this, the facilitator moves the team away from a lose–lose and toward a win–win in small steps, which gradually consolidates support. This gradual building of support seems consistent with Weick's (1984) call for a series of "small wins" when embarking on a big change.

> Proposition 7: Identifying lose–lose, win–lose, and compromise actions before seeking win–win actions improves the prospects of a transformation.

To initiate this search, the facilitator has the developmental team identify what can happen if no action is taken using a group process such as the nominal group technique or NGT (Delbecq et al., 1986). This suggests a lose–lose result such as a vicious cycle of cost cutting that amplifies job stress, as noted above. Next, the team divides into two subgroups according to its sympathies with one of the concerns that make up the core tensions, such as cost and job stress in the Ford example. The cost and job stress subgroups use a group process to identify actions that can deal with either the stress or cost containment concern and produce the valued outcome. The subgroups prioritize their ideas and then report their suggestions to the other subgroup. Each subgroup, after hearing what the other subgroup proposes, lists what it would have to give up to realize its priority actions and fashions a compromise. The list of "give up" to "get" actions is then prioritized by each subgroup to find compromises that the group is willing to make. This creates the basis for a negotiation to identify a compromise position.

Enlarge the Arena. Constraints often emerge that narrow the scope of search when people problem solve (Guilford, 1976). Opening up the search effort to new possibilities follows widely accepted maxims derived from studies of problem-solving effectiveness and expert practitioners (Schon, 1983).

> Proposition 8: A broader search improves the change of finding the creative actions needed to realize a transformation.

We uncover valued outcomes to guide the search for win-win actions. A valued outcome is similar to an objective; that is, it indicates a hoped-for result. People often have difficulty setting aside their preferences for action to set objectives (Nutt, 1984). To deal with this, we have our team members go directly to uncovering actions, indicating the valued outcome of each action that they suggest. We use a ladder technique to capture these valued outcomes and array them in scope from narrow to broad. This coaxes people to adopt a valued outcome of a larger scope that expands the arena in which the search for win-win action is conducted (Nadler, 1981; Nutt, 1992).

The valued outcomes, identified by subgroups as they formulate their win action list, are used to form the ladder. To illustrate this, consider the Ford example. A compromise that trades off pay with reduced job demands provides a place to start (see Figure 1). To construct a ladder, the facilitator looks for the valued outcome of this trade-off: Why compromise by adding people and cutting salaries? An answer in the valued outcomes identified by the subgroups might be to reduce job stress. This identifies the most basic valued outcome. The same question is posed again: Why reduce job stress? An answer from the subgroup's valued outcomes might be to motivate middle managers. By continuing in this way, a ladder is created from the valued outcomes identified by both of the subgroups, as shown below:

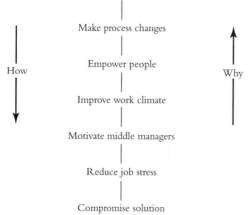

The ladder addresses why and how questions. Moving up the ladder answers the why question (reduced stress produces more motivated middle managers). Moving down the ladder answers the how question (one motivates middle managers to help rid them of job stress). One motivates to improve climate (why), and an improved climate can motivate (how). Improved climates empower (why), and empowerment improves the climate (how), and so on down the ladder.

By moving up the ladder, team members are shown larger and larger spaces in which actions can be sought. The bigger space is better because it has fewer constraints (Rothenberg, 1979). The members of a developmental team who see how a broad scale outcome can open up the search process to more possibilities are more apt to adopt the broader valued outcome to guide their efforts (Nutt, 1984). The developmental team explores the scope of action open to it and selects the valued outcome that will guide its efforts to find a win-win action.

Context Reversal.   To guide the search for a win-win, concerns that make up the core tension are reversed by subordinating each concern in the core tension to the other. If the core tension involves equity transition concerns, the search is directed to find transition possibilities in the equity concerns of key people and equity concerns in the transition possibilities being considered. In the Ford example, the search seeks ways to cut cost in the expressions of job stress made by middle managers. Ways to cope with job stress in options being considered to reduce costs would also be considered. Note how the win-win action in Figure 1 meets *both* concerns in the tension. This approach reverses figure and ground, as called for by problem-solving approaches in Gestalt psychology (Guilford, 1976). A context reversal is insightful because it helps people see new possibilities. Such an approach is also supported by the dictums of creativity: make the familiar strange and the strange familiar (Gordon, 1969).

Proposition 9: Context reversal helps to uncover innovative possibilities for win-win actions that improve the prospect of a transformation.

FIGURE 1

Strategies for the job stress-profit tension at Ford

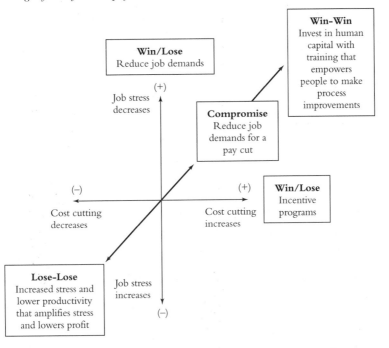

To carry out context reversal, a developmental team must "hold the tension." Holding the tension in the Ford example calls for finding cost-cutting actions that affirm job stress values (e.g., meaningful jobs) and actions to reduce job stress that affirm cost-cutting values (e.g., need to be competitive). Members of the team begin with a job stress action and then add the cost-cutting value to their idea, find a cost-cutting action and add a job stress value, and then repeat for a new set of action ideas. Switching back and forth in this way maintains both values as priorities during the search; it also helps participants to hold the tension.

Creativity.   A group process, such as NGT, is not powerful enough to find highly creative ideas and must be enhanced in some way (Woodman, Sawyer, & Griffin, 1993). To help people visualize creative ideas, the silent reflective phase of NGT can be bolstered by incorporating creativity techniques such as relational algorithms (Grovitz, 1978), synthetics (Gordon, 1961), lateral thinking

(de Bono, 1970), and mental imagery (Anthony, Bennett, Maddox, & Wheatley, 1993).

Proposition 10: Creativity enhancements to a group process increase the prospect of finding innovative win-win actions, which improves the chance of realizing a transformation.

Fashioning a Change Circle

Another set of actions must be crafted to deal with the related issue tensions. To illustrate, a developmental team in a college of business could search the "space between" teaching, research, and service. The key is to find ideas that harmonize and provide a dynamic balance among them, so that each activity supports the other through time, building on a win-win action. The change circle is made up of these complementary actions and the win-win. Synergy is realized when these actions create a succession of steps that, when carried out, manage the core and related issue tensions.

Creating a Circle.   The circle illustrates the complementary nature of an aligned set of actions. We use the spoke and wheel arrangement, shown in Figure 2, to picture this alignment. The diagram serves two additional purposes. It illustrates the relationships between tensions, a win–win action, and related actions with a concrete example (as in Figure 2) and provides a format to locate this same information as it is crafted by a developmental team.

Facilitators present the diagram in Figure 2 to a development team to demonstrate the nature of aligned action, how these actions connect to a win–win action, and how both types of action are derived from tensions. To do this, the facilitator recalls the core issue tension and locates it on the wheel as a spoke. The related issue tensions also are arranged as spokes. The win–win action is located next to one of the concerns that make up the core issue tension. The facilitator then circles the wheel and identifies missing actions that must be uncovered to manage each concern in the related tensions. Drawing on group process and creativity techniques, the facilitator has members of a development team search for these mutually supportive actions that close the circle.

The facilitator uses intervention and amplification to complete the change circle. To *intervene,* the win–win action for the core issue tension is offered. *Amplification* calls for examining the related issue tensions to find actions that can produce the valued outcome, deal with a concern in the next issue tension in the circle, and push along the win–win action.

Figure 2 provides an example, again drawing on the middle management training program at Ford (Spreitzer & Quinn, 1996), in which job stress-cost cutting (equity-productivity) seemed to be the core issue tension. Related issue tensions of control-change (transition-preservation) and individual excellence-teamwork (transition-equity) also were crucial at Ford (Pascale, 1990). To create the change circle, the facilitator has a developmental team look for actions that build on the win–win action, deal with a concern in an adjacent issue tension on the wheel, and help to realize the

valued outcome (e.g., improve the company). To find these actions, the facilitator has each team member work around the wheel, beginning with the first concern, improving individual excellence. Team members identify actions that meet all three requirements (respond to the concern, capitalize on the win–win, and contribute to the valued outcome). The team members work through each of the concerns in this way, developing a list of actions for each concern on the wheel. This creates action sets that are sorted by each of the concerns found in the related tensions. In the Ford example, actions were required to deal with concerns about individual excellence, control, teamwork, and change (see Figure 2). The actions numbered 1 to 5 in Figure 2 identify some possible responses. Reporting out and setting priorities follow the action identification steps.

Figure 2 illustrates what could have resulted. The first action in Figure 2 calls for middle manager empowerment, such as a quality circle, addressing both the desires for individual excellence and the investment in education. Action 2 increases middle manager control over company practices, which amplifies empowerment. Action 3 commits to implementing cost-cutting proposals. This action deals with concerns about company competitiveness and builds on the authority to make changes. Action 4 encourages reciprocity to promote teamwork among empowered managers, which increases the pace of change. Action 5 encourages middle managers to take personal responsibility for their destiny in the company by riding a crest of change that creates new opportunities. By circling the wheel, the win–win action coupled with the complementary actions will begin to manage issue tensions in the wheel.

> Proposition 11: Synergistic actions that respond to concerns in the related issue tensions and amplify the win–win action increase the prospects of a successful transformation.

Institutionalizing Change.   A trip around the change circle, shown in figure 2, identifies steps in an implement action plan. After several successful

FIGURE 2

The spoke and wheel configuration: Ford example

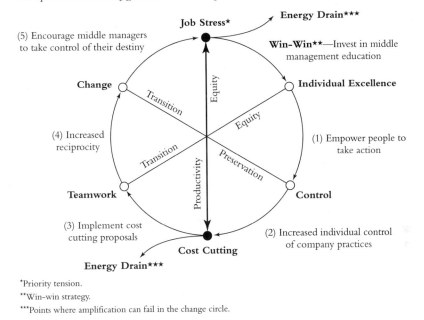

*Priority tension.
**Win-win strategy.
***Points where amplification can fail in the change circle.

cycles, the changes made begin to transcend the issue tensions that make up the spokes of the wheel. For example, if leaders at Ford had moved through several cycles of education-empowerment-personal control-cost cutting-reciprocity-destiny creation, job stress could have been reduced. At the same time, company leaders would produce a number of initiatives to realize their aim of cost cutting. Several cycles must be completed in which these actions are carried out before key issue tensions can be managed. Implementation will also depend on coping with a variety of additional difficulties, such as dealing with people who have something to lose and limited resources. The circle provides direction for an implementation effort but does not overcome all of the difficulties that will be encountered along the way. However, "rolling the circle out" offers an aligned and mutually supportive set of actions to being the change process; it also provides a way to keep the momentum going (Thompson, 1967).

Proposition 12: Several trips around the change circle must be completed before the prospects of a transformation improve.

A strategic change circle produces useful results when all parties receive something of value. This can be assessed by asking participants about their perceptions and by examining the actions contained in the circle to assess strategic change. For instance, in the Ford example, both the middle and top managers seem to benefit from the actions in the circle. The middle managers would be able to recast the jobs, making them more meaningful, and top management would realize cost reductions.

Summary and Implications

Four aspects of organizational transformation that have been neglected in the literature were discussed: the role of a vision, uncovering barriers as issue tensions, ways to fashion win-win actions for a core issue tension, and uncovering and aligning actions for related issue tensions. Vision provides the trigger. A vision offers a strategic and inspiring picture of what the organization can become, indicating whom the organization wants to serve, how this will be done, and the regard and image these actions can produce. This provides the energy to jump to a new level of organized complexity. To make this jump, leaders employ facilitators and developmental teams to uncover how issue tensions can block the vision. The core issue tension and related issue tensions direct the search for actions that produce win-win and amplifying actions, which make up a transformational change circle. Several transformational jumps can be made. The first draws on the leader's vision (Vision 1). The second draws on these ideas and the ideas of key insiders (Vision 2). A still broader vision incorporates the ideas of key outsiders with those of key insiders (Vision 3).

To begin, a developmental team is empowered to search for obstacles that can block a vision. These obstacles arise as concerns that push and pull the organization in several ways at the same time, creating an issue tension. In our approach, issues are formed by noting how a given concern calls forth an opposing concern. These pulls are typically organization specific, shaping crucial issues for that organization. Core issue tensions, which seem to produce the other issue tensions and precede them, and related issue tensions linked to the core tension are uncovered to create the issue agenda.

The developmental team attempts to fashion a win-win action for the core tension. This is accomplished by enlarging the arena (which expands the scope of search), engaging in context reversal to pose the search question, and applying creativity techniques to look for ways to overcome both concerns that make up a core issue tension. Actions that amplify a win-win for a core issue tension, deal with key related issue tensions, and contribute to the valued outcome are uncovered to implement the vision. To begin the process of transformation, leaders take steps to carry out the win-win and align it with the related actions.

Leaders in our approach are "on tap, but not on top." We call for leaders to empower key people and trust them to find ways to realize a vision. A transformation is more likely when leaders delegate these activities to a developmental team. The team, aided by a facilitator, finds issue tensions, uncovers win-win actions for these tensions, and creates a change circle to implement the vision of what the organization wants to become. Success stems from building a change circle to Visions 1, 2, and 3 to "sweep in" more and more stakeholders. This gradually transforms an organization through the implementation of progressively broader visions that incorporate the views of many constituencies. Leaders armed with these tools are positioned to increase their change of realizing a transformation. The process we offer helps facilitators organize their thoughts, pose insightful questions, and mobilize needed support. The hoped-for-result is improved capacity that can take an organization to higher levels of functioning through time.

References

Ackoff, R. (1981). *Creating the corporate future.* New York: John Wiley.

Anthony, W. P., Bennett, R. H. III, Maddox, E. N., & Wheatley, W. J. (1993). Picturing the future: Using mental imagery to enrich strategic environmental assessment. *Academy of Management Executive, 7(2),* 43–56.

Argyris, C. (1982). *Reasoning, learning, and action: Individual and organizational.* San Francisco: Jossey-Bass.

Bateson, G., & Bateson, M. C. (1987). *Angels fear.* New York: Macmillan.

Block, P. (1991). *The empowered manager.* San Francisco: Jossey-Bass.

Cameron, K. S. (1986). Effectiveness paradoxes: Consensus and conflict in perceptions of organizational performance. *Management Science, 32(5),* 539–553.

Carlzon, J. (1987). *Moments of truth.* New York: Ballinger.

Covey, S. (1989). *The seven habits of highly effective leaders.* New York: Simon & Schuster

De Bono, E. (1970). *Lateral thinking: Creativity step by step.* New York: Harper & Row.

Delbecq, A., Van de Ven, A., & Gustafson, D. (1986). *Group techniques for program planning.* Middletown, WI: Greenbrier.

Eden, C., & Radford, J. (Eds.). (1990). *Tackling strategic problems: the role of group decision support.* Newbury Park, CA: Sage.

Fisher, R., & Ury, W. (1981). *Getting to yes.* New York: Houghton Mifflin.

Gordon, W. J. J. (1961) *Synthetics.* New York: Harper & Row.

Grovitz, H. (1978). *Galton's walk.* New York: Harper & Row.

Guilford, J. P. (1976). *The nature of human intelligence.* New York: McGraw-Hill.

Hampden-Turner, C. M. (1990). *Charting the corporate mind.* New York: Free Press

Johnson, B. (1992). *Polarity management.* New York: HRD Press.

Lewicki, R., & Litterer, J. (1985). *Negotiation.* Homewood, IL: Irwin.

Mason, R. O., & Mitroff, I. I. (1981). *Challenging strategic planning assumptions.* New York: Wiley-Interscience.

Morgan, G. (1988). *Riding the waves of change.* San Francisco: Jossey-Bass.

Nadler, G. (1981). *The planning and design approach.* New York: John Wiley.

Nanus, B. (1989). *The leader's edge.* Chicago: Contemporary Books.

Nutt, P. C. (1984). Types of organizational decision processes. *Administrative Science Quarterly, 29*(3), 414–460.

Nutt, P. C. (1992), *Managing planned change.* New York: Macmillan.

Nutt, P. C., & Backoff, R. W. (1992). *The strategic management of public and third sector organizations.* San Francisco: Jossey-Bass.

Nutt, P. C., & Backoff, R. W. (1993). Strategic issues as tensions. *Journal of Management Inquiry, 2*(1), 28–43.

Pascale, R. T. (1990). *Managing on the edge.* New York: Simon & Schuster.

Quinn, R. E. (1988). *Beyond rational management: Mastering the paradoxes and competing demands of high performance.* San Francisco: Jossey-Bass.

Quinn, R. E. (1996). *Deep change.* San Francisco: Jossey-Bass.

Quinn, R. E., & Cameron, K. (1988). *Paradox and transformation.* Cambridge, MA: Ballinger.

Rothenberg, A. (1979). *The emerging goddess.* Chicago: University of Chicago Press.

Schon, D. (1983). *The reflective practitioner: How professionals think in action.* New York: Basic Books.

Senge, P. (1990). *The fifth discipline: The art and management of the learning organization.* New York: Doubleday.

Simon, H. W. (1969). *The sciences of the artificial.* Cambridge, MA: MIT Press.

Spreitzer, G., & Quinn, R. A. (1996). When organizations dare: Organizational strategies for workforce empowerment. *The Journal of Applied behavioral Science, 32,* 237–261.

Thomas, J. (1976). Conflict and conflict management. In M. Dunnette (Ed.), *Handbook of industrial organizational psychology.* New York: John Wiley.

Thompson, J. D. (1967). *Organization in action.* New York: McGraw-Hill

Tichy, N., & Devanna, M. (1992). *The transformational leader.* New York: John Wiley.

Van de Ven, A. H., & Poole, M. S. (1987). Paradoxical requirements for a theory of organizational change. In. R. Quinn & K. Cameron (Eds.), *Paradox and transformation: Toward a theory of change in organization and management.* Cambridge, MA: Ballinger.

Warfield, J. N. (1990). A science of generic design. Salinas, CA: Interscience.

Weick, K. (1979). *The social psychology of organizing.* Reading, MA: Addison-Wesley.

Weick, K. (1984). Small wins: Redefining the scale of social problems. *American Psychologist, 39*(1), 40–49.

Wheatley, M. J. (1992). *Leadership and the new science.* New York: Berrett-Kohler.

Woodman, R., Sawyer, J., & Griffin, R. (1993). Toward a theory of organizational creativity. *Academy of Management Review, 18*(2), 293–321.

"Wrong Road?" Critics fault Ford plan to produce small cars with Mazda of Japan. (1986, June 23). *Wall Street Journal.*

VI EXAMPLES AND SPECIAL SITUATIONS

We believe that organizations and their members are in a decade of continuous/discontinuous change and the challenge for leaders will be to make a paradigm shift to OT and design the dynamically stable organization.[1] This organization of the future is called by many different names. Some of the more popular are the horizontal organization,[2] the knowledge and technology-based organization; the STAR organization,[3] and the learning organization;[4] and the 1993 Academy of Management annual meeting even had the theme of "Managing the Boundaryless Organization."

We believe all of these organizations have more similarities than differences, and, although some authors describe limited successes, these organizations are still in the experimental stages. Figure 1 is an overview of the "old organization" and the "future organization." This model first appeared in *Business Week,* October 23, 1992, and we modified it to include the main patterns from the models listed above. OD and OT is the application of behavioral science theory and practice to help organizations make the paradigm shift to the future organization.

Readings in Part VI

The first article, by Leonard Goodstein and Warner Burke, examines large-scale and fundamental change, often called *organizational transformation.* In this essay, Goodstein and Burke apply Kurt Lewin's model of unfreezing, movement, and refreezing to a major change effort at British Airways. They describe how considerable use was made of all of the usual OD methodologies such as team building, process consultation, role clarification, and negotiations.

The second article, by Anthony J. Rucci, Steven P. Kirn, and Richard T. Quinn, is a thorough description of an organization transforming from the mature (old) design to the future organization (STAR). Further, this article describes how CEO Arthur Martinez, with a strong vision, led the unfreezing process. His vision and values shaped the transformation at Sears toward a learning organization that is a (1)

FIGURE 1

The mature organization and the future (STAR) organization

Mature (Old) Model	Variables to Change	Future Organization (STAR)
Incremental or rapid	Change	Random
Single loop	Learning	Double loop
Top down	Control	Shared
Hierarchy	Organization	Network and alliances
Security	Expectations	Personal growth
Homogeneous	People	Different attitudes and values
Individuals	Work design	Self-directed teams
Extrinsic	Motivation	Intrinsic
Domestic	Markets	Global
Cost	Strategic advantage	Time
Functional	Structure	Process driven
OK	Quality	Few compromises
Money	Focus	Customer
Quarterly rate of return	Values and vision	People I/E
Individual	Rewards	Team based

Source: This is a modification of *Business Week,* October 23, 1992, pp. 62–63, and Robert A. Zawacki, Carol A. Norman, Paul A. Zawacki, and Paul Applegate, *Transforming the Mature Information Technology Organization* (Colorado Springs: EagleStar Publishing), 1995, p. 28.

compelling place to shop, (2) compelling place to work, and (3) compelling place to invest. More than skin deep, this transformation included major changes in attitudes and behavior, metrics that measured this change, and the necessary changes in the human resource systems and processes to reinforce and sustain the new organization. With this strong leadership at the top, each major business unit was given the goal of driving the change effort throughout Sears. The third editor of this book, Zawacki, had the privilege of coaching the Sears information technology unit during its transformation The unit's transformation was led by senior vice president and CIO Joe Smialowski, who used a collaborative approach, entitled "Reaching beyond Technology," to reinforce the change program. Other business vice presidents at Sears used a similar approach. This is truly a remarkable case history of a major transformation of a Fortune 500 company.

The next reading in this part is by Robert M. Frame, Warren R. Nielsen, and Larry E. Pate. It is a description of an organizational transformation (OT) effort at one of the *Chicago Tribune's* printing facilities. After a strike by 1,000 workers, management made a commitment to create a new culture that emphasized operating beliefs, human resource development, and effective use of capital and resources. The results of this OT effort are very positive, and the authors conclude their descriptive case study with guidelines for organizations of the future.

Most of the growth in new jobs has been in small entrepreneurial firms during the past 10 years. We see that pattern of job growth continuing at least for the remainder of this decade. Because of this recent emphasis and interest in small firms, we included the article by W. Gibb Dyer, which articulates an OD framework for diagnosis and intervention in small entrepreneurial firms. Further, Dyer discusses interventions at the start-up, growth, and succession stages of the firm.

Two of the drivers of change in organizations today are time-based competition and reduced costs. Because of these drivers, change agents are working with more and more organizations that are merging with other organizations or are in turn-around situations. Can OD efforts add value to the bottom line of a business during mergers and turnaround situations? The final reading, by Gregory W. Pacton, attempts to answer the question of the applicability of OD during the crises of turn-around situations.

Endnotes

1. Andrew C. Boynton and Bart Victor, "Beyond Flexibility: Building and Managing the Dynamically Stable Organization," from a paper dated June 27, 1991, and forthcoming in the *California Management Review.*
2. "The Horizontal Organization," *Information Week,* August 27, 1992, pp. 32–40.
3. Robert A. Zawacki, "Key Issues in Human Resources Management, *Information Systems Management,*" Winter 1993, pp. 72–75; and Robert A. Zawacki, "Is the Horizontal Organization Already a Dinosaur?" *CASELab Notes* 2:1 (1993), pp. 9–11.
4. Peter M. Senge, "Transforming the Practice of Management," paper presented at the Systems Thinking Conference, November 14, 1991.

READING 35
CREATING SUCCESSFUL ORGANIZATION CHANGE

Leonard D. Goodstein
W. Warner Burke

Buffeted at home and abroad by foreign competition that appears to produce higher-quality goods at lower prices, corporate America has now largely forsaken (at least publicly and momentarily) the traditional analogy of the organization as a machine and its organizational members as parts designed to work effectively and efficiently. Instead, many American corporations are accepting the "New Age" view of organizations as "a nested set of open, living systems and subsystems dependent upon the larger environment for survival."

What is surprising about this quote is not its viewpoint, which has been normative in the organizational psychology and behavioral literature for several decades, but its source: *The Wall Street Journal*. And it is typical to find such articles in virtually every issue of most recent American business publications: articles on corporate culture, on the changing attitudes of American workers, on the need for greater employee participation in managerial decision making, and on the place of employees as an important (if not the most important) asset of the corporation.

We are not suggesting that traditionally managed organizations are now extinct in America. Corporate executives, however, have definitely begun to recognize that managing the social psychology of the workplace is a critical element in the success of any organization.

Organizational Change

Organizations tend to change primarily because of external pressure, rather than an internal desire or

need to change. Here are a few all-too-familiar examples of the kinds of environmental factors requiring organizations to change:

- A new competitor snares a significant portion of a firm's market share.
- An old customer is acquired by a giant conglomerate that dictates new sales arrangements.
- A new invention offers the possibility of changing the organization's existing production technology.

Other examples include (1) new government regulations on certain health care financing programs and (2) economic and social conditions that create long-term changes in the availability of the labor force. The competent organization will be so alert to early warning signs of such external changes that it can move promptly to make internal changes designed to keep it viable in the changing external world. Competent organizations are those that continue to change and to survive.

Thus it is practically a cliché to state that change in organizations today is a way of life. And clearly it is not saying anything new to comment that executives and managers today are more finely attuned to change or that they more frequently view their role as that of change agent.

But even though we often state the obvious and spout clichés about change, this does not mean that we have an in-depth understanding of what we are talking about. We are only beginning to understand the nature of change and how to manage the process involved, especially with respect to organizations. The purpose of this article is to improve our understanding of organizational change by providing both some conceptual clarification and a case example that illustrates many of the concepts involved.

Source: Leonard D. Goodstein, "Creating Successful Organization Change." Reprinted, from *Organizational Dynamics*, Spring 1991. Copyright © 1991 American Management Association International. Reprinted by permission of American Management Association International, New York, NY. All rights reserved. http://www.amanet.org.

It is possible to conceptualize organizational change in at least three ways—levels of organizational change, strategies of organizational change, and more specifically and not mutually exclusive of strategies, models and methods of organizational change. (First we will present the concepts, second the case example, and finally some implications.)

Levels of Organizational Change

A broad distinction can be made between (1) fundamental, large-scale change in the organization's strategy and culture—a transformation, refocus, reorientation, or "bending the frame," as David A. Nadler and Michael L. Tushman have referred to the process—and (2) fine-tuning, fixing problems, making adjustments, modifying procedures, and so on; that is, implementing modest changes that improve the organization's performance yet do not fundamentally change the organization. By far most organizational changes are designed not to transform the organization but to modify it in order to fix its problems.

In this article we address more directly the large-scale, fundamental type of organizational change. (A word of caution: "Organizational transformation," "frame bending," and other expressions indicating fundamental change do not imply wholesale, indiscriminate, and complete change. Thus when we refer to "fundamental change," we do not mean "in any and all respects.")

We are concerned with transformation when an organization faces the need to survive and must do things differently to continue to exist. After polio was licked, for example, the March of Dimes had to change its mission in order to survive as an organization. Although its mission changed from one of attacking polio to one of trying to eradicate birth defects, the organization's core technology—fund raising—remained the same.

A corporate example of transformation is seen in the transition of International Harvester to Navistar. Facing bankruptcy, the company downsized drastically, completely restructured its financial situation, and overhauled its corporate culture.

Although many of the company's technologies were sold off, it, too, retained its core technology: producing trucks and engines. Once internally focused, its culture is now significantly market-oriented—and the company is operating far more efficiently than it did in the past.

Although organizational members experience such transformations as a complete change, they rarely if ever are. Theory would suggest that if fundamental—or even significant—change is to occur with any success, some characteristic(s) of the organization must *not* change. The theory to which we refer comes from the world of individual change: psychotherapy. For organizational transformation to be achieved—for the organization to survive and eventually prosper from such change—certain fundamentals need to be retained. Some examples: the organization's ultimate purpose, the previously mentioned core technology, and key people. The principle here is that for people to be able to deal with enormous and complex change—seeming chaos—they need to have *something* to hold on to that is stable.

Conceptually, then, we can distinguish between fundamentally changing the organization and fine-tuning it. This distinction—which is a matter of degree, not necessarily, a dichotomy—is useful in determining strategies and methods to be used in the change effort. When fine-tuning, for example, we do not necessarily need to clarify for organizational members what will not change—but in the case of transformation, such clarity is required for its successful achievement.

Strategies of Organizational Change

Organizational change can occur in more than one way. In a 1971 book, Harvey A. Hornstein and colleagues classified six ways: individual change strategies, technostructural strategies, data-based strategies, organization development, violent and coercive strategies, and nonviolent yet direct-action strategies. All of these strategies have been used to attempt, if not actually bring about, organizational change. Senior management usually chooses any one or various combinations of the first four and manages them internally. The last two—violent, coercive strategies and nonviolent yet direct-action strategies—are more often than not initiated by actions outside the organization, and the organization's executives typically manage in a reactive mode.

In this article we address some combination of the first four strategies. Yet, as previously indicated, we are assuming that the overwhelming majority of organizational changes are motivated by *external* factors—that executives are responding to the organization's external environment. But even when it is not a reaction to some social movement, organizational change is nevertheless a *response*—a response to changes or anticipated changes in the marketplace, or changes in the way technology will affect the organization's products/services, or changes in the labor market, etc.

This assumption is based on the idea that an organization is a living, open system dependent on its environment for survival. Whether it is merely to survive or eventually to prosper, an organization must monitor its external environment and align itself with changes that occur or will occur in that environment. Practically speaking, the process of alignment requires the organization to change itself.

Models and Methods of Organizational Change

Models of change and methods of change are quite similar in concept and often overlap—so much so that it is not always clear which one is being discussed. Kurt Lewin's three-phase model of change—unfreeze, move (or change), refreeze—also suggests method. Organization development is based on an action-research model that is, at the same time, a method.

More on the model side is the relatively simple and straightforward framework provided by Richard Beckhard and Reuben T. Harris. They have suggested that large-scale complex organizational change can be conceptualized as movement from a present state to a future state. But the most important phase is the in-between one that they label *transition state*. Organizational change, then, is a matter of (1) assessing the current organizational situation (present state), (2) determining the desired future (future state), and (3) both planning ways to reach that desired future and implementing the plans (transition state).

Methods of implementing the change—for example, a new organizational strategy—include the following:

- Setting up a comprehensive training program (individual change strategy).
- Modifying the structure, individuals' jobs, and/or work procedures (technostructural strategy).
- Conducting a companywide survey to assess organizational culture for the purpose of using the data to pinpoint required changes (data-based strategy).
- Collecting information from organizational members about their views regarding what needs to be changed and acting accordingly (organization development strategy).
- Combining two, three, or all of these methods.

The case example we will discuss here illustrates organizational transformation in response to change initiated in the institution's external environment—excluding, however, the violent, coercive strategies and the nonviolent, direct ones. The example, which is analyzed according to Lewin's three-phase model/method, highlights the use of multiple methods for change—in fact, it presents in one form or another a specific method from each of the four other change strategies mentioned earlier.

Case Example

In 1982 Margaret Thatcher's government in Great Britain decided to convert British Airways (BA) from government ownership to private ownership. BA had regularly required large subsidies from the government (almost $900 million in 1982), subsidies that the government felt it could not provide. Even more important, the Conservative government was ideologically opposed to the government's ownership of businesses—a matter they regarded as the appropriate province of private enterprise.

The growing deregulation of international air traffic was another important environmental change. Air fares were no longer fixed, and the resulting price wars placed BA at even greater risk of financial losses.

In order to be able to "privatize"—that is, sell BA shares on the London and New York Stock Exchanges—it was necessary to make BA profitable. The pressures to change thus exerted on BA by the external environment were broad and intense. And the internal organizational changes, driven by these external pressures, have been massive and widespread. They have transformed the BA culture from what BA managers described as "bureaucratic and militaristic" to one that is now described as "service-oriented and market-driven." The success of these efforts over a five-year period (1982–1987) is clearly depicted in the data presented in Figure 1.

This exhibit reflects BA's new mission in its new advertising slogan—"The World's Favorite Airline." Five years after the change effort began, BA had successfully moved from government ownership to private ownership, and both passenger and cargo revenues had dramatically increased, leading to a substantial increase in share price over the offering price, despite the market crash of October 1987. Indeed, in late 1987 BA acquired British Caledonian Airways, its chief domestic competitor. The steps through which this transformation was accomplished clearly fit Lewin's model of the change process.

Lewin's Change Model

According to the open-systems view, organizations—like living creatures—tend to be homeostatic, or continuously working to maintain a steady state. This helps us understand why organizations require external impetus to initiate change

and, indeed, why that change will be resisted even when it is necessary.

Organizational change can occur at three levels—and, since the patterns of resistance to change are different for each, the patterns in each level require different change strategies and techniques. These levels involve:

1. Changing the *individuals* who work in the organization—that is, their skills, values, attitudes, and eventually behavior—but making sure that such individual behavioral change is always regarded as instrumental to organizational change.

2. Changing various organizational *structures and systems*—reward systems, reporting relationships, work design, and so on.

3. Directly changing the organizational *climate or interpersonal style*—how open people are with each other, how conflict is managed, how decisions are made, and so on.

According to Lewin, a pioneer in the field of social psychology of organizations, the first step of any change process it to *unfreeze* the present pattern of behavior as a way of managing resistance to change. Depending on the organizational level of change intended, such unfreezing might involve, on the individual level, selectively promoting or terminating employees; on the structural level, developing highly experiential training programs in such new organization designs as matrix management; or, on the climate level, providing data-based feedback on how employees feel about certain management practices. Whatever the level involved, each of these interventions is intended to make organizational members address that level's need for change, heighten their awareness of their own behavioral patterns, and make them more open to the change process.

The second step, *movement,* involves making the actual changes that will move the organization to another level of response. On the individual level, we would expect to see people behaving differently, perhaps demonstrating new skills or new supervisory practices. On the structural level, we

FIGURE 1

The British Airways success story: Creating the "World's Favorite Airline"

	1982	1987
Ownership	Government.	Private.
Profit/(loss)	($900 million).	$435 million.
Culture	Bureaucratic and militaristic.	Service-oriented and market-driven.
Passenger load factor	Decreasing.	Increasing—up 16% in 1st quarter 1988.
Cargo load	Stable.	Increasing—up 41% in 1st quarter 1988.
Share price	N/A	Increased 67% (2/11/87–8/11/87).
Acquisitions	N/A	British Caledonian.

would expect to see changes in actual organizational structures, reporting relationships, and reward systems that affect the way people do their work. Finally, on the climate or interpersonal-style level, we would expect to see behavior patterns that indicate greater interpersonal trust and openness and fewer dysfunctional interactions.

The final stage of the change process, *refreezing,* involves stabilizing or institutionalizing these changes by establishing systems that make these behavioral patterns "relatively secure against change," as Lewin put it. The refreezing stage may involve, for example, redesigning the organization's recruitment process to increase the likelihood of hiring applicants who share the organization's new management style and value system. During the refreezing stage, the organization may also ensure that the new behaviors have become the operating norms at work, that the reward system actually reinforces those behaviors, or that a new, more participative management style predominates.

According to Lewin, the first step to achieving lasting organizational change is to deal with resistance to change by unblocking the present system. This unblocking usually requires some kind of confrontation and a retraining process based on planned behavioral changes in the desired direction. Finally, deliberate steps need to be taken to cement these changes in place—this "institutionalization of change" is designed to make the changes semipermanent until the next cycle of change occurs.

Figure 2 presents an analysis of the BA change effort in terms of Lewin's model. The many and diverse steps involved in the effort are categorized both by stages (unfreezing, movement, and refreezing) and by level (individual, structures and system, and climate/interpersonal style).

Unfreezing. In BA's change effort, the first step in unfreezing involved a massive reduction in the worldwide BA workforce (from 59,000 to 37,000). It is interesting to note that, within a year after this staff reduction, virtually all BA performance indices had improved—more on-time departure and arrivals, fewer out-of-service aircraft, less time "on hold" for telephone reservations, fewer lost bags, and so on. The consensus view at all levels within BA was that the downsizing had reduced hierarchical levels, thus giving more autonomy to operating people and allowing work to get done more easily.

The downsizing was accomplished with compassion; no one was actually laid off. Early retirement, with substantial financial settlements, was the preferred solution throughout the system. Although there is no question that the process was painful, considerable attention was paid to minimizing the pain in every possible way.

A second major change occurred in BA's top management. In 1981, Lord John King of Wartinbee, a senior British industrialist, was appointed chairman of the board, and Colin Marshall, now Sir Colin, was appointed CEO. The appointment of Marshall represented a significant departure from BA culture. An outsider to BA, Marshall had a marketing background that was quite different from that of his predecessors, many of whom were retired senior Royal Air Force officers. It was

FIGURE 2

Applying Lewin's model to the British Airways (BA) change effort

Levels	Unfreezing	Movement	Refreezing
Individual	Downsizing of workforce (59,000 to 37,000); middle management especially hard hit. New top management team. "Putting People First."	Acceptance of concept of "emotional labor." Personal staff as internal consultants. "Managing People First." Peer support groups.	Continued commitment of top management. Promotion of staff with new BA values. "Top Flight Academies." "Open Learning" programs.
Structures and systems	Use of diagonal task forces to plan change. Reduction in levels of hierarchy. Modification of budgeting process.	Profit sharing (3 weeks' pay in 1987). Opening of Terminal 4. Purchase of Chartridge as training center. New, "user-friendly" MIS.	New performance appraisal system based on both behavior and performance. Performance-based compensation system. Continued use of task forces.
Climate/interpersonal style	Redefinition of the business: *service,* not *transportation.* Top-management commitment and involvement.	Greater emphasis on open communications. Data feedback on work-unit climate. Off-site, team-building meetings.	New uniforms. New coat of arms. Development and use of cabin-crew teams. Continued use of data-based feedback on climate and management practices.

Marshall who decided, shortly after his arrival, that BA's strategy should be to become "the World's Favorite Airline." Without question, critical ingredients in the success of the overall change effort were Marshall's vision, the clarity of his understanding that BA's culture needed to be changed in order to carry out the vision, and his strong leadership of that change effort.

To support the unfreezing process, the first of many training programs was introduced. "Putting People First"—the program in which all BA personnel with direct customer contact participated—was another important part of the unfreezing process. Aimed at helping line workers and managers understand the service nature of the airline industry, it was intended to challenge the prevailing wisdom about how things were to be done at BA.

Movement. Early on, Marshall hired Nicholas Georgiades, a psychologist and former professor and consultant, as director (vice president) of human resources. It was Georgiades who developed the specific tactics and programs required to bring Marshall's vision into reality. Thus Geor-

giades, along with Marshall, must be regarded as a leader of BA's successful change effort. One of the interventions that Georgiades initiated—a significant activity during the movement phase—was to establish training programs for senior and middle managers. Among these were "Managing People First" and "Leading the Service Business"—experiential programs that involved heavy doses of individual feedback to each participant about his or her behavior regarding management practices on the job.

These training programs all had more or less the same general purpose: to identify the organization's dysfunctional management style and begin the process of developing a new management style that would fit BA's new, competitive environment. If the organization was to be market-driven, service-based, and profit-making, it would require an open, participative management style—one that would produce employee commitment.

On the structures and systems level during the unfreezing stage, extensive use was made of diagonal task forces composed of individuals from different functions and at different levels of responsibility to deal with various aspects of the change process—the need for MIS (management information systems) support, new staffing patterns, new uniforms, and so on. A bottom-up, less centralized budgeting process—one sharply different from its predecessor—was introduced.

Redefining BA's business as service, rather than as transportation, represented a critical shift on the level of climate/interpersonal style. A service business needs an open climate and good interpersonal skills, coupled with outstanding teamwork. Offsite, team-building meetings—the process chosen to deal with these issues during the movement stage—have now been institutionalized.

None of these changes would have occurred without the commitment and involvement of top management. Marshall himself played a central role in both initiating and supporting the change process, even when problems arose. As one index of this commitment, Marshall shared information at question-and-answer sessions at most of the training programs—both "to show the flag" and to provide his own unique perspective on what needed to be done.

An important element of the movement phase was acceptance of the concept of "emotional labor" that Georgiades championed—that is, the high energy levels required to provide the quality of service needed in a somewhat uncertain environment, such as the airline business. Recognition that such service is emotionally draining and often can lead to burnout and permanent psychological damage is critical to developing systems of emotional support for the service workers involved.

Another important support mechanism was the retraining of traditional personnel staff to become internal change agents charged with helping and supporting line and staff managers. So, too, was the development of peer support groups for managers completing the "Managing People First" training program.

To support this movement, a number of internal BA structures and systems were changed. By introducing a new bonus system, for example, Georgiades demonstrated management's commitment to sharing the financial gains of BA's success. The opening of Terminal 4 at Heathrow Airport provided a more functional work environment for staff. The purchase of Chartridge House as a permanent BA training center permitted an increase in and integration of staff training, and the new, "user-friendly" MIS enabled managers to get the information they needed to do their jobs in a timely fashion.

Refreezing. During the refreezing phase, the continued involvement and commitment of BA's top management ensured that the changes became "fixed" in the system. People who clearly exemplified the new BA values were much more likely to be promoted, especially at higher management levels. Georgiades introduced additional programs for educating the workforce, especially managers. "Open Learning" programs, including orientation programs for new staff, supervisory training for new supervisors, and so on, were augmented by "Top Flight Academies" that included training at the executive, senior management, and management levels. One of the academies now leads to an MBA degree.

A new performance appraisal system, based on both behavior and results, was created to emphasize customer service and subordinate development. A performance-based compensation system is being installed, and task forces continue to be used to solve emerging problems, such as those resulting from the acquisition of British Caledonian Airlines.

Attention was paid to BA's symbols as well—new, upscale uniforms; refurbished aircraft; and a new corporate coat of arms with the motto "We fly to serve." A unique development has been the creation of teams for consistent cabin-crew staffing, rather than the ad hoc process typically used. Finally, there is continued use of data feedback on management practices throughout the system.

Managing change. Unfortunately, the change process is not smooth even if one is attentive to Lewin's model of change. Changing behavior at both individual and organizational levels means inhibiting habitual responses and producing new responses that feel awkward and unfamiliar to those involved. It is all too easy to slip back to the familiar and comfortable.

For example, an organization may intend to manage more participatively. But when a difficult decision arises, it may not be possible to get a consensus decision—not at first, at least. Frustration to "get on with" a decision can lead to the organization's early abandonment of the new management style.

In moving from a known present state to a desired future state, organizations must recognize that (as noted earlier) the intervening *transition* state requires careful management, especially when the planned organizational change is large and complex. An important part of this change management lies in recognizing and accepting the disorganization and temporarily lowered effectiveness that characterize the transition state.

In BA's change effort, the chaos and anger that arose during the transitional phase have abated, and clear signs of success have now emerged. But many times the outcome was not at all clear, and serious questions were raised about the wisdom of the process both inside and outside BA. At such times the commitment and courage of top management are essential.

To heighten involvement, managing such organizational changes may often require using a transition management team composed of a broad cross-section of members of the organization. Other techniques include using multiple interventions, rather than just one—for example, keeping the system open to feedback about the change process and using symbols and rituals to mark significant achievements. The BA program used all of these techniques.

Process consultation. In addition to the various change strategies discussed above, considerable use was made of all the usual organization development (OD) technologies. Structural changes, role clarification and negotiations, team building, and process consultation were all used at British Airways to facilitate change.

In process consultation—the unique OD intervention—the consultant examines the pattern of a work unit's communications. This is done most often through direct observation of staff meetings

and, at opportune times, through raising questions or making observations about what has been happening. The role of the process consultant is to be counternormative—that is, to ask why others never seem to respond to Ruth's questions or why no one ever challenges Fred's remarks when he is clearly off target. Generally speaking, process consultation points out the true quality of the emperor's new clothes even when everyone is pretending that they are quite elegant. By changing the closed communication style of the work teams at British Airways to a more open, candid one, process consultation played an important role in the change process.

The Research Evidence

Granted that the BA intervention appears to have been successful, what do we know generally about the impact of OD interventions on organizations and on their effectiveness? Over the past few years, the research literature has shown a sharp improvement in both research design and methodological rigor, especially in the development of such "hard criteria" as productivity and quality indices. The findings have been surprisingly positive.

For example, Raymond Katzell and Richard Guzzo reviewed more than 200 intervention studies and reported that 87 percent found evidence of significant increases in worker productivity as a result of the intervention. Richard Guzzo, Richard Jette, and Raymond Katzell's meta-analysis of 98 of these same studies revealed productivity increases averaging almost half a standard deviation—impressive enough "to be visible to the naked eye," to use their phrase. Thus it would appear that the success of BA's intervention process was not a single occurrence but one in a series of successful changes based on OD interventions.

The picture with respect to employee satisfaction, however, is not so clear. Another meta-analysis—by Barry Macy, Hiroaki Izumi, Charles Hurts, and Lawrence Norton—on how OD interventions affect performance measures and employee work satisfaction found positive effects on performance but *negative* effects on attitudes, perhaps because of the pressure exerted by new work-group norms on employee productivity. The positive effects on performance, however, are in keeping with the bulk of prior research A recent comprehensive review of the entire field of OD by Marshall Sashkin and W. Warner Burke concluded, "There is little doubt that, when applied properly, OD has substantial positive effects in terms of performance measures."

Implications and Concluding Remarks

We very much believe that an understanding of the social psychology of the change process gives all of us—managers, rank-and-file employees, and consultants—an important and different perspective for coping with an increasingly competitive environment. Our purpose in writing this article was to share some of this perspective—from an admittedly biased point of view.

The change effort at BA provides a recent example of how this perspective and this understanding have been applied. What should be apparent from this abbreviated overview of a massive project is that the change process at BA was based on open-systems thinking, a phased model of managing change, and multiple levels for implementing the change. Thus both the design and the implementation of this change effort relied heavily on this kind of understanding about the nature of organizations and changing them.

The change involved a multifaceted effort that used many leverage points to initiate and support the changes. The change process, which used transition teams with openness to feedback, was intentionally managed with strong support from top management. Resistance to change was actively managed by using unfreezing strategies at all three levels—individual, structural and systems, and interpersonal. Virtually all of the organizational change issues discussed in this article emerged in some measure during the course of the project.

It is quite reassuring to begin to find empirical support for these efforts in field studies and case reports of change efforts. Moreover, the recent meta-analyses of much of this work are quite supportive

of what we have learned from experience. We need to use such reports to help more managers understand the worth of applying the open-systems model to their change efforts. But we also need to remember that only when proof of the intervention strategy's usefulness shows up on the firm's "bottom line" will most line managers be persuaded that open-systems thinking is not necessarily incompatible with the real world. The BA success story is a very useful one for beginning such a dialog.

As we go to press, it seems clear that many of the changes at British Airways have stabilized the company. Perhaps the most important one is that the company's culture today can be described as having a strong customer-service focus—a focus that was decidedly lacking in 1982. The belief that marketing and service with the customer in mind will have significant payoff for the company is now endemic to the corporate culture. Another belief now fundamental to BA's culture is that the way one manages people—especially those, like ticket agents and cabin crews, with direct customer contact—directly impacts the way customers will feel about BA. For example, during 1990, Tony Clarry, then head of worldwide customer service for BA, launched a leadership program for all of his management around the globe to continue to reinforce this belief.

Yet all is not bliss at British Airways, which has its problems. Some examples:

- American Airlines is encroaching upon BA's European territory.
- The high level of customer service slips from time to time.
- Those who can afford to ride on the Concorde represent a tiny market, so it is tough to maintain a consistently strong customer base.
- Now that BA has developed a cadre of experienced managers in a successful company, these managers are being enticed by search firms to join other companies that often pay more money.

Other problems, too, affect BA's bottom line—the cost of fuel, effectively managing internal costs, and the reactions of the financiers in London and on Wall Street, to name a few. It should be noted that since 1987 and until recently, BA's financials have remained positive with revenues and profits continuing to increase. During 1990 this bright picture began to fade, however. The combination of the continuing rise in fuel costs, the recession, and the war in the Persian Gulf have taken their toll. Constant vigilance is therefore imperative for continued success.

It may be that BA's biggest problem now is not so much to manage further change as it is to manage the change that has already occurred. In other words, the people of BA have achieved significant change and success; now they must maintain what has been achieved while concentrating on continuing to be adaptable to changes in their external environment—the further deregulation of Europe, for example. Managing momentum may be more difficult than managing change.

References

The Wall Street Journal article referred to at the outset, "Motivate or Alienate? Firms Have Gurus to Change Their 'Cultures,'" was written by Peter Waldbaum and may be found on p. 19 of the July 24, 1987, issue.

With respect to levels of organizational change, see the article by W. Warner Burke and George H. Litwin, "A Causal Model of Organizational Performance," in the 1989 Annual published by University Associates of San Diego. These authors describe the differences between transformational and transactional change. Along the same conceptual lines is the article by David A. Nadler and Michael L. Tushman—"Organizational Frame Bending: Principles for Managing Reorientation" (*The Academy of Management Executive,* August 1988, pp. 194–204).

Regarding strategies of organizational change, see Harvey A. Hornstein, Barbara B. Bunker, W. Warner Burke, Marion Gindes, and Roy J. Lewicki's *Social Intervention: A Behavioral Science Approach* (The Free Press, 1971).

Concerning models and methods of organizational change, the classic piece is Kurt Lewin's chapter "Group Decisions and Social Change," in the 1958 book *Readings in Social Psychology* (Holt, Rinehart & Winston), edited by Eleanor E. Maccobby, Theodore M. Newcomb, and Eugene L. Hartley. For an explanation of organization development as action research, see W. Warner Burke's *Organization Development: Principles and Practices* (Scott, Foresman, 1982). The framework of present state–transition state–future state is explained in *Organization Transitions: Managing Complex Change,* 2nd ed. (Addison-Wesley, 1987), by Richard Beckhard and Reuben T. Harris. A recent article by Donald C. Hambrick and Albert A. Cannella, Jr.—"Strategy Implementation as Substance and Selling" (*The Academy of Management Executive,* November 1989, pp. 278–85)—is quite helpful in understanding how to implement a change in corporate strategy.

A point made in the article is that, for effective organizational change, multiple leverage is required. For data to support this argument, see W. Warner Burke, Lawrence P. Clark, and Cheryl Koopman's "Improving Your OD Project's Chances of Success" (*Training and Development Journal,* September 1984, pp. 62–68). More on process consultation and team building may be found in two books published by Addison-Wesley: Edgar H. Schein's *Process Consultation, vol. 1: Its Role in Organization Development,* 1988, and W. Gibb Dyer's *Team Building: Issues and Alternatives,* 1987.

References for the research evidence are: Richard A. Guzzo, Richard D. Jette, and Raymond A. Katzell's "The Effects of Psychologically Based Intervention Programs on Worker Productivity: A Meta-Analysis" (*Personnel Psychology* 38, no. 2 (Summer 1985), pp. 275–91); Raymond A. Katzell and Richard A. Guzzo's "Psychological Approaches to Worker Productivity" (*American Psychologist* 38 April 1983, pp. 468–72); Barry A. Macy, Hiroaki Izumi, Charles C. M. Hurts, and Lawrence W. Norton's "Meta-Analysis of United States Empirical Change and Work Innovation Field Experiments," a paper presented at the 1986 annual meeting of the Academy of Management, Chicago; John M. Nicholas's "The Comparative Impact of Organization Development Interventions on Hard Criteria Issues" (*The Academy of Management Review* 7, no. 4 (October 1982), pp. 531–43; John M. Nicholas and Marsha Katz's "Research Methods and Reporting Practices in Organization Development" (*The Academy of Management Review,* October 1985, pp. 737–49); and Marshall Sashkin and W. Warner Burke's "Organization Development in the 1980s" (*Journal of Management,* no. 2 (1987), pp. 205–29).

READING 36
THE EMPLOYEE-CUSTOMER-PROFIT CHAIN AT SEARS

Anthony J. Rucci,
Steven P. Kirn
Richard T. Quinn

It is no longer news that over the past five years, Sears, Roebuck and Company has radically changed the way it does business and dramatically improved its financial results. Much has been written about the Sears turnaround, detailing the company's strategic shifts and its transition from big losses to big profits. But the Sears transformation was more than a change in marketing strategy. It was also a change in the logic and culture of the business. In fact, the process of altering the logic is what changed the culture.

Led (and pushed) by CEO Arthur Martinez, a group of more than 100 top-level Sears executives spent the better part of three years rebuilding the company around its customers. In the course of rethinking what Sears was and wanted to become, these managers developed a business model of the company that tracked success from management behavior through employee attitudes to customer satisfaction and financial performance. Along with its measurement system, this *employee-customer-profit model* is rigorous enough to serve as an integral piece of the management information system and as a tool that every individual in the company can use for self-assessment and self-improvement. Moreover, the work of creating the model and the measures made such demands on the managers involved that it changed the way they think and behave. That cultural change is now spreading through the company.

The basic elements of an employee-customer-profit model are not difficult to grasp. Any person

with even a little experience in retailing understands intuitively that there is a chain of cause and effect running from employee behavior to customer behavior to profits, and it's not hard to see that behavior depends primarily on attitude. Which is not to say that implementing an employee-customer-profit chain, or model, is easy. One big problem is measurement. Unlike revenues and profits, soft data are hard to define and collect, and few measures are softer than customer and employee attitudes, or "satisfaction." In many businesses, it is difficult to measure even relatively hard behaviors like customer retention, and the inevitable result is that many companies are unwilling to expend the time, energy, and resources to do it effectively. Not surprisingly, many companies do not have a realistic grasp of what their customers and employees actually think and do.

Sears does. By means of an ongoing process of data collection, analysis, modeling, and experimentation, we have developed and continue to refine what we call our Total Performance Indicators, or TPI—a set of measures that shows us how well we are doing with customers, employees, and investors. We understand the several layers of factors that drive employee attitudes, and we know how employee attitudes affect employee retention, how employee retention affects the drivers of customer satisfaction, how customer satisfaction affects financials, and a great deal more. We have also calculated the lag time between a change in any of those metrics and a corresponding change in financial performance, so that when we see a shift in, say, employee attitudes, we know not only *how* but also *when* it will affect results. Our TPI makes the employee-customer-profit chain operational because we manage the company on the basis of these indicators, with remarkably positive results. But the system is a good deal more complex—and a good deal harder to imitate—than this glimpse suggests.

Any retailer could copy the Sears measures—even our modeling techniques—and still fail to achieve an operational employee-customer-profit chain, because the mechanics of the system are not in themselves enough to make it work. It goes without saying that you must be able to measure and manage the drivers of employee and customer satisfaction, and we will explain how we do this at Sears. But two additional elements are indispensable. First, a company must build management alignment around the model and the measures—which, for all practical purposes, make up a single system. Because this system is to be the cornerstone of management decision making, it is critically important that every manager—especially those at the top of the company—understand the system and buy into it wholeheartedly. Second, it is essential to deploy the system properly in order to create a sense of ownership among sales associates and staff. Deployment is easy to shrug off. It looks like a simple communication challenge, but it is a good deal more. It is an issue of trust and of business and economic literacy. Unless employees grasp the purpose of the system, understand the economics of their company and industry, and have a clear picture of how their own work fits into the employee-customer-profit model, they will never succeed in making the whole thing work.

Making an employee-customer-profit chain operational is therefore a challenge in three parts: creating and refining the employee-customer-profit model and the measurement system that supports it; creating management alignment around the use of the model to run the company; and deploying the model so as to build business literacy and trust among employees. At Sears, there was no distinction between parts one and two. Managers themselves created the model and aligned themselves with it as they did so, since people automatically buy into systems they invent. Part three, deployment, followed.

The three together were a radical response to a 10-year business downturn that threatened the survival of the Sears retail business—a 111-year-old American institution.

Turnaround

The year 1992 was the worst in the history of Sears. On sales of $52.3 billions, the company's net loss was $3.9 billion, almost $3 billion of which came from the merchandising group. Worse yet, 1992 was no anomaly but the culmination of bad trends, most of them directly related to the company's lack of focus. For a century, Sears had flourished on the strength of its adaptive ability to understand and serve U.S. consumers and their changing needs and wants. Beginning in the 1980s, however, Sears diversified into insurance, financial services, brokerage, and real estate, while other retailers, notably Wal-Mart, were focusing fiercely on the retail consumer and were capturing market share with remarkable speed. The Sears response was to sell or spin off all its nonretail businesses and return to its roots.

Arthur Martinez arrived in September 1992 to head up the merchandising group. (In August 1995, when Sears had divested everything but merchandising, he became chairman and CEO.) Martinez had been vice chairman and a director of Saks Fifth Avenue, as well as group chief executive for the retail division of BATUS, where he was responsible for Saks, Marshall Field, J. B. Ivey, and Breuners. But no retailer in history had ever succeeded in effecting a turnaround of the kind and scope that Sears required, perhaps even to survive. Martinez and his leadership team needed to make some quick decisions about product lines, store types and locations, strategies, asset allocations—even about the company's basic identity as a retailer. Two factors worked in Sears's favor. First, we would not have to invent a crisis to get the attention of employees, who were hungry for improved performance. Second, the company's heritage was an asset. Research showed, almost surprisingly, that through years of turmoil—and despite specific customer-satisfaction ratings that were very low—American families had maintained a positive, trusting image of Sears as a good, honest place to shop.

Within 100 days of his arrival, Martinez initiated a comprehensive turnaround plan. For decades, the underlying assumption had been that Sears was a man's store, but market data showed that an extremely high percentage of buying decisions were being made by women. Martinez refocused marketing on "the softer side of Sears" and introduced new private-label lines of apparel and cosmetics. He expanded and accelerated existing plans to move into off-mall specialty stores, including Sears hardware stores and HomeLife furniture stores. He slated 113 stores for closing, reducing the number of mall-based stores to about 800; those that remained were to be thoroughly renovated over five years at a cost of $4 billion. He also terminated the 101-year-old Sears catalog, which was losing more than $100 million a year. Store operations were reengineered, with a heavy emphasis on training, incentives, and the elimination of administrative and other nonselling tasks for sales personnel. Staffing was adjusted to put more of the best people in the stores during evenings and weekends, when the best customers were shopping. The company's entire service strategy was revamped to make it more responsive to busy women and their families. Sears began offering Sunday deliveries and a long list of new services, including repairs on any brand of appliance. Martinez decreed that Sears would accept all major credit cards instead of limiting itself to Discover and the Sears card.

The results were spectacular. In 1993, the company's merchandising group reported net income of $752 million, a sales increase of more than 9 percent in existing stores, and market share gains in apparel, appliances, and electronics. Sears as a whole had one of its most profitable years ever. The resurrection produced a total shareholder return for the year of 56 percent.

Transformation

Business turnarounds are remarkable events, but all too often they are only skin deep. They are exciting, certainly. Management introduces a new strategy,

speaks with great conviction about empowerment and customer focus, and lavishes a great deal of attention on the workforce. But few rank-and-file employees ever really understand the point of all the activity or grasp their own role in it. Moreover, the turnaround means a lot of extra work and can tire everyone out. So once the energy and excitement—and the results—have peaked, many companies fall back in relief and reassume bad habits.

We were determined to keep this pattern from repeating itself at Sears. Once the company was making money again, there was a widespread, perceptible sense of "Glad that's behind us," and we realized that success could become our enemy. The task we faced was substantial: to transform the company, turn its short-term survival program into a platform for long-term excellence, and, in the process, engage the creative power of employees in the vital task of shaping the company's future. We knew that Sears had to listen to its customers and respond to their needs. We also understood that no plan we devised and imposed from above was ever going to work. If Sears was to undergo a transformation—if attitudes and behavior were to change and a new sense of urgency and purpose were to spread through the company—senior management as a whole would have to take the lead. As Martinez saw it, his job was to coax or compel his senior managers to come up with a plan.

In March 1993, he called the first of several offsite meetings in Phoenix, Arizona, for about 65 senior managers. (This group, known as the Phoenix Team, grew steadily until it included roughly 150 people—the entire senior echelon.) In an intensive two-and-a-half-day session, Martinez presented five new strategic priorities—core business growth, customer focus ("Make Sears a compelling place to shop" was the way he put it), cost reduction, responsiveness to local markets, and organizational and cultural renewal—and then led the discussions himself. You are the future leaders of Sears, he said in effect, and as you go, so goes the company. Back at Sears headquarters in Chicago, the Phoenix Team continued to meet one Saturday a month to discuss the priorities and work on implementation.

At the November meeting later that year, Martinez wanted to know how the five strategic priorities were progressing, and a general discussion followed. Everyone agreed that the priorities made sense to top-level managers, but the rest of the company thought it was all a lot of "M.B.A. stuff." "They nod their heads when you talk about customer focus," someone said, "but they don't know what they're supposed to be doing different." And then one candid and courageous soul stood up and said, "To be completely honest about it, I don't know what *I'm* supposed to be doing differently." People shifted uneasily in their seats, and a few nodded in agreement. It was a startling moment. Here was the Phoenix Team, whose job it was to design a corporate transformation and generate renewal among 300,000 employees at more than 2,000 locations, and no one seemed to have a clear sense of what, exactly, that might require.

In most companies, in most situations, it is the eight or ten most senior executives (along with the strategic planning department and various consultants) who ask the big strategic questions: What business are we in? Whom do we serve? How do we compete? What is our value proposition? As a rule, the 100 to 200 people in the second management layer take the answers to those questions on faith. What gets lost as a result is cross-functional dialogue, questioning, cooperative planning, creativity, and ownership. At Sears, the 1992 turnaround strategy—as well as the five strategic priorities—were developed and deployed more or less according to the old top-down paradigm, with strong initial results but without the broad ownership and employee engagement that Martinez wanted. In 1992, there had been no real alternative—the company was teetering on the edge. And the turnaround strategy worked. Then, in 1993, Martinez had needed a set of priorities he could use to make a direct, almost personal bid for the hearts and minds of his senior managers. He had won their hearts, it appeared, but he still needed to give them an opportunity and a compelling reason to think outside the old Sears box and figure out for themselves what they should be doing differently.

What followed was more than a year of careful but intense pressure on those senior managers. There were plenty of ideas on the table. The problem was getting members of the Phoenix Team to explore the possibilities until they themselves could develop a plan for Sears that would work because it was their own creation.

We began by asking each member of the team to write a "news story" about where Sears would be in five years and how it got there. At the Phoenix meeting in March of 1994, task forces were formed around four recurring themes in those stories: customers, employees, financial performance, and innovation. The new groups were asked to define *world-class status* in their areas, identify obstacles to achieving it, and establish metrics for measuring progress. The task forces met for two-and-a-half days, then presented their findings to the whole assembly. Martinez told them it was a good start. But since the company was going to bet its future on their initiatives, they would need to spend more time, gather more information, and make specific recommendations.

When the team got back to Chicago, a lot of people complained about the extra workload. They had no time to spend on task forces, they insisted, because they had to run the company. The message came back that they had to do both. They had to find the strategic answers and create an operational strategy. For several weeks, everyone struggled. As the deadline for recommendations approached, the sense of urgency grew. The task forces began meeting weekly, usually at 7 A.M. or earlier. (Months later, when many people wondered if the 7 o'clock grind had to go on forever, they needed to be reminded that no one ever told them they had to meet at that hour, or every week, or at all. Urgency and involvement had scheduled all those early morning meetings.)

The four task forces grew to five: customers, employees, financial performance, innovation, and values. The financial task force built a model of the drivers of total shareholder return over a 20-year period and drew inferences about what Sears would have to do to be in the top quartile of *Fortune* 500 companies. The innovation group did outside benchmarking, undertook a research project into the nature of change, and suggested an effort to generate one million ideas from employees. The values group gathered 80,000 employee surveys and identified six core values that Sears's people felt strongly about: honesty, integrity, respect for the individual, teamwork, trust, and customer focus. The old command-and-control culture was too parental and didn't value people enough. Performance should count more than effort.

The customer task force studied customer surveys going back several years and conducted 80 customer focus groups across the country, videotaping the sessions so that every member of the task force could watch. They asked the focus groups why they shopped at Sears, what they wanted, what they expected, what they disliked. Sears had always talked a great game on customer focus: "Satisfaction guaranteed or your money back" had been a Sears watchword for a hundred years, and "Take care of the customer, take care of the customer" was a kind of Sears mantra. Much of it was hollow, however, and it often seemed that no one at headquarters had been listening to customers. Across the country, the task force heard endless stories about how we failed to meet customers' expectations. Merchandise was out of stock, sales associates were hard to find, returns were time consuming, service was bad. The big surprise was that, in spite of it all, people basically liked Sears. One of our great assets was the American public's persistent wish to see the company succeed.

The employee task force conducted 26 employee focus groups and studied all the data on employee attitudes and behavior, including a 70-question opinion survey given to every employee every other year. What the group heard, again and again, was that employees took a great interest in the company's success. They were proud to be at Sears. "It's not a job," someone said. "It's my life's work."

While the task forces were busy gathering data, we set up an additional group to produce a vision and values statement. It had predictable difficulties. After talking to 80,000 employees, the group came up with a set of values that sounded like the Boy Scout oath. We were going to be the world's leading retailer, practice charity and kindness, end world hunger, and achieve peace in our time. All fine ambitions, but what did they have to do with retailing? We turned to outside professionals, and

they came up with a vision statement that sounded like every other company's vision statement.

Then it struck us that we had been staring at it all along. Early in the process, Martinez had talked about making Sears a "compelling place to shop." We also wanted Sears to be a compelling place to work. And if we could achieve both of those goals, Sears would certainly become a compelling place to invest. So "Sears, a compelling place to work, to shop, and to invest" became not our vision, exactly, but a clear statement of what we wanted to be known for, internally and externally. We called it the "three compellings" and later just the three C's. We combined it with three shared values that we came to call the three P's: "passion for the customer, our people add value, and performance leadership." Some people in the company thought all of this was far too simplistic, but to most of us, simplicity was its strength. The three C's and the three P's were simple, yet they amounted to a wonderfully concise version of the entire employee-customer-profit chain, from motivated employees to satisfied customers to pleased investors. No one would have to carry around a little printed card to remember what Sears was all about.

Measurement

Times of crisis like the ones Sears had gone through make corporate transformation necessary and, ironically, somewhat easier. People know that change is required because they can easily remember when pieces of the sky were raining on their heads. But change to what? Change managed how, especially in a large organization? And change perpetuated how, as a dynamic process rather than as a onetime event?

The task forces had spent months listening to customers and employees, studying best practices at other companies, thinking about what would constitute world-class performance at Sears, and establishing measures and objectives. As a result, they had at least a partial answer to the first question: Change to what? The customer task force had established four goals: to build customer loyalty, to make Sears a fun place to shop, to provide excellent customer service by hiring and holding on to the best employees, and to offer the right merchandise at the right prices. The employee task force came up with three: to build a workforce of involved and empowered employees, to encourage new ideas, and to create an environment in which employees could realize their personal goals and develop their skills and abilities. The financial task force had four goals: to increase operating margins, to improve asset management, to raise productivity, and to grow revenues.

While the separate task forces were formulating those objectives, the Phoenix Team as a whole was beginning to think in terms of a business model that would link employees, customers, and investors into a single logical entity. In fact, it was a short step from "compelling place to work, to shop, and to invest" to the same thought expressed as a formula for the company's success: *work* × *shop* = *invest*. This simple algorithm looked more like a slogan than an operational strategy, but there was more to it than met the eye. In the first place, the formula took into account our conviction that for Sears to succeed financially, we had to be a compelling place *both* to work *and* to shop—that is, *work* × *shop*, not *work* + *shop*. The right merchandise at the right prices would get us nowhere if our employees were poorly motivated. Second, it was a formula made up of leading, not lagging, indicators. It is now a truism that financial results are a rearview mirror, that they tell you only how you did in the last quarter and not how you will do in the next. But few if any companies have ever come up with dependable predictive metrics, and that's what we were after.

The objectives formulated by the task forces gave us a set of preliminary measures, on which the task forces had already begun to gather data. (See the exhibit "The Initial Model: From Objectives to Measures.") We now formed a new team to convert those measures into an econometric model. The measurement team's task was to come up with a kind of balanced scorecard for the company—the Sears Total Performance Indicators, or TPI. But we wanted to go well beyond the usual balanced scorecard, commonly just a set of untested assumptions, and nail down the drivers of future financial performance with statistical rigor. We wanted to assemble the company's vast body of interview and research data—some of it from the task forces, much of it collected routinely over the course of years but never used strategically—then analyze it, draw connections across the data sets, and construct a model to show pathways of actual causation all the way from employee attitudes to profits. We wanted a set of nonfinancial measures that would be every bit as rigorous and auditable as financial ones. To make that happen, we had to take this first version of the employee-customer-profit model and elaborate and refine it until we had tested and proved the measures it was built on.

It was a task that struck many people as utopian, but even the skeptics understood that dependable information about causation would be invaluable if we could get it. Suppose, for example, that we wanted to spend some money to increase sales associates' knowledge of the products they sell. Would customers notice? Would the investment lead to increased customer retention, better word of mouth, higher revenues, greater market share? If so, how long would it take? Or, even more to the point, suppose that we wanted to measure the effects of an improvement in management skills. Because 70 percent of our employees work part-time, and part-time employees have a high turnover rate, we know that management skills are critically important. The model and the TPI could tell us *how* important those management skills actually were, measured in terms of employee attitudes and customer satisfaction. We wanted a chain of causation that would answer all those questions and more—a working model of the employee-customer-profit chain that would help us run the company.

For customers and employees, some of the metrics were brand-new. Personal growth and development was not something Sears had ever measured before, and neither was customer retention. We had to invent the measures and the new

The Initial Model:
From Objectives to Measures

The first step in creating an employee-customer-profit model was to devise a set of measures based on our objectives in our three categories: a compelling place to work, to shop, and to invest.

	A COMPELLING PLACE TO WORK	A COMPELLING PLACE TO SHOP	A COMPELLING PLACE TO INVEST
OBJECTIVE	• Environment for personal growth and development • Support for ideas and innovation • Empowered and involved teams and individuals	• Great merchandise at great values • Excellent customer service from the best people • Fun place to shop • Customer loyalty	• Revenue growth • Superior operating income growth • Efficient asset management • Productivity gains
MEASURES	• Personal growth and development • Empowered teams	• Customer needs met • Customer satisfaction • Customer retention	• Revenue growth • Sales per square foot • Inventory turnover • Operating income margin • Return on assets

measurement techniques that went with them. Once we had defined our new measures, we spent the first two quarters of 1995 gathering metrics of every kind, old and new; in the third quarter, we gave our huge collection of survey and financial data to a firm of econometric statisticians for analysis. The methodology they use is called *causal pathway modeling*—as distinct from regression analysis, which examines data and observes correlations without establishing causation. The experts took our two quarters of data from 800 different stores, compared the results across time and place, and, using statistical techniques like cluster and factor analysis, found linkages and impacts in the data. A month later, they gave us their report, having found some strong and some weak connections, and some connections we had never expected or imagined. We made the appropriate adjustments in our model and went on collecting data for a new iteration at the end of the next quarter.

It was exciting stuff. We could see how employee attitudes drove not just customer service but also employee turnover and the likelihood that

employees would recommend Sears and its merchandise to friends, family, and customers. We discovered that an employee's ability to see the connection between his or her work and the company's strategic objectives was a driver of positive behavior. We learned that asking customers whether Sears is a "fun place to shop" told us more than a long list of more specific questions would. We were also able to establish fairly precise statistical relationships. We began to see exactly how a change in training or business literacy affected revenues.

We also found that two dimensions of employee satisfaction—attitude toward the job and toward the company—had a greater effect on employee loyalty and behavior toward customers than all the other dimensions put together. We still use the 70-question employee survey to gather information about working conditions, satisfaction with pay and benefits, and so forth; but for econometric purposes, a mere 10 of those 70 questions captured the predictive relationship between employee satisfaction and customer satisfaction. Moreover, those 10 questions amounted to a report card on

A Compelling Place to Work

We discovered that responses to these 10 questions on our 70-question employee survey had a higher impact on employee behavior (and, therefore, on customer satisfaction) than the measures we devised initially: *personal growth and development* and *empowered teams.*

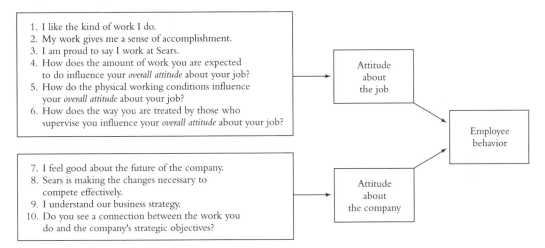

1. I like the kind of work I do.
2. My work gives me a sense of accomplishment.
3. I am proud to say I work at Sears.
4. How does the amount of work you are expected to do influence your *overall attitude* about your job?
5. How do the physical working conditions influence your *overall attitude* about your job?
6. How does the way you are treated by those who supervise you influence your *overall attitude* about your job?

7. I feel good about the future of the company.
8. Sears is making the changes necessary to compete effectively.
9. I understand our business strategy.
10. Do you see a connection between the work you do and the company's strategic objectives?

Attitude about the job

Attitude about the company

Employee behavior

management, which reemphasized the importance of management skills in achieving company goals. (See the exhibit "A Compelling Place to Work.")

Conversely, the statisticians could find no direct causal pathway from two of the measures we had put into our tentative model—*personal growth and development* and *empowered teams* —to any of our customer data. We believe that growth, empowerment, and teamwork matter, but clearly something about the way we measured them was flawed. However important they might be, the measures we had did not lie on a predictive pathway from employee attitudes to customer satisfaction to shareholder value. So in the next version of our employee-customer-profit model, we replaced those initial measures with the 10 questions about the job and the company.

In the 18 months from mid-1994 to the end of 1995, we produced a model, refined it three times, and created a TPI for the company as a whole, but the process of improvement continues. We conduct interviews and collect data continually, assemble

our information quarterly, and recalculate the impacts in our model once a year to stay abreast of the changing economy, changing demographics, and changing competitive circumstances.

The TPI is not a perfect system and never will be, despite our steady improvements. (See the exhibit "The Revised Model: The Employee-Customer-Profit Chain.") It tells us less than we would like to know—and less, probably, than we need to know. The point is that we know vastly more than we once did, that all that information helps us run the company, and that some of it has given us a decided competitive edge. Take the example about the quality of management as a driver of employee attitudes. Our model shows that a 5 point improvement in employee attitudes will drive a 1.3 point improvement in customer satisfaction, which in turn will drive a 0.5 percent improvement in revenue growth. If we knew nothing about a local store except that employee attitudes had improved by 5 points on our survey scale, we could predict with confidence that if

The Revised Model:
The Employee-Customer-Profit Chain

This is the model we use today. The rectangles represent survey information, the ovals, hard data. The measurements in gray are those we collect and distribute in the form of the Sears Total Performance Indicators.

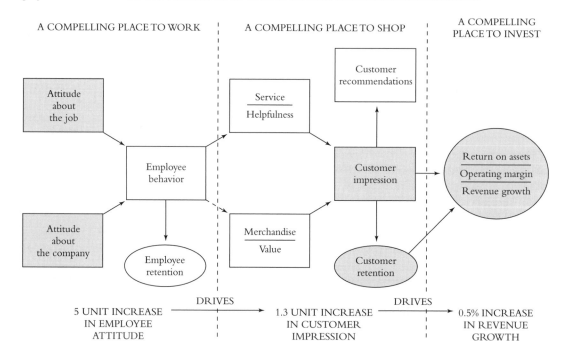

revenue growth in the district as a whole were 5 percent, revenue growth at this particular store would be 5.5 percent. These numbers are as rigorous as any others we work with at Sears. Every year, our accounting firm audits them as closely as it audits our financials.

Deployment

By mid-1995, as we began making the TPI operational, we had invested nearly two years in the transformation of senior management, a group of 100 to 200 people. We now had to build the same kind of ownership and engagement in the entire Sears workforce—a group of 300,000 people—in a much shorter period of time.

As we mentioned earlier, deploying the employee-customer-profit chain and the TPI throughout the company was more than a question of communication. In fact, only a few years earlier, the communication challenge had been the reverse. Before the turnaround, frontline employees sometimes seemed to be the only people in the company who understood that Sears was in trouble with its customers, and somehow they couldn't get the message through to management. Now that the financial turnaround had succeeded, what sales associates needed to be told was not just that the customer mattered but that *they* mattered too—that the company could not survive without their active help and participation. We needed to take our statistical model in all its intellectual purity and bring it down to earth. We needed to change the perceptions and attitudes of our workforce, augment its grasp of how the business worked, and focus every individual's attention on his or her behavior in front of the customer.

To begin with, employees misunderstood what was expected of them, and that was a real barrier to effective change. Consider the experience of a top-level Sears executive who toured stores across the country and asked hundreds of employees, "What do you think is the primary thing you get paid to do here every day?" In more than half the cases, the answer was, "I get paid to protect the assets of the company." For two good reasons, that answer was a serious problem. In the first place, it is not an answer people would give you if you woke them out of a sound sleep at 2:30 in the morning. Someone had taught them that line. In the second place, it is the *wrong* answer. Sears is a retailer, not Fort Knox. The sort of answer we needed to hear was, "I get paid to satisfy the customer." And it needed to come from the heart.

Misunderstanding is also a barrier to trust. The same executive asked people a second question: "How much profit do you suppose Sears keeps on every dollar of revenue that goes through the register?" The median response was 45 cents. The real answer was 2 cents. How could we expect people to react well to a variety of necessary changes if they thought the company was rolling in wealth? We decided to address both misconceptions with a program we called "town hall meetings," which included learning maps, dialogue, and action plans.

Learning maps were not original with Sears—they were developed by a company called Root Learning of Perrysburg, Ohio—but combining them with town hall meetings was our own idea. The combination seemed ideally suited to our needs. Learning maps are easy to use and require no prior training or special skills, yet they draw people into the content, make substantial demands on their analytical reasoning, raise their economic literacy, and increase their understanding of how the company works. Town hall meetings expand that learning and convert it into action.

A learning map is a large picture of a town or a store or, in one instance, a river that leads small groups of participants through a business or historical process. The learning map that [Sears used] was designed to walk people through the changing demographics, economics, and competitive circumstances of the retail trade. [It was entitled "A New Day on Retail Street."] The charts and graphs sprinkled through the picture provide relevant data, and the historical element gives context, but the accompanying questions—for instance, What are the implications for our business and our team?—are meant to stimulate hard thinking about the company's future, not to communicate dogma. Moreover, the maps demonstrate that we trust employees to reach their own sound conclusions.

Every Sears employee from top management on down goes through the learning maps with a group of eight to ten colleagues. Then the group joins other groups for a town hall meeting and action-planning session, which the unit manager opens by saying, more or less, "In light of what you've learned and heard in studying the learning maps, what is one thing we could start doing in this store (service center, warehouse, or office) tomorrow to improve our competitive position? Or what could we stop doing? Or what could we simplify?" The only eligible suggestions are ones that can be implemented at the local level, which automatically excludes anything that company headquarters would have to approve. The goal is to reject as few ideas as possible and to act on the others at once, partly because so many of them are surprisingly good and partly because seeing the company take action on your own suggestion is a very positive experience.

We launched the town-hall-meeting process with the Phoenix Team, which now included 60 district managers, in April 1995. Later, the district managers held town hall meetings for their store managers, who then took charge of cascading the process down to the in-store associates. Every map is rolled out at a town hall meeting in the same manner—from the top of the company on down. The second map, "Voices of Our Customers," came along toward the end of 1995 and dealt with the way consumers see Sears and its principal competitors. Our third map, "The Sears Money Flow," appeared in early 1996 and gave employees a look at where revenues actually go and why it is that even today only about 3 cents of every dollar flows all the way through company operations to emerge on the other side as profit. Quite recently, we rolled out a new map called "Ownership," which leads people through the TPI and helps them see how measurement can enable them to do better and more rewarding work.

Town hall meetings are designed to be part of an ongoing engagement process with employees that goes well beyond learning maps. The goal of learning maps is economic and business literacy— but business literacy in the service of the larger goal of behavioral change. We want managers to change their behavior toward employees, to communicate the company's goals and vision more effectively, and to learn to make better customer-oriented decisions, because we cannot do well financially unless we do well in the eyes of the customer. We want frontline employees to change their behavior toward customers—to become more responsive, take more initiative, and provide better service. (To help them do so, we also give them greater decision-making authority. At Sears hardware stores, for example, sales associates can make refunds and adjustments of up to $25 in value without approval from their supervisors.) The learning maps were only a first step. Full-scale, meaningful, operational deployment of the employee-customer-profit model and the TPI involved three additional initiatives: a concerted effort to alter leadership behavior, changes in our reward and compensation systems, and a new initiative to bring the benefits of the TPI to departments and individual sales associates.

Changing Leadership Behavior. For managers in particular, a grasp of the TPI is indispensable because the TPI is so fundamental to corporate performance—and therefore to management—and therefore to the selection, promotion, and compensation of managers. We have talked a great deal about those 100 to 200 top-level managers because they are the people responsible for strategic implementation, operations, and resource allocation. But there is more to leadership than resource allocation, however strategic and insightful. We need leaders at every level of Sears who take responsibility not only for the company's business performance but also for the culture that keeps the new model alive and working.

In 1995, consequently, we set about creating a leadership model that would incorporate every aspect of the transformation: the employee-customer-profit chain, the TPI, the three C's, and the three P's—plus, of course, operational competence. Our first step in developing the model was to ask the team of 15 executives at the top of the company to list the skills and qualities they looked for in appraising their own direct reports. We pared that list of 35 criteria down to 12, grouped around the three P's. (See the exhibit "Leadership Skills at Sears.") We announced that all of our 19,000 managers would get an annual performance appraisal by their boss and by small groups of their peers and subordinates. These 360-degree reviews, as they're called, rate managers on the 12 criteria. We use the 12 leadership skills as the basis for promotion, we use them in hiring future managers from college campuses, and we use them in training.

On January 1, 1995, we established Sears University, with a central campus in Chicago, seven regional centers around the country, a permanent staff of instructors, and a curriculum of course offerings in every subject we consider essential to the operation of the TPI and the employee-customer-profit model. All courses are also linked to one or more of the 12 leadership skills, which enables managers to identify the programs that will help them meet a specific development need.

Since opening our university, we have trained more than 40,000 Sears managers. We also operate a strategic-retail-management program, which 250 senior executives have attended in groups of about 30 at a time. The program was explicitly designed to create constructive discontent by requiring

Leadership Skills

Every manager at Sears is hired, promoted, and appraised on the basis of these 12 criteria, grouped in relation to the three P's.

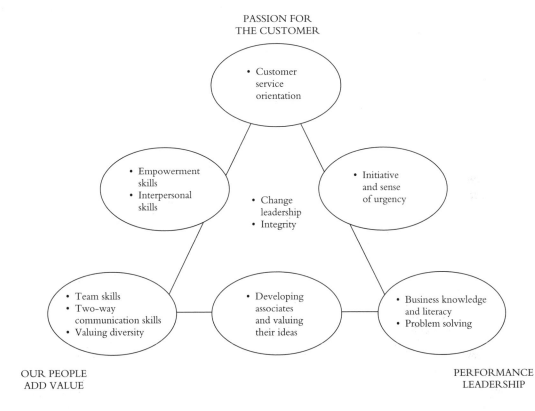

PASSION FOR
THE CUSTOMER

- Customer service orientation

- Empowerment skills
- Interpersonal skills

- Change leadership
- Integrity

- Initiative and sense of urgency

- Team skills
- Two-way communication skills
- Valuing diversity

- Developing associates and valuing their ideas

- Business knowledge and literacy
- Problem solving

OUR PEOPLE
ADD VALUE

PERFORMANCE
LEADERSHIP

executives to do case studies of other retailers that have achieved world-class status on some critical dimension of retailing.

Altering Rewards and Compensation. For the 200 managers at the top of the company, Sears took a truly revolutionary step in 1996 by basing all long-term incentives on the TPI. This means that for the first time in any corporation, as far as we know, long-term executive incentives are based on nonfinancial as well as financial performance—one-third on employee measures, one-third on customer measures, and one-third on traditional investor measures. The board of directors took a leap of faith in agreeing to this plan, which rests on the reliability of the TPI as a leading indicator.

Recognition of the importance of nonfinancial measures has made its way into the annual incentives of nearly all field managers as well. A significant portion of these managers' pay is at risk, based on targeted improvements in customer satisfaction. Moreover, in goal-sharing pilot programs at more than 45 locations, hourly associates are being given the opportunity to earn variable incentive pay that is almost always based on improved customer satisfaction.

Cascading the TPI. Ultimately, if the TPI methodology is to be fully effective, we must make it available at the local unit level. One current step in that direction is a new touch-tone telephone survey that we have now put in place. A random selection of customers receive a coupon worth $5 toward their next purchase if they will call an 800 number and answer 24 questions about their shopping experience. Some of the questions are tied to the performance of the company, store, and department; some relate to the behavior of the sales associate; and all are statistically significant with regard to customer satisfaction and retention. The data are aggregated nationwide, but we are beginning to make them available by district, store, department, and, soon, by individual sales associate as well. (The associate's employee number is on the transaction ticket, and the customer punches it in before punching in answers to the questions.) Our goal is to make it possible for managers and their sales associates to have constructive discussions about individual strengths and weaknesses *as seen by the customer,* and we are currently evaluating various approaches to the use of such information so that we can encourage and empower employees at the same time that we give them insight into how they are perceived.

From Employees to Customers to Profits

In one limited sense, the deployment of the Sears model and measures is virtually complete. We use the TPI at every level of the company, in every store and facility; and nearly every manager has some portion of his or her compensation at risk on the basis of nonfinancial measures. In a broader sense, of course, we still have a long way to go.

Deployment, for example, is an unending effort. Normal turnover rates in the retail industry require continual reorientation of new employees in both the three C's and the economic literacy maps. Even without turnover, communicating with 300,000 employees at thousands of locations is a challenge.

We have been working at this transformation for less than four years, and it seems to us that our track record so far is remarkable. But how much change can a company the size of Sears absorb in so short a time? And does the system work? Are we changing our employees' and our customers' perceptions of Sears?

To answer that question, let's look at some statistics. Independent surveys show that national retail customer satisfaction has fallen for several consecutive years, but in the course of the last 12 months, employee satisfaction on the Sears TPI has risen by 4 percent, and customer satisfaction by almost 4 percent. That may seem a trivial improvement. But if our model is correct—and its predictive record is extremely good—that 4 percent improvement in customer satisfaction translates into more than $200 million in additional revenues in the past 12 months. At our current after-tax margin and price-earnings ratio, those extra revenues increase our market capitalization by nearly one-quarter of a billion dollars. Even more impressive from our point of view is what our model tells us: it is our managers and employees who, at the moment of truth in front of the customer, have achieved this prodigious feat of value creation.

READING 37
CREATING EXCELLENCE OUT OF CRISIS:
ORGANIZATIONAL TRANSFORMATION AT THE *CHICAGO TRIBUNE*

Robert M. Frame
Warren R. Nielsen
Larry E. Pate

Recently, popular research-based books—such as *In Search of Excellence, A Passion for Excellence, Reinventing the Corporation, The 100 Best Companies to Work for in America, Creating Excellence, Change Masters, Thriving on Chaos, The Winning Performance, Megatrends,* and *Leaders*—have documented that increasing numbers of corporations have undergone a transformation in both culture and performance. Many of the values, beliefs, and norms that seemed essential in establishing and building the reputations of successful companies are now being challenged, to the extent that many consider a systematic transformation of those variables necessary for companies to remain viable (Bennis & Nanus, 1985; Hickman & Silva, 1986; Peters & Austin, 1985).

Of course, for years the organization development (OD) literature has discussed change processes for creating healthier lives and healthier, more human work settings (e.g., Beckhard & Harris, 1977; Lippitt, 1982). In the 1980s we have begun to see evidence that the hopes and dreams of many of the "founding fathers" of OD—such as Argyris (1970), Bennis (1969), and Schein (1969)—are becoming realities. Abundant reports indicate that,

despite the slow, evolutionary nature of systemwide transformation (which requires changes in behavior, systems, and structures), movement toward excellence in the work place is not only possible but also measurable (Nora & Stramy, 1986).

This article describes one such organizational transformation effort still in progress at the *Chicago Tribune,* one of the largest and most prominent newspapers in the United States. The event that triggered the *Tribune's* transformation was a 1985 strike involving all five of the production union locals at the newspaper's printing facility in downtown Chicago. We describe below the multiphase transformation effort that took the *Tribune* from crisis to excellence, and some of the results of this effort.[1]

Various conceptual frameworks could readily be applied to aid one's understanding of our research. For example, several organizational (O), change agent (C), and intervention (I) characteristics clearly influenced the results (R) obtained for the *Tribune,* consistent with the OCIR model (Pate, 1979) that postulates that $R = f(O, C, I)$. We speculated, however, that the conceptual framework of the model recently represented by Greiner and Schein (1988) would prove even more useful because *(a)* the transformation effort was intended to move the *Tribune's* system from a traditional bureaucratic model toward a collegial-consensus model and *(b)* the effort prompted a consideration and transformation of the previously existing power dynamics at the *Tribune.*

We thus found it necessary to consider the essential, albeit subtle, difference between the terms *develop* and *transform.* Organization development efforts should be expected to focus more on improvements building on *previous* learning and

Note: The views expressed in this article are those of the authors and do not necessarily represent the positions or policies of the *Chicago Tribune* or any of its subsidiaries. An earlier draft of this article was presented at the meeting of the Western Academy of Management in Big Sky, Montana, in March 1988. The authors are indebted to Dan Spencer and to the three anonymous *JABS* reviewers for their helpful comments.

behavior (i.e., to seek to develop the organization), whereas organizational transformation efforts should be expected to focus more on the desired *future* state the change effort is intended to create (i.e., to seek to transform the organization). We used 10 transformational factors roughly corresponding to the 10 modules of the 20-week training program as a framework for guiding the research discussed in this article.

Stop the Presses: The Walkout at the *Chicago Tribune*

The production printing plant wherein the organizational transformation occurred received its name of the Freedom Center through an employee contest. The largest offset newspaper printing plant in the United States, it produced a daily edition of the *Tribune, USA Today,* a Sunday insert package, a daily insert package, and a national edition of the *Tribune.* The Freedom Center was built in 1981 to house the equipment for state-of-the-art satellite transmissions, computerized type layout, offset printing, plate making, inserting, and packaging. This plant employed about 1,460 persons, of whom 1,250–1,300 worked in production and the remainder in circulation. The center's newsprint warehouse stored as many as 26,000 rolls of newsprint brought in by rail; its computerized prepress operations did not rely on paste-up and other manual operations; and advertising graphics and data were gathered by operations and composed on computer screens. Approximately 60 percent of the newspaper's volume consisted of advertisements.

In addition to contract matters, the primary issues sparking the strike were control over hiring selection and transfers. The key *Tribune* production managers, who had long believed that these issues were crucial to their ability to combine leading-edge technology with advanced, socially responsible management, responded swiftly to the walkout. They sought to fill all vacant positions without rehiring any of the persons on strike. Within days, they brought in a small core of qualified machine operators and press operators, either by transferring

them on temporary assignment from the other *Tribune* operation centers across the country or by hiring them through strategically placed advertisements from other newspapers. For several weeks after the walkout began, management pitched in to help run the presses and the packaging and ancillary equipment to keep the *Tribune* on schedule. During that time, nearly 1,000 new employees—most of them having little or no newspaper experience—had to be screened for hire.

The Freedom Center management, led by a relatively new vice president who had a vision of the production plant's one day being a showcase of technological and managerial leadership, viewed the walkout not as a crisis of survival but as a window of opportunity. In effect, the strike represented a chance to improve the systems of operational and performance management so that they would transcend those characteristic of much of the newspaper industry. Argyris (1974) documents these "restrictive traditions" in describing his own organizational renewal effort for what he calls the *Daily Planet* (which is curiously similar to the *New York Times*). Argyris characterizes the living system of the *Planet* as

> competitive and low in trust, and as operating within win-lose dynamics. Evaluation and control are more important than inquiry and innovation; risky issues and innovations tend not to be discussed; additiveness and coherence in problem-solving activities are low; group discussions are ineffective and group meetings are considered a waste of time; and there is a deep pessimism about changing human nature or increasing the effectiveness of the system. (1974, p. 32)

Argyris's description also fit the *Tribune.* Much of the management group prior to the strike had been promoted on the basis of tenure and politics, rather than managerial skill. Unions exercised significant control over operations. The company had avoided some serious issues, but the executives finally decided that management effectiveness had to be improved so as to change the company's performance. Because the *Tribune* had invested $200 million in the Freedom Center, top management determined that one of the key changes should be making the center become what they had intended it to be: a modern, efficient plant. Thus they initiated modifications in management style, measurement methods, and the level of control workers exercised over the measurement system. The powerful unions that had previously been an integral part of the political environment of the *Tribune* prior to the transformation remained in place afterward, but exerted less influence than before.

The Freedom Center's management team, in response to both the walkout and the hiring of nearly 1,000 new employees needing to learn to operate state-of-the-art production equipment, wished to minimize the pressures and stress accompanying this transitional period. Within nine months of the strike, the management team administered an employee survey, and felt deeply concerned when the results suggested that low morale permeated the main-line production departments. Further analysis diagnosed poor supervision as a primary cause of low morale, which in retrospect seems understandable. The vice president for production observed:

> once we found ourselves in the situation of having hired a thousand new people, we also found ourselves without a lot of people familiar with the way a newspaper operates. One area in particular is the press area, where our pressroom is a fairly complicated area to work in. There are 10 production machines, each of which today would cost $10–15 million. And you have seven or eight people working each one of those presses. It's fairly complicated work. Presses are fairly unforgiving. You either do the job or the press doesn't run. So we found ourselves there with a need for 19 supervisors at the first level . . . supervising groups of 7 people. This in addition to those supervisory jobs filled from outside with experienced people.

Furthermore, the workforce composition had shifted dramatically. The person who was production manager at the time of the walkout noted that supervisors

> went from supervising a group of experienced employees with an average age of 50–55 years to one of

20–25 years old. So . . . in some areas we had managers who stayed only accustomed to a highly structured unionized organization, managing new employees talking about quality circles, progressive communication programs, and career path opportunities.

In short, because the former pressroom supervisors were on strike with their employees and all of the other supervisors had learned to supervise according to the traditional model, the entire workforce was ill prepared to carry out a new vision of leadership concerned with "excellence."

Generating Results-Focused Solutions to the Walkout

At this time, the *Tribune* management recognized the immediate need to initiate training for staff and line personnel, both to standardize procedures for the hundreds of newly hired employees with greatly varying habits, and to clarify the standards and requirements expected within the new Freedom Center organization. Top management solicited proposals from qualified organization development and change consultants for designing and implementing a top-down modular management training program for all levels of management. This request for proposals asked for training addressing 12 basic subjects corresponding to the significant deficiencies identified by the survey analysis. In addition, because the production supervisors in the pressroom units were union members who had walked out along with the strikers, the *Tribune* management simultaneously needed to fill 19 positions for new first-level supervisors.

A consulting group that had done work nationwide was hired to conduct both the management training and the assessment of more than 130 self-nominated candidates for the 19 vacant supervisor positions. Because most of these applicants were new to the firm, no one on the pressroom staff knew them. The consulting group therefore followed an Assessment Center approach (which typically relies on the pooled judgments of others) to screen job candidates. Nearly all of the 130 candidates who underwent the Assessment Center process naturally felt concerned about its fairness, as they did not yet have any reason to trust any system of selection or evaluation other than the more traditional one used throughout the industry (Argyris, 1974).[2]

The Assessment Center method, based on a job analysis that identified skills and abilities required or expected for effectively performing the job of supervisor, included the following basic elements:

- Multisituational measures derived from a series of exercises and simulations, each designed to give the candidate an opportunity to demonstrate her or his ability.

- Multiple assessors, all of them knowledgeable pressroom employees familiar with the job's requirements but not with the candidates they assessed.

- Pooled judgments of the assessors comparing individual candidates' attributes to set performance criteria.

Once the training program and Assessment Center were custom designed and initiated, the top management team met away from the job site with a principal of the consulting firm to engage in an activity known as "future state visioning." For years, the company's top executives had worked off-site on operating plans mostly centered around specific projects. This time, however, the off-site experience focused on developing an entirely new management style for the Operating Department. The vice president for operations later commented that instead of talking about "what we were going to do in 1986," top management discussed "where we wanted to be in 1987, 1988, and 1989." All of this activity took place within a four-month period in the spring and summer of 1986.

One of the authors of this article worked on the transformation effort on a daily basis; one was involved on a few occasions; one took no part in designing or conducting the intervention, but afterward helped examine and interpret the resulting data.

The custom-designed management training program condensed coverage of the 12 subjects (as cited in the request for proposals) into 10 eight-

hour modules, which were addressed one at a time throughout 20 weeks. These modules were:

1. Overview of management.
2. Interpersonal skills.
3. Leadership.
4. Team building and team-oriented leadership.
5. Situational leadership.
6. Problem solving.
7. Time management and delegation.
8. The performance management system.
9. Coaching.
10. Summary and integration.

Based on the feedback and responses of the groups after they began their training, "downstream" modules were modified and refined to meet the participants' primary needs. The traditional management development approach would be to start such efforts with top management and then follow with a top-down "cascade" training sequence (Pate & Nielsen, 1987). In contrast, the consultants asked that members of the top management team undergo training in the basic program principles only *after* their immediate subordinates had covered at least 7 of the 10 modules. The reason for delaying the top group's training was that this would enable the consultants to provide valuable feedback to managers about the organization based on data generated by their subordinates in response to program content—and thus provide a "real-world" organizational context for many of the program's principles and techniques.

Aware of the underlying values associated with the training program's content, the management team spent an additional four days away from the job site—far away, at a *Tribune*-owned setting in the most northeastern area of Ontario, Canada—refining a new vision for the Freedom Center. The core documents initially drafted by the top group included "mission" and "operating belief" statements, which laid out the team's management philosophy and foundation values, and one providing a cornerstone for a new piece entitled "Performance Management System: Key Result Areas" that discussed performance measures for the overall production plant. In addressing basic transformation questions—such as "Who are we?" and "What do we want to become?"—the management team developed a mission statement incorporating commitment to *(a)* providing "printing . . . for Chicago tribune Company and others," *(b)* entering into "a partnership with vendors," and *(c)* becoming "customer driven" in philosophy and orientation. All of these goals represented a marked departure from the *Tribune's* traditional philosophy, direction, and historical definitions for its production plant (e.g., it was not previously "customer driven"). Furthermore, all of these goals are consistent with the focus associated with "excellent" companies (Peters & Austin, 1985; Peters & Waterman, 1982).

The initial drafts of these core organizational transformation documents were refined further by the immediate subordinates of the management team, who also went off-site for several days to do this work. These subordinates refined the mission and philosophy statements and developed Key Result Areas (KRAs) for the 12 major operating production and staff support units of the Freedom Center, which were involved with the following functions:

- Prepress and technical support.
- Newsprint operations.
- Pressroom operations.
- Packaging.
- Plate making.
- Quality/reliability.
- Finance.
- Engineering/maintenance.
- Purchasing/materials management.
- Training.
- Employee communications.
- Administration groups.

Once they had accomplished this transformation work off-site (which included identifying specific KRAs and related performance measures for each one), the consultants began laying the conceptual foundation for a comprehensive process that came to be called the KRA Perfor-

mance Management System, which they introduced during the later modules of the training program. Developed by Edwin Yager (as outlined by Coonradt, 1985), this system employs sports metaphors understandable by nearly anyone who enjoys some form of sports or recreation, and is based on principles identified in response to the question, "Why, in sports and recreation, will people pay for the privilege of working harder than they will work when they are paid?" The answer—clear goals, unchanging rules, effective score keeping, freedom to choose methods, and immediate feedback based on self-administered measurement systems—provides the keys to a comprehensive performance management system applicable in any work place.

Although the terms *key result area* and *measurement* are used to design and conduct OD programs, the *Game of Work* approach actually represents a departure from OD applications of these concepts. The concepts are similar to those of Deming (1982) and Drucker (1986), and focus explicitly on *results,* rather than on tasks, duties, activities, projects, programs, or methods, which the process interventions of an OD program would more likely address (Schein, 1969). This emphasis distinguishes organizational transformation efforts from OD efforts. The concentration on outcomes and results was outlined in the management development segment of the *Tribune's* development effort during classroom training, reinforced through written belief statements of a commitment to using measured performance as the basis for rewards, and applied during the OD segment via natural work group interventions at all levels according to the KRA Performance Management System.

Each natural work group developed additional KRAs associated with the mission statements and identified specific performance indicators (e.g., cost per ton), using what were called "results-to-resources" ratios as measures of each KRA. Team building sessions focused upon obstacles and issues associated with sustaining minimum base-line performance standards, and called for charting measured progress for each team's "field of play" and displaying results consistent with effective charting principles.

The team building activities thus were not oriented toward group process—as would be the case in an OD program—but instead dealt with results and measurement, consistent with the philosophy that "if you cannot measure it, you cannot manage it." Furthermore, consistent with a plantwide KRA of customer satisfaction, when issues and obstacles associated with interdepartmental "interfaces" were identified, intergroup team building sessions were designed according to the measured performance orientation.

As soon as charts reflecting results for both the department and work group levels were developed, the consultants strongly recommended that they be posted, believing that the very act of making them visible would help employees focus their efforts on resolving problems related to production, quality, and cost and making improvements that would be reflected in charted results. This expectation was fulfilled. Employees took an immediate interest in the charts, which typically reflected actual performance on a daily or weekly basis, the base-line minimum performance standard, and a rolling average trend line to discourage overreaction to the peaks and valleys normal for most production performance measurement (see Figures 1, 2, 3, and 4 further below).

Finally, three overall plant KRAs were identified at the off-site meetings:

1. Implementation of the operating beliefs (which were outlined and mailed to each employee in a document labeled PACE, which stood for participation-attitude-communication-environment).

2. Human resource development.

3. Effective capital and expense resource utilization.

After some analyses, the measure for the latter KRA was identified as cost per ton, a measure of "through-put" throughout the entire production process. To our knowledge, no other newspaper publisher has used this particular measure as the key to bottom-line productivity and cost improvement.

The implications of developing an entirely new measuring system are far reaching. The key financial managers supported a review of the previous four years so that a history could be developed, which was a significant contribution. More important, the management team's focus shifted from "budget thinking" to "resources thinking" (i.e., capitalizing on and maximizing resources), with dramatic effects. It was determined that *every dollar spent on cost per ton required five to six dollars of advertising expenditures; thus, a cost savings of a million dollars represented five to six million dollars of savings in advertising revenues.*

Results

Using numbers projected downward to protect confidential company financial data, Figure 1 shows that a goal for annual metric tons of newsprint was established for 1987 for the *Tribune's* Freedom Center. This measure was considered the key economic factor in what was considered an "aggressive" budget for the year, as represented by the "plan" line in the figure and the gap between the "goal" and plan lines. Consistent with the *Game of Work* labels associated with Coonradt's (1985) management process, in this chart and in others throughout the plant, savings above the budgeted goal appear in the area called "paydirt."

Figure 1 reflects savings based on an annual average of 200,000 metric tons of newsprint consumed at $40 per ton ahead of plan through the first four months of the period, representing $8 million in potential "annualized" savings. After applying the *Tribune's* gross profit margin factor, this represents annualized advertising revenue savings of tens of millions of dollars. For three quarters, performance continued at this record level.

Figures 2, 3, and 4 report other results for the first four months of 1987 or for the period after the organizational transformation effort began. Data are based on production records for previous years.

Figure 2 shows data for the budget plan versus actual productivity in the pressroom in terms of thousands of eight-page papers printed. This unit's performance, when extended through the first three quarters of 1987, showed a remarkable 43 percent improvement over the figures for the last quarter of 1986.

FIGURE 1

Cost per ton (cumulative)

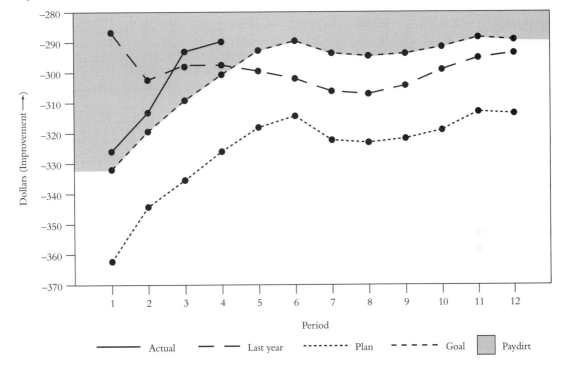

Figure 3 reflects improvement in pressroom reliability performance, according to half-hour production targets met for circulation department delivery schedules. The goal for each paper was 90 percent of scheduled target times, a major achievement. The trend continued well beyond the charted 87 weeks.

Figure 4 reflects improvement in pages-per-hour productivity for the composing unit, which was still operating under the union contract work rules during the first five months of 1987. This unit's productivity increased by almost 25 percent during this period, something never before achieved in the unit's history of more than 100 years.

Incentives

Nearly every experienced trainer, change agent, or manager realizes that rewards and consequences are important elements of any performance management system (Lawler, 1981). Merely installing a performance system does not guarantee that people will follow it. For example, Hope and Pate (1988) suggest that individual compliance and self-motivation are influenced by the extent to which one considers a system consistent with one's own sense of integrity. Furthermore, research on the psychology of compensation and its impact on behavior, performance, and results (e.g., Lawler, 1971, 1981, 1983) has consistently demonstrated that effective performance management depends on people's recognizing the importance of individual differences.

From the beginning of the change effort, the *Tribune's* management realized the importance of these factors. Their plans evolved into a two-pronged strategy. First, a transitional phase was implemented in which the company's ongoing merit pay and performance appraisal process for salaried employees shifted from evaluating personal qualities and behavior toward rewarding contributions to measured results related to the work

FIGURE 2

Labor utilization (productivity in terms of eight-page papers per hour for press)

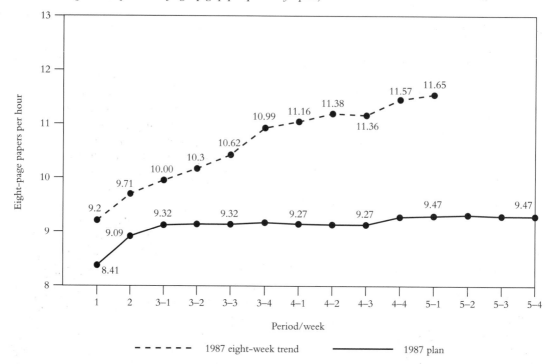

group's key result areas. This transition began at the top with "hours-eligible" managers. Before 1987, each manager was informed that her or his bonus would be tied to KRA performance; this represented an attempt to avoid hoping for one behavior while rewarding another (Kerr, 1975).

Second, middle managers and employees alike were invited to get involved in developing self-funding incentive programs to reward hourly employees and their supervisors for performance. The pressroom group was the first to respond to this invitation. With respect to cost-per-ton as the overall plant measure for effective use of resources, the pressroom management team developed an incentive program whose published purpose was to "elevate the pressroom's level of newsprint yield (reduction of waste) and printing quality to the top of the industry as quickly as possible and to compensate you, the pressroom employees, accord-

ingly." This incentive program recognized that waste reduction and quality control were mutually dependent on one another. Therefore, the team set specific goals for the first three years of the plan for controllable waste, with employees to share in the dollar savings resulting from lowering waste costs. Concurrently, a quality component was devised for determining how to distribute the waste award.

Consistent with the emphasis on internal customer satisfaction, the second department in the production process, packaging, was involved in pulling random copies of newspapers at the start of each production run so that the pressroom management could grade them according to a published quality score sheet. For a given press, a work crew would select a second copy to grade, with these results averaged with those of the pressroom management. This enabled the press crew to work to improve their combined scores. Individual press

FIGURE 3

Daily reliability (Monday through Friday production targets)

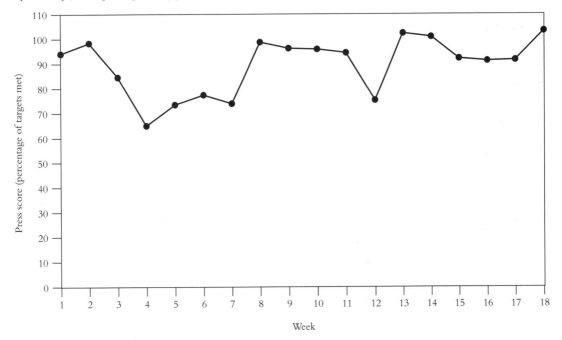

scores were charted and averaged to determine pressroom-wide weekly press quality scores, which were used to make cumulative quarter-to-date averages that were posted in the pressroom and ultimately used to determine the amount of waste savings to which these employees and their supervisors contributed.

At the time we concluded our analysis, the results of these processes had been encouraging and rewarding for all concerned. Although ratios of productivity gains to wage gains are not available, initial awards for hourly employees represented a 10 percent bonus for the two-month launch period. Just prior to the plan's initiation, when productivity and quality "scorecards" were posted for the first press crew, other crews immediately requested their own—even before monetary rewards were announced. The principle underlying this, as taught during the management development segment of the change effort (and shown during

Emery Air Freight's well-publicized experience in obtaining significant performance improvements), is that performance measurement systems indicate to workers what management considers important, and that one can expect performance to increase in response to offering workers appropriate feedback and rewards associated with performance.

As of the completion of our study, the pressroom was continuing to perform well within the "paydirt" parameters for productivity and quality (see Figure 1). If these performance levels persisted—which we have reason to believe they should have—by the year's end the employees would have realized related rewards equivalent to a 15 percent bonus above their base pay. Related contributions to budget plan cost per ton—and hence to the company's bottom line—were significant. Employees in other Freedom Center production departments were completing their own self-funding incentive plans at that time, as expected.

FIGURE 4

Composing productivity (in terms of pages per hour)

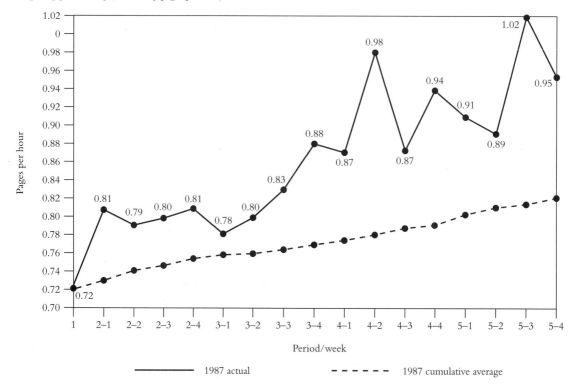

We wish to note that, a week after the first bonus check was cut, quality scores reached 98.5 percent (during some press runs scores of 99.44 percent were obtained). These are significantly better than the industrywide theoretical maximum score of 97 percent, which is based on the assumption that 3 percent waste is normal for a press start-up. Moreover, newsprint utilization scores averaged 90.2 percent.

Discussion

The future of North American organizations continues to be characterized by global competition and a related search for world-class levels of excellence (Peters & Waterman, 1982). Compelling research evidence (e.g., Bennis & Nanus, 1985; Peters & Austin, 1985; Peters & Waterman, 1982) suggests that corporations can increase their odds of competitive success when they develop internal corporate cultures that emphasize human values and human processes and recognize the dignity of individual employees. Such processes promote leadership that provides meaning and inspiration to those expected to be followers, focus on *measuring results* as a means of directing energies and resources toward both products and customers, and demonstrate that motivation for improving bottom-line results can emerge from development at the individual, group, and organizational levels. Several important factors identified in the recent literature on "excellence" include purpose, vision, alignment, leadership, measured results, system structure, personal power, teamwork, customer needs, and the integration of intuition and reason.

Corporate leaders seem increasingly eager to develop more efficient procedures by using the latest available management techniques (Davis, 1988), such as decision support systems. These, however, will not likely mean much to employees who seek inspiration and respond only to that which affects their personal and financial growth. Peters and Waterman (1982) summed this up in their comment that we should not place too much emphasis on markets, because "Markets don't buy products, people do." For example, most rank-and-file employees would not likely be motivated by management's consideration of democratic capitalism versus return on investment, but would understandably be more stimulated by appeals to their self-esteem, spirit, growth, and survival.

To the extent that a vision without a foundation is only a daydream, we management scholars must ensure that our visions of organizations of the future are well grounded in clear, integrated action steps permitting measurable outcomes. A well-conceived, well-grounded vision of what the organization seeks to become, which we found at the *Chicago Tribune,* is the cornerstone of a fast-tracking transformation effort. Such a vision becomes the "master template" through which participants in the transformation process can—individually and collectively—assess and modify their efforts. The vision's goals, combined with a clear performance management system that links rewards with performance, can foster coordination and the will to achieve the desired future for the organization.

The transformation process described in this article and illustrated by the *Tribune's* Freedom Center project is a powerful means of providing such grounding and encouraging its use in other organizations. We wonder, however, about the curious dynamic between crisis and growth. Must crises precede growth—as was the case for the *Tribune*—or can an organization achieve far-reaching, beneficial change without this being externally driven (Greiner, 1972)? Certainly, research is needed to determine how executives and management consultants can encourage dramatic change *without* needing the creative burst of energy generated by dissatisfaction.

Proven OD interventions, such as team building, served the *Tribune* by integrating other segments of the transformation effort as they helped both individuals and work groups work cohesively, systematically, and with a focus on results. This in turn helped align management's internalized philosophy and practices with the pursuit of the vision through performance management.

The *Tribune's* Freedom Center story constitutes both an ending and a beginning. Thousands of organizations like the Freedom Center need transformation, but, unfortunately, most will never initiate this because their top managers lack the necessary vision. Instead, these organizations are more likely to launch numerous projects with fanfare and enthusiasm, only to see them die for lack of comprehensive, integrated change strategies (Lawler, 1983; Walton, 1985). Dedicated, astute management consultants can provide valuable service to the organizations of the future by primarily helping top managers see and follow their visions of what their organizations are capable of becoming.

Creating excellence by fine-tuning a change and development effort can be difficult (Pate & Greiner, 1989). This task becomes even harder when the issue is that of resurrecting a dead change effort. Integrating transformation techniques, even in organizations such as the *Tribune* that have faced crisis as an antecedent condition, can empower firms to turn crises into opportunities. This article demonstrates that the results in terms of performance and savings can be significant.

Certainly, various organizational, change agent, and intervention variables influence the results of an intervention program (Pate, 1979), and we do not intend to overstate the importance of the consultant or to self-aggrandize the role consultants play. In the case of the *Chicago Tribune,* such factors as the union situation, the status of the 1,000 replacement workers, the elimination of restrictive work practices and featherbedding, changes in equipment and process technology, and new manufacturing structures influenced the results we report. Obviously, changes occurred in the workforce management policies, but we do not know the extent to which the organization altered its production and inventory control systems, cost and other information systems, make/buy decision-making processes, and facilities (i.e., the number, size, location, or capacity). Our point is that we can readily indicate the more significant changes and cost savings that the *Tribune* experienced, but some ambiguity exists as to causality. The paradox is that although much research must be done on the dynamics of the transformation process so as to determine causality or to generalize our findings to other settings, the consultant as artist is the one who will interpret these results as a statement of possibilities, and who will weave the threads within them to create additional tapestries of excellence.

Endnotes

1. The *Chicago Tribune* is sensitive, as one might understand, about disclosing important financial information. Thus we had to "generalize downward" some of the cost savings reported beyond merely changing the vertical scale numbers. The savings following the change effort were actually *greater* than indicated in the figures in this article. Moreover, as of this writing, arbitration efforts with the unions are still taking place, preventing us from further elaborating on the details of the strike.

2. About 140–150 candidates initially applied for the supervisor positions, and more than 90 percent of these persons participated throughout the assessment process. When they submitted their applications, candidates were told that the assessment process would be taken quite seriously, that selections would not be based on political considerations, and that the process would necessarily require considerable time and effort. Approximately 12 candidates (fewer than 10 percent) chose to withdraw their applications from consideration, and thus were not included in subsequent assessments.

References

Argyris, C. *Intervention Theory and Method: A Behavioral Science View.* Reading, MA: Addison-Wesley, 1970.

Argyris, C. *Behind the Front Page: Organizational Self-Renewal in a Metropolitan Newspaper.* San Francisco: Jossey-Bass, 1974.

Beckhard, R., & Harris, R. T. *Organizational Transitions: Managing Complex Change.* Reading, MA: Addison-Wesley, 1977.

Bennis, W. G. *Organization Development: Its Nature, Origins and Prospects.* Reading, MA: Addison-Wesley, 1969.

Bennis, W. G., & Nanus, B. *Leaders.* New York: Harper & Row, 1985.

Coonradt, C. A. *The Game of Work.* Salt Lake City: Shadow Mountain Press, 1985.

Davis, M. W. *Applied Decision Support.* Englewood Cliffs, NJ: Prentice Hall, 1988.

Deming, W. E. *Quality, Productivity and Competitive Position.* Boston: MIT Center for Engineering Studies, 1982.

Drucker, P. F. *The New Frontiers of Management.* New York: E. P. Dutton, 1986.

Greiner, L. E. "Evolution and Revolution as Organizations Grow." *Harvard Business Review,* July–August 1972, pp. 37–46.

Greiner, L. E., & Schein, V. E. *Power and Organization development.* Reading, MA: Addison-Wesley, 1988.

Hickman, C. R., & Silva, M. A. *Creating Excellence: Managing Corporate Culture, Strategy and Change in the New Age.* London: Unwin, 1986.

Hope, J. W., & Pate, L. E. "A Cognitive-Expectancy Analysis of Compliance Decisions." *Human Relations* 41 (1988), pp. 739–51.

Kerr, S. (1975). "On the Folly of Rewarding A, While Hoping for B." *Academy of Management Journal,* 18 (1975), pp. 769–83.

Lawler, E. E. *Pay and Organizational Effectiveness: A Psychological View.* New York: McGraw-Hill, 1971.

Lawler, E. E. *Pay and Organizational Development.* Reading, MA: Addison-Wesley, 1981.

Lawler, E. E. "Human Resource Productivity in the 80's." *New Management* (1983), pp. 46–49.

Lippitt, G. L. *Organization Renewal: A Holistic Approach to Organization Development* 2nd ed. Englewood Cliffs, NJ: Prentice Hall, 1982.

Nora, J. J., & Stramy, R. J. *Transforming the Workplace.* Princeton Research Press, 1986.

Pate, L. E. (1979). Development of the OCIR Model of the intervention process. *Academy of Management Review,* 4 (1979), pp. 281–86.

Pate, L. E., & Greiner, L. E. (1989). "Invited Commentary: Resolving Dilemmas in Power and OD with the Four ACES Technique." *Consultation: An International Journal,* 8, no. 1 (1989), pp. 58–67.

Pate, L. E., & Nielsen, W. R. (1987). "Integrating Management Development into a Large-Scale System-wide

Change Programme." *Journal of Management Development,* 6, no. 5 (1987), pp. 16–30.

Peters, T., & Austin, N. *A Passion for Excellence: The Leadership Difference.* New York: Random House, 1985.

Peters, T., & Waterman, R. H. *In Search of Excellence: Lessons from America's Best-run Companies.* New York: Harper & Row, 1982.

Schein, E. H. *Process Consultation: Its Role in Organization Development.* Reading, MA: Addison-Wesley, 1969.

Walton, R. E. "From Control to Commitment in the Workplace." *Harvard Business Review,* March–April 1985, pp. 76–84.

READING 38
ORGANIZATION DEVELOPMENT IN THE ENTREPRENEURIAL FIRM

W. Gibb Dyer, Jr.

Organization development (OD), a field that applies behavioral science knowledge to the problems facing organizations, has been created and shaped by theorists and practitioners whose work has been grounded in large institutions. For example, much of Kurt Lewin's pioneering work at the Massachusetts Institute of Technology (MIT) was based on his efforts to train leaders of various community organizations. Other notables in the field such as Douglas McGregor, Herbert Shepard and Robert Blake, and Richard Beckhard developed their ideas while consulting with Union Carbide, Esso Standard Oil (later Exxon), and General Mills, respectively. And even today, when writers cite companies that practice OD, names such as TRW, Honeywell, General Electric, and other large organizations are frequently mentioned (Cummings & Worley, 1993). Indeed, most of the theories and methods used by OD practitioners are based on the experience of large corporations (Cummings & Worley, 1993; French, Bell, & Zawacki, 1994; Glassman & Cummings, 1991).

In the past decade, however, we have witnessed the rise of the entrepreneurial firm. In the United States there are about 21 million businesses. Of those businesses, only 80,000 employ 100 or more people (Birch, 1987; Dennis, 1993). Small businesses grew faster than the historical trend during the past two decades, and entrepreneurial firms have created more net new jobs during this period than have large corporations (Birch, 1987; Kirchoff & Greene, 1995). In fact, large corporations (more

This article was originally presented as a paper at the Academy of Management Meetings, Vancouver, British Columbia, August 9, 1995.

Source: W. Gibb Dyer, Jr., "Organization Development in the Entrepreneurial Firm" in *Journal of Applied Behavioral Science* (vol. 33, no. 2) pp. 190–208. Copyright © by NTL Institute of Applied Behavioral Science. Reprinted by permission of Sage Publications, Inc.

than 500 employees) have had a net loss of jobs in recent years, ascribable to corporate restructuring and downsizing. The Bureau of Labor Statistics also notes that small business will be the predominant organizational form in those industries projected to grow during the next 10 years (Dennis, 1993).

Given this dramatic change in the structure of American industry, along with similar trends in other parts of the world, we must wonder how well the traditional theories and methods in the field of OD fit these "new" organizations: Do present diagnostic models capture the essence of an entrepreneurial firm? Can interventions such as team building be applied similarly in both large corporations and in entrepreneurial firms? Are change processes similar in large corporations and small, entrepreneurial firms? The purpose of this article is to explore these issues by presenting a diagnostic model and framework for managing change in entrepreneurial organizations. Such a framework comes from others' research and practice as well as my own experience attempting to introduce change into these kinds of organizations.

Theory and Conceptual Framework

The Nature of "Large" Versus "Small" Systems. Before outlining a framework for diagnosing and intervening in entrepreneurial firms, we first need to briefly explore how these new, relatively small, entrepreneurial ventures differ from larger systems that are typically the targets of OD activities. Over the years, numerous scholars have noted how organizational dynamics change and evolve as organizations grow and mature (e.g., Adizes, 1979; Greiner, 1972; Schein, 1985). Indeed, even some of the early OD practitioners recognized some of the differences between large and small systems and defined their practice as "large system change" (Beckhard, 1975; Miller & Rice, 1967). I have summarized the characteristics of large systems and smaller, entrepreneurial organizations in Table 1. Although there may be exceptions, these dimensions reflect the significant differences between the two.

Large systems typically have a history that provides a backdrop for the norms, values, and behaviors of organizational members. Well-developed routines and traditions serve as guides for present behavior as well as orient the organization toward the future. In contrast, new ventures have little in the way of ingrained traditions and routines. In the early stages of an entrepreneurial firm's development, the creation of traditions plays a significant role in organizational dynamics. Moreover, although entrepreneurial firms may have more "freedom" given that they are not bound by tradition, the lack of timeworn routines can also prove to cause inefficiency and a poor use of resources as members of the organization try to develop routines that "work" and are effective.

The leadership dimension also presents numerous differences between these types of firms. Previous work by Schein (1983), Kets de Vries (1977), and others has already outlined how entrepreneurs and founders differ from managers in the way they lead others. Such work suggests that managers lead by using a variety of analytic tools, are conservative in their orientation, and tend to follow the tenets of "professional management." Entrepreneurs, on the other hand, tend to be impulsive, highly emotional, and have high needs for control. They tend to be "visionaries" who have the ability to create excitement and commitment among their followers. Such differences in leadership styles have a tremendous impact on the behaviors and cultures of each type of organization (Kets de Vries, 1977).

Large organizations, by their very nature, generally need more formal systems to coordinate their activities. Because problem solving and coordination generally cannot be done through frequent face-to-face contact as is the case in smaller

TABLE 1

The differences between "large" and "small" systems

Dimension	Large Systems	Small Systems
History	Relatively long history as compared with small entrepreneurial systems; have developed traditions, routines, and so on.	Short history; lack traditions, routines, and so on.
Leadership systems	Led by those with a managerial orientation. Typically have developed formal information, reward, human resource systems, and so on.	Led by entrepreneurs and founders. Informal or no systems.
Structure	Hierarchical and bureaucratic.	Flat, informal, and particularistic.
Ownership	Often dispersed through public ownership, C-corporation. Stock price is important.	Closely held, private, family owned; typically proprietorship, partnership, LLC,* or subchapter S. Stock price not as important as earnings.
Governance	Well-defined board of directors. "Outside" directors often play a role.	Based on founder's decisions. Rarely is there a functioning board.
Family	Little if any involvement by leader's/manager's families.	Family of founders/leaders often work in the business.

*LLC = limited liability company.

systems, large organizations require formal policies and procedures, information systems, and other formal systems to regulate behavior. New organizations generally function by following informal rules of thumb and tend to avoid the creation of formal systems until absolutely necessary. In my own studies of entrepreneurial firms, I have found that founders and employees in these firms preferred informal ways of doing work because they disdained the bureaucratic procedures they had encountered in large organizations (Dyer, 1992).

The structure of large systems also tends to be more hierarchical and bureaucratic than that of smaller, entrepreneurial firms. Much like Weber's bureaucratic model, employees in large systems tend to be evaluated on the basis of merit, rise through a series of relatively well-defined hierarchical positions, and are oriented to a particular career path. An organization chart helps provide the framework outlining hierarchical movement as well as career paths. Entrepreneurial organizations have what is known as a "wheel" or "spider web" structure, with the founder at the hub or center controlling all of the activities of the organization (Dyer, 1992). Evaluation of employees' performance is informal and based on the expectations of the founder. Employees often are required to do several different tasks—they must be generalists rather than specialists—and therefore a clear, formal career path is not possible when an organization is newly founded.

Large systems are frequently public corporations (C-corporations) where the stock is widely held. Shareholders are concerned about the stock price and make a concerted effort to influence the management team to make quarterly goals to maintain or increase the price of their shares. Entrepreneurial organizations are generally proprietorships, partnerships, limited liability companies (LLCs), or subchapter S corporations where the stock is privately held. The reason for using such forms has to do with questions of liability and the fact that the owners avoid the double income taxation of the C-corporations because they are only taxed at their individual tax rate. The number of share-

holders is typically quite small with these forms of organizations, and the stock price is not as critical as earnings because the stock is not publicly traded.

These two types of organizations are also governed quite differently. Large organizations generally have a well-defined board of directors, frequently composed of company outsiders. The board meets regularly and provides overall direction and sets policy for the firm. In entrepreneurial firms, the founder makes all the key decisions and thus a board is viewed as either unnecessary or redundant (Ward, 1991). Founders find outside review of their decisions anathema and therefore avoid using a board that would provide such review and oversight.

Large organizations often have strict policies against nepotism, and with few exceptions (e.g., Ford, IBM) family relations play little role in the firm. In contrast, often family members are the only ones who are willing to work for the new venture and therefore become an important source of labor. However, hiring family members makes relationships complex given that the entrepreneur may not know how to treat family members: Should they be treated like all other employees or like family (Dyer, 1986)? This potentially creates conflicts and dilemmas in managing the firm's human resources that are not found in large organizations.

Having discussed some of the more prominent differences between large and small systems, the reader, it is hoped, will be able to recognize that these organizations do indeed function quite differently and have different dynamics. Given this backdrop, we can now begin to develop a framework that will help to more effectively diagnose the problems and dynamics of entrepreneurial organizations.

A Diagnostic Framework for Entrepreneurial Firms. Traditional diagnostic models such as those developed by Cummings and Worley (1993), Weisbord (1978), Hanna (1988), Peters and Waterman (1982), Nadler and Tushman (1977), and Kotter (1978) focus exclusively on work systems in the context of the managerial hierarchy, describing various organizational systems (e.g., information, structure, reward) and processes (e.g., communications, decision making, leadership). Moreover, most of these systems and processes are assumed to be well developed and routinized, reflecting the dynamics of larger corporations.

However, these diagnostic models are found wanting when it comes to diagnosing the dynamics of entrepreneurial firms. The behavior of entrepreneurial firms is not only a function of firm dynamics but should also be seen in light of the firm's governance structure and also in light of the dynamics of the founder's family (Lansberg, 1983). Indeed, these three interdependent systems: (*a*) business, (*b*) governance, and (*c*) family, and their relationship to one another, must be part of any diagnostic framework for entrepreneurial firms. Even open-systems diagnostic frameworks often do not reflect the dynamics of governance or of family systems because OD practitioners generally assume that a governance structure such as a board of directors is not accessible as a system in which to initiate change, and family dynamics are often assumed to be "nonrational" and therefore should not be a subject of serious consideration or should be merely eliminated (Dyer, 1994). However, those who have attempted to initiate change in entrepreneurial firms have described the importance of understanding these three systems and their interrelationships (Hollander & Elman, 1988: Lansberg, 1983). The diagnostic model presented in Figure 1 presents the basic elements of each of these systems.

The model in Figure 1 presents a skeletal framework outlining a few of the structures and processes that are a part of each of the three systems. In the business system, for example, strategy, structure, technology, and culture are key factors that drive behavior. Reward and information systems, along with communications and decision-making processes, are also key to understanding firm behavior. A diagnosis of the governance system begins with an understanding of what kind of formal structure is in place. Typical forms include the following: (*a*) a proprietorship, (*b*) a partnership, (*c*) an S-corporation, (*d*) a C-corporation, (*e*) a limited-

FIGURE 1

Systems of an entrepreneurial firm

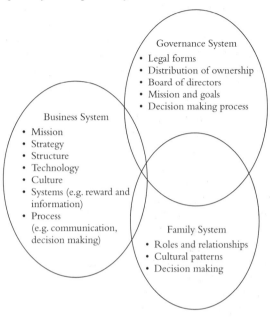

liability company, or (*f*) a trust. Each form has somewhat different issues and dynamics because the distribution of ownership and responsibility for decision making vary depending on the type of governance structure. For any governance system, it is also important to understand who makes what decisions. For example, if a board of directors is established, there are a number of issues related to board composition and decision making that need to be understood (Ward, 1991). In terms of the family system, it is important to understand the culture of the family; the nature of family relationships and decision making; as well as the family's relationship to, and assumptions about, the business and the governance systems (Dyer, 1986). Those consulting with entrepreneurial firms may find the values underlying these systems in conflict. For example, a family exists to develop and support family members, whereas a business exists to generate profits and operate efficiently. Family members are rewarded for who they are, whereas businesses conditionally reward employees on the basis of their performance. Such conflicting value systems often create significant tensions as they clash in an entrepreneurial firm.

Although some entrepreneurs may insist that their family plays no role in the firm, I find that it is important for any diagnosis to examine current and possible future family involvement in the business. For example, in most cases, were the founder to die, his or her ownership in the business would be passed to his or her family. With such an event, the family is thrust into a critical role regarding the business. Thus the family needs to be prepared for such a contingency. Also, as the founder's family grows and evolves, family members may begin to play a significant role in the ownership or management of the business even if they had no role in the founding of the business. Thus family dynamics (or the potential for family dynamics) should be explored in all diagnoses of entrepreneurial organizations regardless of whether or not they are currently defined as "family firms."

Organizational Patterns in Entrepreneurial Firms.   As we examine the systems in entrepreneurial firms, there appear to be common patterns that are largely a function of the founder's personality, experience, and skills. Kets de Vries (1977) and Dyer (1986) have noted that because founders often distrust others, the systems that they create are based on an authoritarian model. For example, in a previous study, I discovered that most entrepreneurial firms I studied had the following systems patterns (Dyer, 1986).

1. The business was paternalistic in nature. The founder "took care" of employees in return for their loyalty. The founder also made all key decisions, supervised employees closely, and carefully controlled all information disseminated to employees.

2. The business was governed by either a "paper" or "rubber stamp" board. These boards existed only on paper or to ratify decisions that the founder had already made. These boards reflected the disdain that the founders had for outside review.

3. The family was patriarchal (matriarchal) in nature. The founder also exhibited an authoritarian presence in the family. Children were taught not to question the founder and were generally left in a dependent relationship.

This particular configuration of these three systems had significant implications for the functioning of these entrepreneurial firms. Innovation and creativity in the firm were often stifled. Little employee development took place. Employees were in the dark regarding company goals and objectives. Little information was shared regarding employee performance. Without the oversight of a board, founders made decisions in a vacuum. Furthermore, their families were of little help because they were also kept in the dark regarding the firm's operations and had to rely almost totally on the founders for direction. Under these conditions, strategic planning, succession planning, or any sort of change planning was either not done or done quite poorly.

Other, less common patterns reflect more professional orientations to running an enterprise. The board may actively advise the founder. Decisions may be based more on formal systems rather than the personality of the founder. The family may not play a role in the firm if the founder decides that merit should be the only criterion used in making employment decisions. Such a pattern has different consequences for the founder and the business. Thus the role of the OD consultant working with an entrepreneurial firm is not only to discover the nature of each system but to see the holistic pattern: to understand the relationships between systems and recognize that the patterns in these systems lead to certain outcomes.

Criteria of Effectiveness in Entrepreneurial Firms.   For OD consultants to function effectively, they must have the ability to work with a client to ascertain the criteria to be used to evaluate the system under scrutiny and to develop normative models to determine what the system should look like in the future. With any organization, developing criteria to determine effectiveness is a difficult issue, but it is a particularly thorny problem in entrepreneurial firms. Common criteria for business success might include such things as stock price, profits, or market share, but these criteria may need to be weighed against such things as family harmony and solidarity, providing employment for family members, and family wealth. Moreover, the needs of family and non-family shareholders may also need to be considered. How to increase shareholder wealth when there is no market for the company's stock is often a difficult question to answer.

Each system tends to have different criteria that determine effectiveness, and unfortunately in many cases they are in conflict. For example, should a founder employ an incompetent family member if this enhances family relationships at the expense of the firm's performance? Unless OD consultants are able to see the "big picture" and work through these issues related to the effectiveness question, they may end up using criteria that meet their own expectations and therefore not serve their clients well.

With these ideas in mind, I will now describe how the framework presented in Figure 1 can be used to diagnose the problems afflicting entrepreneurial firms at various developmental stages.

Methodology for Diagnosis

The "clinical approach" I use for gathering data to diagnose an entrepreneurial firm relies on work done by Berg and Smith (1985), Schein (1987), and McCollom (1990). This approach to data gathering is a process of generating and testing hypotheses through working with members of the organization being studied and by using their categories and systems of meaning to interpret the data. Moreover, with the clinical approach, the consultant becomes the research instrument and therefore should be aware of, and take into account, his or her reactions, feelings, biases, and emotions while gathering the data. Schein notes that the consultant should focus initially on the presenting problem of the client and then organize an inside-outside team to gather and analyze data. In the context of an entrepreneurial firm, such a team is generally composed of the founder(s), the consultant(s), and several key employees, board members, and family members. The process involves gathering data and having the insiders articulate the meaning of the data from their perspective and the outside consultants looking for "surprises" and interpreting the data with their knowledge of behavioral science. On the basis of their analysis, the team develops various hypotheses to be tested and a theory of firm behavior.

I have found the following to be key sources of data:

1. The firm's founders (whether currently working at the firm or not).
2. Family members of the founders or other employees with equity ownership.
3. Key managers—particularly those who joined the firm during the founding period.
4. A cross section of employees from different functions and levels.
5. Company records: articles of incorporation, partnership agreements, histories, organization charts, policy manuals, sales, productivity, or other records.
6. The layout and design of the offices/plant.
7. Regular activities and meetings.
8. The organization's customers and suppliers.

Through interviewing, observation and a review of archival records, the inside-outside team attempts to gather data from these sources. The key to an effective diagnosis, in my opinion, is to initially cast a broad net—gather data from all sources available. What might initially seem irrelevant or unimportant may prove crucial at a later stage of the diagnosis. In my own experience, lengthy interviews (2–4 hours) with the founders tend to provide the best initial source of data. There are often little archival data to analyze and, depending on the organization, little to observe. Thus "getting inside the heads" of the founders is my preferred starting point. The kinds of questions that might be asked in such interviews are described in detail in Dyer (1986, pp. 138–141).

Diagnosis across the Entrepreneurial Life Cycle: Three Case Studies

To illustrate how I have used the diagnostic framework and methods previously outlined, I will describe three entrepreneurial firms and my attempts to help them. I have found that the issues facing entrepreneurial firms are quite different depending on their stage of development. Thus the three firms that I will use for illustrative purposes will be a start-up company, a growth company, and an entrepreneurial firm making a transition from the founder to the next generation of leadership.

The Dilemmas of Start-Ups: The Phillips Company. Entrepreneurial start-ups face a number of problems unique to founding an enterprise. The governance structure needs to be defined and its role delineated. New firms may fail because of the inability of founding partners or board members to develop effective working relationships (Ward, 1991). Because start-ups have a "liability of newness" without established resource networks, only half of these firms survive five years (Dyer, 1992). Moreover, an efficient work system has to be created for the firm to function. Cummings and Worley (1993) suggest that in such "underorganized systems," defining work roles, decision-making processes, authority, and communications patterns is key to organizational effectiveness, and the role of the OD specialist is to help management define these roles. Entrepreneurs often rely on family members to fill positions in their start-up companies because finding personnel is a serious problem. This creates the problem of "institutional overlap" because the norms of doing business that emphasize profitability and efficiency are often in conflict with familial norms of love and support (Lansberg, 1983).

The case of the Phillips company (all names disguised) illustrates how these issues are brought to bear in the founding of a business. The Phillips family had made initial plans to start a small software business. The father, Fred Phillips, a Ph.D. in electrical engineering, had made a decision to leave a firm that he had helped found and start a new enterprise with his sons and son-in-law. However,

as they began to have meetings to launch this new enterprise, conflicts began to emerge in the family. It was at this point that I was asked by one of the sons to intervene to help the family work through these conflicts. Initially, I interviewed the founder, his four sons, his son-in-law, and their spouses. Because my client was strictly the Phillips family, I decided to gather the data myself rather than create a team. Gathering data in this manner would allow family members to be more candid in giving information without another family member present. Upon analyzing these interviews, several business, governance, and family issues emerged.

Business Issues

1. The new business was not going to be capitalized sufficiently for it to succeed. Thus the founder needed to seek additional sources of capital.

2. Fred Phillips' son-in-law had some technical expertise and one son had an MBA degree and some managerial experience, but the other three had little expertise related to software development. It was unclear how they would contribute to the firm.

3. A business plan had not been clearly formulated that examined all of the marketing and production problems that the new firm would face.

Governance Issues

1. Although the family had decided that the new company would be a subchapter S corporation, the composition of the governing board was unclear. Two of the sons wanted all family members participating in the business to be on the board, the father assumed that the board would follow his lead and not play an active role, whereas the son with the MBA degree was encouraging the family to include some nonfamily board members.

Family Issues

1. The father wanted the business to be a "family business" that would help strengthen family relationships. However,

the spouse of one of the sons felt that such an arrangement would "smother" her independence. She wanted to have a life independent of her in–laws and was concerned that if her husband worked in the business with his family, her own family would become a mere extension of her husband's family as well as the business.

2. The son with the MBA degree, who it was assumed would be the general manager, wanted to be compensated on the basis of his position and expertise. This would mean that he and his father would be the highest paid employees in the company. The other brothers and the son-in-law, however, wanted all family members to receive the same salary. All family members are equal, they reasoned, thus salaries should be equal as well.

After gathering these data, I met with all family members and their spouses to present these issues and to discuss ways to resolve them. Given that the issues affected the entire family, I brought the entire family together initially to provide the feedback. In presenting the data to a client, I prefer to start with the less emotionally charged issues first (usually business issues) to allow the client some success in working through a problem and to set some norms for problem solving. In this case, the business issues were relatively easy to manage: The father was able to identify other sources of capital, an organization chart was developed and roles defined, and the son with the MBA degree was able to articulate a clear business plan. However, the family was not able to resolve the family and board issues. Some were adamant that all family members should be on the board, whereas others felt that the board should only include those with experience and outside board members should be considered. The compensation issue caused heated debate, because compensation not only affected their standard of living but was a reflection of one's self-worth and standing in the family. My role in the discussion was to help the family clarify the issues, to understand the options available to them, and to understand the potential

consequences of their actions. As a result of these discussions, the son with the MBA degree decided not to participate in the business and took a job with a large high-technology firm.

Even though Fred Phillips recognized that it would be quite risky to start the business without the assistance of his son with the MBA degree, he decided to start the new venture anyway. Almost immediately the new firm ran into difficulty with product development and manufacturing. Without quality products to ship to customers, the company experienced increasing cash flow problems. As a result, one of Fred's sons and his son-in-law left the business. In a consulting role, the son with the MBA degree has recently attempted to help Fred develop a plan to make the company profitable, but it is teetering on the brink of bankruptcy.

Managing a Growth Company: The Bills Company.   As an entrepreneurial firm expands and grows, a different set of issues and dilemmas emerges for the entrepreneur to grapple with. As the firm grows more complex, the governance structure often must change to include a functioning board that oversees company strategy, capital requirements, and management practices. Few start-up entrepreneurial firms have functioning boards, and those that do often find them relatively ineffective (Schwartz & Barnes, 1991; Ward, 1991; Ward & Handy, 1988). Most entrepreneurial firms are highly centralized, authoritarian systems that are not conducive to growth (Kets de Vries, 1977; Schein, 1983). Hence other forms of control via budgets, information systems, delegation, and shared values may need to be developed (Dyer, 1992). Professional management may enter the entrepreneurial firm as it grows, creating a clash of values and operating system (Dyer, 1989; Schein, 1983). Finally, family members and other employees may become incompetent as the firm develops and higher skills are required. Thus the entrepreneur must make decisions regarding the entry and development of family members who may wish to be involved in the business.

The case of the Bills Company (all names disguised) illustrates many of the problems that afflict the typical entrepreneurial growth company. My involvement with the Bills Company began when I was invited by the director of human resources to help them deal with several problems related to their human resource practices. The Bills Company, a retail organization, had grown rapidly since its inception. The company had been doubling or tripling its size each year, both in terms of revenue and number of employees. This posed some significant problems for the president of the firm, John Larson, and his cofounders. The following is a list of issues that emerged after I interviewed the key founders and a sample of company employees and examined various historical documents. I should note that the interviews were generally conducted with a representative from human resources as part of an inside/outside team effort.

Business Issues

1. Because the firm was hiring so many employees to handle its growth, little thought had been given to the selection and training of these employees (employees joked that all someone needed was a pulse to be hired). Thus many new employees were mismatched with their jobs and, as the firm grew, were unable to perform effectively. For example, no one in the human resource department (about 20 employees) had any formal training in human resources. Although these employees did the best they could under the circumstances, the level of performance needed to improve significantly in human resources in order to support company growth.

2. The company's growth had exceeded the founders' wildest expectations. However, in a volatile industry, they knew that competitors would start encroaching on their markets. Thus company strategy, which had been highly successful, needed to be refined to meet these new competitive conditions. Moreover, the strategy needed to be communicated effectively to employees who often complained that they were in the dark regarding the future direction of the company.

3. As the company expanded into foreign markets, issues related to organizational structure and control began to emerge. The question they were asking was, How much control should be given to the foreign subsidiaries and how much should be left to company headquarters? Moreover, the company now needed managers who had a global perspective, and preparing managers for overseas assignments and keeping expatriates motivated and productive were key issues.

Governance Issues

1. The board of directors, composed of the original founders, met irregularly to discuss company issues. Larson found the board meetings generally to be unproductive and therefore he believed the fewer meetings the better.

2. The firm had no clear succession plan in the event of the death of any of the key founders, particularly Larson. It was also unclear how a stock buyback would be financed in the event of the death of one of the founders—particularly those with large numbers of shares. Thus future control of the firm was uncertain.

Family Issues

1. The Larson family had several family members working in the business in significant positions, whereas other founders had family members as employees to a lesser extent. As the firm grew, most of these family members were reassigned to positions that fit their capabilities, and professional managers were hired to take their places. This "changing of the guard" created some confusion on the part of employees as expectations and demands changed with new management.

2. Larson and the other founders have several children. Although currently young, some of the founders seem to want their children to have opportunities to participate in the business. Thus requirements for the entry and evaluation of family members needed to be developed in the future.

In my role as a consultant, I have spent most of my time helping the firm work on the business issues. Some of the activities that have taken place include the following:

- Developing a strategic plan for continued growth.
- Restructuring several departments and reevaluating their mission.
- Developing management training programs.
- Team building in departments to clarify roles and expectations.
- Clarifying roles between family and nonfamily employees.

Future OD activities will need to focus on helping the company improve the functioning of its board, clarifying its succession plan, and developing a plan to involve future generations of family members in the business.

Exiting the Entrepreneurial Firm: The Williams Company. All entrepreneurs will eventually be replaced as leaders of their organizations through death or retirement. Succession brings a whole new set of dynamics and issues for business, governance, and the family. It is at this stage of the entrepreneurial firm's evolution that the training and development of future leadership become a significant issue; however, "letting go" on the part of the founder often proves to be a most difficult problem to resolve (Dyer, 1986; Lansberg, 1988). As the firm matures, bureaucracy and other related problems of organizational rigidity may inhibit growth and innovation. Thus new leadership and paradigms for management may be needed to transform the firm into a more competitive enterprise. During

succession, the question of governance can become even more problematic because the founder(s) and other key shareholders and board members may be asked to play different roles. Estate planning also becomes a key issue as the entrepreneur attempts to transfer assets and ownership to the next generation of family members.

Several years ago, I was asked by Steve Williams, son of Peter Williams, founder of the Williams Company, to help them manage the success process (all names disguised). Unfortunately, the family had not done any planning regarding succession. The firm had grown rapidly in recent years, growing from 1 small store in the 1960s to 15 stores in the 1990s. The company was known as a "high-end" company, one with quality products that commanded premium prices. Peter Williams's four sons, Alan, Steve, Lee, and Matt, all worked in the business; however, only Steve, who had recently obtained an MBA degree, had expressed much interest and aptitude in taking over for his father. One sister, Jean, had worked in the business briefly but was now staying at home raising her four children. As I interviewed all of the family members and some nonfamily managers, the following issues emerged:

Business Issues

1. There was little coordination and consistency in policies across the various stores. This created some confusion among the store managers and among customers who patronized more than one store.

2. Store managers requested more feedback regarding their performance.

3. Quality control needed to be improved.

4. Advertising programs needed to be coordinated.

5. Employee training needed to be standardized.

6. The company needed to develop a marketing strategy to compete against lower priced competitors that had recently been able to improve their product quality.

Governance Issues

1. Although Peter Williams, his wife, and his four sons were designated as members of the governing board and were, in fact, equal owners, the board did not function. Peter Williams made all of the decisions regarding the business. Thus there was no regular forum for family members to express their concerns regarding the business.

Family Issues

1. The sons did not trust Peter to turn over the business to them. They felt he would still control all the major decisions.

2. Peter Williams, now in his early 60s, did want to turn the business over to his sons but wanted his sons to recognize his contributions to the business and still wanted some input regarding the firm's operations, because the value of his shares and the income he received from property that he was leasing to the business were contingent on the firm's performance.

3. Peter Williams's daughter, Jean, wanted to feel "equal" to the other brothers because she did not own any stock in the business. Family members recognized this inequity but did not know how to resolve it.

4. One son was going through a divorce. His wife was claiming that she should be given half of his stock in the business, thus complicating the governance system.

5. Another son had a substance abuse problem and was having difficulty functioning in his role in the firm.

To deal with these issues, the following steps were taken:

1. A family team-building session was held to deal with the trust issue. This proved to be a very difficult session, but in the end, misunderstandings were clarified, and the trust level was restored.

2. A board of directors was formally established. Peter Williams was named as board chairman, and Steve Williams was named chief executive officer. This arrangement satisfied Peter's need for recognition and some involvement, and Steve felt comfortable because he was given the responsibility for making executive decisions. Board meetings were held on a regular basis and Steve developed financial reports to update each board member on the firm's progress.

3. The board started with strategic planning to deal with the business issues. A comprehensive marketing and operational plan was developed and carried out. As a result, sales reached an all-time high.

4. Working with the accountants and lawyers, along with myself, the family worked out a plan to transfer assets (not ownership) to Jean so she would feel more equal, and a plan was developed to give assets, and not stock, to the one son's ex-wife.

5. Working with a professional counselor, the family confronted the son with the substance abuse problem and was able to get him into treatment. He has made good progress thus far.

As was the case with the previous companies, the diagnosis and intervention focused on all three systems simultaneously. However, in the case of the Williams Company, improvements in the business and the governance system could only be made after trust was restored in the family. Once trust was restored, creating an effective process for governing the firm was the next step. This allowed the family to focus all of its resources and energies in solving the business problems along with the other problems that were afflicting the family.

Managing Change in the Entrepreneurial Firm

Managing change in an entrepreneurial firm also presents some unique challenges. Typical models for managing change suggest that the change agent, whether a manager or consultant, needs to build broad support in order to initiate change (Beckhard & Harris, 1977; Cummings & Worley, 1993; Quinn, 1980). In the context of entrepreneurial firms, however, the key figures are the founders. Their support is critical to achieve success. Moreover, because they generally are involved in all aspects of the business, they are in a position to implement any plans for change. Thus the role of the change agent is to prepare entrepreneurs and coach them in the art of managing change. In entrepreneurial firms, key people in a change effort may not even work in the business. Family members and board directors may be able to help to initiate change or could serve to undermine any change effort. Thus, by looking at all three systems, the change agent can better plan for change by identifying those people whose support is critical.

As the field of organization development emerged, one of the primary technologies was "process consulting" pioneered by Edgar Schein (1988) of MIT. The assumption underlying process consulting was that the consultant need not have any specific knowledge about an organization's products, markets, technologies, and so on but needed only to have an understanding of what constituted effective organizational processes such as decision making, communications, or problem solving. If consultants were to help clients improve these processes, then clients would be more effective at solving other, more technical problems facing them. What I have found in working with entrepreneurial firms is that their leaders need both process and content consulting. Consultants need to be able to provide entrepreneurs with road maps regarding how to solve specific problems, such as succession planning or the creation of a board of directors, along with helping them improve organizational processes. Also, the problems related to the family are often highly emotional and sensitive. Thus they may require more expertise than a typical OD consultant might have. Hence Swartz (1989) has argued that interdisciplinary consulting teams are needed when working with entrepreneurial firms and family businesses. In my own work, I have worked jointly with lawyers,

accountants, financial planners, family therapists, and clinical psychologists when working with various clients because many of the problems facing these clients fell outside my level of expertise. Working with other professionals who operate from different paradigms can be somewhat frustrating, but if the members of the consulting team can collaborate successfully with each other, the results can be excellent. For example, I recently helped the founder of a family business work through several business and family problems related to his divorce. His wife wanted joint control of the business, which would have made governing the business very difficult because they had different goals for the business: He wanted to grow the business, whereas she wanted to take funds out of the business for her personal use. A financial consultant who had worked with this family and myself were able to work out a plan with the founder and his wife to leave the founder in control of the business while leaving his wife sufficient assets to ensure financial security for her. Through this plan we were also able to find significant tax savings for the founder. Such a plan would not have been possible unless I had worked with the financial planner to develop this plan.

The types of interventions employed by the OD consultant often require modification (Dyer, 1994). For example, consultants may find themselves conducting team-building and role clarification sessions that include members of the same family or members of the board of directors. These individuals may have long, dysfunctional histories with each other in nonwork contexts, and therefore the issues that emerge may be difficult to resolve. Also, because employees in entrepreneurial firms may have roles in each of the three systems, clarifying their roles and their goals and objectives can prove a daunting task. Strategic planning is also done quite differently when one is attempting to satisfy the goals and demands of both business and family (Ward, 1987).

The kinds of interventions employed by consultants also change as the entrepreneurial firm evolves (see Table 2). In early-stage entrepreneurial

TABLE 2

Interventions in entrepreneurial firms

	Stage of Development		
System	*Start-Up*	*Growth*	*Succession*
Business	Business planning	Strategic planning Structural change Team building Career development	Strategic planning Succession planning
Family	Family council	Family strategic planning Career development Family therapy	Asset management board Estate planning Conflict management Family therapy
Governance	Partner relationship interventions	Board of directors interventions	Ownership and board transition planning

firms, interventions designed to improve the company's business plan, to define roles for those governing the firm, and to help the entrepreneur's family work through the stress of a new business start-up are often used. Growth firms generally require changes in organizational structure and in clarifying roles. Training and career development needs become more important along with developing new forms of control through better systems. Thus structural change, career development, clarifying corporate strategy and values, and helping to engineer new information systems often become the interventions of choice during the growth stage. During the growth stage the family may also need to engage in family strategic planning (Ward, 1987) to plan for family involvement in the firm. Particularly in dysfunctional families, therapy may be the best option. I have also found that the creation of an effective board of directors during the growth stage can help the founder gain the insight and support needed to manage growth successfully. Succession and estate planning, whether or not to sell the business, leadership development, and culture change and renewal are the issues facing entrepreneurial firms making the transition to the next generation. These complex issues require the con-

sultant to have considerably different types of expertise to help founders, organizations, and their families manage these changes successfully. Strategic and succession-planning interventions are generally needed along with interventions to manage the founder's estate and the potential conflicts that accompany such planning. Firm ownership and board composition often change during succession, and therefore planning needs to take place to ensure a smooth transition.

Conclusion

The purpose of this article has been to suggest that the models and methods typically employed by OD consultants do not necessarily apply to entrepreneurial firms. More complex theories and diagnostic models are needed that take into account the dynamics of the business, the governance system, and the family. Consultants often find themselves working in and between these systems and therefore need to develop interventions that are appropriate for each system. Also entrepreneurial firms are not all the same. Depending on their stage of development, the issues they face are very different, requiring very different types of expertise.

Thus interdisciplinary consulting teams may be needed. Finally, the consultant needs to be aware of the pitfalls of managing change in these complex systems. Although the entrepreneur is generally the focal point for any change effort, one must also consider the power of individuals in the others systems as well. I have found consulting with entrepreneurial firms to be an extremely rewarding enterprise because change can occur more quickly than in large organizations and therefore it is somewhat easier to test one's theories about organizations and change. Working with entrepreneurial firms can also be very frustrating because of their complexity, but it can also be a highly rewarding learning experience.

References

Adizes, I. (1979, Summer). Organizational passages— Diagnosing and treating life cycle problems of organizations. *Organizational Dynamics,* pp. 3–25.

Beckhard, R. (1975, Winter). Strategies for large system change. *Sloan Management Review,* pp. 43–55.

Beckhard, R., & Harris, R. T. (1977). *Organizational transitions: Managing complex change.* Menlo Park, CA: Addison-Wesley.

Berg, D., & Smith, K. (1985). The clinical demands of research methods. In D. Berg & K. Smith (Eds.), *The self in social inquiry.* Newbury Park, CA: Sage.

Birch, D. (1987). *Job creation in America: How our smallest companies put the most people to work.* New York: Free Press.

Cummings, T. G., & Worley, C. G. (1993). *Organization development and change* (5th ed.). St. Paul, MN: West.

Dennis, W. J., Jr. (1993). *A small business primer.* Washington, DC: The NFIB Foundation.

Dyer, W. G., Jr. (1986). *Cultural change in family firms: Anticipating and managing business and family transitions.* San Francisco: Jossey-Bass.

Dyer, W. G., Jr. (1989). Integrating professional management into a family owned business. *Family Business Review, 2* (3), 221–235.

Dyer, W. G., Jr. (1992). *The entrepreneurial experience: Confronting career dilemmas of the start-up executive.* San Francisco: Jossey-Bass.

Dyer, W. G., Jr. (1994). Potential contributions of organizational behavior to the study of family owned businesses. *Family Business Review, 7* (2), 109–131.

French, W. L., Bell, C. H., Jr., & Zawacki, R. A. (Eds.) (1994). *Organizational development and transformation: Managing effective change* (4th ed.). Burr Ridge, IL: Irwin.

Glassman, A. M., & Cummings, T. G. (Eds.). (1991). *Cases in organizational development.* Homewood, IL: Irwin.

Greiner, L. E. (1972, July/August). Evolution and revolution as organizations grow. *Harvard Business Review,* pp. 37–46.

Hanna, D. P. (1988). *Designing organizations for high performance.* Menlo Park, CA: Addison-Wesley.

Hollander, B. S., & Elman, N. S. (1988). Family-owned business: An emerging field of inquiry. *Family Business Review, 1* (1), 145–164.

Kets de Vries, M. F. R. (1977). The entrepreneurial personality: A person at the crossroads. *Journal of Management Studies, 14,* 34–57.

Kirchoff, B. A., & Greene, P. G. (1995). *Response to renewed attacks on the small business job creation hypothesis.* Working paper, New Jersey Institute of Technology, Newark, NJ.

Kotter, J. P. (1978). *Organizational dynamics: Diagnosis and intervention.* Menlo Park, CA: Addison-Wesley.

Lansberg, I. (1983). Managing human resources in family firms: The problem of institutional overlap. *Organizational Dynamics, 12* (1), 39–46.

Lansberg, I. (1988). The succession conspiracy. *Family Business Review, 1* (2), 119–143.

McCollom, M. E. (1990). Problems and prospects in clinical research on family firms. *Family Business Review, 3* (3), 245–262.

Miller, E. J., & Rice, A. K. (1967). *Systems of organization.* London: Tavistock.

Nadler, D. A., & Tushman, M. L. (1977). A diagnostic model for organizational behavior. In J. R. Hackman, E. E. Lawler III, & L. W. Porter (Eds.), *Perspectives on behavior in organizations* (pp. 85–98). San Francisco: McGraw-Hill.

Peters, T. J., & Waterman, R. H., Jr. (1982). *In search of excellence: Lessons from America's best-run companies.* San Francisco: Harper & Row.

Quinn, J. B. (1980). Managing strategic change. *Sloan Management Review, 21*(4), 3–20.

Schein, E. H. (1983). The role of the founder in creating organizational culture. *Organizational Dynamics, 12* (1), 13–28.

Schein, E. H. (1985). *Organizational culture and leadership.* San Francisco: Jossey-Bass.

Schein, E. H. (1987). *The clinical perspective in fieldwork.* Newbury Park, CA: Sage.

Schein, E. H. (1988). *Process consultation* (2nd ed.). Reading, MA: Addison-Wesley.

Schwartz, M. A., & Barnes, L. B. (1991). Outside boards and family businesses: Another look. *Family Business Review, 4*(3), 269–285.

Swartz, S. (1989). The challenges of multidisciplinary consulting to family-owned businesses. *Family Business Review, 2* (4), 329–339.

Ward, J. L. (1987). *Keeping the family business healthy.* San Francisco: Jossey-Bass.

Ward, J. L. (1991). *Creating effective boards for private enterprises: Meeting the challenges of continuity and competition.* San Francisco: Jossey-Bass.

Ward, J. L., & Handy, J. L. (1988). A survey of board practices. *Family Business Review, 1* (3), 289–308.

Weisbord, M. (1978). *Organizational diagnosis: A workbook of theory and practice.* Reading, MA: Addison-Wesley.

READING 39
ARE ORGANIZATIONAL DEVELOPMENT INTERVENTIONS APPROPRIATE IN TURNAROUND SITUATIONS?

Gregory W. Pacton

Introduction

Turnarounds vary considerably in the type, the conditions leading to the critical situation, the degree of severity, and the resources available. Turnaround firms are those which have deteriorated beyond the level where they are simply underperforming. They are in need of significant and immediate improvements in their performance levels. "Workout specialists" are frequently hired to manage firms in the more advanced stages of deterioration. These specialists are narrowly focused on "stopping the bleeding"; if the "bleeding" cannot be stopped, these individuals are skilled in maximizing the liquidation value of the firm. Generally, turnaround firms differ from companies which are engaged in renewal or rejuvenation efforts in the respect that turnarounds require crisis management in order to simply survive. Daily business reports and news briefings contain a wealth of information regarding the actions taken by managers in an attempt to accomplish turnarounds at ailing companies. Most of this information is geared toward the investment communities and deals with balance sheet and cash flow issues. The investment community closely scrutinizes the actions of turnaround managers and the short term performance results of these actions as a way to assess risks and credit worthiness. The business community is similarly preoccupied with the strategic and market implications of turnarounds. Much of the attention given to turnarounds is focused on the "hard" financial, strategic, market, and operational business issues.

Source: Reprinted with permission of *Organization Development Journal*. "Are Organizational Development Interventions Appropriate in Turnaround Situations?" by Gregory W. Pacton, vol. 16, no. 2, Summer 1998, pp. 43–53.

Academic and popular business literature abound with case studies of successful OD transformations. Much has been written recently about the rejuvenation of businesses which have been subject to mergers, acquisitions, divestitures, and changes in strategic direction. The volume of popular business literature dealing with this subject would imply a growing acceptance of OD in the business community as an integral and vital element in achieving organizational change and making organizations more competitive. Despite this growing acceptance however, questions remain regarding the applicability of OD during the crises of turnaround situations.

Problem

Turnaround endeavors stand apart from typical business change processes in the respect that the magnitude and rapidity of the changes required are critical to the organization's survival.

The focal point for firms which are essentially sound, profitable, but underperforming, will be different than that for firms which are unprofitable and at the brink of insolvency. The firm near insolvency will be struggling with an acute shortage of critical resources, namely cash and time. Relative to an underperforming company, a turnaround firm will typically require drastic and immediate actions by the CEO to keep the firm solvent. Such actions may include large-scale workforce reductions, elimination of all nonessential spending, wholesale liquidation of inventories, disposal of nonessential assets, restructuring of debt with creditors, and negotiation of extended terms with suppliers.

The underperforming firm is analogous to a person whose health might be characterized by obesity, high blood pressure, and a general lack of fitness. This person's condition has seriously deteriorated, and though not life-threatening at the moment, may become life-threatening in the future unless actions are taken to improve the situation. The turnaround firm is analogous to a person who has suffered cardiac arrest, is in cardiac intensive care, and requires immediate bypass surgery. The cardiac patient, like the turnaround firm, must first be stabilized before the journey back to wellness can begin. It makes little sense for the turnaround firm to concern itself with longer term activities such as R&D or capital investment if the firm cannot survive the immediate crisis. It would also seem to make little sense for the turnaround firm to be concerned with OD efforts which may have long term benefits but do not aid in immediate crisis survival.

The CEO, as doctor of the ailing firm and its chief change agent, must provide selective and intensive attention to the few critical elements which will provide immediate improvements in the firm's" condition. This paper explores several questions regarding the relevance and applicability of OD under turnaround conditions. Should OD efforts be part of the selective and intensive focus of the turnaround CEO? Are OD interventions applicable and appropriate to turnaround situations? Does OD contribute materially toward achievement of the turnaround? Does OD improve the likelihood of success or the rate at which success is achieved? What kinds of OD interventions might be appropriate for turnaround situations?

Prior Research and Literature Review

Before the applicability of OD to turnaround situations can be addressed, it is necessary to establish an operational definition of a turnaround. There is a wealth of literature dealing with organizational decline. Unfortunately the definitions of organizational decline, and more specifically, of turnaround situations vary considerably. Sloma (1985) takes a broad perspective that turnarounds include any initiatives aimed at improving the

company's performance. His definition includes companies who are facing imminent bankruptcy as well as those who are currently profitable but have hints of an impending future problem.

A broad but more clinical view of a company turnaround is taken by Pant (1991) in her definition of a turnaround effort as one which strives to achieve "a substantial improvement in the firm's return on assets relative to the average return of its industry." Her research found that of 835 firms which had ROA's in the bottom quartile for their industries during the period 1970 through 1976, only 64 successfully executed a turnaround by improving their ROAs to the upper quartile during the ensuing four year period. Of the remaining firms, 369 remained in the lowest quartile while 402 indicated some improvement but still well short of a successful turnaround. Pant's work focuses on technical aspects of turnarounds but illustrates that a large percentage of companies which undertake turnarounds do not achieve the desired results. Of those which are not successful, some demonstrate improvement but remain underperforming companies, some continue to barely survive, and others are liquidated.

In the Weitzel and Jonsson (1989) model, organizational decline progresses through five stages of increasing severity. The first two stages in their model are characterized by decreasing margins, profits, and capital investment. The third and fourth stages are characterized by operating losses and cash flow crises respectively. The final stage is liquidation of the firm's assets and beyond the point of potential turnaround. Winn (1993) adds a dimension to the five-stage decline model by proposing that the type of turnaround can vary, with each type incurring a different degree of difficulty. Companies which are operating in stages one and two are considered underperforming, whereas only those companies which have deteriorated to stages three or four are considered turnaround situations. Her research indicates that a successful turnaround will generally require one to five years depending upon the type and degree of decline.

The need to immediately address financial issues is confirmed by Hoffman's (1989) extensive research on turnarounds. He found that most successful turnaround managers rank cost control as first in importance, followed by changes in employee attitudes. Successful turnaround managers aggressively and actively managed financial, strategic, marketing, and operational issues with the objective of accomplishing very short term improvements in the firm's performance. He also found that these turnaround leaders actively engaged in making political and symbolic changes within the firm, developed new team members, and consulted with large numbers of the organization's members. Schaffer and Thomson (1992) found through their studies of numerous companies that turnaround situations required management to shift away from activity-centered efforts to a results-driven focus. They concluded that only a results-driven approach will yield the desired bottom-line business results in the timeframe required. Their work suggests that turnaround efforts aimed at establishing organizational development processes such as widespread employee training or team-building may be misdirected because these processes will not yield the immediate and tangible results required. Their work, however, indicates that a results-driven approach may be the basis for reorienting the organization for its future existence.

Finkin (1985, 1988) also stressed the requirement to address both strategy and control of operating costs, but acknowledges the importance of addressing the "drastic psychological and cultural changes" in a turnaround. He argues that employees must feel a sense of urgency, cooperation, involvement in achieving the turnaround, and certainly commitment to the turnaround. Finkin also points out that successful turnarounds are not accomplished by consensus; although employees must be involved, the radical changes necessary require a strong leader with the will to do whatever is necessary to assure the success of the turnaround effort.

Unfortunately, as organization deterioration continues, many incumbent CEOs are unable to make the drastic changes required for a turnaround. Levinson (1994) found that many incumbent CEOs in declining businesses either failed to grasp the firm's situation or were unable to bring themselves to making the radical changes required. Similarly, Castrogiovanni's (1992) research indicates that as the organization progresses to more severe levels of deterioration, the potential benefits of changing the CEO increase. The benefits of such an action are all related to gaining the support of the organization stakeholders. New CEOs can provide a fresh perspective on the business and its environment, provide a skill set or competency needed to navigate the turnaround, and to provide a signal to the organization that change is imminent. Castrogiovanni argues that long term change strategies are irrelevant if the business is not able to survive the short term crisis. His work indicates indirectly that OD intervention efforts become less applicable as the stages of organizational decline become more grievous. When a company's situation becomes sufficiently serious to necessitate a turnaround specialist, OD change efforts become subordinated to other issues such as cost cutting, financial restructuring, large scale downsizing, and maximizing the business' liquidation value.

Implementing the financial and operational changes required in a turnaround requires a strong willed CEO capable of making difficult decisions. However, there are far too many detailed actions for an individual to carry out single-handedly. Therefore, widespread involvement of employees would intuitively provide the vehicle for accomplishing a rapid turnaround. Reger, Mullane, Gustafson, and DeMarie (1994) point out a flaw in this intuitive conclusion. They argue that other members of the organization may not share the CEO's mental model about what must be done, the actions required to accomplish such, and the time frame in which the results must be realized. Turnarounds require actions which challenge members' basic assumptions and beliefs about the organization and its business. However, Reger, Mullane, Gustafson, and DeMarie also imply that the fundamental and radical levels of business change typically required in turnarounds cannot be accomplished without a deliberate organizational development effort.

Similarly, Tushman, Newman, and Romanelli (1986) argue that concurrent "frame-breaking" organizational changes may be required in strategy, structure, people, and processes for firms in a turnaround situation. Frame-breaking changes are revolutionary and involve discontinuous changes throughout the organization. They argue that rapid frame-breaking may be healthier than slower evolutionary organizational efforts because the old organization including its culture, practices, perspectives, are dismantled faster than they can reform. This creates a void in the organization which primes it for new attitudes and behavior, and provides the basis for establishing a new organization. The preponderance of research literature regarding organizational development deals with the broad topic of change, e.g. the need to become something different and perform differently in the future. However, there is little in the prior research which addresses the applicability and relative importance of OD as an integral component in time-critical turnaround efforts. The applicability of OD change initiatives would seem to be obvious for underperforming firms. The applicability of organizational development change efforts in or approaching the crisis stage of organizational decline and the relative contributions of OD to actually achieving a successful turnaround are less clear.

Implications for Organization Development

The five-stage model of organizational decline proposed by Weitzel and Jonsson (1989) can be adapted to provide a framework for discussing the relevance of OD in a turnaround situation. The first stage of decline may yield symptoms that a problem exists in the form of decreasing product margins, increasing inventories, and decreases in capital investment. Company profits may remain stable and mask the symptoms. The second stage of decline will generally occur because management does recognize the symptoms and does not perceive that a problem

exists. This stage involves an initial decrease in company profit levels which management erroneously interprets as a one time event due to extraordinary circumstances. The third stage is characterized by a pattern of declining profits and possibly occasional operating losses. It is at this stage that it is recognized that the business is in serious trouble and that deliberate actions to correct the situation are required. Companies in the fourth stage of decline begin to experience problems with cash flow. The organization has reached the crisis stage where it is now at the brink of insolvency and must take immediate and radical steps to preserve its existence. The fifth and final stage in the organizational decline model involves liquidation of the firm's assets. Obviously turnaround efforts and organizational development do not apply. Businesses which reach this final stage are no longer viable concerns and are beyond the point of salvage.

All companies in any of the first four stages of decline would provide fertile ground for OD work. However, as businesses progressively deteriorate from the first to the fifth stages, their condition becomes increasingly critical, and greater levels of attention need to be given to the fundamental financial, strategic, and operational aspects of the business. In early stages of deterioration, cash flow may not yet be a problem. The firm may still be profitable even though signs of imminent distress are beginning to form on the horizon. It is not likely that a firm at this stage would be considering radical steps such as liquidation of nonessential assets which might be required of firms at the brink of insolvency. Firms at the early stages of decline would not require severe remedial actions because their condition is not yet life-threatening.

It is at these early stages that organizational development change efforts would be most appropriate as preventive actions aimed at avoiding further decline and ultimately reversing it. Recognizing the early signs of trouble gives the company additional time to react and avoid becoming a turnaround candidate. Recruiting the workforce as participants in the change effort takes time. Sharing the vision of the future, development of a supportive constituency among the stakeholders, gaining trust and buy-in of organization members will require time—a critical resource which may be in very short supply as the business approaches the final stages of decline. Unfortunately, when a firm reaches levels three and four, the firm may be in such a critical state financially, that nearly all of the available management resources must be focused on financial issues. If the firm cannot pay its creditors, organizational development becomes irrelevant. The value of OD efforts would seem to diminish as the firm approaches these latter stages of decline. Figure 1 provides a graphical model depicting the relative importance of financial management issues versus organizational development in the various stages of decline.

For firms which have already reversed the momentum of decline and which are beginning to realize the financial benefits of a turnaround effort, OD becomes a more valuable tool in continuing and reinforcing the turnaround. Management has more latitude in the reallocation of their time and effort; management of financial issues becomes less demanding thereby allowing increased attention to change interventions which will propel the firm toward its renewal. The need to first focus on cost controls until the firm is back on safe footing is supported by Hoffman's research (1989). Only after the business is again financially viable can the CEO begin to work on employee attitudes and behavior.

However, it seems that for all but the most severe cases of deterioration, focusing only on financial, strategic, or operational issues may "stop the bleeding" but does not necessarily prepare the firm to again become successful. The cardiac patient may have survived the coronary crisis, but survival is not synonymous with fitness or wellness. It would therefore appear that some other type of managerial impetus will also be required to move the organization back to health. Organizational development change efforts are the logical therapy. The turnaround firm, like the cardiac patient, must begin a rehabilitation program which involves significant changes in attitudes and lifestyle. Conversely, OD alone does not appear to be sufficient to save the most critically ill firms; OD efforts are irrelevant to

bankrupt firms. The most effective approach to achieving material results quickly appears to be a combination of aggressive management of business issues and focused short term organizational development efforts. The correct combination will depend upon the circumstances and the many variables at noted by Winn (1993). It may be helpful to examine this model via case studies.

The priority of financial concerns over OD in a turnaround effort was illustrated in Clausen's (1990) turnaround methodology at BankAmerica Corporation. From 1981 to 1986, the company's situation deteriorated rapidly as a result of several environmental forces. In 1986, when his turnaround efforts began, the company was losing money at a rapid rate, had suspended its common stock dividend, was facing a hostile takeover attempt by First Interstate Bankcorp, and was being pressured by regulators to address its deteriorating capital structure. He employed a five-step approach in his efforts—three of the steps were focused at producing immediate and tangible results in business performance while the remaining two steps focused on organization development.

The severity of BankAmerica's financial situation required short term actions to "stop the bleeding" including the sale of assets to improve capital ratios. Assets were reduced by $9.6 billion, from $113.8 billion to $104.2 billion, in a 78-day period from September 30 to December 31, 1986. Clausen was also able to raise $425 million to improve primary capital ratios by offerings of notes, warrants, and convertible preferred stocks to Japanese financial institutions. Further, the organization's cost structure required immediate reductions in expenses. Expense reductions were accomplished by a reduction in employment of 21,700 people (30 percent) and closure of over 200 branches to reduce occupancy costs from $513 million to $420 million. The corporation returned to profitability in the third quarter of 1987, within one year after he began his turnaround efforts.

Though the financial aspects of the turnaround efforts capture most of the publicity in the popular press, BankAmerica employed several actions

FIGURE 1

Model of relative importance between financial management issues and organizational development efforts during progressive stages of decline

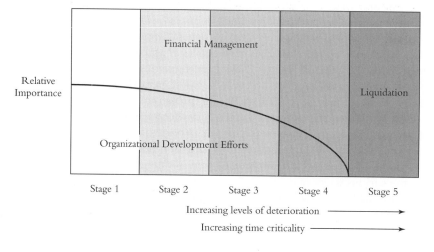

specifically aimed at organizational development issues. A new management team of outstanding performers was formed. Clausen noted that the management skills required in a turnaround situation differ from those needed under normal circumstances. Clausen indicated that success would be achieved only as a team and that every employee needed to fully understand the corporation's objectives and to feel personally involved in the recovery. Specific programs such as the "one new customer" program were aimed at improving the corporation's customer base and at simultaneously involving every employee in the effort. As the turnaround effort progressed and yielded results, the corporation awarded each employee 10 shares of stock in the company. Clausen noted the value in such an action as a symbolic recognition of those who were instrumental in the turnaround and in creating a stronger sense of ownership in the corporation's future. OD efforts were apparently a component of the turnaround strategy at BankAmerica, but significant attention to organizational development issues were not undertaken until the financial issues had been adequately addressed. The relative importance of OD efforts

(vs. technical business) and relative contributions of these efforts to the eventual success are unclear.

The immediate attention to financial issues is also illustrated in Navistar's recovery. In their case study, Borucki and Barnett (1990) examined the role of organizational development in the turnaround and renewal at Navistar Corporation. In the early 1908s International Harvester was nearly bankrupt. The firm was characterized by a lack of cost controls, obsolete manufacturing processes and equipment, excessive debt, and widespread mismanagement of fundamental technical business elements. A series of environmental factors including a workforce labor strike, high interest rates, poor conditions in the farm segment of the economy, and trucking industry deregulation pushed International Harvester to the edge of near extinction. Corporation sales in 1983 were less than half of the levels from four years prior; the firm had also accumulated losses in excess of $2 billion during the same period.

Immediate actions were required to avoid imminent bankruptcy. First, IH was able to negotiate restructuring of its debt with more than 200 lenders. However, many of Harvester's business units were still losing money. IH also restructured in order to reduce operating costs and generate vital revenues. The turnaround effort at IH suffered a near fatal blow in its first start toward recovery. Archie McCardell was initially given the assignment of leading the firm back to prosperity. He embarked on a cost-cutting program which alienated employees and resulted in a 180-day strike. His focus on cost-cutting blinded him to fundamental restructuring of the market and industry, and by 1980, pushed IH to the brink of extinction. Don Lennox was subsequently given the assignment to salvage IH, which had deteriorated even further under McCardell. Radical and immediate change was necessary. One of the most visible and difficult decisions was the divesture of the agricultural business operations. This particular action resulted in the sale of approximately one-half of the company and its original founding heritage. Facilities were reduced from 42 to 7. Corporate employment declined from 95,000 to 13,000—an 86 percent reduction.

Technical actions which yielded substantial impact in both magnitude and speed were required for IH to survive. It was apparent to top management that the required transformation could not be accomplished on technical actions alone. IH made OD an immediate and integral part of its survival strategy. IH provided outplacement services, severance packages with extended health and life insurance, job search assistance workshops, retraining services, relocation financial assistance, and a variety of other benefits to ease the transition of exiting employees. IH spent a total of $5.2 million to aid displaced workers.

Fortunately, Don Lennox had a more global perspective on the company's situation than his predecessors. As part of his initial turnaround efforts, he commissioned a study of the company's policies, management practices, and culture, to determine to what extent these factors would inhibit the turnaround efforts at IH. The conclusion of this study was that the hierarchical style and bureaucratic management would stifle the turnaround efforts unless dealt with. Business divestitures, downsizings, and plant closures were quickly undertaken. The firm

also undertook OD efforts to aid the survivors in the form of team-building training and team effectiveness workshops. These type of efforts were aimed clearly at the short term adjustments required of survivors. Concurrently, Navistar undertook longer term organizational development initiatives, including decentralization of operating authority to the business unit levels, a formalized effort among top management to manage corporate culture, a name change from IH to Navistar, and a formalized mission statement to aid the firm in its transition to a new identity. By 1987, five years after its initial turnaround efforts in earnest, Navistar had successfully navigated beyond its pure survival concerns. Borucki and Barnett concluded that OD efforts were vital to Navistar's short term turnaround and longer term renewal.

The OD interventions employed at Navistar included the development of a corporate values statement, redefinition of the HR function to move it toward a pro-active, service oriented group, decentralization of decision making, implementation of a dynamic strategic planning process with involvement down to the operating levels. After the company was stabilized, additional OD interventions were employed with an eye toward renewal and revitalization. The company established team-building and team facilitation initiatives which evolved into Continuous Improvement Teams. A process to address issues of employment security and competitiveness was installed. New performance management methodologies were introduced. A formal mission statement was also developed.

In their case study, Sorensen, Head, Scoggins, and Larsen (1990) cite OD interventions as a critical element in the SAS turnaround. SAS lost market share between 1975 and 1980 in an increasingly turbulent environment. In 1981, the company lost $8 million and recruited Jan Carlzon to lead the turnaround. Carlzon's technical changes were heavily focused on creation of market niches which would attract business passengers. Specific programs included the creation of the "Euro-class" of travel, increased passenger seating space, dramatic improvements in on-time performance, and differentiated pricing structures to attract new leisure travelers.

They also found that from the onset of the turn-around effort, SAS began a transition from a bureaucratic culture to a service-oriented one. Carlzon replaced 13 of 15 of the top managers in the company as a way of communicating to the workforce in a very visible way that the firm had moved beyond its old approaches. He used top management behavior and symbolism as vehicles to demonstrate change. The rewards and performance appraisal systems were modified to reinforce the desired behaviors throughout the workforce. SAS also used extensive employee training to develop a favorable self-image, to cultivate the desired service orientation among all employees, and to establish a culture with a bias toward achieving results versus simply engaging in processes. SAS was returned to profitability in a little more than one year. It is noteworthy that SAS was able to reverse its financial plight within a very short period of time without reducing its total employment. In fact, employment increased and 25 percent of administrative personnel were redeployed to areas of direct customer service. Sorensen argues convincingly that OD interventions were a vital component in the turnaround endeavors and the speed with which the turnaround was accomplished.

In a more recent case, Gil Amelio (1996) led the turnaround at National Semiconductor. Amelio claims that the transformation was accomplished in two steps. The first step required nursing the company back to financial health with "tactical actions" such as plant closures, aggressive cost slashing, and downsizing the workforce. Once accomplished, the company could then divert its attention to transformation of the organization into a "great company." Unfortunately, he left National Semiconductor after concluding only "Phase 1" to join Apple Computer with a similar challenge.

Amelio (1996) asserts that "You cannot save your way into success." Cost-cutting measures alone will not achieve a turnaround. At best, such actions may stop the deterioration and stabilize the company, but will not restore it to levels of outstanding performance. Amelio argues that the aggressive financial management must be supplemented with other initiatives in order to achieve organizational transformation. Some of these initiatives are strategic in nature such as development of a thorough understanding of customers' needs, knowing your own firm's core competencies and competitive advantages. Other turnaround initiatives are clearly OD oriented. Among the initiatives he believes need to be immediately undertaken in a turnaround are the creation of a clear vision of the company's future, inviting employees to share in the vision and to contribute to it, clearly defining what constitutes success, identification of critical success factors, taking bold steps to reverse the negative momentum, and active communication of the new direction to all employees.

Does the needed attention and priority to tactical turnaround issues imply that ignoring OD initiatives during early turnaround efforts is appropriate? It appears that the answer is "no." All of the aforementioned turnarounds engaged in some type of OD change intervention during the initial turnaround actions. All of the OD change interventions were geared toward simultaneously modifying the firms' cultures, attitudes, and behaviors in parallel with the changes occurring in the financial, strategic, and operational elements of the businesses.

Is there a pattern in the type and application of OD interventions used in successful turnarounds? There does appear to be a pattern. Table 1 provides a comparative view of the tactical/financial actions and the OD intervention employed in each of the turnaround case studies discussed. Clearly, all firms utilized OD interventions. Would the turnarounds have been successful without the use of these OD interventions? It is impossible to say if each would have otherwise been successful. However, the chief change agents in each situation make a convincing case for OD efforts as a key component in the turnaround initiative.

Conclusions

The empirical evidence would seem to indicate that OD efforts do complement turnaround efforts and to a degree improve the likelihood of success

TABLE 1

Comparison of the financial and OD turnaround actions of four successful companies

Company	Turnaround Financial/Operational Actions	Initial Organizational Interventions	Time to Achieve Turnaround (return to profitability)

Bank America	Aggressive cost-cutting
	Location closures
	Sale of assets
	Suspended stock dividend
	Issued preferred capital
	Workforce reductions
		CEO replaced
		Established new
		  management team
		Aggressive communication
		  campaign
			1 year

Navistar	Plant closures Downsizing Debt restructuring Strategic market realignment Divestitures	CEO replaced Corporate values statement Redefinition of HR function Install dynamic and participative strategic planning process	7 years

SAS	Focused on market niches
	Differentiated pricing structures
		CEO replaced
		Replaced 13 of 15 top managers
		Modified rewards and
		  performance appraisal system
		Extensive employee training
		Redeployed 25% of
		  administrative workforce
			1 year

National Semiconductor	Plant closures
	Downsizing
	Workforce reduction
	Aggressive cost-cutting
	Realignment of
	  manufacturing plants
		CEO replaced
		Active communication to
		  employees
		Creating clear vision of future
		Define key success factors
			2 years

in all but the most severe situations. The firm must first survive the immediate financial crisis for OD to be effective.

Case studies of successful turnarounds acknowledge organizational development efforts, but it is difficult to ascertain the relative importance of these OD efforts to the success. Conversely, case studies of failed turnaround efforts usually cite the cause of the failure as the inability to stem the firm's liquidity problems. Although cost-cutting and aggressive financial management may be able to forestall bankruptcy, it appears that such actions need to be supplemented with other strategic and organizational changes in order to materially move the firm back toward rejuvenation and renewal.

Future research might be appropriate to statistically validate whether deliberate inclusion of OD interventions in the turnaround effort yields a greater likelihood of success. Future research might also explore whether turnarounds are achieved faster when supplemented by OD change efforts despite the generally accepted wisdom that OD change efforts take time.

References

Amelio, Gil, & Simon, William L. (1996). *Profit from experience: the story of National Semiconductor and transformation management.* New York: Van Nostrand Reinhold.

Borucki, Chet, & Barnett, Carole K. (1990). Restructuring for self-renewal: Navistar International Corporation. *Academy of Management Executive, 4*(1), 36–49.

Castrogiovanni, Gary J., Baliga, B.R., & Kidwell, Roland E. Jr., (1992). Curing sick businesses: changing CEOs in turnaround efforts. *Academy of Management Executives, 6* (3), 26–41.

Clausen, A.W. (1990). Strategic issues in managing change: The turnaround at BankAmerica Corporation. *California Management Review, 32,* 98–105.

Finkin, Eugene F. (1985). Company turn around. *Journal of Business Strategy, 6,* 14–24.

Finkin, Eugene F. (1992). Structuring a successful turn-around. *Journal of Business Strategy, 13,* 56–58.

Hoffman, Richard C. (1989). Strategies for corporate turnarounds: What do we know about them? *Journal of General Management, 14* (3), 46–66.

Levsinson, Harry (1994). Why the behemoths fell: Psychological roots of corporate failure. *American Psychologist, 49,* 428–436.

Pant, Laurie W. (1991). An investigation of industry and firm structural characteristics in corporate turn arounds. *Journal of Management Studies, 28,* 623–643.

Reger, Rhonda K., Mullane, John V., Gustafson, Loren T., & DeMarie, Samuel M. (1994). Creating earthquakes to change organizational mindsets. *Academy of Management Executive, 8* (4), 31–46.

Schaffer, Robert H., & Thomson, Harvey A. (1992). Successful change programs begin with results. *Harvard Business Review, 70,* 80–89.

Sloma, Richard S. (1985). *The turnaround managers handbook.* New York: Free Press.

Sorensen, Peter F., Head, Thomas C., Scoggins, Helen, & Larsen, Henrik Holt (1990). The turnaround of Scandinavian Airlines: An OD interpretation *Organization Development Journal, 8* (1), 1–6.

Tushman, Michael L., Newman, William H., & Romanelli, Elaine (1986). Convergence and upheaval: Managing the unsteady pace of organizational evolution. *California Management Review, 24* (1), 29–44.

Winn, Joan (1993). Performance measures for corporate decline and turn around. *Journal of General Management, 19* (2), 48–63.

VII CHALLENGES AND OPPORTUNITIES FOR THE FUTURE

Organization development and organization transformation are beset with issues and challenges that will greatly challenge practitioners and scholars in the years ahead. This is partly because it is a young field and partly because of its eclectic nature. Contemporary OD & T practices borrow from social psychology, counseling psychology, organization theory, family group therapy, human resources management, systems theory, group dynamics, management, and other disciplines. Any attempt at an amalgamation of insights from such a spectrum of fields to develop effective interventions for ongoing organizations is bound to create many challenges. For example, how nondirective can the OD consultant afford to be if the client is talking about establishing benefits or privileges in one group without being cognizant of potential perceived inequities by other groups? Counseling psychology has something to say about the utility of a supportive nondirective consultation style, but human resources management and social psychology have something to say about cognitive dissonance and inequity. Reconciling the two conflicting action implications may be difficult in such a situation. How does OD relate to various movements or contemporary areas of emphasis like "quality of work life" or the learning organization? Is OD the same thing? Different? How can one articulate the differences or similarities? What are the consequences of not doing so?

But OD & T practices are also beset with many problems and issues because they inevitably affect people's lives, and sometimes deeply. We would like to think that people are usually affected positively, and we believe this to be so; but questions of ethics, of values, of what is helpful and what is hurtful, must and do arise. How much manipulation is there in the particular OD intervention in the particular context; that is, to what extent is there a hidden agenda in the use of the intervention, or to what extent is the nature of the technique or its consequences kept from the participants? What should be the depth of an intervention in order to be both efficacious and at the same time not harmful? Should the consultant attempt to interpret and surface resistances? Under what circumstances is feedback constructive? How much, or should, the OD consultant be aligned with the exercise of power in the organization? What should the OD consultant's training be? And how does one know when a consultant is qualified to practice? These are not simple matters.

Other issues have to do with the relationship of OD to culture. For example, what forms of OD bring about a deep change in the culture of an organization and what forms result in only modest changes in organizational functioning? What are the costs either way?

Readings in Part VII

Additional emerging issues are discussed in the selections that appear in this part.

In the first essay, "Empowerment: The Emperor's New Clothes," Chris Argyris notes that empowerment of employees is much talked and written about, but little has been done in the way of implementation. He asserts that many change programs are riddled with inner contradictions and that even CEOs, while espousing the values of empowerment, in subtle ways undermine its emergence. Argyris makes a distinction between *external commitment,* in which tasks, behaviors, and goals are defined by others and which does not lead to empowerment, and *internal commitment,* in which employees are much more in charge of their own destinies and which is essential for empowerment. He then provides some recommendations to help executives "think more sensibly about empowerment." While Argyris is quite pessimistic about the extent to which change programs have resulted in employee empowerment, we believe that team building, in particular, has resulted in considerable empowerment in those situations when authentic behavior is encouraged and rewarded. This may be an important area for future research.

In the second essay, "Ethics and Organizational Change," Warren Nielsen, Nick Nykodym, and Don Brown emphasize that along with pressures for change have come critical questions about the ethics of change. These issues, they assert, must be acknowledged and confronted by those involved in change processes. One of the most provocative questions they raise is the following: *"Is it ethical to hold on to the nondirective philosophy?"* They go on to say that "organizations recognize the need for process consultants, but, because of external pressures for change, need consultants who can also function in the task and expert areas."

The third essay, "Re-Energizing the Mature Organization," by Richard Beatty and David Ulrich, discusses one of the key challenges of this era. The authors note that during the decades since World War II, many organizations grew, reached maturity, and then began to decline. Their article describes the necessary steps to take after downsizing (people) to motivate the remaining employees to design the organization for the future that will have a sustained competitive advantage.

In the fourth essay, "Managing Discontinuities," C. K. Prahalad describes major discontinuities he sees facing *all managers* as the world moves into the next millennium. Trends we have seen in the past may be interrupted, or will be juxtaposed with conflicting trends that must be accommodated, or will converge to crate major new challenges and opportunities. While Prahalad does not refer to OD & T directly, some

of the challenges he mentions certainly cry for OD-type help, for example, dislocation of employees, mergers, the creation of teams from several different cultures; the
formation of temporary alliances; speed in disseminating and absorbing new knowledge; the introduction of new skills into organizations; the need for "processes that
improve the ability of teams to develop special skills," and dealing with four levels of
diversity: "race, gender, cultural, and intellectual."

In the fifth essay, "Seven Practices of Successful Organizations," Jeffrey Pfeffer
describes seven dimensions he sees as characterizing "most if not all of the systems
producing profits through people." All are congruent with successful OD & T efforts;
some like "self-managed teams and decentralization of decision making" may be outcomes of OD & T efforts. Pfeffer's seven practices are "employment security," "selective hiring of new personnel," "self-managed teams and decentralization of decision
making" "comparatively high compensation contingent on organizational performance," "extensive training," "reduced status distinctions and barriers, including dress,
language, office arrangements, and wage differences across all levels," and "extensive
sharing of financial and performance information through the organization."

John Nirenberg, in the sixth essay, "From Team Building to Community Building," sees the next logical step after the development of self-managing teams to be
building what he calls "workplace community." He sees community as a form of
organization, "a structure of relationships, a process of working with one another, and
as a mechanism for establishing personal and group expectations, it encourages fruitful participation by each member of the organization." The most immediate requirement in building workplace community, according to Nirenberg, is the matter of
"peer relationship building." He concludes the essay with 13 conditions that are necessary for an organization to move from self-directed teams to workplace community.

W. Warner Burke, in his "The New Agenda for Organization Development,"
reminds us that OD traditionally has emphasized such values as human development,
fairness, openness, choice, and balance of autonomy and constraint. He goes on to
say, "A number of senior practitioners in OD, i.e., those with 20 or more years of
experience, believe that the profession has lost its way—that its values are no longer
sufficiently honored, much less practiced, and that the unrelenting emphasis on the
bottom line has taken over." In particular, Burke finds these values largely absent in
reengineering and downsizing practices and discusses the appropriate role for the
OD practitioner when the client is contemplating moving in one or both of these
directions. Of even more importance, Burke believes, is for OD practitioners to
become involved with the deep issues of "community," the "employer-employee
social contract," the concept of "employability," "trust," "culture clash," and "corporate power."

Reading 40
Empowerment: The Emperor's New Clothes

Chris Argyris

Considering its much touted potential, it's no wonder that empowerment receives all the attention it does. Who wouldn't want more highly motivated employees to help scale the twenty-first century? As one CEO has said, "No vision, no strategy can be achieved without able and empowered employees."

Top-level executives accept their responsibilities to try to develop empowered employees. Human resource professionals devise impressive theories of internal motivation. Experts teach change management. Executives themselves launch any number of programs from reengineering to continuous improvement to TQM. But little of it works.[1]

Take reengineering for instance. Although the rhetoric of reengineering is consistent with empowerment, in reality it is anything but that. Both research and practice indicate that the best results of reengineering occur when jobs are rigorously specified and not when individuals are left to define them. Even the GE workout sessions had their greatest success when the problems resolved were relatively routine. Reengineering has led to improvements in performance, but it has not produced the number of highly motivated employees needed to ensure consistently high-performing organizations.

Few executives would deny that there has been little growth in empowerment over the last 30 years. But why that is so remains a riddle. The answer is complex. The change programs and practices we employ are full of inner contradictions that cripple innovation, motivation, and drive. At the same time, CEOs subtly undermine empowerment. Managers love empowerment in theory, but the command-and-control model is what they trust and know best. For their part, employees are often ambivalent about empowerment—it is great as long as they are not held personally accountable. Even the change professionals often stifle empowerment. Thus, despite all the best efforts that have gone into fostering empowerment, it remains very much like the emperor's new clothes: we praise it loudly in public and ask ourselves privately why we can't see it. There has been no transformation in the workforce, and there has been no sweeping metamorphosis.

Two Kinds of Commitment

To understand why there has been no transformation, we need to begin with commitment. Commitment is not simply a human relations concept. It is an idea that is fundamental to our thinking about economics, strategy, financial governance, information technology, and operations. Commitment is about generating human energy and activating the human mind. Without it, the implementation of any new initiative or idea would be seriously compromised. Human beings can commit themselves in two fundamentally different ways: externally and internally. Both are valuable in the workplace, but only internal commitment reinforces empowerment. (See the exhibit "How Commitment Differs.")

External commitment—think of it as contractual compliance—is what an organization gets when workers have little control over their destinies. It is a fundamental truth of human nature and psychology that the less power people have to shape their lives, the less commitment they will have. When, for example, management single-handedly defines work conditions for employees, the employees will almost certainly be externally committed. That

Source: Reprinted by permission of *Harvard Business Review*. From "Empowerment: The Emperor's New Clothes" by Chris Argyris, May–June 1998. Copyright © 1998 by the President and Fellows of Harvard College; all rights reserved.

How Commitment Differs

External Commitment

Tasks are defined by others.

The behavior required to perform tasks is defined by others.

Performance goals are defined by management.

The importance of the goal is defined by others.

Internal Commitment

Individuals define tasks.

Individuals define the behavior required to perform tasks.

Management and individuals jointly define performance goals that are challenging for the individual.

Individuals define the importance of the goal.

---

commitment is external because all that is left for employees is to do what is expected of them. The employees will not feel responsible for the way the situation itself is defined. How can they? They did not do the defining.

If management wants employees to take more responsibility for their own destiny, it must encourage the development of *internal commitment*. As the name implies, internal commitment comes largely from within. Individuals are committed to a particular project, person, or program based on their own reasons or motivations. By definition, internal commitment is participatory and very closely allied with empowerment. The more that top management wants internal commitment from its employees, the more it must try to involve employees in defining work objectives, specifying how to achieve them, and setting stretch targets.

We might well ask whether everyone must participate in order for empowerment to exist in an organization. In principle, the answer is "yes"; in reality, there is a "but." It is unrealistic to expect management to allow thousands of employees to participate fully in self-governance. The degree to which internal commitment is plausible in any organization is certainly limited. Moreover, the

extent of participation in corporate goals and aspirations will vary with each employee's wishes and intentions.

At SmithKline Beecham, in one of the most far-reaching programs for employee participation that I know of, management used a merger as an opportunity to build empowerment. Throughout the entire organization, more than 400 task forces were created. Yet to this day top management does not believe that internal commitment has been generated throughout the entire company. Their realistic assessment is that not even all the employees on the task forces feel empowered.

To be fair, it is important to remember that empowerment is a goal that organizations approximate but never quite reach. The fact is that it is possible to have various levels of commitment in an organization and still get the job done. Curiously, employees have no trouble understanding the need to keep within bounds. In all my work, I have yet to find employees who make unrealistic demands about empowerment. For top management, then, the essential thing to know is that there are limits to internal commitment. Employees do not understand—in fact, they usually resent—executives preaching internal commitment while continuing to demand external commitment from the rank and file. Indeed, a great source of discontent in organizations is that top-level managers continually risk their credibility by espousing empowerment too glibly.

Clearly, if it is internal commitment that provides the kind of outcomes that CEOs say they want, then they must be realistic and judicious in their demands for it. But the problem goes deeper because the framework that most organizations are now using to transform themselves discourages employees from actually taking responsibility in their jobs.

Change Programs Increase Inner Contradictions

Major change programs are rife with inner contradictions. By this, I mean that even when these programs and policies are implemented correctly, they do not—and cannot—foster the behavior they are meant to inspire. If the inner contradictions are brought to the surface and addressed, they can be dealt with successfully; that is, they will not inhibit the kind of personal commitment that management says it wants. But if the contradictions remain buried and unacknowledged, as they usually do, they become a destructive force. Not only do they stifle the development of empowerment, they also sap the organization's efficiency by breeding frustration and mistrust.

To illustrate, consider the advice that currently represents best practice for implementing and promoting organizational change. That advice breaks the process down into four basic steps:

- Define a *vision*.
- Define a competitive *strategy* consistent with the vision.
- Define organizational *work processes* that, when executed, will implement the strategy.
- Define individual *job requirements* so that employees can carry out the processes effectively.

The underlying pattern of these instructions is consistent with what change researchers and practitioners have learned about effective implementation over the years. Start with a clear framework—

a vision—and progressively make it operational so that it will come alive. So that no one will have any doubts about how to align the four parts of the process, management is advised to speak with one voice. This process makes sense. It is rational.

Yet the process is so riddled with inner contradictions that change programs that follow it will only end up creating confusion, particularly at the implementation stage. Given that all the steps have been so precisely described through a set of instructions, the advice actually encourages more external than internal commitment. Clearly, when employees' actions are defined almost exclusively from the outside (as they are in most change programs), the resulting behavior cannot be empowering and liberating. One immediate consequence is that employees react to the change program by quietly distancing themselves from it. Thus the change program is successful in terms of improving performance because it helps reduce mistakes, as in the case of TQM, or because it helps employees embrace best practices. But at the same time, it undermines internal commitment. In short, the advice for implementing change simply does not provide the new source of energy that many executives want.

But the real danger is that change programs end up poisoning the entire corporation with long-lasting mixed messages. Internally committed employees interpret these messages as "do your own thing—the way we tell you." They reluctantly toe the line. Employees who prefer external commitment will also pick up the mixed messages; however, these people will be relieved because they feel protected from having to take any personal responsibility. In this way, the very working habits that executives do not want to see continued in their organizations are strengthened and reinforced. The result is invariably more inner contradictions and more inefficiency and cynicism, all of which get in the way of real change.

CEOs Undermine Empowerment

CEOs work against empowerment both consciously and unconsciously. Surprisingly—at least to our outsiders—executives do not always seem to want what they say they need. Consider a few typical remarks that I came across during my research. These remarks—excerpted from a roundtable discussion of executives from world-class companies—indicate very clearly the ambivalence of CEOs toward internal commitment and empowerment. The first CEO noted that with "well-defined processes where the variances are small and the operating limits are well defined," you no longer need the old command-and-control approach. Workers are now empowered, "provided they respect the process," he said. The second CEO agreed that these "processes are liberating," while the third observed that many employees have a tough time understanding what it means for processes to be "reliable, respectable, and in control."

Let us stop a moment and ask ourselves how there can be empowerment when there is neither guesswork nor challenges—when the job requirements are predetermined and the processes are controlled. For employees operating in such a world, the environment is not empowering; it is foolproof. This is not a milieu in which individuals can aspire to self-governance. On the contrary, as long as they buy in and follow the dictates of the processes, the employees in the companies just described will only become more externally motivated.

The enthusiastic use of champions in virtually all contemporary change programs sends a similar mixed message from CEOs to employees. Top management is well aware of the dangers of piecemeal implementation and eventual fade-out in major change programs. They strive to overcome those problems by anointing champions. The champions pursue performance objectives with tenacity, managing by decree. They have generous resources available to ensure compliance, and they monitor employees' progress frequently. Altogether, these behaviors reinforce the top-down control features of the external commitment model. The single voice of fervent champions leads employees to feel that management is in control, and it drives out the sense of internal responsibility and personal empowerment. How can employees feel empowered if someone is always "selling" them or controlling them from the top down? Indeed, such champions would not be necessary if employees were internally committed.

The result of all these interventions is disarray. Managers and the change programs they use undermine the empowerment they so desperately want to achieve. Why does this occur? Could it be that today's top-level managers don't truly want empowered employees? In truth, they are probably unsure. At the same time, employees do not hold executives to task for their behavior. Employees have their own mixed feelings about empowerment.

Employees Have Their Doubts

External commitment is a psychological survival mechanism for many employees—it is a form of adaptive behavior that allows individuals to get by in most work environments. How that survival mechanism works is illustrated quite dramatically today in the former East Germany.

When the Berlin Wall came down, a routine way of life for East German workers came to an end. Most workers had learned to survive by complying. For 40 years, most plants were run in accordance with the dictates of central planners. If many East Germans had pushed for greater control over their destinies, their lives might have been endangered. As a result, East German workers over the years learned to define performance as doing the minimum of what was required of them.

After the fall of communism, I participated in many discussions with West German executives who were surprised and baffled by the lack of initiative and aspiration displayed by the East Germans. What those executives failed to understand is how bewildering—indeed, how threatening—it can be for people to take internal commitment seriously, especially those who have lived their entire lives by the rules of external commitment. As I listened to the West German executives who wanted to make East German employees more internally committed, I thought of several cases in the United States and elsewhere where similar problems exist. Again and again in my experience, prolonged external commitment made internal commitment extremely unlikely, because a sense of empowerment is not innate. It is something that must be learned, developed, and honed.

The question, then, is, How do you produce internal commitment? One thing for sure is that the incentive programs executives have used—for instance, higher compensation, better career paths, "employee of the month" recognition awards—simply do not work. On the contrary, in all my years as a change consultant, I have repeatedly witnessed how offering employees the "right" rewards creates dependency rather than empowerment. Inevitably, the power of such methods wears off with use, and all that has been created is more external commitment.

Consider one company with substantial financial woes. In that case, the CEO decided at considerable personal sacrifice to raise his employees' salaries. But his own research later showed that the employees merely considered their raises to be in keeping with their equity in the labor market. Internal commitment had not increased. Employees continued to do only what was asked of them as long as the rewards were increased. They followed the rules, but they did not take any initiative. They did not take risks, nor did they show the sense of personal responsibility that management sought. The CEO was surprised, but I thought that these results were entirely predictable for two reasons. First, pay, like other popular incentive schemes, often advances external commitment while creating a bias against internal commitment. Second, and more fundamental, many employees do not embrace the idea of empowerment with any more gusto than management does. For a lot of people, empowerment is just too much work. Like the workers in East Germany, almost all employees have learned to survive by depending on external commitment.

When it comes to empowerment, executives and employees are engaged in shadowboxing. Management says it wants employees who participate more; employees say they want to be more involved. But it is difficult to know who means what. Is it just a charade? Employees push for greater autonomy; management says the right thing but tries to keep control through information systems, processes, and tools. Employees see vestiges of the old command-and-control model as confirming their worse suspicions—that superiors want unchallenged power. Management just wants to see better numbers. Thus the battle between autonomy and control rages on, and meanwhile, as companies make the transition into the next century, the potential for real empowerment is squandered.

Change Professionals Inhibit Empowerment

During the past decade, I have had the opportunity to work with more than 300 change experts in different organizations. Such individuals differ in their practices and their effectiveness, of course, but more striking than the differences are the patterns that recur.

Caught in the middle of the battle between autonomy and control, the change professional has a tough assignment. The role of the change professional, whether internal or external, is ostensibly to facilitate organizational change and continuous learning. In their own way, however, the vast majority of change professionals actually inhibit empowerment in organizations.

To understand how that occurs, consider what happens as Tom, a change agent, tries to work with Jack, a line manager. (Both are composite figures typical of those I encountered in my research.) Jack is told by his boss to work with Tom, who is there to "help" Jack empower his organization. The change program begins with a series of meetings and discussions. Tom talks passionately about openness, honesty, and trust as the foundations of empowerment. Many employees leave these meetings feeling hopeful about the direction that the company is taking toward more open communication. A month into the program, however, Tom observes that Jack has fallen back into his old style of management. He decides that he had better confront Jack:

Tom's unspoken thoughts:	What Tom and Jack say:
Tom: *Things aren't going well.*	Tom: So how's everything going?
	Jack: Things are going pretty well. There's

a lot of pressure from above, but we're meeting the numbers.

Tom: Great. Super. But I was also wondering how well we're doing at getting people more committed to their jobs. How empowered do you think people feel?

Jack: Well, I think we're doing okay. If there are problems, people come to me and we work it out. Sure, some people are never satisfied. But that's just a few people, and we can handle them.

Tom: Look, Jack, if you solve all their problems, how are we going to empower our employees?

Tom: *Oh great. All Jack cares about is the numbers. Empowerment isn't even on his agenda.*

Tom: *Just what I feared. Jack's not "walking the talk." He just doesn't get it at all.*

Tom: *This is hopeless! There's got to be an easier way to make a living. I'll never get through to him. I wish I could tell Jack what I think, but I don't want to put him on the defensive. I've got to stay cool.*

Jack: Well, to be honest with you, Tom, the signal I'm getting from above is that my job is to produce the numbers without, you know, upsetting people. To be fair, I think I'm doing that.

What's happening here? The change program that began with great enthusiasm is clearly in deep trouble. It's a pattern I've observed over and over again. After the initial excitement passes, reality inevitably settles in. Put aside the nice rhetoric of empowerment, employees *will* have problems. They *will* ask their managers for help, and their managers *will* tell them what to do. That is how most work gets done and how organizations meet their numbers. And in many cases, there's absolutely nothing wrong with this, except that it goes against the theory of empowerment.

What does Tom do when he observes Jack telling his employees what to do? Instead of figuring out whether Jack is doing the right thing in this situation, change experts like Tom will almost always be dismayed, because the managers aren't walking the talk of empowerment. Rarely have I seen a change professional help a manager deal effectively with being caught between a rock and a hard place. Even more uncommon is a change agent who offers practical advice to the manager about what to do.

Not only is Tom unwilling to acknowledge the real problem Jack is having, but he papers over his own thoughts. He tries to act as if he still believes the program can be successful when, in fact, he has given up hope. Tom himself is guilty of not walking the talk of openness, honesty, and trust.

In my experience, line managers are far more willing to acknowledge the inner contradictions of change programs—at least, in private. They will admit to distancing themselves from the soft stuff—two-way participation, internal commitment, and discontinuous thinking—to focus instead on the numbers. Managers like Jack often conclude—rightly, I'm afraid—that the change agent does not know how to help them. So Jack listens politely as Tom warns him about the dangers of backsliding and exhorts him to be more persistent. And then Jack goes on about his business.

In the end, everyone is frustrated. In theory, empowerment should make it easier for organizations to meet their numbers. But when change programs are imposed without recognizing the limitations of empowerment and when managers and employees are not helped to deal effectively and openly with them, the organization ends up worse off than it was to begin with. Empowerment too often enters the realm of political correctness, which means that no one can say what he or she is thinking: this is just nonsense. In this scenario, if you challenge the change agent, you become an enemy of change.

So instead of feeling more empowered, people throughout the organization feel more trapped and less able to talk openly about what's really going on. Is it any wonder that change programs don't succeed and that they actually undermine the credibility of top management?

What Is to Be Done?

Despite all the rhetoric surrounding transformation and major change programs, the reality is that today's managers have not yet encountered change programs that work. As we have seen, the reasons for that are complex. Although managers share some of the responsibility for undermining internal motivation in their organizations, the change programs that could create high levels of internal commitment and empowerment in corporations do not yet exist. That is why I believe it is time to begin the research and experimentation that is required to find some viable answers. But for now, let me begin with some recommendations that may help executives think more sensibly about empowerment.

• Recognize that every company has both top-down controls and programs that empower people, and that some inconsistencies are inevitable and must simply be managed. When these inner contradictions become apparent, encourage individuals to bring them to the surface; otherwise, a credibility gap will be created that can pollute the organization for many years to come.

• Don't undertake blatantly contradictory programs. For instance, stop creating change programs that are intended to expand internal commitment but are designed in ways that produce external commitment. Make sure that what is being espoused will not contradict what actually happens.

• Understand that empowerment has its limits. Know how much can be created and what can be accomplished. Know that empowerment is not a cure-all. Do not evoke it needlessly. Once it has been created, do not misuse it. Be clear about who has the right to change things. Specify the likely limits of permissible change.

• Realize that external and internal commitment can coexist in organizations but that how they do so is crucial to the ultimate success or failure of empowerment in the organization. For instance, external commitment is all it takes for performance in most routine jobs. Unnecessary attempts to increase empowerment only end up creating downward spirals of cynicism, disillusionment, and inefficiencies. As a first precaution, distinguish between jobs that require internal commitment and those that do not.

• Establish working conditions to increase empowerment in the organization. If you want to help individuals move away from external commitment, encourage them to examine their own behavior. It has been my experience that many employees are willing to become more personally committed if management is really sincere, if the work allows it, and if the rewards reinforce it.

• Calculate factors such as morale; satisfaction, and even commitment into your human relations policies, but do not make them the ultimate criteria. They are penultimate. The ultimate goal is performance. Individuals can be excellent performers and report low morale, yet it is performance and not morale that is paramount. When morale, satisfaction, and sense of empowerment are used as the ultimate criteria for success in organizations, they cover up many of the problems that organizations must overcome in the twenty-first century.

• Help employees understand the choices they make about their own level of commitment. One of the most helpful things we can do in organizations—indeed, in life—is to require that human beings not knowingly kid themselves about their effectiveness.

Finally, remember that empowerment can run contrary to human nature, and be realistic about how to achieve and use it. To paraphrase Abraham Lincoln: You can empower all of the people some of the time and some of the people all of the time, but you can't empower all of the people all of the time. In the last analysis, nobody should expect more than that.

Endnote

1. For a description of the similarities and differences in employee-involvement, reengineering, and TQM programs, see Susan Alberts Mohrman, J. R. Galbraith, and Edward E. Alwair, *Tomorrow's Organization* (San Francisco: Jossey-Bass, 1998); J. Hendry, "Processing Reengineering and the Dynamic Balance of the Organization," *European Management Journal*, vol. 1:3, no. 1, pp. 52–57; T. Eccles, "The Deceptive Allure of Empowerment," *Long Range Planning*, vol. 26, no. 6, pp. 13–21; and B. G. Jackson, "Reengineering the Sense of Self: The Managers and the Management Gurus," *Journal of Management Studies*, 1996, vol. 33, no. 5, pp. 571–590.

READING 41
ETHICS AND ORGANIZATIONAL CHANGE

Warren R. Nielsen
Nick Nykodym
Don J. Brown

Introduction

Within the United States we are seeing the demise of once large and powerful organizations; the rapid birth, growth and death of many high technologically oriented organizations; large numbers of mergers in an attempt to diversify or generate a stronger financial base; the introduction of, and growth of franchises offering some market stability; and the attack on the once unquestioned military/industrial complexes.

With these changes in society and organizations have come numerous individuals, groups, and fields of study, which offer assistance to organizations in both managing and instigating internal change. The successes, failures, contributions, and inadequacies of management consulting in providing organizations with methodology and technology to improve organizational effectiveness and health and improve the quality of work life for employees have been reviewed in the literature for nearly 20 years.

In any approach there are a number of ethical issues which have been previously considered by Walton and Warwick (1973), Miles (1979), Frame, Hess, and Nielsen (1982), the OD Institute (1985), Nykodym, Nielsen, and Christen (1985), and Nykodym, Ruud, and Liverpool (1986). Unfortunately, many involved in the field of organizational change have been so busy collecting data for research, attempting to have a positive impact so consulting operations may continue; or trying to

Note: The authors would like to acknowledge the comments of two anonymous reviewers and those of Larry Pate, Colleen Bement, and Rachel Call on previous drafts of this paper.

Source: Warren R. Nielsen, Nick Nykodym, and Don J. Brown (1991), "Ethics and Organizational Change," *Asia Pacific HRM,* vol. 29, no. 1, pp. 82–93; reprinted with permission of *Asia Pacific Journal of Human Resources.*

develop and implement new change strategies, that little real attention has been paid to the ethical issues involved in the process of change.

The purpose of this paper is threefold: first, to review the ethical issues which have already been raised; second, to outline some new considerations which have developed over the past few years; and finally, to make some suggestions relative to the ethics of organization change for both the researcher and the practitioner.

In drawing attention to ethical issues already raised, an attempt to not re-invent the wheel will be made by drawing upon Walton and Warwick (1973), Miles (1979), and the OD Institute (1985). The framework used to specify the issues will be to separate them into issues faced before, during, and after the application of any change intervention(s).

Before Intervention

A major ethical issue facing those involved in organizational change is actually engaging in a discussion of the ethics that will provide the overall parameters within which the client, practitioner, or researcher will act. Such action appears to be relatively simple, but experience to date would indicate that it is seldom done. Too often ethical issues are raised during the project, frequently in a conflict situation, when major work must be set aside until differences are resolved. Even whole projects which had great potential for positive impact on organizational effectiveness, health, and quality of work life have been discontinued because of ethical issues between clients, practitioners, and researchers not dealt with before the project began. It may be that some of those involved in organizational change may be reluctant to openly examine the change objectives of the practitioner because of fear that the client would not be willing to proceed if they were known. On the other hand, it may be that the client's ethics regarding change are not examined because of the belief that the change process itself will change them sufficiently so that they will be consistent with the project and/or the underlying values and beliefs of the strategy being applied.

By far the most important ethical issue that should be dealt with before any change strategy is implemented is that of defining the goals, behavioral outcomes, or expected change objectives. Those involved in the field of organizational change are, at times, painfully aware of the vague unspecified goals used to launch an organization change effort. Probably, over the years, most practitioners have been, at one time or another, so anxious to get a major project started and underway that they have deluded themselves and their clients that the work is an 'emerging' process and that the goals will become clear as more and more is learned regarding the organization. Though it would be foolish to imply that all goals could be established before the change process is undertaken, it would be a breach of ethics to not do everything possible to insure that the client and practitioner know where the change process is likely to lead. Too often, attempts at organizational change appear as the proverbial "Christopher Columbus voyage." Kubr (1986) emphasizes the need for the client and consultant to define the problem together. The clients, immersed in the situation, may be too involved to see the problem objectively. Consultants will make greater progress if they work directly with the client on problem definition. From this basis, clients and consultants will be able to effectively work together to clarify what results are desired from the consulting process.

Another critical issue is that of who will be involved in the establishment of the goals and behavioral objectives. Walton and Warwick (1973), Miles (1979), and the OD Institute (1985) all warn of not solely relying on the higher level managers and administrators to establish the goals. They argue that, since most organizational participants could, at some time, be dramatically impacted by the process, those lower in the organization should also have input. Philosophically, it is difficult to argue with such a position, particularly given the underlying values of the field of organizational change. The difficulty with this issue is the ability to get real involvement on the part of all participants, particularly if the change project is in a very large system. When the authors first began working with one large automotive corporation, that organization employed over one million individuals. To even take a sample of what the employees believed should be the goals would have been a major undertaking and would have taken so long that the change effort would never have been undertaken. Also, in some organizations in which unions exist, and where there is a strong adversarial relationship, consultants and researchers may not be permitted to talk to employees at lower levels.

The authors' feeble solution to this issue is to start with overall goals developed primarily by the top, but with an agreement that new, though consistent goals would be established as each new part of the organization becomes involved. Also, in large projects, we have built in provisions for goal review and modification on at least a quarterly basis. As we have struggled with this issue, we found ourselves coming to the position that as many of the participants as possible should be involved in setting goals; however, the value of high involvement must be considered against the possibility of the occurrence of more serious organizational problems developing during the goal-setting process. To move quickly on goals established by only part of the organization and to have positive impact on the organizational variables that will insure a positive position and provide greater flexibility may be more ethical than attempting to involve the entire organization (at least at the beginning) in the goal-setting process.

Another issue that needs to be considered is that of the process utilized to determine the initial targets for intervention. Should top management make the decision or should it be made with input from the rest of the organization? If people have input there is more support; however, given certain information and perspective, the top may, in fact, be in a better position to establish the target area. The size of the organization also affects this dilemma. In a small organization, it may be relatively easy to get input from all potential participants; whereas, in a large organization, this is much more difficult. In either case, the issue needs to be discussed and the reason for how an area is selected should be made very clear.

Prior to the activation of a change process in any organization, the practitioner or researcher should confront some very personal ethical questions such as:

- What are my own personal values, and how will they impact on this project?
- What are my skills and abilities, and are they sufficient to promote the required change?
- Am I willing to accept the responsibility for the consequences of my decisions and acts upon the organization?
- Am I willing to share all "need to know" data with the client?

It is the authors' perception that the whole field of organizational change would be more effective and would have had a greater positive impact on organizations over the past 20 years had these questions been asked and dealt with honestly. It should be noted, however, that clients can also put pressure on change practitioners to accept and direct projects which are beyond their skill level. The authors are acquainted with a current case where the external consultant does superb team building and has a very positive image with the division management group of a particular manufacturing corporation. This consultant, because of the relationship, was forced upon the management of one of the corporation's assembly plants by division management. The assembly plant, if it is to continue, requires an extensive sociotechnical transformation. Unfortunately, the plant is now involved in a great deal of team building which will likely have little, if any, impact on the real

problems of the organization. In addition, the plant has been given a three-year period to move from a negative to a positive position in nearly every measurable organizational performance indicator. If such a turnaround does not occur, the facility is to be sold. The sale of the facility could result in the termination of approximately 4,000 employees.

Another issue that needs to be clarified prior to the initiation of a change project is the projected costs involved. For this issue to be adequately deal with, the practitioner needs to be very clear with the prospective client regarding fees, travel expenses, material costs, and lost-time cost for participants who will have to be away from their normal work assignments. Currently the authors are involved in a project in Mexico where the travel expenses far exceed the daily fees. Fortunately, the possibility of this situation occurring was openly discussed and agreed to prior to the initiation of the project.

Another crucial issue facing the field of organizational change is that of claims made by practitioners and, to some degree, researchers. Unfortunately, there are few descriptions of failures in the literature, but most practitioners and researchers know of at least several. Too often, those interested in the field, and prospective clients, are faced with the problem of exaggerated claims relative to the viability of organizational change methodologies. If the claims had been more realistic, would the field today have greater credibility in the eyes of prospective clients? Also, would there be more opportunities of learning how to change organizations had the exaggerated claims not led to the demise of many projects? The authors have found high-level managers and administrators more willing to experiment when they were aware, prior to the beginning of a project, that untested interventions and methods were to be utilized.

Miles (1979) and the OD Institute (1985) raise the issue that all organizational participants should have a choice in launching an organizational change process. They argue that all participants should have full information relative to outcomes and costs prior to committing to a full-scale organizational change project. As with the development of change goals, an ethical statement or position such as this sounds appropriate, but becomes very difficult to accomplish in an organization of any size. Certainly, an attempt to keep everyone up to date through the use of newsletters, group meetings, etc., can and should be made. However, in a large organization the process is likely to be weak at best and may break down and become a deterrent, rather than a help. No doubt, most practitioners and some researchers would question the validity of trying to inform all organization participants prior to intervention and may argue that, to do so, might generate expectations or resistance which could not be dealt with adequately. Many of those involved in change strategies argue for intervening into the organization one part at a time. There may be cases where informing the whole organization could be disruptive to the specific project.

Because change projects can go very well or very poorly, depending on numerous situations, circumstances, and decisions, a specific question needs to be raised for the protection of both the client and practitioner—"How can the relationship be discontinued?" The authors have very strong feelings that, if a project is going very poorly, due to reasons outside the consultant's control, the consultant should not be forced to continue an effort which is clearly doomed. On the other hand, the client should not have to continue an effort which is seen as harmful to the organization, its employees, and cash flow. Based on the above, the authors always utilize a contract which allows either party to withdraw with a 30-day written notice. The result has been a greater level of trust between the parties and an assurance that both will genuinely try to make the project a success.

During the Activity

As is the case before intervening in a system to produce change, once a project is launched ethical issues arise which need to be recognized and dealt with by both practitioners and researchers.

Relative to issues during a change project, Walton and Warwick (1973), Miles (1979), and the OD Institute (1985) all focus on the collection and use of data which is obtained from organizational participants. They raise such questions as:

- What data are collected?
- What format is utilized?
- What happens to the data?
- Who gets the data?
- Is the autonomy of the providers protected?

There are still pertinent ethical questions that need to be asked and resolved prior to the collection of any data. There is no question that data can be used to punish organizational participants, and steps must be placed in the process to help prevent such behavior. On the other hand, it is possible that the questions above reflect an old bias from the days of sensitivity training and the use of team-building models which were very interpersonal in nature. In today's setting, some slightly different questions need to be asked, such as:

- Will the data be collected and processed in such a manner that the source(s) of problems can be recognized?
- Will the data be given to individuals who can best solve the problems?
- Will the format used facilitate an understanding of the data (allowing those who furnished the data to explain what it means)?
- Will the format facilitate the obtaining of further data which could more specifically define the problems?

Surely practitioners and researchers must be beyond the point of collecting data where anonymity is guaranteed, and the data are processed solely for the review by upper-management personnel who can make little sense of the data and have great difficulty in trying to resolve any issues that may be contained therein.

A few years ago, the authors were involved in a major organizational change project with a large engineering organization. The organization employed nearly 3,000 engineers and support personnel and was part of a multinational corporation. The project was directed by a steering committee made up of individuals from all levels and functions. The steering committee wanted to collect some data utilizing a format which would insure that the data could be acted on. The result was a survey instrument designed to identify data by work group and through which the providers of the data could explain their perceptions and be involved in problem resolution. The survey also provided an opportunity for the respondents to sign the questionnaire if they so desired. All of the employees were brought into a meeting where the purpose of the format of the survey was explained and questions could be asked. The participants were told that problems could only be solved if it was possible to discern the location of the problems, and the individuals in those areas had an opportunity to develop and implement solutions. The survey was given out and each employee was asked to complete the form and mail it to the consultant's office several states away. We have always believed that it was very significant that 100 percent of the questionnaires were returned, and 95 percent were signed.

The point of the above illustration is that the wrong questions relative to data may be being asked. Rather than asking, "Will anonymity be protected?" the question should be, "Will the data make it possible for the organization to act on and solve problems, whether they be technical, social or interpersonal?"

Another issue that is raised, but often ignored, is that of "Who is the client?" Most change practitioners and researchers are brought in, given access to various aspects of the organization, and paid by the senior management of the organization. Argyris (1970) and Beckhard (1969) take the position that a change effort should, in fact, be directed by the top of the organization. On the other hand, Kubr (1986) realizes that those whose work will be affected by the change process should also be taken into consideration. While guidance from upper-level management is necessary, implementation will require cooperation of the workers. Walton and

Warwick (1973) also raise the issue as to the freedom of individuals to participate in the change process. They discuss the necessity of informed consent, lack of coercion, lack of manipulation, and avoiding the misuse of data. Though these issues may be relevant, they again seem to apply more to the highly interpersonal interventions of the past. As change consultants attempt, as they are now, to facilitate large-scale systems change, these issues seem to fade somewhat. in fact, if large-scale systems change is to be accomplished, all organizational participants must participate in the process and cannot have the option of sitting on the sidelines and watching. Also, there simply may not be sufficient time to insure every individual the freedom of choice in the change process.

One model for dealing with some of these issues has been initiated in the General Motors Corporation (GM) where the change teams consist both of salaried employees and employees represented by the United Auto Workers Union (UAW). Before launching change projects at any particular location, there is an agreement that approval will be given both by GM and the UAW. This model may have great potential in dealing with the issue of freedom of participation; however, it has not been in place a sufficient length of time to determine the real results and impact.

Another issue which has particularly faced practitioners using primarily interpersonal change models has been whether the client system is really interested in change or just the achievement of stability. If the practitioner is restricted to interpersonal models, real change is unlikely to occur (Pate 1979). This being the case, the practitioner could be entrapped into a situation where the real reason for the project is to appease or mollify employees in the organization. Therefore, two factors appear to be critical. First, the practitioner and client must come to a firm agreement that actual change is the goal, and its achievement is to be monitored on a regular basis throughout the project. Second, the project must be so designated that it is not limited to a single organizational variable. Given the interdependencies between organizational variables, work on one area may produce short-run change, but in the long run the organization will most likely return to its prior condition or state.

While working as consultants within a large U.S. insurance firm, the authors became aware of a particular situation which was most troubling and appeared to be a major issue of ethics in organizational change. As change consultants, we were becoming so enthralled with the process of change that we were actually pushing the client system into a position of overplanning and overintervening. The question of how the organizational participants could plan and implement major change and, at the same time, continue the accomplishment of regular tasks and processes, was not asked. As the project continued, it became apparent that pushing the organization to change too many things at one time was leading to failure. In this situation, organizational participants who genuinely wanted to plan for and initiate change were becoming overloaded to the point where they gave up on change plans and went back to doing only their normally assigned tasks. The ethic then is: *Don't push an organization for more change than that which can be handled within the organization's parameters and constraints.* This is not to say that, in a large transformation effort, normal tasks and duties may not be set aside completely and total attention, time, and skills given to the change effort.

The practitioners must assist those ultimately responsible for the change process to establish specific but attainable goals and priorities within realistic time periods. In addition, these goals, priorities, and time frames need to be carefully monitored to insure that there is consistency between goals and the organization's ability to attain those goals.

The argument has repeatedly been made that an organization is an open system and, therefore, change methodologies and technologies must be based on a systems approach. Unfortunately, an examination of consulting projects (Pate, Nielsen, & Bacon, 1977) shows little evidence that a systems approach to organization change has been utilized. Most projects have focused on one or two variables

at the most. In working with client systems, the authors have used a particular descriptive model of organizations to assist those directing the change process in recognizing all the variables which will require anywhere from major change to slight modification. The model is illustrated in Figure 1.

Using the model with clients has helped to insure that a systems approach is taken and that sufficient variables are changed which will, in turn, produce real measurable organizational change.

As a project moves down through an organization, particularly one of any size, another serious question with major ethical implications must be asked and answered. The question is—"How much say will those who are directly or even indirectly affected by the change(s) have in the direction of the change?" It would appear as though this concern is currently being more appropriately dealt with by consultants than in the past. Most current projects with which the authors are familiar require and have built-in mechanisms to involve organizational participants in planning and directing the required change at their level. Again, the joint GM/UAW consulting team is a good illustration of getting all levels of an organization involved and participating in the process. One of the most significant factors in the design of GM's highly acclaimed Saturn project was the extensive planning involvement of the manufacturing facility system and culture, by individuals from all organizational levels.

The last issue which needs to be mentioned is that of the length of the project itself and how long the organization will need to rely on outside resources. One of the original purposes of organizational change consulting was to build an organization capable of continually monitoring the need for and initiating appropriate change to respond to changing environments. The ethic of assisting the organization in its attempts to change, but not building dependent relationships, still seems appropriate today. Greiner and Metzger (1983) point out that dependency between the client and the consultant is inherent in long-term relationships. The client depends on the consultant's availability and

FIGURE 1

Interaction of organizational variables

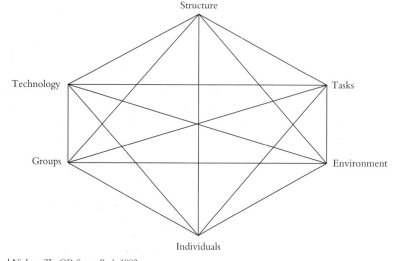

Source: Frame, Hess, and Nielsen. *The OD Source Book,* 1982.

advice, and the consultant depends on a steady income. But when the consultant begins doing work that could be performed by the client, or when the consultant depends solely on the client for income, the situation is unhealthy and should be discontinued. Kubr (1986) emphasizes that consultants can cause problems by both leaving too early or terminating too late, and that they should discuss withdrawal with the client before intervention and continue discussions periodically throughout the assignment.

After Major Change Interventions

If those who intervene in organizations for the purpose of producing real organizational change have faced and adequately dealt with the ethical issues prior to and during the effort, there are few issues left once the practitioner has left the system. Having said this though, there are some issues that need to be considered by both practitioners and researchers.

One such issue was raised by Miles (1979)—that being possible harm occurring to individuals who have participated in the project. It appears that practitioners who have been in this field for any length of time have made a real effort not to have change strategies primarily utilized for the purpose of reducing headcount, or simply implementing plans which enable fewer people to do more work, thus creating an excess of employees who are subject to employee reductions. Unfortunately, this issue may not be raised prior to intervening in a system and assurances obtained from top management that reduction of employees would not be the primary goal of the change activity. If practitioners are successful in improving the organization, there may well be less employees required, and individuals who lack necessary skills may be identified. In the past, this problem was primarily experienced at the lower levels of organizations; but as practitioners and consultants have become more proficient, the impact of change strategies, as noted by Naisbitt and Aburdene (1985), is being felt by large numbers of middle managers. A conclusion that may be drawn is that, when starting change projects, practitioners and researchers should insist that this issue be brought into the open and that the organizations involved develop and implement effective outplacement programs or changes in retirement programs so that a potential reduction in force is not a devastating experience for organizational participants.

The second issue noted, which has ethical ramifications, is that of unintended negative results. An illustration may serve to clarify this point. Several years ago the authors were involved in a change effort in a large manufacturing firm with approximately 5,000 employees. The early stages of the project were focused primarily on the production manager and his immediate staff. Through the change activities, the production group became more and more effective and more organizationally powerful. The effect was that other interdependent departments began to interact less and less with the production group. The other departments felt powerless in relation to the production management team and, out of fear, decreased the necessary interaction and supply of services to them. The answer to this problem may be considerably oversimplified, but it appears as though, if potential negative consequences are identified and discussed, plans can be developed to avoid or reduce them.

The problem which has continued to cause the authors the greatest concern over the years is that of working with an organization, seeing great benefits come from the effort, and then, from a distance, watching the organization revert back to previous patterns and outcomes. One such project has been of particular concern. In brief summary: through a great deal of work, the authors, with other outside consultants, were able to bring a major function of one of the world's largest corporations from the position of being the worst to the best on every performance measure and to significantly assist in obtaining a $14 million savings. Unfortunately, today the function has lost at least 50 percent of the gain obtained. The issue that

must be dealt with is that of maintenance. Those involved in organizational change could be subject to criticism for not including actions and procedures which adequately maintain and protect gains.

The way in which the authors have attempted to deal with this dilemma is not to accept contracts which do not include the assurance from top management that an appropriate number of internal resource personnel will be hired or trained to work with the authors and to assure the necessary follow up and maintenance.

One final concern is directed at those involved in research and evaluation. The field of organizational change continues to lack appropriate evaluation and assessment. Data regarding success or failure continues to be primarily anecdotal in nature. Closely controlled, rigorous studies are needed if practitioners are to be able to evaluate their effectiveness, make necessary modifications, and develop new interventions and strategies. Kubr (1986) proposes that evaluation of the consultation process should be a joint effort between client and consultant. He points out that by evaluating specific benefits to the client, such as new capabilities, new systems, and behavior, and new performance, interpretations of the outcome become clearer. Evaluations are also needed which do not stop after one intervention measurement. Evaluations are desperately needed which track the impact of our work with organizations over a significant time.

Current Issues

As mentioned at the beginning of this paper, most companies and industries in the United States are facing the critical need to change quickly. In the last few years, once-strong organizations have disappeared and whole industries have become very weak because of their inability to compete with both domestic and foreign entities. This environmental condition has raised questions for which solutions are required.

First, those involved in changing organizations must focus on more than the human variable.

Though few would argue that the human variable is extremely important in the total change process, this is not the only variable which must be changed. Therefore, if practitioners, executives, and researchers are to be successful, they must have skills in dealing with and changing many organizational variables simultaneously. Therefore, three of the current ethical questions that need to be asked by practitioners, consultants, and researchers are:

- Am I ready and do I have the skills to work with numerous variables?
- Am I prepared to obtain and utilize support of other professionals in areas of the change project where I lack the necessary skills?
- If we take on projects without the necessary skills in this new environment, are we being ethical relative to clients, organizational participants, communities, and maybe even societies?

Second, foreign competition has become so fierce that U.S. organizations, if they are to survive, must change and change quickly. This very need for speed in the change process brings current needs into conflict with some of the older ethical statements, such as that everyone in the organization should be informed of the process so they can "have" free choice in terms of participating. A particular ethical issue that may supersede the above mentioned is:

"Am I, as a consultant, researcher, or manager, prepared to do as much as possible in a short time frame to enable organizations and, possibly whole industries to survive?"

Third, whereas ethical concerns of the past have focused primarily upon the organization involved in the change process, growing interdependencies are mandating a broader view. The issue of the potential impact of change interventions on communities, geographical areas, other organizations, and society need to be acknowledged. In addition, as change efforts are initiated which involve multiple organizations and possibly whole industries, the following ethical question needs to be asked: *"Are*

organizational change practitioners helping to establish new ethics and values in society, and is that their role?"

Certainly we are bringing about value shifts without getting input from all those impacted upon by our work.

Fourth, organizational change, in the past, has been a relatively slow, deliberate process. Practitioners were facilitators and operated primarily out of a nondirective model. However, the question that can now be raised as the need for fast and extensive change becomes more and more the need of organizations is: *"Is it ethical to hold on to the nondirective philosophy?"*

It may be possible that the ethical question now is whether or not the practitioner has the skills and is ready to provide facilitative content, as well as expert roles. The authors' recent experience would indicate that organizations recognize the need for process consultants, but, because of external pressures for change, need consultants who can also function in the task and expert arenas.

Fifth, current organizational change requirements are pushing those involved in the field to not just talk about systems approaches but to actually use system models in their change activities. No longer can having done teambuilding or conducted experiential training in all parts of the organization be, in any way, considered a systems approach.

Sixth, there is a growing need for consulting teams made up of individuals who are particularly trained to provide options for impacting on specific variables. The question to be asked is: *"Is a change team being utilized which provides for dealing with and impacting on several variables simultaneously?"*

Seventh, overall change strategies with goals, objectives, time frames, change targets, responsibilities, and assessment methods must be developed and utilized. OD practitioners and consultants have had the luxury, in the past, of implementing one phase of a change effort and then determining the next phase or steps. Given the enormous pressure on organizations, a one step at a time process is inconsistent with the needs. This is not to say that flexibility and a commitment to appropriate modification through the change process should be abandoned. However, to enter into a major organizational change effort with a change strategy is, indeed, unethical.

Suggestions and Conclusions

In conclusion, the authors offer a series of suggestions to both the practitioner and the researcher. This is not intended to be an exhaustive list but, rather, a small base upon which others might build.

Relative to practitioners, seven suggestions are offered. First, be aware of and sensitive to the ethical issues in the field of organizational change, as well as the source and strength of these issues. Second, include a discussion and obtain agreement from the client relative to the ethics which will guide the change effort. Third, recognize that the ethics and ethical questions of the past may not fit the current need for rapid and extensive change and that new ethics are emerging. Fourth, discard old variable change models. They may have fit and produced positive results in the past, but are totally inadequate in our current environment. Fifth, insist on more assessment of the impact of interventions. The field of organizational change has once again moved into a time frame where new interventions and approaches are being developed, utilized, and nearly being marketed as the "cure-all" answer to the problems of change. As practitioners and consultants, do not allow a repeat of the past by becoming dependent on anecdotes and continuing to use interventions that have little or no value. Sixth, develop and be able to use the skills necessary to build organizational change strategies. Seventh, stop talking about and begin to truly utilize systems models to produce actual and measurable organizational change.

To the researchers, the authors include some suggestions as well. Again, these are not offered as an exhaustive list but, rather, some areas which need work and which could lead to more and improved assessment. First, produce quality, valid research on organizational change in terms of impact on various variables, intervention effectiveness in accomplishing stated objectives, and identification of real and potential negative consequences as a result of change projects. Second, be willing to provide more than just assessment studies. Assist practitioners by becoming more familiar with organizations in order to provide useful input into the design and implementation of change projects. Third, provide comparison data on the impact of organizational change where different change strategies have been utilized. Fourth, develop longitudinal studies which will provide insights into why particular change projects remain viable and effective over time, while others diminish or die.

In conclusion, the field of organizational change is extremely value-laden. Clients, practitioners, and researchers come into change projects with both individual and organizational values. Interventions come out of values. Interventions in the organization are nearly always based on some value judgment, and the way our results are assessed is often the result of the researchers' value regarding what organizational measures should be assessed.

Those in the field of organizational change are being called upon more than ever to assist organizations to survive and become viable once again. What is done in organizations may have profound impact on society. Those involved in organizational change must acknowledge, deal with, and test the underlying ethics that affect every change project undertaken.

References

Argyris, E. *Intervention Theory and Method.* Reading, MA: Addison-Wesley, 1970.

Beckhard, R. *Organization Development: Strategies and Models.* Reading, Mass.: Addison-Wesley, 1969.

Bermant, G.; Kelman, H.C.; and Warwick, D. P. *The Ethics of Social Intervention.* Washington: Hemisphere, 1978.

Frame, R. M.; Hess, R. H.; and Nielsen, W. R. *The OD Source Book: A Practitioners Guide.* California: University Associates, 1982.

Greiner, L. E., and Metzger, R. O. *Consulting to Management.* Englewood Cliffs, NJ: Prentice Hall, 1983.

Kubr, M. *Management Consulting: A Guide to the Profession.* Geneva: International Labour Office, 1986.

Miles, M. B. "Ethical Issues in OD Interventions." *OD Practitioner* 2, no. 3 (1979).

Naisbett, J., and Aburdene, P. *Reinventing the Corporation.* New York: Warner Books, 1985.

Nykodym, N.,; Nielsen, W. R.; & Christen, J. C. (1985) "Can Organizational Development Use Transactional Analysis?" *Transactional Analysis Journal* 15 (1985), pp. 278–84.

Nykodym, N.; Ruud, W. N.; & Liverpool, P. R. (1986) "Quality Circles: Will Transactional Analysis Improve Their Effectiveness?" *Transactional Analysis Journal* 16 (1986), pp. 182–87.

O.D. Institute. "A Statement of Values and Ethics for Professionals in Organization and Human System Development." Organization Development Institute, April 1985.

Pate, L. E. "A Longitudinal Study of the Intervention Process within an Insurance Firm Using Quasi-Experimental Research Designs." Unpublished thesis, University of Illinois, 1979.

Pate, L. E.; Nielsen, W. R.; and Bacon, P. C. "Advances in Research on Organization Development." In *Contemporary Issues in Human Resource Management.* Schuster F. E., Reston Publishing, 1980.

Walton, R. E., Warwick, D. P. "The Ethics of Organization Development." *Journal of Applied Behavioral Science* 9, no. 6 (1973), pp. 681–98.

READING 42
RE-ENERGIZING THE MATURE ORGANIZATION

Richard W. Beatty
David O. Ulrich

Globalization, reduced technology cycles, shifting demographics, changing expectations among workers and customers, and restructuring of capital markets made the 1980s a "white water decade," rapidly introducing changes for both public and private organizations.

The greater the forces for change, the greater the competitive pressure; and the greater the competitive pressure, the greater the demand for change. This seemingly endless cycle of competition-change can become a vicious circle if executives cannot discover novel ways to compete.

Traditional ways of competing have reached a level of parity in which businesses cannot easily distinguish themselves solely on the basis of technology, product, or price. The ability of an organization to conceptualize and manage change—to compete from the inside out by increasing its capacity for change—may represent that novel way to compete. The universal challenge of change is to learn how organizations and employees can change faster than changing business conditions to become more competitive. That is, to change faster on the inside than the organization is changing on the outside.

This need to understand and manage change is salient, particularly for mature firms where the long-established norms of stability and security must be replaced with new values, such as speed, simplicity, unparalleled customer service, and a self-confident, empowered workforce. The purpose of this article is to explore how mature firms can be re-energized. To do this, we will describe the unique challenges of creating change in mature

firms, detail principles that can be used to guide change, and identify the leadership and work activities required to accomplish change.

The Challenge of Change and Organization Life Cycle

Organizations evolve through a life cycle with each evolving stage raising change challenges. We shall use an hourglass to portray the process of organizational life cycles and change challenges.

As illustrated in Figure 1, organizations in their entrepreneurial stage focus on the definition and development of new products and markets. During this life stage, the change challenge is primarily one of defining and learning how to penetrate a market or niche. Managers who translate ideas into customer value overcome this *niche challenge* and proceed to the growth stage.

In the laundry equipment industry, for example, the entrepreneurial stage developed in the early 1900s when over 60 appliance makers entered the market to provide more automated equipment for doing laundry. These autonomous (and often small) appliance makers served local markets with their specialized machines.

During the growth stage, businesses proliferate. This evolutionary stage could become corporate nirvana—if it persists. Unfortunately, as more firms enter a market, meeting the change challenge becomes necessary for survival. Over time, small firms frequently join together to form large firms; firms that cannot compete either merge or go out of business. Between 1960 and 1985, a major shakeout occurred in the North American appliance market. From over 60 major appliance makers, the market shrank to five major companies that, together, held over 80 percent of the market.

471

FIGURE 1

Organization life cycle and change challenges

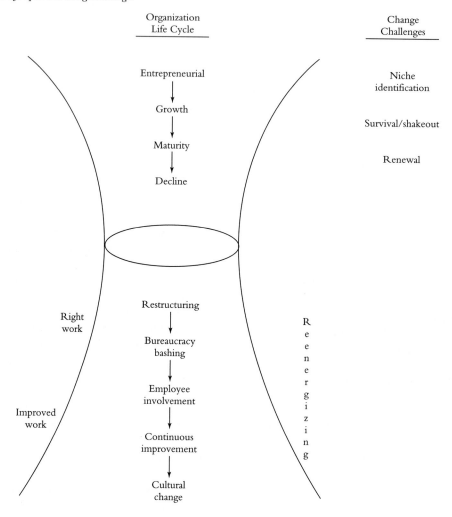

Each of these five major appliance makers faced and overcame the shakeout change challenge.

As organizations overcome the niche and shakeout challenges, they develop standard operating procedures. This third evolutionary stage is maturity. Organizations in the mature stage face a significant renewal change challenge. The presence of established norms that once helped accomplish past success may lead to complacency and managers may become too dependent on these for future success. These calcified norms then become irrevocable patterns of behavior that eventually lead to structural inertia as would be evidenced in the way they affect structure, systems, and processes. Not only do they create inertia but the insulation they provide leads to an avoidance of challenges that can lead to success.

In the appliance industry in the late 1980s, renewal became a major agenda. For example, Whirlpool changed its century-old functional organization into business units and formed a joint venture with Phillips to enter markets outside North America. General Electric spent over $1 billion refurbishing plants, technologies, and management systems. These efforts at renewal, still under way, will predict which firms will emerge as winners in the next century. Organizations that fail the renewal change challenge enter a period of decline, during which they slowly lose market share to firms that have renewed.

In many ways, the renewal change challenge is more onerous than the niche identification or shakeout challenges. To overcome the niche and shakeout challenges, managers in successful organizations were able to focus on customers and develop products and technologies to meet customer needs. During the maturity phase, product and technological parity is likely to emerge. Competitors offer customers similar product features at comparable costs. Given a technological and financial parity, managers facing a renewal challenge must identify additional capabilities to meet customer needs. They must learn to compete through competencies; they must develop the ability to compete from the inside out—to build internal organizational processes that meet external customer requirements.

Organizational Mindsets and Life Cycles

Perhaps the greatest effort involved in overcoming the renewal challenge is to change the mindset of employees at all levels of an organization. The mindset represents a shared way of thinking and behaving within an organization. Mindsets are reflected in "accepted behaviors and attitudes"—customer service at Nordstrom, quality at Ford, and speed, simplicity, and self-confidence at General Electric. Mindsets are often institutionalized in vision, value, and mission.

It takes time for mindsets to be instilled. By the time an organization becomes mature, it has likely established a relatively fixed mindset. Employees self-select into the organization because of its particular set of norms. They are rewarded by

promotions, salary increases, and enhanced job responsibility when they embody the mindset. Mindsets become very powerful means of gaining unity and focus. Students of Japanese service organizations have argued that this unity of mindset becomes a means of gaining competitiveness. The mindset provides a common focus and therefore increases the intensity of work done.

In mature organizations, a shared mindset can be a liability and its intensity may hinder the ability to change. Since employees come to accept, adopt, and associate with the mindset of a mature company, the renewal process requires letting go. To accomplish renewal, traditional control measures must be replaced with an empowered workforce that is more self-directed, self-managed, and self-controlled, thus reducing the need not only for strong competencies in managerial control but for large numbers of managers and supervisors as well. Thus a truly empowered workforce is one that acts out of commitment to purpose without the traditional boundaries and narrow mindsets of mature organizations. In Figure 1, the more open end of the hourglass represents the more open and flexible organizations; the closed end of the hourglass represents the constraints of mature organizations. The hourglass analogy shows this movement from more open and flexible (top of hour glass) to closed and inflexible (center). In this model, renewal becomes the change challenge that allows a firm to go through the "neck" of the hourglass and rediscover a vitality and energy that move the mature firm out of the decline trap and into a revived state of activity.

Principles of Renewal

Responding to the renewal challenge is difficult at best, and unlikely in most cases. Few organizations successfully accomplish renewal from within. Rather than renew, organizations that perpetuate outmoded mindsets become prey to consolidations, acquisitions, or mergers—external pressures that *impose* renewal. We propose that the probability of renewal of mature organizations increases if four principles are understood and practiced. If the managers recognize these principles, they may be able to help overcome the renewal challenge.

1. *Mature organizations renew by instilling a customer perspective and focusing on customer demands.* To begin to overcome the renewal challenge, a company and all its employees must be completely devoted to gaining a sustained competitive advantage. Competitive advantage comes from understanding and meeting customer needs in unique ways.

One of the most difficult challenges of renewal is the ability to recognize whether existing mindsets and practices are inconsistent with current customer requirements. When the mindset within an organization becomes a way of life, embedded in employee work habits, it is even more difficult to acknowledge or change. By examining the organization from a customer perspective, employees may better understand the internal processes and practices that reinforce existing mindsets. Hewlett-Packard, one of the first organizations to adopt such a practice as a part of its renewal effort, did this by incorporating internal and external customer satisfaction into its performance appraisal system.

A more detailed example of this practice is provided by a company that, in working through the renewal challenge, experienced at first mixed results. While employees enjoyed participating in innovative self-managed work teams and preparing vision statements, over a period of time each new activity that appeared promising fizzled, and employees went back to business as usual. To encourage and advance renewal, a workshop was held in which the employees were asked to examine their organization and four of its major competitors, pretending they were buyers of the product. As customers, they talked about why they would pick one supplier over another. They explored the images each of the five companies communicated and examined reasons why customers picked one competitor over another. After performing this analysis, they were able to articulate, from a customer's perspective, the perceived mindsets residing within each of the five competing organizations.

Having done this customer assessment of the competitors, the employees were able to decipher and enunciate the mindset within their own company and distinguish how their company's mindset differed from those of their competitors.

Becoming devoted to customers comes from employees spending less time thinking about internal company policies and practices and more time interacting with and worrying about their next customers. Companies that compete through service seek creative and extensive ways to involve customers in all activities. Customers may become involved in product design, in reviewing vision statements, in attending and making presentations at training and development sessions, and in doing employee reviews. The more interaction there is between customers and employees, the more a customer perspective is instilled within the organization. By taking an active role in meeting customer needs, employees in mature organizations may begin the conquest of the renewal change challenge. They can in effect change their performance expectations from meeting demands vertically dictated, to focusing horizontally on the process requirements in order to meet internal and external customer requirements. When meeting customer needs becomes more important to the organization than preserving political boundaries, employees will be more willing to renew themselves and their company. There are several reasons for this, including the freedom from autocratic directions by giving autonomy to those whose services are dependent on it.

Mature companies seeking to renew have engaged in a variety of activities to ensure customer commitment. At Hewlett-Packard, engineers who design products spend months meeting with customers in focus groups, in laboratories, and in application settings to ensure that new products meet customer requirements. When the mini-van was first announced at Chrysler, several senior executives were not supportive of the concept. They believed the vehicle was neither a truck nor a passenger car and would have no market. However, after extensive meetings with customers, the executives became convinced that this vehicle created an entire new niche.

At an oil service company, sales personnel were trained to interview and work with customers to identify their needs, rather than to sell products. As these sales personnel spent time with customers and became aware of their current and future needs, the oil service company experienced dramatic market share growth.

The principle of customer-centered activity is consistent with the extensive work on quality done by a number of management researchers over the years. It encourages employees to define their value as a function of customer requirements, rather than of personal gain. It replaces old practices with new ones that add value to customers. It refocuses attention outside to change inside—that is, toward the ultimate and the next customer.

2. Mature organizations renew by increasing their capacity for change. Most individuals have internal clocks, or biorhythms, that determine when we wake, when we need to eat, and how quickly we make decisions. Like individuals, most organizations have internal clocks that determine how quickly decisions are made and activities completed. These internal clocks affect how long it takes organizations to move from idea to definition, to action. It has been argued that a major challenge for organizations is to reduce their cycle time, which means to change the internal clock and timing on how decisions are made. For mature organizations to experience renewal, their internal clocks must be adjusted. Cycle lengths must be reduced and the capacity for change increased.

Typically, the internal clocks of mature organizations have not been calibrated for changing erratic and unpredictable business conditions. To enact and increase a capacity for change, managers need to work on alignment, symbiosis, and reflexiveness.

"Alignment" refers to the extent to which different organization activities are focused on common goals. When organizations have a sense of alignment, their strategy, structure, and systems can move more readily toward consistent and shared goals.

Aligned organizations have a greater capacity for change because less time is spent building commitment, and more energy and time are spent accomplishing work. To calibrate alignment, a number of organizations have sponsored "congruence" workshops where the degree of congruence between organizational activities is assessed.

"Symbiosis" refers to the extent to which organizations are able to remove boundaries inside and outside an organization.

General Electric CEO Jack Welch describes any organizational boundary as a "toll-gate." Any time individuals or products must cross a boundary, an economic, emotional, and time toll is paid. When organizations have extensive boundaries, tolls can be direct and indirect expenses. Direct boundary costs result in higher prices to customers because of extra costs in producing the product. Indirect boundary costs occur from each boundary increasing the time required to accomplish tasks. Boundaries, and the tolls required for crossing, set an organization's internal clock and impair capacity for change. Increasing cycle time and creating symbiosis mean reducing boundaries and increasing capacity for change and action. The Ford Taurus has become a classic example of reducing boundaries and increasing capacity for change. By forming and assigning a cross-functional team responsible for the complete design and delivery of the Taurus, boundaries were removed between departments. The time from concept to production for the Taurus was 50 percent less than established internal clocks.

To ensure that a capacity for change continues over time, individuals must become reflexive and have the ability to continue to learn and adapt over time. "Reflexiveness" is the ability to learn from previous actions. Organizations increase their capacity for change when time is spent reflecting on past activities and learning from them.

The capacity for change principle expedites renewal. When individuals and systems inside an organization can so change their internal clocks that decisions move quicker from concept to action, renewal occurs more frequently. In this way, organizational cycles differ from individual biorhythms: Cycle times are not genetic and intractable but learned and adjustable. By adjusting cycles, the capacity for change increases, which may lead to renewal of mature organizations.

3. *Mature organizations renew by altering both the hardware and software within the organization.* Management activities within an organization may be dissected into *hardware* and *software.* Management hardware represents issues, such as strategy, structure, and systems. These domains of activity are malleable and measurable and can be heralded with high visibility—for example, timely announcements about new strategies, structures, or systems. Also, like computer hardware, unless they are connected to appropriate software they are useless. In the organization, software represents employee behavior and mindset. These less visible domains of organizational activity are difficult to adjust or measure, but they often determine the extent to which renewal occurs.

Most renewal efforts begin by changing hardware—putting in a new strategy, structure, or system. These hardware efforts help mature organizations to turn around or to change economic indicators. They do not, however, assure transformation; this comes only when new hardware is supported by appropriate software. Organizational renewal efforts that focus extensively or exclusively on strategy, structure, and systems engage in numerous discussions and debates. These discussions are necessary but are not sufficient to make any difference. At times, in fact, these discussions consume so much energy and resources that too few resources are left to make sure that employee behavior and mindset match the changes. Just as many companies have storage rooms filled with unused hardware, many organizations have binders of strategy, structure, and system changes that were never implemented.

For renewal in mature organizations, changing strategy and structure is not enough. Adjusting and encouraging individual employee behavior and working on changing the mindset are also critical. In one organization attempting to examine and modify software, the focus was not on strategy, structure, and systems but on work activities. Groups of employees met in audit workshops to identify work activities as done by suppliers for customers, then to examine each set of work activities to eliminate whatever did not add value to customers and to improve whatever did. The key to the success of these work audit workshops was that participants would leave with work inspected and modified in a positive manner. As a result of the workshops, participants have changed some of the existing behaviors and beliefs within the business.

For organizations seeking to increase the probability of renewal, new mindsets must be created that will be shared by all employees, customers, and suppliers. For suppliers, this commonly is a shared perspective that leverages competitive advantage. Xerox, between 1980 and 1988, reduced its number of suppliers from over 3,000 to 300. By focusing attention and certifying qualified suppliers, Xerox has built a shared mindset among its supplier network. Ford Motor Company has done similar work with suppliers. A team of Ford executives must accredit each Ford supplier on a number of dimensions of quality, delivery, and service. Without passing the accreditation test, the supplier cannot work with Ford. By maintaining this policy, Ford builds its vision and values into its supplier network, and Ford suppliers mesh their vision and values with Ford. These types of activities build the software that reinforces the hardware, or system changes that eventually lead to renewal.

4. *Mature organizations renew by creating empowered employees who act as leaders at all levels of the organization.* Shared leadership implies that individuals have responsibility and accountability for activities within their domain. Individuals become leaders by having influence and control over the factors that affect their work performance.

Organizations that renew have leaders stationed throughout the hierarchy regardless of position or title. Employees are trusted and empowered to act on issues that affect their work performance. Leaders have the obligation of articulating and stating a vision and of ensuring that the vision will be implemented. Leadership can come either from bringing new leaders into the organization or building competencies into existing leadership positions.

When Michael Blumenthal became chairman of Burroughs, he changed 23 of the top 24 managers within his first year. His assessment was that the current leadership team was so weighed down with traditional vision and values that they could not develop a new leadership capability, capacity for change, and competitiveness. Blumenthal could change the top echelon of his organization, but he could not replace the 1,000 secondary leaders throughout the organization. These leaders needed to be developed to induce a renewal within the company.

Primary and secondary leaders must be able to communicate the new mindset, articulating the vision and values in ways that are not only readily understandable and acceptable to all employees but that are inspirational, also. In other words, the employees must believe that it is worth giving extraordinary effort to make the vision a reality.

In addition to communication, leaders are expected to possess the competencies members perceive as necessary to lead the organization to the heights of its vision. Although some of these competencies may be functional, others are clearly the management of human resources, especially the effective use of measures both positive and negative following the actions of all employees. While the use of alternative reward strategies has become extremely popular in the last few years, leaders should be able to confront employees who are unwilling to perform at levels necessary for making a substantive contribution to competitive advantage.

Finally, leaders must be credible. Members must be able to trust in the word of their leaders; if they cannot, they will be unwilling to accept the vision or the values—and certainly be unwilling to marshal the level of energy necessary to accomplish higher and higher levels of performance. The credibility of leadership cannot be overestimated when trying to energize the organization's human resource.

In brief, we have proposed four principles that can increase the probability of renewal for a mature organization. By understanding these four principles, managers may engage in a series of activities that make this renewal possible.

Leadership and Work Activities

Having identified a need for mature organizations to overcome a renewal challenge, and a set of principles on which renewal is based, we can identify specific leadership and work activities which accomplish this effort. Generally, the process for re-energizing mature organizations follows the five steps shown in Figure 2, although these may not always be in sequence, as some steps may occur simultaneously.

Stage 1: Restructuring. Organizational renewal generally begins with a turnaround effort focused on restructuring by downsizing and/or delayering. Through head-count reduction, organizations attempt to become "lean and mean," recognizing that they had become "fat" by not strategically managing performance at all levels. Organizations continue to improve global measures of productivity (sales or other measures of performance per employee) by reducing the number of employees. At General Electric, staff reductions removed approximately 25 percent of the workforce between 1982 and 1988. This reduction came from retirements, reorganizations, consolidations, plant closings, and greater spans of control. Such a head-count reduction can save organizations billions of dollars and initiate renewal. At J. I. Case, the implement manufacturer, well over 90 percent of the top-management group was replaced as the organization faced a substantial change in how it was to do business in a highly competitive global environment.

The leadership requirement during restructuring is clear: Have courage to make difficult decisions fairly and boldly. No one likes to take away jobs. It will not lead to great popularity or emotional attachment of employees. However, leaders who face a renewal change challenge must act. They must implement a process that ensures equity

FIGURE 2

A process for reenergizing mature organizations

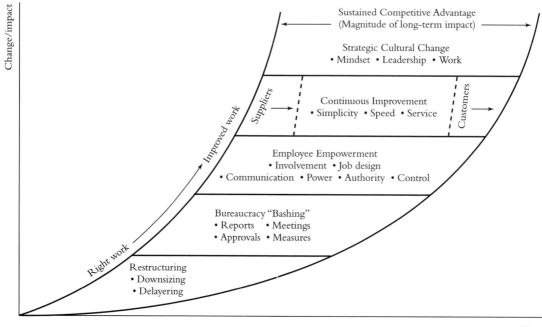

and due cause to employees. By so doing, leaders start the renewal process by turning around an organization through restructuring.

Stage 2: Bureaucracy Bashing. "Bureaucracy bashing" follows restructuring. In this stage, attempts are made to get rid of unnecessary reports, approvals, meetings, measures, policies, procedures, or other work activities that create backlogs. By focusing on bureaucracy reduction, employees throughout the organization experience changes in how they do their work. Often, sources of employee work frustration come from being constrained by bureaucratic procedures and not being able to see or feel the impact of their work. Bureaucratic policies and processes that consume energy and build frustration may have been developed in older work settings, causing more harm than good; these need to be examined and replaced.

In the restructuring stage, mindsets of corporate loyalty are shattered. Employees who believed in

lifelong employment and job security may be angered by restructuring activities. Many companies that go through the restructuring phase eliminate corporate loyalty but fail to replace the employee contract with the firm. As a result, employees feel that their contract with the firm is one-way and short-term. They are giving their psychological commitment to the firm, but only for short-term monetary gains. To resolve this imbalance, employees may reduce their commitment. Executives must learn to sustain employee commitment by replacing loyalty with some other means of employee attachment.

In one company, employee contracts based on loyalty were replaced with opportunity. The chief executive of this company was honest with employees. He told them that there were no guarantees. Job loyalty, as known in stable work settings, could no longer be an economically viable alternative. However, he promised each employee that

loyalty would be replaced by opportunity. He personally promised each employee that the organization would guarantee that each of them had the
opportunity to develop his or her talents, to participate in key management actions, and to feel that
they belonged to a part of a winning team. To
guarantee this opportunity, bureaucracy had to be
removed. Employees were able to identify the
bureaucratic blockages in their jobs, to discuss
these blockages with their bosses and peers, and to
suggest how they could be removed. By so doing,
employees could feel and see the value of opportunity in their work.

The bureaucracy bashing stage is necessary
because, even though the head count may have
reduced costs, the workload still remains, and
adjustments must be made to meet the work volume requirements with the reduced head count.

At General Electric, Jack Welch has talked about
reducing the workforce by 25 percent but not
reducing work. As a result, employees are faced
with the burden of doing 25 percent more work,
which over a period of time may lead to malaise
and lower productivity. Unnecessary, non-value-
added work must be removed to gain parity
between employees and their work load.

To get rid of bureaucracy requires getting rid of
work that adds little value to customers. Continuous
improvement programs that focus on meeting needs
of internal and external customers may be designed
to yield higher quality, speed, and greater simplicity
in how all suppliers service the organization.

A process developed by one of the authors and
shown in Figure 3 focuses on bureaucracy "busting." A work audit is conducted using two questions: (1) To what extent does this work activity
add value to customers? and (2) To what extent are
these activities performed as effectively as possible?

The first question is answered by inviting customers to share their views on the value added by
work activities performed by the supplier. This dialogue between suppliers and customers may occur
exclusively within a company (internal sup-
plier/customer discussions) or between a firm and
its external customers. One company began invit-

FIGURE 3

Developing a customer focus in bureaucracy bashing

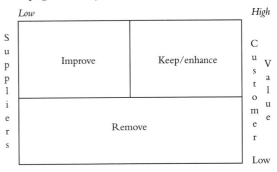

ing customers to training programs in an effort to
understand customer needs and to ensure that
work activities proposed within the company met
customer requirements. Activities which add little
value to customers were moved. This two-step
process attempts to determine the "right" of the
organization to leverage its competitive advantage
and that of its customers.

Activities that add great value to customers
become subject to the second question. This question is answered by developing an improved process
to perform the work. Auditing work processes
encourages specific analysis to ensure that quality in
work activities is improved.

However, leaders must first model the bureaucracy busting they advocate. They must be willing
to let go of work systems that were implemented
but that have added little or no value to the
processes' next or ultimate customer. Reports or
procedures that may add value to the leader, but
that may be seen as bureaucratic blockages to
employees, must be identified and leaders must be
willing to concede their pet projects for the sake
of removing these blockages. Leaders must demonstrate flexibility and listen to all reasonable requests
(as long as they add value to customers and fall
within legal and ethical boundaries). Finally, leaders need to encourage and reinforce risk taking
among employees who initiate bureaucracy busting activities. A single equation predicts the
propensity for risk taking. We see risk taking as a

function of the will to win, divided by fear of failure. If the numerator is high, by selecting and developing committed employees, then leaders have the responsibility of reducing the fear of failure quotient.

Stage 3: Employee Empowerment Stage. Bureaucracies empower top managers. Bureaucracy busting empowers employees. Removing barriers between employees and managers builds openness and dialogue in ongoing management processes and begins to change the nature of the organization. Self-directed work teams, employee involvement processes, and dialogue should be built into the fabric of the organization. Without employee involvement and a fundamental new approach to management, costs may be reduced, productivity increased, and bureaucracy eliminated—but the results will not be long lasting if employees are now empowered for organizational improvement.

Many work activities encourage employee involvement. In a Japanese firm, newer professional employees have the opportunity and obligation to make the first drafts of important business proposals. By asking new employees to make these first drafts, the employees learn more about the overall business, feel empowered to have an impact on the business, and build relationships with colleagues in preparing the proposals. Pepsico has involved and empowered all employees by announcing profit sharing for all. Federal Express has institutionalized employee involvement by guaranteeing employees access to the senior management meeting held each Wednesday. Employee complaints may be directed to this forum by employees without fear of any retributions by their immediate bosses. IBM assures employee involvement by allowing employees to work through a corporate ombudsman who can represent the employees' views to management without fear of reprisal or having to undergo subordinate appraisals. Amoco has initiated an extensive employee involvement program where employees are formed into teams to discuss ways to improve work and to get subordinate appraisals of their managers. These examples of employee involvement mark a fundamental change from the traditional work contract of hierarchical mature organizations to a more fluid, flexible, mutual work environment.

Traditional models of power and authority came from position and status. Power and authority in a renewing organization should come from relationships, trust, and expertise. Empowerment is a movement away from leader and expert problem solving to a system where everyone is continuously involved in improving the organization in order to leverage its competitive advantage through speed, simplicity, and service. Leaders must learn that sharing power builds a capacity to change, commitment, and competitiveness.

Stage 4: Continuous Improvement. Employee empowerment builds employee commitment. This initial commitment must be translated into long-term processes so employee involvement is not tied to any one individual but is part of a system.

Continuous improvement efforts began in mature companies by focusing on error detection and error prevention. In these efforts statistical tools—for example, flow charting, Pareto analysis, histograms, studies of variance, and operational definitions—were used to ensure that errors could be taken out of work procedures.

The continuous improvement required for this stage includes, but also goes beyond, this error focus. Continuous improvement is changing not only the technical tools of management but also the fundamental approaches to management. The continuous improvement philosophy overcomes the practice. The focus on continuous improvement must be upon the "right" work that was identified through restructuring and bureaucracy bashing. The philosophy must be one of service to customers through speed and simplicity in work processes. As this philosophy is understood throughout an organization, it becomes the rallying cry, ensuring an ongoing commitment to improve work processes.

Generating this philosophy becomes the major leadership requirement at this stage. The leader must manage through principles. The leader must articulate and communicate the principles that will govern the organization. These principles must be sensitive to each of the previous stages—restructuring for productivity, bureaucracy busting for flexibility, and employee involvement for empowerment. By instilling a philosophy of management that can then be practiced according to the specific needs of the business, leaders are able to set a direction, motivate, and steer a company through renewal.

Stage 5: Cultural Change. The final stage of renewal is really an outgrowth of the other four. Fundamental cultural change means that employees' mindset—the way they think about their work is shifted. Employees do not feel part of a "mature" company, but they see themselves as having faced and overcome the renewal change challenge. They feel the enthusiasm and commitment of trying new approaches to work and, as a result, they bring more desirable changes into the organization.

We would agree with many others who have studied these issues that accomplishing cultural change takes many years. Our rule of thumb is that, for mature organizations, the cycle time for creating fundamental cultural change is twice the cycle time it takes for introducing a new technology. Some technologies change more rapidly than others—say, for example, genetic engineering as opposed to utilities. In more rapidly changing technologies, there is more receptivity to cultural change. These organizations seem to have a more external focus. In industries with slow changing technologies, the cycle time for cultural change is extended, since these industries probably have a greater structural inertia. The latter are more internally and vertically focused.

In the re-energized organization, every leader would be judged by his ability to persevere, and how strong an advocate he is of the new culture. But it is also necessary that he exhibits tolerance since culture changes require time to take effect.

More importantly a leader must constantly and demonstratively be a model and a cheerleader of the culture he hopes to implement.

At General Electric, Jack Welch has committed the entire company to a cultural change. He con-stantly talks about his commitment—to financial analysts, to investors, to shareholders, to employees, and to public forums. He has defined a set of principles and has frequently asked managers to spend time implementing these principles. Welch has also asked his managers to provide him with feedback on his personal behavior. At GE he has become the nucleus of encouraging employees to commit energy and time to understanding and adopting the new work culture.

In short, the five stages in Figure 2 indicate a sequence for adopting changes to re-energize a mature organization. By first defining the right work to do, then finding ways to improve that work, companies may make simple, short-term changes that can have major, long-term impact. These five stages are based on the four principles we have identified.

Making It Happen

We have put forward a very simple argument in this paper: Mature organizations must face and overcome the renewal change challenge; they must change; they must redefine how work is done and recreate work cultures consistent with changing customer demands.

How do we anticipate that these changes will occur? It will happen because organizations and leaders at all levels have developed a new vision of strategy and culture. Organizations are becoming far more strategic, far more purposeful, and far more customer oriented. It will happen also because of new tools that are focusing more and more closely upon performance and that are raising difficult questions about the value of work and of the customer requirements within the organization.

Most mature organizations will sooner or later have to face the renewal change challenge. They will then have to find ways to change their culture; their vision will have to actually be translated into specific actions, and managers must be prepared to help employees improve, to observe their progress, and to give them feedback. Employees also must seek responsibilities, strive for continuous improvement, and change the organization's culture by making each effort add value to its customers and investors strategically and continuously.

The role of the leader is to challenge the value of each process for its contribution to customers and investors, encourage a shared vision and values, and enable employees to act by encouraging greater customer and cost consciousness, adaptability, initiative, accountability, and teamwork. To accomplish these goals, managers must model the way and immediately recognize the contributions of employees as they take risks in changing established work habits and attempt to continuously improve and enhance their contributions.

If the renewal change challenge can be overcome, an organization may move through the neck of the hourglass (see Figure 1). At the other side of the hourglass is the ability to become re-energized and meet customer needs through innovative, resourceful, and bold customer-focused initiatives.

References

Several pieces have appeared recently which explore the broad range of activities and values of interest to us. One is "Why Change Programs Don't Produce Change" by Michael Beer, Russell Eisenstadt, and Burt Spector in *Harvard Business Review,* November–December 1990. It demonstrates how most change programs fail because they are guided by a fundamentally flawed theory of change. The authors claim many change programs assume that change is a conversion experience that requires an attitude change. We agree that real change requires a change in attitude and in the fundamental roles, responsibilities, and relationships that should provide the alignment of the appropriate

behaviors. However, our major focus is that change occurs because work and work relationships have been redesigned to leverage the organization's human resource competitive advantage.

Another piece that is consistent with our approach is Randy Myer's "Suppliers Manage Your Customers," in *Harvard Business Review,* November–December 1989. He points out that "customer-back" organizations are successful, because, to satisfy the next and ultimate customers, you must be provided by suppliers who treat you as important customers.

A significant piece on the leader's role appeared in the *Sloan Management Review* in 1990. The article by Peter M. Senge was entitled "The Leader's New Work: Building Learning Organizations." This is a major piece that focuses on the leadership role in transforming organizations. It recognizes that becoming heuristic is essential to successful transformation—that is, an organization must learn and build the internal capability that enables it to return to viability, regardless of the level of environmental turbulence. The article stresses two leadership styles that have emerged over the years: traditional (plan, organize, and control) and transformational (vision, alignment, motivation). But a third type of leader, the leader of the future, is one who is a designer of work, a teacher, and a supporter of change—in essence, the ultimate change agent companies have been alluding to for years but is seldom seen represented.

Finally, a corollary piece appeared in *Harvard Business Review* in January–February 1991 by Robert G. Eccles, entitled "The Performance Measurement Manifesto." It suggests performance measurement is an essential missing element from many organizational change efforts and certainly from discussions on re-energizing mature organizations. Identifying the right work is essential but so is measuring the right work. Clearly, if organizations are to survive, customers need to be prioritized and processes need to be clarified. Both require measures to assess their effectiveness and to test whether they are aligned with organizational goals and objectives.

READING 43
MANAGING DISCONTINUITIES: THE EMERGING CHALLENGES

C. K. Prahalad

As we move into the next millennium, all managers will face a new set of competitive challenges—challenges that represent *major discontinuities*. The critical managerial tasks are more than just becoming good (e.g., TQM), fast (e.g., cycle time) or lean (e.g., agile). Managers recognize that these attributes are necessary but not adequate goals for survival in the next millennium.

Increasingly, the ability to recognize the impending discontinuities and learning how to be innovative are becoming the real challenges for senior managers. Most firms do not have good track records. To the contrary, there is evidence that established firms are not very adept at coping with or managing discontinuous change.[1]

Discontinuities translate some core competencies into core rigidities.[2] At the same time, new core competencies have to be built to exploit the new opportunities that emerge. Managers have to simultaneously "forget" selectively and "learn" aggressively. This is the challenge.

This article outlines the basic discontinuities that all firms will face during the next decade. Next, the critical managerial challenges and tasks that result from these discontinuities are described. The creation of new competencies by integrating the old processes with newly acquired knowledge and skills follow. Finally, the basic steps for building a program to implement the new competencies are provided, along with the nature and impact of the new demands on the maintenance of a corporate core competency profile.

Source: C. K. Prahalad, "Managing Discontinuities: The Emerging Challenges." Reprinted from *Research Technology Management,* May–June 1998, pp. 14–22. Copyright © 1998 Industrial Research Institue, Inc.

The Emerging Competitive Landscape

The eight discontinuities described below constitute the emerging competitive landscape. Taken one at a time, they do not tell the whole story. What is not obvious is the collective pressure these discontinuities exert on a management group.

1. *Global.* During the 1980s, "global" meant new and aggressive competition from Japan and South Korea. Increasingly, it also means global customers, as is the case of the auto industry.

During the last decade, over 3 billion people abandoned the ideology of a planned economy and moved toward variants of a market economy. This generated new opportunities for established firms. However, global expansion also produces geographical asymmetries in growth patterns. China and India may be growing at 7–10 percent per year, while Western Europe may be growing at less than 2 percent. Asymmetrical growth can lead to dramatic shifts in resources within a multinational (MNC) firm. By the year 2010, it would not be surprising if most of the Western MNCs had more than 50 percent of their assets in China, Southeast Asia and India. This would have a dramatic effect on how products are developed and how human resources are managed within the MNC. Needless to say, the composition of the top management in these firms will also be different.

Further, there is an emerging geographical focus to industry expertise. For example, Taiwan produces more than 50 percent of all computer monitors, 72 percent of all mouse, and about 60 percent of all the motherboards.[3] The California Bay area (Silicon Valley) remains the heart of the software industry. London and its environs dominate the video game software development industry. Movies and music industries are still dominated by the United States and the United Kingdom. This geographical foci means that firms must be present in the "place where the music is made" to keep themselves up-to-date.

It is not surprising that all high-tech firms—European, Japanese or South Korean—have made investments in the Bay area. While these investments, initially, tended to be small and of a "sensing post" variety, increasingly they represent significant investments. For similar reasons, most electronics and financial services companies are also investing in Bangalore and other centers in India to access software talent. Thus, globalization will have a significant impact on both the resource and skill configuration of the MNC.

2. *Deregulation and Privatization.* There appears to be an unstoppable trend toward deregulation and privatization. Starting from the breakup of "Ma Bell," the trend is clear—in both the developed and developing countries.

Telecommunications, utilities, airlines, financial services, and health care are but a few of the traditionally regulated industries that are undergoing traumatic change. For example, in most of these industries, mergers and acquisitions are endemic. There is a race to extract value out of the inefficiencies that are inherent in regulation-induced local and regional monopolies. There is also a race to globalize. For example, utility firms such as Enron are expanding into other countries. Relieved from local regulatory restrictions, these industries (e.g., power, telecommunications) are rapidly becoming global. Further, there is a significant amount of de-verticalization of the industries—separating, for example, power generation from transmission and marketing. There is also an emerging spot market for power. Recently, there has been an attempt to differentiate and brand products and services, such as power, which have been traditionally managed as commodities.

In tandem with deregulation, there is a significant move toward privatization of public sector firms. This trend is obvious worldwide—from China, India, Chile, Poland, France, and Germany. Privatization produces a significant amount of social disruption as the inefficient public sector firms shed obsolete assets, consolidate their businesses and resize their firms. These efforts significantly impact capital flows, unemployment and the need for growth to absorb the workforce rendered surplus by the restructuring of the public sector.

The implications of deregulation/privatization are:

- Most industries that were local will become regional, national and global.
- The economics of these businesses will change dramatically.
- There is likely to be significant unemployment generated by these efforts to rationalize regulated industries. The U.S. and U.K. telecommunications industry demonstrates the level of resizing that may be required worldwide in a wide variety of industries.

3. *Volatility.* Almost all industries are experiencing a new level of volatility—the need for scaling up and scaling down and significantly reducing the cycle time for product development.

Volatility and seasonality combined create a new set of demands on management. For example, it is hard to justify "focused factories" dedicated to a single business line when that business is subject to great volatility. As the demand for products and services fluctuates, focused factories will have to dramatically scale up or be closed down. This dilemma is increasingly forcing firms to create "flexible factories" that can serve multiple, related business units.

Further, privileged access to suppliers is also becoming a major source of concern. Firms must maintain a close relationship with their suppliers to ensure that they will support the marketplace volatility of their end products.

4. *Convergence.* The convergence of multiple technologies represents a major discontinuity. Although the convergence

of computing, communications, consumer electronics, and entertainment is often cited as an example, convergence is a lot more pervasive. For example, increasingly:

- Personal care products such as shampoo and face creams will have to incorporate the disciplines of pharmaceutical technologies, including clinical trials. Hair growth and anti-aging, for example, will change the nature of the personal care products industry. The fashion industry must marry science.
- Soybeans, corn, potatoes, cotton, and other "commodity" products will have to contend with new developments in plant genetics. Monsanto's introduction of Roundup, for example, along with pest-resistant seeds, brings a new level of technological sophistication to a traditional business—in the application of fertilizers and insecticides, as well as in primary processing.
- Chemical and electronic technologies are co-mingling. Digital cameras, printers and copiers are interesting combinations of material science, chemistry, electronics, and software.
- Automobiles are a combination of "engineered" materials, electronics and software combined with traditional mechanical engineering.

A large number of similar convergences can be identified. The key issue is that very distinct "intellectual heritages" will have to be managed and seamlessly integrated. For example, a company such as Kodak, steeped in chemical imaging, can find managing such a transition (chemical engineering + electronics + software) to be daunting. Revlon, Procter & Gamble and others have to manage an equally difficult transition—from traditional fashion to "cosmaceuticals," and from traditional food to "health and wellness diets," respectively.

Digitalization has probably had the most profound significant impact on all types of industries, from movie-making to financial services. There is not one industry that can postpone the need to understand and exploit the benefits of digital (information) technology.

5. *Indeterminate Industry Boundaries.* As a result of such convergences, many of the traditional industry boundaries are changing. For example, the dividing line between personal computers and television is uncertain. So too is the boundary between communication and computing or entertainment. The distinction between what constitutes a professional business and a consumer business is increasingly hard to delineate. Microsoft, AT&T, Sears, Sainsbury, or Tesco could all be the next competitors in the financial services industry. These indeterminate sector boundaries suggest:

- There are no clearly identifiable competitors.
- Competitors will approach selected opportunities from their own vantage points. For example, Dell computers can see the opportunity as PC–TV, while Sony or Philips see it as TV–PC, reflecting their different starting points. Therefore, there will be multiple migration paths—Dell and Philips may not approach the migration to a PC–TV the same way, much less Microsoft or Intel. The same can be argued for banks—insurance firms, banks, retailers, and communication companies will not approach the market the same way.
- Competition for "migration paths" may be as critical as the end game itself.

Traditional analytical tools used to determine where value is created may be inappropriate in this new and emerging industry environment.[4] For example, in the traditional view of strategy, we have associated size with market influence. In the emerging competitive landscape, size does not lead to industry influence. Similarly, incumbency provides no rights; indeed, it may be a disadvantage.

One cannot assume clear industry boundaries. The boundaries between suppliers, competitors, customers, and collaborators are very porous. There are no permanent competitive positions. The structure of these industries is in a state of constant flux. The strategic question is not about optimizing but retaining the *capability for flexible and quick response*. The goal is to create a robust competitive position.

As the resource configurations of individual firms tend to be inadequate to meet the growing and changing demands, a wide variety of collaborative arrangements have become the norm in most industries. Increasingly, firms large and small have a higher propensity to form alliances. Many of them may be temporary. As industry structures evolve, the importance of an alliance does change. Firms will form new alliances and opt out of old ones. Forming and learning from alliances and disbanding those that are no longer strategic may be a learned skill itself.

6. *Standards.* New industries produce new standards as markets evolve. What are the standards for DVD or Minidisk? What are the standards we need for security and privacy before E-Commerce can flourish? What are the communication standards for creating a seamless exchange of images and video over the Internet? Questions such as these are critical in the evolution of markets. Increasingly, issues of this kind are resolved by market forces, not by governmental mandates. Several interesting phenomena created by these changes are:

- Competitors collaborate to establish standards. Vendor standards do not become industry standards unless one standard gains enough market power to implicitly enforce it. This means that a coalition of firms subscribing to the standard proposed by one vendor (e.g., Java by Sun) will have to support it over other vendor standards (e.g., NT by Microsoft). This is "inter-coalition" competition.

- Multiple industry standards may coexist for some time, and this is very expensive, creating uncertainties for both the consumer and the firms. Over time, one dominant industry standard evolves.

- Inter-coalition competition for setting standards is different from "intra-coalition" competition for profits. For example, while Philips and Sony collaborated in creating the DVD standard, they also compete for profits in the DVD business.

Standards can evolve through market-based competition (as against standards imposed by public policy). Such market-based standards involve competition between a cluster of firms supporting a standard against another cluster supporting an alternate standard. In an important sense, this competition is about competition among coalitions of firms. All firms involved in this process will have to take a position on the basis for supporting one standard over another. For the firm proposing the standard, the question is "What makes the standard attractive to the largest number of firms? What core competence can be used as a bargaining tactic with potential supporters?"

7. *Disintermediation.* In almost all industries, the distance between the producer and the end-user is shrinking. The multiple distribution steps—wholesalers, dealers and retailers—are being reduced to a single distribution step. New channels are emerging. The World Wide Web provides an opportunity for producers to go directly to the end-user. This phenomenon is pervasive, be it in brokerage (e.g., Charles Schwab), garments (e.g., Levi Strauss) or computers (e.g., Dell, Gateway).

With the proliferation of manufacturers offering their wares electronically, there is unlikely to be a dearth of information available to the end-user. However, information, by itself, does not guarantee the ability to make good decisions. It is likely that a new form of intermediary—the expert—will emerge. Experts (electronic equivalent of Consumer Reports) will act as intermediaries who will verify quality and cost and make recommendations.

The process of disintermediation has significant implications for the traditional cost structure of industries, especially the selling and administrative costs. Disintermediation will also have an impact on the levels of finished goods, inventories and accounts receivable required for a unit of revenue.

The implication is that there will be both profit and loss and balance sheet impacts. Firms will have to fundamentally rethink their business models.

8. *Eco-Sensitivity.* This will become a major issue in the next millennium. Firms will move away from a compliance-oriented perspective to a business-opportunity-driven viewpoint of environmental issues.

For example, the growing affluence of mainland China will influence the mix of food consumed. (Invariably, affluence is associated with more meat and sugar consumption.) China has a shortage of water and arable land. Therefore, most of the additional demand for food—in the form of corn, chicken or hogs—must be imported. This implies that China will become a major importer of food during the next decade. This is ecologically sensible; China gets all the food it needs, without straining its scarce water resources. The abundant water resources and land in the Americas get used. This is an ecologically sensible solution for the world as a whole.

The New Economy

Any of the individual discontinuities can be managed. But the New Economy is about all these forces impacting the firm simultaneously (see Figure 1). Businesses will be affected differently; however, all of them will be subject to the impact of a subset of these forces. Taken as a whole, these discontinuities will force all firms to:

• Be concerned about doing business worldwide. This implies that all firms will have to worry about multiple locations, multiple cultures, multiple skill sets, and multiple business perspectives.

FIGURE 1

Eight discontinuities are shaping the New Economy

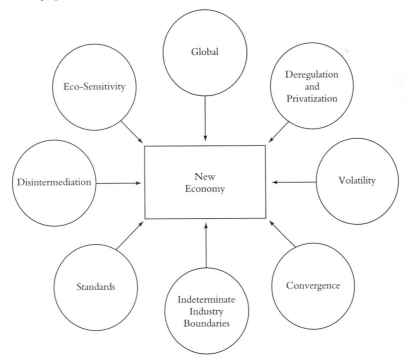

- Be concerned about temporary alliances—alliance and collaborative agreements that are designed to transfer skills across firms. In these alliances, learning is as important as protecting critical intellectual property, demanding that people be open to new ideas while protecting vital company interests.

- Focus on speed as a major issue—not just speed in product development, but also in knowledge transfer across markets and businesses. To remain competitive, companies will have to absorb this new knowledge and reconfigure their businesses accordingly.

- Reevaluate the business model used in the developed world. Current beliefs about the "capital intensity" of a business or the "profit model" associated with it may not be sustainable. The business model needs to be reevaluated and adapted to meet the requirements of the New Economy.

The discontinuities that constitute the New Economy will demand new skill sets among management teams.

Revisiting Core Competencies of the Firm

The idea is widely accepted that in addition to being a portfolio of distinct businesses, the diversified firm is a portfolio of core competencies.[5] Core competencies are a combination of:

- Multiple technologies (hard and soft).
- Collective learning (multilevel, multifunctional).
- Capacity to share (across business and geographical boundaries).

A core competency can be represented as a multiplicative function of these three elements. To manage competitive discontinuities, managers will be confronted by new, complex challenges. They will have to:

- Incorporate new bundles of technologies—new to the traditional businesses of the firm.

A bundle of related technologies, or a *knowledge stream,* such as software, needs to be blended with more traditional technologies (e.g., electronics and software in a chemical firm). This means that managers must recognize that they have to work with a new logic (e.g., electronics in a traditional chemical firm).

- The composition of teams will also change. Globalization requires that team members *from multiple cultures* must learn as a group.

- The redeployment of core competence across a number of applications at high speed will force firms to *collaborate and transfer knowledge across multiple business units and geographical locations.*

The task of managing competencies in the new global market place is complex. There are at least five distinct tasks:

1. *Gaining Access to, and Absorbing New, Knowledge.*

The most obvious way to gain access to the new knowledge stream is to recruit people with the required (new) knowledge (e.g., mathematicians in a bank, geneticists in a traditional pharmaceutical firm, or software engineers in a hard-core manufacturing firm). Anyone who has been through this process of new skills acquisition knows how hard it is to have these new skills accepted and made welcome in an organization. While bankers have to learn the new tools that mathematicians bring to the game, mathematicians also have to learn banking.

This two-way knowledge transfer is critical before a useful blending can occur. However, the tendency in most organizations is to reject these new skills—similar to the response of an immune system to an invading virus. Left to its own devices, the organization is unlikely to absorb these new skills. Therefore, one of the critical roles of senior management is to create legitimacy for the new knowledge. Top managers must not only constantly present the strategic direction of the firm to all employees, but also identify the new knowledge that will help to create that future. Further, several levels of the organization must learn and apply the "culture" of that new knowledge. For example, software has a different culture from manufacturing.

The intellectual heritage limits and restricts what a management team can do. For example, why do we not have software upgrades in automobiles? It is equally difficult for those who have operated in a regulated environment to understand the culture and discipline of the capital market. One senior manager from the Eastern bloc, perplexed by the changes in the stock prices on a daily basis, asked: "Which organization fixes the price?" In his country, governmental agencies fixed all prices until recently.

It is not enough that the need for new knowledge is recognized and steps are taken to acquire them (including alliances), but fundamental legitimacy and urgency must be assigned to that task. In order to be successful, the progress of the task of instituting and melding the new knowledge into the different traditional intellectual cultures must be continually monitored.

2. *Integrating Multiple Streams of Knowledge.*

Acquiring new knowledge is a difficult process, and actively integrating it into traditional knowledge to create new business opportunities is even harder. For example, at Kodak, knowledge of chemical imaging must be integrated with electronics and software knowledge to create new hybrid products. Photo compact disks and digital cameras demand a seamless and careful integration of multiple streams of knowledge. Over time, the commingling of these streams creates a new competence.

Organizations learn by doing. Therefore, it is critical that top managers set up specific, bite-size projects. Projects are the carriers of new learning. They focus the organization's attention on solving the problems of integrating the new knowledge with the old. Project teams with cross-disciplinary membership are critical for successful learning and application.

3. *Sharing across Cultures and Distance.*

While the focus thus far has been on intellectual diversity—the culture of various knowledge streams—in a global firm, there is yet another dimension to cultural diversity. This is a result of *multiple country cultures.*

Different cultures have different implicit priorities. For example, the product development philosophy—the priorities placed on quality, cost, time, safety, and performance—among U.S.-trained, European, Japanese, and Chinese designers is likely to be different. No manager lives in a vacuum. She/he lives in a culture that values some characteristics more than others. This is a result of deep socialization. In some cultures, for example, learning is a linear process. It is primarily analytical and based on individual effort. In other societies, learning is much more sequential, experiential and a team-oriented effort in which intuition plays an important role.

When collaboration is initiated in the context of evolving knowledge, across multiple cultures (i.e., collaboration with teams from three different continents), conflicts and misunderstandings emanate. A deeper and explicit understanding of the socialization patterns of groups involved becomes a necessity. Moreover, managers must avoid stereotyping the other groups. Cross-cultural collaborative activity is emerging as a critical skill in the New Economy.

4. *Learning to Forget.*

It is easy to exhort an individual or an organization to learn. But forgetting may be equally important.[6] The dominant logic of the firm,[7] or the recipes people use to learn, can become a major impediment to learning. Firms (managers) must first learn to forget, and forgetting is more difficult than learning. In most organizations, the forgetting curve is flat; in an age of discontinuities, a flat forgetting curve is a serious problem.

For example, it takes an enormous amount of effort to move from a "cost plus" view of the business to a "price minus" view of the business. The two formulas are: (1) Cost + Profit = Price; and (2) Price − Profit = Cost.

The traditional Department of Defense (DoD)–type businesses are characterized by mindsets, processes and skill sets appropriate to (1). Commercial businesses are characterized by (2). The transition for DoD-driven firms to the commercial arena has been one of deep frustration, with few successes. Participants in this different business culture need to forget their old patterns and replace them with new ones.

A similar situation exists in deregulated industries. Previously, the market was the "regulators"; some would argue that competition was also the "regulators." Senior managers paid a lot of attention to regulators, and the process of regulation made most of the firms in the industry look and act the same. The genetic variety, if any, was minimal. In market-based competition, the game is about consumers, differentiation, price-performance, innovation, and competition. This is a very different competitive milieu. To compete in the New Economy, it is essential to forget the old patterns.

5. *Deploying Competence across Business Unit Boundaries.*

The more that the large organizations move toward business unit (BU)–based strategies, measurement systems such as EVA, and rewards, the harder it is to focus on sharing across BU boundaries. The motivation for sharing is removed from the BUs and the competence base becomes fragmented.

In order to have a system of deployment of competencies, all BUs must have a common understanding of the patterns of market and technology evolution. Without such understanding, the conceptual framework for sharing does not exist.[8] But a conceptual framework, without organizational support systems, is unlikely to work. Many firms invest time and energy developing perspectives on the future while clinging to administrative systems that reinforce the BU orientation to the exclusion of all others. It is as if we were approaching the fourth-generation strategy with a third-generation knowledge base, second-generation managers, and first-generation administrative systems. There is a clear mismatch between "desire," rhetoric and reality in most firms across this dimension.

Composition of Competencies

The creation of new competencies by integrating a firm's existing knowledge base with new knowledge streams creates the need to reevaluate the elements that collectively create the system of competencies. Two broad elements can be recognized:

1. People-embodied knowledge—both tacit and explicit.[9]
2. Capital-embodied knowledge—both proprietary and vendor-based.

It is the combination of both people-embodied and capital-embodied knowledge that represents the totality of the competence base within an organization. In many industries, such as semiconductor manufacturing, access to vendor-based knowledge (and learning to work with them creatively) tends to be as important as the internally-generated proprietary knowledge (see Figure 2).

The relative importance of the various elements in the overall composition of a firm's competence profile is important to understand, in order to manage it effectively. The balance is likely to be different between:

- Established and new firms in the same industry (e.g., General Motors and Samsung).
- Traditional and new industries (e.g., cement manufacture vs. digital imaging).
- Firms with one location and multiple locations around the world (e.g., the tacit-to-explicit balance is critical in managing multiple locations, which demand more explicit knowledge).
- Dominant and multiple cultures (e.g., if most of the development work is done in one dominant culture, say in Japan, then the group can work with more tacit knowledge).

Needless to say, the balance between the elements is a moving target. As the discontinuities in the competitive landscape evolve, they will have an impact on the nature and composition of the elements of the competence base of the firm. Senior managers will have to constantly evaluate and calibrate these shifts and adjust their focus accordingly.

It is the combination of both people-embodied and capital-embodied knowledge that represents the totality of an organization's competence base

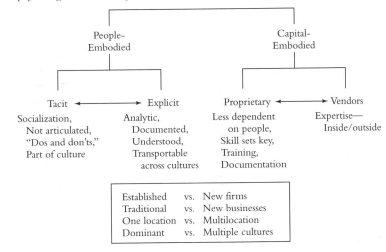

Competence Progression

Competence development is about learning, but learning takes place at three levels: (1) individual; (2) family groups; and (3) the firm as whole. The focus of learning is not just analytical, but also processes and values. Process and behavioral learning are as much a requirement as the analytical or scientific capabilities of individuals. The concepts of a team and a family group are embedded in the framework of competence. Therefore, processes that improve the ability of teams to develop special skills are critical.

Deploying competence into creating new "white space" opportunities embraces the idea of inter-team transfer and sharing. Therefore, individuals, teams (family groups) and the total organization (inter-team collaboration) are important aspects of competence management. But the cornerstone of the concept is the quality and the centrality of individuals.

The development of a new competence must explicitly recognize the role of individuals, teams, the whole organization, and the process by which individual excellence, scientific knowledge, creativity, and imagination are transformed into team

expertise and organizational capability. The competence progression is illustrated in Figure 3.

The challenge to senior managers is to develop specific managerial steps to manage this transformation. While many of these steps will be somewhat firm-specific, there are some universally beneficial steps.

Building New Competencies: First Steps

Building new competencies and selectively leveraging and protecting existing competencies are difficult organizational tasks. The difficulties are as much organizational as intellectual. A minimum program would include:

1. Investment in extensive socialization within the firm. Extensive international travel and job assignments help managers become more culturally sensitive. In addition to training in interpersonal competence, there should be training in intercultural competence. Managers during the next decade will have to deal with four levels of diversity: race, gender, cultural, and intellectual. Each aspect of these areas needs training.

FIGURE 3

The challenge to senior management is to develop specific
steps to manage the competency development process

Competence Progression

Technology	×	*Collective Learning*	×	*Sharing across Boundaries*
1. Individuals		Teams		Organization
2. Tacit/explicit		Tacit/explicit		Explicit/tacit
3. Personal excellence		Team expertise		Organizational capability
4. Scientific knowledge		Understanding specific applications		Building competence
5. Creativity and imagination		Projects/special capabilities		New way to build businesses, and compete

2. Development of language skills. European firms do a better job than U.S. firms in language training, at least of their expatriate managers. Language will be a critical aspect of competence transfer. It is easy to recognize that tacit knowledge cannot be easily transferred across language barriers. As the tacit component of the competence profile increases, language skills become critical.

3. Extensive documentation—not a bureaucracy—is critical to transfer from the tacit to explicit. This means that there must be a concern for standards and standardization, such as a commitment to a common CAD system, common IT architecture, common and shared glossary of terms, and a common design philosophy. Basically, there is a need for a common, shared managerial framework. Top managers must clearly identify what is not negotiable within the firm. But left to their own devices, they are likely to have, for example, incompatible CAD systems or quality processes—a common occurrence in highly decentralized firms. This makes sharing impossible.

4. Extensive commitment to training, in both the analytic and experiential side of management.

These four areas are a basic framework for constructing a program to manage new competencies in the New Economy that is forming. This New Economy will dominate the competitive landscape for the foreseeable future. This competitive landscape is being shaped by major discontinuities. These provide immense opportunities for firms that are alert. Firms will have to rethink the nature of their core competencies and acquire new competencies that will shape their future.

The future belongs to the imaginative, those that have the courage to overcome the discontinuities and reshape their firms to meet the challenges of the New Economy.

Endnotes

1. Christensen, Clayton M. *The Innovator's Dilemma: When Technologies Cause Great Firms to Fail.* Harvard Business School Press, 1977.
2. Leonard-Barton, Dorothy. "Core Capabilities and Core Rigidities: A Paradox in Managing New Product Development." *Strategic Management Journal,* Vol. 13, Special Issue, Summer 1992 (pp. 111–125).
3. See for example, Chin Chung: "Division of Labor across the Taiwan Strait: Macro-overview and Analysis of the Electronics Industry," in *The China Circle.* Barry Naughton, (ed), Brookings Institution Press, 1997.

4. See Porter, M. E. *Competitive Strategy: Techniques for Analyzing Industries and Competitors,* Free Press, New York, 1980.

5. Prahalad, C. K. and Gary Hamel. "The Core Competencies of the Corporation," *Harvard Business Review.* May–June, 1990.

6. Hamel, Gary and C. K. Prahalad. *Competing for the Future* (Chapter 3), Harvard Business School Press, 1994.

7. Prahalad, C. K. and Richard Bettis. "Dominant Logic: A New Linkage between Diversity and Performance."

Strategic Management Journal, Volume 7, Number 6, November–December 1986 (pp. 485–501).

8. The need for such a framework, a strategic architecture, is discussed in C. K. Prahalad and Gary Hamel: *Competing for the Future,* (chapter 5), Harvard Business School Press, 1994.

9. People-embodied knowledge has received a fair amount of attention with the increasing focus on knowledge management. I. Nonaka and H. Takeuchi: *The Knowledge Creating Company,* Oxford University Press, New York, 1995.

READING 44
SEVEN PRACTICES OF SUCCESSFUL ORGANIZATIONS

Jeffrey Pfeffer

Effective management of people can produce sub-stantially enhanced economic performance. A plethora of terms have been used to describe such management practices: high commitment, high performance, high involvement, and so forth. I use these terms interchangeably, as they all tap similar ideas about how to obtain profits through people. I extract from the various studies, related literature, and personal observation and experience a set of seven dimensions that seem to characterize most if not all of the systems producing profits through people.

- Employment security.
- Selective hiring of new personnel.
- Self-managed teams and decentralization of decision making as the basic principles of organizational design.
- Comparatively high compensation contingent on organizational performance.
- Extensive training.
- Reduced status distinctions and barriers, including dress, language, office arrangements, and wage differences across levels.
- Extensive sharing of financial and performance information throughout the organization.

This list is somewhat shorter than my earlier list of sixteen practices describing "what effective firms do with people,"[1] for two reasons. First, this list focuses on basic dimensions, some of which, such as compensation and reduction of status differences, have multiple components that were previously listed separately. Second, some of the items on the previous list have more to do with the ability to implement high-performance work practices—such as being able to take a long-term view and to realize the benefits of prompting from within—than with describing dimensions of the practices themselves. It is, however, still the case that several of the dimensions of high-performance work arrangements listed, for instance employment secu-rity and high pay, appear to fly in the face of conventional wisdom. This article outlines these practices, provides examples to illustrate both their implementation and their impact, and explains their underlying logic.

Employment Security

In an era of downsizing and rightsizing—or, as Donald Hastings, CEO of Lincoln electric, called it in a speech to the Academy of Management in 1996, "dumbsizing"—how can I write about em-ployment security as a critical element of high-performance work arrangements? First, because it is simply empirically the case that most research on the effects of high-performance management sys-tems have incorporated employment security as one important dimension in their description of these systems. That is because "one of the most widely accepted propositions . . . is that innovations in work practices or other forms of worker-man-agement cooperation or productivity improve-ment are not likely to be sustained over time when workers fear that by increasing productivity they will work themselves out of their jobs."[2]

This was recognized long ago by Lincoln Elec-tric, the successful arc welding and electric motor manufacturer that has dominated its markets for decades. Years ago, it began offering guaranteed employment to workers after two (and now three)

Source: Reprinted by permission of Harvard Business School Press. An excerpt from *The Human Equation,* by Jeffrey Pfeffer, entitled "Seven Practices of Successful Organizations," which appeared in *California Management Review,* Winter 1998.

years on the job. It has not had a layoff since 1948. Nor is it the case that this is just because the company has never faced hard times. In the early 1980s, a recession and high interest rates caused Lincoln's domestic sales to fall about 40 percent over an eighteen-month period. Nevertheless, it did not resort to layoffs. One thing the company did to avoid laying off people was to redeploy them. Factory workers who had made Lincoln's products were put in the field with the task of selling them, in the process actually increasing Lincoln's market share and penetration. Over the years, Lincoln has enjoyed gains in productivity that are far above those for manufacturing as a whole, and its managers believe that the assurance workers have that innovations in methods will not cost them or their colleagues their jobs has significantly contributed to these excellent results. Similarly, when General Motors wanted to implement new work arrangements in its innovative Saturn plant in the 1990s, it guaranteed its people job security except in the most extreme circumstances. When New United Motors was formed to operate the Fremont automobile assembly plant, it offered its people job security. How else could it ask for flexibility and cooperation in becoming more efficient and productive?

Many additional benefits follow from employment assurances besides workers' free contribution of knowledge and their efforts to enhance productivity. One advantage to firms is the decreased likelihood that they will lay off employees during downturns. How is this a benefit to the firm? In the absence of some way of building commitment to retaining the work force—either through pledges about employment security or through employment obligations contractually negotiated with a union—firms may lay off employees too quickly and too readily at the first sign of financial difficulty. This constitutes a cost for firms that have done a good job selecting, training, and developing their work force: Layoffs put important strategic assets on the street for the competition to employ. When a colleague and I interviewed the Vice President for People at Southwest Airlines,

she noted that the company had never had a layoff or furlough in an industry where such events were common. When we asked why, she replied, "Why would we want to put our best assets, our people, in the arms of the competition?" Seeing its people as strategic assets rather than as costs, Southwest has pursued a careful growth strategy that avoided overexpansion and subsequent cuts in personnel.

Employment security policies will also lead to more careful and leaner hiring, because the firm knows it cannot simply let people go quickly if it has overestimated its labor demand. Leaner staffing can actually make the work force more productive, with fewer people doing more work. The people are often happy to be more productive because they know they are helping to ensure a result that benefits them—having a long-term job and a career. Furthermore, employment security maintained over time helps to build trust between people and their employer, which can lead to more cooperation, forbearance in pressing for wage increases, and better spirit in the company. Herb Kelleher, the CEO of Southwest, has written:

> Our most important tools for building employee partnership are job security and a stimulating work environment . . . Certainly there were times when we could have made substantially more profits in the short term if we had furloughed people, but we didn't. We were looking at our employees' and our company's longer-term interests . . . [A]s it turns out, providing job security imposes additional discipline, because if your goal is to avoid layoffs, then you hire very sparingly. So our commitment to job security has actually helped us keep our labor force smaller and more productive than our competitors'.[3]

For organizations without the strategic discipline or vision of Southwest, a guarantee of employment security can help the firm avoid making a costly decision to lay people off that has short-term benefits and long-term costs.

If you want to see just how costly such layoff decisions can be, consider Silicon Valley. Executives from the semiconductor and electronics industries often write newspaper and magazine articles and testify before Congress in favor of permitting immigration of skilled workers. These executives favor immigration because they manage companies that are frequently short of necessary talent. The executives complain about their difficulty in recruiting qualified personnel in their expanding industry.

What you won't see in their articles or testimony, but what you will find if you look at newspapers from a few years ago, is that many of these very same firms laid off engineers, technicians, and other skilled workers in some instances just two or three years—or even less—before subsequently complaining about labor scarcity. Think about it. My friends in the valley have perfected the art of buying high and selling low. When times are tough in the industry, common sense suggests that that is exactly the time to recruit and build your work force. Competition for talented staff will obviously be less, and salaries need not be bid up in attempts to lure people from their existing jobs. By hiring when times are poor and developing a set of policies, including assurance that people will be retained, a firm can become an employer of choice, and the organization will not have to enter the labor market at its very peak to acquire the necessary work force. Instead, many firms do exactly the opposite. They lay people off in cyclical downturns and then, when the entire industry is booming and staff is scarce, they engage in often fruitless bidding contests to rehire the skills that they not that long ago sent packing.

Employment security can confer yet another benefit, in that it encourages people to take a longer-term perspective on their jobs and organizational performance. In a study of the financial performance of 192 banks, John Delery and Harold Doty observed a significant relationship between employment security and the bank's return on assets, an important measure of financial performance: "The greater the employment security given to loan officers, the greater the returns to banks."[4] Why might this be? In a bank that hires and lays off loan officers quickly to match economic fluctuations, the typical loan officer will worry only about booking loans—just what they have typically been

rewarded for doing. With employment security and a longer-term perspective on the job, the bank officer may be more inclined to worry as well about the repayment prospects of the loan and about building customer relationships by providing high levels of service. Although a specific loan officer's career may prosper by being a big loan producer and moving quickly from one bank to another, the bank's profitability and performance are undoubtedly enhanced by having people who take both a longer term and a more comprehensive view of their jobs and of the bank's financial performance. This is likely to occur, however, only with the prospect of long-term continuity in the employment relationship.

The idea of employment security does not mean that the organization retains people who don't perform or work effectively with others—that is, performance does matter. Lincoln Electric has very high turnover for employees in their first few months on the job, as those who don't fit the Lincoln culture and work environment leave. Southwest will fire people who don't provide the level of customer service the firm is well-known for delivering and don't want to improve. Employment security means that employees are not quickly put on the street for things, such as economic downturns or the strategic mistakes of senior management, over which they have no control. The policy focuses on maintaining total employment, not on protecting individuals from the consequences of their individual behavior on the job.

The idea of providing employment security in today's competitive world seems somehow anachronistic or impossible and very much at variance with what most firms seem to be doing. But employment security is fundamental to the implementation of most other high-performance management practices, such as selective hiring, extensive training, information sharing, and delegation. Companies are unlikely to invest the resources in the careful screening and training of new people if those people are not expected to be with the firm long enough for it to recoup these investments. Similarly, delegation of operating authority and the sharing of sensitive performance and strategic information requires trust, and that trust is much more likely to emerge in a system of mutual, long-term commitments.

Selective Hiring

Organizations serious about obtaining profits through people will expend the effort needed to ensure that they recruit the right people in the first place. This requires several things. First, the organization needs to have a large applicant pool from which to select. In 1993, for example, Southwest Airlines received about 98,000 job applications, interviewed 16,000 people, and hired 2,700. In 1994, applications increased to more than 125,000 for 4,000 hires. Some organizations see processing this many job inquiries as an unnecessary expense. Southwest sees it as the first step toward ensuring that it has a large applicant pool from which to select its people. Similarly, Singapore Airlines—frequently listed as one of Asia's most admired companies, one of the most profitable airlines in the world, and consistently ranked quite high in ratings of service quality—is extremely careful and selective in its recruiting practices. Flight attendants are an important point of contract with the customer and one way in which Singapore Airlines differentiates its service. Consequently, senior management becomes personally involved in flight attendant selection. Prospective generalist staff, from which the ranks of mangers will come, must pass a series of tests and clear two rounds of interviews, including interviews with a panel of senior management. "From an initial pool of candidates, about 10 percent are short-listed and only 2 percent [one out of 50] are selected."[5]

Nor is such selectivity confined to service organizations. When Subaru-Isuzu opened its automobile assembly plant in the United States in the late 1980s, it received some 30,000 applications for employment. The Japanese automakers have consistently emphasized selecting good people as critical to their success, and they have been willing to expend the resources required on the selection

process. It has always fascinated me that some people see selectivity on the part of elite universities or graduate schools as a mark of the school's prestige but see the same selection ratios on the part of companies as a waste of resources. It isn't.

Second, the organization needs to be clear about what are the most critical skills and attributes needed in its applicant pool. The notion of trying to find "good employees" is not very helpful—organizations need to be as specific as possible about the precise attributes they are seeking. At Southwest Airlines, applicants for flight attendant positions are evaluated on the basis of initiative, judgment, adaptability, and their ability to learn. These attributes are assessed in part from interviews employing questions evoking specific instances of these attributes. For instance, to assess adaptability, interviewers ask, "Give an example of working with a difficult co-worker. How did you handle it?"[6] To measure initiative, one question asks, "Describe a time when a co-worker failed to pull their weight and what you did about it."

Third, the skills and abilities hired need to be carefully considered and consistent with the particular job requirements and the organization's approach to its market. Simply hiring the "best and the brightest" may not make sense in all circumstances. Enterprise Rent-A-Car is today the largest car rental company in the United States, with revenues in 1996 of $3 billion, and it has expanded at a rate of between 25 and 30 percent a year for the past eleven years. It has grown by pursuing a high customer service strategy and emphasizing sales of rental car services to repair garage customers. In a low wage, often unionized, and seemingly low employee skill industry, virtually all of Enterprise's people are college graduates. But these people are hired primarily for their sales skills and personality and for their willingness to provide good service, not for their academic performance. Dennis Ross, the chief operating officer, commented "We hire from the half of the college class that makes the upper half possible . . . We want athletes, fraternity types . . . people people." Brian O'Reilly interpolates Enterprise's reasoning:

The social directors make good sales people, able to chat up service managers and calm down someone who has just been in a car wreck . . . The Enterprise employees hired from the caboose end of the class have something else going for them. . . a chilling realization of how unforgiving the job market can be.[7]

Fourth, organizations should screen primarily on important attributes that are difficult to change through training and should emphasize qualities that actually differentiate among those in the applicant pool. An important insight on the selection process comes from those organizations that tend to hire more on the basis of basic ability and attitude than on applicants' specific technical skills, which are much more easily acquired. This has been the practice of Japanese organizations for some time. "Japanese recruitment seeks to find the individual with the 'proper character whom it can train.' . . . Instead of searching for applicants with necessary skills for the job, the focus is on social background, temperament, and character references."[8]

Sophisticated managers know that it is much more cost-effective to select on those important attributes that are difficult or impossible to change and to train people in those behaviors or skills that are more readily learned. At Southwest Airlines, a top pilot working for another airline who actually did stunt work for movie studios was rejected because he was rude to a receptionist. Southwest believes that technical skills are easier to acquire than a teamwork and service attitude. Ironically, many firms select for specific, job-relevant skills that, while important, are easily acquired. Meanwhile, they fail to find people with the right attitudes, values, and cultural fit—attributes that are harder to train or change and that are quite predictive of turnover and performance. To avoid having to retrain or resocialize people that have acquired bad habits at their previous employers, companies like Southwest prefer to hire individuals without previous industry experience. Many also prefer to hire at the entry level, obtaining individuals who are eager to prove themselves and who don't know what can't be done.

It is tempting to hire on the basis of ability or intelligence rather than fit with the organizations—so tempting that one occasionally observes firms trying to differentiate among a set of individuals who are basically similar in intelligence or ability while failing to distinguish those that will be well suited to the organization from those that will not. One of my favorite examples of this is recruitment at Stanford Business School. Stanford has a class of about 370 MBAs, selected from an initial applicant pool that in recent years has exceeded six thousand. These are obviously talented, motivated, and very intelligent individuals. Distinguishing among them on those criteria would be difficult, if not impossible. But many firms seek to do the impossible—they try to get around the school's policy of not releasing grades in an effort to figure out who are the smartest students and to assess differences in ability among a set of applicants through interviewing techniques such as giving them problems or cases to solve. Meanwhile, although many job recruits will leave their first job within the first two years, and such turnover and the requirements to refill those positions are exceedingly expensive, few firms focus primarily on determining fit—something that does vary dramatically.

Two firms that take a more sensible and pragmatic approach to hiring are Hewlett-Packard and PeopleSoft, a producer of human resource management software. For instance, one MBA job applicant reported that in interviews with PeopleSoft, the company asked very little about personal or academic background, except about learning experiences from school and work. Rather, the interviews focused mostly on whether the person saw herself as team oriented or as an individual achiever; what she liked to do outside school and work; and her philosophy on life. The specific question was "Do you have a personal mission statement? If you don't, what would it be if you were to write it today?" Moreover, the people interviewing the applicant presented a consistent picture of PeopleSoft as a company and of the values that were shared among employees. Such a selection process is more likely to produce cultural fit. A great deal of research evidence shows that the degree of cultural fit and value congruence between job applicants and their organizations significantly predicts both subsequent turnover and job performance.[9]

Firms serious about selection put applicants through several rounds of interviews and a rigorous selection procedure. At Subaru-Isuzu's U.S. manufacturing plant, getting hired involved going through multiple screening procedures including written tests and assessment center exercises and could take as long as six months or more. The fastest hire took nine weeks.[10] Such a lengthy selection process has several outcomes. First, it ensures that those who survive it have been carefully scrutinized. Second, it ensures that those eventually hired into the firm develop commitment. Applicants selected become committed as a consequence of having gone through such a lengthy and rigorous process—if they didn't really want the job, why would they go through it? At Subaru-Isuzu, the selection process "demanded perseverance," ensured that those who were hired had "the greatest desire and determination," and, since it required some degree of sacrifice on the part of the people, encouraged self-elimination and built commitment among those who survived.[11] Third, this type of process promotes the feeling on the part of those who are finally selected that they are part of an elite and special group, a feeling that causes them to enter the organization with a high level of motivation and spirit. Laurie Graham's participant observation study of Subaru-Isuzu concluded that "the fact that so much money, time, and effort went into the selection of employees reinforced the belief that the company was willing to go to great lengths to select the best."[12]

Rigorous selection requires a method, refined and developed over time through feedback and learning, to ensure that the firm can identify the skills it is seeking from the applicant pool. At Southwest Airlines, the company tracks who has interviewed job applicants. When someone does especially well or poorly, the organization can actually try to assess what the interviewers saw or missed, and why. It is puzzling that organizations will ensure the quality of their manufacturing or service delivery process by closing the loop on that process through feedback, while almost no organizations attempt to do the same thing with their recruiting process. Sources of applicants, scores on tests or interview ratings, and other selection

mechanisms must be validated against the subsequent performance of the people selected if there is to be any hope of improving the effectiveness of the process over time.

The following list summarizes the main points about how to go about selective hiring to build a high-performance organization.

- Have a large number of applicants per opening.
- Screen for cultural fit and attitude—not for skills that can be readily trained.
- Be clear about what are the most critical skills, behaviors, or attitudes crucial for success; isolate just a small number of such qualities and be as specific as possible. Simply seeking "the best and brightest" frequently doesn't make sense.
- Use several rounds of screening to build commitment and to signal that hiring is taken very seriously.
- To the extent possible, involve senior people as a signal of the importance of the hiring activity.
- Close the loop by assessing the results and performance of the recruiting process.

Self-Managed Teams and Decentralization as Basic Elements of Organizational Design

Organizing people into self-managed teams is a critical component of virtually all high-performance management systems. Numerous articles and case examples as well as rigorous, systematic studies attest to the effectiveness of teams as a principle of organization design. One researcher concluded that "two decades of research in organizational behavior provides considerable evidence that workers in self-managed teams enjoy greater autonomy and discretion, and this effect translates into intrinsic rewards and job satisfaction; teams also outperform traditionally supervised groups in the majority of . . . empirical studies."[13]

In a manufacturing plant that implemented high-performance work teams, for example, a 38 percent reduction in the defect rate and a 20 percent increase in productivity followed the introduction of teams.[14] Honeywell's defense avionics plant credits improved on-time delivery—reaching 99 percent in the first quarter of 1996 as compared to below 40 percent in the late 1980s—to the implementation to teams.[15] A study of the implementation of teams in one regional Bell telephone operating company found that "self-directed groups in customer services reported higher customer service quality and had 15.4% higher monthly sales revenues."[16] In the case of network technicians, the implementation of self-directed work teams saved "an average of $52,000 in indirect labor costs for each self-directed team initiated."[17] Moreover, membership in self-directed work teams positively affected employee job satisfaction, with other factors that might also affect satisfaction statistically controlled. "More than 75% of surveyed workers who are currently in traditional work groups say they would volunteer for teams if given the opportunity. By contrast, less than 10% who are now in teams say they would like to return to traditional supervision."[18]

Teams offer several advantages. First, teams substitute peer-based for hierarchical control of work. "Instead of management devoting time and energy to controlling the workforce directly, workers control themselves."[19] Peer control is frequently more effective than hierarchical supervision. Someone may disappoint his or her supervisor, but the individual is much less likely to let down his or her work mates. At New United Motor Manufacturing (NUMMI), the work process is organized on a team basis with virtually no buffers of either in-process inventories or employees. As a consequence, "all the difficulties of one person's absence fall on those in daily contact with the absentee—the co-workers and immediate supervisor—producing enormous peer pressure against absenteeism."[20] Team-based organizations also are largely successful in having all of the people in the firm feel accountable and responsible for the operation and success of the enterprise, not just a few people in senior management positions. This increased sense of responsibility stimulates more initiative and effort on the part of everyone involved.

The tremendously successful natural foods grocery store chain, Whole Foods Markets, organized on the basis of teams, attributes much of its success to that arrangement. Between 1991 and 1996, the company enjoyed sales growth of 864 percent and net income growth of 438 percent as it expanded, in part through acquisitions as well as internal growth, from ten to sixty-eight stores. In its 1995 annual report, the company's team-oriented philosophy is clearly stated.

> Our growing Information Systems capability is fully aligned with our goal of creating a more intelligent organization—one which is less bureaucratic, elitist, hierarchical, and authoritarian and more communicative, participatory, and empowered. The ultimate goal is to have all Team Members contributing their full intelligence, creativity, and skills to continuously improving the company . . . Everyone who works at Whole Foods Market is a Team Member. This reflects our philosophy that we are all partners in the shared mission of giving our customers the very best in products and services. We invest in and believe in the collective wisdom of our Team members. The stores are organized into self-managing work teams that are responsible and accountable for their own performance.[21]

Each store is a profit center and has about ten self-managed teams in it, with team leaders and clear performance targets. Moreover, "the team leaders in each store are a team, store leaders in each region are a team, and the company's six regional presidents are a team."[22] Although store leaders recommend new hires, teams must approve hires for full-time jobs, and it takes a two-thirds vote of the team members to do so, normally after a thirty-day trial period. Through an elaborate system of peer store reviews, Whole Foods encourages people to learn from each other. By sharing performance information widely, the company encourages peer competition. "At Whole Foods, pressure for performance comes from peers rather than from headquarters, and it comes in the form of internal competition."[23]

Second, teams permit employees to pool their ideas to come up with better and more creative solutions to problems. The idea, similar to brainstorming or group problem solving, involves pooling ideas and expertise to increase the likelihood that at least one member of the group will come up with a way of addressing the problem. In the group setting, each participant can build on the others' ideas, particularly if the members are trained in effective group process and problem solving. Teams at Saturn and at the Chrysler Corporation's Jefferson North plant "provide a framework in which workers more readily help one another and more freely share their production knowledge—the innumerable 'tricks of the trade' that are vital in any manufacturing process."[24]

Third, and perhaps most importantly, by substituting peer for hierarchical control, teams permit removal of layers of hierarchy and absorption of administrative tasks previously performed by specialists, avoiding the enormous costs of having people whose sole job it is to watch people watch people who watch other people do the work. Administrative overhead is costly because management is typically well-paid. Eliminating layers of management by instituting self-managing teams saves money. Self-managed teams can also take on tasks previously done by specialized staff, thus eliminating excess personnel and, just as important, putting critical decisions in the hands of individuals who may be closer to the relevant information.

The AES Corporation is an immensely successful global developer and operator of electric power and steam plants, with sales of more than $835 million and six thousand employees in 1996. A 1982 investment in the company of $10,000 would be worth more than $10 million in 1996. The company "has never formed corporate departments or assigned officers to oversee project finance, operations, purchasing, human resources, or public relations. Instead, such functions are handled at the plant level, where plant managers assign them to volunteer teams."[25] Front-line people develop expertise in these various task domains, including finance, and receive responsibility and authority for carrying them out. They do so effectively. Of course, mistakes get made, but learning follows.

The AES structure saves on the cost of management—the organization has only five levels—and it economizes on specialized staff. The company developed a $400 million plant in Cumberland, Maryland, with a team of just ten people who obtained more than thirty-six separate permit approvals and negotiated the complex financing, including tax-exempt bonds and ten lenders. Normally, projects of this size require "hundreds of workers, each with small specific tasks to perform within large corporations."[26] The savings and increased speed and flexibility of the AES team-based approach are clear and constitute an important source of the firm's competitive advantage.

At Vancom Zuid-Limburg, a joint venture in the Netherlands that operates a public bus company, the organization has enjoyed very rapid growth in ridership and has been able to win transport concessions by offering more services at the same price as its competitors. The key to this success lies in its use of self-managed teams and the consequent savings in management overhead.

> Vancom is able to [win transport contracts] mainly because of its very low over-head costs. . . . [O]ne manager supervises around forty bus drivers . . . This management-driver ratio of 1 in 40 substantially differs from the norm in this sector. At best, competitors achieve a ratio of 1 in 8. Most of this difference can be attributed to the self-managed teams. Vancom . . . has two teams of around twenty drivers. Each team has its own bus lines and budgeting responsibilities . . . Vancom also expects each individual driver to assume more responsibilities when on the road. This includes customer service (e.g., helping elderly persons board the bus); identifying problems (e.g., reporting damage to a bus stop), and active contributions (e.g., making suggestions for improvement of the services).[27]

How can moving to self-managed teams, possibly eliminating layers of administration and even specialized staff, be consistent with the earlier discussion of employment security? Eliminating positions need not entail the elimination of the people doing these jobs—those individuals can be redeployed to other tasks that add more value to the organization. In the case of Lincoln Electric, recall that, at least temporarily, factory workers became salespeople, something that Mazda Motors also did when it faced a production employee surplus because of low sales in the 1980s. At SAS Airlines, staff that formerly did market research and planning were moved to positions where they had a more direct effect on customer service and operations. At Solectron, a contract manufacturer of electronics, institution of self-managed teams meant that managers, who typically had engineering degrees, could spend more time rethinking the overall production system and worrying about the technology strategy of the company—activities that added a lot more value than directly supervising $7 per hour direct labor. Often many tasks, such as the development of new products and new markets and the evaluation and introduction of new production technologies, require the time and strategic talents of managers, and these activities and decisions add much more value to the organization by using the knowledge and capabilities of the people. Consequently, a move to self-managed teams is consistent with maintaining employment when other, often more important, things are found for supervisors and specialized staff to do.

Even organizations for which working in formal teams is not sensible or feasible can benefit from one of the sources of team success: decentralization of decision making to front-line people, who have the knowledge and ability to take effective action. The Ritz-Carlton Hotel chain, winner of the Malcolm Baldrige National Quality Award in 1992, provides each of its people with discretion to spend up to $2,500, without any approval, in order to respond to guest complaints. Hampton Inn Hotel, a low-priced hotel chain, instituted a 100 percent Satisfaction Guarantee policy for its guests and permitted employees to do whatever was required to make the guests happy.

> A few years ago while working as a guest services representative at a Hampton Inn Hotel, I overheard a guest at our complimentary continental breakfast complaining quite loudly that his favorite cereal was not available. Rather than dismiss the person as just another disgruntled guest, I looked at the situation and saw an opportunity to make this guest happy. I gave him his money back—not for the continental breakfast, but for the cost of one night's stay at our hotel. And I did it on the spot, without checking with my supervisor or the general manager of the hotel.[28]

These policies may seem wasteful, but they're not. Ritz-Carlton mangers will tell you that a satisfied customer will talk to ten people and an unhappy customer to one hundred. Spending money to keep clients satisfied is a small price to pay for good advertising and encouraging guests to return. Similarly, at the Hampton Inn, "company research suggests that the guarantee strongly influences customer satisfaction and loyalty to Hampton Inn, and that guests who have experienced the guarantee are more likely to stay with Hampton Inn again in the future."[29] It is important to realize that successful implementation of guest satisfaction programs or, for that matter, programs to use the ideas and knowledge of the work force require decentralizing decision making and permitting people at all levels to exercise substantial influence over organizational decisions and processes. All of this requires trust, a commodity in short supply in many organizations that have become accustomed to operating with an emphasis on hierarchical control.

High Compensation Contingent on Organizational Performance

Although labor markets are far from perfectly efficient, it is nonetheless the case that some relationship exists between what a firm pays and the quality of the work force it attracts. It is amusing to see firms announce simultaneously that first, they compete on the basis of their people and that their goal is to have the very best work force in their industry, and second, that they intend to pay at (or sometimes slightly below) the median wage for comparable people in the industry. The level of salaries sends a message to the firm's work force—they are truly valued or they are not. After all, talk is cheap and many organizations can and do claim that people are their most important asset even as they behave differently.

I sometimes hear the statement that high compensation is a consequence of organizational success, rather than its progenitor, and a related comment that high compensation (compared to the average) is possible only in certain industries that either face less competition or have particularly highly educated employees. But neither of these statements is correct. Obviously, successful firms can afford to pay more and frequently do so, but high pay can also produce economic success.

When John Whitney assumed the leadership of Pathmark, a large grocery store chain in the Eastern United States in 1972, the company had about ninety days to live according to its banks and was in desperate financial shape. Whitney looked at the situation and discovered that 120 store managers in the chain were paid terribly. Many of them made less than the butchers, who were unionized. He decided that the store managers were vital to the chain's success and its ability to accomplish a turnaround. Consequently, one of the first things he did was to give the store managers a substantial raise—about 40 to 50 percent. The subsequent success of the chain was, according to Whitney, because the store managers could now focus on improving performance instead of worrying and complaining about their pay. Furthermore, in a difficult financial situation, the substantial raise ensured that talent would not be leaving for better jobs elsewhere, thereby making a turnaround more difficult. Whitney has consistently tried to pay a 15 percent wage premium in the many turnaround situations he has managed, and he argues that this wage premium and the resulting reduced turnover *facilitates* the organization's performance.

The idea that only certain jobs or industries can or should pay high wages is belied by the example of many firms including Home Depot, the largest home improvement and building supply company in the United States, with about 8 percent of the market and approximately 100,000 employees. The company has been successful and profitable, and its stock price has shown exceptional returns. Even though the chain emphasizes everyday low pricing as an important part of its business strategy and operates in a highly competitive environment, it pays its staff comparatively well for the retail industry, hires more experienced people with building industry experience, and expects its sales associates to provide a higher level of individual customer service.

> At Home Depot, clients can expect to get detailed instruction and advice concerning their building, renovation, and hardware needs. This requires a higher level of knowledge than is typical of a retail sales worker. Management considers the sales associates in each department as a team, with wide discretion over department operations. Associates also receive above average pay for this retail segment.[30]

Contingent compensation also figures importantly in most high-performance work systems. Such compensation can take a number of different forms, including gain sharing, profit sharing, stock ownership, pay for skill, or various forms of individual or team incentives. Wal-Mart, AES Corporation, Southwest Airlines, Whole Foods Markets, Microsoft, and many other successful organizations encourage share ownership. When employees are owners, they act and think like owners. Moreover, conflict between capital and labor can be reduced by linking them through employee ownership. Since 1989, Pepsico has offered a broad-based stock option plan available to 100,000 people, virtually its entire full-time labor force. Publix, a supermarket chain with 478 stores in the Southeastern United States, earned 2.75 percent on net sales in 1995 in an industry where the average is 1 percent. The company has enjoyed rapid expansion. It is important to note that the sixty-four-year-old company "has always been owned entirely by its employees and management, and the family of its late founder. . . . Employees become eligible for stock after working one year and one thousand hours . . . [E]mployees . . . wear name badges proclaiming that each is a stockholder."[31] Home Depot, the number one rated *Fortune 500* service company for profit growth, makes sure its managers own stock in the company. At Starbucks, the rapidly growing coffee outlet chain, 100 percent of the employees, even those working part-time, receive stock options in the company.[32] But such wide-spread encouragement of stock ownership remains quite rare. Hewitt Associates, a compensation consulting firm, estimated that in 1993 "only 30 large companies now have stock option plans available to a broad range of employees. Instead, most companies simply give stock options to employees once they reach a certain level in the corporation. Many workers then exercise the options and sell the stock in a single transaction. . . . They do not acquire a stake in the company"[33]

As various schemes for encouraging employee stock ownership have become increasingly trendy, in part because they frequently have tax advantages and, more importantly, are relatively straightforward to implement, it is critical to keep two things in mind. First, little evidence suggests that employee ownership, by itself, affects organizational performance. Rather, employee ownership works best as part of a broader philosophy or culture that incorporates other practices as well.

> An employee ownership culture is . . . a high-performance workplace in which each employee becomes an owner who is afforded certain rights in exchange for assuming new responsibilities. Such a culture is achieved by following the "working for yourself" thrust of employee ownership in conjunction with a battery of practices intended to create a non-bureaucratic, less hierarchical organization focused on performance.[34]

Merely putting in ownership schemes without providing training, information sharing, and delegation of responsibility will have little effect on performance because even if people are more motivated by their share ownership, they don't necessarily have the skills, information, or power to do anything with that motivation.

Second, many organizations treat stock options and share ownership as psychologically equivalent, but they are not. An option is just that—the potential or option to acquire shares at some subsequent point in time, at a given price. If the stock price falls below the option price, the option has no value. As Bill Gurley, one of the Wall Street's premier technology analysts, has argued. "The main problem with stock options is that they do not represent true ownership." Gurley goes on to describe the two potential negative effects that follow from the option holder's being given the upside but protected from the downside:

> There is a huge incentive for option holders to take undue risk [and] there is an incentive for [people] to roam around. Try your luck at one job, and if it doesn't pan out, move on to the next one. . . . [A]n aggressive stock-option program has many of the same characteristics as leverage. When times are good, they are doubly good . . . when times turn bad, the effects of stock-option compensation can be quite devastating.[35]

If, by contrast, someone purchases stock, even at a slightly discounted price, that person has made a behavioral commitment with much more powerful psychological consequences. The person remains an owner, with psychological investment in the company, even when the stock price falls. Consequently, share ownership builds much more powerful commitments and psychologically binds people to their organizations more than do options, even when the economic consequences of the two schemes are largely similar.

One worry I sometimes hear voiced about share ownership concerns inevitable declines in stock price. When I asked AES people working at the power plant in Thames, Connecticut, specifically about this issue, I was told that people do watch the stock price, but when it goes down, most employees want to buy more. One person stated, "We feel we're part of the entrepreneurs. The fluctuations in stock price reinforces the fact that we're responsible. If there were only upside, we're taking a free ride. The fact that the stock price fluctuates and that people gain and lose accordingly makes people feel like they are more of an owner of the company."

A number of organizations use profit sharing to great effect, particularly when it extends throughout the organization. At Southwest Airlines, profit sharing causes its people to focus on costs and profits because they receive a percentage of those profits. At Hewlett-Packard, quarterly profit-sharing payments are greeted with anticipation and excitement. The enthusiasm of vice presidents and secretaries alike, the excited talk pervading the organization, makes it clear that when profit sharing covers all employees the social pressure to continue producing good results becomes both powerful and widespread.

Profit sharing also makes compensation more variable, permitting adjustments in the labor bill without layoffs. At Lincoln Electric, profit sharing averages around 70 percent of individual employee salaries. When business falls, profit-sharing payments fall and labor expenses decrease—without having to break the firm's commitment to employment security. This variable component of wage costs, achieved through profit sharing, has permitted Lincoln to ride out a substantial sales decrease without laying off anyone covered by its guaranteed employment policy.

Paying for skill acquisition encourages people to learn different jobs and thereby to become more flexible. Gainsharing differs from profit sharing in that it is based on incremental improvements in the performance of a specific unit. Levi Strauss, for instance, has used gainsharing in its U.S. manufacturing plants. If a plant becomes more efficient in its use of labor and materials, the people share in the economic gains thereby achieved. They share in these gains even if profits in the firm as a whole are down. Why should employees in a plant in which they have achieved efficiency gains be penalized for problems in the general economy that have adversely affected sales or, for that matter, by the performance of other parts of the organization over which they have no control?

For a number of reasons, contingent compensation is important. First, simply, it is a matter of equity and fairness. If an organization produces greater returns by unharnessing the power of its people, justice suggests that some proportion of those gains should accrue to those who have produced the results as opposed to going solely to the shareholders or management. If people expend more effort and ingenuity, observe better results as a consequence of that effort, but then receive nothing, they are likely to become cynical and disillusioned and to stop trying.

Second, contingent compensation helps to motivate effort, because people know they will share in the results of their work. At Whole Foods, a gainsharing program "ties bonuses directly to team performance—specifically, sales per hour, the most important productivity measurement."[36] Teams, stores, and regions compete on the basis of quality, service, and profitability, with the results translating into bonuses. At Solectron, the implementation of self-managed teams positively affected quality and productivity. But when bonuses based on team performance were instituted, productivity and quality improved yet again.

Managers sometimes ask how to prevent employment security from turning into something resembling the civil service, with people just marking time. The answer is by coupling employment security with some form of group-based incentive, such as profit or gainsharing or share ownership. The organization thus unleashes the power of the team, whose economic interests are aligned with high levels of economic performance. Explaining Whole Foods' exceptional performance record, their CEO, John Mackey, stated the following:

> Whole Foods is a social system. . . . It's not a hierarchy. We don't have lots of rules handed down from headquarters in Austin. We have lots of self-examination going on. Peer pressure substitutes for bureaucracy. Peer pressure enlists loyalty in ways that bureaucracy doesn't.[37]

Peer pressure is stimulated by profit sharing and stock ownership that encourages team members to identify with the organization and to work hard on its behalf.

Training

Virtually all descriptions of high-performance management practices emphasize training, and the amount of training provided by commitment as opposed to control-oriented management systems is substantial. Training in steel minimills, for example, was almost 75 percent higher in mills relying on commitment as opposed to those relying on control. The previously cited study of automobile assembly plants showed that training was substantially higher in flexible or lean compared to mass production systems. Training is an essential component of high-performance work systems because these systems rely on front-line employee skill and initiative to identify and resolve problems, to initiate changes in work methods, and to take responsibility for quality. All of this requires a skilled and motivated work force that has the knowledge and capability to perform the requisite tasks.

> [H]aving a work force that is multiskilled, adaptable to rapidly changing circumstances, and with broad conceptual knowledge about the production system is critical to the operation of a flexible production system. The learning process that generates these human capabilities is an integral part of how the production system functions, not a separate training activity.[38]

Training is often seen as a frill in many U.S. organizations, something to be reduced to make profit goals in times of economic stringency. Data from the worldwide automobile assembly plant study, in this instance, from fifty-seven plants, are particularly instructive in illustrating the extent to which U.S. firms, at least in this industry, underinvest in training compared to competitors based in other countries. Table 1 presents information on the amount of training provided in automobile assembly plants operating in various countries and with different ownership.

The data in the table are startling. In terms of the amount of training provided to newly hired production workers, U.S. firms operating either in the U.S. or in Europe provide by far the least. Japanese plants in North America provide about 700 percent more training, and plants in newly industrialized countries such as Korea, Taiwan, and Brazil provided more than 750 percent more training than do U.S. plants. Only the amount of training provided in Australia compares with U.S. levels. Similar, although not as dramatic, differences exist in the training provided for experienced production workers. Once again, the United States and Australia lag, with Japanese firms operating in Japan

TABLE 1

Amount of training for production workers in automobile assembly plants

Ownership/Location	Hours of Training in the First Six Months for New Workers	Hours per Year for Those with > 1 Year Experience
Japanese/Japan	364	76
Japanese/North America	225	52
U.S./North America	42	31
U.S./Europe	43	34
European/Europe	178	52
Newly industrialized countries	260	46
Australia	40	15

Source: John Paul MacDuffie and Thomas A. Kochan, "Do U.S. Firms Invest Less in Human Resources? Training in the World Auto Industry." *Industrial Relations* 34 (1995): 156.

providing more than twice as much training to experienced workers. It is, of course, possible that U.S. firms' training is so much better and so much more efficient that it accomplishes just as much with a small fraction of the effort. This explanation cannot be definitively ruled out because the study did not measure (which would be almost impossible in any event) the consequences or the effectiveness of training. Although this explanation for the differences is possible, it is not very plausible. Rather, the differences in training reflect the different views of people held by the different firms and their corresponding production systems. "The Japanese-owned plants appear to train a lot because they rely heavily on flexible production, while the U.S.-owned plants in Europe and the Australian plants appear to train very little because they follow traditional mass production practices and philosophies."[39] U.S. automobile plants serious about pursuing profits through people show substantially larger training expenditures. Workers coming to Saturn initially "receive between 300 and 600 hours of training and then at least 5 percent of their annual work time (92 hours)" goes to training.[40]

The difference in training levels also reflect differences in time horizon—the Japanese firms and

Saturn, with their policies of employment security, intend to keep their people longer, so it makes more sense for them to invest more in developing them. This illustrates a more general point–that the returns from any single high-performance management practice depend importantly on the entire set of practices that have been implemented. A firm that invests a lot in training but considers its people to be expendable costs to be quickly shed in times of economic difficulty will probably see little return from its training investment.

Studies of firms in the United States and the United Kingdom consistently provide evidence of inadequate levels of training and training focused on the wrong things: specialist skills rather than generalist competence and organizational culture. For instance, a case study of eight large organizations operating in the United Kingdom found one, W. H. Smith, a retailing and distribution organization, in which less than half of the people received *any* training at all in the past year. Furthermore, in only two of the organizations "did more than half the respondents indicate that they thought they received the training they needed to do their jobs well,"[41] and less than half of the organizations had a majority of employees who felt they were encouraged to develop new skills. What training is provided frequently focuses narrowly on specific job skills. "One Lloyds Bank senior manager said, 'People's perceptions of development would be that it is inadequate. But of course they are looking at being developed as generalists and I want them to be specialists more and more.'"[42] And all of this is occurring in a world in which we are constantly told that knowledge and intellectual capital are critical for success. Knowledge and skill *are* critical—and too few organizations act on this insight.

Training can be a source of competitive advantage in numerous industries for firms with the wisdom to use it. Consider, for instance, the Men's Wearhouse, an off-price specialty retailer of men's tailored business attire and accessories. Because four of the ten occupations expected to generate the most job growth through 2005 are in the retail trade sector, and in 1994, 17.9 percent of all American workers were employed in retail trade, this industry has some importance to the U.S. economy.[43] Yet the management of people in retailing is frequently abysmal. Turnover is typically high, as is the use of part-time employees, many of whom work part-time involuntarily. Employees are often treated poorly and subjected to arbitrary discipline and dismissals. Wages in retailing are comparatively low and are falling compared to other industries, and skill and career development and training are rare. The industry is characterized by both intense and increasing competition, with numerous bankruptcies of major retailing chains occurring in the last decade.

The Men's Wearhouse went public in 1991 and in its 1995 annual report noted that since that time it has achieved compounded annual growth rates in revenues and net earnings of 32 and 41 percent respectively. The value of its stock increased by approximately 400 percent over this period. In 1995, the company operated 278 stores with a total revenue of $406 million. The key to its success has been how it treats its people and particularly the emphasis it has placed on training, an approach that separates it from many of its competitors. The company built a 35,000 square-foot training center in Fremont, California, its headquarters. In 1994, some 600 "clothing consultants" went through Suits University, and that year the company added "Suits High and Selling Accessories U to complement our core program."[44] "New employees spend about four days in one of about thirty sessions held every year, at a cost to the company of about $1 million."[45] During the winter, experienced store personnel come back to headquarters in groups of about thirty for a three- or four-day retraining program.

The Men's Wearhouse has invested far more heavily in training than have most of its competitors, but it has prospered by doing so.

> Our shrink is 0.6 percent, only about a third of the industry average. And we spend zero on monitors in our stores. We have no electronic tagging and we spend nothing on security ... We feel that if you create a culture and an environment that is supportive of

employees, you don't have to spend money on security devices. . . . My sense is that our rate of turnover is significantly lower than elsewhere.[46]

Not only does the typical U.S. firm not train as much, but because training budgets often fluctuate with company economic fortunes, a perverse, procyclical training schedule typically develops: Training funds are most plentiful when the firm is doing well. But, when the firm is doing well, its people are the busiest and have the most to do, and consequently, can least afford to be away for training. By contrast, when the firm is less busy, individuals have more time to develop their skills and undertake training activities. But that is exactly when training is least likely to be made available.

Training is an investment in the organization's staff, and in the current business milieu, it virtually begs for some sort of return-on-investments calculations. But such analyses are difficult, if not impossible, to carry out. Successful firms that emphasize training do so almost as a matter of faith and because of their belief in the connection between people and profits. Taco Inc., for instance, a privately owned manufacturer of pumps and valves, with annual sales of under $100 million, offers its 450 employees "astonishing educational opportunities—more than six dozen courses in all,"[47] in an on-site learning center. It cost the company $250,000 to build the center and annual direct expenses and lost production cost about $300,000. Asked to put a monetary value on the return from operating the center, however, the company's chief executive, John Hazen White, said "It comes back in the form of attitude. People feel they're playing in the game, not being kicked around in it. You step to the plate and improve your work skills; we'll provide the tools to do that."[48]

Even Motorola does a poor job of measuring its return on training. Although the company has been mentioned as reporting a $3 return for every $1 invested in training, an official from Motorola's training group said that she did not know where these numbers came from and that the company is notoriously poor at evaluating their $170 million investment in training. The firm mandates forty hours of training per employee per year, and believes that the effects of training are both difficult to measure and expensive to evaluate. Training is part and parcel of an overall management process and is evaluated in that light.

Reduction of Status Differences

The fundamental premise of high-performance management systems is that organizations perform at a higher level when they are able to tap the ideas, skill, and effort of all of their people. One way in which they do this is by organizing people in work teams, a topic already briefly covered here. But neither individuals nor teams will feel comfortable or encouraged to contribute their minds as well as their physical energy to the organization if it has sent signals that they are not both valuable and valued. In order to help make all organizational members feel important and committed to enhancing organizational operations, therefore, most high-commitment management systems attempt to reduce the status distinctions that separate individuals and groups and cause some to feel less valued.

This is accomplished in two principal ways—symbolically, through the use of language and labels, physical space, and dress, and substantively, in the reduction of the organization's degree of wage inequality, particularly across levels. At Subaru-Isuzu, everyone from the company president on down was called an Associate. The company's literature stated, "SIA is not hiring workers. It is hiring Associates . . . who work as a team to accomplish a task."[49] It is easy to downplay the importance of titles and language in affecting how people relate to their organization—but it is a mistake to do so.

> The title "secretary" seems subservient, Wilson [a consultant at Miss Paige Personnel agency in Sherman Oaks, California] said, "whereas administrative assistant sounds more career-oriented, and they like that." . . . Paul Flores . . . said employees at the Prudential Insurance Co. of America treat him better

because of his new title. . . . When he moved to the supply unit, he became a SIMS (supply inventory management system) technician. . . . [I]nstead of people saying, "I want it now," they say, "Get it to me when you can."[50]

At NUMMI, everyone wears the same colored smock; executive dining rooms and reserved parking don't exist. Lincoln Electric also eschews special dining rooms—management eats with the employees—as well as reserved parking and other fancy perquisites. Anyone who has worked in a manufacturing plant has probably heard the expression, "The suits are coming." Differences in dress distinguish groups from each other and, consequently, help to inhibit communication across internal organizational boundaries. At Kingston technology, a private firm manufacturing add-on memory modules for personal computers, with 1994 sales of $2.7 million per each of its three hundred people (a higher level of revenue per employee than Exxon, Intel, or Microsoft), the two cofounders sit in open cubicles and do not have private secretaries.[51] Solectron, too, has no special dining rooms and the chief executive, Ko Nishimura, does not have a private office or a reserved parking space. Parking has become quite tight as the company has expanded, and shuttle buses ferry employees in from more distant parking lots. Ko Nishimura rides these same shuttles and has said that he learns more riding in with the employees than from almost anything else he does. The reduction of status differences encourages open communication, necessary in an organization in which learning and adaptation are encouraged.

Status differences are reduced and a sense of common fate developed by limiting the difference in compensation between senior management and other employees. Whole Foods Markets, whose sales in 1996 were over $800 million and which has enjoyed substantial growth and stock price appreciation, has a policy limiting executive compensation. "The Company's publicly stated policy is to limit annual compensation paid to any executive officer to eight times the average full-time salary of all Team Members."[52] In 1995, the CEO, John

Mackey, earned $130,000 in salary and a bonus of $20,000. Nor does Whole Foods circumvent this restriction on executive compensation through grants of stock options or by giving executives shares in the company. In 1995, Mr. Mackey received options at the market price on four thousand shares of stock.

Herb Kelleher, the CEO of Southwest Airlines who has been on the cover of *Fortune* magazine with the test, "Is he America's best CEO?" earns about $500,000 per year including base and bonus. Moreover, when in 1995 Southwest negotiated a five-year wage freeze with its pilots in exchange for stock options and occasional profitability bonuses, Kelleher agreed to freeze his base salary at $395,000 for four years.

> Southwest's compensation committee said the freeze, which leaves Mr. Kelleher's salary unchanged from his 1992 contract, "is pursuant to a voluntary commitment made by Mr. Kelleher to the Southwest Airlines Pilots' Association." . . . The . . . compensation committee said the number of options granted Mr. Kelleher, at his recommendation, was "significantly below" the number recommended by an independent consultant as necessary to make Mr. Kelleher's contract competitive with pay packages for rival airline chief executives.[53]

Sam Walton, the founder and chairman of Wal-Mart, was typically on Graef Crystal's list of one of the most underpaid CEOs. These individuals are, of course, not poor. Each of them owns stock in the companies they manage. But stock ownership is encouraged for employees in these companies. Having an executive's fortune rise and fall together with those of the other employees differs dramatically from providing them large bonuses and substantial salaries even as the stock price languishes and people are being laid off.

Clearly, practices that reduce status differences are consistent with rewards contingent on performance—as long as these contingent rewards are applied on a group of organizational level so that the benefits of the performance of the many are not awarded to the few. Reducing status differences by reducing wage inequality does limit the organization's ability to use individual incentives to the extent that the application of individual rewards increases the dispersion of wages. But this is not necessarily a bad thing. Many managers and human resource executives mistakenly believe that placing *individual* pay at risk increases overall motivation and performance, when it is actually the contingency of the reward itself, not the level at which it is applied (individual, group, or organizational) that has the impact. Contingent rewards provided at the group or organizational level are at least as effective, if not more so, than individual incentives and, moreover, they avoid many of the problems inherent in individual merit or incentive pay.

Sharing Information

Information sharing is an essential component of high-performance work systems for two reasons. First, the sharing of information on things such as financial performance, strategy, and operational measures conveys to the organization's people that they are trusted. John Mackey, the chief executive of Whole Foods Markets, has stated, "If you're trying to create a high-trust organization . . . an organization where people are all-for-one and one-for all, your can't have secrets."[54] Whole Foods shares detailed financial and performance information with every employee—things such as sales by team, sales results for the same day last year, sales by store, operating profits by store, and even information from its annual employee morale survey—so much information, in fact, that "the SEC has designated all 6,500 employees 'insiders' for stock-trading purposes."[55] AES Corporation also shares detailed operational and financial information with its employees to the extent that they are all insiders for purposes of securities regulation. But Whole Foods goes even further, sharing individual salary information with every employee who is interested.

> The first prerequisite of effective teamwork is trust. . . . How better to promote trust (both among team members and between members and leaders) than to eliminate a major source of distrust—misinformed conjecture about who makes what? So every Whole Foods store has a book that lists the previous year's salary and bonus for all 6,500 employees—by name.[56]

This idea may at first seem strange. But think about your organization. If it is anything like mine, where salaries are secret, when it's time for raises people spend time and effort attempting to figure out what others got and how their raise (and salary) stacks up. This subtle attempt to find out where you stand takes time away from useful activities. Moreover, individuals frequently assume the worst—that they are doing worse than they actually are—and in any event, they don't have enough information to trust the salary system or, for that matter, the management that administers it. John Mackey of Whole Foods instituted the open salary disclosure process to signal that, at least this company had nothing to hide, nothing that couldn't be seen—and questioned—by any team member.

Contrast that organization with *Fortune* magazine, where a now-retired senior editor told me that after the Time-Warner merger when the company was saddled with debt, senior personnel were called together and told to "cut expenses by 10 percent." When the editor asked to see the expense budget and how it was allocated, he was told he could not. He resigned soon after. What message does an organization send if it says "Cut expenses, but, by the way, I don't trust you (even at senior levels) enough to share expense information with you?"

A second reason for sharing information is this: Even motivated and trained people cannot contribute to enhancing organizational performance if they don't have information on important dimensions of performance and, in addition, training on how to use and interpret that information. The now famous case of Springfield ReManufacturing beautifully illustrates this point. On February 1, 1983, Springfield ReManufacturing Corporation (SRC) was created when the plant's management and employees purchased an old International Harvester plant in a financial transaction that consisted of about $100,000 equity and $8.9 million debt, an 89–1 debt to equity ratio that has to make this one of the most leveraged of all leveraged buyouts. Jack Stack, the former plant manager and now chief executive, knew that if the plant was to succeed, everyone had to do their best and to share all of her or his wisdom and ideas for enhancing the plant's performance. Stack came up with a system called "open-book management" that has since become a quite popular object of study—so popular that SRC now makes money by running seminars on it. Although the method may be popular as a seminar topic, fewer organizations are actually willing to implement it.

The system has a straightforward underlying philosophy, articulated by Stack:

Don't use information to intimidate, control or manipulate people. Use it to teach people how to work together to achieve common goals and thereby gain control over their lives.... Cost control happens (or doesn't happen) on the level of the individual. You don't become the least-cost producer by issuing edicts from an office. . . . [T]he best way to control costs is to enlist everyone in the effort. That means providing people with the tools that allow them to make the right decisions.[57]

Implementing the system involved first making sure that all of the company's people generated daily numbers reflecting their work performance and production costs. Second, it involved sharing this information, aggregated once a week, with all of the company's people, everyone from secretaries to top management. Third, it involved extensive training in how to use and interpret the numbers—how to understand balance sheets and cash flow and income statements. "Understanding the financials came to be part of everyone's job."[58]

Springfield ReManufacturing has enjoyed tremendous financial success. In 1983, its first year of operation, sales were about $13 million. By 1992, sales had increased to $70 million, the number of employees had grown from 119 at the time of the buy-out to 700, and the original equity investment of $100,000 was worth more than $23 million by 1993.[59] No one who knows the company, and certainly not Jack Stack or the other managers, believes this economic performance could have been achieved without a set of practices that enlisted the cooperation and ingenuity of all of the firm's people. The system and philosophy of open-book management took a failing International Harvester plant and transformed it into a highly successful, growing business. Similarly impressive results have been reported in case studies of Manco, a Cleveland-based distributor of duct tape, weather

stripping, and mailing materials; Phelps County Bank, located in Rolla, Missouri; Mid-States Technical Staffing Services, located in Iowa; Chesapeake Manufacturing Company, a packaging materials manufacturer; Allstate Insurance; Macromedia, a software company; and Pace Industries, a manufacturer of die cast metal parts.[60]

If sharing information makes simple, common sense, you might wonder why sharing information about operations and financial performance is not more widespread. One reason is that information is power, and sharing information diffuses that power. At an International Harvester plant, "the plant manager's whole theory of management was 'Numbers are power, and the numbers are mine'"[61] If holding performance information is the critical source of the power of a firm's leaders, however, let me suggest that the organization badly needs to find some different leaders.

Another rationale for not sharing information more widely with the work force is managers' fears that the information will leak out to competitors, creating a disadvantage for the organization. When Bob Beck, now running human resources at Gateway 2000, a manufacturer of personal computers sold largely by mail order, was the Executive vice President of Human Resources at the Bank of America in the early 1980s, he told his colleagues that the organization could never improve customer service or retention until it shared its basic business strategy, plans, and measures of performance with its entire work force. When his colleagues on the executive committee noted that this information would almost certainly leak out to the competition, Beck demonstrated to them what ought to be common knowledge—in most instances, the competition already knows.

When organizations keep secrets, they keep secrets from their own people. I find it almost ludicrous that many companies in the electronics industry in the Silicon Valley go to enormous lengths to try to keep secrets internally, when all you have to do to penetrate them is to go to one of the popular bars or restaurants in the area and listen in as people from different companies talk quite openly with each other. When people don't know what is going on and don't understand the basic principles and theory of the business, they cannot be expected to positively affect performance. Sharing information and providing training in understanding and using it to make better business decisions works.

Conclusion

Firms often attempt to implement organizational innovations, such as those described here, piecemeal. This tendency is understandable—after all, it is difficult enough to change some aspect of the compensation system without also having to be concerned about training, recruitment and selection, and how work is organized. Implementing practices in isolation may not have much effect, however, and, under some circumstances, it could actually be counterproductive. For instance, increasing the firm's commitment to training activities won't accomplish much unless changes in work organization permit these more skilled people to actually implement their knowledge. If wages are comparatively low and incentives are lacking that recognize enhanced economic success, the better trained people may simply depart for the competition. Employment security, too, can be counterproductive unless the firm hires people who will fit the culture and unless incentives reward outstanding performance. Implementing work teams will probably not, by itself, accomplish as much as if the teams received training both in specific technical skills and team processes, and it will have less effect still if the teams aren't given financial and operating performance goals and information. "Whatever the bundles or configurations of practices implemented in a particular firm, the individual practices must be aligned with one another and be consistent with the [organizational] architecture if they are ultimately to have an effect on firm performance."[62] It is important to have some overall philosophy or strategic vision of achieving profits through people, because an overall framework increases the likelihood of taking a systematic, as contrasted with a piecemeal, approach to implementing high-commitment organizational arrangements.

Clearly, it requires time to implement and see results from many of these practices. For instance, it takes time to train and upgrade the skills of an existing work force and even more time to see the economic benefits of this training in reduced turnover and enhanced performance. It takes time not only to share operating and financial information with people, but also to be sure that they know how to understand and use it in decision making; even more time is needed before the suggestions and insights implemented can provide business results. It certainly requires time for employees to believe in employment security and for that belief to generate the trust that then produces higher levels of innovation and effort. Consequently, taking a long-term view of a company's development and growth becomes at least useful if not absolutely essential to implementation of high-performance organizational arrangements. One way of thinking about various institutional and organizational barriers and aids to implementing high-performance management practices is, therefore, to consider each in terms of its effects on the time horizon that characterizes organizational decisions.

Endnotes

1. See chapter 2 in Jeffrey Pfeffer, *Competitive Advantage through People: Unleashing the Power of the Work Force* (Boston, MA: Harvard Business School Press, 1994).
2. Richard M. Locke, "The Transformation of Industrial Relations? A Cross-National Review," in Kirsten S. Wever and Lowell Turner, eds., *The Comparative Political Economy of Industrial Relations* (Madison, WI: Industrial Relations Research Association, 1995), pp. 18–19.
3. Herb Kelleher, "A Culture of Commitment," *Leader to Leader,* 1 (Spring 1997): 23.
4. John E. Delery and D. Harold Doty, "Modes of Theorizing in Strategic Human Resource Management: Tests of Universalistic, Contingency, and Configurational Performance Predictions," *Academy of Management Journal,* 39 (1996): 820.
5. Ling Sing Chee, "Singapore Airlines: Strategic Human Resource Initiatives," in Derek Torrington,

ed., *International Human Resource Management: Think Globally, Act Locally* (New York, NY: Prentice Hall, 1994), p. 152.

6. "Southwest Airlines," Case S-OB-28, Graduate School of Business, Stanford University, Palo Alto, CA, 1994, p. 29.

7. Brian O'Reilly, "The Rent-a-Car Jocks Who Made Enterprise #1," *Fortune,* October 28, 1996, p. 128.

8. Laurie Graham, *On the Line at Subaru-Isuzu* (Ithaca, NY: ILR Press, 1995), p. 18.

9. See, for instance, C.A. O'Reilly, J.A. Chatman, and D.E. Caldwell, "People and Organizational Culture: A Profile Comparison Approach to Assessing Person-Organization Fit," *Academy of Management Journal,* 34 (1991): 487–516; J.A. Chatman, "Managing People and Organizations: Selection and Socialization in Public Accounting Firms," *Administrative Science Quarterly,* 36 (1991): 459–484.

10. Ibid.

11. Ibid.

12. Ibid.

13. Rosemary Batt, "Outcomes of Self-directed Work Groups in Telecommunications Services," in Paula B. Voos, ed., *Proceedings of the Forty-Eighth Annual Meeting of the Industrial Relations Research Association* (Madison, WI: Industrial Relations Research Association, 1996), p. 340.

14. Rajiv D. Banker, Joy M. Field, Roger G. Schroeder, and Kingshuk K. Sinha, "Impact of Work Teams on Manufacturing Performance: A Longitudinal Field Study," *Academy of Management Journal,* 39 (1996): 867–890.

15. "Work Week," *The Wall Street Journal,* May 28, 1996, p. A1.

16. Batt, op. Cit., p. 344.

17. Ibid.

18. Ibid., p. 346.

19. Ibid., p. 97.

20. M. Parker and J. Slaughter, "Management by Stress," *Technology Review,* 91 (1988): 43.

21. Whole Foods Market, Inc., *1995 Annual Report,* Austin, TX, pp. 3, 17.

22. Charles Fishman, "Whole Foods Teams," *Fast Company* (April/May 1996), p. 104.

23. Ibid., p. 107.

24. Harley Shaiken, Steven Lopez, and Isaac Mankita, "Two Routes to Team Production: Saturn and Chrysler Compared." *Industrial Relations,* 36 (January 1997): 31.

25. Alex Markels, "Team Approach: A Power Producer Is Intent on Giving Power to Its people," *The Wall Street Journal,* July 3, 1995, p. A1.

26. Kirsten Downey Grimsley, "The Power of a Team," *Washington Business, The Washington Post,* February 12, 1996, p. F12.

27. Mark van Beusekon, *Participation Pays! Cases of Successful Companies with Employee Participation* (The Hague: Netherlands Participation Institute, 1996), p. 7.

28. Rhonda Thompson, "An Employee's View of Empowerment," *HR Focus* (July 1993), p. 14.

29. Ibid.

30. Thomas R. Bailey and Annette D. Bernhardt, "In Search of the High Road in a Low-Wage Industry," *Politics and Society* (1997, in press).

31. Glenn Collins, "In Grocery War, the South Rises," *The New York Times,* April 25, 1995, p. C5.

32. Verne C. Harnish, "Company of Owners," *Executive Excellence* (May 1995), p. 7.

33. Mary Rowland, "Rare Bird: Stock Options for Many," *The New York Times,* August 1, 1993, p. F14.

34. David Jacobson, "Employee Ownership and the High-Performance Workplace," working paper no. 13, National Center for the Workplace, Berkeley, CA, 1996.

35. Bill Gurley, "Revenge of the Nerds: The Stock Option Square Dance," World Wide Web, www.upside.com/texis/Columns/atc/article.html?UID= 970314003, March 14, 1997.

36. Fishman, op. cit., p. 105.

37. Ibid., p. 104.

38. John Paul MacDuffie and Thomas A. Kochan, "Do U.S. Firms Invest Less in Human Resources? Training in the World Auto Industry," *Industrial Relations,* 34 (1995): 153.

39. Ibid., p. 163.

40. Shaiken, Lopez, and Mankita, op. cit., p. 25.

41. Catherine Truss, Lynda Gratton, Veronica Hope-Hailey, Patrick McGovern, and Philip Stiles, "Soft and Hard Models of Human Resource Management: A Reappraisal," *Journal of Management Studies,* 34 (1997): 60.

42. Ibid., pp. 60–61.

43. Bailey and Bernhardt, op. cit., p. 5.

44. Men's Wearhouse, *1994 Annual Report,* Fremont, CA. p. 3.

45. Michael Hartnett, "Men's Wearhouse Tailors Employee Support Programs," *Stores* (August 1996), p. 47.

46. Ibid., p. 48.

47. Thomas A. Stewart, "How a Little Company Won Big by Betting on Brainpower," *Fortune,* September 4, 1995, p. 121.

48. Ibid., p. 122.

49. Graham, op, cit., pp. 107–108.

50. Suzanne Schlosberg, "Big Titles for Little Positions," *San Francisco Chronicle,* April 29, 1991, p. C3.

51. "Doing the Right Thing," *The Economist,* May 20, 1995, p. 64.

52. Whole Foods Market, Inc., *Proxy Statement,* January 29, 1996, p. 15.

53. Scott McCartney, "Salary for Chief of Southwest Air Rises After 4 Years," *The Wall Street Journal,* April 29, 1996, p. C16.

54. Fishman, op. cit., p. 106.

55. Ibid., p. 104.

56. Ibid., p. 105.

57. "Jack Stack (A)," Case 9-993-009, Business Enterprise Trust, Stanford, CA, 1993, pp. 2–4

58. Ibid.

59. Ibid., p. 5.

60. Tim R. V. Davis, "Open-Book Management: Its Promise and Pitfalls," *Organizational Dynamics,* 25 (Winter 1997): 7–20.

61. "Jack Stack (A)," op. cit., p. 3.

62. Brian Becker and Barry Gerhart, "The Impact of Human Resource Management on Organizational Performance: Progress and Prospects," *Academy of Management Journal,* 39 (1996): 786.

READING 45
FROM TEAM BUILDING TO COMMUNITY BUILDING

John Nirenberg

A guy visits a friend who lives on a farm. As he drives up he notices a pig with one peg leg. Later he asks his friend about it. "That pig is incredible," his friend says. "He's friendly and obedient, and one time while we were asleep, he saved our home by tapping on the bedroom window when he saw a fire start outside."

"That's fantastic," said the visitor, "but what about the peg leg?"

"Come on now," reproached the friend. "A pig that special you don't eat all at once."

This joke, told by Oren Harari, an associate of Tom Peters, is a rich commentary on the times. When applied to most organizational settings, it illustrates how downsizing, reengineering, and forced-ranked performance appraisals cut up and demoralize the workforce while seeking commitment, brilliant work, and self-sacrifice. *Fortune* magazine reported a case in point:

> "Listen to US WEST's Jerry Miller, whose team of billing clerks in Duluth, Minnesota, got downsized out of existence last month: "When we first formed our teams, the company came in talking teamwork and empowerment and promised we wouldn't lose any jobs. It turns out all this was a big cover. The company had us all set up for reengineering. We showed them how to streamline the work, and now 9,000 people are gone. It was cut-your-own-throat. It makes you feel used." US WEST, which argues that in the long run reengineering will enhance teamwork, admits that for now, "people's stress levels will be high, and some people will be sad and angry."

Today, teams are all the rage. Team building and work redesign have proven to be very effective innovations for companies willing to do more than just glom on to the new craze. But as with other sweeping new management ideas, there is still more talk than real action and many of the early adopters fail to adequately apply the concept. When teams are formed a very powerful force is set in motion that will have an impact far beyond the productive efforts expected from its members. Teamwork requires a new way of being.

The Center for Effective Organizations at the University of Southern California reports that while 68 percent of Fortune 1,000 companies declare they are using teams, only 10 percent of workers are on such teams. Walking the talk still remains a problem. American business hasn't yet begun to tap the full potential of groups of people working together toward a common goal. It has given mere lip service to the ideas of team building and sharing a common purpose, or vision, in the workplace. In reality, the U.S. workplace is still designed for individual performance and to provide the bulk of benefits to some, while others are "managed"—controlled and dominated—to accrue those benefits to investors and managers. With stress levels at epidemic proportions and job security at a post-depression low, morale and productivity suffer. In an era requiring more initiative for each individual to add value to the productive process while being constantly threatened with downsizing, organizations are self-destructing. Today, may people are questioning the legitimacy of that system and are searching for ways to create an equitable, productive, and satisfying workplace.

Building a sense of community in the workplace seems to be a reasonable, even obvious, solution to this national malaise, especially since work has become so stressful and often demeaning for too many people. Developing a sense of community in the workplace promises to revitalize organizations and unleash the creative energies of the American workforce once again.

Source: "From Team Building to Community Building," John Nirenberg, *National Productivity Review,* Winter 1994–1995, pp. 51–62. Reprinted by permission of John Wiley & Sons, Inc.

When organizations turn to all of their members and tap the innate creative insights of people wanting to do their best, they rediscover a long-standing, almost forgotten, uniquely American approach to building effective organizations: self-managing teams. But the companies now struggling with this concept are clearly at a crossroads. They can take the high road and pave the way for real community building in their workplaces, thereby creating living organizations, or they can take the low road and hope for a quick fix while exploiting the good intentions of their workforce.

Taking the High Road

Because community, as a concept of social organization, carries with it such a long and checkered attachment to various failed or, at best, unusual social experiments, it is important to dispel some preconceptions about what community really means. Community does not assume everyone is equal in aptitude or ability. It does not mean that achievement, intelligence, entrepreneurial drive, or creativity is found equally among all people. It is not a device to stifle individuals or to attribute to them qualities that they do not possess. It is not a matter of putting everything to a vote or insisting on a group mediocrity at the expense of individual expression or organizational risk taking.

Rather, community is a form of organization. It is enabling. As a structure of relationships, a process of working with one another, and as a mechanism for establishing personal and group expectations, it encourages fruitful participation by each member of the organization. It also establishes management accountability to the managed (the entire workplace community) as well as to the owners. It is not a mandate. It is a matter of individual choice. It obviously isn't something that everyone wishes to engage in routinely, because it demands that people attend to interpersonal processes and take responsibility for the organization's success. Yet, implementing the concept of workplace community in our organizations offers the possibility of enormous increases in productivity and employee satisfaction.

Workplace communities encompass a set of values and a way of being that is only now being applied in the business world. The nature of organizational life is becoming more and more team-based; meetings, conferences, and corporate events requiring the collaboration and cooperation of many individuals are now routine. They are the precursors of workplace community. Using self-managed teams and other collaborative opportunities as a platform for change, it is possible to transform existing organizations into workplace communities.

Experience at Lesher Communications. Don Jochens, production director at Lesher Communications, a newspaper printing company employing 1,100 people in northern California, is doing just that. Six years ago he made a commitment to develop self-managing work teams. He was convinced that workplace democracy and employee participation was not just the right thing to do but also would lead to a more productive, more efficient, and more satisfying work experience. Two years after beginning team building and training in self-management, a new plant provided the opportunity to fully test his personal convictions, the new design, and its effectiveness.

Caught in the recession, the plant experienced an almost 7 percent drop in productivity after the first year of operation. Had the company not been financially healthy or had a more skeptical manager been responsible for the experiment, the self-managing work teams may well have had to disband. But the company stuck with it. The second year found the plant besting its baseline year. The third year continued the gains. The plants' crucial measure was cost per ton, which dropped from the baseline of $222.78 to $197.47, even though total work and tonnage increased over the same period. Given current figures, plant managers anticipate dropping the cost-per-ton figure to $150, thanks to the success of the plants' self-managing teams. Now, they are expanding the concept throughout the entire company.

Start with Self-Managing Teams. Self-managing teams are the first step in a process that leads to community building. Community is established when teams truly acquire the skills and are empowered to make all necessary decisions regarding their own work. And, through their representatives on a board of stakeholders, decisions are made regarding the future of the company and matters of governance.

Community conveys a concern for the success of the organization and the individual members in it and that concern is felt at a fundamental and personal level. Community is inclusive. The group must justify exclusion—of saying no—rather than justify inclusion. There is a sense of personal efficacy in the role one plays by participating in the creation of the ends toward which the community strives. Commitment, the willingness to coexist and to give of oneself fully, is crucial. Each person in collaboration with others determines how she or he will serve the community. They also determine the means through which they will achieve their personal responsibilities. All roles are necessary and there is no hierarchy of importance, even through at times some jobs are more pressing, more fun, more visible, or more central to the fulfillment of the organization's goals than others. This level of responsibility doesn't come immediately. People must be taught how to work in the new structures. By taking several years to develop its teams, Lesher learned it takes time and training to help people behave in new more responsible and creative ways. Community requires continuous learning.

Workplace community is the culmination of highly evolved self-managed teams becoming a living organization. Its main task is knowledge-based: the sensing, gathering, interpretation, processing, and reevaluation of information, concepts, and ideas. The operative environment that is established is inclusive, responsive, and created and re-created by its members for the purpose of doing their work effectively.

By encouraging individuality, community can never be totalitarian; it strives to move beyond democracy to consensus, yet it focuses on realism, accommodating multiple perspectives and dealing with dissent. There is decentralization of all authority. Community strives to become a group of all leaders; managers or facilitators of projects may serve for the duration of the project or for a designated period of time after which the position rotates or the group re-appoints them.

There are no sides or cliques and a group can disagree gracefully without creating a win/lose situation. However, a grievance system with trained mediators presides over interpersonal and organizational/personal disputes and is independent. This is a backup to be used when work groups find that internal conflicts result in a stalemate or to settle general grievances against the organization.

Community develops a structure that provides avenues for the expression and resolution of conflict and protects the existence of diversity of thought. Power is task-centered, not person-centered. Unilateral veto powers, if they exist at all, are assigned by the workplace constitution, as are other rights and responsibilities, while a separation of powers and checks and balances are built into the process.

Each member can be as involved in additional responsibilities as he or she chooses and is encouraged to serve on administrative, policy, and maintenance committees. A community forum exists for decision making in these areas. Each person is directly or indirectly involved through the election of representatives. Operating rules and the community-building process are either determined by work groups or designed by the forum(s).

Community allows the full, authentic expression of ones' whole personality and encourages complete and honest communication. It also encourages humility, self examination, and vulnerability—the ability to truly be oneself. This violates the traditional business norm of pretended invulnerability where one must always be correct or covered in the eyes of fellow workers.

In an era where menial/routine work is declining and where technology can be purchased by anyone worldwide because knowledge is freely and instantly available, the only competitive advantage remaining is building an organization that can add value, act appropriately, and move fast to achieve its goals and meet customer needs. Creating community provides the vehicle to do this because it alone overcomes the inherent barriers of the traditional organization that interfere with the utilization of information; free, open, and honest communication; and the creativity of its members.

Experience in Santa Clara County. Judith Robinson, manager of training and staff development for Santa Clara County, California, points out how even a government bureaucracy needs to recognize and act upon the new realities. "We're building a culture of support and creating the feeling of partnership among our staff. Everyone makes a difference and we need to acknowledge that. We're reorganizing work. We are no longer the typical civil service. In fact we have begun to redesign work so that we act more like full-service, one-stop teams and cut through the red tape." Hardly the words of a bureaucrat. Santa Clara, as well as other governments, has turned a corner. After massive budget cuts and a painful, though thoughtful, downsizing, the county is rethinking the way it serves the public and is becoming very creative in dealing with a difficult situation. And while necessity is the mother of invention, taking steps toward team building and self-management leads logically to teams developing community-like characteristics. Eventually, if nurtured, a workplace community emerges and a living organization is created.

Becoming a Community

For an organization to become a community, certain conditions must prevail. Each person who is selected by and freely joins the organization is expected to be involved in decisions affecting their day-to-day work and the governance and maintenance of the organization. The form may be direct or representative involvement.

Community means mutual aid, cooperation, respect, friendliness, individual efficacy, responsibility, and good treatment of strangers—those we don't work with directly but who are part of the organization. Larry Quadracci of Quad/Graphics in Pewuukee, Wisconsin, tries to create this kind of environment through his belief that management, like marriage, "is a close personal relationship that is worked at daily." That means no layoffs or personnel policy changes without consultation and involvement. Representative bodies of employees—of everyone through the CEO—deal with these

and other issues in an effort to keep everyone in the governance process and informed. The work group or representative body (forum) also decides issues regarding hiring, socialization of new members, performance expectations, assignments, scheduling, benefits, rewards and punishments, and dismissal. It also arranges for the mediation of disputes between individuals and handles grievances rooted in organizational policy, rules, or structure. These ideas are beginning to be instituted quite successfully by companies embracing self-managing teams. Even situations that were believed to require laying off people have been turned around through imaginative "pain sharing" programs. Robert Rosen reported in *The Healthy Company* that, "When the computer chip manufacturer Intel, Inc. was forced to reduce personnel costs, it chose progressive salary cuts according to employee's individual paychecks. Pay cuts ran from none to 10 percent, with the lowest-paid workers losing nothing from their pay checks." Hewlett-Packard and others are known to have a similar policy.

Many more imaginative ways involving shortened work weeks, voluntary leaves without pay, and early retirements help ease the blunt edge of the cuts. But when that still isn't enough to meet the economic needs of the moment and re-deployment of talent to potential growth areas or other parts of the organization is not possible, it shows enormous respect for those involved to ask if they would like to be part of the solution instead of simply treating them as part of the problem. Inviting employees to be involved in the process of cutting back empowers them with an opportunity to save the company as well as their jobs. If even after that possibility is exhausted, executing the layoffs based on a pre-determined formula would certainly demonstrate fairness and at least show respect for all of those affected.

Community means inclusion, acceptance, efficacy, freedom of expression, and having social as well as organizational goals legitimated. It is also being able to communicate openly and freely and to observe all constitutional rights in the organizational context.

The individual's acceptance by, and usefulness to, the organization is assumed. Personality and relationships issues are dealt with separately from competence and task-related issues. This requires the individual's willingness to recognize and to commit to the legitimacy of the fundamental values and associated requirements of the employment agreement. Each person accepts responsibility to make the agreement work and accepts a given process for changing the agreement to meet their mutual needs as the organization evolves. Just as the U.S. Constitution has an amendment procedure, companies such as Perot Systems offer corporate policy statements that suggest that they are moving in this direction. Motorola, S.C. Johnson, Lincoln Electric, and New United Motor are a few U.S. companies that still have a no-layoff policy. Their regard for the employee places them on many lists of best places to work and they are committed to employee participation in creating a suitable work environment.

To be accepted, the individual must live up to his or her role, responsibilities, and group function. In return, the individual takes part in determining the organization's objectives and in pursuing his or her own career objectives within the workplace community. The community stimulates its own growth and group development by creating a learning environment and providing opportunities for individuals to develop fully.

Consciously building community means deliberately creating a system for the good of all stakeholders. It means empowering each member to participate meaningfully in the creation and evolution of an effective organization. Community adds attention to the interpersonal as well as workflow processes—the software—of building an effective organization. It focuses on both task and human interactions. Members learn to accept others and take responsibility for the larger whole, not just their immediate role. In community, self-managed work teams would operate autonomously within the organization, much like a state does within the federal structure of the United States. Indeed, the widespread adoption of self-managing

work teams is an intermediate step clearing the way toward full-scale workplace community.

The transformation of organizations into communities is quite possible because the new technologies and contingencies of work support these changes and because it is likely to enhance competitiveness. It is also likely if everyone is to be involved in the pursuit of efficiencies and become responsive to customer and colleague alike. The time is ripe to take the initiative in creating the kinds of organizations most suited to our present circumstances and future needs.

Toward a Post-Managerial Era

Eventually, everyone will execute managerial responsibilities and be accountable to each other in work groups. The changing conditions required of workplace community also suggest that we are at the dawn of a post-managerial era. Since workplaces will eventually be restructured into networks of teams, one's typical assignment will be team-based, characterized by new personal responsibilities and shared leadership.

Computers and telecommunications services will provide each person with all the information necessary to act independently and to coordinate their work and that of their work group's with others in the work-flow process. In this kind of workplace environment with a flattened hierarchy and a huge lateral base of networks, the community model of organizing seems most appropriate. And the community model provides a perfect structural basis for collegial and peer group coordination to deal with complex problems and unique customer demands. This is especially so in a turbulent environment requiring the need for frequent interaction.

A Basic Blueprint. In a survey of residential communities, the most demanding and challenging form of community building, *The New Age Community Guidebook* found that to be successful organizations should nurture several important qualities that facilitate the transformation to community:

1. A willingness to think and act in terms of the good of the whole not just in terms of personal needs and opinions. This is a willingness to grow toward unselfishness, and make a commitment to identify and live organizational values.

2. Tolerance for differences and open-mindedness toward different points of view.

3. A willingness to work out conflicts, having a realistic belief in the possibility of resolving differences to mutual satisfaction.

These qualities can be developed and supported throughout the change process. The concept of building workplace community and its benefits to the individual and the organization should be discussed. The buy-in process should emphasize individual concerns, examining both barriers and facilitating forces.

Don Jochens of Lesher Communications found that it is not enough to have a philosophy that is supportive of democracy and community in the workplace. The way you express it determines if you can implement it successfully. During a change effort at another firm, he simply suggested to some members in his department that they merge sections. Thinking nothing of it, he was surprised that they took it upon themselves to discuss possibilities at the next meeting, and at the next meeting, and at the next meeting.

It was not long before a reorganization plan was suggested to the entire group by the planning committee, but Jochens was sure that those not on the planning committee would be surprised and not buy into the idea. He was wrong. Everyone bought in and all went like clockwork. The reason? The planning committee members had been going out to everyone affected and getting their input and tweaking the reorganization plan with their suggestions. Ultimately, though unwittingly, everyone had been included in planning for and implementing the change.

In a different situation, on another occasion, but facing the identical need to change, Jochens tried to tell people that his reorganization plan would be effective and good for everyone. It turned into a miserable experience because people resisted him. They resented being "done to" instead of "done with."

When he introduced the redesign at Lesher he was fully inclusive from the start and sought out volunteers, making clear the exploratory and vital nature of the change. In addition, the process evolved with each participant playing an important role from the outset and taking responsibility for the design and outcome of the effort. Be prepared to take some time, but as the Japanese say, "Sometimes you need to waste time to save time." Patience and communication up front will save delay, chaos, and failure down the road.

Organizations seeking to move toward community will find the following steps helpful:

1. Establish a membership planning committee with representatives of all groups. Guarantee employment during the process to ensure active participation and support. This group first develops the personal skills required to create community, and develops an appropriate process to spread the learning throughout the organization.

2. Assess the organization's ability and willingness to proceed with an extended change program, given present conditions.

3. After having determined the organization's vision and values, decide on the appropriate depth of the community concept to be implemented; the degree of personal participation; the areas for involvement in organizational policy making; the structure of the community; feedback processes and goal setting procedures; and a time frame for accomplishing implementation by phases.

4. Assess personal and work group needs to sustain the change effort; institute a continuous training, education, and feedback program.

5. Establish action committees throughout the organization to take over specific implementation from the original membership committee. Each action committee is taught the skills required to guide the change process in their specific areas.

6. Create a catalog of baseline measure; measure all key variations in performance, both in terms of job output and interpersonal issues (climate, culture, morale); look at communications processes—particularly the difference between espoused and actual patterns; and assess satisfaction/dissatisfaction of all members of the organization as groundwork is laid and implementation of the change program begins. Wage and salary review should reflect changes as well; perhaps a reformulation of compensation and other rewards should include a plan for gain/pain sharing at this point.

7. Have the target group draft its own program for change. It should address training employees in multiple skills to handle different work roles in autonomous groups. Instruction and reinforcement of group-centered personal leadership techniques also would be useful.

8. Institutionalize the change. Commit to the changes by establishing supportive policies and procedures.

9. Foster feedback and learning through community-wide diffusion of results.

Creating a Strategic Plan and Change Opportunities

Before a company vision statement can become a viable axiom for each member of the community, it must be continually reinforced and applied every day in individual thinking and action. When each member of the community is trained to manage, serve as a pivot, and perform leadership functions and is capable of running meetings for the group, as well as playing other necessary roles, the sense of personal efficacy is reinforced, which motivates action for the good of the community. The core skills required to build a workplace community are:

Interpersonal
- Meeting facilitation
- Dispute resolution through mediation
- Peer supervision and coaching
- Process observation

- Role clarification and self-assessment
- Team building (including the use of survey feedback and action research techniques)
- Creative problem identification and solving
- Consensus-building methods
- Mastering half-day or full-day "think-ins"

Personal
- Identifying and living up to one's own and one's organization's values
- Development of self-confidence/esteem
- Commitment to keeping agreements
- Being authentic
- Suspending judgement
- Communicating honestly
- Being able to use creative, holistic (and interdisciplinary) thinking
- Giving and receiving feedback (positive and negative)
- Able to be self-disclosing
- Able to actively listen/empathize
- Capacity for self-reflection about behavior in interpersonal contexts
- Honoring and knowing how to stimulate inquiry and dialogue
- Keeping everyone informed
- Anxiety and stress reduction

However, nothing short of a reformulation of the social contract can work to reduce the major factors contributing to work-related anxiety. According to an American Management Association survey, these factors are:

- Inadequate support from superiors
- Ineffective performance by superiors
- Inadequate performance from subordinates
- Not knowing precisely what is expected on the job
- Not receiving credit/recognition when due
- Inadequate information about career advancement requirements
- Not being able to depend on the word or actions of managers

Having the skills and being able to use them are two different issues. Reducing anxiety and building a sense of place, purpose, and psychological safety for the individual increases the use of these skills.

Guaranteeing the security of one's position and providing clear expectations can do much to reduce anxiety in the workplace and clear the way for unfettered individual contributions to the work at hand. Though security of one's position is impossible to guarantee because of shifting economic conditions, the security that one may speak freely and at a peer level is vital to achieve and unrelated to the economic issue.

Management at Lesher Communications realizes that people were employed under a set of assumptions that are now being altered. Putting people through this kind of stress requires that the organization be sensitive to those who are unable to make the transition. This means finding the right place for people, respecting their struggle, helping them cope, and giving them opportunities to learn.

While some individuals resist or choose not to embrace the new structures and dimensions of the workplace, they do not derail the process. Although an individual at Lesher may not buy in to the new emphasis on teams and choose to remain a strict individualist, he or she must still turn to the team for decisions that were previously handled by a supervisor. Thus, no one is forced to participate, but they must eventually realize that it's in their best interest to do so. If scheduling is determined by the team, one will want to participate in the decision-making process to receive a favorable work schedule. Although this may seem coercive, the intention is not to force participation. Rather, the intention is to invite everyone to take full responsibility for their work lives.

Thus, building workplace community requires immediate attention to the issue of peer relationship building. Communication skills and community will develop when they stem from a total way of being within an appropriate and respectful organizational context that stimulates authentic and honest interactions.

Organizations that have self-directed work teams and endeavor to build workplace community must ensure that:

- A safe communications environment is guaranteed.
- Work is team-based and customer-centered (internal and external).
- All individuals have responsibilities and are empowered to accomplish them.
- All employees enjoy the same rights and protections.
- Each person plays a role in the maintenance and governance of the organization.
- A vision is jointly created or accepted upon recruitment.
- There is a mutually determined quality of life bottom line.
- On-the-record third-party mediation and grievance procedures are available when requested.
- There is a willingness to revisit and reengineer the way work gets done by the people doing the work.
- Gains and pains are shared equitably.
- There is a commitment to job security.
- A public plan exists to deal with separations.
- The individual chooses to be in the community and the organization chooses the individual.

Modern complex organizations are living human systems that require an understanding of and attention to the relationships and well-being of each participant. By fashioning workplaces with and striving to truly embody the aspects listed above, today's organization indeed promises to become a living organization surviving well into the twenty-first century.

READING 46
THE NEW AGENDA FOR ORGANIZATION DEVELOPMENT

W. Warner Burke

Founded on a value base circa 1960 that emanated from the human relations movement, in general, and the sensitivity training (T group) movement, in particular, organization development (OD) has always operated within a framework of humanistic and ethical concerns for people. Although not all practitioners would agree on the specific values that guide the field, most would concur that OD has tended to emphasize such concerns as:

Human development—It is worthwhile for people in organizations to have opportunities for personal learning and for growth toward a full realization of their individual potentials.

Fairness—It is important that people in organizations are treated equitably without discrimination and with dignity.

Openness—It is imperative that communication in organizations be conducted with forthrightness, honesty, and integrity.

Choice—It is critical that people in organizations are free from coercion and the arbitrary use of authority.

Balance of autonomy and constraint—It is significant that people in organizations have autonomy and freedom to perform their work responsibilities as they see fit, yet execute these responsibilities within reasonable organizational constraints. The OD practitioner's responsibility is to see that these two forces—autonomy and constraint—are in balance.

While this list may fall short of expressing the value system that guides OD, it likely comes close.

The problem we face today is not so much agreeing on the specifics, but rather living the values we do espouse.

A number of senior practitioners in OD, i.e., those with 20 or more years of experience, believe that the profession has lost its way—that its values are no longer sufficiently honored, much less practiced, and that the unrelenting emphasis on the bottom line has taken over. Moreover, such management techniques—fads, if you will—as reengineering and downsizing have taken the country by storm, hurt people, and violated the values associated with OD. In the meantime, OD practitioners have stood on the sidelines and watched—or themselves become victims. Regardless of how valid these observations may be, it does seem true that OD has lost some of its power, its presence, and perhaps its perspective.

The purpose of this paper, then, is to address some of these issues, first by examining what we know about the efficacy of reengineering and downsizing and, second, by articulating a current and future agenda for OD practitioners with respect to these techniques. reengineering and downsizing were selected for examination as opposed to, say, total quality management (TQM), because the former represent a greater challenge to the practice of OD—they more directly impact the field's underlying values.

To be clear about the direction of this paper: It begins by examining reengineering and downsizing to determine the OD practitioner's agenda vis-à-vis these two interventions, but it does not leave it at that. The overriding purpose is to propose a deeper agenda for OD and to consider six additional intervention domains—community, the employer-employee social contract, employability, trust, culture clash, and corporate power.

Reengineering, Downsizing, and Organization Development

To begin, let's review what is known about the efficacy of reengineering and downsizing and, for each, ask if the technique should even continue to be used. Answering these questions allows us to focus on the implications for OD practitioners, i.e., the agenda.

Reengineering—Does It Work?

Even though reengineering as we know it today (similar practices were previously labeled "business process redesign") has been in evidence for about a decade, we do not as yet have enough research to draw sound conclusions about its validity. Part of the problem is that reengineering has taken on the trappings of a fad—a rapid surge in popularity in the early 1990s, fueled by Michael Hammer and J. Champy's book on the subject, which rode the best-seller list for months. Organizations rapidly initiated reengineering projects; then, faced with disappointing early results, abandoned the effort just as quickly. Likely, the results would have been better had companies stayed with the ship longer. Most of the evidence so far (much of it anecdotal) builds a case for a low success rate. Some recent evidence provides encouragement, but the jury is still out.

Reengineering—Should It Be Done?

There's nothing inherently wrong with the idea. To consider a set of workplace activities and processes at their most basic levels in an effort to improve the activities, eliminate them altogether, and/or add new procedures and processes can be highly beneficial. Like so many other organizational change ideas, the problems come with implementation.

Typically, these problems arise for several reasons. Rather than fine-tune work processes, reengineering has focused on a radical redesign of work—a reinvention of how tasks get done. By emphasizing the details of specific procedures, the designers lose sight of the bigger picture—how changes at the work unit level will affect the larger business or organizational unit. In addition, reengineering has frequently been associated with downsizing and therefore vehemently resisted by many organizational members, much to Michael Hammer's dismay.

The Agenda for the OD Practitioner.

If reengineering is a passing fad, why bother to set an agenda? There are two answers to this.

First, much of what is involved in reengineering is not new. Its roots can be traced to Frederick Taylor, and before that, to the very foundation of industrial engineering. This discipline, after all, has been around for 90 years. Its fundamentals are basic to any and all work organizations and, moreover, are not likely to pass from the scene. Other labels for the practice may come into vogue, just as "reengineering" superseded "work redesign," but the knowledge of how to redesign work processes, even radically, will remain useful.

Second, reengineering means change, and there is much to be said for starting with a clean slate and redesigning work for the good of workers and the organization. It should even be alluring for OD practitioners. Moreover, OD practitioners are in a position to contribute. In their study of 20 organizations involved in reengineering (at least three of these achieving successful implementations), Gene Hall, Jim Rosenthal, and Judy Wade identified six crucial organizational elements, or depth levers as they call them, that must be the focus of change if reengineering is really going to work: roles and responsibilities, organizational structure, measurements and incentives, shared values, skills, and information technology.

With the possible exception of the last item, OD practitioners provide (or should provide) ballast for all these levers and thus play a key role in any reengineering effort. And by being organizationally focused (as opposed to working exclusively with certain individuals and selected work processes), the OD practitioner can be highly useful in keeping the larger business or organizational units, and their intricate relationships, in mind. To the extent that OD ignores or, even worse, challenges reengineering, it loses an important opportunity to make an impact and to be true to its values.

Downsizing—Does It Work? The short answer is "no." The amazing fact about downsizing is that, in most cases, the action produces the opposite of what is intended. Consider, for example, cost reduction—a primary goal for most downsizing plans. Although this may occur in the short run, a longer term scenario usually shows either no cost reduction or, in a number of instances, actual cost increases.

Another typical goal, productivity improvement, proves equally elusive. The evidence shows either no improvement or even a deterioration in productivity!

To add to the evidence, research by R.E. Cole found nine additional organizational problems resulting from downsizing: loss of personal relationships between employees and customers, increases in rules and procedures (therefore addition to bureaucracy), and loss of a common organizational culture, to name three. And a study of over 200 organizations by Kim Cameron and his colleagues added a dozen other problems to Cole's list.

The toll taken on individuals is immense. For a flavor of the consequences on individual and family lives, see the recent *New York Times Special Report: The Downsizing of America* and David M. Noer's book, *Healing the Wounds*. The pictures painted are not pretty. In fact, our American experience with downsizing is similar to cancer; practically every family we know has been touched.

The history of downsizing, now 16 or so years in the making, has left its legacy. The American workplace will never be quite the same.

Downsizing—Should It Be Done? We might well ask if there is ever any justification for downsizing. The short answer is maybe.

We know that most large organizations employ people with "non jobs" and continue to support useless if not downright wasteful activities. There is some evidence that when downsizing is done carefully it can have positive consequences. Poor outcomes result from poor implementation and a lack of supporting activities such as counseling, training, severance packages, and outplacement. The way downsizing is carried out seems to be more important than the decision itself. Also, downsizing is more likely to be associated with positive outcomes when it works as part of an overall strategic plan.

Regardless of the potential for positive results, many would argue that downsizing is harmful to the economy, devastating to both its victims and the corporate survivors, and plainly and simply immoral. But not everyone would so argue.

In a carefully crafted and balanced article in *The New Yorker*, John Cassidy points to evidence supporting a net gain over the past decade in American jobs rather than a loss. He refers to two important reports, one by Joseph Stiglitz, chairman of the Council of Economic Advisors, the other by Princeton economics professor Henry Farber. These two reports independently concur that downsizing has not had the dire consequences on our economy and the country as a whole that the popular press and other anecdotal writings would lead us to believe.

Cassidy points out that these reports "should permit a more dispassionate discussion of downsizing." He goes on to emphasize that downsizing is real, that there are victims, and that these victims should not be ignored. Furthermore, layoffs and downsizing have been with us a long time, as our economy ebbs and flows. Ask any blue collar worker.

The two reports by Stiglitz and Farber on which Cassidy relies suggest "that what is really new about the downsizing phenomenon is not its absolute scale as much as its impact on the upper echelons of society. An increasing number of its victims are middle-aged, educated, and affluent." Labor Department statistics show that while displacement has indeed occurred, there has been little change in overall job stability in the United States. Job loss, then, while serious (just ask a recent victim), does not appear to be any more serious today than 10 or 15 years ago.

And to quote Cassidy one last time: "The ability of the United States economy to create jobs at a rate matching its rapid population growth distinguishes it sharply from many other industrial economies, especially those in Europe. . . . While

American commentators worry about downsizing, the talk in Paris and Berlin is about how best to mimic American job creation."

So perhaps what we are experiencing is not "the downsizing of America" (the title of *The New York Times* book) but the "job shifting of America." And maybe we are not losing our middle class, but rather our middle class is changing its work affiliations, from the bulk employed by large corporations—each person for an entire career—to a more dispersed and diverse group of Americans. This group may include more people than before working in small to mid-size companies (many starting their own enterprises), more working in nonprofit organizations, and some living off their severance packages or working in temporary situations until they discover what they want to do next with their lives.

The Downsizing Agenda for the OD Practitioner.   It's tempting for the OD practitioner to want absolutely nothing to do with downsizing. After all, downsizing hurts people, and the act itself can border on (if not blatantly constitute) immorality.

Yet, if OD practitioners are employed by or contracted to work with an organization, are they not obligated to help? If they are capable of providing help, are they not obligated to do so? Isn't this provision to help a value of higher priority than avoiding involvement in a situation where people may be hurt, if not treated immorally?

These queries beg the question of what we mean by *help*. For the good of the organization and its individual members, consultative help may mean confrontation, questioning, and challenging.

Let's consider downsizing from a different point of view, namely, why so many executives stick to their decision to reduce headcount in the face of so much negative evidence regarding the outcomes. William McKinley, Carol M. Sanchez, and Allen G. Schick provide insights on this issue. Building on institutional theory from sociology and simplifying the language, they cite three social forces that support an executive's downsizing rationale: "constraining," "cloning," and "learning."

Constraining forces pressure executives to conform to what is the "right thing" to do at a particular time. Although previously associated with decline, a negative force, downsizing is now seen as "the right step." Large organizations mean bureaucracy, rigidity, and resistance to change. Today's fashion is to be lean, mean, and nimble, and thus more competitive. To capture the essence of this social force, the authors refer to a *Fortune* article in which the writer stated that "The chiefs of America's biggest companies seem caught in the grip of what might be called wee-ness envy—my company's workforce is smaller than yours."

Organizational cloning can take a number of forms; for example, mimicking other organizations with respect to such management techniques as TQM, reengineering, self-directed groups and, of course, downsizing. Cloning is particularly prominent within industries, each company wanting to mimic what the best in its field is doing. And when executives want to measure how well their cloning process is going, they call it benchmarking.

Learning occurs via educational institutions and conferences sponsored by professional associations, as well as by finding "lessons" in the actions of apparently successful peers at other companies. Academic courses in cost accounting, for example, teach (at least by implication) that downsizing is an efficient form of doing business. And when one CEO sees another turn companies around with a "slash and burn" strategy (e.g., Albert J. Dunlap, previously at Scott Paper and [at the time of this writing] at Sunbeam), there is a temptation to duplicate the practice.

McKinley et al. go on to identify four conditions that enhance the power of these social pressures for downsizing: (1) dependence, (2) ambiguous standards, (3) uncertain core technologies, and (4) frequent corporate interaction patterns. In other words, the more dependent a company is on other organizations for resources, especially when those other organizations are dominant partners, the greater the ambiguity regarding what should be proper performance. Also, the greater the uncertainty about what a company's core technologies are, and the more interactive a company is with its constituents and competitors, the more susceptible that company is to conformity, cloning, and learning. And the more likely to downsize, if that is what others are doing.

The point, then, is as follows: When an OD practitioner's client is contemplating downsizing, the intervention of choice is to test the wisdom of such a decision. Testing the degree to which the potential decision seems to be a response to the social forces that McKinley et al. define (and within the context of their four conditions that enhance the power of these forces) would be highly appropriate—because this testing, or intervention, would be grounded in relevant theory and would confront forces to which the client may be oblivious.

There are other reasons for challenging a potential act of downsizing. Consider, for example, the consequences in terms of organizational memory loss and erosion of valued skills and experience. Service companies are highly susceptible to such loss. An example:

One insurance group, having slimmed its claims department, found itself settling larger claims both too swiftly and too generously. Belatedly, the group discovered that it had sacked a handful of long-term employees who had created an informal—but highly effective—way to screen claims. The company was eventually forced to reinstate them.

Moreover, there are alternative models to follow. For example, Sara Lee, under the leadership of its CEO, John Bryan, seems to compete quite well in a tough business and to do so globally without laying off hundreds or thousands of people when times are tough. Sara Lee takes pride in being socially responsible, a good corporate citizen.

For corporate leaders, perhaps the model regarding downsizing is Bill Flynn, the former CEO, now chairman, of Mutual of America. Mr. Flynn stated at an annual employee meeting that if the company ever had to institute a corporate layoff policy, it would not be because someone in the mail room had made a mistake. Rather, it would be because he had made a mistake—and he would put his name first on the layoff list. Not surprisingly,

Flynn's statement earned him the trust of the employees attending that meetings.

OD practitioners have a twofold role to play in the downsizing arena. First, to challenge a potential downsizing decision by asking "why" and to test for the impact of social forces. This includes searching for other ways to control and reduce costs and to become a key player in implementing those alternatives. Second, if other options have been thoroughly explored and downsizing is the only remaining choice, to push for dignity, humane treatment, and ultimate fairness in how the victims and survivors are dealt with.

The OD Practitioner's Deeper Agenda

Rather than become obsessed with reengineering and downsizing, it is more important that practitioners understand and become involved with issues that are deeper, longer lasting, and more critical to the bigger picture. Six issues in particular merit attention.

Community.   Each summer, we conduct a two-week conference for public school superintendents at Teachers College, Columbia University. Participants come from all pockets and corners of the United States—large, medium, and small districts from urban, suburban, and rural areas. My colleague, Professor Tom Sobol, runs the program. In his summary report of the 1996 summer conference, the following paragraph was a jolt:

> It's not easy being a public school superintendent these days, so cataloging their mutual problems was easy: lack of money, too many conflicting public demands, public hostility, uncertain tenure. But surprisingly, once these matters were acknowledged, they were not what superintendents wanted to spend time on. The problem that gripped their attention was the decline of community in America—the role of the public school in creating and sustaining that community.

I suspect that the assessment is accurate. Downsizing may hurt victims much more today than a few decades ago when communities were stronger.

Support now comes from professionals (e.g., out-placement counselors), not so much from friends and neighbors. More of the burden is placed on one's family, and some families have not survived the ordeal. Moreover, downsizing has hit the white collar worker harder and, compared with a layoff of hourly wage earners, is more permanent. And white collar workers have no labor union for support, to help serve in the community's role of providing sustenance.

This lack of community is not likely to change anytime soon. As a culture, we Americans are clearly an independent lot. This independence seems to have become more pronounced in recent years, in part because of two trends. One is an apparent increase in self-orientation, the "what's in it for me?" syndrome. Christopher Lasch has written about the syndrome in his 1978 book, *The Culture of Narcissism*. Similarly, a national survey by Donald L. Kanter and Philip H. Mirvis identified what they subsequently labeled "the cynical Americans"—a group that made up 43 percent of those surveyed. Consider, also, that 58 percent of the survey respondents agreed or strongly agreed with this statement, "People pretend to care more about one another than they really do."

A second trend, growing stronger as technology marches onward, is that for daily living, we literally do not need other people as much as in the past. We can live alone quite comfortably, thank you, especially in large urban areas. We can have almost anything—from a mattress to pizza—delivered. And with Blockbuster Video, who needs friends for entertainment? Besides, we have the Internet.

There are, no doubt, other trends that help explain the decline in community—crime, geographical dispersion of family members, and less personal time, to name a few. Suffice it to say, the superintendents are probably right.

Agenda for the OD Practitioner: Organizational effectiveness depends on interactions and interrelationships among employees at all levels. The OD practitioner plays a significant role by bringing people together. This means initiating and arguing for, if not calling and conducting meetings

themselves—not just facilitating them. This means, especially, promoting activities such as cross-functional teams and helping self-directed groups to actually self-direct.

Is it not true that the lack of community in society carries over into the organization? Also, employees today are incredibly busy just keeping up with their individual tasks and responsibilities. They spend considerably more time with a computer terminal (with troublesome software and poor interactive systems) than with people. They are reluctant to get together; they have too much to do. By promoting community via small and large group meetings, the OD practitioner helps with organizational effectiveness and also improves individuals' quality of worklife.

The Employer-Employee Social Contract. We know that the relationship between employer and employee has changed. Company loyalty—especially in large corporations—is a thing of the past. True, in small and family-owned businesses, loyalty may still be strong. But with the pervasiveness of downsizing, and with the message that one can no longer expect a lifetime career with a single employer ringing clear, the weakening of the bond between the organization and its employees comes as no surprise.

In fact, a recent study by Chip Walker and Elissa Moses shows that a "self-navigation" subculture has emerged in America, representing about 26 percent of those sampled, half of them being under the age of 35. Members of this group hold strongly to the value "I must take care of myself." They tend to reject tradition and conformity and are more likely to start their own businesses.

The self-navigators, however, are not the majority. A far larger number of workers would prefer to stay with their companies, if possible, yet feel insecure about the prospects. The popular press continues to report that in spite of low unemployment and a strong economy, people continue to express an unease about the security of practically any workplace. Even the Federal government (e.g., NASA) and employee-owned companies have downsized.

In addition to doing away with loyalty, downsizing has affected another aspect of the employer-employee social contract. A new work relationship falling under the banner of "rent an employee" has recently emerged. The so-called contract worker has been around for a long time but many of the new contracts return former employees to their old jobs, some as consultants, others as employees of temp agencies or leasing companies. Approximately 20 percent of those who were victims of downsizing fall into this category, another version of the changing employer-employee relationship in which the two parties feel less obligation to one another. As *The New York Times* reported,

> Not having careers to advance, some praise the liberation from enervating office politics, and from the stress of competing for raises and promotions. They talk of a greater flexibility to work when they please. But their altered status cuts at their self-esteem. They are sometimes shunned by co-workers. They are often less effective than they had been. Many find themselves no longer going the extra mile to get a job done or acquire a new skill.

The new arrangement is attractive to companies because they can immediately place experienced workers into their former jobs, sidestepping the need for training. But these workers are not likely to be as motivated as before. Consequently, productivity suffers. If the rental employee trend continues, productivity will be adversely affected nation-wide.

While most of these "rental" workers reported that they enjoyed their increased freedom, they regretted the loss of pension and health benefits. Although portability is not fully in place as yet, it looks as though employees will be able to carry these benefits from one employer to another sometime in the near future. This kind of portability should help bolster their feeling of security. But rental employees will have to find other means for their benefits.

Agenda for the OD Practitioner: The agenda for the OD practitioner in this domain concerns at least the following:

1. *Expectations.* The greater an employee's ambiguity regarding the employer's expectations related to role and task responsibilities, the more likely the employee is going to experience feelings of job insecurity, if not reduced motivation. OD practitioners can help by cajoling and coaching managers to be clear with their people about goals, objectives, and task requirements and about what they as managers want.

2. *Performance Feedback.* The absence of feedback also contributes to insecurity and reduced motivation. Again, urging and coaching managers to provide feedback to their people will help clarify employees' understanding of their social contract with the organization.

3. *Reward Systems.* If employers want to keep their above-average performers but cannot guarantee long-term employment, then they must make it worthwhile for these employees to stay with the organization. OD practitioners can help with the development and sustainability of a true pay-for-performance system. What discourages employees is a reward system that (*a*) does not base pay appropriately on the level of work and/or skills required, and (*b*) provides incentives based on some seemingly arbitrary process.

Employability.   A recent opinion survey of bank employees, conducted by our organization, revealed very clear attitudes concerning training and development. These employees, the survey showed, want opportunities for training and development and are very likely to take advantage of these. Consider this in the context of the "employability clause" many companies are adding to the social contract, along the lines of "if we have to let you go some time in the future, we will ensure that you are employable." If these bank employees are representative, they intend to hold their employer to that promise.

Whether employees work for a large bank, General Motors, or for a variety of companies as contract labor, they need to think of themselves as self-employed in the sense that they are in charge of their own careers. As Edward E. Lawler III recently put it:

. . . individuals must be able to develop marketable skills, assess and compare their skill levels with those of others, and manage their own careers.

In other words, few employers today and in the future are going to take responsibility for career management.

Agenda for the OD Practitioner: The employability arena is, of course, all about career development, but not exactly as we have known it in the past. Rather, it is about one's career per se, as a professional, as a specialist, as an expert, regardless of organizational affiliation. The OD practitioner's job is to help individuals understand more clearly what they (*a*) are good at, i.e., their unique set of skills and talents; (*b*) want in their work life, e.g., one career, multiple careers, etc.; and (*c*) feel about the balance of work and other activities in life, e.g., family, hobbies, community service, etc.

It would behoove us as OD practitioners to revisit such sources as Edgar Schein's writings on career anchors; J. Kotter, V. Faux, and C. McArthur on self-assessment and one's career; Herb Shepherd's life planning exercise; Morgan McCall, Michael Lombardo, and Ann Morrison's "lessons of experience"; and Warren Bennis's "invented life." In addition, we can help individuals by being knowledgeable about continuing education and distance learning opportunities as well as the broad array of training and development programs.

Trust.   In a consultant's private interviews with employees sooner rather than later, the subject of trust (or more accurately, distrust) is likely to surface. This topic rarely appeared in my interviews a dozen or more years ago. Today, the issue seems pervasive. Why? While there are multiple reasons, three stand out: (1) the widening gap between "haves" and "have nots," (2) a diminished congruence between words and deeds, and (3) a lack of openness.

1. As we know, there is an increasing disparity between the wealthy and the poor in our society. Corporations clearly contribute to this: the disparity between a CEO's compensation and the

average worker's has, in some instances, reached the incredible ratio of 140 to 1 in the United States. This gap remains regardless of the CEO's or the organization's performance. And with a merger or acquisition, the CEO and others at the top become multimillionaires while the rank and file continue to worry about their jobs, pensions, and health insurance. In time, the tremendous wage gap may begin to deflate, but the damage to trust has been done.

2. Not unrelated is another gap that I hear about time and again in my consulting interviews—the difference between what managers and executives say and what they do. We Americans cannot abide hypocrisy.

On this issue, Warren Bennis refers to the special case of empowerment, that is, executives espousing empowerment on the one hand and downsizing on the other. He puts it this way:

> . . . empowerment is an increasingly Orwellian term, not simply a lie, but an infuriating inversion of the truth. A demoralizing sense of powerlessness is what many jobholders are feeling (as they worry about being downsized) . . . How can you have workplace empowerment in the absence of trust? . . . Empowerment and restructuring are on a collision course. It's impossible for a company to reengineer and empower at the same time, even though many firms are attempting it.

3. And, finally, distrust comes from a lack of openness. Executives rarely believe that it is wise to tell employees anything about an impending change until they have all the facts in hand and their ducks in a row. Yet I have never encountered an organization where executives are accurate in their assessment of what employees know. Invariably, employees know more than executives think they do. So, when executives delay or communicate in an ambiguous manner, they breed distrust.

Agenda for the OD Practitioner: The trust issue is fundamental. Trust, after all, is an outcome, a result of certain behaviors. But the prime behavioral precursor to trust is openness, and openness is one of the fundamental values guiding OD. We practitioners must espouse and push for openness in the organization(s) we serve. We might begin by modeling the behavior ourselves. And, of course, coach and provide feedback for executives on this dimension of their behavior.

Culture Clash.   Attempts to integrate very distinct organizational cultures as part of a merger or acquisition is not uncommon today and will become even more prevalent in the future. Even though the merging companies may be in the same business, the difference in their respective cultures can be remarkable. Putting the two cultures together is a monumental task and will take years, not mere months.

A merger or acquisition provides an obvious example of the cultural issue. Not so obvious is, say, outsourcing, often a result of downsizing or some other form of restructuring. The outsourced unit is not a formal member of the organizational family, but the relationship has to be nurtured and managed nevertheless. And the relationship is not dramatically different from the partnering dynamics of a strategic alliance or joint venture.

The ability to recognize and manage the effects of cultural differences constitutes a strategic advantage in today's environment. Culture influences the negotiation process, management in general, performance monitoring and control, and work and information-sharing norms. Cultural differences can be assets or liabilities, depending on the strategic goals for the interorganizational relationship. Cultural characteristics should therefore be considered as important determinants of relationship viability when assessing the potential partner's compatibility.

Several revealing insights on this subject emerged from a recent interview with a group of seven senior bank executives. The executives had been through a merger some 18 months earlier and were about to enter a second, considerably larger and more complicated merger. I asked what they had learned from their previous experience that, when applied, would make this upcoming merger more effective. The following is a synopsis:

1. First and foremost, they stressed the importance of having a vision of what the merged bank should be. This emphasis is similar to what social psychologists refer to as a superordinate goal, that is, a goal that can only be achieved through the cooperation of the two parties.

2. People in the merged organization need to understand the "why" behind the vision—the rationale for the merger and how individual action supports and contributes to a realization of the vision.

3. Related to the previous point, they talked about the importance of employee communications, especially being open and truthful with all employees. For example, if people are going to be forced to leave the firm and find jobs elsewhere, the sooner they can be told, the better.

4. Establishing relationships with one's merged partners beyond the workplace is helpful: for example, having lunch together, going to a ballgame together, etc.

5. The executives believed that having a few off-site meetings together early in the process to work on critical issues was highly useful. Getting together on neutral territory and away from the daily grind of their respective offices expedited the communication and decision-making processes.

6. These executives also believed that proximity was key. Being in separate geographical locations was detrimental to a successful merger, they maintained.

7. Also key was rapid decision making, particularly in the early days of a merger. These executives believed that "getting on" with the new organization as rapidly as possible, even though some corrections might have to made later, was more important because people needed clarity and structure to begin the long and arduous process of making the merger work.

8. Again on the theme of openness, these executives stated that in order for them to gain the respect of their people in the merged organization, they had to "walk the talk," that is, say what they mean, mean what they say, and be highly congruent in word and deed.

9. Most importantly, the executives stressed that the customer must not be forgotten. Prior to and in the midst of a merger, everyone becomes insular, discussing in great detail the new organization and forgetting the business, especially the customer.

This list of nine principles comes from these executives' collective experiences and does not constitute research. Yet in the area of interorganizational relations, practice continues to outpace research. It is therefore sensible that lessons from experience such as these should guide both practice and research about interorganizational relations.

Agenda for the OD Practitioner: Instead of focusing on organizational culture change as I advocated back in 1982, the work of OD should now emphasize the interrelationships of cultures. To some extent, this is an extension of our diversity work at the interpersonal and group level. But at the same time it is different, in that culture, from an organizational perspective, is related more to general systems theory, social psychology, and organizational sociology than to interpersonal psychodynamics and the dynamics within and across small groups.

I do not mean to advocate an either/or scenario here—either culture change or emphasis on cultural interrelationships. Rather, there needs to be a different theoretical perspective and consequently a difference in certain action steps. For example, an early step in a merger is putting together two, usually different, compensation systems. This requires expertise of a different order from what an OD practitioner would normally bring to the table, although the OD person could contribute by helping participants become aware of the assumptions and values that underlie the two systems.

Back to the main point. The agenda for the OD practitioner is *inter*, working in between persons and systems. OD skills that need to be honed, therefore, include negotiation, mediation, conflict management, and conflict resolution. Add to this a good dose of understanding about organizational cultures for good measure. Increasing our knowledge about cross-cultural dynamics, general systems theory, and organizational psychology and sociology would help as well.

Corporate Power.   My final agenda item is simply to call attention to two important books: David Korten's *When Corporations Rule the World* and Ralph Estes' *Tyranny of the Bottom Line.* Our agenda here is to read these books and to think about values. Our actions, whatever they may be, will come later. My urging at this stage is to read, think, and feel.

With strong credentials and considerable documentation, Korten contends that global corporations are become more powerful than nation states and, therefore, are not sufficiently monitored or regulated. Driven predominantly by financial goals, global corporations contribute significantly to (1) widening the gap between the haves and have-nots throughout the world, (2) destroying the middle class, and (3) weakening local economies. With all the hype about globalization, Korten's perspective is sobering. Not everyone agrees with Korten, particularly global executives—see, for example, a book by a former global company executive, Henry Wendt, titled *Global Embrace: Corporate Challenges in a Transnational World.* In any case, as you read Korten's book, think about where you stand vis-à-vis the issues he raises, especially if you work with a global corporation.

Even those who have not as yet read Estes's book can predict much of its content—corporations being driven by short-term profits and working to please stockholders more than customers and certainly more than employees. Estes makes these points and more. He addresses the fundamental purpose of a corporation, raises the question of who controls the corporation and, of course, discusses accountability. Again, not all would agree with Estes. But he raises the right questions— important questions for us to consider and . . . use in determining our own position.

It is equally important, as we read Estes, to clarify for ourselves what the primary causal factors are for a positive bottom line—what organizational behaviors contribute to profitability, which hinder. Our job is to determine the antecedents, then decide which ones we should get behind, which ones to fight against.

This final agenda, then, is one that confronts our values. My purpose has been to raise awareness.

Exhibit 1

Summary of organizational consulting issues and the OD practitioner's agenda

Organizational Consulting Issue	OD Practitioner's Agenda
Reengineering	Focus on specific change target that are critical to the success of a reengineering effort, e.g., roles and responsibilities, the larger systemic picture, etc.
Downsizing	Confront reasons for decision and test for constraining, cloning, or learning forces; push for humane treatment, dignity, and fairness.
Community	Bring people together; initiate meetings, not just facilitate them.
Employer-employee social contract	Seek clarity regarding task expectations and goals/objectives; help to provided feedback for employee; promote reward system based on merit and perhaps pay for performance.
Employability	Foster career development by helping people to understand what they (a) are good at, (b) want in their work, and (c) desire concerning balance of work and other aspects of life. Review career development literature and related sources.
Trust	Espouse and live the value of openness; provide coaching and feedback for executives regarding the congruence of their words and actions.
Culture clash	Place emphasis on the interrelationships of cultures and consult in the domain of "in-between-ness."
Corporate power	Read the two books by Korten and Estes, and think about the implications for OD work and feel the values that are confronted.

Joining a picket line, a march on Washington, D.C., or storming the gates of a global corporation *is* your business.

Exhibit 1 provides a summary of the eight organizational consulting issues that have been covered, plus brief statements of the OD practitioner's agenda.

The Tao of OD

There are at least two primary criteria for a professional practice. One is to have a theoretical basis for the practice and the other is to act within the bounds of a set of ethics.

The way for OD is in place. It is more a matter of owning the theories and values of OD and, with strong commitment, putting them into practice. As we say to our clients: "If you own the decision, you're likely to implement it."

And, finally, back to the purpose of this paper, that is, to argue in favor of a deeper agenda for OD. In an attempt to be relevant to "real" business issues, such as downsizing, we have neglected many of the fundamental values of our field, values that are integral to community, the organization-individual interface, the development of people, trust, interorganizational relations, especially concerning cross-cultural dynamics, and how power is addressed and exercised.

It is time—indeed, past time—for OD practitioners to challenge issues and actions that we know to be wrong, to run counter to the very foundation of our field, and to cause us to wake up in the middle of the night and question ourselves.

References

This paper is based on a presentation given for the combined preconference on "Restructuring, Reengineering, and Downsizing: A Crossroads for Society" and "The Bottom Line: Defining Our Values for the Future" at the Annual Conference of the Organization Development

Network, Orlando, Florida, October 5, 1996. I am grateful to Billie Alban, Dennis Gallagher, Len Goodstein, Dick Powell, and Lisa Tolliver for their feedback on an earlier draft of this paper.

The wave of reengineering began with M. Hammer and J. Champy's book, *Reengineering the Corporation: A Manifesto for Business Revolution* (New York: Harper Business, 1993). Some case examples of successful and unsuccessful reengineering have been described by G. Hall, J. Rosenthal and J. Wade in a 1993 *Harvard Business Review* (Vol. 71, No. 6, pp. 119–131) article, "How to Make Reengineering Really Work," but more comprehensive reviews have been provided by Kim Cameron, "Techniques for Making Organizations Effective," a chapter in D. Druckman, J. E. Singer, and H. P. van Cott (eds.) *Enhancing Organizational Performance* (Washington, D.C.: National Academy Press, 1997) and by J. P. Womack and D. T. Jones in their 1996 book, *Lean Thinking* (New York: Simon & Schuster). The *Economist* article recording Michael Hammer's defense of reengineering was in the November 5, 1994 issue on page 70.

For articles showing the ill effects on productivity as a result of downsizing, see A. Bennett, "Downsizing Doesn't Necessarily Bring an Upswing in Corporate Profitability," *The Wall Street Journal*, June 6, 1991, pp. B1, B4; R. E. Cole, "Learning from Learning Theory: Implications for Quality Improvements of Turnover, Use of Contingent Works, and Job Rotation Policies," *Quality Management Journal*, 1993, Vol. 1, pp. 9–25; and R. Henkoff, "Getting Beyond Downsizing," *Fortune*, January 10, 1994, pp. 58–64. Kim Cameron's work concerning downsizing is published in a number of sources; the one referred to in this paper is K.S. Cameron, S. J. Freeman, and A. K. Mishra, "Best Practices in White-Collar Downsizing: Managing Contradictions," *Academy of Management Executive*, 1991, Vol. 5, No. 3, pp. 57–73. For a current and more extensive coverage, see his chapter in the Druckman et al. book referred to above. And for yet another review, see Wayne Casio's article, "Downsizing: What Do We Know? What Have We Learned?" *Academy of Management Executive,* Vol. 7. No. 1, pp. 95–104. For publications about the effect of downsizing on individuals, victims, and survivors, see the 1996 book, *New York Times Special Report: The Downsizing of America* (New York: Times Books, Random House), and David M. Noer's book, *Healing the Wounds: Overcoming the Trauma of Layoffs and Revitalizing Downsized Corporations* (San Francisco: Jossey-Bass, 1993). For a recent article claiming that downsizing is not over, see L. Uchitelle's piece in *The New York Times,* "Despite Drop, Rate of Layoffs Remains High," August 23, 1996, pp. 1, D2.

Studies showing the importance of *how* downsizing is implemented and demonstrating the possibility of some positive outcomes include S. W. J. Kozlowski, G. T. Chao, E. M. Smith, and J. Hedlund, "Organizational Downsizing: Strategies, Intervention, and Research Implications," *International Review of Industrial & Organizational Psychology,* 1993, Vol. 8; J. Brockner, S. Grover, T. Reed, R. DeWitt, and M. O'Malley, "Survivors' Reactions to Layoffs: We Get By With A Little Help From Our Friends," *Administrative Science Quarterly,* 1987, Vol. 32, pp. 526–554; G.D. Bruton; J. K. keels, and C.L. Shook, "Downsizing the Firm: Answering the Strategic Questions," *Academy of Management Executive,* 1996, Vol. 10, No. 2, pp. 38–45; and Cameron's chapter in Druckman et al. (see above). *The New Yorker* article by J. Cassidy was in the April 22, 1996 issue, pp. 51–55.

For information on the ebb and flow of the American middle class, at least from an economics perspective, see the article by E. Kacapyr, "Are You Middle Class?" *American Demographics*, 1996, Vol. 18. No. 10, pp. 30–35.

The W. McKinley, C.M. Sanchez, and A.G. Schick article is "Organizational Downsizing: Constraining, Cloning, Learning," *Academy of Management Executive*, 1995, Vol. 9, No. 3, pp. 32–42. The "wee-ness envy" article is by L.S. Richman in the September 20, 1993 issue (pp. 54–56) of *Fortune* and entitled, "When Will the Layoffs End?"

The articles about the downsized insurance group and the CEO of Sara Lee are both from *The Economist*: the former "Fire and Forget," April 20, 1996, p. 51, and the latter "The Cecil Rhodes of Chocolate-Chip Cookies: How to Be a Good Corporate Citizen in a World of Globalized Markets," May 25, 1996, p. 74. The anecdote about Bill Flynn comes from an article by the current CEO of Mutual of America—T. J. Moran, "What Leaders Owe," *Leader to Leader*, 1996, Vol. 1, No. 2, pp. 15–17.

The "me-syndrome" was expounded in Christopher Lasch's book, *The Culture of Narcissism: American Life in an Age of Diminishing Expectations* (New York: Norton, 1978), and the cynical Americans in the D. L. Kanter and P. H. Mirvis book, *The Cynical Americans: Living and Working in an Age of Discontent and Disillusion* (San Francisco: Jossey-Bass, 1989).

The "age of self-navigation" study is by C. Walker and E. Moses and reported in *American Demographics*, 1996, Vol. 18, No. 9, pp. 36–42. For an article about downsizing in employee-owned companies see L. Uchitelle, "Downsizing Comes to Employee-Owned America," *The New York Times*, July 7, 1996, p. E3. Also by Uchitelle is *The New York Times* article about rental employees, "More Downsized Workers Are Returning as Rentals," December 8, 1996, pp. 1, 34.

Ed Lawler's thinking and advice about career self-management can be found in his latest book, E. E. Lawler III, *From the Ground Up: Six Principles for Building the New Logic Corporation* (San Francisco: Jossey-Bass, 1996, Chapter 12). And sources for OD practitioners regarding careers and career development include E. H. Schein's *Career Dynamics: Matching Individual and Organizational Needs* (Reading, MA: Addison-Wesley, 1978); the book by J. Kotter, V. Faux, and C. McArthur, *Self-Assessment and Career Development* (Englewood Cliffs, NJ: Prentice Hall, 1978); a description of Herb Shepherd's life-planning exercise can be found in Chapter 13 of W. L. French and C. H. Bell, Jr., *Organization Development: Behavioral Science Interventions for Organizational Improvement*, 5th Ed. (Englewood Cliffs, NJ: Prentice-Hall, 1995); "lessons of experience" is recorded in the book by M. W. McCall, M. M. Lombardo, and A. M. Morrison, *The Lessons of Experience: How Successful Executives Develop on the Job* (Lexington, MA: Lexington Books, 1988); and the "invented life" is W. G. Bennis' *An Invented Life: Reflections on Leadership and Change* (Reading, MA: Addison-Wesley, 1993).

The quote from Warren Bennis about empowerment comes from an article in the February 20, 1996 *Los Angeles Times*.

With respect to interorganizational relations and culture clash, see W. W. Burke and N. W. Biggart, "Interorganizational Relations," in D. Druckman, J. E. Singer, and H. P. Van Cott (eds.) *Enhancing Organizational Performance* (Washington, D.C.: National Academy Press, 1997). In 1982 in W.W. Burke, *Organization Development: Practices and Principles* (Boston: Little, Brown) I argued that OD practitioners should focus on culture change.

With respect to corporate power, see D. C. Korten, *When Corporations Rule the World* (West Hartford, CT: Kumarian Press, and San Francisco: Berrett-Koehler, 1995) and R. Estes, *Tyranny and the Bottom Line: Why Corporations Make Good People Do Bad Things* (San Francisco: Berrett-Koehler, 1996). A counter-argument is provided by H. Wendt's *Global Embrace: Corporate Challenges in a Transnational World* (New York: Harper Business, 1993).